Stumbling Down the Shamanic Path

Mystic Adventures and Misadventures

Michèle Burdet

iUniverse, Inc.
New York   Bloomington

iUniverse books may be ordered through booksellers or by contacting:

iUniverse
1663 Liberty Drive
Bloomington, IN 47403
www.iuniverse.com
1-800-Authors (1-800-288-4677)

Because of the dynamic nature of the Internet, any Web addresses or links contained in this book may have changed since publication and may no longer be valid. The views expressed in this work are solely those of the author and do not necessarily reflect the views of the publisher, and the publisher hereby disclaims any responsibility for them.

ISBN: 978-1-4401-5206-1 (sc)
ISBN: 978-1-4401-5208-5 (dj)
ISBN: 978-1-4401-5207-8 (ebook)

Cover art by Gwen Sepetoski

Graphics by Eric Balmer

Printed in the United States of America

iUniverse rev. date: 04/05/2010

CONTENTS in SYNOPSIS

Channel - Wessex - Glastonbury, hedgehog, Abbey - the Abbott's ghost - Windmill Hill crop circle - Stonehenge - Woodhenge - Silbury Hill - West Kennett Long Barrow - Devils' Den dolmen - the rock helmet - buckshot in the bean field - six-pointed star under Milk Hill - Wells - "who is buried where?" - the black jaguar

PREFACE

Writing another book in this lifetime was not in my mind, much less on my agenda, until a distinguished professor of anthropology urged me to do it. We were at dinner in the village of Aguas Calientes, beneath Machu Picchu, and he glanced up from his beef kebab to propose (approximately):

"You should write a book of your long spiritual path, with all its ups and downs. It could be useful to people who are just starting out, maybe hesitating, uncertain if they should make the effort."

That is the purpose of this book, to show how a spiritual life can evolve out of nowhere, moving ahead and growing in a seesaw way on a path that sometimes flowed and other times tripped, stumbled, and blocked. To encourage you to make the effort.

I dedicate these pages first to those of you who can identify with an obstacle-strewn itinerary.

My considerable thanks go to the professor, Juan Nunez del Prado of Cusco. He seeded the notion, and I am eternally grateful for Juan's friendship and counsel.

I was enjoying the relative flexibility of life in what are sometimes called "the golden years" when a gifted astrologer, Carol B. Willis, mentioned that my near-term planetary aspects were favorable for writing.

"Do you have a literary project in mind, something that hasn't gotten out of the starting blocks?" she asked. I admitted there was one, and she urged me to launch it immediately. Apparently Sagittarius was ideally positioned to build a fire under my Virgo-ish love of polishing prose. Thank you, Carol, for striking the match.

Without further waffling I began to write, understanding that these first pages told the middle of the story. Three chapters boiled out of my head, my fingers racing over the keyboard. After reading what emerged from the computer printer, I grew excited. I discussed the project with my favorite metaphysician, Dr.(Hom) Eileen Nauman, and she was enthusiastic. She agreed with Juan's idea that the story would be valuable and she offered all the moral support I would need to complete the project. With Eileen's slosh of life-giving water on the warmed seed, I went back in time to write the beginning. It took me two years to catch up to those three chapters in the middle.

This is a true story, with real-life characters and events that really happened, most of it very vivid in memory. Knowing that memory can be treacherous, I have relied heavily on my daily journals and my three filing cabinets of correspondence and information to nail down and verify the vagaries of fugitive detail. To protect privacy I have changed the names of a few of my companions on this path.

So here it is, one woman's trudge up (or down, I'm not sure which) the spiritual path into unsuspected and rewarding domains.

— Michèle Burdet

Chapter One

MY GOAT LADIES

It all began with an enigma. At first I had no idea what was happening. Invisible forces of which I was unaware had some kind of a plan for me, but in the beginning I knew nothing of all this.

In January of 1976 one of my dearest friends, a kind of a distant cousin, became very ill after an unusually tough slog through the snows of New England. Being a faithful Christian Scientist, she did not normally give in to illness. (This church claims to practice healing by the same spiritual principles used by Jesus — for them illness is primarily a metaphysical problem.) This time she had the good sense to call an ambulance, and at the hospital they diagnosed pneumonia. And it turned into congestive heart failure. Her convalescence was slow.

Cecilia was 69 at the time, working as secretary to the city manager, loving what she was doing. And suddenly her spinster world began to fall apart. There was no e-mail in those days, just winged snailmail (the concept amuses me), and thus it was quite a while before her story emerged from her customary reserve.

"The visiting nurse is still coming to the house, and I visit the hospital for checkups," she wrote, "but my strength isn't returning as it should. Luckily I have had sick leave days to spare, as I had never used them before."

What should she do? She was alone in the world. Robust health had kept her sailing through a busy, productive life. She lived alone in the old family home, which she had bought from her parents' estate, and she rented out a couple of upstairs rooms to young men of good character. She had an excellent job at which she was good and felt herself well-paid. Now this tidy little universe was crumbling at the center.

We had a rather special relationship. When I had moved to Boston to pursue a master's degree, I had looked up my family name in the telephone book. It was an unusual name, an English deformation of a French name, and there aren't a lot of us in the world. I found Cecilia in one of the suburbs, we met, and we figured out that we might be something like fifth cousins.

Cecilia became a bulwark for me in a time of need. She shored me up during a long emotional crisis and later — despite her Christian Science faith — she got me to the right kind of doctor in a medical emergency. She was a generation older than me, but we became good friends and often saw one another for a supper "out" or a little weekend excursion, like Cape Cod or Gloucester. We became bound together by a bond of affection which continued to grow.

Then I'd left the country for a good position, later married a Swiss gentleman, and for the last half dozen years we'd kept in touch through letters, hers neatly hand-written, mine always typed in my usual wall-to-wall margin format. Now she began to confide in me, rather slowly, as if she was pulling her own teeth to talk about herself and her problems. For some unfathomable reason Cecilia seemed to trust my judgement.

As is usually the case, her future was clearer to me than to her. Her energies were not snapping back as they do in youth. I foresaw that she would have to retire from her work, sell the family home in order to raise some capital, and learn how to relax on her old-age pension. This logic was crystal-clear to me, but I was not blind to her emotional investment in how life had been before January 15. Are we not all alike in this respect?

"Everyone has been marvelous but I'm still not ready to go back to full-swing work, and that is the only kind they deal out at the Town Hall!" These lines she wrote in March summed up the situation neatly.

My mode of response tried to be jaunty.

"Give Nature time," I counseled. "You've been overdrawing at the energy bank and now the note is due. Pay up. I'll bet there are lots of books you've never quite had time to read."

"Plant a few seeds in the garden if there is a warm afternoon," I added, "and wear a sweater, yes?"

Then I told her I would be there for a pair of fleeting visits. I would be visiting the United States for the first time in five years, landing in Boston, and I would see her upon arriving in May and just before departing in June.

My own health had been battered by a series of colds, asthma and bronchitis, but I was going to make that trip to see my husband's family in the Northeast, my adult children and my mother in California, with a neat little week sandwiched in to tour the southern Rockies with my daughter in her mini-bus.

One of my stepsons met me at Logan Airport and took me directly out to see Cecilia. It was a hot day and she offered us lemonade in the garden.

Cecilia had innate elegance. She carried herself like a queen and dressed with exquisite good taste, which in New England meant lots of well-cut suits. She was not beautiful nor even pretty in the Hollywood sense. There was a twinkle in her eyes, not in total harmony with the rather aristocratic nose. She somehow managed to look like champagne while dressing on the equivalent of a "beer budget".

Her appearance this day shocked me. She was gray and haggard, her slender frame gone skinny. And she wore a plain polo shirt over nondescript pants. It was a warm sticky day, but she was dressed as if she felt a chill. My earlier assessment of her future received reinforcement.

She offered us lemonade, and Allan carried the tray for her, out to the side garden.

She said she was hoping to go back to work, and I said she was crazy. There was none of the usual strength, the usual twinkle could not quite make it to the surface. We talked about her recuperation, her ideas about the future. One thing was clear, she could not face the idea of leaving her home. She did not need to remind me of her emotional investment in its supercargo of family memories.

As gently as I could, I said "you must know in your heart that it is inevitable. Better to do it by choice while you can rather than have it forced on you later."

She sighed. "I suppose you are right, but....." Her voice trailed off.

"You need to move to a warmer climate," I pointed out. "Sharpen your pencil and we'll talk about how that can be done when I come back in six weeks."

And that's how the first part of the enigma took shape.

On my return to Boston I was recovering from another bout of bronchitis but continued with a full schedule, trying to cram a week's worth of meetings into thirty-six hours. One of my failings. It was late June by now, and I'd been on the road since mid-May. The last event before heading out to Logan Airport for my night flight was to meet with Cecilia. I picked her up in my rental car and we headed out to the western suburbs, selecting a sunny hotel terrace for a summer supper.

She looked a lot better and was in good spirits. It was reassuring to see the sparkle back in her eyes. The doctor had told her she could go back to work and this had lifted her morale considerably. I told her my instinct was that it was too soon medically but probably a good thing spiritually.

"Being involved in your work is much better for the morale than sitting around waiting for a reluctant body to percolate," I proposed.

"Yes, and I'm going to put the house on the market," she replied. "That businessman I trust agrees entirely with your point of view, and I am going to follow your joint advice."

We talked a bit about the businessman and the real estate man and the discussions about price. In her usual old way, she was hesitating to be frank about important facts, but she did let drop the best news of all.

"It looks as if there is a way I will be able to move to Florida after the house is sold," she confided. "But I can't yet tell you much about it."

My heart gladdened with these words, and I beamed approval. We lifted our glasses of rosé and drank to the future. The conversation turned to my trip and what I had seen and done in Connecticut, Maine, New York, New Mexico, Colorado, Arizona, California and Arlington, just outside Washington.

And it all did work out for Cecilia. She retired from her job in December and the Town Hall gave her a nice party. The house was sold and she cleared enough to create some bond income on top of her pensions. And she did move to Florida, lodging in the home of friends.

"Naples is the finest place in Florida," she wrote much later. "Perfect weather all seasons, and very lovely people live here and love it."

Four years after the first illness she had congestive heart failure again. From then on it was all downhill. In her last letter she had clearly hoped I could somehow come physically to the rescue. All seemed to be confusion and uncertainty and she could no longer cope with it. She was ill again and the family who had rented her a room was going through major crisis, and she would have to move.

"I could see some of all this coming up but didn't know what or when or how," she wrote in January of 1980, "and I thought perhaps you could get away for a quick flight."

There was urgent need for money, and I was able to help that much but no more. She acknowledged its receipt with a brief, grateful telegram, and that was the last word I ever had from her. My own family responsibilities had become heavier and heavier, so that a trip to visit her would have been dereliction of duty on this end. My husband needed me too, and he had priority.

After months of failing health and uncertainty of which I have only the vaguest idea, she died in the fall of that year. I learned that much only many months later, and I have never learned the details of that final stage of her life, or even the exact date of her death. We never saw one another again after that summer supper on the hotel terrace, a circumstance whose recollection reawakens sadness.

My flight across the Atlantic after that last meeting was difficult, and I arrived worn-out and ill. Bronchitis had me in its grip over and over again that year.

Soon after returning home I met my friend Odile for one of our regular Thursday lunches. She was in a state of great agitation. Something had happened.

This is when the second piece of the enigma first appeared. I still had no idea there was any kind of a pattern, blissfully unaware that anything unusual was happening to me.

Odile was not as stingy with hard information as Cecilia had been, but she did dish out fact in a rather elliptical way. It was sometimes like pulling teeth to bring one of her loops around to its essential element.

What was the problem? Why was she shaking like a leaf, lighting one cigarette from the final coals of its predecessor?

"Jean-François has brought *her* here. He's carrying betrayal one step further. I can't sleep, I can't eat, I can't stand being shut up in the apartment with him," she complained.

"Wait just a minute, who is *her*?"

Odile began to reel out more loops, from which I extracted some essential facts. Her husband had maintained a long-term liaison with a much younger woman (news to me). Following their move from Belgium to Switzerland he had gone back there frequently on business trips, keeping his illicit romance alive at the same time. And now, Odile believed, the girl was right there in Montreux, continuously available to Jean-François. He was always enforcing great economy in their household expenses and in what he gave her for herself, and now he was (probably) paying the girl's rent in a modest hotel.

"Well, at least there will be fewer travel expenses," I quipped.

"Oh no," she moaned, "now he's taking little trips and I'm sure she goes along."

"What do you intend to do?" I asked.

"What can I do? He controls the money. I haven't got a bean. I'm a prisoner," she pouted.

Was she considering a divorce? Or couldn't she force him to provide separate maintenance?

"There's not really enough money for that. And I would need a lot of proof," she complained. She lit another cigarette.

"Yes, certainly, evidence would be essential. That's why there are so many private detectives," I pointed out. "If you get the evidence, the money is for him to worry about."

"Oh, it's all such a bloody mess!" she wailed.

My heart went out to Odile. There didn't seem to be anything I could say or do that would help her situation. Her emotions and her thoughts were in a tangle and my instinct told me to stand aside from this classic snarl. It seemed to me her story hung on a series of unverified suppositions. Fanciful notions, a smart defense attorney would sneer.

We met again the next Thursday and she continued her litany of woes, one cigarette after another. More historical details emerged, bit by bit, from the cat's-cradle of her chaotic mental state.

She'd been born in the Congo, daughter of a French planter. When war broke out in 1940 she'd been on a visit to her grandparents in southern

France. She had escaped across the Pyrenées to Spain and Portugal, and from there she finally got to London, the nearest safe haven to which she could gain passage. Some of this I had known, but not all of it. My friend was a handful of years older than I and her curly hair had turned white already. She was neat and attractive, with regular features and she would have been very pretty as a young woman, possibly even stunning. Both an asset and a liability in a dangerous time.

Culturally and climatically she was a fish out of water in England, but she made the best of it by volunteering in the women's auxiliary forces. Ultimately she was assigned to a radar control room in a basement of the War Ministry, and that is where she met the handsome Belgian officer, Jean-François.

It was not love at first sight, but their affair did bloom. He had a wife who had fled with their children to the countryside outside Bruxelles. He claimed they were already separated in spirit but that a divorce was out of the question, both of them being Catholic.

Odile and Jean-François were together much of their leisure time, military schedules and obligations permitting. They could not live together but they could occasionally take leave and go off to a country inn for a few days. Toward the end of the war she became pregnant. Most inconveniently.

Week after week she was serving me generous helpings of this unpalatable meal. By stern questioning I managed to keep her somewhat on track, but boredom threatened to overwhelm my affection for this faithful friend. Something drastic needed doing, for it was clear she was simply wallowing in a muddy mess that went round and round in her head, morning, noon and night.

Inspiration struck.

"You know what you should do?" I queried, during the fourth consecutive Thursday of unrelieved anguish.

"No, what?" she asked.

"I propose that you begin to write all this down. Every bit of it."

"Oh, I'm not that much of a writer," she protested.

"You don't have to be a professional writer. Think of it as a letter to me." I paused, reflecting on how far I could push her. "Go back to your beginnings. Trace the essential phases of your life. Then, when you get to the time of Jean-François you will have an analytical habit put into place."

"I wouldn't dare do that. He would find the papers and then there would be hell and all," she grumbled.

"Don't keep the manuscript at home. Bring it with you every Thursday. After I've read it I will put it in one of my filing cabinets, against the time when you want it back. You will only have one week's worth of pages hidden in your room."

I knew I was letting myself in for a long siege of holding her hand, but this seemed like a way to defang the situation, to make it a little more interesting. She would be forced to become her own therapist. Our little luncheons could gradually get back on an even keel. I would be able to resume my previous habit of sometimes meeting other friends after her dependence on my sympathetic ear, which was suffering considerable wear-and-tear, began to lessen.

Miracle of miracles, she took my recommendation to heart. She began to write her autobiography in secret, the weekly collection of papers carefully hidden from Jean-François' curiosity. They were no longer sleeping together, she had a separate room and therefore some privacy.

The next week she had a sheaf of papers for me, six sheets closely written. I tried to conceal my sense of triumph. This was going to work.

"This is excellent," I said. "You have really buckled down to the task."

"I don't dare be caught writing this while he is home," she said. "The only times are when he goes out for his morning stroll and to buy his newspaper. Sometimes he stays away for a couple of hours, not always."

In this way we began a process in which I read her material closely, in the quiet of home, and then asked questions the next week. We were gradually shifting the focus of our dialogue. She could not keep totally away from the day-to-day nastiness of her situation, the occasional bits and pieces that confirmed her suspicions about what was going on behind her back.

"I saw her," she told me one time. "And I'm sure she saw me. There was a kind of a smirk on her face."

"Come on now," I cautioned, unwilling to listen to any superfluous wallowing. "Are you absolutely sure? I mean, how often have you seen this creature in the past, in Belgium, and how can you be sure it's the same person, here, now?"

"Oh, I *know*", Odile insisted.

I left it there. Her previous installment of "the story" had left me with some questions, and I turned the conversation quickly to them.

And so it went on. Odile's life story was, as a matter of fact, rather interesting. Growing up on a plantation carved out of the jungle did not lead to an ordinary childhood. Infrequent visits to the "mother country" did not cement a sense of identity. Becoming a war refugee was unusual, to say the least. And deciding, as a young woman, that salvation lay in joining the armed forces of a foreign country, in a language not her own, was not only extremely original, but it took courage. These elements of her story were so very intriguing, in their own right, that my attention was easily held.

The rest of the story was less entertaining. Abortions were not easily available as World War II wound to a close. There had been long months of difficulty, physical and economic stress, social opprobrium, and the continued agony of not knowing how well her lover would stand by her. He did, in the end, acknowledge the child as his own. He went home to Belgium after being mustered out and sent her money, barely enough. How she managed to keep the pressure on him is a story in itself, and it probably goes a long way to explain the genesis of the present imbroglio.

In spite of their Catholicism, which seems not to have been as devout as advertised, there was a divorce. Ultimately he married Odile and took her home to Belgium, and that is where they stayed for the next twenty-five years. She raised their son, Marc-Antoine, and Jean-François pursued his engineering career with a certain success. He seems also to have pursued other women with some assiduity. It was not an ideal marriage but somehow they stayed together. And here they were now, living in a small retirement apartment on the shores of one of Switzerland's most famous lakes. And he was still playing games.

On one occasion I asked why she smoked so much. It was hard sometimes to be at table with her, my own allergy to cigarette smoke being a continuing problem.

"Aren't you worried about having cardiac problems?" I asked.

Her reply shocked me.

"That's not a worry. If it happens, so much the better," she said.

"Are you trying to provoke a heart attack?" I asked, incredulous.

"Well, not exactly. But it wouldn't upset me. I haven't all that much to live for."

"Then it's a kind of programmed suicide?"

"Um. That's putting it a little strongly," she murmured. "But.............." her response trailed off.

Having read enough of her life by then, her ingrained pessimism came as not a real surprise. And then, I reflected, there are a lot of smokers and drinkers out there who are committing suicide, whether consciously, unconsciously, or subconsciously.

As the weeks turned into months, and as the months began to add up, Odile completed her autobiography. I read it all, asked questions, made a few marginal notes, and then filed it away. We agreed I would hand the manuscript to Marc-Antoine should he ever ask for it.

Writing her life story did have a calming effect on Odile. It helped to situate her own tormented journey within the perspective of the long, tortuous path of twentieth-century European history. She could see some of the ways in which she had possibly failed to help Jean-François adjust to the difficulties of the choice he had made on her behalf.

Bit by bit, and without totally abandoning Odile, I organized my Thursdays to lunch with a variety of friends. She and I had been thrown together because of our husbands, but I was much more outgoing, more interested in expanding my circle of friends. The problem with the young Belgian woman gradually evaporated, without actually healing. Odile and Jean-François continued their strained life together, a civilized truce.

And tobacco did ultimately kill her. Not a heart attack, as she had imagined, but lung cancer. It was a long slow process, with surgery and all the rest that medical science has invented to camouflage the gaps in its knowledge. She died twelve years after beginning to write her autobiography at my behest, and I still have it in the filing cabinet. Marc-Antoine has never asked for it and I have lost track of him.

But Odile was still busily writing her story when Ulla rang me up.

My husband's life as an oil painter meant that we moved in a circle of fellow artists, gallery owners and dealers. We were invited to a great many *vernissages*. At one of these affairs we had met Ulla, a promising young portraitist from Austria. Because my husband sometimes executed portrait commissions and had, in his earlier days, studied under a noted portraitist, he had a lively interest in comparing notes with compatible souls. Ulla was not one of our intimate friends, but we met her often at these affairs and had received her in our home.

Her telephone call to me had nothing to do with art. She wanted my advice and asked to come talk with me privately. Well, yes, of course, I told her to come ahead.

That's when the third piece of the enigma bubbled to the surface.

Ulla asked me to help her cope with an uncomfortable personal problem. In brief, her lover beat her. But she could not tell this story briefly. She had to paint it for me verbally, with all the ups and downs, flashes of color, the shadows, the little brush strokes that accented character.

Fortunately I had foreseen a pot of tea. This was going to take time.

She was petite and blond, vivacious, loquacious. I had only heard of her Giorgio and didn't really know what he was like. He seemed to be the son of a woman in the village with whom I had a nodding acquaintance. Later someone pointed him out to me, and I recognized a curly-haired Neapolitan type, with rough good looks.

According to Ulla he was magnetic and fascinating, with great charm. But she had discovered a streak of violence running close beneath the surface, and he could explode in an instant. Much of the time he was tender and considerate, generous, helpful, in so many ways an ideal companion. Then, in the wink of an eye, he would fly into a rage.

His magnetism captivated her. The slaps and blows bruised and pained her. All might be lovely for several days, even a week, she could even imagine marrying him. The moments of violence came out of the blue, frightened her, left her blooded, swollen, and sobbing.

Finally she shored up her courage and told him on the telephone not to come, to leave her alone once and for all. Enraged, he arrived at the door, broke in and pummeled her thoroughly before raping her. Which, of course, in his eyes was not rape but simply disciplining his woman.

What in the world did she expect me to do about all this?

"Well, this all sounds rather difficult," I ventured. "How can I possibly help you? I have no wish to get involved with your Giorgio. He sounds like a really macho type. There is no room in my life for dealing with violent people."

"Just try to help me know what to do," she pleaded.

"It seems to me you need at the very least some kind of a social worker to talk to. But with all the physical violence perhaps you really need the police."

"Oh, I couldn't do that!"

"Then what do you really want? Do you want this man out of your life, or don't you? Do you want him punished, or don't you?" I couldn't help but feel rather testy.

She hesitated. It seemed as if she did not know what she wanted.

"I just want him to stay away," she said. "And he won't."

"What claim does he have on you? You're not married. Has he given you gifts, like jewelry?"

"It's more his animal magnetism. He's like catnip for me. He's a marvelous lover, and when he's in a good mood we have a wonderful time being together."

It began to dawn on me. He had enslaved her sexually -- she both wanted her freedom and did not.

A light bulb went on in my mind.

"Have you thought about getting a restraining order?" I asked.

"I don't know what you mean."

"You know, a legal order requiring him to leave you alone, forbidding him to bother you," I explained. "Such a thing is a court order. With that in your favor, if he comes around, you call the police, and they remove him from the premises."

"That might be a good thing," she mused. "How do I go about it?"

"Do you have an attorney?" I asked.

"No, and I don't have money for one either."

Another idea popped into my mind.

"Go to the consumer's association," I proposed. "They have free legal counsel available."

She brightened up at that idea. I agreed to research the telephone number, dates, and place where this service was available.

"I'll call you as soon as I have the information," I offered.

We finished our tea talking a bit about her art and her next show. Then she left me to make good on my promise.

The next day I got the consumer people on the telephone and found out about their free legal service. After communicating the details to her, I got busy packing my valise. My husband and I were going off for several weeks to visit friends and family in the Netherlands. I had no more time for Ulla and her brutal lover.

The next time I heard from Ulla she had been to see the consumers' lawyer and been told what she had to do to keep Giorgio away from her. She did nothing about the situation, letting it drag on and on, getting beaten from time to time, falling back into his arms after a reconciliation, going around and around in this infernal love-hate cycle.

Then one day she appeared at the door.

"Please excuse my coming unannounced, I've come to say goodbye," she said.

I invited her in, cautioning that I had only a handful of minutes before doing something with my own resident artist.

"So, are you leaving this part of the world?" I asked, after we had sat down.

"Not entirely. But I am going home to see my parents in Austria, for at least three months,"

"Do you think that will solve your problem?" My skepticism was not quelled.

"I've told Giorgio that if he doesn't leave me alone I will take legal action," she declared. "I've seen that legal counselor again and gotten the addresses of several attorneys who could help me."

"Do you really mean that this time?"

"Absolutely. It's come to a showdown between having my life in a constant turmoil because of him or getting back to painting well again. That's the true focus of my life and I have to get back to it." Ulla's tone was emphatic.

I wished her luck, and we said a temporary goodbye. And that's how it worked out. While Ulla was away in Austria her Latin lover found another dolly, and when she came back he didn't bother her again.

Some months later I was lunching with Madeleine, who was studying astrology. We got talking about how people come into our lives, how relationships shift and alter. And I told her about how this year had been for me one of counseling people, a totally new thing in my life.

"This is a kind of an enigma to me," I pointed out.

"Have you looked at their birthdays?" Madeleine asked. "It could be that you and they had some intersecting transits. Planetary aspects could have something to do with it, you know."

"Well, I know one of them was born in early January, but I don't remember the date offhand," I said.

"That's Capricorn," Madeline said, "and you were born in Virgo. Both Earth signs. You have quite enough in common to spark a relationship. See what I mean?"

Yes, I did see what she meant. This was an amusing idea.

At home later that day I took down the birthday book from its spot on my reference shelf. I turned to the January pages in the front of the book, because I knew Cecilia's date was inscribed there. Indeed it was, she had been born on a January 7. This little book came from an art museum, there were reproductions opposite every page of dates, and famous artists' names were associated with each date of the year. Cecilia shared her birthday with Albert Bierstadt, whose fabulous paintings of the American West as the explorers saw it fascinated me.

My eye scanned the page automatically, and to my surprise I found Odile's name on the line below that of Cecilia: Odile had been born on January 8!

Suddenly excited I picked up the telephone and dialed Ulla's number.

After the customary pleasantries I asked for her date of birth.

"Why do you want to know?" she asked.

"I have this birthday book with the names of famous artists for every date, and I wondered where you fit into it."

"I'm not a famous artist," she said, "but I was born on January 9."

It took willpower to conceal my excitement, which I simply could not share with Ulla. "That's fun," I replied. "You have the same birthday as William Powell Frith, an English painter of the nineteenth century."

"Never heard of him," she said.

"Neither have I," I admitted. "How about the French sculptor Nicolas Coustou?"

"Don't know that one either."

"Seventeenth century," I pointed out. "Well, thanks for satisfying my curiosity. I'll try to remember to send you a card."

Alone with my thoughts, I was dazzled. What a wild coincidence, January 7, 8 and 9! What did it mean? My three Capricorns were not at all born the same year, far from it, but the concatenation of these dates struck me as having some kind of deep significance.

Three women, linked only by their birthdays, brought me their deep, life-shattering problems, and sought my help. Why should they come to me, of all people? I was not a professional counselor of any kind, brought no qualifications or credentials to the table. There must be some astrological explanation, I thought. But I was not then and still am not enough of an astrologer to be able to find the interpretation.

In the rarefied world of astrology Capricorn is the sign of the Goat. There are qualities of stubbornness, patience, perseverance, prudence and — certainly relevant here — surefootedness in treacherous environments. In this light my three Capricorns were Goat Ladies, without dispute.

And beyond astrology, was there another answer to this enigma?

This question began to bubble in my mind.

Chapter Two

SEARCHING

My search for meaning in all this followed a leisurely pace.

It was relatively easy to understand that for some unknown reason "invisible forces" out there, or whatever, had chosen to send three women to me for advice, comforting, counseling. In one word: help. It was less easy to comprehend the astrological significance.

My friend Madeleine was a student of this arcane science but she did not feel qualified to research all the aspects of this unique conjunction. She spoke of transits and progressions but said she had not yet learned how to do all that. It appeared there was a lot of daunting mathematics involved. Computerized astrology did not yet exist.

Nor did I have any clearly developed ideas about those invisible forces. About the only thing certain for me was that conventional notions about something called God rubbed my fur the wrong way. I was not an atheist — I did believe there was "something" — maybe I was an agnostic? These labels did not really have useful meaning to me.

My parents had brought me up in the Episcopal Church, the USA version of the Church of England. My father was the prime mover in this religious orientation. He had been brought up in what was known as "high" Episcopalianism, which seemed to be almost indistinguishable from Catholicism in practice. He was a believer, he had "faith", whatever that is. And we children were to go to Episcopal Sunday School while our parents were in the regular Church service. As pre-adolescents we had to go to catechism classes, after which we were "confirmed" and from then on took communion beside our father.

Mother seemed to be a passive participant in all this. It always seemed to me that she simply went along to keep peace in the family but that there was no fervor in her. She submitted as we did. Many decades later I received some insights into her attitude — or lack of attitude, if you like.

My own attitude was one of silent skepticism. During catechism classes I asked one question, and one question only, of the Reverend Parker. He was talking about the Holy Trinity — Father, Son, and Holy Ghost — and I asked him to clarify what was meant by the Holy Ghost.

Do not ask me to recall how he replied. His explanation was couched in a kind of flabby vagueness, which exemplified for me most of what they were trying to teach me. His exact words were not sufficiently to the point to have survived the more than sixty-five years since that day.

I felt like a perfect hypocrite at the time of the Confirmation. I had to go through with it because I had no alternative. What arguments could I possibly have mustered had I chosen to defy my father and express what I really thought? "This is a load of rubbish," is what I was thinking. There was no way I could say that without starting a war within the family, a war I would lose. I had no weapons, no ammunition, nor was I the least bit warlike. I was an intellectual prisoner. It is in this state , unfortunately, that most of us start life.

At eighteen years of age I left home to pursue university-level studies at one of the better four-year colleges in Southern California. From that time on my connection with the Episcopal Church sank out of sight. Neither religious studies, nor church, nor chapel was compulsory at my college, although all were offered. Sometimes I drifted into Tuesday morning chapel because they played interesting classical music. Whenever there was some kind of Bible reading I used such moments to consider the studies ahead of me that day and, most important, what might be served for lunch.

When my daughter reached school age we found that most of her schoolmates were going to Sunday School. She seemed vaguely interested in doing what they were doing, so we sent her to the Presbyterian Sunday School for a few weeks. That was where her school chums went, and the only other choice in our small town was the Catholic Church.

She began bringing home little leaflets with pastel illustrations of a kind of a soft, effeminate Jesus. We looked at one another with distress and agreed to remove our child from that Sunday School. This was a gut reaction.

Not long afterward I was talking to our friend Joyce about this situation. She told us about something called the Unitarian Church, which was without dogma and totally unconnected with Christian teachings. She and her husband took their boys to that Sunday School and went to the Sunday services themselves. As she described the nature of the services, it sounded to me like a perpetual study in comparative religion. We joined them in this venture.

And comparative religion is what it was. The minister, who was a molecular biologist, drew his texts from everywhere: Buddhism, Taoism, the vast array of semi-suppressed Christian documents known as the *Apocrypha*, the Dead Sea Scrolls, Ralph Waldo Emerson and the Transcendentalists, and an impressive number of famous philosophers and poets of many centuries. Ethics and the true nature of morality were part of the agenda. While this was going on upstairs, our children were getting something similar downstairs. They spent a whole year on the spiritual life of the Native American tribes.

We loved this universal approach to spiritual thinking. This church was not even a member of the National Council of Churches, which was resolutely Christian. And Unitarians did not identify with any rigid belief.

This spiritual exploration served us well for those few years. Life changed; there were physical moves and quite a lot of nomadism for a series of years. In several environments I found the Unitarian Church a happy place to be from time to time. While in Boston, during the time that Cecilia and I had become close, one of the Unitarian ministers, John Hammon, was of considerable help to me in working through my problems during a time of personal crisis.

One time, years later, when I was visiting John and Oressa in their retirement home on Puget Sound, he uttered the definitive Unitarian question. In the course of conversation I happened to use the word God, and his reaction was jovially explosive:

"Who?" he asked, with a broad grin.

"I was referring to that entity, that creative spirit, which a lot of people call God," I explained.

"Who?" he repeated.

Against this background, and in light of startling new information that had come forward, my mind often reflected on what the events of 1976 were supposed to mean.

For there was soon fresh information in the spiritual world. A medical doctor in Virginia, Dr. Raymond Moody, published *Life After Life*[1]. This little volume laid before the western world the stories of countless people who had died, been pronounced clinically dead, and then been resuscitated.

They came back to life all telling similar stories of being sucked out of their bodies, zooming through a tunnel, and ending in a kind of "light world". There they met relatives and friends who had already died, and finally they encountered a shimmering Being of Light who dealt with them gently. This personage sometimes led them through a review of their lives, but It explained that it was too soon for them to die physically, that their work was not finished on this side. And, zoom again; there they were back in their bodies, recovering painfully from the illness or accident that had seemingly killed them.

Moody's publication was not simply fresh information, it was a strong breeze blowing out of the stale corridors of human spirituality. In a stroke it blasted the centuries-old fears of purgatory, fire and brimstone that underlay Christian churchdom.

It was more of a gale-force wind roaring through my perceptions. Cobwebs disappeared as if by magic. In an instant I knew that Moody's hundreds and hundreds of cases represented truth, that they opened perspectives only vaguely hinted at in what claimed to be Holy Scripture. Twentieth-century medicine, in its ability to revive people who once would have died, had unwittingly opened the doors to a new way of looking at the relationship between life and death.

Meanwhile, Dr. Elisabeth Kübler-Ross was pursuing similar researches from the viewpoint of a medical professional helping the terminally ill. Moody says she told his publisher that she could have written a similar manuscript based on her own work, adding up to several hundred cases. She had already published *On Death and Dying*[2], a landmark study of patients approaching death.

Suddenly death and its hereafter was no longer such a shadowy realm. It sounded positively agreeable. Death might be a source of problems for those one left behind, it could cut short one's plans and projects, but the event itself need not be feared.

My casual searching had not gone very far when I stumbled across a little book entitled *A Search for the Truth*[3], by a certain Ruth Montgomery. As a well-known journalist, a syndicated columnist traveling the world, Montgomery was a skeptic about the supernatural. Her words brought to mind my own journalistic career. Skepticism had to be one of the reporter's first tools, underlying the digging and questioning that established the veracity of a news story.

It led me to remember one evening in the early 1950s when two young men came into the editorial room of the morning newspaper where I worked. They presented a couple of snapshots of what they said was a flying saucer. We looked at the photos. Yes, there was a resemblance to the shape of a flying saucer, at that time a relatively new concept in the public mind.

"Where did you get these pictures?" I asked.

"On the Pines-to-Palms highway, at the big lookout point," one of them replied.

I knew the place, hours away, where the mountain highway began its plunge to the desert floor. There was a wide curve and a big space to pull off and admire a panorama of the colorful desert mountains and the deep canyon at one's feet. The city editor and I looked at one another quizzically.

"Your flying saucer looks like a Cadillac hubcap," I suggested. "And that spot is a marvelous place to whirl one out into space, like throwing a discus."

We didn't print the picture.

The same kind of skepticism echoed through Montgomery's pages as she became acquainted with spirit mediums and discarnate entities who brought messages from "the other side". Frequently they introduced friends and relatives of those assembled.

Her innate skepticism began to crumble when a medium brought through her deceased father with intimate information that no one except herself could have known. And then some of her husband's deceased family came through with more correct facts mixed into their declarations.

Montgomery's search brought forth a lot of lore about extra-sensory perception, psychic visions, automatic writing — which became her preferred method of investigation — and the afterlife. One by one I read several of her books, some of which seemed to leap off bookstore shelves into my uncertain hand.

All these stories of the afterlife led logically to an adjacent slice of the spiritual world: reincarnation.

Montgomery's books after *A Search for the Truth* began to focus more and more on this phenomenon. *A World Beyond*[4] introduced me to tales from the afterlife of her recently deceased friend, the medium Arthur Ford, and to the concept of higher planes of consciousness. *The World Before*[5] talked about the creation of human souls as sparks of cosmic energy; it gave details about Atlantis and Lemuria. Edgar Cayce had talked about these concepts, and here they were again, coming through from the afterlife via channeling. Later books delved deeper into the past lives of famous people, the notion that many of them were "walk-ins" (advanced souls who enter a mature physical body in a time of crisis), extraterrestrials and their visitations to this planet, and an endless series of psychic experiences by ordinary people.

Perhaps more important to my own search for the truth was the concept that we each have our spiritual Guides — discarnate beings who accompany us through life and try to help, guide and protect us. None of that work can get very far until we reach a point of acknowledging that we have Guides, that they are there and we can learn to communicate with them. Montgomery made it perfectly clear from the outset that her "psychic" books after *A Search for the Truth* came through a process called "automatic writing", in which she basically took dictation from her own Guides.

These readings opened to me the idea of comprehending the arrival of "my three Capricorns" as a form of spiritual guidance. Three people astrologically compatible with me were brought forward to give me a kind of mission. Was I being taught to use my worldly experience as a means of helping others? Did this mean that I had spiritual Guides who were trying to nudge me along a certain path? It was not quite that clear to me in those days, but Montgomery's reportings from "the other side" most definitely pried open my mind and made me receptive, even warmly receptive, to these ideas.

I had already read about the famed trance medium Edgar Cayce in *The Sleeping Prophet*[6]. I now call this little volume "the grandfather of a whole school of contemporary prophecy." Cayce went into deep trance-like sleep and spoke aloud, bringing through healing information for thousands of patients. Many of his sleep-talking sessions were charged with prophecy for the future of the world, filling books of which I have read only a handful. There is a generous helping of reincarnation among the more than 4'000 transcripts of Cayce's sleeping "readings."

At this point in time, the late 1970s, my explorations began to spread into this rather enchanting domain. Thus I came across the works of Sylvia Cranston and Joseph Head, compilations of writings reflecting on the matter down through the ages. Their two works, *Reincarnation, an east-west anthology*[7] and *Reincarnation, the Phoenix Fire Mystery*[8] overflow with the writings and sayings of philosophers, poets, scientists, doctors, psychiatrists, psychologists, statesmen and religious thinkers of numerous countries, traditions, and eras of history. Cranston completed these studies in collaboration with Carey Williams in *Reincarnation: a new horizon in science, religion and society*[9].

In those pages I came across a discussion of the painter Paul Gauguin's mysticism. He is famous for his Tahitian paintings in the late nineteenth-century, in which he frequently included idols and giant heads, the latter reminiscent of Easter Island. Gauguin meant something to me, for my husband was a working artist and our life together focused on the world of painting in its many dimensions.

"Whence Do We Come, What Are We, Where Do We Go?" is a giant canvas more than twelve feet wide and four feet high. Even from reproductions one senses the emotion which prompted the work and the questions posed in the title. Gauguin painted this in 1897 during his second sojourn at Tahiti, a handful of years before his death in the Islands, and it can be considered his spiritual testament.

Against a fantastic panoramic background painted in a muted palette Gauguin depicts a dozen Polynesians in various stages of repose and quiet activity, such as strolling through the background. There is an idol in the style of an Asiatic god depicting Taaroa, the supreme deity of the Maoris, the creator of the world. There are an elder meditating, a dog resting, cats playing, and birds walking and grooming themselves in harmony with humanity. The central figure is reaching to pick a fruit hanging at the top edge of the picture, the position of his arms forming an arrow reaching for the sky, while contrasting with the arms of Taaroa. It is all very low-key and relaxed.

Contemplating this painting sent me back in time, to the first painting which deeply moved me.

In the fall of 1941 a large oil of a broad landscape riveted my attention. While visiting the Los Angeles County Fair for the first time in my young life, I had wandered through the barns full of combed and curried farm animals, marveling over the variety of goats. My heart went out to the brown

Nubians. A whole new bucolic world opened up to the sheltered suburban college girl, just turning 18. And then I found myself in a hall full of paintings by contemporary California artists.

I stood hypnotized before *"The Wind That Blew the Sky Away"*. It evoked other dimensions, The sky above a pleasant countryside was literally ripped open, peeled back, and the artist somehow managed to convey the notion of a fathomless void. A new sensation, a whiff of spirituality entered my being, a new concept bursting upon my consciousness. *"The Wind That Blew the Sky Away"* invaded the spirit of a young college girl in a way that years of exposure to Sunday Services could not. Try as I may, I cannot recall the name of the artist.

If ever a seed was planted, it was that painting, still alive in memory. During the year that followed my brain was stuffed with anthropology, geology, mineralogy, chemistry, spherical trigonometry and the German language, but that meta-artistic image never got obliterated. It simply went underground, and it took the spiritual testament of another painter, Paul Gauguin, to bring it back to the light.

During this period of the late 1970s I began to study astrology, hoping to glean some insight into the meaning of my three encounters. "How to do it" books accumulated on my work table, rudimentary charts took form, hours were plowed into extracting planetary positions from an ephemeris, more hours were invested into fathoming the intricate calculations. Or trying to fathom them.

I found this work slow and tiresome. Despite my mathematical brain this was real drudgery. It was evident to me that professional astrologers only reached that status as the result of long studies. To repeat what I said at the beginning of this chapter, computerized astrology for the amateur did not yet exist. How could it? Personal computers did not yet exist either.

Complete understanding of the "three Capricorns" syndrome was put on hold.

In the years immediately following their appearance in my life the impulse to know, the searching instinct brought me many new ideas. Windows began opening onto previously unglimpsed spiritual vistas. There was, however, no real answer to the question they had planted in my mind.

Three years down this uncharted road, in late 1979, we went to the Caribbean to escape the rigors of the alpine winter.

[1]   Raymond A. Moody, Jr. M.D., *Life After Life*, 1977.
[2]   Elisabeth Kübler-Ross M.D., *On Death and Dying*. New York: Macmillan, 1969. 289p., bibliography, paper. LC 69-11789.

[3]   Ruth Montgomery, *A Search for the Truth*. New York: Ballantine Books, Fawcett Crest, 1966. 256p. ISBN 0-449-24530-6.

[4]   _____., *A World Beyond*. New York: Fawcett Crest, 1971. 176p. ISBN 0-449-24085-1.

[5]   _____, *The World Before*. New York: Ballantine, Fawcett Crest, 1976. 288p. ISBN 0-449-20319-0.

[6]   Jess Stearn, *Edgar Cayce — The Sleeping Prophet*. New York: Bantam, 1968. 287p.

[7]   Joseph Head and S.L. Cranston, *Reincarnation, an east-west anthology*. New York: Julian Press, 1961, and Wheaton, Ill.: Theosophical Publishing House, 1981. x+342p., preface, appendix, index. ISBN 0-8356-0035-1

[8]   _____, ;*Reincarnation: The Phoenix Fire Mystery*. New York, Julian Press, 1977, 1979. xix+620p., notes, index. Foreword by Elisabeth Kübler-Ross, M.D. ISBN 0-517-56101-8

[9]   Sylvia Cranston and Carey Williams, *Reincarnation, a new horizon in science, religion and society*. New York: Julian Press, 1984. xiv+385p., notes, index. ISBN 0-517-55496-8.

Chapter Three

THE ENORMOUS WAVE

Basking on the sands of Guadeloupe, soaking up the hot sun as 1979 slid into 1980, I watched the bathers in the little harbor. Several swimmers were setting up sailboards. A trim lady in a pink bikini, her hair set in a perfect bubble hairstyle, carried a sailboard down to the water's edge, quickly rinsed the sand off it, stepped on, picked up the sail and breezed straight out of the harbor. No fuss, no muss, just like that.

"I ought to be able to do that", I said to myself.

Thus I had a chat with Xavier, the beachmaster, and began to have lessons in sailboarding. It wasn't easy. The board proved to be programmed genetically to wobble with each muscular twitch. Learning to sail a board proved to be an exercise in maximizing one's control over muscular twitches. Bit by bit I got the hang of it and pretty soon I was sailing around the little lagoon with aplomb — as long as the wind stayed steady and the limits of the lagoon did not dictate a change in direction. On such occasions I frequently found myself in the water.

Xavier assured me that it would get better with lots of practice. And it did, sort of. My technique was not as smooth and effortless as the blonde in the pink bikini, but I had hopes.

Then we moved on to St. Martin, and the board I rented there wanted to sail out between the anchored yachts. We did that, which gave me more opportunities to refine my technique for clambering back on the board after a dunking.

Then we moved on to St. Barthélemy, an island even smaller than St. Martin. You get there by landing on a "white knuckles" airstrip — meaning it is short and if the pilot overshoots the plane ends up wallowing in the Baie de St. Jean. Passengers too.

This Bay of St. John echoes the shape of a crescent moon, and we were lodged in rooms attached to a restaurant on a big rock at the other end of the crescent from the airport. Convenient for observing the light planes fluttering in over the mountain and plunging quickly down to the tarmac. We never saw one take a bath, but I heard that it has happened.

A long sandy beach rimmed the bay, and on its shores I found a place that would rent me a sailboard. The bay was very attractive and sailboards

22

evolved over its waters every day. One lovely afternoon, on St. Valentine's Day in February, 1980, I rented one of those boards.

It was a fine place to practice, with a very light breeze paralleling the beach, and I was getting an acceptable workout. Still working on my technique, which was far from perfect. My built-in stubbornness, becoming legendary, allowed me to nurture hopes that an athletic nature could conquer this rather esoteric new sport. There was a lot of inner pressure to do so. After all, hadn't the first sailboarding world championships been held at Guadeloupe just before our arrival on that island? Hadn't we become friends with the local champion, a comely lass named Yolande? These were all true, and they nourished my ambition to glide over the waters as casually as the pink bikini.

While I was sailing along parallel to the beach the wind shifted. Suddenly I found myself being pushed out to sea by an offshore breeze that was stiffening by the moment. My efforts to counteract this caprice of the elements put me back in the water fairly often. There came a moment when I realized I would be better off in the water, pushing the board while swimming, than trying to control that sail from a standing position. I went deliberately into the water and began to swim toward the shore.

The current, however, had other ideas. It would only permit movement parallel to the beach, and that wasn't the way I wanted to go. The people who ran the beach installation seemed to be preoccupied with these new characteristics of wind and current, for I could see them preparing to launch a motorboat. They sped away from the shore and headed straight out to sea. Yes, I could see there was a sailboarder far out, really far out, and having difficulty. They were en route to rescue him and did not even notice me, about one hundred yards downbeach from their tack.

Still swimming, still trying to orient my board and waterlogged sail toward the beach, and not succeeding, I heard a roar behind me. I looked around.

A gigantic wave was bearing down on me. It looked like a surfer's nightmare, seemingly ready to break right on me. And it did.

Board, sail and Michèle were flung in three different directions. I never saw those two again but learned later they'd been found on the beach.

Whereas I had been flung into the seaward edge of a coral reef. Painfully. I pushed against the jagged surface with one foot and tried to swim seaward in order to get around this obstacle. No such luck.

Another big wave slammed me right back into the reef. Had the wind shifted again, now blowing onshore? This was an academic question which flittered through my mind as I struggled to launch myself once again and swim out and around.

No, I was pushed relentlessly back into the coral. I was being badly cut up but there was no time to think much about that. Coral has ten thousand teeth and they were all biting me. From the waist down I was being scraped and scratched with each movement. I simply had to keep trying to swim away from the reef, and the breakers were not permitting me to do that.

Three times. Four times. And I realized that my life was in danger, that there was every chance I could die right there, against the coral reef. The water swirling around me, pounding me into the rock, said that it wanted my life. Therefore I needed help and should call for help.

I could not.

What? Don't know how to call for help? Here was another surprise. I had run up against an unrecognized quirk of my character. It appeared I had become so fiercely independent -- by the force of life circumstances -- that I had a kind of pride about being able to accomplish everything by myself. Because as a child, and despite every material advantage, I had not been helped as the inner me needed to be helped.

All this was racing through my mind with the speed of light as I wrestled with this incapacity to admit defeat, to call for help. Once I had faced this inner wall and recognized its fatal qualities, there came a kind of reluctant liberty. The life force rose to the occasion. I could now call for help.

And I did. There was a sailboarder about fifty yards away. He heard my cries and drew closer, staying well clear of the end of the reef, which was marked by one thumb of rock showing above the water.

"Swim out," he called, "I can't come any closer. I could be caught like you."

"I can't", I yelled back, "the sea won't let me."

"You have to."

He was right. I had to. And the sea was becoming less aggressive. In my youth on the beaches of Southern California my fellow body-surfers had talked about the "seventh wave", how the waves build up in size and force in a regular rhythm. The big one was said to be the seventh, then they decline for a while before building up again. I had been caught by a seventh wave. And now they were declining.

On the fifth or sixth try I was able to push off once again. My left foot went down into a hole seeking a point of support, and it went right into a bed of needles. Later I was told that I had stepped into a bunch of sea urchins, but at that time it was simply additional pain before I could finally launch myself.

The launch finally succeeded, I swam out, bleeding from hundreds of cuts and worried about attracting sharks, but I managed to swim the thirty-odd yards to the friendly sailboarder. I pulled myself onto the tail of his board and he sailed me to the beach.

Taking inventory was not a pretty job. From the waist down I was a mass of blood. None of the wounds seemed very deep but my legs were heavily lacerated. So was my lower abdomen and so were my hands.

The beach people had rallied around by then and they proposed to take me to the doctor. Yes, that seemed like an appropriate idea. I thanked my benefactor, whose name I never learned, and the wife of the couple who rented the boards drove me into the only town on the island, Gustavia.

She took me to the doctor, the only doctor. And this one was a young vacation replacement, it was late Saturday afternoon, and it was clear my appearance on his doorstep was a great inconvenience. He had obviously washed up and put on a fresh shirt and was ready to enjoy an evening on the town. Correction: on the village, for Gustavia is tiny.

I stood there in the vestibule of his clinic. bloody and sandy and still dripping salt water. He turned around me, looking at my battered body from a respectful, hands-off distance.

"You don't need sewing up," he said.

He turned to my escort. "Take her to the Sisters," he said. So much for the Hippocratic oath.

The beach lady drove me around to the infirmary run by some Catholic Sisters. The place was scrubbed clean, mopped down, dried up, tidy, and the white-clad nun who greeted us looked at me with disdain. She peered suspiciously at this tall, middle-aged woman in a blue bikini, with a towel over her shoulder, covered with blood and sand, dripping on her clean floor.

"Go have a hot shower with strong soap, and then use mercurochrome. That's all you need," she said. She didn't exactly slam the door in my face, but it was clear that, in her eyes I was an irrecuperable sinner for whom there was no place in the church.

"Take me back to my car," I asked the beach lady.

We drove back to the beach in silence. Before I got into my jeep her husband told me they'd found the board and the sail. My vehicle was still there. Nobody steals cars on little St. Bart, there's nowhere to go. This was an Australian product, called a "mini-Moke" and resembled an American wartime Jeep, completely open and topless. I drove back to our inn on the rocky promontory, the shifting of gears and the pushing of pedals painful for my lacerated palms and soles.

As I parked the Moke and started up the steps of the inn I realized that my appearance could be upsetting, possibly even disgusting, to others. My loving husband was one of those "tough but oh so gentle" types, an artistic outdoorsman, very considerate of others. He had a big, generous heart, especially toward me, and I did not relish shocking him. He was in the bar, which I had to pass en route to our room. He was certainly startled when he saw me but did not go into shock.

"What in the world happened to you?" he exclaimed, his brow wrinkling with concern, a hand reaching for mine.

I gave him the brief, one-paragraph explanation, watching those bushy white eyebrows arch higher and higher as he shook his head slowly.

"Let me get cleaned up," I pleaded. "I'll meet you here in a bit."

I brushed off the sand before entering our room, then stepped into the shower. Scrubbing with hot water and soap was very unpleasant. It hurt. Everything I did hurt. After the shower I painted my body with red mercurochrome, because that was the only disinfectant available. It stung, igniting a new layer of hurt. Then I pulled a loose cotton muumuu over my smarting body, put on some sandals, combed my hair, applied some lipstick,

In the bar I ordered a double whiskey, neat. Then I told Will in detail what had happened. We agreed that was the end of my career as a windsurfer.

"Try not to be so intrepid," he suggested kindly.

"I'm not intrepid!" I wailed.

It was time for another double whiskey, neat.

Then we went into the dining room, where I demolished a very large, pink beefsteak.

Then I went back to the room, fell into bed, and slept the sleep of the physically wiped-out.

***

In retrospect I can see that my husband's reaction was a model of restraint. No reproaches, no chipping away at me to be careful, don't do this, don't do that. He was a generation older than me and although a miracle of strength for his age, a real force of nature, he was — we soon discovered — teetering on the brink of delicate health. He depended totally on me to manage our complicated itinerary of wintertime island-hopping, and to lose me would have placed him not only in mourning but in a very vulnerable and complicated situation from a practical standpoint. I handled the reservations, paid the bills, organized the transport, supervised our substantial load of baggage, maintained our communications with family and sources of money. In February we could not foresee that in April I would bring him home to Switzerland in a wheelchair.

In this light his gentle admonition "try not to be so intrepid" could be thought of as a caress.

In any event, further intrepidity was out the window for the time being. My aching, smarting carcass would not allow me even to swim in the salty sea for more than a week. I continued to pilot the Moke up hill and down dale over the island, but for the next few days Will had to shift the gears because of the cuts in my right palm. This bizarre teamwork would have been dangerous on a metropolitan freeway, but on pokey little St. Bart' it gave us more chuckles than grumbles.

My left leg was swollen for several days and I limped for a couple of weeks. The big cuts on the left calf under the knee — which should indeed have been sewn up — healed more slowly than the rest. I still have those scars as a souvenir of misdirected ambition. I treated the rest of the hundreds of cuts and scrapes as one would a burn, with lots of creams and unguents prescribed by the doctor I finally saw when we hopped back to Guadeloupe. Slowly the lesser marks began to be absorbed into my substantial coat of Caribbean tan. Later that year a kind of a bubble scar above my umbilicus had to be excised by the dermatologist back home.

Sea urchins can be dangerous and those I stepped on with the left foot definitely injected me with some kind of poison. Three places on that sole turn red and itchy in our alpine winters when I spend too much time in furlined boots. More than twenty years afterward this effect seems to have diminished only slightly.

In the days following this disaster there was another matter weighing on my spirit, something more important than the gradual healing of my physical body.

"Why was I saved?" I asked.

Not believing in any kind of an anthropomorphic God, my mind sent this silent question out over the airwaves in general. It wasn't a matter for breakfast-table discussion; it was a major topic of inner debate. One could argue that I had saved myself, but deep inside that explanation didn't hold water. Inner toughness is not always sufficient when the force of the sea is beating a mere human to death.

Why was I saved? Intuition told me that I had fully deserved to die out there on the coral reef, clobbered between giant surf and ten thousand stone-animal teeth.

Spirit wanted desperately to know the answer to this existential puzzler. Several years of probing into matters of the afterlife, other dimensions, the many reincarnations of the human soul had sharpened my yen to understand what the churches shrank from discussing.

Thus, why was I saved?

And then, one day, the answer came as a kind of illumination.

"Because your work is not yet done."

Yes, I could see that.

There was no question but that I was fully engaged in shepherding an aging oak of a man toward his own mortality. This was a major responsibility and I took it seriously. It was informed and stimulated by conjugal love, but it went much beyond that. I wanted to have him with me as long as possible. And he counted on me. Also, there was a large loving family around us, literally dozens of people we enjoyed together, a family he had given me ready-made, who had welcomed me to their collective bosom, and I owed them much of my happiness. They counted on me too.

Yes, my work was not yet done.

It seemed a sensible answer, as far as I could define it. For the time being I had to leave it at that. Intrepidity was out the window.

Chapter Four

THE BLUE WHALE

My life changed dramatically. This did not happen overnight. There are some passages in life where priorities war among themselves.

Once back in Switzerland all my attention focused on restoring the normal pace of life. There was no time for ruminating on metaphysical questions, and there was a surplus of things to do.

Inner reflections on the implications of my narrow escape on the coral reef were not allowed to occupy much of my energies. Our life seemed to grow more and more complicated. The next long clump of months began its own, invisible snowball effect. Catalysis lay down the road, but the road had to be traversed and its destination was invisible.

We had been in the islands until mid-April of 1980, and our travel plans for the trip home had to be changed because my husband had a sudden health alert. The leisurely freighter was out, the air travel he detested was in, complete with wheelchairs in the airports. Ten days after our return he had another crisis, and his doctor diagnosed gallstones. This defined the new variable in our lives. It was a sneaky little tide which ebbed and flowed. We knew there was a crisis somewhere on or over the horizon. What no doctor could or would tell us was when.

Will still painted most days. In fact, most of the time he felt quite well and enterprising. So much so that we made little trips of two or three days, and at regular intervals we received visits of family, his and mine. Every once in a while there would be a little upset with its day of bed rest and its visit from the doctor

The pressure on me began to build up insidiously. My days and weeks were devoted first to coping, managing household and the large garden, trying to keep the income flowing and the expenses under close rein, keeping our daily life on an even keel. Reading before sleep was the only time I could devote to my search for more answers, ever more answers. Books were my principal resource.

In the search for respite from the sometimes harsh alpine winter we fell upon a new destination in the sun: southern Spain. After talking with friends who had been there in the winter, we chose to go to Marbella on the Costa del Sol, almost within sight of the great rock of Gibraltar.

It took us five days to get there by car, including time out while he recuperated from another mini-crisis in a luxurious casino-hotel near Valencia. That was the time I learned Spanish in a hurry.

After that worrying start, our winter under the Spanish sun grew into a delight. He painted, I played tennis three times a week, and we made a lot of little excursions. We made a few friends -- I met a lot of people at the tennis clubs -- and it was an agreeable life. Health problems remained beyond the horizon for the most part. Will had another minor upset but the local doctor was soothing and nothing came of it.

There was even a sharing of intellectual interests with some of my tennis friends — I'm thinking of Gloria and Ron — seasoned with a dash of mystical questioning. I could tell them about what had happened during the previous winter. Gloria passed along to me a little volume entitled *The Cycles of Heaven — cosmic forces and what they are doing to you*[1]. Responsive chords twanged all through my being, and we had one or two lively discussions about the astonishing smorgasbord of fringe science its authors had pulled together.

Guy Lyon Playfair and Scott Hill marshaled scientific evidence from numerous disciplines to demonstrate how environmental forces can affect humanity physically, emotionally and spiritually. The effect of sunspots and solar flares — which I knew to have had an important effect on the tumultuous financial markets of the preceding winter — was thoroughly outlined. Their interweaving of these energies with planetary movements intrigued me, for I could see the implications for the study of astrology as well as astronomy. There was a lot about electromagnetism, the weather, earthquakes, and human cycles of many kinds. Energy was an underlying theme.

All these concepts began reverberating through my being in ways that this little summary above cannot more than suggest. At home later in that year of 1981 I ordered ten copies of the book, then four more, all of which I distributed to friends on both sides of the Atlantic. *The Cycles of Heaven* struck me at that time as one of the most important dissertations I had ever read. I needed to share it.

There was not a lot of time for such considerations as Will's simmering malady began asserting itself. He was ill for a couple of days in July, and his doctor came twice. He was ill again in late August, and this time there was talk of an operation to resolve the problem once and for all. Will, as usual, did not want to hear of anything like that. As long as he could get back on his feet in a day or two.....

Stress began to pyramid during those months as I recognized it was also becoming imperative to visit my mother in California. Not only did she need some physical help but there was urgent family business to deal with. And would it not be lovely to see something of my daughter and my son, then respectively 31 and 29?

"I consider this trip to be urgent, given Mother's age and collection of infirmities, but I am even more bound to take care of Willy first," is how I expressed the dilemma in a letter to David, a favorite cousin.

Part of the uncertainty lay in the matter of who would be at Will's side, taking charge of the household and simply "being there." Over the years I had called upon an astonishing array of ladies to perform this function: friends of his, friends of mine, a niece, a granddaughter, his daughter in South Africa — it was frequently complicated and more than once these trips had to be postponed and repostponed until the chips fell into place.

On this occasion the blockage suddenly resolved itself with a sequence of three companions for him: two elderly widows and his sister, equally elderly. With this rickety support net in place, and with Will in seemingly stable condition, feeling energetic and positive, I zoomed off to California for four weeks.

That month of September was utterly mad, but everything got done. The legal business and the family visits, and two trips between Los Angeles and San Francisco, one of them by air and the other by motorcar.

Mother longed to visit a niece and a nephew, who happened to be my two favorite cousins. At 83 and with a bad back, an uncertain heart, and the beginning of cataracts in the eyes, there was no possibility of her making such a trip alone. We did it together, with me at the wheel of her ageing car, and it was a great success. She loved it all, was invigorated by the whole thing, and I had the satisfaction of knowing that I had fulfilled an important mission.

October was only marginally more leisurely. Will's health had held up in my absence but he now accepted there should be surgery. My next letter to David, after our visit to him, outlined what lay ahead:

"Willy will enter hospital Monday, October 26, unfed and therefore surly. Extraction of an offensive gallbladder is projected for the 28th. We plan to leave for Spain in mid-December."

His surgeon, who had operated on his stomach ulcers twenty years earlier, did the job as scheduled. That was the easy part. Recovery from that particular operation has a bad reputation, and in light of what we endured in the following weeks that reputation is accurate.

But it wasn't just his physical recuperation which was difficult. In addition to helping him through that, I found myself confronted with a shocking event: we were robbed at home. Specifically, a large diamond solitaire ring, an heirloom that Will's mother had worn, disappeared from my bedroom one day while I was visiting him at the hospital in Lausanne.

The previous day a telephone company technician had appeared at the door, just as I was preparing to make the daily trip to the hospital.

"We've come to change your telephone system," he announced.

It was true that we had, much earlier, ordered a major transformation of the system in the chalet. We had too many telephones, a switching-center box, and a cumbersome ringing sequence. All this had to be transformed and simplified. And here they were to do it, without warning.

"You cannot work here today," I told him bluntly "You haven't made a date with me for this work, and I have no one to be here in my absence."

With considerable grumpiness, the technician agreed to bring back his crew the next day. And I had to organize someone to house-sit while I made the daily trip to Lausanne. One more distraction in life was not really welcome, but it had to be accepted.

Thus four men came the next day. I had my cleaning lady on duty in the house for the whole day, to keep an eye on things. Three men worked in the house, upstairs and down, all the doors were open, and the fourth man, the driver, was in and out carrying supplies for his comrades.

When I got home that afternoon Will's masseuse was waiting. We had agreed she would do me instead of him, for I was becoming very tense and tied in knots. Loosening up the carcass with massage might just loosen up the mental-emotional kinks. I went upstairs to undress. And then I saw the gaping empty spot in the jewel box.

What do you do in such a circumstance? I talked first to the house-sitter, the telephone foreman, and the masseuse. Then I called the police.

Their investigation was cursory, dragged on, and proved to be totally ineffective. Their attitude was that the telephone people, having been hand-picked, could not fall under suspicion. They concentrated on my housekeeper and the masseuse, two ladies of impeccable character I had known for years. Weeks later I was invited to read and sign the file created by the district attorney, to which I appended a blistering handwritten criticism of what I considered sloppy and inadequate police work.

After several months the insurance company paid off. The matter was legally settled, but its unsettling aspects lingered much longer.

Will recovered and I brought him home.

"Hospital food nearly did him in," I wrote to my daughter. "It was so grim he thought he had been sent back to the Swiss Army equivalent of boot camp. The surgeon said Will was the only patient he had who was on a hunger strike."

Having sampled some of his leavings I understood completely. Here at home he began eating regularly and happily, in small quantities. He'd lost ten per cent of his body weight and ninety per cent of his vitality.

There was a lot of post-op care, and I was grateful for the daily visits of the visiting nurse, who took care of things like drains and bandages.

"It's hard having an invalid at home, but it's easier on me than going daily to Lausanne," I told Carol. I had put two thousand kilometers on the car in fifteen days.

And all this was beginning to tell on me.

"Last Friday afternoon I reached a peak of stress reaction," I wrote to her on November, 13, "with incipient chest pressure and rising blood pressure. Shades of newspapering days!"

At that time he had been home four days and it was beginning to look as if life would smooth out. Wrong again!

A loud crash awoke me at three o'clock the next morning. He had fainted while going to the toilet. In spite of his weight loss he was still too heavy for me and I could not lift him. But he regained consciousness and was able to help himself sufficiently that we got him on his feet and back to bed.

Two hours later it happened again. I found him lying on the bathroom floor in a pool of blood. Untrained medically, I still knew a hemorrhage when I saw one.

The next quarter-hour on the telephone was one of the most frustrating I have ever passed. Two of our three doctors were taking low-season vacations, which lots of people in this tourist-oriented community do. The third doctor was ostensibly on duty, holding down the fort, but in fact it appeared he had gone off to a folk-music festival. I left a message. He was on the verge of retiring, I learned later, and his replacement was already in residence but few people knew of his existence.

The visiting nurse came rapidly and confirmed the gravity of the situation. And the two of us could not lift my husband.

At my wit's end, I called the Gendarmerie. In short order two strapping policemen, in full uniform for the occasion despite the predawn darkness, picked Will up off the tile floors and carried him to his bed. One of them was the sergeant in charge of the robbery investigation, but this was not the moment to begin yammering about that. They asked if they should call an ambulance and I agreed with alacrity.

As they were leaving, and shortly before the ambulance arrived, along came the new young doctor. There was now nothing for him to do and we had a brief, amiable chat. Then the ambulance arrived. I raced down the mountain behind it.

At the hospital in Aigle an alert young doctor, in his first year of residency and alone on duty this Saturday morning, saved my husband's life with numerous pints of blood.

I stayed with him for quite a while, drove the quarter-hour back up the mountain to be home for a few hours, then went down again for another visit. He was holding his own; it looked all right.

Home again, like a yo-yo on that mountain road, it was time to do some major telephoning around the family, starting with my stepsons. My composure remained superficially intact, but distress was eating me around the edges. I grabbed several handfuls of nuts and then, totally uncharacteristically, I took a bottle of aquavit, Danish schnapps, out of the cellar refrigerator. I've never been much of a drinker, but there needed to be some kind of reinforcement — however false a friend alcohol really is — before I began dialing those numbers and passing around the crisis news.

At six-thirty the next morning the hospital was able to report Will had passed a quiet night and seemed a little stronger. I seized the opportunity to move slowly for a few hours before going down the mountain late in the morning.

Yes, he was resting comfortably, had some color, was able to appreciate and discuss his narrow escape. I lunched alone in our favorite restaurant. Friends who lived nearby gave me some hospitality, a place to sit and relax for an hour. And the fall colors were becoming glorious, inspiring a few moments of photography. Back to the hospital for another visit. He seemed to be all right although understandably tired, with which I could both sympathize and empathize. I was worn out and did not linger at his side. My vision of the immediate future involved bed and a good book to cool the spirit for sleep.

Banking matters grabbed me that Monday morning before I had finished my late breakfast. There were urgent decisions to be taken, and I had to spend time on them before leaving once again for Aigle.

All was not well down there. Will had begun to bleed internally again. The medical chief was very concerned. They would have to operate again. There appeared to be a stress ulcer which had to be staunched in one way or another.

"You can surely do this here?" I asked.

"Yes, we have a competent surgeon available," the boss doctor said.

"All right, let's do it here," I agreed. "I don't want him taken back to Lausanne. He doesn't want to go through that again,"

Will had made that clear to me.

"Let's keep it simple and get it over with," I insisted.

Heads nodded. It would take a little while to arrange matters, but it was doable.

"I'll go home for lunch while you make the necessary arrangements," I said. "Then I'll call you to find out when you are going to do it."

Simple, trusting me!

When I telephoned they told me he'd been taken to Lausanne in an ambulance. I blew my top, was furious, demanded to talk to the head doctor. He told me they had felt that Dr. S., Will's "habitual" surgeon, knew his stomach better, having been there twice already. And that Dr. S. had agreed to take care of him.

Thus, in white heat, boiling mad, I packed an overnight bag. The sense of betrayal was raging within me. Before leaving the house I called Colette to see if I could sleep there. Yes, of course.

That I got to the cantonal hospital without an accident was a miracle. That I did not attack the structure with a pickaxe is another miracle, because when I got to Dr. S's service and demanded to see him, they told me he wasn't there. A certain level of embarrassment seemed to reign among the ladies in that office.

"He's just left on vacation," they told me.

"Then who in the hell is going to operate on my husband?" I roared.

"Dr. B. He's waiting to talk to you."

Dr. B. was also embarrassed. And worried. He was the senior surgical assistant in this service, he was greying at the temples, apparently of Algerian origin, and he had a very kind and gentle manner. It was clear he understood that his boss, in handing off to him, had left him with a prickly doctor-patient relationship.

But his worry was mostly medical.

"I'm afraid of this case," he confessed. "Tell me about your husband. After all, he's eighty-seven years old!"

Suddenly it was up to me to reassure this surgeon, who I hadn't wanted, in a hospital I had not wanted!

"My man is like an oak tree," I said. "He's constitutionally very strong. If anyone can get through this ordeal, he can."

Thus it went ahead. They gave me telephone numbers to call during the evening in the intensive care recovery room, where he would pass the night. And I gave them Colette's number.

Colette and Jean-Jacques were old friends and they gave me a comfortable haven in their home high on a hill just outside Lausanne. From there, swaddled in friendly solicitude, I was able to keep in contact with the hospital through the evening until it was clear that Will was surviving. That news made it possible to eat and drink with progressive relaxation and then to pass a restful night.

The next morning I was at Will's bedside at eight o'clock. It looked all right, but he was terribly weak. Of course. After six hours of vigil I went downtown for a decent meal, and after that I went across the square to the main Post Office and telephoned my stepson René.

He lived in Maine but he arrived in Switzerland the next day, and he stayed a week. His presence was of inestimable support.

From this point the pressure began to ease off, but life remained complicated. Worse for my husband than for me. His recovery was slow but steady.

It was, however, my painful duty to contact the Belgian owners of the apartment we had agreed to rent in the Spanish sun.

"There is no question of us traveling to Spain this winter," I told Madame on the telephone. "My husband is too weak to travel and we don't dare be so far from his doctors." All quite true, without dwelling on how much we had looked forward to it.

Eleven days after surgery I was able to move him to Valmont, a clinic and rest home high above the lake at Montreux. This served as a "halfway house" between hospital and home. He began to be up on his feet a bit, dressed for the day, eating in a dining room, and having some light physical therapy. Valmont was neither as high nor as cold as up home.

It was easier for me too. Travel time was only half as much, and this was important because the snows began in earnest and driving daily to Lausanne would have become ever more difficult. It was possible to visit him daily for lunch, see to his comfort, make sure of his reading material.

At the end of two more weeks I brought him home, to our mutual joy. It was December 11 and snowing nearly every day; the roads were becoming treacherous. Four-wheel drive passenger cars were not yet a commonplace as they are now. I had had to wrestle with the tire chains more than once. There was also snow to clear at irregular intervals. Will had done this, using an old hand-guided snow blower. Now I took up this chore, a heavy job because the machine was creaky, broke down often, was clumsy to maneuver and hard to start. But I did it.

Bit by bit life returned to something approaching normal. At Christmas his other son, Allan, came to share with us his bubbling nature and inexhaustible supply of jokes. Not only that, but the South African grandson Peter came with his family. Thus the yearend holidays were gay and animated, and we both benefited hugely from the infectious good nature that surrounded us. And they were all gone again a few days into the New Year.

We turned the corner into 1982 with him definitely, but slowly, on the upgrade. He tried to resume some activities too soon. Thus the first time he tried to lunch with his club he had to leave before the meal was served. The second time he almost fainted on the sidewalk afterward, had spots in his eyes for an hour, and rested in the car while I completed the necessary shopping. The third time he was so tired I brought him home immediately and had to come down another day for the shopping. The fourth time it finally worked all the way.

Meanwhile, I began to have my own problems. That I felt overtired seems reasonable, almost an understatement. I became very nervous and could not concentrate on our business affairs. There was not just the daily supervision but there were also some structural problems that needed a creative solution. And I was simply not up to it.

My ancient stomach ulcers, quiescent for a long time, flamed into activity, provoking a whole chain of other reactions throughout the system. And my blood pressure, usually on the low side, soared.

All this was obviously a kind of psychosomatic reaction to months of strain and stress, one little catastrophe building on another. I had met each situation with calm and self-control, only blowing up once (at doctors, of course). And now the calm and the self-control had evaporated. The reasons for stress were disappearing, but the after-effects now began to manifest. I had tons of mental work to do, and my brain wanted out.

The doctor gave me Tagamets for the ulcers and did some cultures to unmask the bacteria that were bugging me. Physical remedies were thus placed on the rails, but the medical art (I refuse to call it a science) tends to neglect the emotional-psychological components.

Early in the year I had resumed contact with Marina, a friend and former professional colleague in New York. We had failed to connect during the winter in the Caribbean, when her flights had been cancelled and her baggage stolen, never to return. Now we exchanged letters and had a long telephone chat. It became quickly apparent that she'd been going through a series of personal crises of her own and thought she had found a solution.

Marina proposed that I try Transcendental Meditation. She felt she had been helped by this mystical practice taught by the Maharishi Mahesh Yogi.

"Over the summer I took an advanced course in TM which makes me a Siddha," she explained. "It has an effect upon my life which is one of harmonizing and bringing together disparate parts of myself. One sees more clearly, but of course it is not a panacea."

"Be forewarned that I am predisposed against maharishis," I replied. We had a step-grandson who had squandered his youth at the feet of one of these charismatic characters. "It seems to have made him a confirmed ski bum who now cleans houses in winter resorts in order to feed himself," I added.

Marina persisted gently, declaring that "the results on my own life within the last year since I began this practice are integrative, bringing calm, assurance, and good vibes around me."

She suggested a handful of books, among which were "*The Cycles of Heaven*" and another one by my old friend Ruth Montgomery. And I declined to read two others written by the Maharishi Mahesh Yogi. That left two titles on her list which she offered to send immediately. I accepted, with gratitude for her generosity and willingness to be of help.

All this talk about meditation set me to wondering. Might this be something I would want to do? But then, wasn't it, after all, rather crazy to sit and try to commune with another dimension? Just a little bit silly? Yet there was the testimony of Marina, verifying that it had been of benefit in her life. And from our few times together in New York I knew her to be thoroughly professional, well-focused, and hard-headed when it came to judging people and their actions.

Somewhere in my reading I had learned that one way to meditate was to concentrate on an object. I decided to do this. With some hesitation.

It took me a couple of days to work through this hesitation, this balkiness at a plunge into the unknown. Then, finally, one gloomy afternoon in mid-March of 1982, I overcame this hesitation --- these fears? --- and took the plunge.

In the crowded room which served as my library and office I pulled the curtains together, closed the door, and placed Beethoven piano sonatas on the turntable at soft volume. There was just enough room for me to sit on the carpet with my back to a bookcase.

My hips would not even then permit getting into the famous lotus position, but I managed to fold my legs into something approximating it. Not too uncomfortably.

Then I took a few deep breaths and began to study my little blue whale, made of deep blue glass, almost indigo. This jaunty little creature was the gift of a dear friend, and he seemed to be smiling. He sat neatly on my palm, flipping his tail skyward.

I studied him intently before setting him on the floor and then closed my eyes. My idea was to meditate on an object, a mandala, and my blue whale was the mandala. Concentrating hard on what I had seen before closing my eyes, I began to view the whale in my mind's eye.

It turned out to be much easier than I had imagined. It was startling to discover rather quickly that I could hold the Blue Whale in the center of the mental eye. I turned and rotated him through every conceivable axis, always maintaining an accurate perspective. I could see him perfectly from any angle. This fact boggled me, when I thought about it later.

I continued this exercise for about a quarter-hour, and there was little trouble holding the concentration. All the while he was on the floor, next to my thigh, and my vision of him was directly in front of my forehead. The image appeared to be perfectly faithful to his shape and proportions, no matter how I turned and twisted him.

And then there was a knock on the door and the spell was broken. It was not easy for me to have total peace for any length of time, what with my husband's needs and the frequent interjections of a very loquacious cleaning lady.

Nevertheless, I had meditated. I was impressed.

I had broken that invisible barrier and entered a new dimension. Not once had I felt that self-consciousness which had been a stumbling block. Not once had I felt that I was doing something silly. I understood better what Marina had been trying to pull me into.

From that moment I knew that meditation would become part of my life.

[1]   Guy Lyon Playfair and Scott Hill, *The Cycles OF Heaven, Cosmic forces and what they are doing to you.* London: Souvenir Press, 1978. 368p., references, index. ISBN 0 285 623354.

Chapter Five

EXPLORING

That first meditation impressed me deeply. It had been absorbing, instructive, eye-opening. It had broken the ice. However, I was not tempted to repeat the experience. One meditation did not an addiction make.

Books were on their way from Marina, I knew, and I was content to wait for the instruction they might bring. And there were other new things happening in my life. I was determined to shake up the routine, recover a measure of my old tranquillity and --- why not? --- open new personal horizons.

Over the years I lunched occasionally with Nini while our husbands were at their Thursday club meetings. I counted her as my first friend in Switzerland, and in the latter part of 1981 I confided to her my desire to find some kind of a social context which would expand on the rather limited possibilities I was finding up in our mountain village.

"Why don't you join our Soroptimist Club?" she proposed. She went on to explain that she was going to be the next president of the club in Vevey, and that she could easily invite me. Soroptimists, it appeared, were business and professional women who met regularly to pursue a double-barreled program of performing benevolent, philanthropic services in the community and of inviting speakers who could broaden their minds. And in the process of working together they expanded their mutual friendships and so enhanced their lives. I liked the sound of it. It appeared that my professional career in journalism, libraries and financial management, the latter still going on, provided more than adequate qualifications for becoming a Soroptimist.

In December I attended my first meeting, to test the waters, and in January I became a member. At that meeting I was asked to give a talk about myself and my life. I held the floor for three-quarters of an hour, explaining the migrations that led a California girl to become a Swiss housewife. They loved it, applauded warmly, complimented me on my French, and made me feel right at home in their group of diversified personalities and vocations.

The process of writing this little discourse, essentially autobiographical, helped me put my life into perspective, to see where I'd been, what I'd done. What I did not tell them was the inner puzzle I was working to solve.

Soon it became apparent that this new affiliation was bringing me more than I had expected. There were some stimulating serendipities. I had not yet caught on that there are no coincidences in this life.

Nini, who had been a teacher, was now an astrologer. Another new member was Agnès, a reflexologist with a deep metaphysical bent. And I found myself sitting next to Blanche, who had founded a research institute in a new science called geobiology.

Intrigued, I asked Blanche to explain just exactly what was involved in that discipline. She began by explaining that there were energies running over and through the earth. They had form and structure in the patterns they made across the landscape. Their interaction with each other and with such phenomena as underground water could affect human health.

"There is a gridwork of magnetic energy covering the Earth," she explained. "There are north-south lines and east-west lines, and there are diagonal systems of energy — all interacting."

"How does one know all this?" I asked.

"This is a kind of *radiesthésie*," she said. "We use a kind of antenna held in the hands."

Bells began to clang in my head. This information made a curious echo in my soul, as if some knowledge I had once had was suddenly rising to the surface. "Radiesthésie" translates in English as "dowsing", in other words, the kind of thing done by "water witches" who used a forked stick to discover where to dig a well. I was avid to know more, at the same time instantly knowing that somewhere in the shadowy past I had known more.

"This network forms a vast invisible whole, like a precisely-woven net spread over the entire surface of the globe," Blanche went on. "This gridwork, when its crossing-points are afflicted, can have great importance for the health of a human being."

Blanche had my full attention, but the evening's program interrupted. I was jittery with impatience to know more about this subject which had suddenly tweaked my neurons. However, it was necessary to wait for the publication of her book to learn more of this subject which struck home so deeply[1].

During this period I was also shopping for a personal computer, going to the trade shows, reading the technical magazines, talking to anyone and everyone who might contribute to my knowledge.

"There are times I desperately need a secretary," I told my daughter. "but I can't afford one and have no space for her to work. So I'm looking for the right machine to become my 'elecretary'."

Finding my 'elecretary' was taking a long time, and in the meantime two books arrived from America.

Marina's package contained *Joy's Way*[2], by a young medical doctor named W. Brugh Joy, and a rather technical-looking book on transcendental meditation entitled *TM; discovering inner energy and overcoming stress*[3], by a team of four authors, one of them a doctor.

These books arrived two weeks after my first experiment with meditation, and I plunged into them eagerly.

Brugh Joy's development seemed a bit slow and heavy to start with, so I switched to Dr. Bloomfield and his team. This was rather interesting here and there, relating the various physical benefits of Transcendental Meditation as taught by the Maharishi Mahesh Yogi and his army of teachers.

It appeared there were dramatic effects on respiration, oxygen consumption, the heart rate, and the metabolism in general. Biochemical and brain wave changes were noted.

All this was reasonably interesting, but it did not tell me how to meditate. For that you had to find a TM center and be trained in the technique. This did not appeal to me, for I felt allergic to getting involved with spiritual organizations or anything "New Age-y".

I went back to Joy's book and began plowing into it. He was a young medical doctor who had discovered healing sensitivities in his hands. He could feel certain unmapped energy centers called "*chakras*", a Sanskrit word which is now so commonly used in the metaphysical world that it is no longer foreign. He had already quite a metaphysical education from his mother, all of which became walled away when he studied medicine and then practiced that art. Ultimately he felt deeply impelled to abandon his medical practice in order to explore the mystical side of life.

Halfway into the book he unveiled some meditational techniques to reward my patience. *Joy's Way* became my preferred bedtime reading, and one Sunday morning in mid-April — having read him late the night before, I decided to try some of his suggestions.

I propped myself up in bed with an extra pillow for the back, wrapped myself warmly in a cozy bathrobe, closed my bedroom door but left the window open, switched off the lamp, and began to convert myself into melted butter.

It's a rather effective relaxation technique, becoming melted butter. You start by imagining yourself to be a block of butter fresh out of the refrigerator. Then you melt yourself. You can learn to do it much faster than it would happen in a warm kitchen.

When I thought I had just about become a blob on the saucer, then I went to work pinning golden numbers on a black curtain. This was another of Joy's techniques, learned from his own teacher Eunice Hurt, and it isn't easy.

In your mind you create a pile of large cards numbered consecutively from one to one hundred. One at a time you pick up these large golden numbers, sharp and clear, and you pin them to the black curtain. With your eyes closed, of course. You hold the golden image, sharp and clear, wobble-free, for at least five seconds, and then you put down that card and pick up another.

I added an extra wrinkle to this program. I had been studying a book entitled *Drawing on the Right Side of the Brain, how to unlock your hidden artistic talent4*. Having already dabbled quite a bit in painting and drawing, now married to a fulltime working artist, sometimes badgering him into giving me a little help in this domain, I was intrigued by anything that could help improve my extremely modest skills. And the author of this book, Betty Edwards, applied scientific principles derived from study of the human brain to the fostering of creativity. Focusing closely on the contrasting functions of the two cerebral hemispheres, she taught how to use the nonverbal, intuitive, global functions of the right hemisphere to learn how to draw images better.

Working with Edwards' ideas, I had already worked a bit at comparing and shifting images from one hemisphere to the other. Thus it came naturally to mind that applying these principles to the posting of numbers might be a clever idea.

In the meditation, after becoming a pool of butter, I picked up each card and sought first to make the image sharp in my mind's eye. When I discovered the figures weren't as distinct as I wanted them, I moved the number card from dead-center to the right side, and then shifted them back and forth, left and right, between the hemispheres of the brain. Of course, this was not a pure rendering of the technique as Joy had explained it. Because of this extra work I was conscious of exceeding the standard count of five for holding the image.

And something exceptional happened.

I had started melting myself down at six-fifteen in the morning. Before six-thirty I began posting the numbers and thought I would simply do that for about fifteen minutes, then read some more before rising for the day.

After posting, moving, fixing clearly, and then putting down five numbers, I was getting tired and decided to see how long I had been working.

The bedside clock read twelve minutes past seven o'clock.

What?

Where had I been? How was it possible that working with only five numbers could have taken three-quarters of an hour?

This was my introduction to what I began to call "time warp" in meditation. I had been there, not here, but where was there?

Wherever "there" might be did not really matter. This thing called meditation had me thoroughly hooked. Curiosity had led me up to a frontier, and my blue whale had swum me over it. Most people, it seems to me, fear crossing this frontier — I suspect they fear losing control of their sanity, or is it life itself that seems threatened? With the curiosity of a natural-born explorer, I had to know more. Meditation did not yet become a daily habit, but I went on with sampling the techniques Brugh Joy had described.

In the middle of the ensuing week I meditated again — my notes do not tell me what I did — and the next Sunday evening I consumed a big, ambitious menu of inner goodies.

Joy had described a type of breath control which made a good preamble to meditation, so I opened by doing a lot of that. A cycle of controlled breaths begins by inhaling slowly through the nose until your lungs are fully expanded. Then you hold your breath while counting to seven. Exhaling is done equally slowly, with the tongue raised toward the palate so as to produce a hissing sound. The idea is to expel the last bit of air by squeezing from the abdomen up. You repeat this routine ten times to complete the cycle.

I did this enthusiastically before beginning the meditation proper. Once again I melted myself into a pool of liquid butter, then I undertook what Joy calls a spiral meditation.

This involves the chakras, a series of energy centers in the human body which seem to have been defined in Hindu philosophy thousands of years ago. In Sanskrit chakra means wheel, and in metaphysics it describes the spiraling action of subtle energy centers or fields in the human body. Western science has trouble with the concept, for the chakras — like the acupuncture meridians — cannot be found in the autopsy of a human cadaver. In terms of western anatomical science, the chakras cannot exist. However, it becomes clear in spiritual practice that the chakras do indeed exist and play a powerful role in regulating human energies as they spin.

The seven major chakras lie along the spiral column, starting with the root chakra between the pubis and the coccyx. From bottom to top, the majors are found in the lower abdomen, the solar plexus, the heart, the throat, a point just above and between the eyebrows, and the crown of the head. There are dozens of minor chakras; Joy claims to have identified forty. In his spiral meditation he works with these seven major chakras plus the mid chest, spleen, palms, elbows, shoulders, knees, feet and a point above the head which he calls the transpersonal point.

Thus, from my buttery state, I began to visit these chakras in a spiral unwinding from the heart. It proved to be hard to reach the top without losing concentration somewhere along the line. And I "lost time" somewhere up there between the crown chakra and the transpersonal point. *That* again.

After coming down from this exercise I was still "up" for more, so I posted a few numbers and then simply contemplated those chakras for a bit.

There was suddenly the sensation of a pretzel untying itself, moving up through my neck, chin and causing my lips to wriggle snake-like and involuntarily.

Another little snake simply turned and twisted a little bit in my body, and then my fingers began to tingle.

Instinctively I understood these phenomena to be expressions of my inner stress unwinding. It hadn't occurred to me that perhaps I was pushing it a little, plunging ahead rather recklessly.

This realization crept in during the following week. Here's how I summed it up in a letter to Marina:

"I did breathing exercises so enthusiastically eight days ago that I got a spasm near the left lung, well to the left, even in the ribs perhaps, which moved back to the center and has been slow to recede. The spasm did not arrive immediately but the following day, and I can't imagine any other cause. Strange, because I'm very strong in the lungs. Felt something wiggle during meditation."

Not in any way discouraged, I resumed my ad hoc explorations within a few days. On Friday of that week I did more breath control and melted my brick of butter. Two days later I began daily meditation, sometimes twice daily. In these sessions I began the repetition of a mantra of my own invention, a one-word sound with onomatopoetic effect in the mind.

"Strong tingling sensations began developing in my hands and fingers when I meditate," I told Marina. "I am able to sense the forehead chakra but really can't isolate the others."

By this time I was looking for a teacher, a "guru", who could help me thread through this fascinating inner world. With lessening reluctance, I had written to a TM office I'd found in the telephone book. It was my hope they would have a facility closer to my location. And there was.

They informed me that there was an "academy" over in the village of Nextmountain on a sunny, treeless range north of here. I telephoned for an appointment.

A charming young woman, all smiles and serenity, met me at the door. I shall call her Nora, because that is not her name. We sat in a sunny veranda while she explained what TM was all about.

"Maharishi teaches us that anyone who can think can meditate," she told me. "It should be gentle and easy. It should be effortless."

I knew already that TM involved the use of a mantra, a word or phrase which is repeated over and over again. This is a device to quiet the mind. Nora pointed out that the verbalization of the mantra gradually fades into a kind of passive awareness of its presence, which keeps the mind occupied in a way which it finds charming. I was to discover that this word "charming" came up frequently in writings about the method, Maharishi's point being that the mind has to be charmed into not wandering.

Nora explained that this process of turning gently inward, without forcing, would lead into a level of deep rest. This would be more beneficial to the body than sleep in terms of dissolving the accumulated stress which had led me this far. This seemed to echo the Bloomfield book.

It was obvious that this method of meditation would be quite different in style from the exercises Joy's writings had inspired me to pursue. There was a moment of hesitation while I reflected on this contrast, for I had been enjoying these new adventures.

Then the explorer's curiosity got the better of me once again. I made a date with Nora for my initiation into Transcendental Meditation two days later, because I was too impatient to wait for the next group initiation about a month hence. She instructed me to bring a few pieces of fresh fruit, some flowers, and a clean white handkerchief to be used in the ceremony. To learn TM would cost me three hundred francs (somewhere near one hundred dollars at the time), which seemed reasonable.

On Sunday afternoon, May 9, I sat with Nora in a little nook with a small altar around which my fruit, flowers, and handkerchief were disposed. Incense informed the air. She instructed me to close my eyes while she went into meditation, then began to sing a little song in Sanskrit. After a bit I was aware that her chant was in fact the constant repetition of a polysyllabic word which had a Sanskrit ring to it.

I glanced at her with one eye, she returned it significantly and I understood she was bringing in my new mantra, and I was supposed to start pronouncing it. Which I did, keeping my eyes closed and meditating. It seemed as if I was looking into a black box or a dark cavern. I don't know how long we kept this up, perhaps ten minutes. There was a kind of heaviness in my brain.

Afterward I realized there was also a kind of cosmic ringing in my ears, especially the left ear. It has never gone away. That is to say, this tinnitus — for that is the medical name — is still with me more than twenty-five years later. I have grown accustomed to it, but for quite a long time I sought an explanation for why I had it. No one could or would tell me. The TM people told me that it was nothing important and that it would go away. Not true.

This was not the only new phenomenon in my life. Meditation with the Maharishi's technique brought me a wide variety of sounds, sights and sensations.

The next morning after the initiation I went right to work with the new technique. Once again I seemed to be in a kind of space resembling a dark box or a cavern, murky, obscure, a kind of lake in the cavern into which I floated gently toward the bottom. Toward it, but never all the way there. Intruding thought skeins blocked my descent, as I lost and regained the mantra.

Again there was that fatigue in the same region of the brain as the previous day: center right, in what I thought might be the upper part of the limbic zone. And the ringing in my ears was always there, from the moment of awakening.

I was simultaneously relaxed but heavy. A little spasm erupted in my chin and wiggled up to the mouth. And then another one. And still another, reaching my upper lip.

"My body seemed to be made of a kind of leaden jelly," I wrote in a little note for Nora. I was without strength after this meditation and went back to bed. My body was very tired but I was happy. After a quarter hour of rest everything was fine and I rose to meet the day.

"It is difficult for me to describe the little waves, the near-heaviness, the sense of pins and needles crawling over my skin," I told her in that note. "The brain fatigue disappeared with that little rest, and I feel very happy, full of smiles. The recent grouchiness is gone, I find myself to be gentle and kindly."

Throughout that morning my body seemed to be gently radiating something, to the point where my work was less efficient than usual.

After initiation into TM there is a phase of "checking", in which teacher and student meditate together, the former making sure that the latter is doing it correctly. For this purpose I went back to sit with Nora for ten minutes the next two afternoons.

Meditation was giving me headaches those first few days of TM.

"I am not a headache person, being rarely afflicted," I wrote to Marina, "but I have had more headaches in the last week than in a normal six months."

Gradually, however, this phase passed, and other things began happening. On the third afternoon after the initiation I played tennis with Barbara, my usual adversary.

"This is my fiftieth summer of tennis," I told Marina, "so you will understand it is significant when I say I have never had such concentration."

Barbara noticed that right away.

"What is it with you today?" she called across the court.

What it was, was that I seemed to know in advance where her balls were going to bounce on my side of the net. What was really happening was that my concentration was so sharp that I detected its trajectory almost from the instant it left her racket.

We had always played fairly evenly, which made for good sport. Neither one of us could count on defeating the other. Now that began to change. That day I demolished Barbara. I was always where I needed to be in plenty of time to hit killing shots, and the points she won came from my infrequent errors.

From then on the pattern of our friendly rivalry changed. Mostly I began to win rather easily, but this seemed to depend on how good my meditation had been.

Change was steady in meditation, in a kind of ascending zigzag pattern. On the sixth day there was a clear sense of evolution. The mantra seemed to return more spontaneously, and the brain hemispheres began swapping places. The right lobe, clear and light, swapped position with the fuzzy left lobe. Then they returned to the original order with a lightning-like flash and crack across the connecting cables (the corpus callosum). And I was absent for a tiny bit, knowing this only after coming back. Another time warp.

"Is this the beginning of transcendance?" I asked myself, not really knowing how to recognize that state if it arrived.

My sister-in-law Elise came over from Grindelwald that weekend for my husband's birthday, which we celebrated with a fine luncheon on the lakeshore at Montreux. Late that Sunday afternoon Elise and I took a digestive stroll up the ravine, enjoying the spring greens illuminating the trees, listening to the burbling of the stream in the bottom of the canyon.

As we turned around and started back down toward home my brain began to move, as if asking to meditate. We sat on a bench to admire the colors and let the percussion of the rushing waters rumble strongly in our ears. As soon as we were at home I excused myself and went up to be alone with the inner me.

It was lovely, all somersaults and waves and swellings like trampolines in slow motion. It was easier following the stray thoughts out, easier following the mantra back in. My head was less heavy afterward, with no headache, and I felt refreshed and energetic.

And my concentration was intense, acute. I prepared the evening meal as if inspired, preparing three different menus for we three different people in twenty minutes. While cooking my thoughts turned to our cousin Jim across the mountains in Chateau d'Oex. Five minutes later he telephoned. That little psychic "hit" got my attention.

From the beginning I kept a journal of my meditative experiences, just a few lines to follow the evolution. This habit has proved invaluable, enabling me to reconstruct the story so many years later.

Gradually my practice of meditation settled into a comfortable routine. I was able to organize life to respect the twice-a-day schedule. Mostly it was steady, quiet diving with the mantra, losing it to a thought, allowing that to flow gently back to the mantra, this cycle repeating itself over and over again for the twenty minutes or more of each session.

In those early days I was troubled by noise: the traffic on the highway fifty yards from the house, a door slamming, voices, the sound of the grass-cutter in the garden, ordinary household commotion. Later it became possible to meditate in noisy environments like trains and buses and waiting rooms, but at first everything disturbed me.

"Phenomena" crept in from time to time, an intriguing diversity of sensations and happenings.

For example, I seemed to be simply puttering along for the next three days after the lovely inner excursion inspired by the stream in the ravine. Then a late-day meditation, going smoothly despite outside noises, was punctuated by two well-separated, involuntary spasms. These were long and deep, moving vertically from the bottom up. At that time I knew nothing of the Kundalini phenomenon, which these sensations surely were.

This is an energetic flow starting from the coccyx and rising toward the brain. In Eastern metaphysics Kundalini is sometimes called the "serpent of fire", symbolized by a tiny snake coiled tightly inside the coccyx and waiting to be awakened. It can be calm and gentle, or it can swoop up smoothly, or it can explode with violence, causing neurological damage. There is a wide spectrum of possibilities and the literature is cautionary.

It seemed to be awakening in me at that time, but I was ignorant of the process. Years later I came back to my journal entry for this day, read it carefully, and immediately inscribed "Kundalini" in red ink in the margin. Fortunately my first experience with the little snake was smooth and gentle. Indeed, as it has subsequently and always been.

In between the moments of simply letting thoughts flow and then lead me back to the mantra, other things began to happen. Irregularly, not in any structured way. There was the sensation of pulsations and waves, sometimes oceanic in feeling. A sea of rollers and roll-overs.

One afternoon there came inside my head a vision of the center and lower shell of my brain as a hollowed-out coral fan, a shell-gridwork in dark lilac, and suddenly that was wiped away by a hard, ragged crack of lightning.

Such entertaining phenomena did not come every day.

As I told Marina, "Most of the time it's just plain stress-processing, chasing the elephants out of the underbrush. Sometimes they look back at me, trunk raised angrily, ears flattened, and give a good glare as I boot them on the backside, then they shuffle off and let the mantra come back."

And come back it did, reliably. It returned quietly, as a pulsation moving deep inside me. It had a sound, but it wasn't necessary to speak it. The cells of my body both pronounced it and heard it. There were moments when they were it.

"The mantra is...........a vehicle on which the attention rests and which leads it down to the subtler levels of thinking," is how another TM teacher, Peter Russell, expresses it[5].

That word "stress" is important. It was slowly moving out of my life. It is claimed that meditation accomplishes this easily, without forcing the issue. And certainly it was happening to me that way.

"The sounds used in the TM technique are ones which resonate with the nervous system in a soothing harmonious manner," says Russell.

Certainly this was true for me. My nerves were quieting, my concentration on my work was better, my mood was happy. My husband observed that my recent irritability and impatience seemed to be dissolving, giving way to the calm, even-tempered wife I had once been. And I was able to observe that his health and strength were returning. The many months of mutual stress were fading away behind us.

Those subtler levels of thinking were still eluding me, but something good was going on and it never occurred to me to eliminate this meditative dimension from my life.

"TM has a grip on me," I wrote to Marina. "When it's fine, you couldn't buy it from me for a hundred million."

[1] Blanche Merz, *Les Hauts-Lieux cosmo-telluriques; leurs énergies subtiles méconnues.*
     Genéve: Librairie de l'Université, Georg, 1983. 200p., glossary, bibliography. ISBN 2-8257-0104-01.
[2] W. Brugh Joy, MD, *Joy's Way; A Map for the Transformational Journey; an introduction to the potentials for healing with body energies.* Los Angeles: Tarcher, 1979. 290p., index. ISBN: 0-87477-085-8 (paper).
[3] Harold H. Bloomfield, MD, Michael Peter Caine, Dennis T. Jaffe, and Robert B. Kory, *TM: discovering inner energy and overcoming stress.* Foreword by Hans Selye, MD, and introduction by R. Buckminster Fuller. New York: Dell, 1975. ISBN 440-06048-195.
[4] Betty Edwards, *Drawing on the Right Side of the Brain, How to unlock your hidden artistic talent.* Los Angeles: Tarcher, 1979; London: Souvenir Press, 1981. 207p,, glossary, bibliography, index. ISBN 0-285-62468-7.
[5] Peter Russell, *The TM Technique, a Skeptic's Guide to the TM Program.* Boston: Routledge & Kegan Paul, 1976. 1977. xi+191p., references, index. ISBN 0-7100-8672-5.

Chapter Six

BLOWING FUSES

"Imagine that you are standing in the city of Los Angeles on a clear, silent night, about three miles from the Olympic Coliseum at Exposition Park. And imagine that the Coliseum's 103,000 seats are filled with people all blowing police whistles in unison," I wrote to Carol.

"That's about what I hear, 103,000 massed police whistles, at a distance of three miles."

This is the first thing that Transcendental Meditation brought me, ahead of various benefits, ahead of various other phenomena. As I mentioned in the previous chapter, this ringing in my ears began with the first initiatory meditation. And it has never left me.

In a lighthearted way, I have often referred to this sound as my own personal electrical substation. It can rise or fall in volume (voltage?), and in the early months of TM it rose frequently during the meditation, merging with a kind of vibratory envelope that surrounded me at those times.

The medical arts call this condition "tinnitus", and they seem to be quite disarmed before it. They can't explain it and they can't cure it. My experience has been that they don't really want even to talk about it. Or perhaps I have yet to press the right button.

However, this sound does not really bother me. It did not seem initially to interfere with my hearing, it did not get in the way of listening to good music or good conversation, it did not prevent me from sleeping. But it never left my consciousness. And that is still the case.

Over the long term there has been one change: it did ultimately interfere with my hearing. There is no particular tendency toward deafness in my heredity, but there has been a gradual loss of hearing in the left ear, in which the ringing has always been the strongest. In more than twenty-five years of meditation the acuity of that ear has diminished by fifty per cent, and what remains is, for want of a better word, "fuzzy". It is this latter quality which rendered a hearing aid useless, and I gave up on that option after a four-month trial. In ordinary life I sit so that my still-perfect right ear is toward the voices with whom I am chatting. In crowded rooms with bad acoustics I suffer. In communication with the cosmos it doesn't seem to matter.

TM people stonewall this situation. Like the doctors, they don't want to talk about it. Their usual answer boils down to something like "Oh, that's nothing. It's not important, and it will go away soon."

No, it did not go away. It took about ten years for me to realize that there was the beginning of a loss of hearing connected with this phenomenon. By that time my spiritual practice had moved far beyond TM, its practitioners, and its Maharishi. As you will learn.

On another level, ignoring the purely physiologic context, one can describe this ringing as a kind of cosmic music, possibly the sound of electrons discharging in the air around us. My visual reference for this phenomenon is found in a fascinating picture book entitled *The Invisible World*[1], full of microphotography and electrophotography or Kirlian photography, after the pioneering Russian scientist Semyon Kirlian.

There is a full-page photograph of air, captured by a technique called energy imaging photography. This picture shows the form that electrical discharges take in the air, and what you see in it is a fantastic garden of fan-like plant designs with trunks, branches and long needles which might be found on a particularly exotic medicinal herb or a pine tree yet to be invented.

It takes only a small leap of the imagination to conceive of all those myriad little submicroscopic needles vibrating at ultra-high speed. And the sound they produce, as perceived by a human ear which has somehow been sensitized, could be a ringing.

For sensitized I had been. It was apparent within a month that my being was connecting rather rapidly with another level of energy.

I've already mentioned the sense of pulsations and various cerebral acrobatics such as waves and oceanic roll-overs. In my pre-World War II youth we used to do bodysurfing in the Pacific Ocean. Now I'd found a new way to ride the waves, with much less expenditure of energy, and one never came up spitting sand.

At the end of May, three weeks into the practice, there was a group meditation at the academy. Later experience in that house leads me to believe that I was sitting on an energy hot spot -- the kind of thing Blanche had been talking about -- for that first meditation in a group. In that seance a strong sense of my aura began to envelope me, accompanied with more of those pulsations and eventually a feeling of "centering". I cannot explain how that feels, it just is. Nicely.

In meditation a couple of days later my brain began tingling. This sensation spread to my hands and feet, which continued to tingle for a quarter-hour after I'd finished.

I had sat for this meditation immediately after showering, and I am willing to believe the waterfall effect could have switched the ionization around me and within me from positive to negative. Studies in ionization of the atmosphere identify a buildup of positive ions as stressful and tiring, while a surge of negative ions is perceived as refreshing and stimulating. As after a rainstorm.

There was a wide variation from session to session. Aside from the frequent intrusion of phenomena, the mantra would drift downward by itself, sinking easily into the pool from which thought arose. It could stay down, centering, with respiration almost at a standstill and scant perception of the passing of time. These moments were undramatic but very restful and refreshing. Light, floating, not many thoughts to "process", perhaps the illusion of some mental flexions but no pyrotechnics. This was the essence of transcendental meditation for me. It rarely got any better than this, and it didn't need to.

Sandra, one of our step-granddaughters, arrived in early June, 1982. She had done some TM in college but had let it slide over the years. She told me the mantra given her seemed incompatible with her nature, and her teacher, a fellow student, had been unhelpful. The two of us had a very agreeable relationship, enjoying doing things together in spite of a full generation of age difference. It was easy to lure her onto the tennis court, and the fact that I demolished her with ease perked up her interest in resuming meditation.

She accompanied me up to Nextmountain one afternoon for my "checking" with Nora. Sandra had agreed to take care of her grandfather for a few days, so there and then I made a room reservation with Nora for a brief "retreat", to start a week later.

Meanwhile, just having another meditator — even a "backslid" one — in the household seemed to stimulate my own practice. New things happened.

The morning after Sandra's arrival I began to see objects in meditation. This was qualitatively different from simply tracking thoughts to their exit. Dreamlike images rose up. First there was a net full of vegetables, then there was a kind of a giant artichoke occupying my brain.

Two days later Sandra meditated with me at day's end, in my husband's studio where the vibrations were so good. I experienced a very strong sense of being "in", of being enveloped by magnetism, especially around the head and shoulders. And more images welled up. There was a parade of caricature masks, dream-like. They seemed to represent people who seemed familiar but who I could not place in memory. Paradoxically, all this was very refreshing.

There was now almost always in meditation a sense of the vibrational field around me, of that pulsation which seemed to merge with and be a part of the sound in my ears. Frequently I "went away" for a handful of time; one of these "black-outs" lasted nearly half an hour.

The day before I was scheduled to go on my little retreat there was a completely new phenomenon. The vibrational field embraced me lovingly, after a few "flashes", one of which sped through a circuit of my head, arms, and fingers, powering the chakras in those body parts.

The previous evening I had risked a thimbleful of a coffee-flavored liqueur, and it had gotten me up four times during the night and my bladder was still "nervous" during this morning meditation. That reconfirmed a long-standing intolerance to caffeine.

This power coursing through my arms and down into my fingers seemed custom-made for healing work. I placed my tingling fingertips firmly over the lower abdomen and held them there. The power penetrated, I could feel a sense of tension dissolving, and from then on there was no more trouble with that kind of urgency. TM had brought me a healing! Would wonders never cease?

My retreat at Nextmountain commenced on a Sunday afternoon. Sandra drove up there with me, took the car back home, and would come to fetch me after forty-eight hours.

After getting me settled into my room upstairs, Nora outlined a program.

First she drew me a couple of pages of stick figures in exercise positions, which she explained were Hatha Yoga movements, the whole set being called an "asana".

Next she taught me how to do nostril breathing. In this technique you inhale through the left nostril, holding the right nostril closed with a finger; you hold that breath at the top of the nose for a time equal to the time of inhalation; then you close the left nostril with a finger and exhale through the right nostril. Then you return, right to left. The tip of your index finger on the forehead serves as a kind of fulcrum for the fingers doing the opening and closing of nostrils. One does this gently, not with gigantic breaths, and one observes an equal time count -- usually about four counts, but longer is fine -- at each step of the process.

She called this exercise "pranayama". In Sanskrit this translates to "breath control" or "energy control". Prana means breath or breathing, but it means energy too, because the action of irrigating the body with oxygen through the lungs is considered a primary form of energizing. "Yama" is control.

Nora instructed me to do four "cycles" a day while in retreat. A cycle began with the asana exercises. Then one sat for meditation, beginning that practice with pranayama. After the twenty-minute meditation would follow a short period of rest lying on the bed.

There was one other instruction: I was not to leave the house unescorted.

To my lifted eyebrows she explained that people doing a retreat had sometimes been found wandering aimlessly in the village or sitting on a bench staring at the cosmos, totally spaced-out. These events sometimes created a problem of incomprehension in the community, not a good thing. Such as, "who are those kooks, anyway?" When not doing my four cycles I was invited to browse through the extensive videotape library of Maharishi giving lectures.

Meditating four times a day in this cycle format was rather powerful overall but it took a while for my work with the mantra to gain the upper hand over the phenomena. The house felt alive with energy. I was almost always aware of the vibratory envelope which I began to call a "field", sometimes strong, sometimes light. My mantra process rose and fell within this energetic context. A cycle would leave me happy but exhausted, and I would need that time of rest afterward.

All kinds of things happened. There was a pop in my ears one time when the mantra came back from chasing thought elephants. Another time my body was receiving horizontal charges of energy, in what I noted in my journal as "dot-dash twinkling", leaving me quite revved up.

Interspersed with all this crackling there also arrived some wonderful, lucid, open spaces in my consciousness, a sense of cosmic presence. The two halves of my brain experienced this differently. The left half was white and light gray in a hemispherical shape, while the right side was very clear and had a kind of parabolic lift-off approaching its right edge. A calm trance-like state of transcendance accompanied this vision of my inner landscape.

It had been my hope that being at the "Academy" for a couple of nights would enable me to extract from Nora and her husband some answers to the numerous questions raised by all these phenomena. What I wanted was a thorough discussion of all the "nuts and bolts" of what was going on. My mind had created a long list of questions about the significance of the sometimes weird sights and sensations coming to me.

But no one wanted to talk about what I felt to be basics. Nora had a knack for turning away my questions. Typical is the following exchange:

"What I want to know is, on the basis of these phenomena, where am I in the process?" I asked.

"You are where you are," she replied with a sweet smile.

On several occasions she let slip guarded remarks to the effect that I seemed to be rather advanced.

What that appeared to mean was that I was already a candidate for siddha training, for which you are eligible after practicing TM for six months. Whereas I had been doing it for less than six weeks.

Marina had mentioned this phase of TM. She had taken this training about six months before recommending meditation to me.

So what are all these siddhis which you learn in order to become a siddha? The answer seemed to be: take the training and find out.

Much later and from other sources I learned a tiny bit about the siddhis. They are basically yogic powers, subtle powers, achieved through the awakening of spinal energy and its chakras. A large measure of self-mastery as a primary power is implied.

It is said that mastering the siddhis makes of one a siddha, a perfected being. Great yogis, accomplished siddhas, can apparently perform amazing feats, such as practicing bilocation --- being physically and being seen by others in two widely-separated places at once. Clairvoyance and mindreading could be child's play to a siddha.

The only siddhi that I could learn about at this time was levitation. Years later Marina told me that she had practiced this art, and I surmised that my hosts at the Academy levitated regularly in a special room in the basement. I've seen photographs of a siddha levitating in some kind of an open-air pavilion, before the era of easy computer manipulation of images.

After siddha training one was expected to expand one's meditational practice to one-and-a-half hours twice a day, the minimum time necessary to consolidate and exploit these arts.

In our discussions it began to emerge, somewhat like osmosis, that siddha training would provide all the answers to my questions, everything would become crystal clear.

So how much does it cost to become a siddha? "From two thousand to four thousand francs," was the rather vague answer I received. That was two thousand dollars in the money of that period.

From other conversations I deduced that these fees were the principal source of revenues for the local centers, such as this Academy. Nora's husband had a job in the village which paid the rent for this large house. Beyond that they lived from the instruction and the lodging they provided, and the Maharishi's palatial headquarters at Seelisberg over in central Switzerland took a percentage.

In other words, it was a commercial operation, a kind of a franchise business like a fast food restaurant. Of course, it had to be somewhat commercial in order to survive and exist so that it would be there when we needed it. I came away with the clear impression that the answers to my questions came with a hefty price tag.

My old allergy to organizations began to itch again.

Several years later I came across a passage in a book that provided a different perspective on the siddhis.

"Siddhis, attainment of powers of all kinds, is a great temptation in the life of an initiate," says Pandit Dr. Arya in his book *Mantra and Meditation*[2] (pages 179-180).

There are two dangers in pursuing the siddhis, in his learned opinion.

One is that "at the slightest appearance of some hunch or some prediction coming through, and so forth, one begins to imagine himself as a siddha, an adept," he says. And the other is that "one becomes tied down to the desires for such powers and dreams of subtle ego."

"The siddhis are not in fact any kind of attainments in the sense that they are additions to one's personality..... they are simply the unblocking of power," he continues.

Reading this several years later confirmed for me what had been happening back in those early days of TM: not only was I discharging stress, but I had been unblocking power.

And to sum up, Dr. Arya comments that "the recent trend in certain meditation circles to popularize siddhis and to sell them for a certain fee, is highly frowned upon by the masters of the Himalayas."

These lines from Dr. Arya offered vindication for my reluctance to get enmired in deeper practices. I already had all I could handle, and I was looking for answers, not powers.

At home again after the retreat my meditation reverted to twice a day as before, but I now prefaced my practice with pranayama nostril breathing. In the mornings I incorporated the hatha yoga exercises into my existing program of calisthenics, and did them all first, so that meditation became a "cycle".

One time during my retreat Nora had spoken to me of a phenomenon she called "soma". It could occur and if it did I should be pleased rather than disturbed, she said, because it was a good sign. She told me that soma was a fluid which could manifest in the mouth without being the same as saliva. It could possibly drip down from the back of the mouth. Something that seems to fit what she was talking about occurred in me about twenty-four hours after returning home.

While in my evening meditation, which was evolving pleasantly within a quiet energy field, my mouth opened involuntarily and there was a light flow of a vaguely sweetish fluid under the tongue. This secretion continued for quite some time and it was indeed pleasant, as Nora had suggested. It did not overflow and drool, which would not have been pleasant.

In ancient Indian rituals one sometimes drank soma, identified as the juice of a mysterious plant. There was a deity and a cult surrounding this practice. And in human endocrinology one speaks of a hormone called somatotropin, produced by the pituitary gland in the base of the brain and not far from the back of the mouth. But my rivulet came from under the tongue and I had not yet experimented with mysterious plants.

Whatever it was, this variety of "soma" manifested once and never again.

Transcendance was gradually moving into my meditations. It was almost as if one tried to learn how to remember not to think about anything when it happens: that's a good trick! For me it was something like the opening of a camera shutter on a kind of circular scene. Click, open: a few seconds of something promising, then click, shut.

Three days after returning home I was meditating in my husband's studio when disaster struck.

During the late-day session the window of transcendance was opening nicely. The second time it came seemed long and tantalizing, I was deeply absorbed in a powerful field, sensing that this was going to be a big one. Just at that split second the telephone rang.

My head exploded. The top of my head blew off. My intense state magnified the sound of the ringing, and it was as if I were standing in the tower of Notre Dame de Lausanne surrounded by huge bells just when the sacristan began to pull their ropes. It was physically painful. My meditation was shattered.

I moved to pick up the receiver, a few steps away. It was Sandra calling from the railroad station at Aigle, where she had gone to meet some friends from Paris. At this time our telephones were not yet on plugs that could be disconnected, but until now I had never been disturbed in such a way.

It was quite disorienting. It was as if my personal electrical field had short-circuited, almost an electrocution. Trying hard to reconnect, to settle back into my lovely state, I succeeded only partially in restoring calm. There was lots of stomach gurgle. I was goggle-eyed, spaced-out, and felt a strong desire to lie down and rest. I had blown a fuse.

---

[1]   *The Invisible World; sights too fast, too slow, too far, too small for the naked eye to see.* London: Secker & Warburg, 1981. 160p. ISBN 0-436-37680-6.

[2]   Pandit Usharbudh Arya, D.Litt., *Mantra and Meditation, Superconscious Meditation, Volume 2.* Honesdale, PA: Himalayan International Institute of Yoga Science and Philosophy, 1981. xxxiii+247p., appendix. ISBN 0-89389-074-X.

Chapter Seven

UNTANGLING THE WIRING

What do you do when a light bulb snaps and one of the house circuits blows a fuse? Well, you go down to the fuse box and reset the appropriate circuit-breaker. The lights come on again, and everything goes on as before.

It wasn't quite that simple to restore order in my meditational world, but it wasn't as chaotic as I had thought it would be. Stubbornly, I kept on meditating. In retrospect I find that remarkable. Something would not allow me to consider giving it up.

TM had plunged me into a cosmoelectricmagnetic environment which had been entertaining and sometimes exciting, but now these effects seemed muted.

This riveting event led me to lean back and take a look at where I had been and where I might be going. In a handful of months meditation had rather quickly changed my life. It was perfectly evident to me that I had found powerful tools in the kind of exercises that Brugh Joy had presented and in the kind of meditation that the Maharishi called "transcendental."

My original goal had been to tame the stress in my life and find a level of tranquillity. This objective had been met, and handsomely. Joy's philosophy and techniques had ushered me into a new dimension of life. He had put me on a path, absorbing and full of promise. TM had diverted me into a stream, equally absorbing and full of promise. It gave me an inner canoe in which I had begun gliding neatly down a lazy river, within a fascinating landscape. It was a lovely trip. Then I hit a rock and capsized.

It didn't occur to me then to abandon ship, seek another current. I beached the canoe long enough to empty the water, then resumed paddling, meditating as before. But there were subtle differences.

The energy field I had begun to inhabit so comfortably had been given a hard shake but had not completely disappeared. The mantra dove pretty well most of the time, with irregularity. In about a month the inner work began to regain a comfortable level.

First, close the eyes, slowly and gently. Tip of the right index on the forehead chakra, close the right nostril with the thumb, take in fresh energy in a long, slow stream through the left nostril, counting to four. Hold it at the top for a while, count of four. Close the left nostril with the middle finger, lift the thumb, exhale slowly and completely toward the right, squeezing the gut to get out all the air, counting to four. Hold there, on "empty", count of four. Then reverse the process. And repeat that for three "roundtrips".

The mantra begins to pronounce itself internally, worming its way toward the cellular level. Let it sink, slowly diving. Oh, I'd better not forget to buy eggs....follow that thought as it squiggles out to the right and evaporates. Mantra, mantra, mantra, diving toward the depths of the pool. Is there enough butter in the fridge? No, I refuse to have industrial margarine in the house, it's got to be butter.......bye, bye, thought, see you later. Mantra, mantra... diving clearly and easily, going deep. I'm in my center, there's an urge to "find" a place calling to me -- to get both inside and outside the brain --- a darker mass of energy. Snapped twice into a clean, light window of nothingness, here comes thinking again. Out to the clear exit on the right, always the right. I feel a pulsation as the field flows around me, vibrating softly. Mantra. Silence. Mantra. It wants to come up. Let it. Open one eye slowly. Close it, Try the other one. Close it. Open them both, close them. Open. Exhale. Take a deep breath.

How long was that? Look at the wristwatch. Twenty minutes. Well, time to be up and doing again.

That's kind of how it went. There is no such thing as a typical meditation, but I have just lived one with you.

It was working. It wasn't always like this. Sometimes the whole process was sluggish, and thought skeins went on forever before the mantra came back. Occasionally the diving and centering led me into a silent space for an indeterminate length of time, out of which I would suddenly snap, fully alert. There were endless variations, but there were no more fireworks. At first I thought more than just that was missing, that it was not as fluid and easy as it had been. Whatever traumatic after-effect there had been now dissolved slowly. There were a lot of "good" meditations and a certain number in which the mantra battled with thought processes. Before the summer was over a gentle rhythm was evident.

"I have a feeling of idling in low gear," I told Carol. "I need to be wound up again like a clock."

The circumstances of daily life kept getting in the way but finally I got back to Nextmountain for another "checking" in October. The meditation part of this was satisfactory; I could feel the greater power of the vibrational state of that old house, compared to my home chalet. There was a more intense field of energy.

Once again Nora stonewalled me. I related the blown fuse episode to her, and she immediately changed the subject. Apparently Maharishi had not given his teachers instructions on how to respond to such a story. I had sought guidance and found none, not even a glimmer of counsel.

In the opening lines of this personal history I said "Invisible forces of which I was unaware had some kind of a plan for me." This was still a rather skeletal notion, with scarcely any meat on its bones. My three Capricorns first raised the question without providing anything approaching an answer. Reading Ruth Montgomery's books nudged open a spiritual doorway, just a crack.

It took the nearly-fatal accident on the coral reef to open my mind to the notion of some kind of divine intervention. I had asked why and I had received an answer — "because your work is not yet done" — which proved to be the case over the ensuing two years.

Delving into Brugh Joy's evolution further pushed into that doorway. At some point in these explorations a spiritual component crept into my quest. Joy's experiences placed the inner debate on that level, but I had to read one hundred of his pages before actually encountering the word "spiritual". He spoke of awareness, energy, transformation, mind, metaphysics, "psi" phenomena, and higher or expanded consciousness without once speaking of spirituality.

Similarly, I found the same avoidance when reading some of the Maharishi's prose. His Preface to his translation and commentary of the Bhagavad-Gita never refers to spirit or spirituality[1]. (In fairness, one can cite four instances of the word "God" in nine dense pages.)

Peter Russell offers an explanation. Maharishi founded the Spiritual Regeneration Movement in 1958, in Madras, but when he arrived in the West he found distrust toward anything smacking of spirituality. What a sad commentary on so-called "Christian" religions! People were put off by the name of his Movement, so he created a new one, the International Meditation Society[2].

His organization has carried on in this vein. In my possession are several copies of his gilded, gleaming "World Government News", which were given me at Nextmountain in response to my request for basic theoretical information about TM. The inside front cover is devoted to a detailed outline of his "World Government of the Age of Enlightenment". In about one thousand words of fine print one reads continually of "enlightenment", "consciousness", "natural law", "creative intelligence" and "the physics of unity". Spirituality had been abolished because it would scare away the people he wanted to attract.

I found all this glittering and frequently vacuous prose quite off-putting, but it was all I had to work with until Sandra gave me her battered copy of the Bhagavad-Gita.

"See if you can make sense of this," was her offhand remark.

Ultimately, in an appendix to this tome, I found an imprecise description of the technique[3].

TM works through "turning the attention inwards towards the subtler levels of a thought until the mind transcends the experience of the subtlest state of the thought and arrives at the source of the thought. This expands the conscious mind and at the same time brings it into contact with the creative intelligence that gives rise to every thought," Maharishi explains.

"The expanded capacity of the conscious mind increases the power of the mind and results in added energy and intelligence. Man......begins to make use of his full mental potential."

Simply put, the technique of Transcendental Meditation deals with consciousness, taming it for the benefit of mind and body. That's the theory, and that pretty much explains why I stuck with it. My impetus to take up meditation had been to soothe jangled nerves and hence smooth my days. The practice had brought some results which seemed indeed to benefit mind and body. Beyond that my powerful physical reactions during the early meditations appeared to reinforce, in my psyche, the sense of the spiritual. I had been enjoying the pursuit of this blossoming. There was a lot of static accompanying the process, but that too was fairly entertaining except for the blown fuse.

"I am more or less on a kind of plateau where change comes slowly," I told Carol, after five months of twice-daily meditation. "However, I seem to transcend frequently, if I understand correctly what the Maharishi was saying when he responded to a question on 'how do I know when I am transcending?'"

"Meditation has helped me a lot," I went on. "Before starting I was really a very unhappy person. I felt weighed down with problems and jobs to be solved and I felt most unhappy with my environment. TM has changed me. I am more or less serene without being tranquillized in the narcotic sense."

"And," I added, "I sleep much better. This is a principal breakthrough."

Near-death on the reef had led to a illumination of sorts. Brugh Joy had been slow to acknowledge the spiritual nature of his approach, and TM evaded the issue. My experiences with both approaches appeared to contain spiritual seeds, yet all these teachers shied away from it. Early rejection of my father's religion seemingly denied any spiritual leanings I might have, by conventional definitions of the time. Now the lack of explanations for psychological phenomena was troubling me at another spiritual level, this one unconventional. The right path still eluded me.

Finding helpful sources became a preoccupation. I began looking for books and articles which would talk about the physical things one feels during meditations, what really goes on in the brain which is felt, which results in sensation.

"I mean the vibrations and pulsations and waves, the sense of being plugged into an electrical power network that I regularly sense," I said in a letter to my daughter (thinking partly of my continuously 'massed police whistles'). "The literature of Maharishi's organizations does not delve into all this."

Too many unanswered questions left me impatient and dissatisified, I told my catalyst friend Marina.

"There is far too much circular blah-blah and far too little down-to-earth talk," I complained. "No one wants to discuss with me what happens and I no longer bother to try to have a dialogue."

Marina had told me of a protective aura which would block the sensation of electrical fields. This appeared to be intrinsic in Maharishi's method and teachings, something that everyone received automatically.

"I do not know meditation without electrical fields," I wrote her. "To me, they come with TM. My 'massed police whistles' began with the first meditation. I have associated them as being integral with TM, and Nora has not disabused me of this notion."

"Should she have done so?" I asked. "When the mantra set up a neural pulsation, it had an electrical feeling. You seem to be saying that TM should protect me from this. In my case, it has created more and made it a part of my life, not protected me."

Within these ruminations I could not forget that new adepts who went on retreat at Nextmountain were instructed not to stroll alone in the fresh air outside the house. They might "space out" and become an embarrassment in the village. Sitting on a bench staring at the cosmos was potentially dangerous. The fact this kind of thing happened appeared not to merit explanation. Why did it happen? What did it mean? No comment.

Against this background I went again to Nextmountain in December for a "checking" meditation with Nora. This time I felt that everything moved more slowly, to the degree that a notion of slow and fast can apply to meditation. And, in contrast to the previous visit in October, this time the energy field was less intense than at home.

There was, as usual, no response to my remarks on any of these subjects. The refusal to answer my questions, to require that I simply accept, was too much like the blind Christianity I had fled. It aggravated my rebellion against structures but reinforced my curiosity about what lay beyond. An untapped potential awaited enlightenment.

That was the last time I went to Nextmountain. Spirit, with a strong push from intellectual frustration, was leading me into a quiet separation from Maharishi's movement, as distinguished from his meditational technique. That I still liked, and to it I clung as a kind of handrail on a slippery path.

Interesting new bushes began to grow beside that path.

In September, six months after my first experiment with meditation, I somewhat hesitantly told my mother about this new element in my life.

Her reply shook me.

"Oh, that's very interesting!" she exclaimed. "My father used to meditate."

"Grandfather Hardy used to meditate?" I stammered, momentarily almost speechless.

"Yes, he used to get up at five o'clock in the morning, take a shower, and then he would meditate."

"Tell me all about it," I implored.

"Well, there's really not much more. Sometimes on Sundays he would take us all out to the Uplifters Ranch to hear talks by a swami."

Mother really hooked me with this bit of family history. There had always been a tendency for close-mouthed secrecy that had been an aggravation to me, but now my news had turned a key in a lock. For the next minute or so I tried out the names of various swamis and gurus who had landed in Southern California during the first quarter of the century, but none of them rang a bell in her memory.

"So what was Granddad's spiritual orientation?" I asked. "Did he have a church affiliation?"

"Um, not exactly. He used to send us to the Theosophical Sunday School."

You could have knocked me over with the proverbial feather.

Quickly I scanned memory, rewinding back to my childhood, searching for a clue. And, of course, it was right there in front of my face. Mother accompanied us to church, docilely, but she rarely spoke about the service, the sermon, the minister, much less anything the least bit theological. She simply went along because it was required of her. Like me. And Theosophy was so distant from the anglican Episcopal Church[4]. Had this never bothered her?

"Tell me more about your time in Theosophy," I asked. "I've read a little about that. How much of it carried over for you into adult life? Did you like it?" I was brimming with enthusiasm at what appeared to be a promising new factor in our sometimes creaky relationship.

"Oh, you know, I would much rather have gone to the Presbyterian Sunday School with my classmates."

That was a bucket of cold water poured over my head. Some years later I tried once more to winkle more information from her, without success.

Her story had a powerful effect on me, despite its disappointing end. It told me there was a genetic reason for my spiritual explorations. The link between me and my grandfather is strengthened by the fact I am tall like he was, the tallest of his grandchildren, and that at age twenty-one I looked like a feminine version of him at the same age. The old photograph revealing this resemblance startled me the first time I saw it.

These links helped me understand for the first time why I had incarnated into the family. For otherwise I was a misfit in every sense. The compilations of Head, Cranston, and Williams had pretty well convinced me of the validity of this controversial theory[5]. And the tragedy is that Granddad and I never made a "connection". Not once did we ever have a private conversation, although he lived until I was twenty-five years old.

About this time a Canadian friend sent me a little book, as kind of a gag, she confessed[6]. *The Star People* by Brad and Francie Steiger was all about extraterrestrials living among us, flying saucers, angelic encounters and the like.

In the middle of this little volume there is a chapter about dreams. Until that moment I had paid very little attention to my dreams. Chapter Thirteen: "Dreams of Remarkable Encounters", changed all that. The Steigers snagged my interest by evoking the role of dreams in relating to cosmic intelligence.

"The dream and the trance-like states offer particularly good times for our angelic beings to interact with us, " Francie Steiger said.

"Setting aside time for meditation will permit one to reach a state of consciousness to receive awareness, but the dream-state will still provide one of the most productive areas in which to receive teachings[7]."

Inasmuch as some other writers had spoken of dreams as a clue to past lives, I decided to follow the Steigers' simple little system of recording my dreams. I installed a supply of 3x5 file cards in a bedside drawer, with a ballpoint pen at hand. First thing in the morning I began to jot down what I could remember of my dreams. Occasionally I would switch on the light in the middle of the night to record an episode, but mostly I avoided this because getting back to sleep again is often difficult for this very light sleeper.

This meant I was missing a lot of dreams, even though the faculty of remembering —requested aloud before going to sleep — began to function immediately.

There were, and still are, times when I tell myself that a dream will be remembered in the morning, and it isn't. So often they go skittering away, wisps of brainwork that float away on the morning breeze.

The file began building inexorably, and the small file box had quickly to be replaced with a longer one, complete with alphabetical dividers. I have registered as many as four dreams from one night, although that is exceptional.

The variety of topics astonished me. Certain patterns began to emerge, and within six months there was a fantastic spectrum of dreamwork. Here is the first half-year of dream recording: animals (4), axis tilt, baggage, bedshaking, bodyguard, children (2), clothing, computing, conflict including war (5), crime (2), destitute, directory (of dreams!), dreaming, Düsseldorf (where I had worked for a while), dwelling (13), entertainment, esthetics (as in the intriguing dream skein I titled "sex and esthetics"), evolution, food (2), genealogy, "going places" as distinguished in degree from "traveling" (5), hesitation, hospital, land and tenants, late, librarian (I had been one), mail box key (it was lost in the dream and earlier really had been lost), marriage (3), metaphysics (3), money, specific people (7), photography, politics (2 — one in which I was a presidential advisor), prisoners, robbery, rock-climbing, searching, self-defense, sex (9), sport, spy story (2), subway, Switzerland (2), taxes, and traveling (14 — once with my old white tomcat, the mighty hunter, passed on decades ago).

The recurrence of certain themes is obvious. Traveling and Going Places together made for a major preoccupation, and it still goes on. "Sex" proves my vital juices haven't slowed down. "Dwelling" deals with houses and apartments that I have known and not known, including one floor plan that recurs frequently in various settings. This involved an extra room behind a bedroom, a kind of secret, private sanctuary. My dream space?

The very first two dreams recorded had to do with sex, and I will not dwell here on the raunchy details. Apparently some reflections of this basic drive had to be purged before my subconscious could liberate itself and range widely.

The three dreams relating to metaphysics reflect rather well the thrust of what I have been saying in this chapter.

The first one I recorded is brief: "Impossible to recall dream. Only image is one of an elliptical collection of dots, gray on gray, which suggest electrons." This dream appears to relate vaguely to some of the early "fireworks" experiences in meditation, but in its vision of electrons it was a precursor of things to come.

In the second such dream, early in the new year of 1983, "I was attending some kind of an institution where one studied occult and exotic subjects. There seemed to be an underlying menace of becoming an inmate/prisoner rather than being a student on a good intellectual footing with the masters. Details fuzzy other than study tables in a large room, good windows on one side. My first spouse was present but not interested, whereas I was considerably interested and began to read and recite passages to an approving colleague/master."

In the third of these dreams I was in a "heated discussion with (a friend) on the amount of time needed for TM and on what I have derived from it. Question not resolved."

It doesn't take much brainwork to link the last two to meditation and my prickly relationship with the Maharishi's organization.

Let me close this chapter with a dream experienced one year later.

"In a time of darkness or little sun, perhaps winter, or in the shade of a mountain, I was in company with people in some way depending on me. In the final episode, in a house before a departure, I felt called upon to aid the youngsters, and I did this by beaming waves from my brain to the brain of the nearest child, and through him to the brain of the next."

This dream, in early 1984, was clearly premonitory but it would be years before its link with eventual reality could be seen. My dreamworld was racing far ahead of my quibbles with the TM people.

1   Maharishi Mahesh Yogi, *On the Bahgavad-Gita, a New Translation and Commentary*, Chapters 1-6. Penguin Books, 1969. 494p.

2   Russell, op.cit. , p. 13.

3   Maharishi Mahesh Yogi, op.cit., p.470.

4   Helena P. Blavatsky founded the Theosophical Society in 1875, with the objective "to collect and diffuse knowledge of the laws which govern the universe." Soon afterward she wrote the mammoth Isis Unveiled, an encyclopedic survey of ancient mysteries and modern science and theology. It is said that she received this compendium through a variety of spiritual channeling, writing at blinding speed. Many notable people interested themselves in this movement. Blavatsky moved the Society to India. A later book, The Secret Doctrine (1888), presented a survey of sacred writings of Hinduism. Spiritual practices of Blavatsky and her successors, Charles Leadbeater and Annie Besant, included psychic channeling, clairvoyance, astral travel, the study of auras, and work with discarnate masters. In the 20th century Besant's successors, still based in India, discovered a brilliant child and, as the youth Krishnamurti, groomed him for a Christ-like role. As a young man Krishnamurti refused this role and struck out on an independant path, becoming a highly respected spiritual teacher until his death in 1986 at the age of ninety.

5   See citations in Chapter Two.

6   Brad and Francie Steiger, *The Star People*. New York, Berkley, 1981. 200p., index. ISBN 0-425-05513-2.

7   Steiger, op.cit., pp. 126-27.

Chapter Eight

PLAYING WITH ENERGY

Questions of meditation aside, that summer of 1982 offered a bumper crop of ups and downs in the practical, everyday world.

We had trouble finding a steady garden man that season, which meant there was no one to cut one thousand square meters of hay, most of it on steep slopes. With more bravura than good sense, I put on my hiking boots and tackled the job with a long-handled scythe. I'd been watching the farmers do it, observing their rhythmic movement, so once again I said "I can do that."

This time I was on solid terra firma, my element, instead of being on a board wobbling on the water. Indeed I could do it, but I was a lot slower than the farmers and it took an eternity to slice down that stand of hay. The job got done, without elegance, but it got done.

My vegetable garden produced a bumper crop of raspberries, cauliflower, green beans, salad greens, spinach, carrots, radishes, onions, potatoes and zucchini. We ate fresh, untreated vegetables daily, and I prepared all the rest for the freezer.

Except it wasn't really a freezer. We were using an old refrigerator turned up high, because freezers were expensive and, being in a cash crunch, we had been trying to postpone major purchases.

One afternoon I returned home from a shopping trip down in the valley to discover that the "freezer" had given up the ghost. And all my lovingly cultivated produce was lost. Thus we ended up buying that freezer anyway. I found a cheap one at the supermarket, which was still running twenty years later when I replaced it for a larger one.

My ulcer was burning too. This was one stress symptom that meditation had not completely tamed. Also, my elderly husband had been having occasional bouts of jaundice, despite the gall bladder operation that had created so many months of chaos for both of us. In addition to that, we learned one of his retinas was full of pinholes. His vision was declining, and painting was becoming nearly impossible for him. His driving license had to be surrendered. This was a disaster to his ego, but it was a relief for me.

Ever since the episode of the cow I had become progressively more apprehensive when he was at the wheel. As we sped down the mountain one day I remarked nervously on a black-and-white cow crossing the highway about one hundred yards ahead.

"What cow?" he demanded.

Do I need to say more?

This matter of Will's vision had a big effect on our life. Not only did he have to abandon his passion for work at his painter's easel, but reading became very difficult. He used a magnifying glass to read, and we got him a subscription to the large print edition of *Reader's Digest*. And I began to read aloud to him, at least half an hour every day, until my voice-box began to grate. We began with books about the Alps and alpinists, a passionate subject for both of us.

These were "downers", but there were "ups" beyond the mutual pleasure we discovered in this reading experience.

One of my objectives had been to join the computer age. I could see how a computer could enable me to write faster and thereby keep words flowing onto the page at a rhythm closer to my brain's ability to conceive them. And having once worked on the academic, publishing side of the computer field, I was itching to start having "hands-on" experience.

After doing a lot of looking and asking of questions at a computer trade exposition, I settled on a basic Hewlett-Packard machine for my "elecretary". This was a "CP/M" model, at least two generations before the first "Windows" computers. It used the large five-inch "floppy" discs, and you had to have two of them in the twin disc drives to get anything done.

Innovation lurks in my character, thus for a printer I chose an Olivetti electronic typewriter. Some "garage tinkerers" over in Neuchâtel had developed a modem which deluded the typewriter into thinking it was a computer printer. And it worked. Even the man who sold the Olivetti was impressed.

There was a "downer" in this otherwise sunny picture. The HP "crashed" and was out of service for six weeks while their technicians fussed over it — under warrranty fortunately. Ultimately it come home again and gave me no more trouble for quite a while. On this eccentric configuration I was able to produce two books in the next five years. To say nothing of a voluminous correspondence famous for its "wall-to-wall" margins, as a former professional colleague described them.

When the year began "coincidence" had placed me at the dinner table next to Blanche, the lady who appeared to be an expert on earth energies. She had answered just enough of my questions during a meeting of the Soroptimist Club to start my brain cells racing. Her research institute sounded relatively modest in size and scope, but her knowledge seemed to be vast.

Two months later she was the speaker of the evening, telling us about cosmic-telluric interplay in some of the sacred sites of India. Earth energies followed gridlike patterns across the landscape. Their intersections with each other and with phenomena such as faults and underground watercourses created peaks and hollows of high and low energy, she explained. The interplay of these invisible lines and points could exalt the human spirit, but they could also lead to human health problems.

So how do you know which is which? I asked myself. The answer was forthcoming, but not fast enough for my impatience.

Blanche talked about how this system can affect us in our work and in our sleep. Placement of one's bed, it turned out, was a vital decision which could affect energy in the short-term and overall health in the long-term. This energy system seemed instantly familiar to me, as if I had worked with it at some time in the deep past. Thus in mid-August I persuaded her to survey our home for these geopathic zones about which she had been so eloquent.

Blanche came late one morning and accomplished most of her analysis before we sat down to an amiable lunch with my husband Will. She went over the whole house with a brass antenna, concentrating on the rooms where we spent the bulk of our time. This dowsing wand was formed from one continuous rod of brass, shaped to resemble vaguely a fish. She held her "fish" by the points of its tail, her two index fingertips balancing it lightly. I watched almost as if hypnotized, my spirit saying "I can do that, I can do that."

It was bemusing to discover that Will, who built the house and lived in it for ten years before my arrival, had unconsciously chosen to roost on spots that are neutral. His bed, his desk, his easel, his favorite spot on the sofa — all of these were exempt from undesirable energies. None of them was located on a grid intersection.

Although Will was now a working artist, a painter, he was basically a man of the land. Earthy, in most senses of the word. He had grown up in the bosom of nature, roaming the heath and sand dune country of his mother's western Holland and hiking his father's beloved Alps. He'd graduated as an agricultural engineer and had worked as a forester, as a horticulturist and landscaper, as the director of a nature reserve, and as the director of a large farming enterprise. The garden he created around our chalet testified to his sensitivity to the land and what would grow on it. Indeed, it was that sensitivity, demonstrated during a morning stroll in a Dutch forest so many years earlier, that had won my heart.

In this light I understood perfectly why he had gravitated — unconsciously but quite naturally — to live on the most harmonious spots in the house.

In contrast, and without foreknowledge or malicious intent, he had left me the energetic crumbs. As I lay in bed my torso was in a grid intersection.

So was my desk chair. My place on the sofa, next to him, was just touching a hot spot.

Just what is this mysterious configuration?

During her lecture to our Club Blanche had explained that the basic grid she worked with is rectangular, with the lines of force roughly 2.3 meters apart north-to-south and 2.5 meters east-to-west. The lines themselves are about twenty-one centimeters (eight inches) wide. Where they intersect you have an eight-inch square of micro-voltage electricity which can upset your personal wiring.

This effect can be more intense, or less intense, depending on polarity. An important quality of the intersections is that they exhibit polarity — either positive or negative — and this polarity normally alternates from point to point. The grid can be warped by other influences, principally subterranean groundwater but also seismic faulting and heavy electrical installations. There is more than one grid, it turned out, and I was not to learn much more of any of this until a few months later.

After lunch Blanche and I prowled around the outside of the house. Sometimes she put aside her antenna and walked around with her hands deployed like little wings at hip-height.

Blanche found the chalet free of subterranean water, except at the extreme northeast corner, where the refrigerator sat. Sure enough, that was also where the builder had installed little vents in the foundation to dry out the walls. There is an underground stream in the region cutting that corner and flowing at an angle out into the garden.

In this space the trees are warped and plants grow badly. Nothing thrived or even survived in one planting bed. Now I understood why, and eventually my horticulturist husband began reluctantly to accept this rather original explanation.

Before Blanche left us that day in August I picked up her brass wand, with which she had located the currents in the house. After one or two ineptnesses at holding it with just the right balance between firmness and delicacy, I moved around and found that indeed it turned ninety degrees for me too, just as it had for her, whenever I bumped into one of the invisible currents. Once or twice it even whirled in a circle when I lingered on a crossing-point.

One of my observations over the years here on our mountainside had been that I seemed almost overstimulated by the environment. I had boundless energy and felt marvelous. Living at high altitude was salubrious for this former asthmatic, and the mountain air was positively tonic. Now I was receiving an additional explanation: I was living and sleeping predominantly on grid intersections. This stimulation threatened to become over-stimulation, with possible cardiac consequences.

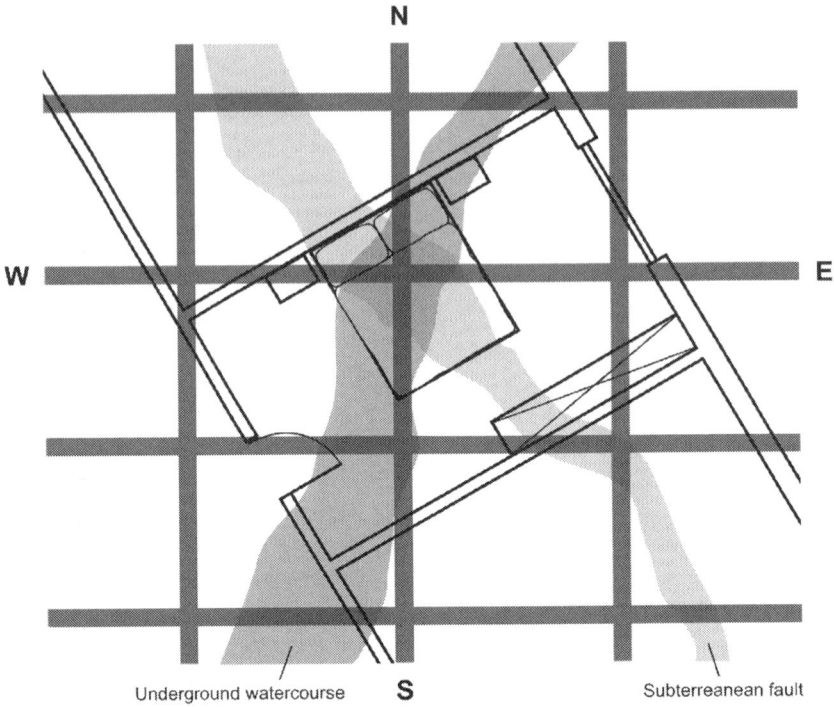

Underground watercourse   **S**   Subterreanean fault

EXAMPLE OF A GEOPATHIC ZONE --- The rectangular Hartmann grid overlays human living arrangements, as shown here by the black lines atop a bedroom. In this case the bed lies directly over an intersection of the energy grid (heavy lines), an underground stream and a fault line (shaded areas). This is an exaggeration designed to illustrate a "worst case" scenario. Fortunately, this rarely happens!

An immediate consequence of Blanche's work was that I moved my bed and rearranged my study. Until I had started TM and moved my bed (just shifted about two feet to the side) I had not had one eight-hour sleep during the year. Now it began to happen frequently, and the times when I slept badly diminished from about fifty per cent of the time to about five per cent of the time.

Confirmation of the overstimulation I had been receiving came in an unexpected way.

My bedside clock had always lost time during the week and had to be advanced up to five minutes when I wound all the timepieces on Sundays. Now, this little clock suddenly began gaining five minutes a week, instead of losing them. It had not been repaired or adjusted. It had only been moved to sit on the night table at a place where my breast used to be before the bed was moved. The clock demonstrated that earth energies had been racing my internal motor.

In these ways Blanche's visit proved to be another turning point for me, in a year already rich with new departures. The earth energy dowsing I had just seen — just tried — impressed me deeply. I was drawn to it atavistically. I knew this capacity had been part of me in some other time, and now I wanted desperately to explore it anew.

At the same time I had sensed that Blanche hesitated a moment before allowing me to take her antenna in my hands and move around our living-room. She did not let me prolong the experiment. She had not been happy to see me do this.

Three months later she organized a seminar through her Research Institute in Geobiology. On a brisk Saturday in mid-November I drove to her village of Chardonne, in the vineyards high above the lake.

Intellectual vitality animated the small civic hall. It was filled with architects, engineers, builders, doctors, nurses, and lay people like myself who wanted to learn about this budding science. The air practically bubbled.

During the morning session Blanche gave a tutorial on her method of analysis, which derived principally from the work of two German scientists, Dr. Ernst Hartmann and Dr. Manfred Curry.

Hartmann began to find correlations between earth energies and illness during the 1950s, and in the 1960s he began to describe the electromagnetic structure now called the Hartmann network or grid. Dowsers also refer to it as the "global" because it is found almost everywhere on the planet -- on the surface, underground, and at elevation.

Hartmann received his medical training at the University of Heidelberg and practiced in the village of Waldkatzenbach, near Eberbach-am-Neckar. His early research focused on the interplay of the environment and human beings. In 1961 he created the Study Group in Geobiology, and began to publish a quarterly journal titled *Wetter-Boden-Mensch* (Weather-Earth-Humanity).

His first book cumulated the sum of these early research articles[1].

Hartmann's grid is organized in a north to south, east to west pattern. Curry, publishing a few years earlier, had identified a gridwork of larger dimensions. Curry's lines ran northwest to southeast, northeast to southwest, and his grid is familiarly called the diagonal, as compared to the Hartmann.

Blanche did not give us much information on the Curry system, except to emphasize that where the two systems nestle closely atop one another, the effects of crossing-points are magnified.

On this day we learned the Hartmann network. It is omnipresent and easily related to human activity. It is the principal grid with which Blanche worked. Hartmann had designed the fish-shaped wand she used, which he called a "lobe" antenna. We received a broad outline of the system which is explained in greater detail in her first book (still in press at the time of this seminar, described later in this chapter).

One could say Hartmann had designed a technique for navigating within the earth's natural electromagnetism.

In fact, there is always electricity in the air and without it we could not live. This was only one of the numerous points brought out by an electrical engineer who Blanche had thoughtfully added to the program. This gentleman told us about the absolutely wild variations that can prevail in all kinds of EM fields. He confirmed that the human environment is saturated by a wide spectrum of fields, some natural, some artificial. There is a tiny EM field along the tracks of an electrified railroad, barely perceptible, but in extreme cases its presence can be felt twenty kilometers distant. This example stuck in my mind.

The engineer's mass of dry detail served a purpose: he made it easy to comprehend that electromagnetic fields lace our environment. The existence of grid-like systems such as those identified by Hartmann and Curry fitted easily into this picture of chaos surrounding us.

White tapes outlined a fragment of a grid system on the floor in a corner of the hall. My eyes riveted on this testing ground from the first moment, but Blanche did not invite us to work there until the end of the day's program.

When she finally proposed that anyone interested could try their hand at dowsing the taped corner, I waited quietly, taming my impatience. One after another people picked up the wand, walked across the test corner, and got nothing. It was interesting to me that not everyone wanted to try.

Then I took the lobe antenna between my fingertips and moved slowly across the sample grid. I could feel the energy that visibly swung the brass fish as we crossed the invisible lines of force. It was remarkable to me that I was the first experimenter to get these reactions.

At day's end Blanche announced she had a small supply of antennae available for sale. If you think I didn't leap at this occasion you haven't been paying attention! One of the brass lobes came home with me and is still a basic tool in my dowsing kit.

It was not lost on me that there ought to be some kind of connection between this telluric (terrestrial) energy and the electrical phenomena of my early meditations.

Several tangential elements bubbled up in my mind: meditation, electromagnetic activity in the brain, earth-rooted electromagnetism surrounding our daily life, and the potential for spiritual manifestation. These notions milled around in my thought processes like a herd of wild horses in a corral. The perfect synthesis eluded me. Spirit roamed the fringes of this theorizing, trying to lasso a concept.

Winter was upon us. It snowed here the day after the seminar at Chardonne, and within a week I was roaming the nearby trails on my crosscountry skis. My skill and equilibrium at this sport were not such that I could wander slopes and fields freely with a dowsing wand in my hands instead of reassuring ski poles.

My early work with the antenna took place inside the house, and only when snow melted temporarily could I work with it outside. Rather quickly I surveyed our living space, confirming what Blanche had found. This gave me courage to expand my field of inquiry, and I began to map the Hartmann network throughout the house.

Earlier I had wondered about how to tell the difference between a beneficial point and one that was inauspicious. Quickly my work at home brought the answer: the antenna reveals the polarity intrinsic to each intersection. When I held it over a crossing-point it revolved between my fingertips. Its spin -- until it spun out of control and fell to the floor! -- was either clockwise or counter-clockwise. Clockwise was clearly positive, hence beneficial. Clockwise could be stimulating and potentially healthful (as long as you didn't sleep over it, as I had been doing.) Counter-clockwise was negative, hence draining, hence fatiguing to the human organism.

I loved to meditate in my husband's big red leather armchair in his studio. It was there that I experienced so much the sense of being immersed in an energy field.

Dr. Hartmann's brass fish quickly told me why: in that chair I was sitting on a crossing-point of positive polarity. Aha, something learned!

There wasn't very much more I could do with the antenna at this point, but more food for thought was on its way. Blanche's book appeared in 1983 and I ordered a copy as soon as I heard about it[2].

Her title alone promised to open some doors. "Hauts-lieux" means "high places", but they also translate to mean "sacred sites". The term means somewhat more than that. Rome is the haut-lieu of Christianity just as Machu Picchu was a haut-lieu for the Incas, and as Jerusalem is for three religions.

Blanche leads her readers on a tour of Egypt, India, Ladakh, Chartres, Santiago de Compostella, and a variety of less imposing sites studded across Western Europe. She took along her Hartmann lobe antenna, a Geiger counter, and a mysterious little device she called a Bovis biometer. This appeared to be nothing more than a flat calibrated stick used in combination with a pendulum. Such a simple instrument permitted the dowser to take a reading of the vibratory intensity of a place, or object or, in fact, anything.

Everywhere she went on this itinerary had spiritual importance. She was using the brass fish to map out the Hartmann network in temples, monasteries, cathedrals and megalithic sites. Then this Bovis technique for measuring vibrations enabled her to isolate and measure the points of highest spirituality within a site.

All of it fascinated me, but quickly I saw that my lobe antenna was just a starting point. With it you could find all the lines of force according to Hartmann, which in some of these sacred places were jammed together in a tight power structure, and with it you could identify the points of high and low polarity. However, with it you could not easily locate underground water, and with it you could not find the interlocking Curry network (which she did not invoke in her book). I suspected she relied on those supersensitive hands to find the underground streams. And she did not want to complicate the picture with the Curry network, for the purpose of the book was to reveal key ideas to the general public.

I could now see how it might be possible to herd my wild horses into a coherent structure linking spirituality with geobiology, geopathic zones, and geography. And I saw also that I did not have all the tools.

These dowsing techniques do not just scout out the electromagnetic fields that lace our environment. They lead toward the sacred, as does a meditative practice that also interlocks with the telluric power structure.

Clearly, I could not go very far in this search seeking only the Hartmann network. It is not the only system that can be found and isolated by competent dowsers. In subsequent years my own studies gave me more of an overview of the various networks which have been studied. I went about seeking more tools, especially the Bovis biometer.

It was exciting to find myself puttering around on the cutting edge of new science. It was frustrating not to know more, to be able to do more, right away. More seeking was clearly ahead of me. There were more books to ferret out and read, and some already on my shelves needed to be studied again. The scientific documentation was slowly being built up into a respectable body of evidence. All of this beckoned. I wanted to see it.

[1]   Dr. med. Ernst Hartmann, *Krankheit als Standortproblem* ("Illness as a Problem of Location"). Heidelberg: Haug Verlag, 1967.

[2]   Blanche Merz, *Les hauts-lieux cosmo-telluriques, leurs énergies subtils méconnues* (Cosmic-terrestrial sacred sites, their unrecognized subtle energies.) Genève: Librairie de l'Université, Georg & Cie S.A., 1983. 200p., glossary, bibliography. ISBN 2-8257-0104-1.

Chapter Nine

VISIONS

She was on the arm of her husband, coming up to his right shoulder. They were moving to my left. She wore her long dark hair parted in the center Indian-style and there was color in her cheeks. A grave expression chiseled her classic features as she moved ahead at a deliberate pace. She wore a green blazer over a white blouse, above a dark skirt. She looked straight ahead, not at me. Nothing at all registered about him.

A few weeks later I planned the defense of a Mediterranean pueblo against pirates, later displaying their severed heads on poles.

These are early samples of the visions I began to receive while in meditation. Typically I would begin in the usual way, a bit of breathing work before I began to follow the mantra as it dove. Random thoughts would skitter away. Slowly the sense of an energetic field would form around me. It might pulse a bit. And then I would be away.

Why did the dark-haired woman appear? She resembled no one I knew. Had I known her in a past life? Would she eventually become a spiritual contact of some sort? Questions without immediate answers.

Nothing in our winter in Spain, two years earlier, had led me ever to reflect on pirate attacks on those glistening white pueblo villages lining the Mediterranean coast. That such events might have historical basis was not part of our touristic education. And that I should be the person organizing defenses against such attacks was totally original. It came out of nowhere.

Correction: it came out of somewhere, out of some dimension with which I was unfamiliar.

The act of beginning to record my dreams at the end of 1982 seemed to have set in motion a new facet of my meditational processes. Soon I began to note little passages such as "thoughts like dreams" and "dreaming images". In the days just before "seeing" the dark-haired woman I felt "wrapped in spirit". The sense of the energy field and its coming pervaded my meditations. Thoughts emerging as I dove with the mantra seemed to be on an astral plane.

The Spanish pueblo scene came while I was staying overnight with dear friends Gudrun and Reinhard in their home halfway between Frankfurt and Wiesbaden. I meditated and slept in an attic guest room, with nice energies gathering under the peaked ceiling. The next day I would be off to America for another visit to my family.

The need for this trip had grown in my spirit with the arrival of winter. My mother was nearly 85 and we needed to visit possible retirement homes in the Los Angeles area. There was also the prickly problem of helping her reorganize her finances in a "low maintenance" mode. Before getting that far west, it was highly desirable to visit Vera in Atlanta. New friends met in Boston, she and her husband had been pillars of strength, help and hospitality while I lived there. They had left the severe climate of New England for the warmer South, and I had visited them once soon after they moved to Atlanta. Now he had moved on to other dimensions, and Vera was grieving sorely.

Several times during the winter season I had tried to organize the necessary companionship and caretaking for my Will, without luck. And then suddenly it fell into place. Three caretakers materialized one after the other, giving me a clear signal to go now, not earlier, but now. Meaning late March, 1983.

My first stop after Frankfurt was Atlanta. This was a joyous reunion with Vera and her daughter Carrie. We had a lovely time, seeing spring colors, shopping, dodging the panicked traffic in a freak, six-inch snowfall, but mostly just enjoying one another. For the last time, as it turned out, and I think back often to this time together. Vera and her Bill had given me much support when I had needed it, and later it had been my privilege to help them through their own bad patch.

In Los Angeles we quickly became three to undertake a serious tour of Mother's favorite restaurants. My daughter Carol came down from Ventura the day after Mother collected me from the airport bus. And we became four whenever my uncle Oliver joined us. Mother had grown closer to her younger brother in her years of widowhood, and he had become her frequent escort for the theater, or little trips, or just plain out to dinner.

In the ensuing days we went to visit a retirement home in suburban Pasadena, and I spent one whole day working over her accounts. A gallant cousin living in that city agreed to set up appointments for me to meet several financial managers who could conceivably be trusted to look after Mother's little capital.

One day she came home from the beauty salon with a scratchy throat, and she was angry about having caught her stylist's "bug". The next day she was sniffling and coughing. The day after that she could not get out of bed, needing assistance to get to the bathroom.

Carol and I looked at one another, nodded simultaneously, and I picked up the telephone to dial Mother's doctor. Dr. Wallace did not like the sound of that at all, and he came rather soon. His examination was brief but thorough.

"Grace, I want you in the hospital right away," he said, folding his stethoscope and standing up. "You have a bad case of pneumonia."

We packed a little bag for her, bundled her into her warmest bathrobe and into the car, and I drove us to the Good Samaritan. Once she was installed in her hospital bed, receiving care, and falling asleep, Carol and I headed for the nearest restaurant.

My own reaction to all this was clear, and over lunch I confided my sense of the situation to Carol. In addition to being my daughter, she was a kindred soul. She wasn't a meditator and she wasn't following any kind of a spiritual path that I knew about, but she was rapidly becoming a favorite sounding-board for my mystical musings.

"You and I were meant to be here, at this time, now," I pointed out. "In January it was impossible for me to find the people to stay with Will. And nothing jelled in February either. Then early last month it all fell together for me to be here now, on April 2, when she needed help."

"Are you saying some kind of a guiding hand has been at work?" Carol proposed.

"Yes, clearly. If we had not been on hand this morning, Mother would have died in her bed, helpless. She would not even have been able to reach the telephone. She would have slipped into coma and no one would have known about it. By the time Uncle Oliver wondered why she wasn't answering the phone and came to check up, he might have found a corpse."

This was all hypothetical, of course, but I was convinced of it. Once again those "invisible forces of which I was unaware" had intervened.

And this wasn't the first time Mother had awaited my arrival in order to let incipient illness take control. A few years earlier I had returned from a side trip to San Francisco to find her lying weakly on the sofa. That time she had ended up in the cardiac care unit.

Mother had not taken to Theosophy in her youth, despite paternal nudging. At least, she had seemed to indicate an indifference to that spiritual bent. Had some of it sunk in anyway? Was she subconsciously more tuned-in than she admitted? On some deep level heard by Spirit could she have known there would be a health crisis, leading her to express a psychic wish that Michèle could be there?

At an earlier time I would have dismissed such a train of thought as ridiculous pipe-dreaming. Now I opened to the possibility.

"You know," I mused aloud to Carol, "this is a kind of a reminder for me. It is telling me to pay attention, that I am on some kind of a path. I don't see where it is leading, but there are marker stones along the way. This event is another one. Being here at this moment is no coincidence."

Mother's hospitalization threw cold water on the joy we three had been sharing, but it was possible for me to go on with the rest of the trip as planned.

This involved flying to the north, staying successively with my two favorite cousins, one in San Carlos, one in San Francisco, meeting Carol again at the airport, and traveling with her up to Santa Rosa. We spent a couple of days visiting my son, her brother Neil, jointly working on a harebrained — harebrained? No, not so harebrained — idea I had about acquiring a piece of property big enough for all three of us. In the end, nothing came of it.

All this time I was trying to maintain a meditation schedule, sometimes against daunting odds. In Atlanta it had been totally impossible. Time was short, the dynamic Vera wanted every waking minute of my time, and my room was too cold because of the unseasonable snow. In Los Angeles it had been possible to meditate in the mornings but not thereafter.

On the trip north I began feeling poorly, some kind of a respiratory infection was sapping my energy. Maybe the cold that felled my mother? Well, it could have played a role, but I knew the core of the problem lay elsewhere. It was simply that my body was supersensitive to the air pollution of the Los Angeles Basin. Growing up there had been difficult although eased after we moved out of the city to a higher, drier suburb. The air quality began to deteriorate seriously during World War II, and after the war I began moving farther and farther from the metropolis. The brown wall in the sky kept inching its way eastward, and finally we picked up our brood and moved north of San Francisco. This was better, much better, and the fresher air of the North Bay reinvigorated me, gave me new wings for all phases of life including my news work. It cannot be accident that following my nose led me to a home in the Swiss Alps.

Now I was learning that about four or five days was my limit in Los Angeles and environs. Then I had to get out for a while, blow out my lungs elsewhere, before plunging back into the morass. This time I had been there more than ten days before taking the programmed side trip. Thus respiratory it was, but not basically Mother's vicious cold. Six nights up north was not the cure I needed, but it was a necessary breather.

Back in Los Angeles again I could resume my spiritual practice, such as it was, on an every-morning basis. TM was not being easy. Instead of helping me dissolve the stress of travel and fatigue, the mantra was becoming progressively more elusive.

Mother's recuperation from the pneumonia was slow. Her age was holding her back, but at least she was recovering from a malady that frequently kills people of her years. I visited her in the hospital at least daily, and one day I went to Pasadena to interview those potential financial managers for her. Dr. Wallace kept her in the hospital and she was still there when I flew to Washington on the last leg of the journey.

My dear friend Kay — we had been great buddies in New York — made me comfortable in her suburban bungalow on a quiet tree-lined street. She found it amusing that I had taken up meditation and was beginning to talk a lot about offbeat subjects.

"I grew up with all this metaphysical stuff," she said.

"What do you mean?" I asked. "You never mentioned it when we both lived in New York. Tell me."

"It's just that my mother was gifted in this direction. She had some talent as a psychic. Sometimes there were meetings in our house. That kind of thing. We meditated."

"What about now?" I asked.

"Well, you know, I don't feel any compulsion in that direction. It's enough to go occasionally to the Unitarian Church or the Church of Religious Science," she observed.

What a long arm of "coincidence" there is in our lives! My friend had become a scientist, with a doctorate in physics and an international reputation in her research specialty. But I knew that she consulted astrologers too. It almost seemed that every time I turned around someone of my entourage turned out to have had some kind of brush with the mystical world.

My meditation program was suffering with all the travel. Theoretically, and it had been my experience somewhat in the beginning, one should be able to perform transcendental meditation anywhere, anytime. But this trip demonstrated to me that such was not the case. Was there some flaw in my technique? Had the mantra become inadequate?

Nora gave me this polysyllabic Sanskrit word during the initiation ceremony. Where did she get it? Every TM practitioner was supposed to have their own, you were instructed not to reveal it to anyone, it was yours. I knew, however, that Sandra's mantra was not polysyllabic but monosyllabic, and that she didn't like it and had drifted away from meditation for that reason.

How did the teachers select mantras for their fresh initiates? Was there a little black book, a dictionary, with a protocol for making the choice? It was a deep, dark secret. I suspected that astrology had something to do with it, but Nora simply smiled sweetly with a little negative movement of her head. Which meant what, no to astrology or no, she wasn't telling? Maharishi required his teachers to operate under strict rules about answering questions. In the face of that, it didn't make sense to me that he would allow them the freedom to make psychological assessments leading to mantra assignment.

Mine had functioned beautifully for a full year, leading me gently into the inner depths, coming back again and again after thought strings played out, producing deep relaxation and a distinct sense of being in an energy field.

More and more this was not the case. In Kay's home I could meditate in the living room early in the morning the first couple of days before she stirred. One time it was nice, the next time it was too much troubled by outside noises, and after that I could only snatch five minutes here and there.

Then came the trip home, during which I made several attempts to "get in", but nothing seemed to work very well. Home again in late April, the first meditation was good, the mantra tracking well. After that not so good. Yet I did not dream of giving up because earlier there had been so much satisfaction. My brain, my whole nervous system, had been satisfied.

Overseas travel by air is, of course, very hard on the physical body. And this trip had been chopped up by my tendency to try to cram in too many visits, too many destinations. My health had suffered, with the pollution-inspired cold sliding into either influenza or bronchitis, for which I seemed to have a constitutional weakness despite alpine air. The return flight was supposed to go to Zurich, yet at the crack of dawn on a lovely day we found our plane landing in Munich for reasons never explained. And we waited, and we waited, and we changed planes and finally took off. From Zurich I could telephone to warn my household that I would be on a later train crossing the country from east to west.

Martine, number three on the caretaker team, was at the station in Aigle to meet me in the late afternoon. Up the mountain again, and after snuggling a while with my loving Will, I pulled on some stout shoes and announced a walk in the pre-dusk freshness. My man was too lazy to join us, but I was able to drag Martine toward the sidehill track to Curnaux. Wisely she did not ask a lot of questions, I was too busy learning how to breathe again. The light mountain air worked like a tonic in my lungs. Synchronizing my respiration with the "new" air began to heal spirit and body. This half-hour hike restored me to the land of sentient beings. All parts of me rejoiced; we were home.

There was an interesting letter waiting for me. Before leaving for the United States I had begun writing to people on the cutting edge of the psychological world -- writers and editors -- asking them to explain tinnitus. I wanted to know more about my "massed police whistles". Now a West Coast editor had replied, the only one who ever did, and I am eternally grateful[1].

"The brain has reference sounds which we don't always hear," my correspondent wrote. "Many people find these tones reflect a pattern in psychic perception or widened awareness."

This echo of my own sense of what the noise meant brought a heaping helping of inner relief. A few short lines returned me to the mainstream.

Extrapolating those words ever so lightly told me that TM had brought to the surface of my perceptions something that had always been present.

"The TM people generally don't discuss phenomena except in advanced courses," said my savior. "I think it's too bad that they are not more open about the phenomena. As I understand it, Maharishi wanted the teachers trained uniformly and to not say more than they were told to say."

There it was again -- the TM stonewall.

Enclosed with the letter was a photocopied reference to the "nadas", with the suggestion these could be of interest. It was an entry from the *Yoga Dictionary* compiled by Ernest Wood[2], from which I feel impelled to quote, for it told me that what I heard could be compared to the "song of the cosmos".

"Sound has to be thought of as everywhere," he says, "just as in the springtime there is a simultaneous movement, and everything breaks into song."

"In the soul or mind of the yogi there is such a movement, and the noises of chaos are to be replaced in all respects, by the songs of cosmos..........only in the hearing of the song of cosmos is there attainment."

Wood points out the yogi must listen to his inner voice in several ways. The kinds of sounds mentioned in his various Buddhist and Hindu sources include the nightingale, a silver cymbal, the sound in a conch shell, stringed instruments, a bamboo flute, a trumpet, a bell, a lute, drums, tinkling ornaments, horns, the sea, clouds, waterfalls, bees and thunder.

All of these are nadas, and it was easy for me to insert my whistling-buzzing-ringing into this spectrum of yogic phenomena. Wood adds that nada can also describe the prolongation of a sound such as the recitation of "Om".

Related concepts began to emerge from other sources. I had been reading *The Aquarian Conspiracy* by Marilyn Ferguson[3]. She explains that brainwaves reflect fluctuations of energy.

"Meditation, reverie, relaxation, and other assorted psychotechnologies tend to increase the slower, larger brainwaves known as alpha and theta. Inward attention, in other words, generates a larger fluctuation in the brain," she wrote. "In altered states of consciousness, fluctuations may reach a critical level, large enough to provoke the shift into a higher level of organization[4]."

In these lines Ferguson explained for me the occasional oceanic movements in my brain during meditation, as well as the vibratory, pulsating sensations that signaled the energy field which often seemed to surround me.

Two weeks later I began to shake up my meditation technique. My reading had also taught me about the existence of a very old Hindu mantra, one dating back millenia. I liked the way "Om Mani Padme Hum" sounded in the body, and I loved its translation (one of several, I have since learned): "The All is a jewel in the bud of the lotus which blooms in my heart."

My meditations began with breath control in the form of alternate nostril breathing, the Pranayama technique I had learned during the retreat at Nextmountain. From there I slipped easily into the new-old mantra, Om Mani Padme Hum. I loved its rhythm, its resonance. It led me into pleasant energy fields, and it lent itself to the "diving" that is central to the TM method. Within a short time I was happy again with my meditations. I don't know how to define the quality of a meditation in simple words, but the quality was improving rapidly. Once again I emerged from my sessions with a renewed sense of refreshment and clarity.

Late one afternoon about a month later I was enjoying a nice vibrational state when suddenly I found myself running alongside a giant wingless bird.

One could compare it to a female pheasant that was gray in color and seemingly without plumage. A group of us were running with it across a flat meadow. We came only to its shoulder and we were nude or nearly so. I stopped for breath and watched my companions as they followed the bird across the plain. It seemed to be a hunt but none of us had any weapons.

The image of this great bird without wings and almost without plumage -- a giant plucked chicken-- haunted me for days and weeks to come. This was so totally out of contact with my everyday world. It seemed prehistoric, yet I was there.

I asked myself: "*where did that come from?*"

A week later Om Mani Padme Hum led me into a nice hollowed-out space that mutated into a fearful vision in a tunnel before returning to a pleasant state. The next afternoon I began a period of switching back and forth between Om Mani Padme Hum and the original TM mantra. The latter immediately took me into a quiet space where I saw a faint flower in bloom.

Something I had read or heard about gave me the notion of trying to meet my Inner Advisor. I gave several meditations the mission of helping me meet It, but all I got out of that was a vision of a string of railroad freight cars labeled "F&NT" in big white letters. This label did not correspond to any railroad line I had ever heard about. Another mystery for my growing collection!

A few weeks later along came something else for my catalogue of anarchic scenes: a shining pink amorphous form, outlined with light, loomed on the screen inside my forehead. Geometric forms came next, about a week later. There was a circle with a dot in the center, and then there was a triangle, both of them in light.

All during this period there were other new things in my life. I had decided to give up waiting for my husband to go hiking with me. He opened the summer with a jaundice attack; coming a year-and-a-half after the traumatic gall bladder episode it was worrisome to me and inspired laziness in him.

I began learning our mountains on my own. Will's son came with his family and we did some modest hiking itineraries. We visited Will's sister in Grindelwald, and she introduced me to a lovely series of trails in that spectacular region. In midsummer, a few days after chasing the giant wingless bird, I led a young Dutch woman up the Haute-Corde, a modest little (7'627 feet) pyramidal peak accessible by trails.

From its summit one overlooked the fabled Miroir de l'Argentine. As seen at distance from our windows this huge steep cliff resembled a mirror, hence its name. Looking down on its upper reaches from the Haute-Corde I could see that there was a vast network of holes and crevices corrugating the surface. Even so, at that time I had no ambition to try climbing it. It looked awesome.

Will had shown me the itinerary for this nice hike on a topographic map, and leading it without the slightest difficulty opened vast new perspectives to my adventurous spirit and my ageing but still athletic body.

The summer brought me yet another opening: my introduction to alternative medicine. My friend Elisabeth received the impromptu visit of three young women from California, two of them professional acupuncturists. To respect their privacy, I have changed their names in the following account. Anna and Rose had been taking an advanced training course from their professor in Oxford, and their friend Josy, a dietician, was along for the fun of the trip. I guided them over some alpine trails and we did an excursion to touristy Gruyères. And all the while I was discreetly pumping them about acupuncture, which had long made theoretical — and instinctive — sense to me without my ever having had any experience of it.

They offered to work on me and I accepted eagerly. For some months I had been troubled by a stiff neck and frequent tightness in the shoulders, as well as a kind of phantom toothache that manifested about four or five o'clock in the morning. After the first treatment I noticed nothing for a couple of days, then I was surprised to find that my hemorrhoids had suddenly shrunk a bit. This, Anna and Rose informed me, was due to the needling in the feet.

The second treatment was small and had little effect, except that I did feel very well and energetic afterward, which at that particular moment was not a change.

The third treatment made a convert of me. I told Anna about a whole set of little problems that I felt might just be related, asking her to work from a holistic viewpoint. She needled the wrists, the hands, the shoulders and the feet.

During the following days I observed that the burning pain which started in my right shoulder and went down the upper arm had been suppressed. The early morning toothache, which had gone on for many months, disappeared. And my meditations were especially good for about three days afterward.

Anna, Rose and Josy returned to California, but I was privileged to visit all of them over the years.

This adventure blended with another beginning at the same time. A friend who had been crippled for years with osteomyelitis in the hip asked me to chauffeur her over the mountain to a chiropractor in another village. After her treatment we were chatting with the therapist and I wondered if her chiropractic technique could help me. She asked what troubled me and I mentioned the neck and shoulders.

"Yes, and the jaw too," she said. She was looking at me from more than a meter away when she made this observation. You can imagine that said jaw dropped in astonishment.

The shoulder pain began to return about three weeks after the needles had relieved it, and now my acupuncturists had gone. So the next time I drove my friend over the mountain to her chiropractic doctor I had some therapy too. Her manipulations and massage did relieve the neck for a couple of days, but only that. But after this first session she insisted that I see my dentist.

Which I did. And this was conclusive. An x-ray showed an infected root canal. This was the consequence of emergency work done by another dentist while mine was on vacation. Dr. W. ripped out his colleague's expensive crown and began to treat the infection. Overnight the neck and shoulder pain subsided, evaporated, and disappeared forever.

These adventures left me with a profound respect for the talents of so-called "alternative" practitioners. The acupuncture had provided first-class pain relief, sparing me going to a medical doctor who would probably have given me muscle relaxants and injections — all of which had irritated my ulcers in the past. The chiropractor was reputed to have a "gift", and her correct diagnosis of a problem in the jaw — from a distance — proved it, leaving me speechless with admiration. She had *seen* the invisible, and after one treatment she had the integrity to push me in another therapeutic direction.

On the mundane but still lively side of life Will and I threw a party in late September, 1983. By setting up an extra table in his painting studio, we were able to wine and dine a dozen of the closer friends, gathered to help us celebrate two anniversaries: ten years of our "July-November" marriage, and my sixtieth birthday.

In mid-November another vision entered my meditation. I got completely absorbed in this scene of two long-headed African women wearing colorful long gowns. They/we were in a timeless native village. One of them had a black face and the other a paler face, and both of them wore coifs in a pointy-head style that seemed to complement their dolichocephalic faces.

About a month after that I began a determined effort to meet my "inner teacher" in meditation. This mythical personage proved to be as totally elusive as "higher self". Images of lots of men I had known came in over the next days, but Inner Teacher wasn't tempted.

As the year ended I resumed this quest, trying to find or hear my Guide with the help of Infinite Intelligence and Divine Will. These high concepts, like many of the others proposed in metaphysical literature, proved equally unhelpful. Other interesting notions popped up out of the usual nowhere, such as the idea of geopathic zones, leading me to wonder if my Guides wanted me to meditate in a more neutral zone. Another time Om Mani Padme Hum took me into a very strong field of the etheric body surrounding the physical body. It felt like I could almost float upward, lift off.

Infinite Intelligence and Divine Will floated pleasantly enough through the breathing routines and the mantra (sometimes one, sometimes the other). This effort continued fruitlessly through January, but by then more visions began to pile in.

Sitting up in my bed early one morning, praying to Infinite Intelligence and then chanting Om Mani Padme Hum internally, I was shown a view of California's vast aqueduct crossing the desert, carrying water from the Sierra Nevada mountains hundreds of miles south to Los Angeles. I saw that this monster pipeline had been breached by sabotage south of Lone Pine, leaving Los Angeles "a helpless giant".

Four days later the TM mantra carried me directly to a dear friend whose death seven years earlier had shocked me, and from there I went into a startling scene. *Two spectral figures, hooded like the Grim Reaper with their faces in shadow and not visible, marched in front of me carrying torches on long poles. Moving toward my right, they passed between me and a haystack, advancing toward a large home, maybe a small castle. I had the impression of a large thatched roof, mostly hidden by bulky trees in the background and a small yellow field lying between the haystack and the trees. The lighting was that of a long summer dusk, with deep shadows, and the sun already gone. Then the building was in flames.*

Six days later came a long and complicated dream with a surprising dénouement. *In this dream, at my then age of sixty, I had to go back to work and took a job in a library down at Villeneuve on the lake shore. I was one of about four on the staff. This library (which in fact does not exist) occupied an elevated loftlike space, opening onto an overview of a café half a floor below. Uncertain of my tasks and lacking instructions, I tried to follow a kind of work list written on a scrap of silk. What was wanted seemed unclear, but, wishing to be effective, I called on old skills and began to do some cataloging. I hoped that, in the absence of precise instructions, that would satisfy. After all, I have been a head librarian in several work environments.*

In the café below I could see my favorite cousin David sitting in a booth with his back to a window, thus facing my way. I worked a little more and then went down to greet him.

Then it was lunchtime and I expected to join David but found him surrounded by male friends. He tried to introduce me but there was too much hubbub. They were moving to a well-known restaurant down the street. I tried to follow but couldn't find him again.

The head librarian, a short, chunky, woman with reddish-brown hair and glasses on her round face, proposed that I lunch with her. We couldn't get adequately served, and she plunged off in search of a better place. I followed but couldn't find her. Because she was short and rather stocky, I worried that she might become ill — heart trouble came to mind. She wasn't in the first or second dining areas, and I thought she might be in the third one, farther back.

On my way there I passed a group of women crowded into a semi-circular booth; they thought they knew me. One jumped up and greeted me as "Theona", as if I were someone not seen in a long time, but I demurred. "I'm Michèle," I told her. Theona? Who's that?

Still trying to join my head librarian, I never succeeded. I had missed David entirely but later, outside on the street facing the embarcadero, I met two youths who were part of Dave's crowd. One of them may have been his son. They befriended me and offered to help.

In my personal dreamworld this story is remarkable for its length. And for its message: the name Theona.

The women in this sequence were all familiar faces in my daily life. A "librarian" alongside whom I worked is often seen in the village. The "head librarian" owned a fabric shop in a nearby town. The one who called me Theona worked for many years for a big supermarket down in the valley.

Was I named Theona in another life? I could not recall ever hearing this name before, although I have known one or two Leonas. Some research in my own reference shelves persuaded me that the name was a feminine version of "Theon".

History tells us of two Theons. There was Theon the satirical poet of ancient Rome, noted for his acid wit. And there was Theon the Greek mathematician and astronomer of the fourth century A.D., whose version of Euclid's *Elements* was the only known interpretation of the master's work until modern times.

I can identify with both of these thumbnail descriptions. Both had qualities which are not foreign to me.

While the name Theona resonates well within me, the Greek mathematician Theon named his daughter otherwise: Hypatia. She was born in Alexandria in 375 A.D. and became a famous philosopher, mathematician, astronomer scientist and teacher in that Egyptian city during its peak as a center of learning. Her intellectual brilliance, combined with eloquence and beauty, drew students from all around the Mediterranean. She was the acknowledged leader of the Neoplatonic school of philosophy, which drew the ire of the Bishop Cyril. He stirred up a riot against heathen philosophy, and Hypatia was hacked to death at the age of forty by monks among a Christian mob.

Ancient history thus poses a question: would I rather have been the fatally brilliant daughter of Theon, or might it not have been more restful to simply be a Theona in some quiet backwater?

Whatever, four days after dreaming of Theona, I was looking upward at a tall Egyptian idol. This was not a dream but a meditation in which the mantra Om Mani Padme Hum stimulated some brain wave rollovers before I slipped into the vision. This statue was at least fifteen feet high, standing at the end of a shadowy hall, and it was a real center of attraction. The statue was mostly deep turquoise with some very discreet gold trim, especially around the stylized headdress.

We received a lot of slick-paper advertising for books and organized voyages to Egypt, but I could not recall ever having seen an illustration of this statue. I went through piles of old clippings and brochures looking for this one and did not find it. In other words, I tried to confirm the possibility of memory sticking to a particular image seen in print. But no, careful research could not demonstrate that I had ever seen a picture of that statue.

Three days later I awoke in the morning with the name "Udaipur" running through my mind. There was no recollection of a dream involving that place in India. Was this place prominent in the dreams already forgotten, or was my subconscious presenting me with some choices? For example, telling me to go there, or reminding me that I had once been there (not in this lifetime, in any case), or to seek and reread a book in which I had seen the name?

Obviously, in considering such choices, I am automatically excluding the notion that irrelevant information simply pops up out of nowhere. No longer could I believe in "out of nowhere". Everything was "out of somewhere".

Some of my dreams turn out to be baffling excursions with only the vaguest of mystical significance. Not long after "Udaipur" surfaced I took a nocturnal ramble to Far Rockaway. I had never visited this place on the exurban fringe of New York during the three years I lived in that city, back in the 1960s. Mind sought to correct that omission, I guess. *In the dream state*

I was on the distant edge of the metropolis, and we were looking at a lavishly-fitted-out car that turned out to be a house. We went on to look at another house, to occupy it briefly, then we were at a sports club. I offered to join in a both-sexes football game but they politely pointed out they were playing only six to a side, and I saw they wore uniforms. Fretted momentarily about the contents of my handbag. After watching this football game briefly, a bit enviously, we started out to find the way home.

We emerged onto a road where there were two women, and we asked for their help. There came the impression they helped only Socialists, which we were not. One of them did offer to help but could not find a map.

Walking again through the long grasses, avoiding the wet places, as dusk fell we came to a massive wood-and-stone structure, and through a passage we saw the glimmer of bay water. I heard the rumble of trains overhead. Eureka! this must be Far Rockaway.

Upstairs in a social group, I was led to point out I must have been in Far Rockaway in a previous lifetime, because (quoting from the old notes) "I had no way of knowing it from this one." That didn't make any more sense than the meaningless address the girl sitting next to me showed me.

Ten days after this bit of nonsense came a lengthy dream which has stayed with me all these years. I indexed it under "Conflict and War", but it was much more than that. It was the climax of and the most violent of a conflictual, warring series which had started many months earlier.

In this other dimension I was doing some kind of research for my country of Switzerland. I found that a given document which had strayed into my hands was really intended for a person who was secretary of a subversive organization for another country. When he appeared on the scene, I redoubled my efforts to make my superiors realize how important, how potentially dangerous was this seeming non-entity.

Suddenly there were sounds of fighting from the airfield. I rushed toward another building where my cameras were in a locker. Others were on similar missions, but we were brought up short by furious fighting on my half-right. A powerful wedge of enemy troops charged down a hill and punched savagely into the forces protecting us. The shock of the assault by this "dark" force plunging down the slope was frightening. It looked catastrophic. The clash foretold of worse to come; it was panic-inspiring. It was like a battle of centuries ago, with lances shimmering above the tumult of colliding shields and bodies.

This infamous secretary was sitting on a kind of bleachers watching with satisfaction. He had changed face and looked differently. I asked him what they were up to. He insisted they would not harm us, that they were there simply to help.

They set up a big gun that stuttered bullets all over.

I started to move away rapidly. He followed, changing to yet another appearance, still insisting there was no harm for us. Formerly he had been stocky, with a black brush moustache; now in the third embodiment he was tall and thin. Then he was shot, and his body lay on the pavement. I expected the next bullet to be for me, in the back.

Finally, I was standing in the alleyway between hangars, looking first at the body of the man, in his rumpled raincoat of the third embodiment, then down at my own body sprawled on the tarmac.

Was this a kind of out-of-body experience? Was my subconscious reminding me I had died that way once yet still lived? Or that it was still to happen?

Interesting dreams were coming thick and fast at this period. Had they always been coming thick and fast or was it simply that now I was writing them down?

With striking visions in meditation, and with dreams like these, I did not need adventure books, motion pictures, or television for entertainment. My notes were recording a fabulous variety of "home movies", beginning about fifteen months after first becoming a meditator.

These visions always seemed to come at a point when consciousness had altered and I was suddenly "away" somewhere — on another plane, or in another world. I always had the sensation of being a participant or a close spectator in these scenes. Because some of them appear to have an archaic setting, I suppose them to be glimpses of past lives.

One such occurred about a month after that dream of conflict and death. The meditation had been light to begin with, then slipped into a fragile vibrational state, then there was a sudden shift and I was "in" a scene.

A young woman with long blonde hair, some corkscrew curls, danced out of a crowd toward me with an expression of glad greetings. Her gait was effervescent and her face wore a gay expression, as if she had been photographed in the middle of a word and a step.

She wore an eighteenth-century dress in a kind of a gold-ochre-dark yellow polished cotton. The sleeves were short with a bit of ruffle, her decolletage was ruffled, and there was a hint of ruffled petticoat peeping out at the ankles. She wore a kind of straw picture hat.

This young woman did not quite resemble anyone I knew, although there was a vague impression of a fleshier version of the face and nose of my English friend Martine, who had looked after my Will. There was a young man in knee breeches, a brocade weskit over his full-sleeved white blouse --- he seemed to watch over her. And I, the spectator, was simply me. No distinguishing characteristics.

These long scenarios seemed to taper off as we went into the spring of 1984. There was an interesting double view of a lake and a boatman, somewhere in

Europe. The lefthand view was a pastel painting of the righthand view, which was in vivid colors. Another time I was moving through a series of strange places not seen before, and then I observed three dancer-like figures in front of a Moslem arch.

My meditations began to bring me large blotches of amethyst color. They would open and close, sometimes revealing a scene of a structure or a rock, the scene closing quickly like a camera lens being stopped down.

One evening in June the head of a strange toothy creature appeared. It had a long face, a big mouth, a big nose, long ears and human-looking skin, but it wasn't recognizably human by any definition familiar to me.

A couple of mornings later the mantra was visible as a caravan descending the opposite slope of a small valley, and then it became a machine as it climbed the near slope toward me.

This incredible variety of visual phenomena kept me well entertained. More than that, it kept me meditating. And it kept me pondering and searching too.

Some of these scenes certainly suggested past-life experiences. Purely subjective criteria singled out the giant wingless bird episode, defending the Mediterranean pueblo, the chateau going up in flames, and the eighteenth-century girl as being "videoclips" from previous lifetimes. What a span of history they implied!

At least two of these episodes seemed to have a prophetic weight, as if I had been given the gift of precognitive vision. The matter of the sabotaged aqueduct fits this schema, and so does the dream of the battle scene ending in an out-of-body view on my own corpse. That one brought together diverse elements of both ancient and contemporary history, it was certainly life-threatening and seems clearly to propose a violent death. In the past or in the future?

One of the most compelling for me was the episode in which I returned to a former profession, librarianship, and through it received a name: Theona. This one stays with me. Another that sticks is the chase of the giant wingless bird. It is impossible for me to discard that scene -- it happened, millenia ago, and I was there.

Do we carry memory of past lives buried deep in our brain cells? Or do we occasionally gain access to that immense spiritual memory bank called the *Akashic Record*?

As well as understanding what these phenomena meant to me, I wanted to know how they fit into what might be called the mystical mainstream. My resources for digging into these questions were rather limited. Reading and meditation were my only contacts with esoteric currents past and present. TM was still the core of my meditational practice, despite trying out another mantra, but I had given up trying to get helpful answers from the Maharishi's organization. My letter to his research director in the United States, about the ringing in my ears, lay unanswered.

On the other hand Marilyn Ferguson's book had provided helpful information about this phenomenon. I'd also discovered her *Brain/Mind Bulletin* and become a subscriber. It offered engrossing reading, helping me sense where the various mainstreams were flowing. Reading *BMB* for half a year began to show me that the so-called "mainstream", like the Amazon river, was composed of an almost infinite variety of currents coming together.

Ferguson's newsletter was helping me comprehend the dazzling sprawl of disciplines that wove the connections between science, psychology and metaphysics. It was a metaphysical lifeline. And then she printed an interview with a man named Robert Monroe that captured my attention. It sent me racing to find the file of publications I had brought back from the previous spring's trip to California.

[1]   Unfortunately this source must remain unidentified, for repeated letters over recent years failed to reestablish contact. Friends helped in the search, a publisher's office was found, but there was no answer. Dead, or simply doesn't want to be quoted?

[2]   Ernest Wood, *Yoga Dictionary*. New York: Philosophical Library, 1956. Pp. 104-105.

[3]   Marilyn Ferguson, *The Aquarian Conspiracy, personal and social transformation in the 1980s*. Los Angeles: Tarcher, 1980. 448p, references and readings, index. ISBN 0-87447-191-9 (paper).

[4]   *Op.cit.*, p. 168-169.

Chapter Ten

MASSAGING THE BRAIN

In one of my very first meditations I had tried to promote the harmonization of the two hemispheres of my brain. The immediate inspiration for this was a desire to tap the creative right side. My ability at sketching, although not bad, was not, to my perception, fluent enough, and I wanted to unlock eye-hand fluidity. I had been reading *Drawing on the Right Side of the Brain*[1] when I received Brugh Joy's book[2] from Marina. There was a remarkable "time warp" when I combined techniques from both authors into one of my earliest meditations.

A few months later, just before the episode of the blown fuse, I had spoken in a letter to my daughter of "wanting to integrate better the two halves of my brain, and I think that some of the cerebral hi-jinks that occasionally come along are signs of harmonization taking place."

It is pertinent here to explain that I am left-handed and left-footed. When I went to primary school back in 1929 they tried to break me of this vile, incorrect, anti-social and probably immoral perversion. The immediate result was that I "spaced out" and became intellectually frozen in that first classroom. We lived right on the borderline between two school districts, so it was easy for my parents to transfer me at the semester break to another elementary school. There they began again to try to make a right-handed writer of me. And, of course, instead of creating someone with "normal" handwriting they created a stutterer.

The campaign continued, as it did in those days, and very quickly they had on their hands a child who both spoke badly and wrote badly. Finally, unable to break me of my neurological perversion, they let me start writing with the left hand. However, they insisted I do this in the classic position of right-handers. This didn't go down very well either, and finally they surrendered and let me do what comes naturally to a left-hander. Most of us "southpaws" write with the hand hooked around so that the fingers holding the pen are above the line. Of course, this leads to smudging of the ink text and a nice stain on the heel of the hand.

My handwriting was execrable throughout school days and has only improved modestly with maturity. The stuttering stopped, but it was years before I could respond orally to questions without an instant of hesitation. It was as if my neurological responses had been damaged by the attempt to make of me a right-hander.

Brain/Mind Bulletin returned my attention to this earlier preoccupation by publishing an interview with a man named Robert Monroe[3]. Among other things, he claimed to be harmonizing the two halves of the brain. Except that he called it Hemi-Sync, a patented process derived from the term "hemispherical synchronization".

Monroe's first claim to fame was a well-sharpened ability to travel "out of body" during sleep. This occurred involuntarily to begin with, but with some psychological guidance he allowed it to develop and became very experienced in this unusual mode of travel. Monroe was a production executive in the radio industry, having a scientific and engineering background. Over time he developed electronic gear which enabled volunteers to experiment with their own possibilities in this bizarre direction. To do this he used sound patterns mixed on stereo channels.

"We discovered that if the brain hears a certain frequency, it tends to imitate it — the 'frequency following response'. These sound waves are too low to be picked up by the ears, but they can be heard by the brain by playing slightly different wave lengths to each ear. The brain then assimilates the two frequencies and hears the difference between them," he explained in the *BMB* interview.

In order to send a low alpha wave such as ten cycles per second to the brain, Monroe played a 100-cycle sound wave in one ear and a 110-cycle wave in the other. The brain hears both waves, makes its own calculation, and receives a ten-cycle signal. Monroe covered these patterns with the sound of ocean waves, also inserting verbal instructions to his human experimentees, who he called "explorers."

This interview send me racing to the pile of papers I had brought back from the last trip to California, just one year earlier. I remembered an article about Monroe in a magazine I'd picked up in an esoteric bookshop. After a bit of rummaging around, "Altered States of Consciousness" rose to the surface of my personal ocean of not-always well-filed documentation[4]. The writer described a week of the "Gateway Program" at the Monroe Institute of Applied Sciences in the Blue Ridge Mountains of Virginia. Participants spent most of the day in and out of a CHEC unit (Controlled Holistic Environment Chamber), listening to and interacting with Monroe's series of tapes. Apparently most participants were hoping to travel out of body but relatively few did.

Reading carefully, filtering out the out-of-body chit-chat, I learned that a personal program of signals could be tailored to individual goals, such as learning to sleep better, or stay awake better, play better golf or tennis, improve your motor skills, improve your powers of concentration. Monroe had told *BMB* that "we now use twenty-three operating frequencies with consistent, predictable results." His tapes had been used to help stroke victims, surgical patients, and autistic children. And, of course, to learn —- maybe — how to travel out of body.

Monroe's auditory work intrigued me. Hemispherical synchronization sounded like a good thing to me. My childhood problems with left-right, my interest in improving my ability to sketch and paint, and now the new matter of the ringing in my ears — my "massed police whistles" stemming from immersion in TM — all led me to imagine something like the Gateway Program could be of benefit.

Without further ado I sent off to the Monroe Institute my order for the first unit of the Gateway Program, the "Discovery" tape set, and a copy of Monroe's first book, *Journeys Out of the Body5*.

When "Discovery", Wave One in the Gateway program, arrived it proved to be a series of six tapes with a small manual. I knew in advance that I would need a stereo cassette player with headphones for these exercises, and I had ordered a small portable stereo player. The headphones I had already. When the tapes arrived I was of course impatient to get started with this intriguing new process, but my dealer in the village had not yet received the little machine.

With some hesitation, I decided to go ahead and start the program using the monaural cassette player in hand. This was mid-July, 1984.

At the beginning of every session one commences by repeating the Gateway Affirmation, which I liked immediately and which has lent inspiration to other affirmations I have created for myself over the years.

The Affirmation opens with "I am more than my physical body. Because I am more than physical matter, I can perceive that which is greater than the Physical world."

Looking back at my first encounter with these words, it is amazing to realize how much of an opening they created at that time. For until that moment I had never thought of my relationship with my body in such terms.

Yet I knew from the vibrational shells with which TM had surrounded me that there was more. The Affirmation placed that outer presence as part of me, within a greater me. It wasn't just something that sprang up and flowered when I meditated. Robert Monroe was telling me the vibrational stuff around me was actually part of me. And it made sense instantly. But why couldn't the Maharishi have instructed his teachers to tell us that when we experienced it, instead of leaving us in the dark?

There was much more to the Affirmation:

It continued with: "Therefore, I deeply desire to Expand, to Experience, to Know, to Understand, to Control, to Use such greater energies and energy systems as may be beneficial and constructive to me and to those who follow me. Also, I deeply desire the help and cooperation, the assistance, the understanding of those individuals whose wisdom, development and experience are equal or greater than my own. I ask their guidance and protection from any influence or any source that might provide me with less than my stated desires[6]."

Completeness flowed through these declarations, creating a kind of reassurance.

After your Affirmation, the first Discovery tape teaches you how to create a box with your mind, into which you stow all the disturbing factors in your life, such as money matters, photos of people who are a source of worry, the next appointment with your dentist, a misunderstanding with someone near and dear. Rather quickly my first box began to overflow and I had to make a regular trunk with a padlock. This sometimes got so full I had to sit on it, hold it closed with my body weight while I snapped the lock. Monroe calls this an "energy conversion box", and it is a useful device which I have used often over the years.

After stuffing and securing the ECB, a "resonant tuning" chant guides you into breathing exercises which you vocalize, spreading energy everywhere within and around yourself. The sound of ocean surf masks the Hemi-Sync tones being played into your brain.

With the second tape you are introduced to a state called "Focus 10", in which your physical body goes into deep sleep while your consciousness remains wide awake and alert. And with the third exercise you learn how to create your Resonant Energy Balloon, an energy field which flows out of the top of the head like a fountain, falling all about you and reentering through the soles of your feet. Then you shift the flow pattern of this "REBAL" into a spiral that winds around the physical body. It creates an energetic shield and filter, preventing the intrusion of vibrational patterns lower than your own.

Subsequently I have encountered this kind of energy visualization a number of times. Numerous spiritual teachers employ variations on these themes. But they were all new to me at the time.

Impatience to get started led me to do the opening exercise twice that first day -- once before preparing supper, once before settling into the night's sleep.

My journal says that "as the exercise progressed I gradually relaxed into a state not unlike that of a meditation but without the problem of runaway thoughts." I found the level of vibration different than in meditation, it was more subtle, less "buzzy". I felt concentrated but somehow "thinner".

A few days later I was able to borrow the empty apartment of a friend in order to find greater isolation from the sounds of household and highway.

"Focus 10 developed a kind of detached vibratory sensation, semi-hypnotic," I wrote in my journal. "As it matured I felt once again that sense of my body narrowing, at first into almost a hollow tube or tunnel, from which I felt briefly as if I could lift off or out."

This proved to be a most refreshing experience from which I emerged bright and bouncy.

My stereo machine still had not arrived some days later but the shop loaned me one. And this made a clear difference.

"More tones are perceived and hemi-sync is now fully heard as it should be," I scribbled. And, significantly, "my existing tinnitus is audible during most of these sounds. It is strong after the tape." No suppression then, no magical melting away. Was my phenomenon impervious to these techniques?

During these early days in Gateway the time commitment was such I could not always fit in my ordinary meditative practice. From time to time I would slip in a TM session, and a few times I blended the mantra into the tape exercise. Monroe's "resonant tuning" included breathing exercises which resembled the pranayama I had been doing.

Eventually my new little machine arrived and provided a more intense listening experience, fuller tones, deeper perceptions. One heard more.

Within ten days (according to my journal) I was receiving vibrations in my hands, then "they began to spread, starting with the torso. Each sound of his (Monroe's) voice was a resonating stimulant. By the end of the countdown the vibrations were cresting on each sound."

A few more days and I received a brief vision. I saw the old Arroyo Vista Hotel, in its shining bisque color, standing in its place at the end of the Colorado Street Bridge leading across the deep arroyo and into the city of Pasadena. This was not hard to understand, for my mother was now living in the retirement community we had visited in that city. All this snapshot proved was that thoughts of her lurked in my subconscious.

In spite of that, and after a bit more than two weeks of work with the tapes, I could write that "with Hemi-Sync I do not feel the difficulty of great mind-wandering that goes with TM."

After another week or so I began to have new sensations. "I wondered if there was an earthquake, for I was conscious of lying on quaking jelly," I noted. A few days after that "I began to have sensations of rolling or falling or drifting backwards, weightlessly. This happened repeatedly, and that sense of narrowness was briefly present."

These sensations of falling back, or rocking, or feeling ready to separate came along frequently, especially as I progressed through the set of six tapes. Often enough there would be a fugitive sense of floating. By the time I began to work with Tape Six I would feel "as if lift-off was not far away."

However, I never did achieve an out-of-body state. Such had not been my first objective at all, but as one continues with this sound therapy one begins to experience all these sensations of "almost" going out and up, until the goal shifts insidiously. After a month of this kind of exercise, and working in the most advanced tapes of the set of six, the following quotation from my journal sums up what frequently manifested.

There is a "vague sense of floating, without separation and always with a sense of still being in physical body, given a boost by Monroe's last suggestion to float."

Frequently there was vibrational tingling in my hands and arms, sometimes elsewhere in the body. The vibrations were just as strong as in TM, but of a different quality. And I could not define that difference, simply acknowledge it. Both methods stimulated waves of energy. TM released a considerable amount of electromagnetic energy in irregular bursts, without acknowledging such was part of the program. Monroe's system, on the other hand, was designed to work with these energies in a deliberate, coherent fashion.

Sometimes there were phenomena similar to both systems. At the end of a TM meditation I would "see" colored circles opening, evolving and dissolving. They were usually a sort of purple color but could move toward a kind of orange. I began getting the same thing with Hemi-Sync. The circles formed and reformed, waxing and waning continuously against a panorama of a myriad of dots. These thousands of atoms seemed to dance against a brindled green background. Sometimes there were strange light waves curlycuing on this inner screen. Sometimes I would black out for a few minutes.

Much of the time I was mixing Hemi-Sync/Discovery with TM during the course of a day -- one time one technique, the next time the other.

In mid-September I was working with an "energy conversion" tape. Then the next morning, unable to sleep after four-thirty in the morning during Full Moon, I was reading Edgar Cayce on reincarnation when a kind of bright little storm cloud invaded my brain, a bit of fluffy turbulence. It seemed to be a call. So I had a quick wash, then went down to my husband's studio for some Transcendental Meditation.

After getting into it, I began giving progressively more precise instructions to my subconscious to produce memories of my last life. I fell into a deep vibrational state, no mantra, no thoughts, no visions, simply a state of molecular activity, an extension and inward deepening of the tinnitus. There was extreme sensitivity and resonant reaction to outside noises (some early morning highway traffic beginning). Coming out because of this, I was somewhat dazed in a cellular sense. Altered consciousness, to be sure, but no pastlife memories.

More little visions began piling in during Tape Six of the Discovery package. I saw myself standing on a precipice atop the Mannlichen above Grindelwald, and I was looking down toward Wengen and the deep cleft of the Lauterbrunnen when a big military helicopter passed opposite me at slow speed. Soldiers leaned negligently against the open door and one of them waved to me. They were Americans, not Swiss, against that background of snowy peaks, and this troubled me.

One of the objectives in this exercise was to have a look at the most recent past lifetime. It was disconcerting to see a big shaggy dog, which I was scratching behind the ears, but soon after that I was a short woman pulling on a shrimp pink sweater top. These informations did not overwhelm me.

Vibrational effects continued to build up. Monroe's "Focus 10" state would put my body physically asleep, but my hands, arms and lower torso would be strongly energized.

Then the postman delivered the next six tapes from the Monroe Institute. Entitled "Threshold", they introduced a state called Focus 12. This is described in the accompanying leaflet as a "state of expanded awareness, a high-energy state where one becomes more conscious of inner resources and guidance."

Typical of Monroe's counsel with all the exercises is this advice: "you need not know the way to guidance; guidance knows the way to you." These words, I might add, can be and should be applied to any other consciousness-expanding technique one might explore. They teach "let it happen, don't make a big effort, don't over-concentrate, go with the flow." This would be useful counsel for anyone using TM, and I have found it repeatedly valid in subsequent years of spiritual exploration.

Threshold introduces "color breathing", yet another widespread and useful technique. While his special soundtrack is coming through your stereo headphones, Monroe tells you to "inhale vibrant, sparkling energy." Once you've inhaled it, then you hold it and color it emerald green (for cleansing), red (recharging), white (energizing), or purple (healing), and then in exhalation you push it through the physical body. The first time I did this particular routine I got lost in the explanation phase and could not hold green or red, and I really never achieved anything at all during the tape. Other spiritual disciplines assign other functions to these colors.

The next time I tried it, early one Sunday morning in October, the color breathing worked quite well. I could feel the white light pulsing in the palm chakras of my hands. Green and purple were effective, but for some reason I did not do red. Focus 10 became strong and pleasant. I did not feel much while going up to Focus 12, but Monroe points out over and over again you don't have to make any effort, his tape leads you there. Once in Twelve, and trying to do the patterning he had taught earlier, I found myself thinking about "preparing" my husband. For what, I wondered? Death? I had asked for news of my Guides but received this instead.

Then I was back down in Focus 10, which became so delicious a state I did not want to leave it when Monroe called for coming down all the way. I held on against instructions and into the closing tones. Then I twiddled my fingers, the technique for coming out.

After the end tone there is usually a long tail of blank tape, but when it ran out this time I heard brief Morse code signals. I hadn't heard those signals ever before on these tapes, so I played it back to find them, but they weren't there. So where did all that come from?

My notes concluded "this has been one of my most successful tape sessions." So successful, in fact, I received a strong after-effect, described in this footnote in my journal:

"At the end of this session, which moved me as much or more than a powerful meditation, I felt a wish to go to church. Which I did. During the service I was gradually invaded by a sense of vibrations around me, reinforced by the acoustic resonance of the pastor's voice and the organ. This was persistant (underlined in my notes). Before the service I did Green and Purple, then popped a Resonant Energy Balloon."

It is necessary to understand that I was not a devoted churchgoer, and I did not emerge from this service somehow "converted". In no way. As I have explained earlier, the Christianity into which I was born was incompatible with me. Our local pastor had a special magnetism which made his sermons sometimes interesting, and I enjoyed talking with him, but I always tried to filter out the Biblical background in order to locate the kernel of his thought.

Being drawn to the church in this way and on this day was most exceptional. It seems evident that the passages through Focus 10 and 12 had set up some kind of a spiritual resonance.

The next day I went back to the preceding Threshold exercise in order to work on Focus 12 without other influences. Focus 10 was light but gradually deepened, then I was in Twelve.

I posed this question, inspired by my reading: "Who are my Guides and how can I reach them?"

Soon I received the image of myself standing in the middle of a small vineyard we had once considered buying in Provence. I could not fit this scene into any notion of a clear answer about my Guides. Rumination led to a couple of auxiliary views around that village of Cadenet.

Again I tried, this time placing the question in a small rocketship or space capsule and pushing it out to float deeper into the outer reaches of my mental space. No answer came back.

One more time I framed the question, placing it into a dinghy and floating it out once again. There was no apparent answer, but I concluded it could come at some later time, on a later tide.

When I tackled Threshold Four new things happened. There was a different style of sound with a pronounced quaver of large amplitude. It was blatant rather than subtle as the Hemi-Sync tone had always been. Very quickly I noticed a broad field of striped waves flashing before my closed eyes in the dark room. These waves moved upward lengthwise, not like the ocean, and they were dark and light, blue zebra stripes. They kept flashing until I blinked my eyes while installing Focus 10. That state went in easily, and then Twelve felt more intense than usual. The movement from one state to the next is difficult to express in words. It's a neurological process of following cues and concepts which Monroe installs along the way. I lost the thread numerous times and had a hard time stating and pushing my meagre "pattern"— again the matter of gaining fruitful contacts with my Guides.

The vibrations this time were the strongest I had ever felt in the Gateway program, very strong, and less "electric" than in TM.

During the next days I alternated between TM and this powerful Threshold Four tape, sometimes mixing methodology in a small way. I had found Monroe's "resonant tuning" technique could be an agreeable introduction to a regular meditation.

One morning in late October I did the resonant tuning, then my pranayama, and then plunged with the mantra. I dove like a duck with folded wings down a long tube in the dark, three times. There were few thoughts but much resonance.

In fact, "resonance" was becoming a regular participant in my meditations. The vibratory field would resonate to outside stimuli. My skin developed radar-like antennae for distant noises. The sound of a spoon dropped in the kitchen, two rooms distant and behind closed doors, could shock me and start the waves moving through the field. The phenomenon became a regular visitor. A garden tool striking a stone in the rockery, the rattle of a tea cup across walls and doors, any sharp noise could start the waves rolling.

That evening I plugged into Threshold Four again, and something new came in. During the early "surf" portion I noticed a "silent sensation", something swishing rapidly from side to side soundlessly. One could say a "tone" felt but not heard. Green waves piggybacked on the resonant tuning process, then irregular lines wavering and flickering. Both Focus 10 and 12 claimed me but there was a lot of instability, lots of little surprise effects and a sense of "bubbling tension."

One of the surprise effects was the sight of an old aircraft, a pre-WW2 biplane hovering about fifty feet above the meadow in front of the house. This was a clear and vivid vision but it was gone again in a flash.

Two days later TM floated me into an extraordinary state. My brain was being massaged. Its top surface was being stroked gently, there was a kind of squeezing movement, mixed with a motion similar to flexing, giving a delicious caress to the upper convexity. I wondered if pleasure hormones were being released. Whatever, it was euphoric and asexually orgasmic. And it was divine. Squeezing and flexing simultaneously --- what acrobatics!

There had been hints of this sort of phenomenon in the early months of meditation but never as intensely developed. Nowhere had I read references to such inner pleasures. I didn't "do" drugs, and now I could quip "with meditation, who needs drugs?"

Later on some confusion arose with the positioning of the headphones. One was supposed to listen to Bob Monroe with the right ear, but on a few occasions he had come through the left ear. Checking the headphones, I had made no mistake. I reversed them a few times, and the exercises worked but with tiny differences. Harking back to my primary-school problems with left and right, noticing the subtle differences when reversing the headphones, observing that my tinnitus (strongest in the left ear) was as exuberant as ever, I felt there was a possibility for confusion that the Gateway instruction brochures did not elucidate.

From then on I made a special effort to make sure the tape was playing in the right ear. And everything did go along gently. The Gateway sessions were agreeable, frequently with strong vibrations but without the TM "buzz". The sound of ocean surf covered the Hemi-Sync frequencies, and then other sound frequencies accompanied the movement into Focus 10 and 12.

All kinds of little visions snapped in from time to time. Once I had the impression of a large blonde face peeking in at me through the decorative hole in the window shutter. Another time I saw my cousin Shirley sitting on her sofa in California. When I snapped my fingers she looked up at me. Telepathic connection? A couple of days later there was an old-fashioned orange-red racing car roaring around a city curve, with crowds lining the streets. That was a strange one, because I don't watch automobile races.

It seemed clear that the Gateway sound program, fluctuating between remarkable effects and purely routine sessions, was somehow powering-up my TM meditations. Toward the end of November I awoke early one morning with a point of light trying to break into my consciousness by entering the brain at upper left. So I set up the tape but nothing much happened.

That evening, however, my meditation went immediately into a long vision culminating in a scene of medieval dancers forming a large ellipse in a square or large courtyard. There was a tall king with long blond braided hair and a gold crown. It was all Nordic in feeling, and I was both part of the scene and spectator.

Meanwhile visions continued flooding in during both Threshold tape sessions and meditations. In the next days my "home movies" brought me:

-- *some swashbuckling characters in eighteenth-century costume for a cape-and-sword French "western";*

-- *a large car-and-trailer rig pulling out of the cemetery parking lot three hundred yards down the road;*

-- *a tall, handsome middle-aged man wearing tropical slacks and a bush jacket, in a murky street scene;*

-- *in a landscape of bright earth tones, I saw a sitting rifleman crumple as he was shot; he was like a Spanish or Mexican peasant in dark clothing, seated against an orange-brown dirt wall, cradling a rifle, when the bullet hit him in the belly and he collapsed forward;*

-- *in answer to the question "who are my Guides?" there came a tall man who looked rather Armenian, dressed all in black, jacket like a Navy peacoat, mariner's cap, graying hair and mustache, metal-rimmed glasses, and he looked directly at me; he was vaguely Christ-like in appearance, with a prominent nose and a long face;*

-- *while I was wandering mentally in the town of Vevey, four young people of both sexes waved vigorously to me from a hilltop far above the church of St-Martin; they were gay and personable, even at that considerable distance, and they were trying hard to attract my attention;*

Some months later, in Threshold, I asked again about my Guides and cast the question like a vast fish net toward a widening horizon. Within the next few minutes I "saw" all of the following:

-- *a line of dark-clad peasants walking in single file beside a paved road, in hilly country with nothing except brown grass; it felt like Italy;*

-- *standing outside the Villa Castagnola art museum in Lugano, I met a husky, barrel-chested young man; he was tall and clean-cut but heavyset, an earnest florid complexion; he wore a rust-colored shirt and greeted me with a warm handshake;*

-- *then came a woman with blonde hair in Afro style, white blouse, black skirt, and she was exhorting me about something;*

-- *and finally I saw a young woman, with long brown hair; she wore an ivory wool turtleneck and jeans, and she was sitting at a long wooden table, gazing at me with a calm, serene smile across a bowl of soup.*

Could all these people be my spiritual Guides? It seemed to me that if they were, then they would come again when invited. I conceived of my meditative states as being the times when my own spirit was most open to continued contacts, the time when messages from "out there" could most easily be received.

But no, none of them ever came again. Their perceived fickleness leads me to suppose that my altered state of consciousness was letting in a variety of discarnate beings from other planes, possibly the so-called "astral". In this period there were no durable contacts. It is, of course, possible that I was not capable of recognizing good contacts and filtering out the not-so-good.

Threshold Five introduces a new gimmick: an "energy bar tool". Bob Monroe compares it to the light sabers of the "Star Wars" series, the staffs of Moses and Abraham, Merlin's magic wand, or King Arthur's sword Excalibur.

Creating an EBT or personal power stick happens in Focus 10. You draw a dot of light into a bar, turning it on and off until it is pulsing like a strobe light. You can speed it up or slow it down, make it thicker or thinner. My energy bar tool realized itself fairly well and changed colors easily. I could sense the energy tingling and radiating. Were these sensations coursing through my physical body or were they limited to the altered state? Impossible to say.

As 1984 rolled over into 1985 my regular meditations, somewhat modified, were taking over from my seances with the Gateway auditory process. I found that Monroe's "energy conversion box," "resonant tuning" and "resonant energy balloons" made excellent entries into Transcendental Meditation. My work with the mantra seemed enhanced, the phenomenon of resonance was occurring frequently and helping to deepen the meditative state. Vibration was often noticeably present.

My journal frequently contained remarks such as "a nice state of expanded, resonant consciousness." And more and more there were brief episodes of that lovely brain massage sensation. My notes on that are brief but eloquent:

-- *"working into the back side of a lobe, feeling of `turning under', deep, like turning over a clod in a field; resonance"*;

-- *"conceived idea of mantra as a hand gently massaging the brain, which TM made me aware of as an organ having sensation"*;

-- *"sensing contact of mantra with brain-organ, gentle pleasant sensations"*;

-- *"light state of brain awareness; resonance -- an exterior noise popped me into a quiet center"*;

-- *"beginning of brain massage"*;

-- *"gentle energy envelope surrounding a pleasant brain state, generating thought"*;

-- *"resonant thrills in brain and neck"*.

These sensations marked the gradual emergence of another level in my spiritual life. I did not know what they meant, but I certainly enjoyed them.

There seemed to be mysteries within mysteries, like an endless set of Russian boxes. Perhaps they were a symptom of hemispherical synchronization taking place?

At the same time I sensed the end of a cycle. Working with Robert Monroe's sound tapes brought me fascinating interior experiences. They had brought me some new spiritual ideas, new meditational tools and intensities. Frequently they seemed to lead me to the absolute edge of lifting out of my body, and it was a mystery to me why that phenomenon had not occurred.

In addition to working with the taped exercises, I had been listening to Monroe's "Explorer" series. He had edited a set of two dozen cassettes recording the experiences of a group of volunteers who had learned to voyage to other dimensions while lying comfortably in one of the CHEC isolation booths. These people went from advanced sound states such as Focus 21 into other realities and/or out of body. They reported their experiences orally as they traveled or as they met other entities in other dimensions.

All this was fascinating, a great spur to continuing one's own explorations. I was particularly taken with the experience of an explorer who met a pleasant little man in a rather bland landscape. This fellow was familiar with Planet Earth and many of its facets. It turned out that he preferred to be a vegetarian when visiting down/over here with us.

"Could you tell me your favorite vegetable?" the Explorer asked.

"Oh yes, it's the rutabaga."

This statement, which has its humorous side, tantalized me. I realized I had never eaten a rutabaga. It took several months before I found a garden shop which had rutabaga seed, after which I began to grow them in my *jardin potager*. And, of course, eat them. Their unique flavor pleases my palate, and now rutabagas grace my dinner plates regularly. They go very well with turnips, celery root and the stems of broccoli too.

My notion that Monroe's Hemi-Sync might have an effect on my tinnitus had proved to be overly-optimistic. Nothing much had changed in that domain. Later correspondence with his staff brought me the following lines:

"....we really don't know anything about this ringing or buzzing in the ears.......It almost sounds like your tinnitus is a form of energy that is enhancing your experiences[7]."

This was pretty much the conclusion I was reaching in that winter, which was taking on aspects of a key turning-point. Working with their Gateway program had made it very clear that I was indeed more than my physical body and that, from time to time, I could "perceive that which is greater than the physical world".

After six months with the Gateway tapes my practice with them began to space out and become infrequent. I was using some of what they had taught me in my daily meditations, with evident benefit. I had ordered their third Wave entitled Freedom, but when it came I did not exploit it with that earlier enthusiasm and diligence.

This third set of tapes went deeper into interesting techniques, including preparation for traveling out of body. In spite of that bait I grew impatient with the stereo-and-earphones approach at a time when exterior pressures began to accumulate. Bit by bit I set these promising cassettes aside for that moment in life known as "later".

The physical world was ganging up on me again. Change was looming in several directions. Without giving up meditation, which was becoming rooted in my being despite the numerous uncertainties and frustrations, I needed desperately to respond to new pressures on my time.

[1] Betty Edwards, *Drawing on the Right Side of the Brain,* op.cit., Chapter Five
[2] W. Brugh Joy, *Joy's Way,* op.cit., Chapter Five.
[3] "Robert Monroe: update on journeys out of body," *Brain/Mind Bulletin,* March 26, 1984, p.3.
[4] "Altered States of Consciousness", by Pat Stone, *The Mother Earth News,* March-April 1983, pp. 88-91.
[5] Robert A. Monroe, *Journeys Out of the Body.* New York: Doubleday, 1971, Anchor Books, 1977. 280p. ISBN 0-385-00861-9.
[6] From the pamphlet *Discovery, an Introduction to the Gateway Experience,* copyright 1981 by the Monroe Institute of Applied Sciences.
[7] Personal correspondence, The Monroe Insitute, September 28, 1987.

Chapter Eleven

TRANSITIONS

My work with the Gateway Hemi-Sync program evolved against a backdrop of burgeoning stress at home. My husband's health began to deteriorate soon after his ninetieth birthday in 1984. There were moments when the alarm bells rang urgently, followed by periods of tranquillity for both of us.

Commentators love to say that "we live in a time of transition", which may gradually wind down until another time of transition replaces it. The concept becomes banal. It could easily be said that for most people life is continual transition, continual change, although there may be periods when it goes underground, operating at the cellular level.

Transition began to knock on our door more frequently. Sometimes it was benign, other times it was chaotic. We began to experience a full measure of both. And their nature was ultimately transformative.

"Will has had a series of liver crises since his birthday in May," I wrote to my daughter Carol. "Two in the month following. Three in August. Two in September, and the second time was a humdinger."

That one came the week after my own birthday, and we came within twenty-four hours of losing him.

"I took him to the hospital in Aigle by ambulance the night of the 27th," I told her. He had a high temperature, was much dehydrated, in great physical weakness, and his blood pressure sank to 80. They diagnosed a triple infection and stuffed him full of appropriate antibiotics.

"Three days later he wanted to come home, refused medical advice to stay another day, at least, and home he came."

The doctors threw up their hands in dismay and made him sign the equivalent of a "hold harmless" affidavit.

Three years earlier I had brought him home from the Caribbean in a wheelchair and we'd had that wild season with the gall bladder, hemorrhaging and two operations. The stress from that time had propelled me into meditation, whose value as a tranquillity tool was now being tested again. This time it was well-established, and the need to maintain this particular discipline was a major reason for not giving all my spiritual time to the Gateway voyages.

Of course it was a disappointment that the gall bladder episode had not put an end to problems of this nature. He had shown some jaundice then, and now it became a regular visitor. First he would have the period of pain and crawl into his den to suffer it away, very much like the wild creatures of whom he was so fond. Overnight he would feel better, emerge from his hole, and then would come the jaundice, the outward sign of the disease. And he would be up and about, stubborn old warrior that he was.

"Last week one would have thought he might not survive until Christmas," I told Carol in mid-October. "This week he is enterprising and demanding."

One of the consequences in my life was the slow-motion decision to taper off plowing through the Gateway program. This immersion in brain-stimulating sound required large chunks of time. Counting "set-up" time and a few minutes of slowly coming back to reality afterward, each session took at least an hour. As Will and I moved through this new phase of his life I needed more meditation time just to "keep my cool". Fully exploiting the possibilities of the Gateway Freedom "waves" was no longer a reasonable option.

Another facet of life was reopening. Two book projects loomed on the horizon. In my first years of residence in our chalet I had completed a long library reference book project, five years in the making, finished in 1973 and published under my professional name in 1974. What lay ahead was different, but still would call upon all my editorial skills.

For more than a decade my husband had fretted that a family history he wanted to share with his children and grandchildren did not exist in the English language. His mother's family was prominent in the Netherlands and a number of articles about various of her ancestors had appeared in historical journals, later to be compiled into a small volume. This was published just about the time I moved into the chalet and became a member of the family. Will had quickly obtained from the historian who was the author his permission to create an English translation.

The permission was easier to acquire than the translator. A woman commissioned to perform it in 1974 disappeared without a trace, carrying with her our only spare copy of this out-of-print work. With his English- and French-speaking descendants clamoring over the years, my husband brooded over this affair in his own Taurean way. With me in the wings muttering "why in the world don't you do it? I'll edit it for you so that it reads well in English."

During the winter -- between bouts of jaundice -- he made the mistake of bleating about it again, and I leaped on him.

"What else do you have to do with your days? So you're half-blind? So do a sloppy job and Michèle will mop up. Do two pages each day and in two months it will be done." These were small pages, two of them equivalent to one normal book page.

This time he rose to the challenge.

He passed the month of February 1985 bent over his desk, the book, and his aged portable typewriter, squinting painfully as he moved his magnifying glass back and forth. Once he had started, the task fired his enthusiasm and despite the visual handicap he took wings. Instead of just two pages a day, he did four. In a month his rough draft was finished and ready for me.

While he was clacking away on the old portable I was doing my own fretting about my mother. The arthritis in her spine had become very painful, and eventually she consented to surgery. To have calcification scraped out of your vertebrae at age eighty-seven takes spunk. Fortunately she had no shortage of that quality. She went into hospital for her major repairs while Will was bent over his keyboard, magnifying glass in hand. There was, of course, no question of my leaving him in order to look after her. My younger sister could do that.

It would be amusing to have an astrological analysis of this particular period, because at this time there was also some kind of a transition developing in my meditational life.

Late one afternoon TM led me deeply into another reality. I seemed to be involved with a knot of people on another plane. We were standing around a large hemispherical boulder in a gray, lifeless environment, and we were talking in a rather matter-of-fact way. I remember one of the men leaning against the boulder stood with his ankles crossed and his arms folded casually over his chest.

Coming away from that place, I could not orient myself. I didn't know who or where I was except that I existed, in a kind of limbo, neither here nor there. One level of consciousness understood I needed to come back, but I didn't know how. For a long moment I was lost out there, then I remembered Monroe's trick of wiggling the fingers, and I snapped home.

This event was worrisome, especially since about a week later another meditation took me three times to similar other realities.

"That way leads to psychosis," I reflected.

My first reflex was to give up the mantra which Nora had given me three years earlier when initiating me into TM. However, I desperately needed to talk to someone, and there seemed to be no one. And then it occurred to me that Jean could provide a helpful ear.

He was the minister of the local Protestant church. Christian, of course, which came up against my inner wall of resistance. But this man exuded qualities of mind which suggested he could separate spirituality from dogma if need be.

Our neighbor Joan had talked about him so glowingly I had gone with her to hear him one Sunday. He was talking about the need to develop an inner spiritual life. He quoted from mystic and spiritual sources beyond the

Christian Bible, and on that morning he told why the churches were losing "their adepts, their clients". He said it was because they had been making them feel guilty instead of teaching them the joy of spiritual attainment! I wanted to stand up and cheer.

Pastor Jean and I would sometimes chat on the sidewalk in the village, and one time I loaned him Ruth Montgomery's *A Search for the Truth*.

Then Monroe's tape on color breathing had such a powerful effect on me that I wanted to go to church, a moment described in the previous chapter.

Yes, I thought it possible to talk to Jean. It was clear from listening to him that he was something of a mystic himself, over and above what his churchly role required of him. One morning I went to the parsonage, talked at length about my career as a meditator, and described to Jean and his wife this new development in my meditational life. They agreed with me that a mantra could possibly lead into a psychotic state, that it was within the realm of possibility. They were sympathetic to the practice of meditation and did not take a position against TM. Possibly, we decided, I had dwelt too long in the house of one mantra.

Thus it happened that my style of meditation entered a phase of mutation. Before going to visit Jean I had already turned provisionally away from the TM mantra, now I began slipping away from the TM technique itself.

For a few months I went frequently to Jean's church. It became an intellectual challenge to see if his teaching style would dare go beyond the limits of the books of the Christian Bible. Ruth Montgomery had spoken of a few Protestant ministers in America who were opening to a larger view on God, Jesus, reincarnation and allied questions. Ultimately I did not linger long on this branch of the path, for reliance on accepted writ seemed to be ironclad in the Swiss Protestant community. It felt like a straitjacket to me.

Meanwhile, my new cycle of meditational experimentation opened within me. I mixed breathing exercises, Monroe's resonant tuning and/or his resonant energy balloon, with mantras of my own invention. Other than my little blue whale, images did not serve me well as the central focus of meditation. Mantras worked for me, not mandalas.

Om Mani Padme Hum and its concatenation of the "m" vibration remained a favorite, but also I played with rhythmic phrases associated with Jesus. Having shaken off Christian dogma long ago, then having read some very unbiblical versions of his life, my spiritual senses opened to admiration for Jesus as the master teacher and healer he came here to be[1]. "Gospel" and the concepts employed post-mortem to create a church in his name had nothing to do with it.

After several months of these new directions, mostly successful, I felt sufficiently purged that it seemed safe to use my TM mantra again. Just to get a fresh assessment of its value.

And then another new phenomenon came along.

My inner viewing screen, just behind the "third eye" above the bridge of the nose, began to produce interesting panoramas. I began to see circles of light that evolved in three dimensions. Color would swell into a circle, bordered with another color, and then it would start moving away from me, receding into the future. Peaceful sensations accompanied this phenomenon.

Two years earlier I had noted the arrival of "large blotches of amethyst color" in my meditations, opening and closing rhythmically. Now the principal color, at first, was green. Rather quickly it became blue with a green border. These were not geometrically-perfect circles; their edges were imperfect, somewhat ragged, but they were not shapeless blotches. Their evolution was always expanding and receding, expanding and receding. I named this phenomenon "cerevision" because it was cerebral, viewed within the brain.

Cerevision could be accompanied by a flow of energy down through my body, which I sensed as a kind of dance. My hands tingled, felt charged. Energy particles danced. Sometimes I felt them, sometimes I saw them on the little screen. Switching to the mantra Om Mani Padme Hum enhanced the effect and it gradually took over again from the TM mantra. Permanently.

My psyche bathed in rhythmic inner movement, leading to a sense of calm and refreshment. This composure came at a time when it was sorely needed.

True to my promise to my husband Will, I took over the family history when he had finished his heroic labor of making the crude translation. I worked evenings at the computer, cleaning up his text as I entered it into memory. Meanwhile I began badgering relatives for the photos that had appeared in the original book. Many of those illustrations were reproductions of portraits scattered among the Swiss and Dutch branches of the family.

As spring turned the corner into summer I could see an end to the work when, one night, I started getting computer "garbage" while saving my text to external memory. In those days that meant writing from the computer to a collection of "floppy disks". As I pursued this goal "Disk Error" flashed ominously on the screen more than once. Breakdown, a "crash", ensued without delay.

Factory technicians needed two months to put my system back into service. During this time additional material for the book began to come to the surface: two more genealogies and some additional articles which would make good appendices. They would add substantial length to the manuscript and to my editing time, once I could work again. Meanwhile I worried if the part of the manuscript unsaved to floppy disk had been lost. How much more time would be lost repairing the damage?

Even before the computer came home from its hospital we were dealing again with hospitals for humans. In September the doctors ordered a biopsy and ultrasonic radiography, in response to a set of new symptoms. They were not looking at the jaundiced liver but in the prostate area. My husband wanted relief but was otherwise very uncooperative.

"He does not intend to pursue any aggressive treatment to be cured of anything," I wrote to Carol. "He could care less. No hospitals, no operations."

Finally he accepted these examinations on the principal it could be somewhat helpful to know what might be wrong, even though he didn't want to be healed of it. He refused the diagnostics until the doctor agreed to take him in on an ambulatory basis, so he was in at ten o'clock and out at three o'clock, the maximum hospital exposure to which he would willingly submit. It was irrelevant to him that the hospital doctors had saved his life a year earlier. Enough was enough.

He felt well enough and puttered about in a contented way, but his energies were slim and quickly depleted. He would lie on the sofa, pick up the ten-power binoculars and watch the birds -- about five feet away -- attacking the walnut halves he had hung in a net outside the window.

He enjoyed it when I read to him and never got too much of it. We had wonderful discussions about all this reading. It was a kind of conjugal communion, another way of expressing the love we felt for each other.

Meditation twice daily was helping me to maintain near-equanimity against the slowly-accumulating stress, and this intellectual rub together helped both of us. He wondered how a younger woman like myself could love an older man who, he estimated, was fast becoming a decrepit wreck. He feared I might desert him in frustration and disgust. It was necessary periodically to explain to him — and to his anxiety — the multiple faces of love. I suspect many mature couples go through similar processes. We were not exempt, but we rode the crest of it, body-surfing the waves of our mortality.

In our reading we had gone through a mass of books on alpine adventures, then we'd switched to Lawrence of Arabia and Winston Churchill before taking an even more intellectual tack. We were now working on Lytton Strachey's *Eminent Victorians*, and both of us were getting bored with Cardinal Manning's theological idiosyncrasies.

The biopsy report came back positive. The specialists wanted to remove the prostate, which had become nasty. Eight years previously it had been whittled at and eroded in two operations, but a remnant was still there and had sprouted a tumor. That they had not found anything wrong with the liver was a mystery to me. These speculations I kept to myself. As far as Will was concerned, the idea of an operation would not fly. It started with lead in its wings and could not leave the runway.

During the several weeks we had waited for the results of the tests he gave much thought to various means of suicide -- all on the supposition he could look forward to dying from cancer. He wanted to stay away from hospitals, avoid operations, avoid life-support systems, die peacefully at home. This corresponded for the most part to my philosophy and sentiments, but I did not share his notion that life after surgery would not be worth living.

Nor did his personal physician, Dr. G., a very learned practitioner with a deeply compassionate nature. Will continued balking after the biopsy report. He really wanted to let things go and simply decline into a quiet death. His strategy was one of "benign neglect". Dr. G. pointed out it might not be that easy. There would be a danger of uremic poisoning, and he painted a grim picture of the agonies which could ensue.

"Monsieur Burdet," he cajoled, "even though you are rather old, you are programmed genetically for a longer life. You've got a few more years ahead if you accept the inconvenience of this surgery, and you can probably pass them in reasonable comfort with some enjoyment of what each day may bring. If you refuse, you will probably die much sooner. There is a real risk the end could be grotesque and agonizing as the tumor expands to close off the urethra."

My old oak ruminated overnight on this point of view, and then he consented to the operation. He entered hospital the next day, and surgery was accomplished the day following. They kept him two weeks, and when I brought him home it was late November, 1985. His recovery was slow, he was depleted, and Dr. G. had to come more than once.

It became a heavy winter in many respects. Everything I was involved in slowed down. My work of editing the family history, gathering the photographs and compiling the appendices bogged down rather quickly with all the time devoted to nursing and to clearing snow. And early in 1986 came a new kind of transition My husband had the first of a series of what I came to call "mini-micro strokes".

"There was one in February," I wrote to Carol, "and two, perhaps three, in the fortnight following Easter."

These events could be very brief. The first time it was only three minutes before he snapped out of it. They could also be dramatic.

"The hardest one paralyzed his left leg and speech center temporarily," I told her.

I had found him standing with one hand on a dining-room chair, absolutely blocked, his whole being frozen like a statue. I guided him to the sofa, laid him down, and discovered the extent of the paralysis. So I called his doctor, who was not available, and the next one I called was eating his supper but agreed to arrive in a few minutes. And then Will snapped to, the parayalsis melted, he was back among the living, and I could telephone that doctor to finish his supper in peace.

That time his incredible constitution came to the rescue and put everything right within an hour, but there was no mistaking the symptoms and their meaning. For a time there were severe mental problems: memory loss and much confusion. That cleared up, but he needed a lot more coddling. Additional shadows ornamented our future.

"I grapple continually with the problem of trying to help him detach himself from his very earthy preoccupations," I told old family friend Elisabeth. "Sometimes I score with the reading of a particular poem or, as last night, some readings on a spiritual question of which he was unaware. But mostly it is an uphill struggle to turn his attention away from his body."

Meanwhile, my mother got home from her hospital in good time and made a reasonably good recovery. She had lots of physiotherapy and visits from a nurse. My sister had danced attendance during the period, and my presence was not needed. In any case, I could not possibly have been there to help.

Eventually I found a lady who could come in to sit with Will during the afternoons, allowing me to get out for the shopping or a walk. Her presence made it possible for me to resume tennis, a valuable safety valve. I have often referred to my tennis racket as my personal psychotherapist. Smashing the life out of those poor defenseless little tennis balls provides a good outlet for ordinary frustration and the occasional access of rage.

The family book inched along. It began to look like I could really wrap up the whole thing in the fall, permitting me to take on another literary project.

Blanche Merz was looking for a translator for her book *Les Hauts-Lieux Cosmos-Telluriques*[1], and in a reckless moment I said "why not me?" She liked the idea and we agreed on terms.

Existing overload in my life made this a rash decision on my part, but I couldn't bear seeing this particular assignment slip through my fingers. Her *Hauts-Lieux* had opened a new path for me, a path still largely unexplored. But I knew it lay in my future. It felt so absolutely right that I should do her translation for the English-speaking market. Also, it would bring in a tidy little sum of money, never unwelcome.

"Will is living from day to day, sweetly," I told Elisabeth. "So do I live from day to day, although I do try here and there to make a plan."

One of those plans was to indulge my passion for the mountains by going on a weekend hike with the Alpine Club. I had never been able to take part in their rambles before, but this time a lady of our circle who my husband appreciated volunteered to look after him.

Dr. G. urged me to go ahead. "Excellent idea," he said. "It will do you good."

He was right. It did me enormous good. Liberated, I clambered over the craggy 9'000-foot ridge which forms our southern panorama and down the other side, in company with a merry band of instantly likeable companions. This little expedition whetted my appetite for more. More there could not be this summer, but it was the first of many dozens of such excursions I would make with these companions in future years.

Dr. G. had found Will's heartbeat was becoming "distant," to cite his words. And he found a hard mass in the lower abdomen, an evident sign of metastasis. I wondered again about that vulnerable liver — was it touched also? The doctor could not say for sure, and we certainly were not going to have any more tests made. There really wasn't much that could be done at this point. Or said. The question of "how long?" was unanswerable.

My personal defenses lay in meditation, my literary projects and fluctuating amounts of sport, all of them as punctuation to the loving attention needed by my man.

Every once in a while my daily adventures in altered consciousness would provide some entertainment. One time I sensed the environment around me to be shaking. Another time there was a vision of marble faces, a statuary angel, a Borromini-like Mona Lisa. Cerevision was a regular visitor. Brain massage dropped in occasionally for an ecstatic surfing. My tinnitus was, of course, continually present, both in and out of meditation.

"Tinnitus and vibration are the instruments, I am the music. Who is the composer and what does he want to convey? Who is the conductor?" I wrote in my journal after a meditation.

Indian summer teased us along in its soft, dulcet way. Foliage was gradually shifting its vibrational gears, greens going yellow around the edges, announcing the coming of flame. The farmers working the fields in front of us were finishing up the last cut of the season and the land smelled of fresh-mown hay. Cows came down from summer pasture at higher altitudes, the lead cow wearing a floral headdress symbolizing her status as top milker. The clang and bang of their bells marked their passage down the back road. Eight half-grown heifers moved into a sliver of pasture across the road, their smaller bells tinkling continuously as they grazed.

During that sunny autumn I took an unusual step: for the first time in my life I consulted a clairvoyant. Dolores received me in the guesthouse of a farm, hidden away in rolling hills between the mountains and the plain. A friend had told me about her, and she asked me to mail her a copy of my natal planetary chart. "Karmic astrology is my starting-point," she explained.

It was all rather fascinating. She wanted to know right away if I was a doctor, or a nurse, or some other kind of qualified therapist. I explained about my husband, but that was not sufficient for her vision. Her view of my past included a lot of warring as soldier and naval officer, a lot of it in Russia. She told me about a lifetime in Central Asia when I had been a subaltern under Kublai Khan. In sum, I had done a lot of butchering and then, to clean up that karmic burden, had turned to the healing arts.

"Your next incarnation will probably be oriented to medicine", she predicted.

For a kind of double-check when she had finished talking I spread out a handful of nameless photographs. She picked up a little passport photo of my mother and said "she's been Greek". And then she picked up a snapshot of Will and said "you've been together in several lifetimes. You were in the Altai a thousand years ago as husband and wife, except that you were the husband then and he was the wife."

The Altai? Where was that? My atlases showed me that this was a vast alpine region straddling northwestern Mongolia, southwestern Siberia, and northeastern Kazakhstan. Mountains as high as our Alps, forests, and meadowlands. If Dolores was right, it looked very much as if Will and I had already been mountain people, almost born to meet again and enjoy life together in a similar environment once again.

This story amused my husband. His innate skepticism about all things supernatural had been somewhat eroded by my experience with meditation, whose beneficial effects on me had indirectly rubbed off on him. He did not reject out of hand my expanding notions about reincarnation and the afterlife, that we would likely meet again in the world of spirit. He simply observed "I hope you are right." Now the idea that this was not our first time together, and in an alpine world to boot, needed some time to trickle into his thinking.

As the season matured I finished the family history. It topped out at 128 very full letter-size pages, including lots of photographs and the appendices I have mentioned. It had always been my plan to publish it in photocopy, and our man down in Vevey did a superb job of it. The illustrations came out well. The "press run" was only twenty-five copies, but that was all we needed.

We titled it "The Borski Saga", referring to several generations of great-grandfathers on the matrilineal side, believed to have migrated from Catholic Pomerania. His father descended from French Huguenot stock, as did mine, a link which further cemented our union this time around.

This book was my Christmas present to him and our Christmas present to all branches of the family: his children, grandchildren, great-grandchildren, nieces, nephews and cousins. Will loved it and the book was very much appreciated by everyone. His satisfaction and their evident pleasure were full recompense for my effort.

In the midst of all this my never-ending searching turned up some fascinating help on the subject of mantras. And I needed help, for in that autumn of 1986 my meditational practice gradually came under temporal assault. The time set aside for my late afternoon meditation slowly evaporated under the pressure of all that I was trying to do. There were even days when I could not meditate at all. One could say there was too much on my plate. In this difficult situation the book *Mantra and Meditation*[3], which I have already cited in Chapter Six, came to my rescue.

Pandit Arya's deep exposition of how mantras work in the various levels of consciousness and how they are transmitted enriched my bedtime reading. And then one evening I turned a page and fell upon a Sanskrit phrase which he quoted from Patanjali's *Mahabhashya*. "Brahmanena nishkarano dharma" leaped from the page into my soul[4]. It wanted to be with me, to be floated through me, and so it was, starting the next morning. This phrase translates as "A child of God performs the right acts for no reason whatsoever." These words certainly expressed a quality that corresponded with my notions of godliness. To live up to them was an ambition to which I could subscribe.

For the next year "Brahmanena nishkarano dharma" refreshed my spiritual life, just as Om Mani Padme Hum had done several years earlier. It renewed my vibrational world, led me into pleasant spaces in which my cerevision would manifest, and once in a great while, that delightful brain massage. Sometimes I felt so light as to be almost disembodied, ready to lift off. This resurgence of the benefits of meditation refreshed my energies and my ability to harmonize the various levels of responsibility and creativity which were then mine to manage.

Meditation firmed up but had to be limited to once a day, nearly always in the morning before the day's pace became a gallop.

For in this season, along with finishing up the family history, my work on the translation for Blanche had already begun. Her style was hard to translate because she went sailing off into rolling waves of dependent clauses, typical of much French writing. Her book was a popularization of a relatively complex subject. Applying earth energy dowsing techniques to the analysis of the spiritual power of sacred sites was a daunting idea. Intellectually, it was almost virgin territory, for only a handful of English and German geomancers had broken this ground[5]. Blanche's presentation was original and even spectacular, and I felt privileged to be the instrument of bringing it to a larger audience.

In my view this kind of publication was essential to the progress of science. "Establishment science" neglects anything that ventures outside the accepted academic disciplines whose peer-group approval guarantees funding. Progress in nineteenth-century science was dominated by independents and amateurs, even though much of it was derided by the institutions. Blanche and everyone like her were breaking new ground that would be branded "fringe" or "pseudo"-science until enough solid evidence was accumulated. I saw my translation as a tiny contribution to this long-term effort.

Four months of solid work came to a conclusion in mid-March, and the book came out in that year of 1987[6]. The publisher had not accepted my version of what the title should be, and someone in his editorial offices botched a couple of difficult paragraphs to which I had given particular attention. These quibbles aside, the accomplishment brought me a deep sense of satisfaction.

It was clear another sort of conclusion was drawing near. My husband's metastasis took an ugly, highly visible turn. One of the lymph glands in the groin expanded into an external mass the size of a golf ball. It was very uncomfortable for him and it had to be treated and bandaged frequently, eventually several times a day. He needed a great deal of help in all departments of life. Even before I finished the translation we hit an airpocket, when quite suddenly he was no longer independent about things like dressing and undressing.

"The nicest thing that could happen to me now would be to not wake up tomorrow morning," he told me one day at breakfast.

He fell numerous times, especially in the night. He would get up to relieve himself but was groggy because of his sleeping pill. So he fell. And I got up to rescue him. Twice, while trying to get back on his feet, he banged his head on the underside of the washbasin. On one of those occasions the resulting hematoma moved down to blacken his eye, making it look as if I had beaten him. We managed wry little smiles at the joke. Miraculously, nothing except skin was ever broken.

We were quickly in over my head. My ulcers exploded into activity and Dr. G. gave me an ultimatum:

"Surround yourself with help or he must go to a nursing home," decreed the good doctor.

With the help of the Visiting Nurse I was able to find qualified aides, and this program gradually expanded. Some were proposed by a benevolent organization named Pro Senectute, and some were provided through the local chapter of the Red Cross, down in Aigle. All of these services had to be paid, of course, but in sum they were cheaper than an institution, and above all, they meant that he could end his days at home, in his own bed. We could remain together for better or for worse.

Before long we had a sweet lady who came every morning to get him out of bed, washed, dressed, and down to the breakfast table. Morning was his best time, as it was mine, and we managed without more help until after lunch. Then there was another woman who was simply there, to do whatever was needed during that slow time of the day. This was my time to have some respite, to get out of the house.

In April things got tougher, and the Red Cross came up with Josy, a true angel of mercy. She was a delightful lady who took the bus up from Aigle late every afternoon. She looked after him with a wise combination of spoiling and bossing. She massaged his swollen legs, brought him down again for supper, and then took him upstairs again for an alcohol rubdown and into his pajamas.

Before Josy came we were both tired and cranky at the end of the day, and our joint morale was deteriorating. Very quickly she eased the situation. He became serene and my stress level subsided. After she left for the evening I would find him calmly in his bed, or sitting on the edge of it, taking his medicine, and we would end his day in relative happiness and serenity.

In the midst of all this I made a misstep on the steps down into the garden and my back went out. This has been a chronic lifetime problem, my daily exercise program usually kept it under control, and in five days I was back to normal. Just in time to catch a cold brought by one of the visitors. It went into bronchitis, another of my old enemies, and this kept me down for several days.

Word was getting around that he was failing, and a number of people came for short visits. In mid-May we would celebrate his 93rd birthday, and for that event his eldest son Allan came from Connecticut. This was a surprise for Will and there was a highly emotional moment when Allan walked in the door.

Unfortunately he could not stay with us in the chalet. Allan now had a bad heart which no longer supported living up here at our altitude. He tried it for two days, then I had to take him down to Montreux where he had a friend with an extra bed.

The birthday luncheon was a quiet success. In addition to Allan we had Will's sister Elise, his niece Marcelle, and Elisabeth, who was a distant cousin as well as a close friend now living up here. It was cozy and quiet but still an emotional high for my man. He ate a tiny amount of food with evident pleasure, but during the meal he turned gray-green and afterward he was extremely tired and went to bed early.

During this period I had to resort to the employment agencies for additional help to cover all seven days of the week, and we were lucky in the people they sent out. Suddenly I was a personnel office, drawing up schedules and juggling people's availabilities. In the mornings it was now Jacqueline who came to take care of him.

His second son René prepared to arrive from Maine with his wife and two younger children, as soon as their school was out. And Will was now spending a lot of time in bed. He had been "up" for his birthday, now his resolve had left him.

At the beginning of June he was extremely ill. I telephoned Dr. G. and told him we had possibly reached a hospital situation. Bless his soul, he came rapidly, worked some pharmaceutical magic, and the crisis passed. This was a watershed moment, for Will weakened rapidly, eating less and less.

A few mornings later he had an out-of-body experience, right there at the breakfast table while Jacqueline and I were guiding him to his chair. He described it but didn't want to talk about it.

Following that event I was up with him for various reasons three nights in a row. Josy had steadily offered to maintain an all-night vigil when necessary. and on Sunday, June 7, I took her up on it. The day before Dr. G. had looked in at Will's sleeping form and observed "he's ready to leave." That night I took sleeping pills for the first time in years, and Josy sat in his room.

The next morning, before leaving, she told me that he came alive during the night and talked with great lucidity and animation about his life, reliving many facets of it. At three o'clock in the morning he even asked for a "Wienerschnitzel" (breaded veal cutlet) to eat.

When Josy told me all this, I knew it was the end, for his brother René and his cousin Thora had given similar performances the night before their departures. Jacqueline was the day nurse that Monday, June 8, and she roused me from a nap in mid-morning with two words "la mort".

His final agony began then, four hours of battling to breathe while the heart began to fail. He was semi-comatose and not really responding. Hour by hour the breathing became more tortuous. In the last minutes there were several times when we thought it was over, and then there would be a huge gasp and breathing would resume for a bit. I had been monitoring his pulse rate but in the last half-hour it was so faint on the wrist that I kept my fingers on his diaphragm. My fingertips sensed the eventual cardiac arrest, which occurred gently, faintly, like a whisper through a half-closed door.

I sat there for a few minutes, hoping to see a wisp of ectoplasm leave his physical shell. No such luck.

We were handsomely supported in these final days. Elisabeth came the day before to reign over the telephone and to address envelopes. Will's sister arrived the next day, and son René and family arrived on Thursday, the day before our two funeral services. There were lots of people at both. In the Protestant Church (Jean was on vacation and his colleague from a neighboring parish officiated) there were many who came a certain distance, such as the Geneva family, and countless people from the mountain villages, including some of my new Alpine Club colleagues. At the crematorium in Vevey we had another memorial, followed by a reception in a hotel. More family from all around, his fellow Rotarians, some of my Soroptimist colleagues.

The Irish are not so dumb, with their wakes. All this socializing proved to be a good thing, for after the solemn moments we were all able to relax over wine and snacks in a pleasant space.

In her letter of condolence my daughter spoke of Will's "bright inquisitive eyes under those lovely bushy brows" and the "youthful mischievousness" that sometimes glinted from them. Those brown eyes were indeed warm, in harmony with the personality that began working its way under my skin in the forests of the Netherlands Veluwe sixteen years earlier.

Physically he was gone, and I was happy his ordeal was ended. Spiritually he was still with me, but not obsessively. Just after his death I had sobbed a bit in Elisabeth's comforting arms. That kind of grief was short-lived. A page had turned, they like to say here, and one had to get on with life.

In meditation I urged Will's soul to move full speed ahead toward that light which Raymond Moody had so amply documented. My man had completed his transitions for this lifetime, and I wished him bon voyage.

It was, of course, an immense transition for me. I could see only vague outlines of my future. The path stretched before me and it looked reasonably interesting, but I could not see very far ahead. The next six months looked rather cut and dried. Beyond that I could not see. And it did not worry me.

[1] For those who wish to investigate this path, allow me to recommend those titles which were helpful to me:

---Janet Bock, *The Jesus Mystery* ("of lost years and unknown travels"). Los Angeles: Aura Books, 1980. 231 p., appendix "The Legend of Saint Issa", notes, bibliography. ISBN 0-937736-00-7.

---Elizabeth Clare Prophet, *The Lost Years of Jesus* ("on the discoveries of Notovitch, Abhedananda, Roerich, and Caspari"). Livingston, Montana: Summit University Press, 1984. 401 p., notes, bibliography. ISBN 0-916766-61-6.

---Dolores Cannon, *Jesus and the Essenes ("Fresh insights into Christ's Ministry and the Dead Sea Scrolls")*. Bath (UK): Gateway Books, 1992. 272 p., bibliography, index. ISBN 0-946551-92-8.

---Peter Wheeler (compiler of recorded channelings, the medium remaining anonymous), *The Way of Love* ("Joseph of Arimathea tells the true story behind the message of Jesus"). London: The Leaders Partnership, 1996. 255 p., genealogical charts. ISBN 90-75635-01-X. (I have met and spent an afternoon with the medium.)

[2] *Op.cit.*

[3] Pandit Usharbudh Arya, D.Litt., *Mantra and Meditation, Superconscious Meditation, Volume 2*. Honesdale, PA: Himalayan International Institute of Yoga Science and Philosophy, 1981. xxxiii+247p., appendix. ISBN 0-89389-074-X.

[4] *Op.cit.*, p. 154.

[5] Blanche's work was inspired by the medical dowsing of Hartmann and Curry in Germany. In England the leading investigators in her time were John Michell, Tom Graves, T.C. Lethbridge and Paul Devereux, with his periodical magazine *The Ley Hunter* and later the "Dragon Project" and his books. These names represent only the tip of the iceberg, for there were other independent researchers at work in France, Belgium and Switzerland, that I have heard about, as well as numerous Germans inspired by Hartmann's Forschungskreis für Geobiologie e.v.

[6] Blanche Merz, *Points of Cosmic Energy*, translated by Michèle Carter Burdet. Saffron Walden (UK): C.W. Daniel, 1987. 184 p., glossary, bibliography, appendix. ISBN 0-85207-194-9.

Chapter Twelve

GIANT WINGLESS BIRD

In midsummer 1983 I had received the vision of a giant wingless bird. My first attempt to describe this scene dates back to a paper I compiled from my journals. That brief document was created to bring together all the diverse scenes that had been coming into my altered states, and it was primarily a personal record, which I circulated to only two or three close friends. I gave it the title "Other Times, Other Places, Other People -- as seen in dream and meditation", and in one of the entries I wrote:

"Meditation drifting into a light vibrational state with considerable thought evolutions, thence into a vision of a giant wingless bird running across a flat meadow chased and accompanied by running men. The creature was huge --- the men came only to its shoulder --- and it resembled somewhat a female pheasant but gray and without wings. I saw this both as part of the pack (running alongside, at its left) and from a distance (about fifty yards). Was it a hunt? This landscape was rather indefinite in form with pale colors."

The only thing worth adding to that is that we, the chasers-hunters, were all naked or nearly so. We were primitive, prehistoric people, running on a treeless plain. I do not remember any weapons.

This vision haunted me for a long time but was eventually pushed to the background by other scenes coming in as the months rolled on. It was never forgotten but entered into a kind of inner library.

One day six years later I was reading the daily newspaper, turned the page, and — good grief! — there was my bird. The sketch reproduced in the International Herald-Tribune was indisputable[1]. It resembled what I had seen in meditation on July 16, 1983.

There was however, a bit of a problem. The sketch in front of my eyes was derived from prehistoric fossil remains which had been exhumed only two years previously, in 1987, in Antarctica. This giant bird, standing ten to eleven feet tall, had a huge beak -- and I do not remember seeing that beak, but the rest of it conformed to my vision. The science writer did not name this creature, but in subsequent research I found it was called *Phorusrhacus longissimus* and it had lived forty million years ago. And they had just found it.

Not in 1983.

The implications staggered me. Up until that moment my feeling about reincarnation was that it satisfied all my philosophical requirements, as it had obviously satisfied numerous philosophers, writers, academicians, and public figures down through the centuries. Their various reasons were intellectually convincing. The fact that contemporary Christianity preferred a rather vaguely defined phenomenon named "resurrection" struck me as irrelevant. There was a lot of evidence to suggest the fathers of the Church had systematically, and over the course of the centuries, expurgated the generally-accepted notion of reincarnation from their official scriptures.

Now I was confronted with clear evidence: a creature that I saw in meditation had actually existed in prehistoric times, and I along with it. And this particular creature had been discovered four years after I had "seen" it. Science had validated my meditative vision. And that meant that I had lived before, an extremely long time ago.

If that one scene came from a past life, would it not then be reasonable to suppose that many of the visions I was receiving actually provided a glimpse into past lives?

From the moment my mind digested that newspaper report and sketch, my belief in reincarnation became unshakeable. Molecules of lingering doubt melted into the cosmic compost heap, their energy to be broken down, like the human body, and recycled, like the energy of the human soul.

My subsequent research also unearthed the Moa, a huge bird that lived in New Zealand until becoming extinct two hundred years ago. This flightless creature had long, strong legs, a bulky body covered with feathers, a long neck and a big beak, though not as big as that of *Phorusrhacus*. It resembled a wingless chicken, except that it was 11 1/2 feet tall and so could have been my bird. Science called it *Dinornis maximus* ("huge, terrible bird") and said it appeared in the Pleistocene era, which began 1.8 million years ago and ended ten thousand years ago. This was the time of the four great ice ages, it was the time of human evolution, and it saw the appearance of such mammals as the elephant, the horse, and the pig. And the Moa.

So did I really see "only" *Diornis maxima* or did I see *Phorusrhacus longissimus*? I favor the latter, because of the intense shock of recognition when I first saw the illustration in the newspaper. Even if, however, we were running with a Moa, it still had to be centuries ago and thus a memory of a previous life. Moas lived in New Zealand, so under this theory my colleagues and I were probably the ancestors of the very mystical Maori people. What a delightful notion!

---

[1]   Walter Sullivan, "The Reign of the 'Terror Bird'", *International Herald-Tribune*, February 2, 1989, p.7

Chapter Thirteen

THE DAY THE DEER DANCED

During Will's last years I turned more and more to mountain trails for that necessary flow of fresh air through spirit. My physical body loved the gradual trudge uphill against gravity. The senses drank in the air, the sounds of wind and water. Soul exulted approaching the heights.

Heights are all around me here. High mountains create the horizon in every direction, without ever being overbearing or menacing. Behind the chalet a ridge offers protection from the worst of the north wind. On the east, the left, my windows look one kilometer across a canyon toward the neighboring village and the forested ridge behind it. To the south and southwest, directly in front of my meadows, dramatic ten thousand-footers define the horizons.

My viewpoint, my chalet home, stands at 1150 meters of altitude, 3773 feet. It's a comfortable height for year-around living. A major proportion of the mountain villages in Switzerland are found at this altitude and up to about 1300 meters, frequently on benches and plateaus carved by the retreat of glaciation thousands of years ago. Forest is all around, reaching up to about 1700 meters, around a mile high. Above that there are many meadows, but the essential element of the high country is stone.

Deep wooded canyons lie between me and the Argentines, the Muverans and, in the deep distance and absolutely due south, an eastward extension of the French Alps from which rises Mont Blanc (the highest peak in Europe but hidden to our view except at much higher altitude). To the right, southwest, stand the majestic Dents-du-Midi, their seven peaks suggesting a multi-masted schooner sailing regally over the terrestrial seas.

The jagged elements of this powerful panorama are just far enough away to allow the winter sun to stream cheerfully and warmly through the windows. My husband studied the situation carefully before purchasing this piece of land, years before my arrival on the scene. I continue to benefit from his wisdom, for there are many villages in the French, Swiss, German and Austrian Alps which lie in cold shadow during the winter months.

My relationship to mountains must be considered to be primarily spiritual, but this was not at all evident to me before I came to live in the

Alps. Here, in daily communion with these giants of rock, there began to burgeon the sense of finally having found home. Nowhere else did I feel myself to be in such harmony with the world. Just sitting and looking at them elevates my spirit. This simple act becomes a meditation.

In younger years I had simply loved to be in the mountains. That infatuation began early, but spirituality was not a conscious part of those yearnings. Spirituality hardly even existed as a concept in my troubled relationship with religion. I could spell the word but would have been at a loss if asked to define it.

Growing up in Southern California I had mountains almost in the front garden. Brush-covered hills began across the street from the home in which I grew up on the northern fringe of the Los Angeles metropolis. Trails began fifty yards from the door. Their demand to be explored festered in my being.

It was dry country, brushy hillsides choked with sage and manzanita. Quail and lizards were the wildlife most often encountered, plus the occasional gopher snake. We learned early to be on the lookout for the venomous rattlesnakes; their habits, the shape of their fangs and the sound of their rattles were impressed on us at an early age, and I never knew anyone who had been bitten by one.

Our town sprawled at the foot of Mount Verdugo, which to my juvenile eyes seemed to rise in noble proportions to its summit of about 1700 feet. My over-protective parents did not seem to appreciate my longing to hike up to this peak. Nor could I explain why I wanted to do it. Looking backward more than sixty years one could say "aha, a first glimmering of spiritual yearnings!" Perhaps. History can only record that one Saturday afternoon when I was about sixteen years old I went up to the top and told them about it later.

This ascension was a lot easier than I had imagined during the preceding ten years of growing out of childhood. By alpine standards Mount Verdugo is a softly sculpted molehill. By my adolescent standards it was an adventure, following unknown trails, both on the ground and in spirit. There were emotion-tickling discoveries: an interesting rock outcropping, the pleasure of slipping silently through a little wood patch, then a long stretch of trail behind the ridge out of sight of the town. Looking down on the fabled Dead Horse Canyon was kind of a disappointment, for there was nothing special or mysterious about it after all. The cold water of reality dashed away some childhood illusions about this legendary slash in the hills. Finally, the upper reaches of the trail followed a wide firebreak which from a distance resembled a beige stripe down the face of the mountain.

From that lofty eminence I was momentarily mistress of all I surveyed. It was fascinating to see urban geography stretching out at my feet, allowing me to trace with the eye all the usual itineraries, including my bicycle route to high school. Turning to my left, there was a deeper, better look at the long range of the San Gabriel Mountains which closed the Los Angeles basin. The domes of the observatory on Mount Wilson stood more than a mile high but they suggested the incalculable, incomprehensible distances of galactic space penetrated by their telescopes. Deep canyons slashed the San Gabriels like the space between fingers, suggesting mysteries I longed to penetrate. They presented a huge barrier rolling eastward. Beyond them to the north stretched the Mojave Desert, which we rarely visited. Another mystery into which the inner me longed to bite, like a juicy red apple. Why was I the only one in the household who wanted to do such things?

In retrospect, the seed of eventual spirituality was probably planted there, atop this molehill among mountains. Mount Verdugo presented me with a panoramic view toward vast wildernesses, suggesting the ever more profound puzzles of the universe. The matter of my own soul was already a puzzle; I was not yet aware to what degree soul could also be an uncharted infinity.

My earliest experiences with real wilderness centered on my great-grandfather's fishing cabin in the San Gabriel Canyon, whose mouth could be vaguely discerned from my molehill peak. It was there I first met boulder-strewn canyon floors and the rushing waters of a wild river. But I was then a small child whose exploring nature had not yet been unleashed. Mrs. Persinger's cornbread and gingerbread, baked in the oven of the old wood stove, were sufficiently intoxicating to the youngster not yet allowed to ramble the canyon unaccompanied. This doughty little old lady looked after my great-grandfather when he was in residence. Half a century earlier Mary and Bates Persinger had been the true pioneers in the Canyon, carrying all their worldly goods up the rocky riverbed on their backs. She wore full-length blue denim dresses and lived in a cabin about a quarter-mile away. The trail to her home cabin wiggled across the face of a bluff which was a snake clubhouse, and her skill at dispatching rattlers with a long stick was legendary.

In the early 1930s the construction of dams in the Canyon brought the imminent disappearance under the waters of what we called "the cabin". Great-grandfather's retreat of fifty years, originally a fishing club of which he had been a member, would be dynamited and abandoned. Its little bluff would become a shallow place in an otherwise deep lake. He was already past eighty and would simply turn that page of his life. Most of the family seemed resigned to the end of something nice, although somewhat archaic.

Except my paternal grandmother Isabel. She had grown up on a farm "up north" in the Sacramento Valley, and rural life, close to the earth, was in her blood. Marriage to my grandfather had made of her a lady of considerable standing in Los Angeles society of the early twentieth century, but her warm, gracious and considerate nature concealed a deep nostalgia for the great outdoors. She was tall, possibly from her Danish heritage, and carried herself like a queen. She was not beautiful in the classic sense, but she radiated a commanding serenity.

Unhappy with the loss of her father-in-law's hideaway camp in the wild canyon, she began looking for something to replace it. She found it in the San Jacinto Mountains, then a three-hour drive east of Los Angeles. A resort village named Idyllwild nestled in a natural bowl on the sunny flank of the San Jacintos. Many times in the early '30s she took me up to that mile-high hamlet. At first we stayed at the "Inn" in rustic cottages named after birds and wildflowers. "Columbine" and "Blue Jay" remain in memory. I hadn't known she was "shopping" for a replacement cabin, but I was overjoyed when she announced in late 1934 that she had bought "Tahcinto Lodge". The following summer we spent six weeks up there. Thereafter, and for the next half-dozen years until I graduated from high school, she took me there during the school vacations in the winter, frequently in the spring, and often in the summers.

The boundaries of my world exploded. The invigorating lightness of living at altitude, coupled with regular contact with wildlife, unlocked in me a deep attachment to this natural world. If spirituality was seeded atop Mount Verdugo, in Idyllwild it began its long, slow, subconscious germination.

Her "cabin" was more than just a cabin; it was a rustic, shingle-sided house among the oaks and pines. It was rustic because heating was by pot-bellied wood stoves in the bedrooms, the big fireplace in the living room, and the cooking range was nourished by a propane tank. Chopping and carrying wood was part of the daily routine, and she gave me that job after observing that I could wield a hatchet without lopping off a finger. "Tahcinto Lodge" enjoyed a splendid view across the valley to Mount San Jacinto and its neighboring Tahquitz Peak. At 10'804 feet and 8'828 feet these were proper mountains. In winter they were usually snow-covered, and it was there, on the slope below grandmother's cabin, that I taught myself to ski on a pair of borrowed wooden skis. Sliding downhill implied knowing how to climb up again, for there was no such thing as a skilift.

We walked a lot when we were there, winter and summer. The midwinter sojourns -- always the week immediately following Christmas -- involved a lot of studying the sky and consulting the thermometer in hope it would snow, which it sometimes did. Whatever the weather, we always walked. We walked up to the village, along Strawberry Creek, up to Saunders Meadow, or high in Fern Valley underneath Tahquitz Peak and Suicide Rock.

Wildlife was there for those with eyes, ears and patience. Deer abounded in those mountains, and we had a salt lick for them a few yards from the cabin. They came to the lick every evening, timidly, watching me with suspicion. They came also to drink from the little pool she created just below the house. Deer became special creatures within my heart. They seemed to inhabit another dimension to which I craved access. Their big eyes stared at me before they bolted and I wondered if creature-to-creature contact was possible. I would pad slowly and quietly over the forest floor, following their narrow trails through scrub oak and manzanita, hoping to find their hidden home. They exerted a powerful pull on me, but it would be decades before this attraction could be perceived within a spiritual context.

Squirrels romped in the big oaks around the pool and came down to the porch rail to eat nuts from our hands. At night one sometimes caught the aroma of a skunk passing through. We heard about wildcats but it was ten years before I ever saw one.

The winged people — bluejays, redheaded woodpeckers, nuthatches, Oregon juncoes, and mountain chickadees (cousins of the European titmice, the mésanges we have here) — flocked around much of the year.

It is impossible to overemphasize the role this camaraderie with my grandmother played in forming the mountain-dweller and alpinist I was to become forty years later. In her own quiet way she allowed me to enter into and share with her the natural world which was so dear to her, so far from the city in which she was imprisoned. Wittingly or unwittingly, she catalyzed in me a reverence for this side of life, a reverence which I was incapable of feeling toward the religion to which I was exposed every Sunday.

In contrast, my maternal grandfather the Theosophist did not directly pass anything of his philosophy on to me. Yet I now believe the existence of his thread, that genetic tic for the spiritual, had some influence in my soul's choice of a family in which to reincarnate. His influence was subtle, subterranean, genetic. Hers was direct, generous, and warmly concerned.

With the perspective gained over more than sixty years I can see now what was invisible to the teenager: my grandmother was a tower of spiritual strength. Never did I hear her speak of "God" or anything biblical. She didn't talk about religious concepts, but she led the way in setting an example of correct behavior in all one's relationships. She treated each and every person with warmth and consideration. She moved through the world in a christly way without ever once talking about it.

My grandmother took me places, taught me life skills, and never ceased to call my attention to tiny fascinations, be they animal, vegetable or mineral. She taught me to appreciate the sights and smells of her mountain paradise. Right outside the cabin stood a towering Jeffrey pine, and she showed me how to put my nose into the crevices of its bark so as to capture its vanilla-like aroma. Her influence was practical and immediate. Whether it was how to lay a fire, how to drain the water lines so the pipes wouldn't freeze, how to recognize birds, wildflowers and forest plants, she filled my head and receptive spirit with useful lore. Idyllwild was her passionate escape from her urban cage; she gave me an example to follow.

Looking back, I can see that she was right for me at the time. She was a soul companion, but not an overt spiritual worker. Her companionship style of teaching focused on nature and the art of living, qualities which laid a base for making the most of spirituality when it blossomed in me decades later.

Sitting in a church pew, listening to words which made little sense to me, was hostile to my nature. Rules of conduct such as the Ten Commandments resonated with a certain logic. What surrounded them did not hang together, left me mostly puzzled, frequently unconcerned. There was more reality up in the mountains. One was closer to God, whatever that was.

One of our favorite trails led along the South Ridge toward the white forest fire lookout crowning Tahquitz Peak. I always wanted to go up there and see the fire warden in his square hut of windows, but it was supposed to be a very long hike and we never went that far. Our last hike together, in 1952 when she was seventy-five, followed this trail. I get a lump in the throat and misty in the eyes recalling the moment when she said "Well, dear, I think that's enough for me." And she apologized for not being able to continue.

She continued to go to her mountains for another decade but, like a relay runner, she passed the baton to me. She gave me a key to her "cabin" and we went there often until life changes moved me and my young family permanently away from Southern California.

During the year previous to that last hike with her, I had climbed Mount San Jacinto with a friend. We struck off one afternoon from a trailhead near Pine Cove and we got most of the way to the summit before nightfall. We made a little camp up there, at the edge of timberline, somewhere around 9000 feet, cooking a rudimentary supper and then climbing into our sleeping bags early.

At eight o'clock the next morning we stood on the barren summit. The view over the desert was stupefying. Cornell Peak, close by, obstructs the view over the luxurious resort oasis of Palm Springs far below, but the abrupt fall from 10800 feet to the desert floor at sea level is impressive. Falling that far on an eight-mile track makes it possibly the sheerest escarpment of any mountain range in the United States. Across the Cabazon Pass to the north, Mount San Gorgonio's imposing mass blocks the view toward the deserts in that direction. Behind and below us lay evergreen forests. In front stretched a vast emptiness of sand and rock, tumbleweed and cactus, for hundreds of miles. It is the western edge of the great American desert, harsh at any season and dangerous to the unprepared.

That landscape is brown, beige, sand-colored, stretching over barren plains and craggy mountains to the Colorado River, to Arizona, Nevada, Utah and the Rocky Mountains. Greenery is a rarity, clustered around natural springs. The general view includes nothing verdant.

This was my first experience of such a long perspective, much vaster than what I had seen from little Mount Verdugo. Stretching seemingly to infinity, the vista stimulates the imagination as to what lies beyond. This concept of "beyond" plays a role in my life which I have learned not to ignore. Its promise of glimpsing hidden dimensions is a tiny, intangible motor which occasionally propels me into fresh exploration, fresh adventure.

A particular view toward the Weisshorn, as seen from Münster in the Oberwallis, is an important example. Will and I took several brief midwinter vacations in that charming village overlooking the upper reaches of the Rhône River. We went there because of the marvelous crosscountry ski trails stretching for long distances along the river banks. High mountains line the narrow valley floor, and from our hotel room we could see some of the bigger peaks. Especially the Weisshorn, 14'783 feet, Switzerland's third-highest summit. Our hotel balcony offered a long westward view on the Weisshorn, a pyramid of snow and ice standing high above its neighbors. Its southern edge induced in me a sense of "the back of beyond".

There is nothing rational about that impression. That edge outlined against the cosmos faces south, faces toward the spine of the Alps and toward Italy. It never occurred to me even to dream of climbing it. It was too high, too tough, too late in my life, and at that time I still had not become an alpinist. To me that edge outlined in deep blue suggested a jumping-off place, a springboard to "out there" , to the "back of beyond."

In later years several other alpine vistas inspired this sensation in me. Seeing the Weisshorn's other dimension was the first time in which I identified and gave a name to the emotion. It was mysterious. It was tantalizing. It proposed unsuspected portals to unsuspected dimensions. It probably had a lot to do with launching me on alpine trails in search of these other dimensions

Three years before Will left for the other side I made a series of one-day excursions organized by the local tourist office. These were meant to be primarily for summer visitors, but they provided an opportunity to explore the nearby trails which my responsibilities had prevented me from learning. And I was already in my sixties and had not put many kilometers on my legs. The little side-hill itineraries in our immediate neighborhood did not do much to toughen calf and thigh muscles. Out-of-shape me needed to start slowly, and the pace of flatlander tourists suited me perfectly.

These first hikes brought me a more intimate knowledge of the canyons, passes, high meadows, and rocky slopes that were visible from my windows but whose true contours were not fully clear at four, five, six miles distance.

Family excursions had taken me onto the modest Chamossaire, standing behind our villages at 6'929 feet, serving as the top of the ski slopes in winter. In 1983 I had guided myself and the Dutch girl atop the Haute-Corde, 7'628 feet. This is one of the easiest itineraries in the alpine catalog, fun to do as a season warmer-upper.

In that summer of 1984 the tourist office excursions were not much more ambitious. Slogging up the Paneirosse glacier to the Col des Chamois was long and hot, the snow soft and slow under midsummer sun reflecting off the steep walls on both sides. There is a geology lesson imbedded in the walls of the Tsernou ridge on your left: strata laid down over millions of years have been folded into a double "s" curve — a glaring challenge to the scientific posture called "gradualism".

Once at the summit of the glacier your reward is to picnic on a stony saddle, the north Col at 8'714 feet, offering a panoramic view and a growing sense of intimacy with the major peaks. Up that high nothing grows except lichen on the rocks.

This hike also informed me that I needed to do something about my knees. My legs are constitutionally skinny and so are the knees. Going up the Glacier de Paneirosse I had to stop often to let blood pump into the lower legs. This led me to believe the arteries passing through my knees seemed to be poorly developed. For the time being the only thing I could think of to improve that situation was to keep on hiking against gravity.

That season really did give me a fine grasp of the local itineraries. Four hikes under the tourist office leadership armed me for the future. I began the following year's modest agenda with a sense of knowing where I was going. What I didn't know ahead of time was how much Mother Nature was about to bless my inquisitive nature.

The next summer and fall brought me numerous gifts, some of them animal, some of them human, some of them spiritual. Three years into meditation at that point, I walked my path on two levels. Physical eyes observed the trail ahead, placing physical feet where they needed to be. Inner eyes scanned invisible realms in search of a portal, a clue to that "beyond". It had to be up there; I needed to find something that was more than mineral, vegetable or animal.

Our mountain paradise is home to large populations of creatures. Our four-footed fellow citizens and all the winged singers were here long before man built the first chalet. They have had to adapt to our encroachment on their territories, but they hang on as long as possible to their instinctive ways.

For example, the fox who patrols the garden by night. Her tracks in the snow tell me that her itinerary doesn't change: a long more or less straight trail out of the forest and across the meadow, crossing the highway and then resuming over the meadow below our fence. Through the fence, and then an irregular, ziggy and zaggy prowl through the garden, up the rock garden and then, adapting at this point, around the house and back into the garden again, eventually passing through the hedge to visit our neighbors. The same trail punctures the fresh snow year in and year out. Its zigs and zags allow for checking all the traditional mouse holes.

Something about the summer of 1985 caused an explosion in the animal populations, both aerial and terrestrial. There was a kind of a ferment among the wild creatures. They were not just more numerous, but they were more ebullient, even brash. The squirrel, for example.

Squirrels abound in the oak groves lower down the mountain, and they abound in the evergreens higher up. In our immediate neighborhood I had never seen one. So it was all the more extraordinary when Peter and I spied a squirrel galloping toward us as fast as he could. Peter was one of Will's grandsons, just arrived from Colorado at the beginning of June, and to liberate his legs from aircraft compression we had rambled out along the sidehill.

We were on the homeward bight, on a grassy jeep trail which traverses the hillside hayfields, and here came a squirrel scurrying toward us over a nearly treeless mile between two forests. It takes courage for such a small creature to migrate across what must seem a desert to him, I thought. We stopped in wonder, waiting for his moment of fear. He ran almost up to us, then stopped dead ten feet away and for a long moment looked up at us. I felt a kind of contact, reminiscent of feeding nuts to those squirrels gamboling around my grandmother's mountain hideaway. Then his better sense prevailed and our bushy-tailed rodent dashed into the deep grass beside the track.

A month later I was up with the sun and out of the house for a walking meditation in the crisp morning air. Ambling along the sidehill track, I was coordinating measured breathing with an internalized mantra. As I passed the skeleton of a dead fruit tree a kind of fluster-scramble-flutter in the branches startled me from my near-reverie. A hawk was flapping away with a small bird in its talons, apparently snatched not two yards from my head. The hunter sailed into a big fir tree on the forest edge fifty yards away and began to chomp his breakfast, with a branch for table.

Another fifty yards forward I went over a small rise to spot fox cubs at play. Two of them were rolling, tumbling, and wrestling in mock battle in the meadow grass while mother calmly prowled the forest edge in search of mouse holes. They paid no attention to my presence, partially masked as I was by standing close to a bush. This family scene went on for about ten minutes while I stood stock-still, rapt with silent appreciation. Mother fox was concentrated in her search for food; her children were carefree and reckless.

When I got back to the chalet spirit demanded a sitting meditation. No sooner had I launched into Om Mani Padme Hum than my inner screen flashed open and brought back to me the forest edge and my foxes.

The next morning another miracle occurred: our titmice hatched a bumper crop of fledglings and managed to get them all flying. These colorful little birds nest every year in the box we have nailed to a post outside the kitchen window, but most of the time predators snatch some of the babies off the ground before they can get their wings fluttering properly. The big European jays, larger than the California blue jay I had known in my youth, the magpies, and the crows all seem to know almost to the hour when young birds will be launched from their nursery. I have learned to recognize that the jay's chatter in early summer mornings is diagnostic of a fledgling flyout in the offing.

On this particular morning the titmice parents got their brood out of the box in early-morning fog. Our undaunted couple had five young birds in the air, flying, before the predators discovered they'd been hoodwinked. That day, and for several days thereafter, we were treated to the sight of a family of seven yellow-and-black Parus major wheeling and flocking around the garden and from tree to bush and back again. Never before and never since has such a big family come out of that box outside the window.

I repeated my early walk several times in the days that followed but saw no more fox families. Other treats were coming, however. Deer, buzzards and eagles were about to join the festivity.

During the late spring and summer deer come out of the deep forest opposite to munch a particularly appealing variety of herb that grows at the back of the meadow. It is always a moment of joy when I see them for the first time after the winter season. Nine times out of ten one sees only the does and their fawns. Caution is the buck's first instinct, and that caution is thrown to the winds only during the rut, the mating season. This begins in July and is signaled by a change in color of the pelt. They emerge from winter in a brindle-toned coat, but as summer matures and their passions begin to boil the coat veers toward red. Which is why some people call them red deer.

Seeing the deer is a kind of communion for me. Binoculars are always handy near the windows. Long moments pass while I try to determine if there are antlers — only the bucks have them — and if so, how many points. When they raise their heads you cannot distinguish horns from twigs and branches of the forest background.

In this luxuriant summer for animal life it took me several weeks to be sure of what kind of deer I was seeing. At first I thought there were two does and two fawns. It was mid-August before I realized there was one doe with a record three fawns. I could not believe it.

A few mornings later out came the buck, looking gaunt and nervous. His coat was a gorgeous red-brown. With great good luck the binoculars caught a head-on view, revealing he had two points on each horn, one of the horns deformed. In my husband's hunting days in the forests of the Netherlands the state gamekeepers would have selected such an imperfect animal for elimination.

There are magical moments in life, and one of them happened late in the month, my notes say August 29. The buck was out grazing by six-thirty in the morning, just in front of the treeline. Half an hour later the rest of the family emerged. They were all there, buck, doe and three offspring, now growing rapidly.

The three fawns behaved most coltishly, chasing one another in circles and pretending to butt one another. Their mother played with them. My jaw probably gaped — Mother Nature had never before offered such a treat. For a moment even the buck joined in the general fun, feigning antlers-down charges, as they all scampered around. Then the fawns disappeared into the forest — doing as they were told? The doe remained playful and seemed to be trying to seduce the buck, who followed her back into the trees.

This memory of five deer romping around the meadow in playful circles remains the souvenir of a privileged moment. I call it "the day the deer danced." Later my neighbor asked me in excitement "did you see what I saw?" She'd been on her balcony too, hypnotized like me.

At the same season birds of prey are always very much in evidence. Hawks and buzzards hover above the meadows in haying season, waiting for the field mice to start scurrying around in search of fresh cover.

At about the same time as the unusual deer spectacle there seemed to be a pair of large birds spending a lot of time on one of the lower branches of the biggest fir tree at the back of the meadow. There was a lot of crying and calling from one to another, and I began to suspect there was a nest close by. Then I got a clean look at them the same morning the nervous buck first emerged.

They were young golden eagles! Their underwing markings were unmistakeable. They soared around, calling a lot in their typical high-pitched scream. Where were the parents? These birds of prey live up in the crags most of the year, coming down only in summer to exploit the field mouse population. And, I had often suspected, to train their young in the essential art of hunting. This time it appeared that training-time was over, the parents had gone home, and the young were left to look after themselves.

The eaglets stayed in the neighborhood until late in the month. My last sighting was a day or two before the deer threw caution to the winds.

These manifestations of the natural world left a sense of deep satisfaction. They were natural world highlights ornamenting a season that was equally rich in spiritual satisfactions. That these phenomena came in bunches did not leave me indifferent, but I could not intuit a real meaning, if indeed there was a meaning.

Meditation at that time was replete with little visions as well as my own special cerevision, with brain massage coming along with less regularity. The visions themselves were not so spectacular but their frequency spoke of work going on beneath the surface. Taken together, all these phenomena heightened my sense of wonder at the inner world's staggering potentials.

In September we went to Grindelwald to visit my husband's sister at the time of my birthday. Still walking the trails at almost 86, she introduced me to some of her favorite itineraries, Pfingstegg, Stieregg, Milchbach, and she told me how to get from the Firstbahn chairlift to the summit of the Faulhorn (8'796 feet). Which I did, easily, sailing the boulevard-like trails through hordes of other vacationers.

Best of all was the fine, sporty climb up to the Glecksteinhütte, my birthday present to myself to celebrate receiving my old-age pension. The trail passes along the face of a cliff and then turns a corner called Die Enge (the "narrow place" — don't be subject to vertigo!). You enter a world of whiteness. The path heads south toward the sunlit glaciers and snowy peaks, but your attention must remain riveted on the steep fall-off on your right hand (and foot!) Below yawn the vicious-looking crevasses of the Obergletscher, row upon row of shark's teeth carved in dirty ice. After a long, steadily-rising progression in company with this gaping mouth your way finally begins a series of zigzags up grassy-stony shoulders to arrive at the refuge at 7'600 feet. Along the way one might meet the impressive saber-horned bouquetin, the largest wild animal of the high mountains[1]. They are often around the Gleckstein, and on this first trip I met a big one at a little clearing on the downward trail. He regarded me impassively, moved a step to the side, and continued munching the sparse grass.

Grindelwald faces a wall of impressive peaks: the Wetterhorn, Schreckhorn, Eiger, Mönch and Jungfrau. Glaciers slither down between the first three, opening gateways through the wall and into a magical world of ice, rock, grassy banks, sun and Mother Nature's version of a concert. The Gleckstein refuge sits on a high crag offering a loge seat for the spectacle.

Glaciers are musical, I discovered. There is a constant groaning and cracking, punctuated with frequent avalanches. Raw terrestrial power is at work, out of sight in the depths of ancient ice. This mass hundreds of feet thick grinds, slides, slips, inches relentlessly down the surface of a hidden rock base, creeping forward toward the invisible critical break-point.

Seracs -- chunks the size of trucks, houses, office buildings -- split away from steep ice cliffs. These blocks rumble and clatter down to raise a cloud of ice powder. Sometimes you spot a barrow-load of stones tumbling down the side of a slanted crevasse. This debris is sucked from the surface into the glacier's gaping wounds, to become the stuff of which moraines are built in geological time.

One feels great energy vibrating against the pulsing walls of the human aura, but this is sensed, not heard. Water trickles over rock somewhere in the distance. There is no other sound in this wild universe, until the next explosive crashing-off of the breaking ice, bass-baritone chords echoing in the vastness. The blast is followed by a river of blocks and stones cascading downward, rippling trills played on a giant keyboard. One sits, looks, listens and, spellbound, slips into meditation.

[1] The bouquetin, or Steinbock in German, *Capra ibex ibex* for zoologists, is a real heavyweight. They inhabit the rocky heights, their elastic hooves gripping steep slopes, and they descend to the highest pastures late in the day to browse and drink. These are big animals, an adult male weighing nearly 200 pounds and standing nearly four feet tall at the forehead. Their horns are remarkable, heavy curved swords reaching three feet in length for a male in maturity, much less for a female. Their pelt is grayish in summer, turning rust brown in fall. These big creatures, once extinct in Switzerland, have not been hunted since they were reintroduced half a century ago, thus those of the Swiss Alps are less timid than other creatures. One sometimes sees them quite close. Before my first trip up to the Gleckstein my sister-in-law told me of having to hit one with a walking stick in order to get him to move aside on that trail above the gaping glacier. I would not like to be too close to one on a narrow trail along a precipice, thank you.

Chapter Fourteen

VIBRATING WITH THEM

I

My career as a real alpinist probably began that last weekend of July, 1986, when, in my first outing with the Alpine Club, we climbed the Col du Pacheu and then traversed the southern flank of the Muveran massif.

Everything up to then had been one-day hikes without any technical challenges. I had not yet gone anywhere with the Alpine Club. This expedition started with a three-hour climb up a steep trail to the refuge called Cabane du Plan-Névé. Two weeks earlier I had climbed that tough trail one foggy day just to be sure it was within my capacities. It was a stiff climb but my body handled it without any problems, other than being slower than I wanted to be. Still, I was rather apprehensive about my first outing with a group of experienced mountaineers.

My husband Will was very supportive. He'd been up there often, he'd been up the wall of the Pacheu, and he was confident all would go well for me. He approved wholeheartedly of the adventure.

Nevertheless, I was nervous about everything: my first night ever in a mountain "hut", my first climb up a rock wall, my first long alpine expedition, in company with people who were, surely, better than me.

In retrospect I realized they had been equally apprehensive about me. At nearly 63 I was more than ten years older than all but one of those who would do the hike. The leader was asking himself "how will she be on ice? can she climb rock?"

On Saturday afternoon an ebullient lady named Lily and I struck off alone from Pont de Nant, well ahead of the rest of the group. By their design, I knew intuitively. She was peppy, dynamic, lots of fun, and only 50.

My first trip up that trail had been on a cold, foggy day, but this time the midsummer sun was shining in all its glory. It was a hot climb, those one thousand meters seemingly rose straight up. My backpack weighed eighteen pounds, with food for three meals, plenty of water, some extra clothing, camera, binoculars and all the little stuff you tuck in the outer pockets of the rucksack. I hadn't carried so much since that weekend thirty-five years earlier when we camped overnight high on Mount San Jacinto.

On my earlier scouting trip I had enjoyed a long leisurely look at a group of four chamois. These lovely creatures are about the size of a deer but they are really a kind of wild goat, with small straight horns that curl backward just at the top, something like a crochet hook. They are much more timid than the larger bouquetin. On this day Lily and I saw only one or two chamois but we did have a good look at a big marmot[1]. He was sunning himself, sprawled atop a boulder just above our second rest stop six hundred meters above our starting-point.

It was hot that day, it was hard, but gaining altitude creates within me the seed of exaltation. I think this is true of almost all alpinists, even those who don't consciously admit a sense of the spiritual in life.

Each hiker is engaged in a solitary struggle between her/his physical ability and the invisible brake of gravity. This prevails before you add in the dangers of a difficult passage or the superphysical challenge of a major rock climb up where the air is thin. In overcoming these barriers the mountaineer moves his/her consciousness into another dimension. The literature of alpinism suggests that, for some, it is almost like a meditation. There are some mystics who say that, for them, such hiking *is* meditation. My own experience is that moving into a meditational state while climbing with a heavy backpack is not at all easy, but that working with your mantra during this heavy effort can ease the consciousness of physical strain. I have used that technique -- repeating my mantra silently while trudging ever upward -- during the last hour of a particularly rough or steep trail. And it does help.

In three and a half hours we reached the Plan-Névé at 2262 meters. I suspect Lily could have done it much faster without the burden of looking after me. In future years I would be able to knock an hour off that time, but this first season I had not yet "made my legs". We'd started at 1260 meters and thus gained 1002 meters, nearly 3'300 feet. Three hours, one thousand meters, is a typical effort for the first leg of most itineraries, the siting of refuges being determined in part by what is a reasonable approach for most people.

This particular refuge (or "cabane" or "hut") is a stone house seated on a natural platform at the top of a cliff and just below the edge of a small glacier. Sleeping quarters are an upstairs dormitory paved with mattresses and piles of neatly-folded army blankets. In those days the sanitary facilities at Plan-Névé were basic: An outhouse for toilet, and a spring-fed spigot over an outdoor sink for washing. Most of these refuges have guardians throughout the summer only.

Once all the rest of our group had arrived we were fifteen, and I began to meet my companions for the morrow. The guardian and his wife prepared the food we had brought for our supper and we had a gay evening, frequently strolling out onto the clifftop terrace to admire the fantastic panorama of setting sun, then the sparkle of towns and villages illuminating the Rhône valley down to the distant lake shimmering like an oil slick.

Meditating at altitude is fine if I don't have to face strong sunlight. Meditating at a refuge depends for its success on the tranquillity one can find. When you are with a group there is often subtle pressure to remain with them during the long guzzling of beverages. Rehydrating can take a long time at the end of a summer day. Sometimes it is possible to move fifty yards away for a bit of privacy, but the terrain does not always favor this tactic. On this particular occasion I found it impossible to abstract myself sufficiently from the good-natured hubbub. Sitting on a rock ten yards away was inadequate solitude.

At seven o'clock the next morning our leader ("chef de course") Jean-Pierre quietly announced "sac au dos." We all obeyed, swinging our packs onto our backs, picking up our ice-axes, and trudging off across the stony moraine to start the climb up this comparatively small glacier. We had to get to the top of the glacier and onto the rock face early, because as the day wears on (heats up, that is), the danger of rock fall increases. That is why alpinists are always striking off in the early dawn, or even the middle of the night, wearing headlamps. In this case the mountain wall we were to cross lay to the south of us, and this first part of the itinerary lay in cool shadow.

I could see Jean-Pierre eyeing me as we began the tramp up the glacier. He had a rope and ice cleats strapped atop his pack, for emergencies. He was visibly preoccupied, but I was at ease and had no intention of providing him with an emergency.

At the top of the glacier we stepped onto rock at the foot of the passage, a kind of broad cleft in the mountain wall. This was the beloved Pacheu; that's a dialect word meaning "passage". It is about two hundred meters of corrugated rock rising steeply out of the ice, equipped in some places with lengths of chain fixed to the stone as flexible handrails. It tilts toward the vertical at somewhere between forty-five and sixty degrees.

This is a free climb on all fours, hands and feet, and it was a wonderful experience. As youngsters we used to scale a little ten-foot outcropping that rose from the dry creek bed in a hidden gulch about five minutes from home, but I had never before had the opportunity to do a real rock climb.

I went up it like a monkey, exulting in the coordinated movement of hands and feet, loving the contact with the stone. Stimulation surged through my veins, suddenly I was in my natural element, reveling at each new handhold. It was over much too soon. Until that moment I had not known that I was so much at home on rock.

Half the group was already up there, and I received congratulations from all sides, complete with handshakes and embraces. Jean-Pierre was all smiles, visibly relieved.

"You came up like a little cat" he exclaimed.

So I had won my spurs with the climbing fraternity, but I did not feel quite ready for the Matterhorn.

We had climbed five hundred meters from the Cabane, and now leaned or sat against the base of the thumb of rock called the Tête du Pacheu. It is visible from my home, as the passage itself is not. We got up there at eight-thirty, emerging from shadow to bright sun. We stayed half an hour, snacking, drinking, and devouring the eagle's-eye view, savouring our delight at having done it, at being there.

These are moments of elation for all alpinists. It is more than pure kinesthetic satisfaction. Spirit soars. Up among the eagles one sees the world differently. "Down there" takes on another perspective. "Up here" one hobnobs with the peaks and spires that pierce the blue. One is closer to that blue, closer to the cosmos, closer to the traditional realm of gods and angels. Human spirit is brought nearer to that fathomless infinity which I have called the "back of beyond".

From this lofty perch we scrabbled down a steep patch of loose stone, across the top of a névé[2] and then down some more scree before turning westward to traverse the sunny side of the Muverans. It was quickly hot, and the track was neither level nor smooth. Flannel shirts came off and we trekked these small ups and downs in T-shirts and sun cream.

High country magic gradually invaded our senses: there were bouquetin on the Dent du Chamosentse. Almost the same color as the rock, they were at first hard to pick out. We stopped, unanimously choosing this spot for an unscheduled pause, binoculars emerging from our packs along with water bottles. We observed the bouquetins for a long time as they evolved lazily on the rocky shoulder. There were nine of them, we finally decided. Daniel, a state game warden, decreed they were seven females and two young males, both kinds having short horns just a bit longer than a domestic goat. Silhouetted against the sun on the steep edges of this minor peak, they seemed to be posing for picture postcards.

"They're beautiful, and they know it!" Daniel chuckled.

It was true, for they were continually striking poses. Daniel explained that the females and their young lived apart from the males at this season.

It was most of an hour before we saw the males. First we had to cross a little ridge and then trudge slowly up another long névé before reaching the Cabane Rambert (2580 meters) on the southern flank of the Grand Muveran. It took me an eternity to get to the top of this névé, for once again my knees were not letting enough blood through to the lower legs. "Om Mani Padme Hum" did yeoman service during this slow, sweaty effort. I was the last to arrive at the Cabane, resolving that I must absolutely do something to strengthen my legs. Perhaps I could climb rock like a cat, but my toiling up the endless sun-softened snow slope was more reminiscent of a snail.

From the window of the cabane we spotted more bouquetins, a long line of them strung along a ledge high above us. We took turns looking and revising the count. First there were four, then seven, then Daniel counted eighteen. I picked up my glasses and counted twenty-five, then Daniel, the acknowledged expert, made the definitive tally of twenty-seven.

These were the males, with magnificent horns up to a meter in length. They lounged across the flank of the mountain, lords of the Alps taking their ease and gazing down with indifference on those two-legged ants invading their picnic grounds.

Rarely does one see so many of these majestic creatures all in one place.

My most ambitious-to-date ramble over the mountains had brought me a sight that has not been duplicated so far. Sitting high on the back side of my favorite mountain, meeting so many of the wild animals who survive up there all year, basking in the sunny company of like-minded companions, allowed the warmth of enchantment to flow through my spirit. No mantra required.

Forty-five years earlier my heart had gone out to a pen full of brown Nubian goats at the county fair, just before marveling at a painterly version of the wind blowing the sky away. Now heart and soul soaked up the sight of the massive bouquetins etched against crags and crests where the wind tried endlessly to peel the sky away. Now I was higher up, closer to that elusive "beyond". My senses locked onto sky, rock, creatures of the wild, my spirit hungering to see more. Because seeing more accompanied feeling more.

Getting down the mountain was the hardest part -- it always is -- old knees and old ankles complaining every step of the way. And that part of it never got any better in all the subsequent years of alpinism. Three hours down to beer and lemonade, then a bus, then a train back to our starting point.

Down the mountain. Down to earth. My weakening husband had weathered the weekend without me in great form. I'd left little plastic sachets of his medicines for each of the meals, which our cleaning lady had prepared. On Sunday our friend Betty, in the throes of a divorce, drove him to our favorite restaurant.

"I had more interesting conversation in an hour-and-a-half at table with Will than I had in a year-and-a-half with José," she remarked.

That year could offer me no more weekends of such grandeur, but it could still offer some memorable adventures. Two years earlier the tourist office hikes had brought me new friends. Mireille and Carsten, a French-Norwegian couple, were on one of those excursions and we struck up a nice friendship. They were in residence only a few months of the year; thus it was not until late in the 1986 season that she and I struck off on a series of one-day rambles, blessed by enthralling encounters with wild life.

One sunny day in mid-September we met a kestrel eating a rabbit. We were en route to Ensex, a cluster of herdsmens' chalets on a high pasture just over the ridge from here. This soaring hunter, one of the larger members of the falcon family, was dining right on the trail. He was only fifty yards in front of us, apparently ravenously hungry, too much in a hurry to bother flying to a less-conspicuous table. We moved very slowly toward him, halving the distance, and then he did pick up his prey and flew away the same distance, about twenty-five yards. In other words, "you can watch, but don't get too close."

After buying some goat cheese at the hamlet we moved toward Encrenne, a little notch where I had meditated one day on a solitary ramble. We settled for our picnic near a big boulder and found ourselves being scrutinized by a weasel[3]. The supple creature eyed us pertly for an instant, then darted behind the boulder.

Immediately thereafter another weasel scampered uphill, in the opposite direction. A diversonary tactic? Where we too close to a nest of young? I have seen other wild creatures behave similarly.

A few days later we had the chance to get out again and hiked up to the Col des Pauvres, a wasteland pass of boulders and hollows, another point visible from home but requiring the usual three-hour hike to get up there.

Up there, above 2100 meters, one enters into an intimate relationship with the backbone of my Muveran range. The map says it is two kilometers away across the valley of Nant, as the proverbial crow flies, but it looks barely half that. Gaze slightly left and you have the Grand Muveran rising benignly just overhead. Shift your eyes to the right and the two Dents de Morcles, my bats' ears, rise to their peaks out of frightening vertical walls. Between these two major landmarks is a virtual no man's land of rock. The corrugations of these rugged walls are harsh and uninviting.

We had come up the jeep track to the head of the valley, then turned right to zigzag up a long treeless slope to the rock-filled pass. It's the natural picnic site. Now we proposed to climb up to just under the Pointe de Savoleyres and gain the crest, which could be followed all the way back to Pont de Nant.

At the top, the Pointe reveals itself as three towers forming the walls of a tarn or crater choked with jumbled boulders. Wind wailing inside the crater sounded weird chords — Mussorgsky's "A Night on Bald Mountain" comes to mind. Our way led up, around and over these blocks, almost another rock climb. It was careful work, potentially dangerous because of the many rock crevasses and bearpits from which a solitary hiker, if slightly injured, might never get out. We saw one pit, like a bottle, only three or four meters down to a dirt floor but from which one person could not get out even if still in good shape. And then we were up and away from that series of traps.

The crest trail wound around, through and sometimes over a seemingly endless jumble of huge blocks and boulders. It's spectacular but not easy work. We reached a comfortable grassy bank which invited us to sit and slake the thirst generated by this sweaty workout. And then we looked down on the reward of the whole excursion.

One hundred meters below us grazed a large herd of chamois[4]. They were moving lazily within an exceedingly steep grassy bowl, entirely in the late afternoon shade, and we could easily have missed spotting them.

Chamois are extremely shy toward humans, fleeing if you get too close. Unlike the bouquetin, they are not protected and they know that humans will hunt them when October arrives. That's when they seek the highest, most inaccessible places to graze. Chamois have a way of inspecting you from a distance which enchants me. Cocking the head at an angle, they seem to be asking "is that something I need to be afraid of?" Usually they quickly decide in the affirmative and bound away, leaving you with a view of a dark tail bouncing over a white rump.

Mireille and I recognized how privileged we were to have this long, leisurely time of observation, for the chamois were unaware of us. With my small ten-power binoculars we amused ourselves by taking the census. Ultimately we settled on a count of twenty-six.

We could have sat there forever, drinking in the sight of wild creatures in that savage habitat, with the Grand Muveran just across the narrow valley. It was a perfect hour, a perfect situation for meditation, but the crest trail was long and the sun was heading for the Jura Mountains in the northwest. Our golden moment had to end. We picked up our gear and resumed our descent.

Meditating while on the mountains is not as easy as one might think, as I have previously suggested. It is hard to find a comfortable place to sit, unless one just happens to find a grassy spot. The light is often very strong, sometimes aggressively so.

During the summer just concluded I had enjoyed a very nice but short meditation up near Anzeindaz, leaning against a rock in the sun but mercifully not facing it. Cerevision had come, and then spirit took me away to another place for a handful of minutes. Such interludes are rare in my mountainside meditations.

During the winter I found an answer for my poorly-irrigated knees. I bought a stationary bicycle and began cranking out the kilometers on a daily basis. I was determined that the next hiking season would see me sailing up the trails and snowfields.

Pedaling was part of what kept me in shape during that winter and spring. Those were my husband's last seasons in his physical body. When he was gone the mountains beckoned to me as never before. They had been waiting patiently, as mountains do, for my consciousness to reorient its focus.

The day after the funeral we went for a short hike *en famille,* my Swiss-American stepson René, his Swiss wife Katherina, and their children Toby (nine) and Simone (eight). We'd made a ritual of always getting out onto the mountain during their visits from the States, the five of us, and this time would not be an exception. It was a short little outing in the region of Solalex, nothing challenging, just being together in everyone's beloved Alps. We couldn't go higher that day because there was legal work awaiting us at the chalet, and the high country was still clogged with snow.

The Cantonal (State) government has a surefire method of keeping freshly-minted widows from grieving. It hurls paperwork at them. Our accountant and I were furiously busy the rest of the month, and on its last day we met with the justice of the peace to open the estate-settling procedure.

My alpine season really began the next day, July 1. Liberated from the ordeal of accounts and inventories, I pulled on my hiking boots, slung my pack on my back and headed for the high country. From the valley of Solalex I walked up the stony trail to Anzeindaz, a high pasture at 1900 meters, surrounded by snowy peaks. On the way up there I had seen a single chamois, browsing in bracken above the tumultous stream of snow melt at the right of the trail.

Anzeindaz was not in snow but everything around it was. Peaks rise on three sides. All approaches to the sporty little Haute-Corde were impassable. The Glacier de Paneirosse, even higher, was out of the question. The open side of the panorama extends toward the Pas de Cheville in the east. It is another one of those intriguing "back of beyond" vistas, calling to me, but on this day it too was blocked.

Sitting on the terrace of the Refuge Giacomini, I gazed across the water-logged hollow toward the Tour d'Anzeindaz. It's a round-topped loaf with grassy slopes, ordinarily not on anyone's climbing agenda. Choices were limited this day, and the three hundred meters to its summit seemed like a neat little climb. Nothing extravagant, one could say, hardly worth writing about. Almost.

So how to get up there? One would normally approach from the left, borrowing the lower part of the trail for the Haute-Corde. Sorry, too much snow. Well, a frontal assault was all green grass, steep but probably dry. That was what I would do: the east face. And did. It was very steep but provided a fine workout for the legs. No mantra necessary.

The summit offered a handsome view all around: the Haute-Corde and the Miroir de l'Argentine on the left, the Diablerets on the right, a steep falloff to Solalex straight ahead, and the mysterious Pas de Cheville in the other direction. Next I had to decide on getting down again. The south was blocked with snow, straight ahead (west) was a death trap, the steep slope I had come up was boring and uninviting. If I wanted variety only the north side, facing the massif of Les Diablerets, remained as a choice. *Let's go take a look at that,* I told myself, putting feet into motion.

It seemed tentatively practicable, but soon I found myself atop a disagreeable rock barrier that could be described as a cliff. It was a mini-cliff, susceptible to being clambered down but still capable of generating broken bones. Below that lay green slopes, which seemed to lead around to the east, my ultimate direction.

If I went left I could turn around the cliff, so I did that, then followed those green slopes toward the east. I was wandering a little bit, finding my way. There was a kind of shoulder, and when I went around that I found the way blocked by a snowfield.

And a chamois. Well, no, he was well below me and wasn't really blocking me in any way. And chamois don't block, they flee. *Was this the same one I'd seen earlier?* It seemed likely, because his present position was directly uphill from where he had been browsing. He wanted obviously to cross the snowfield but seemed confused by my presence. He was wandering back and forth on the névé, undecided how to avoid me. *Was he waiting for me to signal my route?* Then he decided, taking off rapidly over across the snowy slope, disappearing in the direction I planned to go.

This névé's top was steep and stretched across my path; down at the bottom it seemed to flatten out. At this moment I wished for crampons but I didn't yet own any. It was a north slope, probably icy during the night, but softening quickly under the midday sun.

With my walking stick I could punch little holes that my boots might, with a bit of stamping, enlarge into secure steps. This was my strategy, and I stepped onto the névé. There were only about fifty feet of snow to cross before I would step onto grass again, following the chamois.

It didn't work out that way. After five or six carefully-executed steps the snow slid out from under my feet. Suddenly I was on my backside and sliding downhill at an accelerating rate, a human toboggan. Initial shock became a sense of fun, because the névé curved into a kind of bowl and I would end up comfortably at the bottom, something like sledding down grandmother's hill at Idyllwild onto the schoolhouse meadow. Without a sled.

There was one little glitch, a thin ridge of rock poking up directly in my path. Just a few millimeters of rock edge showing above the snow, and there was no avoiding it. Zip, I skimmed over it and quickly down to the bowl, my backpack bumping along over the snow.

At the bottom I picked myself up, found that my white sunhat had disappeared but nothing else was lost. One doesn't waste time trying to find a white hat on a huge snowfield. Like trying to find a green pea in a meadow. To my right, the eastward track was all grassy and pleasantly undulating. I strolled happily back to the Refuge Giacomini in less than half an hour. When I saw that chamois again he had acquired a companion, and they were far below me.

The young man who served food and drink on the terrace looked at me quizzically.

"Did you have an accident?" he asked.

"No, a nice slide on a névé, but nothing special," I replied. Why did he ask such a question?

"Then why do you have blood on your pants?" he retorted, pointing at my left hip.

With astonishment I saw that he was right. My hiking pants were ripped and there were some bloodstains, but I felt no pain. I had been unaware of an injury; it was surely the work of that little rock edge.

"*Hé*, you're right!" I told him. "*Quelle surprise*!"

Examination in the privacy of the toilet-washroom showed that I had two long parallel slashes down my left hip. They had bled but were no longer bleeding. Twenty years later there were still a pair of finger-length scars, right under the swimsuit seam.

Inner dialogue informed my solitary lunch on that sunny terrace. Looking toward the Glacier de Paneirosse and the snowy world around it, I took psychological inventory.

"*Were you not just a bit foolhardy up there?*" I asked myself. "*Are you intelligent enough to recognize risks when you see them? You think you are not at all reckless but sometimes you do the wackiest things. Remember when Will asked you not to be so intrepid and you complained you weren't that at all? Can you put a brake on your bulllheadedness from time to time and let reason creep into your consciousness?*"

Such thoughts occupied my mind as I ate, but they did not interfere with my digestion. It might seem that I have given more verbiage to this little event than it warrants, but that is because it would return in another form, an intensely metaphysical form, seven years later.

Aside from participating in this moment of self-criticism, Will was often with me. I was not grieving in the conventional sense, for his ultimate departure had been moving toward us so visibly for so long a time that the event was a release for both of us. When he left I had hoped to see the energy envelope move out of his body, but did not. Afterward I continued to hope for some kind of a message, possibly a vision. Nothing had come. So, from time to time, in meditation or just before going to sleep at night, I asked that he find the way to the Light, and go toward it, in case he had not already done so.

Bit by bit that summer became a very rewarding season, helping me move on spiritually. People were kind and considerate. There were lots of hikes with family, with friends, and with the Alpine Club, and each such occasion helped me ground myself in this new role of widow. Wild creatures did their part too, animating luminous moments of communion with their dimension of our world.

Ten days later I went on another Alpine Club excursion. This time four of us climbed a modest summit called the Vanil Noir (7'837 feet). It was a weekend excursion into the mountains looming above the valley of Gruyères. On the Saturday afternoon we had an easy hike up to a jewel of a refuge called Les Marindes. And the next morning our bearded leader, Jean, led Anne-Marie, Adolphe and me up the steep slopes of our pyramidal peak. It's not very high, but it dominates its region, and our climb had its moments.

For a reason I can no longer recall the normal way up was blocked, and we had to skirt the very steep south slope on a narrow path. Jean asked if I wanted the cord. Once again the "chef de course" was carrying a rope, but no one seemed interested in using it. Hmm, I reflected, again that uncertainty about the newcomer. Vertigo is not among my problems, and I declined the cord.

This may have been a rash decision, but no one else on the mountain that morning was roped, and there were quite a few people already up there. It could have been rash because one week later someone died falling down that swooping downslope. At least, that's what the newspaper told me and I believed it.

Once off the awesome south face we got onto the ridgeline. This was fun. We had a lot of entertaining four-footed work with plenty of air on both sides, clambering up grassy slopes to gain the summit.

A week later my daughter-in-law Katharina returned with Toby and Simone. They could stay only two nights, but the intervening day gifted us with a nice ramble to a little, seldom-visited grassy bowl called Plan du Châtillon. With Mireille I had already explored that trail the year before. It's not physically-challenging but you do get quickly into wild country. Our reward was to count forty-three chamois through the binoculars, to our delight and wonderment. The chamois were just up there, perhaps a hundred meters higher, near enough for us to observe their individual movements, distant enough for their own sense of security.

It is thrilling to see so many of these shy creatures, and to be able to show them to my grandchildren was doubly satisfying. We all thought at this moment of their grandfather, who loved his Alps and all their wild inhabitants.

Later in the summer the creatures provided fresh entertainment, and I learned more about the behavior of eagles.

One evening in early August two eaglets were browsing on the freshly-cut meadow across the road. They had been doing a lot of calling in recent weeks. That morning the family had been three: their mother was also in the field, calling to them as if explaining how to hunt mice and find worms. One thinks always of eagles soaring majestically, but the fact is they often hunt by sailing just above the ground, and here they were actually walking around. The young ones remained grounded for long periods those days — up to an hour — and they seemed unperturbed by passing vehicles.

Not long after they took to the air on this evening, disappearing for the night, the deer burst out of the tall grass at the back of the meadow, not yet cut. The buck was quite red now, and he and his doe began to race around in irregular loops. With head and antlers down, he would charge his ladylove, provoking her flight. It wasn't long before this game had its effect and they vanished into the privacy of the forest.

This was the second time in successive years the deer had granted me the rare privilege to see them playing, to witness their courtship dance. Their games with the three fawns of the previous year were still fresh in memory, an exceptional moment which lingered in my spirit like a benediction. This time I could not help but note that we — meaning humans and wild creatures together — would have full moon in four days' time.

A month later they appeared again in the early morning, cropping the tender grass that grows after rains have refreshed the harvested meadow. She had already been out alone a few days earlier, but now her escort came along. His behavior had become quite sober. He looked a little hollow under the spine, as if the rut had been exhausting, but his coat still had the reddish hue. She looked very fit, her pelt already turning toward the brown-brindle color of winter. I permitted myself to speculate on the possibility her comparative splendour might reflect a freshly-conceived fawn informing her body.

On a deeper level I pondered my relationship with the animal world. For I saw that it was changing. On one level they were simply part of the furnishings of the material world, like the trees, rocks and grasslands through which they moved. It seemed as if they were showing me something. I had not grown up on a farm, had not had a dog to teach me a version of the animal life. Deer, weasel, kestrel, foxes, chamois, seemed to be allowing me to establish a connection, to participate in their lives — at a safe distance for them, of course. They had caught my attention and had not fled in terror.

Bit by bit the realization developed that the four-footed world, the wingeds and singers, the swimmers, and the creepers and crawlers can all stimulate our spiritual reflexes. It was hard, at first thought, to understand why this should be so. Yet it was. The wild creatures would not be as docile as farm animals but they were showing me we could have a significant connection on a more etheral plane. My readings during this period about the Native American culture helped in no small measure to appreciate the possible close relationships. Animals were much closer to us in spirit than the earlier me had recognized. Quiet joy marked this growing realization.

This first alpine season of my widowhood was not over, for September's weekends offered me a magnificent series of rambles and encounters.

On the first Sunday of the month eight of us from the Alpine Club explored a *bisse*, an ancient irrigation ditch developed to bring glacier water down to the valley floor. Our neighboring canton of the Valais is very warm and dry much of the year, more mediterranean in climate, and its system of bisses was carved out of the mountainsides to carry water in slow, easy meanders down to where man needed it. This was my first experience of these itineraries, which are relatively easy strolls alongside the ditches, sometimes in forest, sometimes hewn from the rock of overhanging cliffs, sometimes across sunny meadows. We followed "Le Bisse de Saxon" for miles, from Super-Nendaz to Isérables. It was a marvelous day, seeing new country, drinking in the air and sun, and making new friends. Led by Pierre, there were Jean and Anne-Marie from the Vanil Noir climb, Jean-Pierre from the year before, Henri, Christiane and Mike, a lanky Englishman.

The next weekend we penetrated deeply into the heart of the central Alps, starting our hiking at Kandersteg, led by the pipe-smoking Mike. Other faces from the previous week were Christiane, Jean-Pierre, Jean and his Anne-Marie, and there were new ones: René, another Henri and his own Anne-Marie, and another Jean, he who had remained by my side the previous summer when I had toiled so laboriously up that last névé to the Cabane Rambert, pausing so often to let blood flow through my knees.

It is not my intention to fatten these pages with endless lists of names. My point is to demonstrate how rapidly I found myself surrounded with warm-hearted companions. Suddenly a whole new world of camaraderie opened up after years of a social life constructed around family and my husband's old friends. These new friends were welcoming, generous, ready to be helpful during a tricky passage, and I saw that deep bonds of mutual affection had been forged among them. Before I knew it these bonds wrapped around me too. There was hugging and kissing on the cheeks in the continental fashion at the beginning and the end of an expedition. At picnic time dried fruit, nuts, chocolate and biscuits were offered around, and more than one of the men always carried a heavy bottle of wine which was opened at the summit of whatever we were doing that day. I learned quickly to pack a small pewter drinking cup with my picnic gear.

It would be a long time before that hole in my soul created by Will's passage would begin to fill in, but this alpine companionship, experienced weekend after weekend over the years to come, expanded my emotional dimensions so that the hole grew comparatively smaller. Well-being flooded in, emotionally, physically and spiritually. Spirit expanded. I saw these sociable contours of my new alpine life as an extension and expansion of the inner meditational work begun five years earlier. Inner work unfurled outward, like lotus petals slowly opening to greet the light.

We'd gotten to Kandersteg by train. From there we walked into the Gasterntal, a forested valley in the shadow of the Dolderhoerner. At a bend in the valley Mike led us up a trail to a refuge just at timberline. It was full of jolly, boisterous germanic Swiss, and there was a smaller annex reserved for our party, with the usual mattresses and army blankets.

We'd spent the afternoon gradually gaining about 650 meters of altitude. The next morning we began a steep climb up to the Loetschengletscher, and then up this dirty, stony glacier to the pass, 850 meters higher. It amazed me to see that hardy little wildflowers still bloomed in mid-September up there at 2690 meters (8825 feet). Plant life, battered by wind, clung to crevices in this hard, hostile world of stone and ice. My husband had developed rock gardens around the chalet, but our lower altitude was more welcoming. These bits of stubborn color up where bedrock swelled to meet the sky were a tribute to the tenacity of life on a hostile planet. They carried a lesson for me: inner beauty can survive in the harshest of circumstances.

A few days later I drove over to Grindelwald for another visit with my sister-in-law. The mountains were her world, and Elise was on them almost daily. At nearly eighty-eight her hiking was now limited to the easy trails, but her objective was to be up there, in the air, the sun and as close to the peaks as she could easily get. On the day of my sixty-fourth birthday we rode the chairlift up to the First, then enjoyed the long, easy lateral trail over to Grosse Scheidegg for lunch in the sun.

It was a glorious day. Exhilaration filled my being, sitting up there on that grassy saddle with my dear Elise, green slopes flowing away in front of us and to the right, the awesome Wetterhorn and ogre-ish Eiger stretching to our left, great peaks in the distance. No one can truly own a mountain, regardless of what surveyors' boundaries pretend. But we could speak of "her" mountains, those that informed her daily life, on which she walked constantly. And in that sense of possession, her mountains were becoming "my" mountains too.

In this atmosphere of eternal power, for those masses of rock and ice *are* powerful, my grief was melting. Life was good.

---

1   European marmots are chunky, furry, burrowing animals very similar to their North American cousins the woodchucks and groundhogs. In the Alps they

live above 1500 meters altitude and like to construct their dens under boulders. Sometimes they are called "whistling marmots" because their warning signal sounds like a whistle, and it is a sign for alpinists to look around for these elusive creatures. They hibernate in winter.

2   A névé describes a patch or tongue of granular snow which has not yet consolidated into the icy permanence of a glacier. Névés do not normally survive the summer; if one does, it is on the way to becoming a true glacier. The high Alps are studded with these snow patches. Sometimes there is confusion about their identity. The Plan-Névé which we had just climbed is considered to be a true glacier, although small, while the Glacier de Paneirosse which I mentioned in the previous chapter is thought to be really just a very long névé despite its longevity. Science meets linguistics, and both are at sea.

3   About sixteen inches long, so slender as to be almost tube-like, weasels are the smallest carnivorous mammal in the Alps. The males are twice the size of the females and, having a vicious temperament, sometimes kill their mates. They eat mostly mice and field mice but will attack rabbits as well. Those living in the plain remain brown all year; those living at altitude become white in winter, like the slightly-larger ermine.

4   *Rupicapra rupicapra* is a variety of wild goat, about the size of a deer but heavier through the trunk, about half the size of the saber-horned bouquetin. Like the latter, they can live to twenty years of age. They are brown with white bellies, necks and noses. They eat every kind of alpine plant, buds, moss, lichens, leaves, pine needles and even the bark.. They dwell in the high mountain forests, moving up to the higher treeless slopes in summer. An adult male can weigh up to 110 pounds.

Chapter Fifteen

RECEIVING A SPIRITUAL GIFT

The memory of glacial music tugged strongly at me. I wanted to visit the Gleckstein hut again, to sit on the stone wall of its terrace and hear again the ice falls singing. Thus the next morning I took the bus up toward Grosse Scheidegg, which pauses at the appropriate trailhead. Several people on the bus were gabbing in one of the Swiss-German dialects, and one of them got up and asked the driver where to get off for the Gleckstein.

"I'm getting off there," I told her in my version of German. "Follow me if you like."

Soon I was swinging up the stony path, spirits beginning to bound gaily in anticipation of the cliffside trail, the traverse above the shark-toothed Obergletscher, and the possibility of meeting more bouquetin.

I didn't pay attention to how many people got off behind me. Preoccupied with my own pleasurable anticipations, I was not aware of the silence until it was broken.

"Is this the way to the Glecksteinhütte?" a female voice asked me in German. It was the voice of the woman who had spoken to the driver.

"Ja, sicher," I replied, glancing back.

"Is it far? How long does it take?" she asked.

"It's about three hours," I replied, still in German.

After a bit, this voice had another question.

"Are you from around here?"

I explained that I lived in the Alps of the southwestern French-speaking part of the country.

"Oh, that explains your accent."

"Where are you from?" I inquired.

"Well, I'm from Basel now, but I'm originally American," she answered, still in German of course.

Chuckling with surprise, I stopped and turned around to truly see this person.

"Then why in the devil are we speaking German?" I laughed, switching to English.

That's how I met Molly, a raven-haired beauty with a creamy Irish complexion and a big, generous character. We became companions for this hike and before it was over we were close friends. We still are. Molly was divorced from a Swiss, had a small floral business in Basel, and she was half my age. It made no difference. She was another big girl like me, but with an ebullient nature charming away my tendency to be somewhat reserved with new people.

By that time my winter of pedaling and my summer of hiking had done their work: the arteries through my knees had expanded, and I was very fit. Body and soul sailed up the trail without those too-frequent pauses. Having an interesting companion made the day even more successful. Our conversation grew more and more animated as we discovered areas of mutual interest, starting with metaphysical feelings about mountains in general.

From that topic we discovered yet another bond: Unitarianism. It was the only church I had found in which I felt reasonably at home, and Molly was deeply involved in it. She had worked on the staff at the main office of the Church in Boston and even knew one or two of the people who had befriended me during a particularly stressful period of my life. Suddenly there seemed less room for coincidence in this meeting, especially after we discovered a mutual fondness for other kinds of spiritual work. Our dialog raced from point to point with the feverish pace of old friends seeking to retrieve centuries of missed companionship in a handful of minutes.

We got up to the Gleckstein in just under three hours, faster than my time of the previous year. And it was lunch time. I had a few picnic items in my pack, which I planned to round out with a soup from the caretaker's kitchen. Molly didn't know much about these mountain refuges and their resources, so I explained about the possibility of simple meals and simple lodging under army-style blankets in dormitories.

"It's great up here. I need this. I think I'll stay overnight," she said. "What are your plans?"

Sleeping in the hut had not been on my program and I had none of the usual overnight gear in my pack. However, this was blooming into such a warm friendship I decided to ignore my usual Virgo tidiness.

"This was only supposed to be a day trip," I smiled, "but your idea grabs me. After deep thought I can see that the lack of a toothbrush and clean underwear is irrelevant. I'll stay if you do."

Over bread and soup she explained that she had come from Basel the previous day with an acquaintance so as to walk the long ridgeline from Schynige Platte to Grindelwald. They'd taken an early train from Basel, eventually the funicular up from Wilderswil and then tackled the eight-hour hike over endless crests to reach the top station of the Firstbahn, the chairlift connecting to the town below. She had enjoyed that long, tiresome ramble, exulting being on the mountain but progressively irritated by her companion's chronic grumpiness. At the end of that day she had been relieved when the peckish companion took their train for home, but she herself was intoxicated with simply being there. She did not board that train.

"I was seized with a compulsion to stay on," she told me. "It was irrational and crazy. I have no luggage, no change of clothing, nothing but the daypack. It seemed like those mountains..." — she gestured in the direction of the Eiger and the Jungfrau, hidden from our view by the mass of the Mettenberg across the way to the south — "...were tugging at me. I needed to get closer."

She added: "The view of all these mountains around us was a great meal, but the constant complaining in my ears was spoiling the taste. I wanted more, I wanted dessert."

Someone told her about the Gleckstein trail, so she put up in a rustic hotel at the foot of the Obergletscher, washing out her underthings in the basin. The next morning, in the spirit of ordering that rich dessert, she climbed aboard the bus I had boarded five minutes earlier in the town.

My story was brief. After sixteen years of cozy, tight domesticity, happy but demanding, I explained, it was necessary to learn again to spread my wings, to live for myself. This was not a burning of bridges nor a breaking of boundaries. I'd spent the summer hiking with a tribe of alpinists. This trip alone was an expansion.

"I didn't know it was going to bring me a kindred soul," I added.

From the Gleckstein there is almost nowhere to go except up. It is the usual launching pad for the long climb to the summit of the Wetterhorn, rising to 12'142 feet (3701 meters) behind the refuge. It is one of the possible points of departure for crossing the glaciers toward such challenging pinnacles as the Schreckhorn, the Lauteraarhorn, and the frightful Finsteraarhorn, all of them still higher. For a nice unathletic afternoon stroll the Gleckstein could offer us only an informal trail out to a stony point called Beesibaergli, hemmed in by glaciers. Out there, after crossing a raging glacial torrent, we found a sunny spot on some rocks, lovely seats for the afternoon concert. The binoculars passed back and forth as we scanned the glacier faces for the huge avalanches producing each Beethovian crescendo.

We were getting along so famously, like sisters, that an idea popped into my head.

"What is your Sun sign? Do you know your planets?" I asked.

"Aquarius, with Moon in Virgo, " she replied. "And yours?"

My grin started in the brain and spread across my face.

"Virgo, with Moon in Aquarius," I shot back.

And then I explained it to her. We shared a double-mesh of the relationship that the famous Swiss psychologist Carl Jung described as apparently producing compatibility in personal relationships: the Moon sign of one partner in conjunction with, echoing the Sun of the other. At home a few days later my planetary ephemeris showed that our Aquarian aspects were in tight conjunction, less than one degree apart. The aspects were similar to those molding the harmonious relationship I enjoyed with my Aquarian daughter. In other words, Molly and I were born to be friends. The Great Organizer in the Sky had tweaked our itineraries to put us on that bus.

Back on the refuge terrace, waiting for the guardian to announce supper, we slid onto our individual spiritual paths. Molly did her Tai Chi out on a promontory while I meditated on a bench against the stone wall of the building. I was conscious of her slow, graceful, movements, while my Brahmanena mantra led ultimately into a lovely moment of cerevision, all orange and red because I was facing the light. Each in her own way we turned our attention inward, focusing on the ineffable as the day prepared to surrender its power to night.

It was late in the season and we had the place almost to ourselves for supper. A handful of alpinists were talking over their beers, and after supper we fled to the open air. Stars were beginning to fill the sky as night fell. We raced up to the dormitory where we would sleep, snatched some blankets, and brought them down to spread on the terrace.

Never in my life have I seen so many stars. Lying on our backs in the crystalline atmosphere of 7600 feet, we marveled at the incredible mosaic of the heavens. It was almost New Moon, the dark arc of our lunar cycle, we were far from anything resembling city lights, and our vision of interstellar space could not have been more complete. Nothing but starlight. Thousands upon thousands of points of light flashed and winked. The vastness of the universe was hypnotic, leading easily to the consideration of life similar to us existing on invisible planets in the orbit of more than one of those stars. Somewhere up there creatures resembling us might be lying on a terrace looking up at their version of the sky, focusing for a moment on the irrelevant little star we call our Sun, and wondering if friendly life forms whizzed around it on a planet of rock and water.

We were enjoying "Indian summer" temperatures, surface ice on the glaciers might not freeze this night, and their occasional choral crashes accompanied our long communion with the heavens. We lingered under that canopy for a long, long time, finally giving up when the thought of our mattresses upstairs became more compelling than the hardness of the rock beneath our backs.

The next morning at seven o'clock I opened the main door of the refuge, took a look, gasped, and quickly closed it.

"Molly!" I hissed. "Cameras!"

With both of us armed for photography, we opened the door, focused quickly, and began snapping our shutters. Half a dozen bouquetin, females and yearlings, browsed just outside the building. Less than ten feet from the door stood a large waist-high boulder with a natural bowl of rainwater in its upper surface, and a young male was standing atop the rock in order to drink. He posed obligingly, seemingly unperturbed that we had intruded on his morning refreshment. He stood patiently while we snapped great profile shots of his horns, already as long as those of his mother.

It was thrilling to see these fabulous creatures so close. I sense the bouquetin as a mystic animal, inhabiting the heights, the world of stone, lichen and deep snow. How do they survive?[1] Do animals meditate, go into trance?

They began to drift slowly away, not at all from fright, and we slung our packs on our backs. Molly and I had decided not to wait for the guardian to rouse himself and make us the usual breakfast of tea, bread and jam. We headed down the mountain in the morning freshness, reaching the highway soon after nine o'clock. An hour later we were brunching happily on a sunny sidewalk terrace in Grindelwald, plotting our next meeting. Molly had to return to Basel, while I would remain a bit longer to be with my sister-in-law Elise.

Parting was not easy. I was loathe to see her go, and she was torn by the imperative need to get back to her little business. I had found a soul sister. Exactly thirty years younger, she could logically have been a daughter. However the complicity between us was — and still is — that of sisters, and the soul attachment was strong. My awareness in the area of past lives was not yet sufficiently developed to carry the analysis any deeper, but I was aware of having been given a gift.

She was my first spiritual friend. I'd been a solitary explorer for five years. She was not really following a meditational path; her taste in mystical adventures was more eclectic than mine, possibly because she lived in a city with multiple possibilities. She was open to every approach and was free to sample aspects I had only read about. Our conversation was a feast, a kind of mystical smorgasbord.

Molly came into my life when I was ready for her, that's the other aspect of the gift. During Will's last years there was insufficient leisure for me to seek new friends or to explore other branches of the spiritual tree. She came in at the perfect time, three months after his departure, a breath of fresh air. The effect on me was like receiving a springboard toward new levels of inner work. The Angels/Guides who organize "coincidence" outdid themselves on this occasion.

Our next meeting came in midwinter when Molly brought some traveling friends down to my Alps for some snow fun and we had a seasonally appropriate raclette supper at my table. Six weeks later, on my way home from the Netherlands, I found my way — through a baffling tangle of streets I didn't know — to the tall, narrow old townhouse she rented in central Basel. No mountains to climb here, but lots of pleasure exploring the inner city with a guide who really knew her town.

Then one day in the summer - 1988 by now -- she telephoned.

"There's going to be a kind of a spiritual gathering in my home. It may be something for you. I can give you a room, of course."

"What's it all about?" I asked.

"Well, it's supposed to be about something called past-life regression analysis. I did this recently — it was mind-blowing — and the lady who facilitated it for me is going to talk about the process. Gerhard is really organizing the affair. He's the friend who introduced me to Winona. Are you interested?"

Was I interested? Absolutely! I'd read about this work with a certain fascination, I thought it was definitely something for me to explore, and here Molly was opening the door for me.

Thus in mid-July I drove up to Basel on a Saturday afternoon for another of these overnight visits. It's a two-hour trip, which is still within the boundaries of a "quick trip". A warm welcome, a good supper together, and then people began trickling in.

Her spacious, high-ceilinged attic was the conference room. It was the first time I had been with people of a metaphysical bent since the one and only group meditation in which I had participated at Nextmountain six years earlier. I use the word "metaphysical" as perhaps the best grab-bag term to describe the context.

About twenty people, some of them part of Molly's circle of friends and some who were not, sat, lounged and otherwise draped themselves around the friendly space of the attic to listen to Winona. She was an American psychologist who talked about the regression program she was bringing to Basel. Naturally I listened with a certain interest. What she had to say was moderately entertaining, but the lady's overall presentation did not resonate strongly within me. Inner caution held me back. The process attracted me but the person did not. Apparently this was not the right moment for me. Indeed, another occasion lay a few years down the road.

Meanwhile, we had agreed that Molly would come down to my village in four days time for some serious mountaineering.

In the interim there was a lovely walk with Elisabeth's grandson Manolito. This eighteen-year-old Spanish lad, whom I had known since he was a small boy, wanted to have a hike and perhaps see some wildlife. So I led him along the ridge that leads from the Col de la Croix to my favorite little bowl under the Chatillon, where I had taken my stepgrandchildren Toby and Simone the previous summer. And once again Mother Nature blessed the venture. Manolito had a long visit, through my binoculars, with a troop of twenty-four chamois. To be sure, I enjoyed them too. Such communions are a never-ending source of joy.

On the Friday afternoon Molly and I drove to Pont de Nant, the trailhead for our next adventure. From there we trudged the stiff trail up to the refuge at Plan-Névé, which by now I knew very well. Two years earlier I had made that long climb with Lily of the Alpine Club; now she had become — with her husband Joos — guardian of the cabane. We received a royal welcome and some useful advice. For on the morrow I proposed to lead Molly over the Col du Chamois from this, the steep side, and route indications were much to be desired.

My own confidence in doing these scrambles was growing. A month earlier Joos, the husband of Lily, had initiated me into true rock-climbing, with rope, climbing harness, and security techniques on a series of small pinnacles called the Gais Alpins. It was another liberating experience, like the Pacheu two years earlier. Another dimension of life opened to me as this love affair with rock gathered momentum. Previously untapped physical capacities rejoiced in being used. With each such experience my personal "frontier of fear" rolled farther into the distance.

Going over the Col from this side, although steep, was not a dangerous rock climb and we would need no equipment. We set off just after eight o'clock the next morning, crossing glacial moraine scree to the mountain wall, then cautiously following the narrow ledge along the cliff face. This was the most dangerous moment of the day, a fall would be fatal (it's been known to happen there), but neither of us suffer from vertigo and I had already seen abundant proof that my new friend was as sure-footed as I am. After about one hundred yards the way turned abruptly upward, onto grassy slopes up which we toiled for about one hundred and fifty vertical meters. You arrive on the crest of the mountain's shoulder, and we followed this for a bit, then traversed a long bit of stone and scree to reach the bottom of the chimney. This is where the fun began. It's a half-vertical scramble, up a vague kind of rocky staircase for about fifty meters.

There is a snapshot in my mind — I cannot find the photograph — of Molly surmounted by her mop of black hair and standing halfway up the stairs of stone, turning toward me and exclaiming "Isn't this great!"

Indeed it was. "Great" is inadequate to express the exaltation I feel in climbing hand over hand toward a half-perceived edge or crag, etched against the deep blue of the cosmos. At such moments I am intensely rooted in total awareness, completely concentrated, and there is the sensation of being more than my physical body. Spirit is reaching higher along with my hands, spurting beyond them, probing for infinity.

We were at the top, four hundred meters above the cabane, before ten o'clock, gasping with joy. For half an hour we lingered, quenching our thirst, munching a bit of food, and — above all — drinking in the spectacular contours of the mineral world which surrounded us.

Then we scrambled down to the head of the Glacier de Panierosse and strode briskly down this long tongue of snow, passing a towering wall of ancient strata twisted and folded into unreasonable shapes. In three-quarters of an hour we were off the snow and soon at a saddle called the Col d'Essets. To our left stretched the long valley leading down to Pont de Nant, three miles and eight hundred meters lower. To our right, Anzeindaz was an easy one mile northward.

I'd told Molly that if all went well we might hike up to the summit of the Haute Corde from that point, before starting back down to Pont de Nant. And all had gone very well, the weather was sunny and holding for the moment, cumulus clouds rimming the horizon. We seemed to have plenty of time. Getting up the Haute Corde is deceptively long. It's only three hundred meters higher than the Col, but there is a lot of horizontal distance. It took us a full two hours to reach the peak of this delightful pyramid, just visible from my chalet. Once again the panorama was breath-taking, including the vertiginous perspective on the Miroir, immediately below us, as a stone falls.

Starting down, we met a couple from Basel, people Molly knew. That was worth a chat. Burgeoning cumulus clouds began to fill the sky as we continued down toward the Col d'Essets. They were forming telltale anvil forms, some of them looking menacing. Those anvils become thunderheads.

"You know," I told her, "we could get drenched before we get down to the car."

"So what do you suggest?" she asked.

"There is another option. We're only a mile from Anzeindaz; they have simple rooms and good food," I explained.

"You're on. Let's do it."

That's one of the things I like about Molly; she's always game for a spur-of-the-moment alternative!

In another hour we were down at Anzeindaz, its hills and swales populated at this season with more cows than people. The thunderheads were coagulating, but it was still a sublime late afternoon. We took a room at the Refuge Giacomini, showered and were drinking beer on the terrace when the storm broke.

Lightning flashed, the drums of heaven boomed, and a wild wind whipped madly through this high valley. The cows took fright and began to stampede, bawling in panic. The near-hurricane chased us inside but we stood in the doorway as nature raged, terrorizing the cattle. They galloped insanely down all the little slopes to gather in the hollow under the half-dozen stone buildings of this hamlet. We'd enjoyed fabulous luck: fine weather for everything we chose to do on the mountain, and fine shelter against the eventual storm.

Our descent Sunday morning was quick and easy. We took a bus back to the village, walked down to the chalet, collected her car, and drove over to Pont de Nant to retrieve mine. Molly returned to Basel in the afternoon. We were already selecting the next mountain to share, and we thought it would probably be around Grindelwald. Our meeting on the Gleckstein trail the year before seemed to require observance, if not celebration.

The entire alpine season of that year, from June through October 1988, was blessed with wonderful rambles. Ten times I went out with the Alpine Club, sometimes for two, three or four days at a time. Elise asked me to drive her through a favorite itinerary in the Grisons, our mountainous southeastern canton wedged against Austria and the Italian Alps. This delightful trip took most of a week, and soon afterward I was back in Grindelwald again, for my birthday and for more high adventure, in the true sense of the word.

My numerous visits to Grindelwald over the years had riveted my attention on the Wetterhorn. Driving up from the valley floor there is a moment when this *massif* comes into view, like a beacon, and at that moment my heart leaps. It is not the highest of the imposing row of peaks casting their shadow on Grindelwald. From right to left, the massive Jungfrau, the Mönch, the Eiger and its intimidating North Wall, then the equally towering Schreckhorn and Lauteraarhorn looming behind the modest Mettenberg, all stand several hundred meters higher than their neighbor on the left, the Wetterhorn.

But the asymmetrical, Himalayan contours of that mountain call to me, like an old friend, something out of the deep past with which I must absolutely reconnect. It reaches out like a magnet, it radiates a subtle energy to which my neurons respond. My two hikes to the Gleckstein hut on its flanks had been only appetizers. It wasn't long before I hungered for the whole meal, the summit. It was 2200-plus feet higher than I had been with the Alpine Club that summer, than I had ever been on foot, but spirit was whispering to me on the inside, nagging me, telling me to push on, to renew with every crag on that peak.

After the Grisons with Elise I had been home for three nights, then off to the mineral-rich Binntal with the Alpine Club for a weekend of hiking and chipping for crystals. This was a three-day weekend built around the holiday called Jeun Fédéral, a kind of a fasting day when no one fasted. On the third morning I deserted my companions after breakfast. Instead of hiking with them I drove out of the Binntal and followed the Rhône through the

Oberwallis and up to its glacier source, under the Grimsel Pass. This twisting pass road, open only in the summer, reaches 7103 feet before plunging down toward the Haslital. At the pass I hiked up a little knoll for my picnic, overlooking the chilly lake, grateful for my flannel shirt. Then down the north flank into the valley, turning westward to skirt the Brienzersee to Interlaken, and thus up again to Grindelwald. There I settled into my favorite hotel, the Schönegg, for what was going to be at least a week.

My first action, after unloading the car and telephoning Elise of my arrival, was to visit the Bergsteigerzentrum[2], the mountain guides' office. There I discussed the Wetterhorn with Herr Kauffmann, the guides' coordinator, asking him to find me a middle-aged guide. I didn't want a young man with speed in his legs. He gave me bad news: the storms of five days earlier had deposited too much snow at high altitude.

"The Wetterhorn is 'out of condition' to be climbed," he told me. "Perhaps it will be ready in a day or two, if this fine weather holds. You must be patient."

Patience is not my strongest quality, but I have come to the conclusion that learning patience is one of the goals of this incarnation. In this instance, I would have to be doubly patient, for there was another hitch.

"Also, I don't have any guides available for the moment," he added. "They are all engaged, younger and older."

His answer was the same when I stopped in the Bergsteigerzentrum again the next morning. Over lunch with Elise in her apartment on a northern knoll, I outlined my program. She was enthusiastic about an attack on the Wetterhorn, which she had climbed three or four times. She offered to pay half the guide's fee, as a present for my sixty-fifth birthday. There was one other gift: a mass of sixty-five red roses from Molly. Otherwise the celebration of this milestone was quite modest. In the evening we joined Bep, a friend from the Netherlands, for supper in one of Elise's favorite restaurants. And I was able to tell her that she would finally meet the famous Molly in a few days, because she had telephoned to announce her arrival for the coming Sunday afternoon.

Wednesday morning my telephone rang.

"The mountain is 'in condition' to be climbed now, and I have found you a guide," Herr Kauffmann declared. "You leave for the Gleckstein in mid-afternoon."

Rüdi was thirty-eight, not the senior guide I had wanted, but he did not set an impossible pace. My husband had taught me the steady, unrushed but unlazy pace that eats mountain trails, and my companions in the Alpine Club had reinforced the lesson. There was no chitchat with Rüdi, we saved our breath for gaining altitude. We reached the refuge after two hours and forty minutes of even effort, minus a five-minute break to slake our thirst. On the way up we met two bouquetin, a mother and her young one, just starting to grow horns. They paid no attention as I copied their image onto film. That night after supper we checked the batteries of our headlamps, and Rüdi adjusted the fit of my ice cleats on my boots, so all that was ready.

Up at four o'clock, we hit the trail just after five. We trudged steadily up the agreeably adherent gneiss of the slopes above the hut, with occasional patches of grass, and in an hour-and-a-half we reached the lower edge of the Chrinnenglacier. We'd gained five hundred meters in that first leg, good progress. The sun was just illuminating the south faces of the Mönch and the Eiger. Everything below three thousand meters was still in shadow. The alpine world above us began to glow with light, an energetic spur for my spirit.

Here we paused to attach our ice cleats to the soles of our boots and to rope up. In the old days the hike up this glacier must have been very long and tiring, but glaciers have been shrinking all over the Alps for decades. Crevasses and the danger they represent had all but disappeared from the Chrinnen. Our slog up the glacier gradually bent to the right and became a diagonal traverse.

At seven-forty our glacier butted up against a short wall of rock. We clambered up that bit and were at the Frühstuckplatz, the traditional "breakfast place". Off with the climbing irons. We were at three thousand meters now (about 9850 feet) and the rock work would commence. First came the necessary solid snack, then I snapped a few photos. The upper world was now bright and pristine, unspoiled but also totally challenging. The Lauteraarhorn and the Schreckhorn stood across the way, etched against the southern sky, defended by glaciers and a bar of rock and ice. Spirit examined their edges, diagnosed "back of beyond." Up here spirit could be allowed to soar during a moment of repose, but the physical world and its challenges demanded grounding, total focus.

"How are we doing for time?" I asked Rüdi. In fact, I posed this question every time there was a pause, because I was well aware of the time constraints. One has to get up to the top, but one has to get down again too. That task can be dangerous when afternoon sun begins to melt snow and create avalanche conditions.

"We're fine," he said.

For the next three hours we climbed rock. My body moved in suppleness, automatically dosing the muscular force for each push to the next point. Spirit was aware at all times of the glorious panoramas surrounding me on three sides. The fourth side was rock, and concentration glued me to it. This was mostly easy and agreeable four-point (hands and feet) work, rarely very demanding technically. Except for the occasional instant of adrenal rush when brittle rock broke underfoot, requiring quick reflexes.

This part of the climb was simply very long, five hundred vertical meters. We followed the classic itinerary known as the Willsgrätli, a rocky spine named after a certain A. Wills who led the first ascension from this side of the mountain in 1854. It was very sporty, very tactile of course but, as I have said, very long. For three hours we toiled up these denuded vertebrae, a skeletal system which is the centerpiece of the ascension. Here and there were little pockets and patches of snow remaining from the previous week's storm.

Adrenaline flows aside, the Wetterhorn was not charging me with mystical energy. It was extracting its pound of flesh with every buttress surmounted. The mountain has a reputation as a lightning rod, one of the early climbing parties having been struck by lightning on the summit. This particular morning it was giving pleasure — or allowing pleasure to be experienced — but it was not recharging my psychic batteries.

At eleven o'clock we gained the Wettersattel, a little saddle between the Wetterhorn and its neighbor the Mittelhorn. We were only two hundred meters below the summit dome. That dome was covered in a thick mantle of fresh snow. and there was a lot of soft, deep snow ahead of us. Down on the rock, with western exposure, there had been almost no residual snow. Up here, with eastern exposure, very little from the previous week's snowstorm had melted.

For the first time Rüdi introduced worry about time.

"We're late," he said.

How could that be? I wondered. We'd been on time, we'd climbed well, why were we now "late"?

"There's a lot of snow. It's going to be very difficult," he said. "You have to accept that we turn around at twelve o'clock, no matter where we are."

Yes, I knew the rules about staying off steep snow slopes in the afternoon.

Grumpily, I sipped from my water bottle and I tried to eat. At 3500 meters (11483 feet) one doesn't have much appetite, even after a long spell of hard physical work. It is difficult to refuel the body. The Wetterhorn is a kind of energy fetish for me, but it was not recharging me now.

We reattached our ice cleats and began the ascension. Rüdi used his ice axe to chop and dig steps in the deep snow of the dome's steep flank. In spite of that, we sank in to our knees with each step taken. It was very heavy work for both of us and I began to tire rapidly. We were making insufficient vertical headway, only a small fraction of the dome, nowhere near enough.

There came a moment when, at the door of physical exhaustion, with the critical hour of twelve noon upon us, and with the summit still far above our heads, I said.

"We're not going to make it."

"I think you're right," Rüdi agreed. "So, do we turn around?"

This was a bitter pill to swallow, but I had to agree.

We began the descent promptly at noon, and it took more than four hours to get back down to the refuge. The rocks that had been climbed had to be un-climbed, and that kind of work is only slightly faster than going up.

At the Gleckstein I was exhausted, wiped out. I sat on a bench in the sun with a lemonade in one hand and a can of beer in the other. Rüdi was restless to start down the mountain to the bus stop. I didn't want to budge. We agreed that he would go down but I would stay the night in the refuge. There was no more strength in my legs for the trail down. We said goodbye.

Rain, wind and snow whipped the Glecksteinhütte during the night, underlining my disappointment. In the morning the snowline was about two hundred meters above the hut, but the rocks were wet and slippery everywhere else. On the way down I met a large male bouquetin, but he did not respond to my friendly greeting. On the other hand, he didn't butt me over the cliff either.

That evening Elise and I were guests of Katie, a gallant lady from New Zealand who had lived for years in Grindelwald. The ladies were initially surprised at my failure to reach the summit, but my sister-in-law began to analyze the reasons why.

"Why did you start so late?" she asked. "Every time I climbed the Wetterhorn we were up at two o'clock and out of the hut by three. It makes a big difference. And all that fresh snow! Two hours earlier and it might not have been so soft. But it is late in the season. It is possible you should not even have tried it in the first place."

So we all tried to be philosophical about it. My physical body was stiff and sore, but the real hurt was on the soul level. It was necessary to admit to myself that possibly I had bitten off more than I could chew. Not for the first time.

Two days later Molly arrived. Going back to the Gleckstein was not possible for us. She needed to return home the next evening, leaving us only one day to play. We took the cable car across to Pfingstegg under the Mettenberg, then followed the rocky ledge trail that climbs steadily through the narrow gorge of the Untergletscher. You emerge from the neck of the bottle, turn a corner, and that bright world of sun and ice expands to overwhelm the senses. The café at Stieregg sits in a sheltering cove in the base of the Mettenberg, but we continued on the trail that leads to the Schreckhorn hut. There's a point where that trail turns behind the harsh edge of the Banisegg; the last vestige of man's civilization is no longer visible.

We found our box seats for the concert there, facing the two ears of the Fiescherhoerner. Once again we marveled at the crackings, the groanings and then, after a pause, the cannon-like cascade of the ensuing ice avalanche.

Just before time to dust off our backsides and head back down the trail we got a wild idea. Could we possibly touch off one of those avalanches by the power of mind?

We stretched our arms like antennae, aiming at the glacial face which had been splitting off seracs the size of houses. For long minutes we stood there, eyes closed in an intense meditative concentration. But nothing happened. Nothing at all. The mountain was mocking us and our silly little prank.

We shouldered our packs and took our first steps down the trail and -- crack! -- an avalanche roared down behind us in symphonic majesty, a concerto in tumbling ice blocks.

Molly and I stopped dead in our tracks, turned, and saw the icefall had split off from a point adjacent to that we had selected for our mental focusing.

"Our aim was off," she remarked drily.

Our eyes met, and we burst into gales of wild laughter. Whether we'd caused it or not, it was ours!

[1] According to Geneviève Grandjean, co-author of *Animaux de Montagnes, vie sauvage,* (Editions Slatkine, 1992, photos by René Pierre Bille, ISBN 2-88 445-099-8) the bouquetin support the cold very well but large numbers of them die of starvation during the winter. They support the winter cold but do not have a good sense of danger, many being swept away in avalanches. Some of them do descend into the forests and compete for forage with the chamois. They do not hibernate. During the warmer seasons they often leave their rocks and cliffs to browse in the forests after dark.

[2] Translates as "Mountain Climbers' Center".

Chapter Sixteen

MEETING OTHER DIMENSIONS

In that first year of my widowhood the Alps, working through heart, lungs and legs, massaged me into a new rhythm of life. Exploring the mountains brought me fresh exuberance, and in retrospect I marvel at my great good luck in these adventures. The address book suddenly filled with the names and addresses of new companions. Winter and summer alike overflowed with satisfying excursions over the trails. Spirit expanded.

After organizing, slowly and painfully, an adequate level of revenue, the most pressing material problem became one of shelter, a home and hearth to call my own. During my husband's last year of life I had searched the villages for another chalet or at least an adequate apartment. Nothing pleased me. The chalets I thought I could afford were too small and the large apartments all had faults and cost too much. At a critical moment the young Protestant pastor Jean came to visit even though I was not really one of his flock. We talked about this problem of housing, and he took me by surprise.

"Why don't you simply stay here?" he asked.

His idea took me aback. Although I liked the house well enough, parts of it more than others, and the view was unsurpassable, it hadn't occurred to me that I could possibly afford it.

Jean's question had a catalytic effect. It sent me to the accountant. He was reassuring in his turn, but the matter was not simple. I could not inherit the chalet; I would have to buy it from the estate, and because of unique corporate circumstances the Canton would have to approve the price. To my surprise, this worked out more favorably than I could have imagined, and in a year after my husband's death I became the owner of the home in which I had lived for seventeen years. It proved to be an elegant solution, never regretted. Tranquillity crept in.

My spiritual life, still deeply private, still centered on meditation, began to move forward. "Going within" was very much an ineradicable part of my life, but it seemed to demand less time of me. Once a day instead of twice a day provided sufficient depth and intensity for this time of transition.

Another dimension sprouted into being. Earth energies beckoned, proposing that I begin exploring them with my long-neglected Hartmann antenna. Before long I coined the phrase "investigations inside the invisible" to describe these adventures. Of course, my meditational life already fit that definition, with all the places it had taken me and the sights it had presented. That part of my invisible world was high in color.

Dowsing confronts another dimension of invisibility. Instead of receiving visual and auditory information from elsewhere and other times as had often occurred in my meditations, my lobe antenna contacted energies whose apparent source is quite invisible. The work becomes a challenge of tracking and mapping something that is alive and vibrating but leaves no tangible sign.

In the spring of 1988 I learned about a small group of mystics and dowsers gathered around an architect named Pierre. There was to be a "field trip" into the plains and foothills surrounding the lower edge of the lake of Neuchâtel. On a sunny Saturday I joined them for an ambitious one-day itinerary visiting a variety of old churches, as well as a field full of standing stones I had heard about but never seen. Working alongside others was going to be a novelty too.

For the first time in my life I saw menhirs. These are standing stones set in place by our ancestors. Stonehenge in western England is the most notable example in the public eye. I had read a newspaper article about such stones existing in Switzerland, thus it was with buoyant steps that I entered a tree-rimmed meadow on the edge of the lakeshore town of Yverdon. Here in a clearing of perhaps three acres stood forty-two stones of all shapes, first placed there some 4'500 years ago, according to the archaeologists. None were as large as those revealed in pictures of Stonehenge, but there they were, most of them in two long lines, the others in little alignments of three or four. One could stroll around and get acquainted with them in cozy liberty.

Rather than refer you back to earlier chapters, let me offer a quick résumé of this pattern that Dr. Ernst Hartmann brought to light. A rectangular network of invisible and mostly unpalpable microenergy lies over the surface of our planet, in three dimensions. Call it a grid or a mesh if it helps your visualization. These spaces measure approximately 2.5 meters (eight feet two inches) from east to west, and approximately 2.0 meters (six feet six inches) from south to north. The lines have a characteristic width of a bit over eight inches wide, but they can expand during full moon. The grid is subject to local deformation, and it also shrinks as you approach the poles of our globe.

Underground water, earthquake faults, and vagrant electricity are the most frequent sources of deformation. Hartmann found that the corners, the crossing points of the bands, exhibited polarity, and under normal circumstances the polarity alternated from corner to corner. Thus one small rectangle would have a pair of diagonally opposite corners with positive polarity and the other pair would display negative polarity.

It is clear we are dealing with electromagnetism of a very fine quality, imperceptible to most humans without appropriate instruments. However, the human body is sensitive to these energies, and this is what enabled Hartmann to discover that the crossing points were places where one should not sleep, rest habitually for long periods, or choose as a work place. He found many instances of illness associated with negative polarity crossings, especially when water flowed beneath the site at those points. This is the starting-point of a new discipline the good doctor named "geobiology".

My Hartmann antenna quickly demonstrated to me that these menhirs had been sited with respect to earth energies. Many of them stood on crossing points of the Hartmann grid, but that network had itself been tinkered with. The antenna showed that there were many spots in these major alignments where the intersecting lines of force had been brought closer together, so that a space between two stones might harbor energy lines fifty centimeters apart instead of the standard two or more meters. How did they do that? And there were a few places where an aligned stone was not quite intersected, the crossing line just grazing it instead. One might suppose that the human intervention required in our time to replace fallen stones may not have been well-informed in the nuances of earth energies, if at all.

According to my friend and dowsing inspiration Blanche Merz, the concentration of lines in a narrow space occurs over and over again at sacred sites. Sometimes they seem to have been set up as a barrier, other times they appear to enhance the power of a special spot, and this fact was certainly one of her major contributions. She demonstrated this phenomenon repeatedly in her landmark book *Points of Cosmic Energy*[1]. However, she did not reveal (if indeed she knew) how the ancient builders managed this energetic sleight-of-hand. Discovering the mechanics of this trick became an item on my mental agenda. But Merz's principal contribution was to demonstrate that the network had existed for millenia and had been harnessed by the architects of sacred buildings, that it had a spiritual application predating recent discovery of its medical importance.

There were two major alignments in this meadow, one of them indicating the summer solstice and the other the winter solstice. There were also four short lines of three, four or five stones each, standing apart from the solstice lines. These alignments and groups were all straddling lines of the Hartmann grid. How did our neolithic ancestors know how to do this? The extent of their knowledge and perceptive powers raised huge questions.

Until that morning my experience had been largely confined to my home and garden, where I became quickly accustomed to the relatively stable layout of the energies. Working in the menhir park at Yverdon boosted my confidence in the exercise of this peculiar talent. It wasn't just at home that I was a walking antenna, a reliable link between invisible energies and the demonstration of their presence. Quickly I was able to sketch and map force lines manifesting far away from the familiar ones in my bedroom.

You may ask: what happens to give the dowser such information?

An interesting thing occurs when a dowser intercepts energy — her/his instrument moves independently. A Hartmann lobe antenna swings right or left, sometimes spinning in a circle. A forked stick cut from a willow, the traditional tool of the "water witch", bobs up and down. A pendulum gyrates, a blade antenna dips or possibly flips up to smite its operator on the chin. Angle irons either cross or swing wide apart.

This movement is the basic information. Dr. Hartmann's antenna finds the force lines that make up his global grid, and it will swing right or left depending on the polarity of the current it meets. At crossing points it will swing around and around, becoming very difficult to control. This instrument must be held very precisely, poised vertically between the tips of your index fingers. If you press too tightly it cannot respond to telluric signals; if held too loosely it will fall to the ground. Allowed to rotate over a crossing point it may begin to whirl out of control and fall.

For this reason I began to use a pendulum to define and confirm the crossing points and their polarity. In my hand, a clockwise gyration means positive polarity, counter-clockwise signifies negative polarity.

The dowsing instrument reacts to earth energies and the first signal you get is visual. You see it move, so you know something is there. As time goes on you may have other reactions. Some people feel these energies moving through their bodies, others never do, and I suspect that for the vast majority of sensitives whatever does come takes time to develop. As with the other senses, the possibilities cover a broad spectrum.

In those early days I did not feel anything at all, but as I became more attuned to the method some sensations began to creep in. Over time I began to feel energy in my hands when I used the pendulum. When that did happen, it usually felt like a small tingling. As my practice of this art matured that tingling moved softly up my forearm, softer than the purr of a kitten but still sensed.

These standing stones came as a huge revelation for me. If we had done nothing else that day I would have been grateful to Pierre. But he had laid out an itinerary visiting half a dozen churches and abbeys, and we dowsers literally had our hands full keeping alert, testing new situations, and reading the energies. These churches were powerful teaching tools, each one channeling energies differently, each one presenting different internal relationships.

But they all had one feature in common: the principal axis always ran from east-to-west. The main door was always at the west, leading into the nave or public space. Altars were usually found in or just in front of the choir area, which lay to the east. Variations from this basic alignment ran to five or six compass degrees when they did occur — the builders of these ancient spiritual edifices had probably not always enjoyed total liberty in site selection.

Why this particular orientation? It was not evident to me during this first field trip jampacked with rich explorations, the first time I had worked on spiritual sites and inside religious edifices. I began to understand better this compass orientation two years later in France:

One Saturday morning at Paray-le-Monial in May, 1990, I really felt at the cellular level how the rising sun illuminates, warms, and charges the choir and altar first as it moves from east to west. The power of this effect struck with full force in the *déambulatoire* — the walkway around nave and choir inside abbeys and cathedrals. Enraptured with the vibratory energies, I sat on a stone bench and allowed the sunlight streaming through the stained glass windows to wash over me. It was like a slowly-moving tide, creating a play of energies that induced in me a definite meditative mood. It was restful, vitalizing and ultimately enchanting. I have come to believe that the passage of the sun in this way sets up color vibrations which, during the daily east-west flow, can literally charge the spirituality through those windows.

We were not aware of such effects as we moved from church to church that day in the rolling Vaudois countryside. They were all facing the same direction, that was true enough, but each had dealt in a different way with the presence of underground water.

Quickly I discovered a limitation of my lobe antenna: it was perfect for reading the Hartmann grid but it wasn't much good for reading underground watercourses. I noticed that the man with angle irons seemed to locate them rather easily. I asked Pierre for counsel on this point, and he suggested I might simply try walking through the space very fast. This technique would filter out the grid energies, which respond to the dowser's slow, measured pace, and might reveal this other layer: water.

Underground streams seem to be a feature of all early churches and cathedrals. In Chapter Six of her book Blanche Merz points out that the flow of water is literally engineered beneath the great cathedrals of Chartres and Santiago de Compostela[2]. Each of these gothic vessels has fourteen watercourses gathered together from surrounding substrata into a fan-like arrangement coming to a hub beneath the center of the choir. She points out that excavations at Santiago de Compostela demonstrated this work had been accomplished by human hands.

Our little band of dowsers did not encounter anything so lavish. We ended the day at the Abbey of Romainmôtier, nestled in the foothills of the Jura mountains. This is one of Switzerland's gothic treasures. Its construction embraced a thousand years, the first chapel, then successive enlargements and remodelings dating from the fifth to the fifteenth centuries.

The method of walking fast in order to filter out everything except water only worked moderately well for me. But it did function well enough to confirm the known locations of the two underground streams. They cross at the back of the choir and rather off-center.

Romainmôtier has its own distinct charisma, which I have come to appreciate more and more with successive visits over the years. During this first encounter I busied myself mapping the Hartmann grid and how the main pillars were positioned to exploit the crossing-points. For the builders had definitely done that. The fourteen main columns were sited on every other force line, which allowed each column to benefit from positive polarity. This observation informed my subsequent travels to numerous sacred edifices across Europe. Churches and cathedrals were carefully seated on the global energy network so as to maximize their energy intake.

In addition to the choir, much spiritual energy is concentrated in the transept. Cathedrals are designed like the cross of Jesus, with a long axis running roughly east-west and perpendicular to that of a short axis, the crossbar. There is a square space in this transept which is common to both axes, has mighty pillars defining its four corners, and is usually precisely under the cupola of the tower, when there is only one tower.

On this day the spiritual energy was almost palpable in the transept. My wonder grew as I crisscrossed that sacred square, the lobe showing me that the Hartmann lines were concentrated as if pushed closer together.

It was the end of the day, people were tiring, and I had read about the regenerative power of Gregorian chant. Cassettes of that soaring music played regularly in my home and in the car.

I suggested an energizing experiment to my companions. We formed a circle inside this "power square" of the transept, and we began to chant. We were thirteen, if I remember correctly, thirteen voices learning to chant together. Then, one by one, each of us took a turn standing in the center, precisely under the base of the spire in the bell tower, bathing in the vibrational energy of twelve voices raised in chant, stimulating the waves in that sea of spiritual force.

It was splendid. Everyone got something out of it, and some got quite a lot, merging back into the circle in a state of grace.

This day was a springboard for me. Although there was nothing comparable during the rest of that year, Romainmôtier had laid the base for a wide-ranging exploration of sacred sites during the next several years.

Over and over again I have found the greatest measurable spiritual power in the transepts of churches and cathedrals great and small. Not until many years later would I be privileged to work with a team of like-minded souls ready and willing to find new ways of sensing energy.

On this day I did not yet possess the physical tools for measuring spiritual energy. Blanche used a technique called the Bovis Biometer for measuring the vibrational rate of a site or object, but this tool was not yet in my possession. I had seen only hers. Beyond the Hartmann antenna, she worked with her hands as sensors. This skill was not yet in my tool kit either.

A few weeks later I traveled again to California to visit family. Carol and I had conceived of a short tour together through the Mother Lode country, that stretch of Sierra Nevada foothills which had been the scene of the great gold rush starting in 1849. We had only a handful of days at our disposition, starting from Pasadena. Once in the Sierra foothills, our tour really began at Mariposa, and we worked northward day-by-day as far north as Nevada City. We paused one night at Placerville, looking up a friend of mine named Rose and going to supper with her.

I was itching to do some dowsing but didn't know where to start. Our little guide book to the Mother Lode country, the old gold-mining communities, did not provide any clues about possible "sacred" sites or structures that might sound dowsable. Hesitantly, one asks what one hopes do not come across as silly questions.

We had been wolfing down delicious enchiladas and chiles rellenos, and the mood was convivial, so I plunged.

"Do you know of any power points in the area around Placerville?" I asked.

What exactly did I mean, she wanted to know.

I clarified. "You know, a place where earth energies are particularly noticeable, particularly powerful."

Rose thought a minute.

"Yes, you might try Buck's Bar."

Then she explained that this particular river crossing had been the scene of suicides and accidental drownings, but that also a mystic guru from one of the big valley cities was said to have sent his disciples up there to experience the energies. Did he want them to feel tough energies after having sensed elevating waves somewhere else? Life is full of unanswerable questions.

The next morning we followed her directions to the bridge over the Middle Fork of the Cosumnes River. As the road slowly descended from a ridge into the river canyon, we passed a roadside establishment named "Buck's Bar" and then rounded a bend to aproach the bridge. Which came first: the roadhouse or the place name? Was a grizzled miner named Buck the first to pan for gold on a sandbar in the Middle Fork at that point, or did the name originate with a saloon founded by an innkeeper named Buck?

An old concrete bridge crossed at a point where the river narrows. Upstream to our left, it appeared wide and leisurely, almost lake-like, with generous meadows along the banks. Downstream it was a savage gorge of huge boulders and deep pools. Upstream the river meandered; downstream it roared and rumbled. Downstream the right bank is a Devil's toboggan of smooth rock. On the left bank twisted scrub oaks lean through a jumble of mossy boulders.

The deep pools below the bridge would be clearly inviting to bathers during the ferocious summer heat. But what danger also! The rocks afforded only a few places to climb easily out of the pools. Most of the rock was rounded, smoothed and potholed by glaciation.

Starting up the road a bit from the bridge, I walked the lobe antenna toward the crossing. The global network was normal on the approach to the bridge from both directions. Three north-south lines followed the line of the road as it crossed the bridge, and their spacing was perfectly in harmony with the classic Hartmann configuration. In contrast, the east-west lines were doubled up directly above the funnel of flowing water squeezing through the gorge. This was perfectly clear. The narrowing of the gorge increased the speed and turbulence of the current, creating a concentration of energy around the big boulders and in the swirling pools.

It certainly looked like a dangerous place to swim, but also I had learned that waterfalls and rapids charge the atmosphere with a higher vibration conducive to deep meditation. The implied contrast between death and life was striking: one could credit both the reputation for tragedy here and the story of the guru. Both notions were plausible. However, I had no way to measure what was really happening there. I chafed at this limitation of my only dowsing tool.

Unbeknown to us as that moment, three more important bridges lay ahead on our rambling itinerary. Buck's Bar had sharpened the edge of our curiosity, and we paused at each of them.

Bridgeport is a river-crossing on the Pleasant Valley road west of Nevada City. A wooden single-span covered bridge was flung across the South Fork of the Yuba in 1862, at a point where the river traverses a wide and gentle canyon.

It is enclosed, shingle-sided and immensely photogenic; it was closed to heavy traffic and had been replaced with a modern bridge. Three evenly-spaced force lines follow the roadway across the covered bridge, while the wider roadbed of the modern bridge harbors four parallel energy lines. There is tranquil symmetry here, no doubling up of the lines which follow the water under either bridge. Nothing remarkable at Bridgeport.

About four miles upriver a major road, Highway 49, crosses the Yuba in a steep and deep canyon. An old concrete bridge built in 1921, visually a contemporary of Buck's Bar, curves gracefully to negotiate the generous hairpin turn of the road across the gorge. Below are large smooth rocks, potholes and deep pools, as at Buck's Bar, but no moss, no lethal concentration of energy. Bathers were making the most of the swimming on this hot day in May -- it was a scene of sunny, splashy gaiety.

The energy lines following the bridge axis were assymmetrical because of the structure's curvature, but they were evenly spaced in harmony with the Hartmann network. The perpendicular lines, above the flowing water, were also in harmony, not doubled up.

Our work at these three bridges did not help to elaborate any kind of a general rule, especially in contrast to the geobiological anomaly found at Buck's Bar. There the force lines doubled up in the gorge, at these others they did not. This was the specific difference suggesting a true power point.

I'd learned something: I'd worked far away from my usual haunts, and the Hartmann network held fast. Even so, I was dissatisfied. It felt as if I had only scratched the surface of a puzzle. My tools and my knowledge were inadequate. This was a beginning but only that. Frustration simmered.

We had come to the Mother Lode country because of the lure of the old gold mining camps. They had become villages and towns but were still full of antique charm. Energy dowsing had been an optimistic question mark on the agenda. Another question mark, clearly related, lay unprogrammed beneath the surface. And that one exploded.

Our first night on the road found us at Sonora, once a rowdy mining camp, now become a bustling small town with two traffic lights to solidify its status as the seat of mountainous, sparsely populated Tuolumne County. We had planned to charge right ahead the next morning but that plan dissolved when we saw signs announcing a big "Gem and Mineral Show" in the local events hall.

All my adult life I had been a collector of stones, perhaps a logical result of having briefly studied geology and mineralogy at the university. River banks and stony beaches held a particular fascination for me. I never went home without a handful of freshly-washed pebbles and small rocks, gathered eclectically and later scrutinized through my geologist's pocket lens.

Earlier in the year, on the way home from visiting a cousin in the Netherlands, I had detoured to the town of Idar-Oberstein in southwestern

Germany. I went there because of my amethyst ring. In 1977 my husband and I had been in the city of Trier on the Mosel river, and while he was amusing himself with his club colleagues I wandered the back streets and up a flight of stairs to a gem shop. There I'd bought, for what seemed a modest price, an amethyst ring which immediately became my favorite piece of jewelry. I loved to gaze into the depths of this big solitaire stone, simply mounted in silver.

"Where does it come from?" I asked the sales lady (in German, of course).

"Es kommt aus Idar-Oberstein," was her reply.

Idar-Oberstein thus landed on my mental agenda, a place to go some time. Eleven years later, barely two months before this Mother Lode excursion with Carol, I found the town in the bottom of its river gorge. For centuries it had been a center for gem cutting, polishing, and the making of jewelry. The agate and mineral deposits were long since exhausted, but the town remained a center of these skills. Browsing in the shops of Idar-Oberstein's artisans quickly developed my appetite for the wonders of semi-precious stones.

Sonora's show was, like all others of its ilk, a hall full of stands set up by gem dealers, crystal hunters and rockhounds. The exhibitors and their long tables displayed a wide spectrum from enlightened amateurism to sharp-eyed professionalism. We browsed up one aisle and down another, ogling shelves of crystals and boxes of polished stones of every kind. It was a revelation, a breakthrough, a moment when something latent in me suddenly blossomed. We looked, touched, held up to the light, talked to people, collected the cards of dealers along future itineraries. That Sonora mineral show stimulated senses which had lain fallow. I went into the hall as a person whose little boxes and jars of riverbank pebbles had moved from country to country with her; I emerged as a budding mineral maniac, colorful crystals gleaming in my imagination.

We continued northward that afternoon, visiting Columbia, Angel's Camp, Murphy's and onward the next day through Mokelumne Hill, Sutter Creek, Coloma, and Georgetown before pulling into Placerville for the night. Then we'd visited all those bridges too, en route to Auburn, Dutch Flat, Grass Valley and Nevada City.

Crystals stared out at me from the window of the metaphysical bookstore in Auburn, where we paused to fuel ourselves and the car. A few minutes later I emerged with a quartz crystal alleged to be a "record keeper." Holding it to the light one sees the snowy slopes of a phantom Alp. Not bad for twelve dollars, plus tax. People pay more for worse sources of daydreams.

This is the first mineral specimen for which I have a sales slip in the file. The following year, in true Virgo form, I began keeping a record of these acquisitions. Up until now I'd always had trouble passing on the street anything resembling an esoteric bookshop. Now this weakness extended to stone and crystal shops. A passion expanded.

Aside from my ongoing meditation practice, and activities with Molly described in the previous chapter, the rest of that year offered little spiritual fare. Just one more illumination, in the field of art.

After rambling the Alps all summer, mostly with the Alpine Club, at the end of November I drove the three days down to Alicante on the east coast of Spain. It was time to visit an old friend who had also been widowed about the same time as me. On the long road to Spain Will and I liked to sleep at Figueras, just inside the Spanish border with France and lying where the feet of the Pyrenées plunge into the Mediterranean. It's a strategic place to overnight, and we'd never done more than just that, but this time I decided to stay there two nights on the way home. Something about Figueras, a warmth, an atmosphere that beckoned, told me to gift myself with a full day there. It was also the home territory of the artist Salvador Dali. One could visit the Dali museum which he had created, among other more modest attractions.

Salvador Dali's surrealistic art first became recognized in the 1930s and his "dripping watches", which he termed "soft constructions", became the clichés by which he was judged. Certainly, in that season of my adolescence, his images stimulated our sense of humor rather than any nascent esthetic sense. He seemed to be painting for shock effect, and we took it all as a huge joke. This was abetted by the apparent judgement of the artistic world that he was some kind of a charlatan.

At 65, the widow of an artist, my capacities for appreciation had matured several hundred per cent in the course of a half-century. Dali's personal museum astonished and educated me. First of all, its form was, to say the least, very original. Dali had taken over the ruins of the municipal theater, destroyed during the Spanish Civil War of the late nineteen-thirties. Reopened in 1974 as his own *Teatro-Museo*, it resembles a fortress become a wine-colored wedding cake on the outside, capped with a geodesic cupola, and the outer walls topped with lines of giant golden eggs balanced on end. Inside it is a hollow circle within a square, multiple circular levels of galleries around an airy core beneath that cupola.

As I moved through the rooms of paintings, drawings, sculpture, giant "kitschy" objects and bizarre assemblages, it quickly dawned on me that all this was not just the work of a engaging eccentric with solid painterly skills. It was the *oeuvre* of a great master, a consummate artist with a staggering imagination. His technique with oil on canvas was unsurpassed, his skill and precision of color and execution beyond the reach of all but the greatest. The facets upon facets of some of his compositions left me speechless. Even more, so much of his creation dealt with hallucinations and dreams. Dimensions crowded in on one another, layer upon layer. I saw windows opening onto spirituality where others had seen eccentric shock techniques.

While I was visiting my friend down the coast in Alicante we saw on television that Dali had just been taken to hospital in Barcelona, gravely ill. Seven weeks later he died in Figueras, age 84, and he was buried in a secret crypt within his Theatre-Museum.

Modern art criticism admits that Dali "achieved an extraordinary concentration of imagery." Some of his work resembled jeweled objects whose "miniature dimensions are ideal for an image projected from the imagination, analogous as they are in size to the 'screen' of the mind's eye, which we feel to be located just inside the forehead[3]."

In other words, Dali was painting from the "third eye", the forehead chakra (or energy portal) dear to the metaphysical world!

Those few hours devoted to learning Dali in his own museum remain luminous in memory for the expansion of mind they brought me. It was another moment of revelation, comparable to what I felt on viewing *"The Wind That Blew the Sky Away"* and later the painted meditations of Paul Gauguin (both described in Chapter Two.) In some of Dali's works that wind had indeed blown the sky away, revealing a wildly distorted world. I understood why Figueras wanted me to pause there.

[1]   Blanche Merz, *Points of Cosmic Energy* (translated by myself from the French "Hauts-Lieux Cosmo-Telluriques"). Saffron Walden (UK): C W Daniel, 1985. 184p., glossary, bibliography. ISBN 0 85207 194 9.

[2]   *Op.cit.,* pp. 116-121

[3]   William S. Rubin, *Dada, Surrealism and their Heritage,* critique and catalog of a major exhibition which toured in 1968., page 113. New York: Museum of Modern Art, 1968. 252p. LC 68-17466.

Chapter Seventeen

TOUCHING ANCIENT KNOWLEDGE

So much of what I wanted to explore and to experience lay far from home. By this time I had been reading quite a bit about megalithic sacred sites, earth energies, the invisible lines across the landscape called "leys", and the churches and cathedrals that men built on them. My bookshelves are rich with stimulus but they cannot match being there, seeing the stone, smelling the earth, hearing birdsong and touching the energy of the land. Blanche's writings had provoked an inner need to experience some of these sacred sites through the added dimension of my Hartmann lobe antenna.

As 1989 opened this and a pendulum were still the only tools I had but they were to be my indispensable companions on several ambitious, long and varied trips. I had acquired a pendulum soon after the lobe antenna, for this device proved to be highly accurate in defining precise grid crossing-points and their polarity. The antenna led me to them and then the pendulum nailed them down.

In the spring I set out for England and France. My husband's long, slow decline, which quite naturally concentrated my energies on him, had created a kind of deficit of contact with old friends and the English branch of the family. Invitations to pause in half a dozen households formed the framework of my itinerary. There would be a window of time for some long-deferred genealogical research into my own ancestors. Lastly but far from least, there must absolutely be some energy dowsing in new fields. My sights were set on Stonehenge, Avebury, Glastonbury, and any likely-looking old cathedral that happened to be along my path.

The first day on the road was a wet slog, and that night I slept in the Morvan hill country west of Burgundy. Before pulling into my country inn I had time for a quick sprint around the striking basilica of Sainte-Madeleine, crowning the hilltop village of Vézelay. Successively monastery, church, and then abbey, its life began in the ninth century, with the major construction occurring in the twelfth century. The place hums; it conveyed a palpable vibratory state just being there. However, it was rainy and cold and I was tired and hungry, so I postponed all serious work. The next morning was sunny and encouraging, fine for photography and dowsing.

Vézelay's basilica is untypical of what one might call "high Gothic" design. It is long and thin without a "crossbar" transept. At each end rises a short bell tower, neither of them reaching for the sky like most steeples, and they stand on one side of the edifice, not even centered on one another. These towers are out of harmony with the long, slender line of the vault and its flying buttresses. They look like architectural after-thoughts.

Inside, however, Sainte-Madeleine was all harmonious soft color leading toward a blast of light. The nave is unusally long, ten fluted pillars of varicolored stone down each side, tones of sand, bisque and tan rising to support arches in which brown stones alternate with white. Graceful serenity reigns as you amble slowly down the aisle, your energy field massaged by the resonance of gentle, earthy colors.

In the distance you see that the choir, nestled within the abside, bursts with white light. Morning sun illuminates ranks of tall windows, bathing this section in brilliance. The graceful pillars and all the stone and stucco above and around them are whitewashed with light. The whole creates an amazing transformation from dark to light, not experienced again in just that way in cathedrals visited thereafter.

The lobe antenna soon showed me that the construction respected the Hartmann network. The pillars holding up the vaulted roof were precisely two power points apart, and the *déambulatoire* around the sides was also two points wide. Spaced at this interval, the pillars occupied all the available positive polarity. Sending it skyward? The inner choir was closed off from the public, so I could not check for doubling-up of the force lines. On this trip of discovery I was going to learn that these points of central focus are frequently roped off from all except the clergy. It is as if they do not want their flock to get close to the energy which they alone have the right to absorb and transmit. Elsewhere, in other sacred vaults, you can wander at will and soak up the spiritual force of the stone.

The basilica stands on the very crest of Vézelay's hill, so I was not expecting to find underground water. However, I raced around dowsing for water, using the "fast" ramble proposed by Pierre. To my great surprise there seemed to be water up there, lots of it, possibly ten or more watercourses flowing under the choir and nave. How did they accomplish that? It seemed to be super-abundant under the basilica. The north wall was quite damp almost the whole length of the nave. And this on a hilltop! It seemed as if I was going to harvest as many questions as answers.

Onward across the rolling plains of northern France, across the Channel, and into another world. Visits with friends and family led me, stage by stage, up to the Midlands to stay with Harry and Sue near Liverpool. Rhododendrons were in bloom everywhere as they showed me the touristic high spots.

Liverpool's huge Anglican cathedral is breathtakingly vertigious, awesomely vast inside its red sandstone walls, but I did not sense a play of energies. The high ceiling has a gothic form that is not supported in the same way as the medieval vaults; there are few pillars, they are not free-standing, and they are very widely spaced. This cathedral was built only a century ago and is reputed the largest in England. Dowsing might have provided useful information, but circumstances prevented doing the work.

Across on the Wirral peninsula, however, there stands in the village of Heswall a charming small church reeking of ancient, benign energy. St. Peter's respects the Hartmann network despite being about five degrees off true east-west orientation. "Speed dowsing" suggested fourteen underground watercourses, which really surprised me in such a small edifice and in such an unheralded location. Inside I could not find a point where they might converge. Once again the limitations of my gear chafed the spirit.

This church is not large and does not have a vast gothic vault, but there are pillars nonetheless — and they are round on the south side of the aisle and octagonal on the north side. The reason why is lost in the mists of antiquity. St. Peter's dates back to 1300 and, like other very old religious edifices, it has undergone spates of remodeling and reconstruction, in one case after a fire.

Those fourteen watercourses caught my attention, echoing the major cathedrals studied by Blanche Merz. What is magical about the number fourteen in the Christian religion? Bound by the time constraints common to all travelers, I could not linger to dwell on this feature that tiny Heswall appeared to share with huge Chartres and vast Santiago de Compostella. But "fourteen" meant something to the early spiritual builders, whether French, Spanish or English.

Working my way southward again, pausing overnight here and there as programmed, I reached the fabled West Country.

Salisbury Cathedral offered me a long prowl. Built in the 13th century, it is admired for the purity of its architectural style, immortalized by the painter John Constable, its spire soaring above the plain. The inner architecture respects Hartmann's global grid, the whole shifted six degrees off true east-west. However, the transept showed me nothing in the way of energy concentration.

And, as I worked, my legs began to get heavy. It took me a moment to realize that an energy drain was happening. Blanche had described such phenomena on sacred sites. It behooved me to stop, observe, and think. The answer is ridiculously simple: Salisbury Cathedral is built on wetlands, the great vessel nearly floating on soggy soil. Correction: the builders laid a thick bed of gravel on that pudding to create stability. But the foundations were only four feet deep, and the addition of the spire in the early 14th century added to the stress.

In other words, at Salisbury there was not a question of directing a series of watercourses to converge under the choir. It was water, water everywhere.

The site had been chosen because two earlier structures built on the hills two miles away had suffered from a lack of water. First too little, now too much.

Hartmann and his disciples have demonstrated the difficulty of maintaining health and vitality atop underground water where the force lines show negative polarity. Clever builders, by concentrating and focusing what flows beneath, used to be able to overcome that liability and turn it into an energetic, spiritual asset. Heavy legs told me such was not the case at Salisbury.

My guidebook told me the transept required reinforcing in the fifteenth century but the stress continued, with the four big pillars which define that space having noticeably buckled by 3.5 inches. Major repairs have been undertaken in the late twentieth century. Scaffolding embraced the tower at the time of my visit.

Stonehenge lies only a short drive northward from Salisbury. Silhouetted against the juncture of sky and the contours of rolling plain, the ancient stones seem to frame a series of windows on another world. These are mysterious windows, holding secrets. Such as, why are the stones here? Such as, how did man get these massive stones to this site and erect them? Such as, what belief system inspired such a gargantuan human effort?

For these are huge stones. The outer circle, of which about half remains, is made of "sarsens" standing about thirteen feet tall and weighing from twenty-five to forty-five tons. These came from the Marlborough Downs, twenty miles away. They are capped with horizontal bridging stones, called "lintels" and weighing about seven tons. Inside them stood a circle of smaller stones whose original horseshoe formation is now only fragmentary. These stand about six to seven feet high and weigh about four tons. Called bluestones, they were brought from a mountain in southwestern Wales, 240 miles distant by land and sea.

At the center are the remnants of a horseshoe arrangement of taller, heavier sarsens, also capped in pairs. These assemblages are called trilithons and stand up to twenty-four feet high. Inside them there appears to have been another horseshoe formed of the smaller bluestones. These horseshoes opened toward a shorter "heel" stone planted outside the circle, still standing and providing an alignment with the northeasterly point where the sun rises on the day of the summer solstice.

Archaeology cannot really pin down when this mystery was created, much less give more than a vague suggestion of its purpose. They talk about ceremonial use but there is no evidence from which to draw a hypothesis. The experts offer dates ranging from 3050 BC to 1500 BC for what they propose as three waves of construction. Some insist it began much earlier.

The heel stone appears to be the only one sited with astronomical significance, indicating the rising sun on the day of the summer solstice.

There are theories that Stonehenge may have been a lunar observatory. There is little to go on to support this idea, and Alexander Thom did not include Stonehenge in his comprehensive work on megalithic lunar observatories[1].

In our time you cannot approach and touch the stones. There is an official parking lot on the opposite side of the road, you cross through an underpass, and you emerge onto a path which circles the monument. An iron railing keeps spectators about fifty feet away from the stones.

I looked, strolled the circular path, sat on a bench, still looking. Dowsing was not an option. My first emotion was frustration. My sensitive hands needed to touch; the antenna that is my body wanted to mingle with the stones, let their energy bounce and reverbrate with mine. Such was not allowed.

Sixteen photographs record my admiration for these rugged witnesses of another view of the world. Some of them seem carefully tailored, others show jagged corners, runnels, and scooped-out concavities. My camera's zoom lens took me up close so as to appreciate the texture and to wonder at the irregularities. I played with exposures and filters in order to simulate sunrise and moonlight conditions. It is difficult to conduct a love affair at distance.

Those windows on distant horizons tantalized but did not reveal to me their secret landscapes. At this writing I know now that one can make special arrangements to have a private "audience" with the energies inside the circle. On this first visit, not endowed with clairvoyance, it was only possible to appreciate the fact of a powerful enigma.

To create this amazing temple focused on the sun's most northerly point implies a spiritual vision powerful enough to sustain the builders over centuries of incredible physical effort. Archaeology suggests that their conception evolved over many generations, for the nature and components of the structure went through several phases. But what was the driving force?

This first visit to Stonehenge was simultaneously elevating and discouraging. Spirit sensed there was more here than met my eye, but I could not get a handle on it. I turned away with a certain disappointment.

And then came a surprise: leaving Stonehenge, my eye hit on a road sign reading "Woodhenge". I checked the mapbook and saw it was only a mile or so away to the northeast. No one had mentioned this to me, and my guidebook did not speak of it.

Ten minutes later I was there, gazing with fascination at a roughly circular collection of tree stumps. At first glance it looked like a forest sawed down to about thirty inches high. One could imagine segments of telephone poles. Then one sees they are concrete stumps, ostensibly placed where trees once stood. And it wasn't just one circle at all. It was six circles. Much later I found another book by Thom which diagrammed the site, showing the inner ring to be egg-shaped and the outer rings to be ellipses on the verge of being circular[2].

Authors of various guides to British megalithic sites say Woodhenge dates back to 2300 BC. An official guide sold in the Stonehenge shop says that Woodhenge "was probably a temple, a tribal meeting-place, or a combination of both[3]." However, Thom's diagram clearly shows a northeast-southwest axis suggestive of concern with the summer solstice. And Woodhenge lies northeast of Stonehenge, which would seem to underline the significance of the alignment. Thom assimilates Woodhenge into his list of primitive solar observatories. None of this is obvious to the layman arriving unprepared. Thom's measurements show the principal axis of the outer ellipse to be about 120 feet and his design for the site shows 159 stumps, but what you see on arrival is a sea of stumps and it takes a while to discover the pattern.

I did not know what to make of this place. Dowsing with the Hartmann antenna was frustrating — I could not discern a pattern that reconciled the rectilinear Hartmann grid with the ellipses of concrete stumps. Possibly I had "run" more energy at Salisbury and Stonehenge that day than I had realized. Whatever, I hit a metaphysical rock and brought home no readings. Ultimately I learned that too many sacred sites in one day sap the dowsing reflexes, whether they were used or not.

In his slender guidebook Osborne reports that aerial photography in 1925 revealed circles of black spots in a wheat field[4]. Subsequent digging confirmed that wooden posts lay rotting beneath the surface where the spots had been seen.

Woodhenge left me bemused. Here was an additional dimension in the expanding panorama of megalithic phenomena. "Lithic" is not really appropriate, for the term relates to stones, and Woodhenge was all about wood. There had been posts organized into ellipses. Had there been trees before the posts?

Investigating sacred sites was a major feature of this trip, but there was also a family matter to resolve. Specifically, where did we come from? Back in Chapter Two I wrote about my dissatisfaction with the spiritual choices offered in my youth. Paul Gauguin's giant painting entitled *"Whence Do We Come? What Are We? Where Do We Go?"* epitomized my spiritual quest. Around the dinner table during the 1930s there was occasional chat about family origins. We knew that my paternal great-grandfather was the first of his family born in the New World, in Canada to be precise. He had told my father that we came from a place called Frome, but that we appeared to have been Huguenots. That is to say, French Protestants at a time when Protestants were persecuted. No one in the family expressed any thoughts about all this, but I found it intensely interesting to suspect that we were religious refugees.

Huguenots were burned and decapitated, their heads impaled on pikes, always at the behest of Catholic bishops, of course.

Six days before the Henges of wood and stone I had spent an afternoon prowling through the archives of the Genealogical Society in London. I'd found quite a lot on Frome and a little bit on people bearing our unusual name. One of the librarians gave me the telephone number of the churchwarden in Frome, who was supposed to have custody of all the records. Calling that number gave me the churchwarden's wife, who turned out to be the unofficial parish genealogist.

"Oh yes, we have quite a lot on your family," she said.

My blood boiled with excitement. Frome — pronounced "Froom" as I was quickly to learn — lay close to my major megalithic destinations. In fact, if you draw a triangle connecting Stonehenge, Glastonbury and Avebury, Frome lies near the middle. It would be both appropriate and convenient to rest my head a few nights surrounded by ancestors and an outer ring of sacred stones. Two days after the Henges the churchwarden's wife received me at the church of St. John the Baptist of Frome Selwood. The fruits of her research overwhelmed me. She had culled the records painstakingly to create lists of births, marriages and deaths for individual families, even collecting such records from other parishes in the town. That afternoon I left her tiny church office clutching eleven precious pages of photocopy, densely handwritten lists of my forebears.

The next morning I visited the little Frome museum, where an enterprising soul had created a historical timeline which wound around the walls. I began at the beginning, noting the community emerged with the founding of a church mission by the River Frome in the year 685. Slowly I followed the thread of English history as it impacted this small town until I came to 1831. "First emigration to Canada" was noted.

The hair stood up on the back of my neck. There it was!

Man is stubborn and the current of human affairs is relentless. Frome was a textile town during the Industrial Revolution. It sits on the edge of the Salisbury Plain, where sheep grazed by the tens of thousands. After fleeing France my ancestors became wool carders, spinners, weavers, fullers, and dyers. When mechanization loomed, the labor force of Frome turned out en masse to demonstrate against this threat to their employment. The mill-owners neither fought nor gave in. They simply moved north to Manchester, Sheffield, Nottingham, where hungry people were willing to work with machines.

In the 1820s Frome was in full depression, with half the town on the Poor List. The Vestry got together a purse and called for volunteers to emigrate to Canada, following the example of people in the nearby town of Corsley.

Two hundred people volunteered, of them thirteen families were selected. Twelve families actually made the trip, including that headed by my great-great-great-grandfather. My perusal of those eleven pages of photocopy told me that he took the entire family down to the church to be rebaptized during the week before departure on this hopeful but frightening adventure.

Later the churchwarden's wife sent me a copy of a letter written by my great-great-aunt Marianne, then fifteen years old, who told the people left behind in Frome about the journey. It was a horror. The sailing ship was caught in great storms, there was illness and misery, and some people were washed overboard. They landed in Quebec, went on to Montreal, where the baby of the family, two-year-old Caroline, died of cholera. Finally they settled in Bytown, which eventually became Ottawa. Every time I relive this story in the telling my eyes fill with tears.

Before leaving Frome I stumbled across the answer to another little mystery: the spelling of the family name. Until the mid-18th century the church records were showing four different variations for spelling the name of people who were clearly brothers and cousins. And in rationalizing this anarchic situation, the person in authority inserted a "z" we hadn't had before. Now, on a postcard rack, the answer leaped out at me. There was a humorous cartoon card mocking the Somerset dialect, with a man shouting out "Zomerzet!" So that's how we got our "z", by bringing a French name with "s" to Zomerzet.

There was no longer any mystery about how we got to the New World. How we got from France to England was still unknown, although partial illumination came a few months later. A researcher for the Huguenot Society found us in the records of the Huguenot Church in London in the late 1500s. My forebears had come from northern France. I still don't have all the details and possibly never will. Records of new arrivals frequently exist, records of forced departures rarely do. We kept our heads, on our shoulders not on pikes, and we left. Probably by night, and in stealth. Is it any wonder I have problems with organized religion?

Genealogy aside, the church of St. John the Baptist came as a surprise. It should not have, for the principal structure dates back to the 12th and 13th centuries. And it dowsed. Smack on the Hartmann network. Columns frame six gothic-arched bays down the length of the nave, and they stand on the force line crossing points. Once again, the church is sited six degrees off true east-west. There are reputed to be numerous springs on the site, but structural impediments prevented making a complete circuit of the building. I found four of those springs and can believe there are more.

St. John gave me a mysterious gift. My photograph of the western facade produced a floating image of the stained-glass window which stretches high above the main door. Shot from the street in front, the various windows are opaque and dark against the interior gloom — they are not backlit. But an image of the big window floats in full-color well in the foreground, slightly above and offset to the side of its physical place in the facade. The vivid stained-glass projects as a separate entity in the air and in front of the building. Matthew, Mark, Luke and John levitate in the open air, in full color against the ambient grayness. It is remarkable and unexplainable. I've shown the prints and my negatives to professional photographers, who agree that there seems to be no question of a double exposure. Physically, it is what it is. Psychically, I've had to consider the possibility it was a message for me. That colorful window turned and twisted in my mind as I drove the highways.

Frome had brought me more than expected, not just success in the tracing of ancestors but also another church for my collection. So far every one of them I had visited was constructed with respect to Hartmann's map of terrestrial energies. Clearly his discovery was really a rediscovery of old precepts. His application of this science to health and vitality simply expanded the context.

Next on the program had to be Glastonbury, which proved to be about an hour west of Frome, on my way to the next home visit on the itinerary. It was raining. Dowsing on the flat would be possible, but there could be no question of climbing the Tor without adequate boots. All the prowling about with antenna in hand that I would have time for could be supplied on the Abbey grounds, right in the center of town.

Glastonbury has possibly the longest history of any western religious site. It was mostly tidal marsh at one time, perhaps even an arm of what is now called Bridgewater Bay. It is believed to have been King Arthur's fabled Avalon. Legend says that Joseph of Arimathea, the uncle of Jesus, brought a group of family and disciples here after the Crucifixion, obtained a grant of land from the local king, and built the first church of wood, clay and "wattles". Later there was a Celtic monastery and church, which become an important Christian abbey by the tenth century and the richest abbey in the land by the time of the Norman conquest in 1066. It was rebuilt grander, destroyed by fire in 1184, and rebuilt again — a program which took two centuries. Decay began again after the "Dissolution" in 1539, when Henry the Eighth withdrew from Rome's spiritual authority and established the Anglican Church. From this time the abbey-cathedral was allowed to slowly decline into the ruins one visits today.

With the lobe antenna I surveyed what had once been the nave. Stone "footprints" in the shape of diamonds witness the siting of the great pillars which held up the vaulted roof. There are two rows of eight and, surprise, they are sited precisely according to the Hartmann grid. Each pillar stood on a crossing-point of positive polarity. Within each row the pillars were two points apart, the intermediate Hartmann knot being of negative polarity. Three force lines ran between the two rows, so that polarity was scrupulously respected in each dimension.

This was really all I had time to do, but it was an important confirmation. There was now no doubt in my mind that the early cathedral builders already understood this matter of terrestrial energy lines which Dr. Hartmann revealed in our time. Not only did they understand it, they used it as a template!

Glastonbury merited more of my time but the rigid time-table of visits I had constructed would tolerate no deviation. I was expected. England was offering me stunning hospitality. My initial reticence to pilot my lefthand drive automobile through towns and over motorways populated by righthand drive vehicles had long since melted. The experiment was working well and my mind began to tinker with the scheduling of the next such safari.

Three days later the old stones of Avebury brought me an experience quite different from that offered at Stonehenge. Situated about seventeen miles north of Stonehenge, this is/was a much more complex assemblage of great sarsens. A deep ditch protects a vast circular bank enclosing roughly twenty-eight acres, and inside that once stood a "Great Circle" of ninety-nine standing stones. Within that large circle are the remnants of two lesser circles, each more than three hundred feet in diameter, dwarfing the Henges I had just seen. Many of the stones were destroyed, many more had been scavenged for building nearby structures, the people egged on by a puritanical church seeking to eradicate signs of pagan beliefs. William Stukely sketched and described them in 1743 while this destruction was in progress. His book must have been an essential resource when Alexander Keiller undertook restoration in 1930. The second world war interrupted Keiller's work, which was never resumed, and some stones remain buried.

In the words of the 17th century antiquarian John Aubrey, who saw it eighty years before Stukeley, what remains of this giant conception "....did as much excell Stonehenge as a cathedral does a parish church" [5].

This is no exaggeration, echoing my immediate reactions as I strolled through the great stones that still stand. The public has total freedom here, unlike Stonehenge. Despite the depredations of time and man, there are enough touchable stones to stir your energies and nourish your meditations. I saw immediately that this first visit could be hardly more than an introduction, and I made the most of the afternoon allotted by an agenda framed in ignorance.

The circular conception inhibited work with my antenna but it became clear that the builders understood the global energy system. The pendulum proved essential to confirming that all the original stones seemed to be on crossing points of the network. At this point in my rambles around Britain none of this came as a surprise. Some of the smaller stones, which had the air of manufactured substitutes, did not excite the pendulum at all.

Describing these remnants as such robs them of their power. Spiritual energy pervades the fields even now. To me it was an awesome experience to move among the sarsens, letting sensory impressions flood in. Simply being there was a long, ambling meditation within a cosmic force field.

South of the Great Circle a long double line of stones named The Avenue runs toward a burial ground called the Sanctuary. There were originally about one hundred pairs of large stones marching southward down these green fields. On this day The Avenue was sheep pasture and I found it fascinating to see how the sheep loved to huddle around the stones, even on the windward side. Antenna and pendulum confirmed to me that the sheep sought to cuddle as closely as possible to the positive energy knots occupied by the stones.

In the North Circle there still stand two of three stones that formed a "cove", a horseshoe opening to midwinter moonrise, echoing an astronomical function seen at Stonehenge. Otherwise, only four of the original twenty-seven exist in this Circle. The South Circle, once twenty-nine stones, is also fragmentary.

The modern village of Avebury impinges on the circles and two highways intersect between the inner circles. The explorer crosses back and forth more than once, dodging traffic, in hiking the grounds of this wonderful outdoor temple. It was a wrench to tear myself away from the stones of the South Circle, several of which speak to me in mysterious ways. My implacable itinerary insisted, permitting only a pause to gaze in wonder at the nearby Silbury Hill and no time at all for its neighbors the Sanctuary and West Kennett Long Barrow. Part of the overall Avebury landscape, Silbury is Europe's largest manmade hill. It was created about 2600 years ago in a conical form, standing 130 feet high. All these temptations led me to realize I would be back, probably not just once, and with much more time at my disposal.

There were four more visits during the ensuing days before I crossed the Channel and left behind a different idea of England than I had brought to it. Rolling down major highways opens the mind to endless skeins of contemplations. More than three weeks earlier I had left my alpine home to renew old acquaintances and to explore new concepts. There was an abundance of fodder for my brain to munch as the kilometers rolled by. High on this menu pulsed the web of invisible energy I had been finding and verifying everywhere. Blanche's published research told that man had been capturing and channeling this energy for thousands of years, using it to magnify the spiritual power of religious shrines and structures.

My experiences of the recent days confirmed that. The network lay everywhere, in homes and gardens as well as churches and stone circles, and I had demonstrated this to some of the friends I'd been visiting. None of them had accompanied my investigations on sacred sites. Their raised-eyebrow acceptance of what they saw my antenna do in their parlors did not extend to joining me in the folly of fieldwork. The business of sorting out impressions, of comparing Vézelay and Salisbury, pitting Stonehenge against Avebury, occupied my hours at the wheel, when I wasn't watching Frome Selwood's colorful window sail through space.

Late one blistering afternoon I pulled into a tiny village in the hills near Cluny, site of the greatest abbey of them all. But it was not for this ruin that I paused again in Burgundy: I was here to visit Paul and Margaret. He was the son of old and dear friends of my husband, a couple who came to our alps for a few weeks every winter. One year the younger couple had detoured up the mountain to visit his parents, and we had all been at table for a jolly lunch in their hotel. I had hit it off famously with these two, we became instant joking friends, and they'd issued me an open invitation --- knowing full well it would not be taken up until some years down the road. Now was that moment, additionally blessed by the presence of his mother. She and I were good friends; our men had passed on, she no longer came to the Alps, and so we appreciated one another all the more at this sunny season.

The next morning this dear old friend guided me through the remains of the great abbey. Cluny had been the rival of Rome in its heyday but the French Revolution brought its destruction. Work on organizing the remnants was underway, but on this first visit I could not discern a pattern worth investigating. Nevertheless, it was bemusing to contemplate ruins which had been the "mother" church of our Romainmôtier across the Jura Mountains, a blue line in the east.

Before lunch we put my bags into the car, for I planned a leisurely Sunday afternoon drive back to my alpine meadow. This little get-acquainted visit was just enough so that we could really get to know one another.

At lunch under the big spreading tree the talk turned somehow to the subject of ESP — extra-sensory perception — and from there it went to dowsing. They were intensely interested in what I had just been doing.

Paul mentioned a place on the hillside, just outside the orchard gate, where a circle appeared in the grass every summer. My ears grew pointed. Like every other mystic, I had begun to read about the recent emergence of circles in the cereal fields of England.

"Have you ever seen anything like that?" he asked.

"Well," I hesitated, "we have two choices. We can either just forget you ever said that, and I will start off for Chesières in a few minutes. Or else," and I added mock menace, "you invite me to stay another night, we go down to the car and bring up my bags again, and I will bring up my dowsing gear too."

In merriment, we chose the latter course, and fifteen minutes later we were up on the brow of the hill inspecting what Paul called a "neolithic" circle. Yes, there was a perfect circle inscribed dryly in green grass as if by a well-controlled flame. This was very short hillside pasture grass, sheep fodder. It was not anything like a cereal field. Nevertheless, it was a circle.

Nothing I had dowsed or read about had prepared me for the energy system up on that knoll. It was time for me to give them the "ten-minute tutorial" on the Hartmann network, and I began this while beginning to dowse. And then I had to interrupt myself, stop everything and explain, with puzzlement, that I was not finding what I had been describing.

There were no Hartmann force lines, there was no rectangular pattern. It took me only a few minutes to determine that the global network was not present in the circle. It had been purely and simply suppressed from this spot on the globe — suppressed and replaced by a circle. And the perfect brown ring in the grass, six meters in diameter, proved to be only the beginning.

Bit by bit the lobe antenna divulged an expanding set of rings, each one approximately fifty centimeters outside the preceding one. The outer diameter measured about eighteen meters. No energy rectangles as I had learned them were present. These were energy circles, rolling out from their center like the ripples in a pool into which you have tossed a stone. We laid out lengths of string and used stones and sticks to mark what we found. Except for the one in the center, these circles were entirely invisible. Only the dowsing rod connecting through me could *see* them.

Inside that center was a dead calm — nothing at all. It was neutral like the interior of a Hartmann rectangle. For a pendulum on this site I used a heavy brass surveyor's plumb-bob which gyrated at the end of a fifty-centimeter length of twine. Except that it refused to gyrate. Of course: no crossing points, no polarity, hence no gyrating.

Paul called my attention to a spot nearby, asking me to test the polarity there. I dowsed toward it, intuiting that it was another energy center. Yes, more rings, and we laid out more markers. The two systems were contiguous, their centers proving to be nearly eighteen meters apart.

But this second set was different. The pendulum said its center was clearly negative. Paul tried it too, with the same result. He then explained that this second spot had been avoided for generations. The sheep hated it, and humans who had tried to picnic or lounge there had abruptly moved away. Such reactions are commensurate with negative polarity — at least that much of Hartmann's orthodoxy held true here. The pendulum had not lied.

My hosts were eager to get to the bottom of their home-grown mystery, but all of us realized we lacked enough information to go further at this time. Paul had tried his hand with my antenna, and it was clear that he received a dowser's reaction. In other words, he "had it". Making a paper template from my antenna, he proposed to fabricate his own lobe antenna so that he could continue this path of research we had opened.

Bubbling with enthusiasm, they proposed to give me a quick tour of some interesting churches not far away. We piled into a car and Paul drove us up the valley, then up the other side to the medieval village of Brancion perched between two deep ravines. You walk through ancient streets, dominated by a château, and come out to the promontory where the old church squats. There were lots of Sunday tourists in and all around this rather unprepossessing edifice, a discouragement to serious dowsing even if I had been tempted. Brancion is said to be of the twelfth century, but I did not receive good sensations. To me it was squat, dim and dank — I did not want to linger and got out rather soon. The view over the valley from the terrace was the best part.

Arrriving at Chapaize back down in the valley was like returning to the light. I got a lift simply looking at the graceful proportions of this twelfth-century edifice with its soaring tower. Roman-style rather than the convoluted Gothic architecture of the great cathedrals, this was a handsome country church that seemed to glow in the light color of the local stone of which it was built. Two minutes with the antenna was sufficient to confirm what my senses were telling me. Chapaize worked with the terrestrial energy. I put aside the wand and strolled through with hands deployed. This church invited the spiritual seeker. It wouldn't make a Christian of me, but it told me once again that the early builders had found a formula which encouraged the human spirit to soar.

Back on our hillside we enjoyed another summery evening meal under the trees. This reunion had been years in the making and was worth savoring. We talked much about the work we would do here in the future, for they were enthusiastic to unlock the secret that started with the brown ring in the grass.

My trip home the next day took less than four hours, during which mind dialogued with spirit about the mass of impressions received. All the very old religious structures I had visited worked with the earth energies about which I had been learning. The megalithic sites were something else again. To the degree they were approachable, they too seemed informed by the same energies. At Stonehenge the sense of "windows" had touched me profoundly, echoing that vision of "the back of beyond" sometimes apprehended in my Alps.

Then there was this new phenomenon of crop circles in England, where some people were discovering energy patterns (and others were seeing only hoaxing by pranksters.) Paul and Margaret's knoll seemed to be proposing yet another variation in the study of earth energies. No ruins, no standing stones, no cereal fields, just the manifestation of something invisible. *What kind of a story waited to be uncovered up there?*

[1]   A. Thom, *Megalithic Lunar Observatories*. London: Oxford University Press, 1971. 127p. ISBN 0 19 858 132 7.

[2]   A. Thom, *Megalithic Sites in Britain*. London, Oxford University Press, 1967. 174p. ISBN 0 19 813148 8. Pages 47, 68, 74-75, 78.

[3]   Ken Osborne, *Stonehenge and its Neighboring Monuments*. London: English Heritage, 2d ed. 1995. 36p. ISBN 1 85074 172 7 Page 34.

[4]   *Op.cit.,* p. 33.

[5]   Quoted by Evelyn Francis in *Avebury*, a pocket-size booklet of 58 pages jammed with historical facts, sketches, measurements, theories and mysteries. Wooden Books: 2000. ISBN 1 904 263 15 1.

Indispensable. Buy it in the bookshop after you leave the carpark at Avebury.

Chapter Eighteen

SPIRITUAL NOMADISM

From this point new spiritual adventures began piling in. I had begun a pattern of taking long trips to reconnect with long-neglected people, places and preoccupations. At first I managed to sandwich metaphysical explorations in between visits to people, but there were moments when it seemed the balance was tipping the other way.

The foray into France and England described in the preceding chapter proved to be a springboard. During the ensuing five years I went back to France — especially Cluny — annually, to both England and California thrice, Canada twice, and ultimately to Arizona.

Answers were the goal, always more answers. This virtual nomadism focused on finding answers on several levels: the purely mystical, the matter of my ancestral roots, probing for echoes of past lives, and how these questions meshed with the fascinating archaeo-historical aspects of megalithic and sacred structures. My insatiable thirst to know drove the program; my gregarious nature basked in the sunshine of reunions, visits and revisits.

Dowsing for energy was a principal tool wherever I went. Blanche Merz's studies inspired my first forays into cathedrals and ancient churches. After a handful of such experiences it was perfectly clear to me that the builders had created energetic webs for a high purpose, one that enhanced the Christian spirituality they sought to celebrate. That I could not embrace their doctrine, their dogmas, did not diminish my appreciation of how they sought to facilitate — and control — contact with the Cosmic Creator. Dowsing in such vibrant spaces tuned my physical body to be ever more responsive to these subtle energies. They expanded my spiritual outlook, which of course was what the church leaders earnestly desired for their flocks. For them the Gothic cathedral was a powerful working tool with which they could propagate their message. For me each one of these soaring edifices had a personal character, an energetic signature. Each one offered me the challenge of learning its special secret, discovering how it could touch me at the soul level and stimulate a sense of well-being at the cellular level.

Five months after Cluny and after a summer of joyful alpine exploits, I was on the road again. Out in California there were several "aha's". Up in the extreme north of the state Carol and I made the acquaintance of Mount Shasta, a truly magic mountain looming benevolently over vast stretches of landscape. On a chilly day in late October, with fresh snow dusting the slopes, we drove around Shasta's mass toward the northeast, skirted the Tulelake Waterfowl refuge and finally arrived at the Lava Beds National Monument. Fascinated by volcanism and the lava it produces, I had always wanted to visit this remote wilderness of chaotic stone.

The Lava Beds stretch over perhaps fifty square miles of a very sparsely inhabited area, between rugged mountains and barren plains suitable only for cattle. There are tunnels through the lava and chimneys which poke up vertically. It is mostly brown rock and piles of harsh boulders everywhere. There is nothing smooth about this lava. Trails lead through some of the tunnels and we did some exploring. Up above, where it was more or less flat, I unlimbered the Hartmann antenna.

To my surprise the network was extremely hard to find. I found the east-west lines were not nicely spaced at intervals of eight to nine feet as usual. Instead, they were fifty, sixty, even eighty feet apart. And the north-south lines I found were fifty feet apart. The roughness of the terrain prevented testing a large area. In addition to this huge anomaly, polarity was not limited to the infrequent crossing points. Polarity existed on every individual boulder I tested. And, I felt wonderfully vital and happy at this site. There appeared to be something about lava which tweaks both terrestrial and human energies.

Confirmation of that apparently lava-based anomaly came the following year when Carol and I climbed Mt. Lassen, a volcano which last blew off in 1915. It's about one hundred miles south of those lava beds and is more than ten thousand feet high. Thanks to a high-altitude parking lot, the hike to the summit takes only a couple of hours on a trail like a boulevard. One is slowed more by the rapid physical adjustment consequent to commencing the effort above eight thousand feet. The boulder-strewn summit area itself is an essentially level surface about the size of a football field. This was easy terrain for dowsing, compared to the lava beds. Thus there can be no mistake about what I found. Or didn't find.

Up there the antenna picked up nothing at all. No energy lines, no Hartmann network. Nothing. A vast neutral zone.

Subsequently a mutual friend told me that Blanche kept a vacation cottage on one of the Italian islands — a volcanic island — going there for rest and recuperation. I thought to myself *"what does she know about living on lava that she's not broadcasting to the world?"*

In terms of assessing terrestrial energy, this experience on the Lava Beds could only be compared to the experience on the knoll outside Cluny, where the electromagnetic rectangles had been deformed into circles. And, of course, one must compare those anomalies with all those sacred sites where the energy lines had been doubled up and concentrated. It was axiomatic for

Hartmann-inspired dowsers that his global network could be deformed by underground water, by radiation oozing up through earthquake faults, and by strong electrical currents.

To those influences one had to add human manipulations of exceptional and unknown character, and now there was the presence of lava.

Our day on the lava had been enlivened by lots of wildlife encounters. To get there we followed the boundary of a major waterfowl reserve where thousands of grebes, pelicans, mergansers, ducks and coots splashed happily. Then on the lava we met several groups of white-tailed deer who seemed unconcerned about us. Living on a National Monument, they are automatically protected from hunters. Viewing our photographs later we were amused to see how well-camouflaged these deer really were. They blended perfectly into the general color scheme, and if it weren't for those white rumps they would be hard to spot in our pictures.

After this satisfying day, and before leaving the Shasta area for good, we had occasion to exploit a business card we had picked up the previous year at the Sonora mineral show. On the telephone Michael explained how to find his home on the altiplano west of the great mountain. There we were hypnotized by his wonderful assortment of crystals, which seemed to sparkle even more on their tables in the big windows looking toward the magic mountain. An impossible challenge confronted this budding collector: I wanted something of everything. Quartz points and clusters, smoky quartz, amethyst, fluorite, topaz, lepidolite and tourmaline beckoned. Each of them had its own spirit, its own connection to Mother Earth from which it had been (usually) rudely snatched. Held toward the sun shining over Shasta, they gleamed with subtle suggestions of rainbows. I left Michael's home in the sage with a double handful of treasures from whom I hoped to learn some of the secrets of the universe.

My daughter and I were discovering how much fun it was to join forces for these explorations. For me this was a savory part of the spiritual path which had begun unrolling before me, which I now understood clearly to be a path, and which I wanted to share with her. Carol's own spiritual searchings seemed to be taking a different form. We were traveling approximately parallel roads converging from time to time through a section of the inner landscape, and then our paths would diverge again. Our individual radar were swiveling constantly but on different frequencies, yielding data that was different but eminently shareable. During these trips we often took turns reading aloud to one another during the long stretches of boring landscape in California's Central Valley. In this way we both gained new insights. It was at this time Carol introduced me to the books of Mary Summer Rain, an ultimately prolific investigator into the inner nature of the Native American world and its interface with universal metaphysics. We started at the beginning with "Spirit Song"[1]. In this way we both gained new insights.

As the season matured into winter some small logjams began to break up. Before leaving California to return home a friend showed me a pocket-size Geiger counter and how it functioned. It wasn't exactly the kind of break-through dowsing tool I had been looking for, but I was interested in testing the role of radiation in the interplay between terrestrial and cosmic energy. There was no clear notion of how it was going to be put to work, but one of these gadgets came home to the Alps with me.

The last stop on the journey was London, and there in Cecil Court I picked up a handful of books at Watkins', as was becoming my habit. One of them in particular, by a certain J. Havelock Fidler, looked as if it could teach me some useful dowsing tips[2].

Fidler's book attracted me because it appeared to be an earnest, scientifically-oriented investigation of energy lines, especially the major form called "leys". On this basis alone the book merited a detailed perusal in the comfort of home, so I scooped it up along with others.

In an earlier chapter I described how the builders of Gothic cathedrals had moved energy lines around and sometimes crowded them closely together as a means of augmenting spiritual sensations.

"How did they do that?" I wondered in passing. Fidler opened the door to the answer with his experiments in "charging" stones. A retired agricultural scientist, he went to live on the west coast of Scotland and began rambling the steep, rocky hills, dowsing leys and smaller energy lines. He did not seem to have heard of the work of Ernst Hartmann and Blanche Merz, and his book does not mention the former's "global" network. Fidler was going about the study of leys from a different point of view, and he reported his findings in a series of articles published in the *Journal of the British Society of Dowsers*. But he riveted my attention with the following observation:

"If the stone was held in the hand and hit smartly with a hammer, a good imprint was obtained," he explained. "....one could imprint an untouched stone by hammering it on the ground alongside another stone which had been previously imprinted"[3].

My mind reeled with the music, the ringing sound that must have permeated a cathedral construction site, as dozens of medieval stone masons banged away at their stones!

Good scientist that he was, Fidler invented a simple box-like tool called a "gyrometer", which analyzed the gyration of a pendulum so as to measure the charge of a stone or other object. Needing a unit of measure, he devised the term "petron" and defined it in relation to varying pendulum swings. (It's more complicated than that, but it isn't really relevant to our story.) One hundred petrons -- a stone weighing one kilogram and having a charge of 100 petrons -- would be said to have a power of one "lithon".

Fidler estimated the time necessary to charge or imprint a huge stone, like those used to create Stonehenge, would be less that the time needed to cut and shape it. Speaking of the large sarsens weighing up to fifty tons, he said:

"...it would have taken some 50'000 blows with a stone axe to fix fully the charge of the workers' fields. This sounds like a great deal, but I have found that one can, with an easy rhythm, give one such blow per second; so the required number of blows could be given in just under fourteen hours' work.[4]"

(Perhaps the doughty Scots think nothing of maintaining such a rhythm of work, but my own estimates would consider the matter of wrist fatigue.)

Fidler's work contains many corollary notions involving heat, magnetism, sunspots, phases of the Moon, the role of quartz crystals, effect on plant growth, and more, all of them interesting if any reader wants to pursue such a tangent. In my opinion, the overriding importance of what he demonstrated was that energy can literally be pounded into stone and transferred from stone to stone with a mason's hammer. One can visualize this happening on embryo sacred sites. It makes sense. My mind's ear can hear the ringing, leading me to wonder if the "music" itself did not have something to do with the final result.

And the music that is produced in these sacred edifices could well play an essential role in maintaining the intricate web of energies that play through and between the stone pillars.

In late March, with 1990's travel plans taking rapid form, I paid my annual visit to "Med-Nat" — Médecines Naturelles — the exposition of alternative therapies of every imaginable kind. Here is where the rest of the logjam broke open.

In addition to the lobe antenna, Blanche Merz had also used a tool she called the Bovis biometer, with which she was able to read the vibrational rates of sacred sites. I didn't have one and didn't know how to find one, but I found a simulacrum of a Bovis biometer at Med-Nat in Lausanne. At one stand my eye fell upon a small ruler-like object about eight inches long, calibrated from zero to twenty thousand.

"What's that?" I asked the man sitting there, who seemed to offer some kind of service aimed at improving the energies of a living space.

"It's a Bovis biometer," he replied.

My eyebrows shot up, echoing spirit. It was much smaller than the one Blanche had used in our home.

"Really?"

"This is our version, that we use in our work," he answered.

At this point, hungry to find any kind of useful tool, I brought one of those mini-biometers home and began trying to work with it.

Not long afterward a critical book fell into my hands, once again virtually leaping off the shelf to meet me. This one was all about measuring the radiation of various foods, and folded inside it -- as an appendix -- was a heavy sheet of paper bearing the design of a very unusual ruler and labeled "Biomètre de A. Bovis". This time it felt as if I had struck gold. I had fallen upon a spanking new printing of an earlier work gone through numerous editions. It helped educate me on the method Bovis had created.

Between the covers of this book a French electrical engineer, André Simoneton, laid out a system for measuring the force and vitality of the foods we eat. He made it perfectly clear that he was using "an exclusively physical system invented by Bovis, researcher in physics and dowsing, who died in Nice about 1935"[5].

Bovis created his "biometer" about 1930, as a way of measuring the radiation of objects and expressing these values as wave lengths. One version I have heard is that he began by trying to determine the quality of wine by some other means than tasting. The biometer is simply a ruler thirty centimeters long (one foot) calibrated in microns and angströms, the measure of light, instead of the usual measures of length. The object to be measured is placed at the left end of the ruler, and the operator causes a pendulum to swing slowly back and forth over it while progressing from left to right. At some point the pendulum's movement will change direction. That precise point of change is understood to indicate when the power of the object's radiation is no longer strong enough to counter the basic underlying force of Earth's energy as received through the dowser/operator.

"The pendulum turns or it oscillates," the engineer Simoneton explains. "When it turns that means there is the presence of a magnetic field identical to that of a motor. When it oscillates it is because it is attracted as if by the two poles of a magnet."[6] In other words, the pendulum reacts to magnetic fields, and the operator must recognize when a change of field occurs.

Simoneton reminds us that everything in nature is radioactive, including mankind. We are radioactive "necessarily, otherwise we could neither see, hear, nor smell," he points out, citing an expert in nuclear research[7].

Simoneton's own experiments in the testing of foods showed that the vigor of the pendulum's gyrations (once it had met a value) increased in direct proportion to the strength of the wave lengths measured in angströms. Fresh fruits and vegetables gave the highest readings, mostly between 8'000 and 9'000. So did vegetable soups made with a minimum of water and cooked not more than twenty minutes. One of the highest ranking foods on his chart was oatmeal, up around 9'000, and that really got my attention. A steaming bowl of oatmeal was the core of my breakfast at that time, when I was doing most of my mountain- and cliff-climbing. And here came Simoneton confirming what my body had already told me.

It took some time to learn how to manipulate the pendulum correctly to get valid readings. My first attempts took place inside the chalet. The value for "normal" in human life and environment is 6'500, and that was what Blanche had found in the limited Bovis measuring she did in my home. And that is what I found as I moved through the rooms she had tested with her various techniques.

However, she had not been in my late husband's former painting studio, which had a special atmosphere all its own. Under certain lighting conditions the atmosphere there even looked different, almost as if in a church. Thus there was a sense of learning when the pendulum gave me 10'000 in one Hartmann-neutral space in the center of that room.

It's pretty hard to place an object like a room at the left end of any kind of ruler, Biometer or otherwise. One needed another way of finding a standard starting point. After reflection I chose to place the point of 6'500 on the scale -- normal -- just in front of my umbilicus. Following this method I soon began to get some values that seemed reasonable. Normal, 6'500, was nearly everywhere, as one would expect.

Let me provide a table of orientation for understanding Bovis values, as suggested by Simoneton's work, as translated by Blanche Merz[8], and from my own experience:

1000 units - approaching death

2000-3000 - very sick

5000 - illness

6500 - normal vitality

7500-8000 - full vital energy

9000 - threshold of spirituality, found in monasteries, churches, on some ley lines, and being a zone where sound sleep is difficult and short

10'000 and up - increasing levels of spiritual force

A point in the living room centered inside a Hartmann rectangle, hence a neutral zone, gave me 7000 and 7'500. My bedroom gave 8'000 one morning but only 7'000 the next morning. However, both are "healthy". In the painting studio three different Hartmann-neutral zones yielded, respectively, 9'000', 10'000 and 9'000. After meditation in a big chair in the last of those three I found its value had crept up to 9'500-10'000. Early morning on the upstairs balcony yielded 7'000 to 7'500 several times. During one moment, when I concentrated on a major mountain peak as the sun intensified, it shot up to 14'000. This effect came again one evening after sunset. It was late dusk, with a half-moon, and at the very last light the reading soared quickly from 9'000 up to 14'000. The next morning it was back down to 7'000.

These variations suggest that spiritual work or a "high" of some sort can increase the vibrational rate of a place, which makes sense. Thus the reverse should also be true: a place with a high vibrational rate can heighten the sensations of the people who go there. It's what stimulates humanity to build temples. Such a conclusion is perfectly in line with what Blanche Merz had found in applying the Bovis method to her investigations. Her book details the sometimes very elevated Bovis readings she obtained at numerous sacred sites.

Was it possible to work with two different sizes of biometer? This was a question I needed to resolve. The first version I had picked up at the Med-Nat show was only half the size of the original Bovis design which Simoneton had published with his book. Its compactness offered an advantage for someone on the move, and I had begun to work with it immediately. Then, confronted with the "orthodox" version, I tried that too. To my surprise, the results I obtained were identical. It appeared that the device itself did not matter as much as the mental attitude of its operator.

In fact, I had made a kind of convention with the method. I would go into a semi-meditational state before activating the pendulum, and would ask it to give me an accurate reading of the vibrational rate. And it would. Two years later, working on a mountaintop with a colleague using the full-sized Bovis, and standing at some distance from one another, we got identical readings. So I continued over the years to work with the compact size most of the time. I created a biometer on supple cardboard which I could fold, and it slipped easily into a pocket. Measuring levels of spiritual vitality depended more on my immersion into the sense of the place than on the physical tool I used.

Thus armed, I was ready to sally forth on 1990's adventures into both the invisible and the rock-hard tangible. The months of May and June took me back to France, the following three months were jampacked with hiking and climbing in my Alps, and in October I would be off to California and Canada, pausing at London both ways.

My first goals were the great cathedrals of Bourges and Chartres. Central France in mid-May was oceans of rippling grain fields, with enough small forests dotted around here and there to soften the horizon.

The cathedral of Bourges has astonishing grace. The nave is quite long, flanked by two double rows of slender pillars soaring with elegance to create the vaulted space high in the heavens. Working in the 12th and 13th centuries the builders had spaced their columns three Hartmann lines apart, and there was a tremendous flow of positive and negative energy circulating through the three dimensions.

A choral-and-organ concert was in progress when I entered on a Sunday afternoon, and for my second visit the next afternoon the organist simply let her fingers trickle over the keyboards. The sonic effect was progressively soothing and elevating, the slender pillars seeming to resonate like the strings of a harp, making this vaulted space the most natural place to be, a place to rest and let the sense of spirit wash away one's physical boundaries. One could almost levitate, and 14'000 Bovis in the choir stalls confirmed the effect on spirit.

Bourges provided another kind of revelation. Using my small Geiger counter, I established that the baseline measurements -- the "counts per minute" -- for the outside perimeter were close to what my early experiments had come to show as "normal". Inside the cathedral, however, it was another story. The average range was about half of the normal open air count, which on my little machine ranges between fifteen and twenty "blips" per minute. Inside it averaged a bit more than six, with one period of only three (during the organ-and -choral concert).

Why was this? A certain amount of reflection left me with only one theory: the stone walls, pillars and vaulted ceiling offered the congregation some protection against cosmic radiation. Was this simply happy accident or was it yet another sign of unsuspected (by us) scientific sophistication among the builders? What sensory tools did they have to know that an artificial cavern lessened certain kinds of stress on the physical body?

It is very difficult to take such measurements in these very public places. The ideal is to set the counter on a likely spot and simply leave it for an hour. You can't do this either inside or outside any of these major urban cathedrals. There are too many people circulating inside, and outside you have city streets and automobile traffic. It was just barely possible outside Bourges.

A two-hour drive northward took me to Chartres, where the cathedral is another urban island surrounded by tour buses, like whales basking on a cobble-stoned shore. In spite of these problems, I did manage to get some radiation data. Inside the cathedral, six to seven blips of radiation per minute. For a baseline reading I had to depend on my hotel room, one hundred yards away, where the counter gave a range of ten to twenty blips per minute. It began to look like there is an effect worth studying. Unfortunately I cannot claim to have done so in all the cathedrals I have visited.

Chartres is overrun with masses of tourists. During the day there might be up to half a dozen tour groups clustered around their docent at the foot of a famous statue, or under one of the major stained-glass rosettes. The space is kept dim so that these marvelous windows can be appreciated in all their glory.

The pillars are somewhat thicker than at Bourges and slightly farther apart, and more force lines have been crowded together. Along with the sealed-off choir, there is a heavier, more somber feeling, compared to the soaring airiness of Bourges.

The next morning I was there by eight o'clock, and Chartres had regained some of its fabled magic with a night of rest from the hordes. It was quiet, it soared, one steeps in it. Standing on the focal point under the cupola, one receives the color harmonies of the rosettes and the vertical windows in the curve of the abside. Light and color conspire to inspire. It is forbidden to stand on that point in the precise center of the transept, but my early start and a wary eye for the concierge puttering about made it possible. And I did manage to snatch a reading on the biometer: 9'500, on the threshold of the spiritual domain, possibly all one could hope for in view of the various inhibitions imposed on the visitor. It was about the same down at the other end of the nave. People were coming in by that time and I could not weave through the labyrinth in the orthodox fashion, which means following the track that doubles back over and over again. All I could do was go straight to the core, where I did receive reactions at 9'500, 10'000, and 11'000 angström units on the Bovis scale. Truly following the labyrinth to its center would have produced more, as Blanche had found.

Here at Chartres she had found fourteen subterranean streams coming together under the choir, and I suspect she found them thanks to her antenna-like hands. I could not. Traffic obstacles inside and outside the cathedral prevented me from doing the "speed" walk with the Hartmann antenna, and my hands had not yet developed that level of sensitivity.

From Chartres I turned eastward and within a handful of hours was at Sens, whose cathedral is a hymn to the idea that God is light. Those vaulted volumes and strings of stone make a harp of radiance. No one of sensitivity — regardless of spiritual persuasion — can bathe in this atmosphere and remain unmoved.

Begun in 1140, it is the oldest of the great gothic cathedrals of France, and one wonders what impelled later builders to deviate from the sense of clear lightness that prevails. The transept roses[9] are flanked by vertical windows of stained glass. When the sun shines through them the effect is dazzling, warm, inviting, and the townspeople accept this invitation by using the doors under the roses. One of these doors gives access toward the market square, making a quick stroll through the cathedral a popular short-cut.

The choir is fenced-off like a gilded cage -- there is no access for ordinary mortals. However one can stand precisely in the center of the crossing, directly under the cupola, and get a charge of holy energy, 9'000 Bovis worth. One can imagine, in this temple of light, that a much higher vibrational rate would prevail if the "magic point" were not part of a pedestrian thoroughfare.

The energy falls away quickly here: if you choose to sit on one of the chairs just a few feet away the energy drops to a normal 6'500.

Signs of water were everywhere: stains on flagstones, mold at the base of many pillars. My dowsing rod wiggled constantly. I could easily believe there might be anywhere from ten to fifteen streams flowing beneath.

In the back of the cathedral my Geiger counter pinged through a range of three to nine counts, for an average of five to seven. Once again this was roughly half a normal baseline reading, which would be difficult to verify in the bustling town center.

One of the perils of travel is getting a bad meal, and my highly-rated country inn outside Sens served the one I didn't need. Sick all night, woozy and light-headed the next morning, I could not work as intended. I lost a day to the necessity of much rest and some bowls of rice. Restored to health, I returned to Sens the next morning to finish up my measures and diagrams, but time was now pressing on me. I was expected at Cluny that night, thus my plan to visit the cathedrals of Auxerre, Avallon and Autun, and to revisit Sainte-Madeleine de Vézelay en route, could not be carried out.

Only the pause at Vézelay could be salvaged. My first visit had been at a time of wet and cold, now it was warm and sunny. Once again I marveled at the long view down the nave to the brilliant choir and abside, the tunnel of soft light opening onto bright windows and sandblasted pillars, like a great bulb of white light.

Access to the center of the transept was blocked, so I had to seek the vibrational rate on the edge of the area. It measured only 7'000 on the Bovis scale. Puzzled, I tried again halfway down the nave and got the same value. Was it the church or was it me? Considering the recent damage done to my tripes I could believe it was me.

Sainte-Madeleine did have one defect I hadn't noticed on the first visit: the ceiling of the vault high above the choir area was white stucco, not pure stone. Could this be a reason for the higher readings on the Geiger counter? I got a count as low as seven but just as often up in the eleven to fourteen area, very close to usual baseline readings.

Once again I was aware of the stains of dampness on the floor and at the bases of pillars, but it struck me as useless to try to make a survey. And time was short.

Late afternoon was a long sprint down the autoroute eastward. Traffic was light, the road almost straight, and driving was easy. My thoughts dwelt on what I had learned and not learned during this frantic week of meeting gothic cathedrals. It was perfectly clear to me that their medieval builders worked within a framework of earth energies closely resembling what Ernst Hartmann had brought forward in the mid-twentieth century. They built their pillars on power points and moved force lines around in order to concentrate energy where they wanted it. Dowsing in every one of the edifices on my itinerary proved it. It was also clear they knew something about shielding their congregations from a portion of the cosmic radiations which pour down on us. And they exploited underground water, but my efforts to examine this feature in detail were not very successful.

Daily exposure to the play of vibrations inside these stone vessels had also affected me spiritually. It didn't bring me any closer to the concept of God that the clergy professed. Rather it served to magnify my sense that the Supreme Intelligence of our universe is all about waves of light and the flow of energy. My own energetic layers vibrated to the quivering invisible world, reminiscent of sensations experienced in the early months of Transcendental Meditation, described in Chapter Six. Awareness of what surrounds me kept on expanding.

Filled with such ideas, the red Toyota and I pulled up to the big house on the hill just before eight o'clock, and my patient hosts wafted me quickly to the terrace where sustenance awaited. As we dined Paul showed me the lobe antenna he had created from the template made last year, and they told me that a cousin had found a seventh ring around the concentric circles on the hill.

That proved to be only the beginning of a rapidly expanding system. With two of us dowsing and three family members to help with markers, during that weekend we defined a remarkable energetic pattern in the grass of that sheep pasture. There were not only seven rings in that first circular pattern, there were ten of them, just as there were ten rings in the contiguous formation just uphill.

Fanning out, we found a third set of ten rings in perfect alignment with the first two, but farther downhill. In the space between them the rectilinear Hartmann network prevailed, but wherever we found circles it had been suppressed. And we continued to find circles. Reflecting on our alignment, with its longer leg running downhill, we intuited some kind of a cross. And it was there. Quickly we found sets of rings to the right and left of the central system. We had our crossbar. And the dimensions of the affair began to be impressive. The horizontal crossbar measured two hundred seventy feet from end to end, and the vertical axis ran diagonally downslope for about two hundred feet. This short length suggested there might be more farther downhill.

Somehow, at sometime in the dim past, someone had imprinted the form of a cross on this seemingly uninteresting hillside. It was totally invisible except for the first ring at the top, which showed itself in summer. The long axis of the cross ran about twenty-four degrees to the east of true north, and it slanted over the irregular contours of the slope. Threatening weather drove us off the slope late in the afternoon, but we had been "running energy" all day and were sagging. Prudence and hunger took us back to the house.

What we had found was exalting, bizarre, fascinating, inexplicable. How had this been done? And why? Long hours of discussion followed in a "winter garden" veranda, with the thunderstorm drumming down on the glass panes overhead. In the long evening light of late May I explained the principles of the network to the others. Our talk ranged far into the realms of sonics, crystalline structures, and particle physics. Nor did we neglect the circles appearing every summer in the cereal fields of England, especially around Avebury and Stonehenge. We could not see how that phenomenon related to what we had found on the knoll. The cereal fields were flat, rolling country with plenty of rich soil, and the formations appeared from late May through August, when wheat, barley, rye and their cousins were near maturity, standing high and straight. Such were the canvases on which the cosmic artists painted.

In contrast, our little hillside grew short grass on thin layers of soil atop bedrock, and only one of the countless rings was actually visible in the summer season. What we had found seemed to have been imprinted, and this notion is the closest interface to the cereal field formations. Dowsers were finding that many of those circular designs -- and pictograms -- appeared where there was some kind of an energy imprint in the land.

Thus, we didn't understand what we had found, but five lively minds massaged a lot of ideas.

Archaelogical excavation was not an option, Paul pointed out. First, as previously stated, the hill was mostly solid rock with very little topsoil. Second, to commence an archaelogical dig would mean that layers of officialdom would invade the property and virtually confiscate the even tenor of their lives. There was a slump pit near the top of the formation, which could possibly be a place to dig in search of a cave entrance. It wasn't a particularly palatable idea.

Despite those reservations, they urged me to return as soon as possible, and that visit was set for two weekends hence. First order of business at that time would be to discover the vibrational rates according to Bovis, for the rain had driven us off the hill before I could do that.

At the end of the next week a very excited Paul telephoned to tell me he had found three more sets of circles lying in one arc of the presumed cross formation. The following Saturday I drove back to France, arriving in the village in the mid-afternoon. Before switching from driving mode to dowsing mode I needed some cooling-out time. Margaret remarked that I looked pale, almost white, but I felt fit enough after sitting a while at the big table under the tree.

Then Paul and I went out to attack the puzzle on the hillside. Checking his new discoveries, it was clear these blobs of energy were more like lozenges than circles in shape. Strong force lines connected them back to the central system, the original heart of what was unfolding.

Then it was time to see what the Bovis method could tell us, and it did tell us quite a lot.

The original circle, the brown ring in the grass, was the seat of great power, far exceeding everything else on the hillside. As usual, I went into a semi-meditational space before starting the readings. In my hand the pendulum registered 10'000 the first time, then 13'000 a minute or two later. We believed this, but we wanted a double-check, so we returned after supper and took three more measurements, fifteen minutes apart. The first time yielded 10'000 units, then fifteen minutes later it gave the same value again. And a minute later, as dusk deepened, it soared to 15'000.

That first circle, the only one that was ever visible to the human eye, contained an authentic power point. True spiritual power emanated at that point which we had already designated as the heart of the system.

Nowhere else on the hillside displayed such energetic extremes, although one other focal point reached 9'500. That was in the center of the southern group of rings, at the lower end of what we assumed would prove to be a cross. This reading helped to reinforce that idea.

Going to the opposing ends of the crossbar of that cross, the biometer gave me modest readings: 7'000 at the west end and the same at the east end.

Paul's three lozenges were just downhill from that westerly set of rings. The top one measured 7'500, the other two gave 6'500 units.

After two hours of this kind of work I felt totally drained. Margaret was right — I was tired. However, a good supper and some hours of good company under our prandial tree helped a lot, and I was refreshed enough for those evening readings.

The next day we worked at checking and refining everything we had found, then we began to discover embedded stones. First I found four flat stones forming part of an outer ring. Late in the day I found a new circle down near the gate at the bottom of the hill. Meanwhile Margaret found another arc of embedded stones elsewhere at the bottom of the hill.

Testing for significant radiation proved fruitless. I set the Geiger counter in the center of the original circle, the one we dubbed the "heart", and left it running a long time. One hundred and six minutes, to be precise, and the reading averaged out to 16.6 blips per minutes. This is a very normal figure, nothing unusual. Later I let it run for eighty-one minutes in the house, one hundred yards away. The reading averaged to 17.84 blips per minutes.

Once again quite normal. In my experience the difference between these two readings is without significance. Whatever else might be important on our hillside, radiation itself did not seem to be a factor.

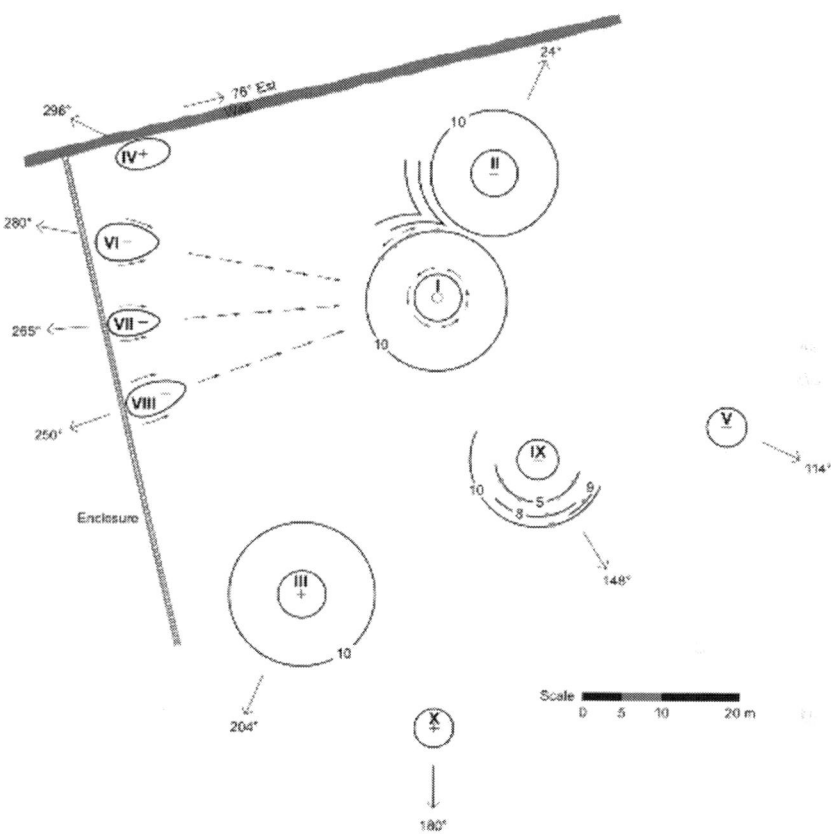

INVISIBLE CIRCLES OF ENERGY --- This constellation of energy circles replace the usual Hartmann grid. Between the sets of concentric circles the Hartmann grid is present. The only visible circle was the inner circle of the set labeled "I". The negative energy was centered in the set labeled "II".

It seemed clear that we were working in some kind of a galaxy or constellation of energetic imprints, but what they meant or how they developed was a total mystery. New possibilities continued to open up. It looked as if we could spend all the summer weekends on the hillside to continue defining whatever it was.

The weather was spoiling again and we supped that evening in the glass veranda. More family had arrived and we were eight to speculate and ponder.

One of the daughters wondered about the top floor where she and her siblings had grown up. So upstairs we went. Up there in the southeast bedroom, where she attested to frequent nightmares, the biometer registered 3'000. Those nightmares became entirely understandable, as well as the fact she had moved her sleeping room.

This day's work had drained me, and I slept like a log. Margaret had seen correctly, my basic energies had been lower than usual on arrival, and "running energy" had been consequently more tiring. This proved to be valuable intelligence for the future. In my late sixties at that time, I could not count on youthful, inexhaustible vigor every day of the year. One doesn't like to learn such lessons, but one must.

These good friends continued to provide warm hospitality over the years. We rambled their countryside, investigating churches, menhirs, hidden clumps of rocks, the remains of Roman hill forts, and quite ordinary-looking pastures.

We didn't work further on our mysterious knoll. It resisted analysis. Paul and I began exploring the region for other energetic power points and the leys that might link them with our network of circles. Taking the long axis of our little galaxy as a guideline we searched the countryside up and down that line trying to fit the whole thing into a ley. That didn't work either.

The following summer he led me along the crest of the knoll and into a forest where we found a number of large tumuli (burial mounds). The Bovis biometer had a field day, offering a huge range of measurements. Some of those mounds gave values up to 9'000 -- a vibrational level common to religious centers -- which to me suggested Celtic priests might rest there. Two of the tumuli, however, initiated me into another register. They insisted on 10'000 units, but with negative polarity. This was a new phenomena for me, in terms of the Bovis method, and I ran several double-checks. Absolute confirmation. And the final double-check was that I began to become very enervated, wiped out. Those negative mounds were draining my energy fast, and we had to get out of there. It took another of those good lunches under the trees, followed by a snooze in the August warmth, to restore my energies. Then we went to inspect the restoration taking place at the once great Abbey of Cluny, back via the ruins of Lournand, a peek into a dead-end cave, and then back to our terrace and nourishing trees. Everyone remarked on how tired I looked, and it is true my legs felt heavy. That lesson about running energies began to take on amplitude.

After this extravagant season of invisible discoveries on the knoll I spent the summer rambling the peaks with the Alpine Club. Dowsing gear can be cumbersome and my first priority was to limit the weight of the pack on my back. The lobe antenna never made these group hikes, the Geiger counter but rarely, and the pendulum almost always. With that I collected an important set of Bovis measurements on many of these excursions, with here and there a discovery.

The vast majority of the places we traversed present a perfectly normal vibratory rate. Occasionally a particular landscape feature might give 7'500 units, or 8'000, and one usually felt fresh and vigorous on such sites even after the effort of getting there.

Readers looking for moments of elation atop such summits as the Matterhorn or Mont Blanc are doomed to disappointment. Our group collected a lot of the secondary, unglamorous peaks which are within the capacities of ordinary middle-aged hikers, places most people have never heard of. Two places in particular captured my interest.

One Sunday morning a dozen of us scaled the Sidelhorn, a 9'000-foot crag south of the Grimsel Pass. In its upper reaches the Sidelhorn is a pyramid of granite blocks and slabs over which we clambered hand and foot. That granite sparkled with quartz, which registered 15'000 Bovis. Quartz is widely used in industry for its electrical qualities, and this granite was unusually rich with quartz. Testing at intervals, the pendulum gave me its 15'000 units three times.

Something else was happening on that summit: the Geiger counter went wild. I let it run for fifteen minutes, deriving a per-minute average of fifty-six counts, nearly quadruple a normal baseline reading. We were out for almost a week of daily hikes and I was able to run this test a number of times. Although most places in these mountains registered up to double the radiation measurable around my home (also in the mountains), nowhere else came close to the interplay of cosmic radiation with the quartz of the Sidelhorn.

Closer to home is the Plan-Nevé. It's a small balcony on the Muveran range, the front edge of a glacial *cirque*, visible from home with binoculars. The stone refuge is open and running full blast during the summer months, under the benevolent eye of a resident guardian, and the steep three-thousand foot hike attracts dozens of hikers on a fine day. I've been up there countless times, sometimes for the day, sometimes for overnight. One feels good on the Plan-Nevé, at 7'421 feet. Hikers arrive, dripping with three hours worth of sweat, wash their faces in the wooden tub, then relax for a moment before tackling the guardian's good soup and their own picnics.

Soon you hear "Gosh, it feels good up here!"

"Yes, I love to come up here, it's so invigorating," someone else will chime in.

After hearing all this repeatedly, and observing the phenomenon within myself, the taking of measurements was imperative.

The Geiger counter did not go wild. It offered a perfectly sober baseline reading. Nothing exceptional.

The Hartmann antenna, however, showed a fine crossing-point with positive polarity smack in the center of the terrace. On that point the Bovis biometer registered 10'000 angströms, and more, many times. One weekend I got values up to 19'000 on that point in the center of the terrace. Those occasions were late in the day and early in the morning -- when there was no one else present. No significant amount of quartz up there, it's a limestone mountain. Explorations elsewhere in the cirque, at least three hundred meters from the refuge, revealed values up to 8'500. The real power, a tonic power for human beings, bubbled on the terrace in front of the *cabane*.

In October I flew to North America again. Carol and I set off on another of our explorations, this one including the climb up Mount Lassen previously described. But first of all we went back to Buck's Bar, Bovis biometer at the ready.

On the way there we passed a difficult night in a famous country inn in one of the nearby mining towns. We slept badly. The next morning I did what I should have done before accepting the room: I dowsed it. The antenna showed that Carol and I had both slept with Hartmann crossing-points on our chests, and the Bovis biometer registered an unhealthy 5'000 units in the room and over the beds specifically. Another lesson learned the hard way.

The gorge of the Cosumnes River at Buck's Bar now revealed its full story, and we understood why it has a bad reputation. Fifty yards away, toward the broad and calm upstream sector, the biometer gave me normal values except for two or three spots where the reading reached 9'000 but with negative polarity. That again! In the center of the bridge, above the narrowing of the gorge, the pendulum reacted at sickly values from 3'000 down to 1'500.

I clambered cautiously down the mossy rocks south of the bridge. At water level, twenty feet downstream from the bridge, the reading was 2'500. Upstream, directly under the bridge, it was only 1'000.

Stated simply, the deep pools in that cauldron of rocks may appear to be an attractive place to swim on a hot summer's day, but the rocks are smooth and hard to climb up on, and the water roils and rumbles. Physically the place is a trap, ideal for psychic fall and death by drowning. Suicide attempts would succeed. The Hartmann antenna had given us part of the picture two years earlier, but the Bovis biometer hammered the nails in the coffin that is Buck's Bar crossing.

A week later we made the hike up Mount Lassen to find an absence of the global energy lines, previously mentioned. Other kinds of vibrations were buzzing merrily. On the summit area the biometer gave me 13'500 units on several points, and on one place it soared to 15'500. At these levels there is a stimulation of the human aura which affects everyone, consciously or not. Meanwhile the Geiger counter blipped away at a rate of about double the baseline measure. I don't see these two types of readings as being interlocking or mutually causative, although I have been nowhere else where I could use both instruments on lava. In other situations they behave quite independently of one another.

It would be needlessly repetitive and certainly boring to report all the readings taken everywhere on these trips. Wisdom reminds us that normal levels of energy prevail most of the time and in most places. What does emerge is that there are simple ways to evaluate those energies in places that we do sense as special and important, as well as those we inhabit continually.

These studies at home and abroad were having a subtle effect on me. It is said that knowledge is power, but the word "power" can be misleading. Knowledge leads to understanding, and my sensations of the world about me were evolving rapidly.

We are surrounded with energies of numerous kinds. In our ordinary daily life we pass through complex structures of vital forces without a thought. Cosmic radiation rains down on us, some of it benign and healthful, some of it not. A bewildering variety of radio, ultra-violet, infrared, gamma, and other waves shoot silently around and through our physical bodies without our knowing it. Two centuries ago humanity's experience of electricity was primarily limited to seeing a bolt of lightning, now it flows through the walls of our homes and offices with unmeasured effects on our physiological processes. For the most part we navigate blindly through this invisible soup.

[1]   Mary Summer Rain, *Spirit Song*. West Chester, PA: Schiffer, 1985. 156p. ISBN 0-89865-405-X.
      This was the first of a long series exploring and relating Native American visions, attitudes and way of life.

[2]   J. Havelock Fidler, *Earth Energy, a dowser's investigation of ley lines*. Northamptonshire: Aquarian Press, 1988. 192p., glossary, references, index. ISBN 0-85030-681-7.

[3]   Fidler, p. 23

[4]   Fidler, p. 71

[5]   André Simoneton, *Radiations des Aliments, Ondes Humaines et Santé, études et hypothèses*. Paris: Le Courrier du Livre, 1949, 1971,1977, reprinted 1990. 300p, charts, appendices, insert: Tableau de Classification des Aliments et Biomètre de A. Bovis. ISBN 2-7029-0058-5.

[6]   *Idem*, p. 61.

[7]   *Idem*, p. 60.

[8]   *Points of Cosmic Energy*, pp. 25-30

[9]   In the great cathedrals the huge stained-glass windows of circular design which illuminate the crossing, the nave and the choir are called "roses".

Chapter Nineteen

VIBRATING HORIZONS

Three years of exploring earth energies on two continents became a fascinating vocation. Spirit and body seemed to buzz with energy.

Moderating all this was the job of daily meditation. In my personal practice breath control is the balance wheel, leveling the playing field for the mantra's game of harmonizing the vibrational environment. Morning became the prime time for this tuning of my receptive fields, before sallying forth to meet the day's challenges. Evening meditation, less frequent, was always different, and usually much more intense. "Going within" at this time of day also serves as a kind of digestive tool, absorbing our reactions to the multitude of invisible influences which have been assailing the layers of our auras.

Meditation has the virtue of being eminently portable, requiring no physical baggage. On the other hand, these travels required much material preparation and impedimentia. My valises were getting dog-eared from being packed and unpacked, loaded and unloaded so often, and the station wagon pleaded with me to keep its overloaded springs well-greased.

Thus an inner sigh of relief swelled out when the next horizon to open up did so quite close to home. Early in 1991 Blanche Merz's research institute launched an ambitious program of seminars spread over the coming two years. There'd been nothing at all like this available earlier in my corner of the world — francophone Switzerland — and I seized the opportunity. With three colleagues, she opened a course of "continuing education" under the umbrella of her Institut de Recherche en Géobiologie. The IRG proposed a vast palette of tutorials on "hard" sciences (astronomy and astrophysics, geology and geophysics, electricity and microwaves) and "soft" sciences (Feng Shui, energy bodies, morphogenetic resonance, and several that I missed while traveling). There would be a field trip to study the strata of quarries and a cave system. In all of this Hartmann's discovery of the energetic gridwork served as pole star, the context against which we measured the subjects presented.

Although the technical material on offer was sufficiently tempting in itself, I was equally delighted at the prospect of meeting other people of similar persuasions without taking long trips. Architects made up one-third of the more than sixty participants, whereas the healing arts and people in the building industry accounted for most of the rest. Aside from Blanche and her trio of colleagues, only two persons identified themselves as geobiologists. One of these became my friend. Violette and I became friendly somewhere in the fourth seminar, while astrophysics was melting into geomagnetism and vagrant electricity. She analyzed earth energies for private clients, diagnosing how the Hartmann network impinged on their living space, how their daily lives were being subtly influenced, and what to do about it. Our friendship blossomed slowly, and as it did so she would ultimately open a door to dimensions I had not suspected.

Before that could happen another ambitious itinerary led me to a score of sacred sites and structures in France and England. Two of them — Paray-le-Monial and Wells — opened wider my perception of what cathedrals can do to stimulate the human spirit, to help focus our inner work. Revisiting some major sites allowed me this time to use the Bovis method to deepen my understanding of their power. These adventures also carried their quota of failures: I left Chichester without having solved its riddles, and at one megalithic site famous for its phenomena I stumbled away empty-handed.

The twelfth-century basilica of Paray-le-Monial is sometimes described as a scale model of the great Abbey of Cluny, which was destroyed during the French Revolution. Half an hour west of Cluny, nestled in hills on which graze the white Charollais cattle, Paray-le-Monial borders a tributary of the Loire River and is home to numerous religious communities. The basilica radiates serenity from the moment one spies it across the slow-moving waters of the Bourbince.

Paray is a vest-pocket cathedral, with only five pairs of pillars between the entry to the nave and the beginning of the abside's half-circle curve. Contrast that to eight pillars at Sens, thirteen at Vezelay, and sixteen double pairs at Bourges. Exquisite inside, it is rich in vibrations, a jewel of quiet power. The Bovis biometer gave me high readings for all the pillars, with the most powerful being the pair at the eastern end, guarding the altar. My pendulum registered from 12'000 up to 22'000 at the north pillar and from 14'500 to 25'000 at the south pillar. The central point of the transept, under the tower, read 14'500 up to 23'000. Paray-le-Monial gave nothing away to its big sisters.

Opposite the south pillar underground water had left its tell-tale seepage patches coming through the wall, and I chose to sit and meditate on a nearby stone bench facing the stained glass windows. The midday sun sent patterns of colored light through the windows onto me and my bench, as bells pealed high noon. At such moments the human spirit is under multiple assault of the most benign nature. The senses reel as sound, light, and the vibrations of artfully-sited old stones resonate on one's auric layers. It was easy to understand how the Christian faith could infuse worshippers in such an environment. I remained there for long minutes, bathing in the sensations. When finally I stood up, the pendulum indicated a rate of 30'000 angstroms. Angstroms are a measure of light, and that raw number truly reflected the glow infusing my being — a glow which lingered as I floated through the town.

Paray-le-Monial is "twinned" with Wells, in the postwar trend of small European cities developing reciprocal cultural relationships with their counterparts in other countries. Nothing could be more appropriate than to link these two spiritual power points.

Wells lies at the foot of the Mendip Hills in Somersetshire and takes its name from the springs flowing abundantly behind the cathedral. It is England's smallest cathedral city but, in my private opinion, the greatest in terms of spiritual impact. Glastonbury, quite a different expression of spiritual power, is only a quarter hour distant by road. From the road descending the Mendips you have Wells at your feet and the Glastonbury Tor is visible across the flat Somerset Levels.

Begun in the late twelfth century, Wells Cathedral was consecrated half a century later but not completed in all major details until the early fourteenth-century. Final touches kept the work going until the beginning of the sixteenth-century. Once again, one must pay tribute to the dogged determination that translated ecclesiastical vision into action for more than three hundred years, for more than a dozen generations of human enterprise. Successive bishops had to raise the money and marshal the forces of their parishioners. How willing were the workers, how willing the Bishop's flock, whose tithes (church taxes) kept the whole thing going?

After entering from the main door of the nave, one's vision is seized by the spectacular "scissors" arches which enclose and brace three sides of the transept. A fourteenth-century architect designed them to correct subsidence which threatened to bring down the oversized central tower, and their work of redistributing weight across the foundations remains successful in two ways.

Although the intent may have been only to reinforce the physical structure, in effect these scissors arches reinforce the spiritual impact of the entire edifice. They can be seen as a set of figure eights, set vertically with the bottom loop buried in the foundations, the top loop coming to a slight point. But a figure eight is also the mathematical sign of infinity, and the architect raised the visual impact by flanking the "waists" of his eights with two great eyes.

The effect is cosmic. This human spirit gasped the first time she drank in the view, and she still gasps on repeated visits. Heart and soul leap. These scissors arches, forming three sides of a square, magnetize the spirit.

Sun shimmers through the interior in endless breathtaking ways, sometimes projecting the colors of the windows on walls and pillars, most notably in the chapel of the apse (abside).

Under the tower, surrounded by scissors arches, I measured 22'000 Bovis units on this, my first visit in November 1991. During visits in later years the more generous summer sun helped send the vibrational rate on this power point soaring to 39'000 on one occasion. The "Lady Chapel", occupying the apse/abside in the eastern end, glows softly from its five windows of stained glass. Under that gracious vault I have measured up to 18'000 Bovis. The entire choir area resonates almost as high.

Wells has an abundance of water percolating down from the Mendips. Six springs bubble up in the gardens immediately behind the structure. They feed a moat surrounding the adjacent Bishop's palace and they contribute to the town's water supply. With such visual evidence all about me, I did not bother to dowse for water under the cathedral. It was enough to note the frequent signs of humidity around and within the edifice. The cathedral was built beside copious water flow, and all the engineering effort seems to have gone into controlling and diverting that abundance.

Wells claims to be England's first true Gothic cathedral, and it is certainly the most beautiful and the most spiritually powerful of those I have seen. It is not, however, the oldest cathedral in the country. The key word here is "gothic". The Norman conquest in 1066 -- a century before construction began at Wells -- was followed immediately by a spate of cathedral building in the so-called "Norman" style, superseding a mode called "pre-Conquest Romanesque."

Wells is at the foot of hills, on the edge of what was once a vast ocean bay. Chichester, by contrast, is a coastal town where one sniffs salt air, another vest-pocket city with a delightful small cathedral right in the center. It lies a few miles inland but an arm of the harbour reaches to the city's edge. This visit -- my second -- came on a mid-November Saturday, sunny and cold. Market day was bustling, I'd had to wait half an hour to park the car, and a good-natured British vitality prevailed.

Chichester presented some puzzles. My notes from two years earlier confirmed "the Hartmann network is alive and well" in the positioning of pillars. This time I was concerned to see what the Bovis biometer might reveal. I was learning that values in these sacred sites could, and usually would, fluctuate considerably, at any given time or day. It became absolutely imperative to repeat measurements at intervals, when time permitted. From a choir area in front of the crossing, through that transept and into the altar space beyond, the readings bounced around between 10'000 and 21'000 angstroms. Was this simply a reflection of the vivacity of the town center just outside? Such an explanation seemed a bit thin, I thought. It was tempting to think that high vibrations might simply be more volatile than the "normal" baseline 6'500 in which we lead the major part of our daily lives. Whatever, the overall atmosphere was very satisfying to the soul.

And that was in spite of a rather chopped-up interior. Here was no sweeping architectural panorama but instead a series of visual obstacles, as if a breathtaking view down the fine nave had to be prevented. And there were some roped-off areas which quite naturally piqued my curiosity.

In the side aisle I stood with my back to a pillar, trying to be discreet as I worked with the pendulum. When I looked up there was an official-looking man staring quizzically at me. Oh dear, this had to happen some day! What do they do to non-clergy caught playing with earth energies in cathedrals? In the days of the Inquisition it would have meant a quick trip to the witch-burning stake, but what more refined tortures had the twentieth-century invented for blasphemers of temples? I could sense my Huguenot ancestors twitching in their graves. Then I realized this gentleman's expression was not menacing; there was the trace of amiability around his mouth, closer to smile than scowl.

"Are you finding out interesting things about our Cathedral?" he asked, in a rather jocular mode.

"Um, yes, there is wonderful energy here," I replied blandly, as unheretically as possible.

The man's blue shop coat with a badge clearly indicated a non-clerical caretaker, a verger or sexton or even a guard, but his strong jaw seemed to be grinning. My momentary sense of alarm faded.

He agreed with me about the energy and then dropped his little bombshell: his father had been a dowser and had explored the cathedral in his own way. Emboldened, I asked about the construction they called the "screen" but which looked a lot like a bridge crossing the nave as if it were a river. This space was roped-off.

"Would you like to step inside?" he asked.

Would I ever! This screen affair was really two parallel partitions composed of three vaulted arches with a space between and the bridge walkway overhead. It crossed the nave just in front of the transept, beyond it was the choir occupying the center of the transept. All this was totally unusual. I accepted instantly. So the man in the blue coat opened the velvet rope to admit me, and then he strode off with a friendly wave.

The puzzle grew murkier. The Bovis method showed a very low reading of 2'500 just in front of the velvet rope, and it gave only 3'000 inside the screen, under the bridge. Why? I could not imagine, for there was nothing else to see, nothing to examine, nothing to dowse in this empty space between the partitions.

Such a low reading might have made sense if there had been a sepulchre, for example, but there was no visible tomb, nothing marked on the floor to indicate something underneath. This was just one of the befuddlements I met in Chichester.

Back of the transept/choir area is a presbytery with the altar, backed by an abstract expressionist tapestry full of movement and an explosion of light. Here was yet another obstacle to a panoramic view down the main axis, but the pendulum gave me readings ranging up to 16'000 Bovis in the presbytery, where a small congregation could sit. My reading soared to 20'000 at the altar, in front of that blazing tapestry. Lots of energy here. There seemd to be a steady increase in vibrational force as one moved eastward from the sickly values inside the screen/bridge. The cathedral builders of the Gothic period knew all about these energies, of this I now had no doubt. Modern clergy frequently make adjustments in the use of space that suggest insensitivity to the vibrational realm, but here in Chichester it appeared they understood how to situate worship services in the place of power.

There were more surprises as I moved toward the Lady Chapel in the eastern end. Two smaller chapels flanked the entry to this luminous apse, and the one on the left, dedicated to St. John the Baptist, riveted my attention. Above the altar and beneath the window of St.John is a *"reredos"*, another kind of screen. In this case it is a painting of mural proportions, created by Patrick Proktor in 1984, only a handful of years before my first visit to Chichester. Cathedral publications declare that the reredos was inspired by works of Grünewald and Poussin, but it reminds me immediately of my old friend *"Whence Come We? What Are We? Whither Go We?"*, Paul Gauguin's spiritual testament of 1897. (See again my Chapter Two.)

Twice as wide as it is high, the reredos depicts the meeting of Christ and St. John, the latter's preaching, the former's baptism. Once again we are in a natural setting flanked by trees, this time with water much in evidence, hills, a mountain and clouds in the background. Greens and flesh tones dominate, as in Gauguin. Twenty people fill the scene, chatting, washing, kneeling, many of them pointing to the baptism, to the preaching, to the crucifixion.

Gauguin's images dramatized the existential nature of his questions. In contrast, Proktor's personnages seem to be concerned with the affirmation of important acts. One of them looks you squarely in the eye and points to John pouring water over a husky young Jesus.

Then, turning into the terminal space of the edifice, the Lady Chapel, one is struck by the light flooding in through the stained-glass windows on three sides. Expecting to find a high vibrational value, I was astonished that the pendulum would not go past 7'000. Then came another velvet rope barring entry to the sanctuary and its altar flanked by candelabra and topped by a splendid arched window bright with color. At their feet is a mosaic inlay, a most unusual mosaic illustrating the signs of the zodiac.

Here, on the planetary mosaic, the vibrational rate leapt upward, to hold at 17'000, the highest reading in the eastern third of the cathedral. How delightful to my heretical sensitivities! Before leaving Chichester I purchased two illustrated booklets from the cathedral shop. Each of them gives the same one-line mention of this astrological design, but neither dares explain its significance.

After my encounter with the verger in the blue coat I had felt emboldened to place the Geiger counter on an inconspicuous ledge while I continued my explorations. Ready to leave now, I retrieved it and calculated the average counts per minute. The figure was 9.3 blips. Outside it gave me a reading of fourteen counts. About a week later the Geiger counter gave me almost identical values inside and outside Canterbury Cathedral. In other words, these great stone vaults shelter their sheep from one-third of the ambient cosmic radiation. What was true in France was equally true in England.

It is satisfying to explore and to learn, to sense phenomena, to feel things *happen*, and it is equally disappointing when things that are reputed to happen don't. My experience at the Rollright Stones is a case in point.

This is a well-known megalithic complex in the deep countryside of Oxfordshire, a few miles northwest of Chipping Norton. Mostly waist-high, about seventy rather nondescript stones — named the "King's Men" — form a circle in a field next to the Cotswold Ridgeway. Across the road the "King Stone" stands isolated inside a fenced enclosure. "The Whispering Knights" are another fenced-in group not far away.

There are endless folktales and traditions associated with the Rollright stones. Some people have experienced electric shocks and anomalies there, as well as light phenomena. There is more than one report of ghosts and fairies. Researchers grouped around Paul Devereux created the Dragon Project to investigate and, if possible, diagnose what was really happening on this site[1].

They used magnetometers, ultrasound receivers, and geiger counters. If I dare make a sweeping generalization derived from Devereux's pages, the sum of the Dragon Project was that ultrasound, magnetic and radiation anomalies did exist on the site. Their detectors clicked away at various times, most often in mornings it would seem, and in varying proximity to certain stones. Magnetic pulsations were observed. I have not followed this project over the years.

Devereux summed up the first dozen or so years of sporadic work in the following terms:

"Rollright's spirit of place, its *genius loci*, has been a patient teacher, and those of us involved in this unorthodox work still make our way to the site from time to time, to learn a little more."[2]

Arriving there a year or so after those lines were published, I can only confirm that the Rollright stones do not display their secrets with any kind of generosity. It was a very cold day in mid-November, just a few degrees above freezing, windy, and my hands were not happy dowsing. Nevertheless I was able to confirm that the Hartmann network was definitely present; it had not been supplanted. Some of the stones were on crossing points, but they did not offer any pendulum reactions.

My compass behaved in a very erratic fashion at thirty degrees east of north. The geiger counter gave a low reading inside the ring, similar to the interior of a cathedral. Out on the road it blipped back up to a normal benchmark value.

To my considerable surprise, Bovis values were generally low in the ring and higher outside. I cannot explain why the pendulum registered a very normal 6'500 angstroms on the circle and inside it but increased to 8'000 when I moved five meters outside (noted on opposite sides). And then five meters farther outside it swung back to 6'500. What was that all about?

This invisible vibrational ring was concentric to the stone circle, which of course suggests a relationship to the galaxy Paul and I discovered on the hillside near Cluny. My ring was outside the stones, but the noted dowser Tom Graves reports finding something similar inside the stones. From the centre of the circle he dowsed seven concentric rings of energy with alternating polarities. He had also found weaker patterns of the same kind in a few other locations in England and had heard of others.[3]

Other than this sniff in the dark — I had not yet read Graves —Rollright defeated me. I knew something was going on, simply because there are so many reports of it. My gear sniffed subtle energies here and there without yielding anything resembling an "aha". I cannot improve on Devereux's cautious judgement.

Ten days later I visited Stanton Drew, a set of stone circles half an hour west of Bath. At 370 feet diameter, the largest of the three is the second largest in England. For me these stones produced much higher Bovis values than the Rollright circle, suggesting the reality of some of the reported electrical phenomena. On the big circle I measured 9'000 and 10'000 vibrations on the compass points, with similar results on the remaining stones of the adjoining northeast circle. This was a dark and cold afternoon, but not as frigid as my midday at Rollright.

Stanton Drew gave me something further to think about in relation to the mystery at Cluny: in the northeast circle my dowsing gave the impression of two inner circles, concentric rings inside the one marked by stones. Added to Tom Graves' findings, here was evidence to support the notion that Paul and I were not wholly insane.

It was getting colder, as one would expect in November. Before setting out for Avebury I had to scrape the windscreen free of heavy frost. Roadside puddles had become ice rinks for the tiny creatures. It was bitter cold among the stones, but their power was up and running -- quite unevenly it turned out. This was my second visit to Avebury but I had not yet acquired the Bovis method on that earlier occasion. This time I made a large tour, measuring, measuring, measuring.

In spite of the cold I could feel the vibrations tingle warmly up into my fingers as I worked. This was a new and recent tendency. There was a wide variety of readings, from subnormal to cathedral strength. In the southwest quadrant, closest to the car park, I found values up to 10'000, usually the taller stones. There was one real anomaly -- a stone that yielded only 5'000 on one side and 4'000 on the other. Disbelieving, I ran this several times, and that 4'000 would not budge. It was as if the pendulum hit a rock wall at that level. What was wrong here? This stone was between mates that ran 8'500 in one direction and 10'000 in the other. I came to a preliminary conclusion that this stone might have been restored to its upright position, possibly on the wrong spot or possibly rotated to a compass angle it didn't appreciate.

At this point I retired to the nearby pub to thaw out my hands around a bowl of hot soup. It was a day made for lounging by a blazing log fire, but the tyrannical schedule pushed me out again. There was only one chance this year to commune with these stones, and I could not dilly-dally.

In the northwest quadrant I measured every stone. There were a few which registered a normal 6'500, which I thought abnormal for here. And there were others which stood proudly at 10'000 to 13'000. There was so much power here that it is impossible to take it all in. The circles are incomplete, having been ravaged in earlier times (as described in Chapter Seventeen), but their conception is vast, dwarfing anything else I had seen.

All these stones contain visible inclusions of quartz, which of course has well-known piezo-electric qualities. This would account for much of the tingling energy people feel here. Let me add that, in my personal opinion, a quartz-bearing granite stone can produce more "punch" — however slight in absolute terms — than a calcium-rich limestone boulder. I think of all nature as alive and vital — to me a standing stone is as alive as a tree.

This attitude underlies Tom Graves' judgement that standing stones are sited with as much care as acupuncture needles. They are placed so as to stimulate Mother Earth's energies. They are her therapy. Graves considers sacred sites in general, not only stone circles and churches, but wells, special trees, roadside crosses and everything analogous to be part of this system[4]. In these few words I do not pretend to do justice to his landmark work.

My own reaction to Avebury after this second visit was that it is one of the world's greatest earth energy centers. Everything I had read about it predisposes to such a judgement, and moving among these masses of vibrating energy confirms it. I flirted with the idea of coming to live in the heart of such energy. Immediately, however, spirit reminded me that my home in the Alps was also an energetic heartland in which I had thrived beyond my wildest dreams.

More of Avebury's power came to me the following day in Bath, via the printed page. After a brief visit to Bath Abbey — from which one of my early Huguenot ancestors had been married in 1605 — I wandered into a bookstore. Metaphysics were upstairs, where I found a knowledgeable young man who quickly put into my hands a new book about English earth mysteries, the tale of a dowser's long ramble from the tip of Cornwall to the Norfolk Coast.

The Sun and the Serpent chronicles the tracing of a major ley, a dominant alignment of sacred sites defining a corridor that stretches three hundred miles across the island[5]. Starting at the farthest southwestern tip of Cornwall, Hamish Miller and his scribe Paul Broadhurst spent several years following Miller's angle irons on the northeasterly tack of the two alignments called "Michael" and "Mary". Twisting and turning around one another, Michael and Mary led ultimately to Hopton-on-Sea on the Norfolk coast. That's where the line points directly to the solar fire of sunrise on May 1, Mayday, called Beltane by the ancients. The alignment passes through multiple churches, sacred rocks and mounts, megaliths and markers of many types, of which the Avebury complex is the center, the mother temple to which all roads led. Taken as a corridor one kilometer in width, the ley passes through sixty-three churches, of which more than half are dedicated to either St. Michael, St. Mary or St. George.

Miller found the Michael and Mary lines to have individual characteristics that enabled him to define their meanderings, a kind of dance around each other. At Avebury the dance becomes complicated, inscribing loops on the landscape before resuming the basic compass directions. I thought how wonderful, how totally intriguing it would be to follow this trace from one end to another. My wonderment and daydreaming had to be tempered by the realities of life: how impossible for me ever to organize such a safari.

However, another point on the alignment lay on my itinerary: Glastonbury. My first visit had been brief and hampered by nasty weather. This second trip was subject to November's vagaries, with schizophrenic cumuli in the skies, uncertain whether they wanted to be dark or bright.

En route I paused to gaze at the Long Barrow at Wellow, on the soggy green slope opposite the village. Barrows are "*tumuli*", burial mounds with sacred aspects. On impulse I hopped out of the car and began the trek to inspect this mound. About halfway there I realized I had forgotten the pendulum and the Bovis scale. Short memories make for long walks, but this little hike over wet meadows and a muddy trackhike was at least interesting. One bridge over a rushing brook, four stiles, a covey of sixteen grouse, hunters shooting in the wood on the next hill, rabbit-eared sheep heavy with wool, and then finally the barrow. The grouse and the sheep were the best part of this little adventure, because the barrow was closed. It was clearly unsafe, the sod and rock roof sagging dangerously. The vibration level around the edges was as one would suspect for a burial mound: very low, hovering around 2'000 units.

Glastonbury, however, made up for this disappointment. The town and the Tor were radiant under clearing skies, and the Saturday afternoon ambiance in the main street was festive. Arthurian legend holds Glastonbury and its Tor to be the Avalon of yore, and this sparkling day reminded me of the tiny port town of Avalon on California's Santa Catalina island, another place that sparkles but in a different way.

Miller traces both the Michael and Mary lines through Glastonbury, the Abbey and the Tor. Not many years after this my second visit the geomancer Nicholas Mann, in the course of tracing King Arthur and his Avalon through the Wessex landscape, revealed an even more powerful alignment[6]. He cites the work of researcher Terry Walsh to the effect that "the sites which comprise the St. Michael Line are on a great circle"[7].

Walsh's research, says Mann, finds eleven great circle alignments passing through Glastonbury. The St. Michael line, he reports, "passes through Zagorsk -- the center of Russian Orthodox Christianity -- and Lake Titicaca", where the Inkan deity Wiraqocha emerged. By widening the line to become a corridor, it could embrace Kailash, the sacred mountain of Tibet, and Uluru, the magic red rock mound of central Australia also known as Ayers Rock[8].

The grounds of the ancient Abbey radiate spiritual calm four-and-a-half centuries after the once-great cathedral was reduced to ruin by the forces of Oliver Cromwell, acting under King Henry VIII during that period of British history called the "Dissolution". Fragments of walls and gothic arches remain to testify to the grandeur that developed slowly over a thousand years, starting from the known Celtic chapel of the fourth century. Legend carries it even further back in time, telling us that Joseph of Arimathea, the uncle of Jesus as well as being a rich man from interests in Cornish tin mines, settled here with a small band of family and disciples a few years after the Crucifixion. Joseph is alleged to have built the first "Christian" church on these grounds, using wood, stone and mud. The wreckage of the Lady Chapel now stands where Joseph built.

One can deduce the form of the Abbey from its remnants, and the bases of the pillars are still there as stone diamonds in the grass. The nave was eight columns long before the transept, and beyond that crossing six more pairs of pillar bases mark the length of the choir-sanctuary up to the high altar.

This was the first time I had surveyed the ruins of a cathedral instead of one still alive and functioning. Thus it was fascinating to discover that centuries of decrepitude have not erased the energy. Those foundation stones of the nave radiate up to 9'000 on the Bovis scale, and the overall layout respects what we now call the Hartmann grid. (One wonders what they called it a millenium ago?) In the center of the transept the vibrational rate rises to 12'500, which value also illuminates the vestiges of the altar. The Lady Chapel measures 10'500 and 11'000, but the sarcophagus on the lower level yielded only 4'500.

On this luminous day there was no mud and rain to hamper my ascension of the Tor. Glastonbury nestles at the foot of this hill, whose summit is crowned by a tower which is the last vestige of a church of St. Michael. Make no mistake about it, this is one of the sacred sites that mark the Michael ley.

It's a pleasant hike up this 500-foot hill, from which one sees a brilliant landscape in all directions. Just a few miles away rises the mass of Wells Cathedral, another point on the Michael alignment. Not too many thousands of years ago the Tor was an island rising from marshes and inlets of the sea, and that seabed is now the Somerset "levels", bounded on the northeast by the Mendip Hills which shelter Wells.

St. Michael's tower sits on what seems clearly to be the intersection of two powerful leys, not just the Michael line but also the Mary line. My only dowsed evidence for this fact at the time was finding that the Hartmann lines are pulled tightly together all over the Tor. Hamish Miller, however, clearly designates an intricate interweaving of Michael and Mary all over the Tor[9]. Inside the structure, which is open to the east and west, there were twelve force lines jammed together and the pendulum showed great pulsation, with Bovis readings of 11'500 and 19'500.

Stone benches line the two solid sides of the tower, and all of us casual tourists who sat there enjoyed a state of grace. When you are basking in 19'500 angstroms you are in total beatitude. People felt friendly, chatty and exalted. A man named Andrew, who said he had dowsed the site twenty years earlier, now mused about organizing an ecological-metaphysical exposition. A dark-haired young man said he walked up regularly "to manifest...to sort myself out." For me, it was simply being gloriously happy to be alive at that crystalline moment in time, a sunny, mild November day with the spiritual beauty of Wessex rippling in every direction, with unknown companions who obviously felt similar emotions. If the whole world could be one vast power point, humanity could not possibly go to war!

That reflection is the appropriate place to end this excursion through English sacred sites. No need to bore you with interesting observations at Gloucester, Bath, St. Albans, Winchester nor Canterbury -- they could not surpass the pure joy of that afternoon atop the Tor.

[1] Paul Devereux, then editor of the periodical *The Ley Hunter*, has detailed the work of the Dragon Project in his book *Places of Power*. London: Blandford (Cassell), 1990., subtitled *Secret Energies at Ancient Sites: A Guide to Observed Or Measured Phenomena*. 224p., bibliography, index. ISBN 0-7137-2064-6.
[2] *Idem*, p.95.
[3] Tom Graves, *Needles of Stone Revisited*. Glastonbury: Gothic Image, rev. ed. 1986 (originally published 1978 as *Needles of Stone*). See page 35 of 227p. Notes, index. ISBN 0-906 362-07-5
[4] *Idem*, Chapter Five, "Needles of Stone", pp. 68-94.
[5] Hamish Miller and Paul Broadhurst, *The Sun and the Serpent*. Cornwall: Pendragon Press, 1989, 1990, 1991. 216 p., index, bibliography, maps and photographs. ISBN 0-9515183-1-3.
[6] Nicholas R. Mann, *The Isle of Avalon, sacred mysteries of Arthur and Glastonbury Tor*. London, Green Magic, rev. ed., 2001 (after Llewellyn Books, 1996). 189p., index, bibliography, appendix, copiously illustrated.
[7] Terry Walsh, *Global Sacred Alignments*. Glastonbury, University of Avalon Press, 1993.
[8] Mann, pp.76-77.
[9] *The Sun and the Serpent*, pp. 153-156.

Chapter Twenty

FREQUENCIES JOIN THE PARTY

Like the bears with whom I feel a deep kinship, winter induces a kind of hibernation. Hunting terrestrial energy takes on another character when the ground is covered with snow. The dowser's response still operates, but it is disagreeable to work with freezing hands. I choose to give such work a rest during the season of clearing snow, skiing and snowshoeing. It's a time for putting order into one's field notes and reading the accounts of those more accomplished researchers who have published.

My fall ramble across southern England had taken precedence over the IRG seminar schedule, so I contacted my new friend Violette to catch up on what my travels had caused me to miss. On the telephone it was clear that she had a lot to tell me, and in turn she wanted to hear in detail about my energy browsings in England. With icy road conditions prevailing on my mountain, and a forecast of fresh snow up here, she didn't want to come here. Instead she invited me to spend a late January weekend in Bern.

During Saturday and Sunday we explored endless facets of geobiology, as well as the IRG sessions, which had focused on architecture. Eye-popping revelation lay elsewhere: in Violette's library of personal notebooks. She allowed me to peruse her archives of interesting sites she had dowsed and analyzed. Using a sophisticated dowsing wand called a "Lecher" antenna she was able to uncover an astonishing range and depth of information. It was calibrated and had a cursor that slid up and down to select wave lengths. Her pocket field notebook was filled with wave lengths — or "frequencies", it's the same thing — identified with all kinds of tangible and intangible matter. She could distinguish between various cultures such as Celtic or Roman; various spiritualities such as Christian or Druidic or Buddhist; various substances such as underground streams or underground pipelines; or various qualities such as victory or defeat, balance or imbalance. The possibilities seemed endless.

This tool looked vaguely like a draftman's T-square whose long blade bore ruler-like calibrations over which the cursor moved. Flat copper wires were imbedded in the transparent blade, and polarity could be switched by repositioning a wire slipped into the hollow handle. This was a Rolls-Royce among dowsing gear, relegating my trusty Hartmann lobe antenna to the status of a Model T Ford. As she explained its operation I could see that it opened up a more refined and powerful method of interrogating almost anything at all, not limited just to invisible lines of force.

We exchanged many stories and studied each other's work, but I was riveted on the idea of this Lecher antenna (named after the man who invented the concept in the 1920s.) How could I obtain such a tool?

"You have to take one of Schneider's seminars. He requires you learn it from him. It's the only way," she informed me.

It appeared that a German physicist named Reinhard Schneider had reworked the original Lecher concept, manufactured the wands and controlled their distribution. You learned it from him, then you could buy it. Following this track wrote itself onto my mental agenda, along with a note to refresh my command of German. I had just begun to speak that language with reasonable fluency at the time of leaving Düsseldorf twenty years earlier in order to marry my French-Swiss painter. In the interval, despite many brief sallies into Germany and our germanophone Swiss cities, my ear for the Teutonic tongue had slowly eroded.

My new friend had other strings to her bow. Getting acquainted with her airy, light apartment I discovered that she was also a sculptress, ceramicist and painter, reviving in me the scent of artists' studios, the tang of expositions, somewhat somnolent in me — but not dead -- since the death of my husband. We found many other points of *rapprochement,* including the satisfaction of meditation but also that we both liked cross-country skiing. We were close contemporaries, born six months apart. She had honey-blonde hair and was shorter than me — most other women are — with an open, welcoming expression on her serene features. She was easy to like. Molly had been my first spiritual companion, Violette became the second.

To finish that weekend we went down into central Bern to visit the Kunsthalle, which was presenting an exposition of the works of the Delaunays, Robert and Sonia. I love major art and have visited hundreds of exhibitions, but it had never occurred to me that one could measure their spiritual effect in a quantitative way. Yet this is surprisingly easy. Violette introduced me to the concept of measuring the vibrations of works of art, using the Bovis meter. If cathedrals, why not fine art? We did not make an exhaustive study that day, but I saw how the wide range of themes interesting to artists could exhibit an equally wide range of vibration. Specifically, I measured only a few canvases, reflecting Bovis rates ranging from 5'000 to 8'000.

More geobiological seminars tempted me as winter melted into spring. The IRG's program was rich and varied. In February there was a controversial presentation on microwaves, contrasting the vehement attack of a renegade biologist against their effect on food with a detailed scientific report demolishing his position. The following month a medical doctor kept us fascinated with information about both the physical body and its interaction with the subtle energies layered about the body, and about Chinese concepts of medicine, including acupuncture.

On seminar days Violette and I lunched together, talking dowsing all the time. My ears twitched madly about the possibilities of using her Lecher antenna to unravel the mystery at Cluny, as just one example. I told her about an interesting energy line in the meadow in front of my house, one that Blanche had tried to interpret, and we agreed on a weekend visit. With the snow season well past, Violette came to my chalet the first weekend in May, bringing her special antenna.

On the highway slanting across the fields down front there is a spot where underpowered cars had trouble, or would boil over in summer. In the early days after my husband had built the chalet, the first house below the village, he had observed all this automotive stress and had toyed with the idea of building a service garage there. Over the years we observed cars hesitating, sputtering, losing power, losing traction in snow, always at that spot. Their electrical systems seemed to cut out right there. Several years before Violette's visit I had observed the spring snow melt was producing a perfect circle in the field just below my fence. I pounded a stake into its center, as a marker. When the thaw was complete I had used the lobe antenna and my pendulum to find a line, and there was one. To my considerable amusement, it crossed the highway at that exact spot, and it seemed to extend some distance towards the east.

To add spice to the situation, one has to understand the geology of this immediate area: one of Switzerland's two salt mines lies deep underground, beneath the canyon that plunges beyond the forest fringe at the far edge of the meadows. The mine is entered via a tunnel in the bottom of the canyon, and the galeries extend and spread deep into the mountain in the direction of our villages at much higher altitude. In the old days miners lived in these villages and hiked up and down the canyon walls to reach their work on a daily basis, snow or not. Some people claim that an old gallery reached high up and was accessible from my village. Of this I am skeptical, the altitude difference is too large. There would have to be more than one thousand feet of vertical shaft somewhere, and I've seen no evidence suggesting that. However, we were willing to believe that our "power loss" point on the state road could be somehow related to the salt mine.

My little story had intrigued Blanche, and she had come up here a second time to examine the phenomenon. Using her Hartmann antenna, she tracked the line across the road as I had done and settled on a point about fifty feet inside the field. Here she sensed — how? — an important anomaly and hypothesized some kind of emanation from the mine far below that could perturb the magnetic field. Her later work inside the mine corroborated this impression.

In the mine, she wrote, "you no longer find the east-west lines of the global network, and the Bovis values fall, oscillating between 2'500 and 4'000 units"[1]. Deep inside the earth she also found an absence of natural radioactivity, whereas aboveground she cited double the natural rate.

Using the Lecher, angle rods, and my lobe antenna, Violette confirmed the point we had found and diagnosed it as a downward spiral of energy. On that point the Lecher resonated to the frequency for salt. She tested for several other elements for which she had wave lengths, with no visible reaction, but the device was definite about salt. She found the point to be on a minor fault line running westward, and at the road it is intersected by an underground stream (probably the same one running downhill just east of my chalet). That alone could probably be enough to interfere with the electrical systems of cars already laboring. Violette tracked the line back toward the point where I had first observed melt, and it seemed to continue its westerly bight (running a few yards below my vegetable garden).

What was impressive to me was the reaction of the Lecher antenna to the faint emanation of salt, but also the discovery of a fault line hidden under the meadows. My existing tools could not give me this level of information. It was clear that I would have to work on my German in order to take that seminar.

Violette pointed out that Schneider spoke rapidly and softly, so I would have to retrain my ear using linguistic cassette tapes. She offered to help me plug the holes in whatever technical concepts that I failed to grasp completely.

Two months later I was in a tiny Austrian hotel on a hillside south of Innsbruck, scribbling Reinhard Schneider's effusions and equations as fast as the limits of my German vocabulary would permit. Fortunately there were lots of printed hand-outs and he worked much from a blackboard. Overnight my German began to come back and I was at ease with my handful of classmates and our professor. His scientific explanations were sometimes hard for me to follow, but the essentials got through. In a nutshell, it was all about translating resonance into wavelengths.

First we trained on a plastic forked wand, also calibrated, and I finally got that to work for me. The Lecher antenna proved to be more stubborn for all of us, and we worked intensively during a long ramble through field and forest. It is necessary to hold the device with a particular grip that is stressful in the hands and wrists until you get accustomed to it. That evening in my room I discovered the stress of these two instruments had created two small hematomas on my wrist, one of which opened and bled copiously.

Schneider droned on the second day, dropping many pearls of wisdom I didn't understand but also dropping tidbits of useful information that I did grasp. He ended the workshop with a convincing demonstration involving four pieces of electronic gear.

He placed us all in a line across the room, firmly holding our new Lecher antennae in the approved fashion. Then he instructed us to set the cursor at a wavelength of 12,45 centimeters. That frequency doesn't correspond to anything I have ever learned about since, but it was tuned to his gear. He told us later that it was set to 35 and 70 megahertz.

Whatever, when he pushed the button on his transmitter, our antennae all wobbled and dipped in unison, like so many electronic chorus girls.

This was very impressive! We just stood there, holding our wands at attention, and the moment he zapped, they dipped. As a demonstration that we could believe in our new tool, it was totally convincing. Physics already dealt with scads of invisible phenomena such as radio waves and cosmic rays. Schneider had devised an instrument which respected scientific rules but could also be used to detect types of offbeat information that entered spiritual domains. In this he was simply following a trend in modern physics that began with Einstein's studies in field theory.

It is worth a few lines to describe my trip homeward from Austria. As the seminar started I began to sniffle, which I passed off as "Heuschnupfen" (hayfever), but I suspect the young Frau Doktoresse with whom I had become friendly was not deceived. Nor was my throat. A cold had me in its grip and it got worse throughout the seminar. By the time of the homeward trip I was sensing this would become another bout of bronchitis.

I had taken two days to get there, enjoying the hospitality of friends overnight on a hillside overlooking Lake Constance, but I was determined to get home as quickly as possible. Health and weather combined to render this long day on the road unforgettable in the sense of "will it ever end?" Threatening clouds were socked in already as I coughed my way up and over the Arlberg Pass and from then on the weather became heavier and heavier. Rain was intermittent but became chronic. Heavy cloudbursts manifested, the biggest one hitting near Châtel St. Denis, only forty-five minutes from home. It was a wall of water, and traffic on this main expressway slowed to a crawl, surfed, and then simply stopped. Along the way I had stopped often, for a bowl of soup, a sandwich, a nap, anything to keep me going and get me home. After eleven hours (550 kilometers) I was there. Bed never felt so good and sleep has rarely been so long and beneficial. The next day, amidst the deepening respiratory symptoms, I observed that, even so, a healing had occurred in Austria: the chronic network of tiny broken veins in my right eye had disappeared. This proved to be temporary, but it did get my attention.

Had our work with all kinds of vibrations somehow touched a frequency critical for the eyes?

Violette called two days after my return to inquire how I got along with Schneider and the Lecher. I told her how hard it was.

"Practice, practice, practice," she urged. Also we consulted our agendas for another meeting and made a tentative date for the fall.

Summer of that year, 1992, saw me on the mountains constantly. It was a season of intense alpinism, during which -- with my Alpine Club companions -- I climbed much rock, learned how to be a "lead" climber on a rope, and ascended the renowed Miroir de l'Argentine for the second time. Rounding out my 69th year, I was at the height of my physical powers and reveling in every moment of it.

In September Violette was at the chalet she and her late husband had built on the alpine balcony of Jeizinen hanging precipitously above the upper Rhône valley. He had been a medical doctor who became a dowser and geobiologist, they had worked together and had chosen this site in the rocks with care. Early in the month I interrupted my alpine exploits to accept her invitation for a very brief visit. It was time to get back to work.

My arrival at supper time gave us an evening to recapitulate my adventure at the Schneider workshop. She had a dowsing program in mind for we had only one full day at our disposal. Wet weather threatened, and we awoke to thick fog. It began to lift in the late morning, and we left her 5'000-foot perch to roam the heights directly above.

One has to wonder sometimes, what drives people like us to such exotic, esoteric undertakings. It was cold and windy, thick clouds billowing overhead, playing tag with the peaks. We wore fleece-lined jackets and gloves (which we removed when working with our instruments).

My dowsing so far had been concerned with the energies that flow in and over the earth. In working with standing stones my knowledge and gear limited me to measuring the force of those energies. The physicist Schneider put into my hands a tool with which I could seek to find out what else was imprinted in the alleged inanimate world. Now we were en route to study a unique rock.

Perhaps right here is the place to evoke the concept of imprint. Psychotherapists and psychiatrists tell us that events and emotions leave an imprint on the human psyche which can range from beneficial to disabling. We are marked by what happens to us, and these therapists try to help us discover and uproot the sources of our distress. Spiritual relief is the goal.

Indigenous peoples, tribal cultures all over the globe, know/accept/ consider that Mother Earth and everything on her are equally alive and subject to lasting impression. It is only the blindsidedness of western man that calls them inanimate objects. Because a rock cannot move of its own volition does not make it dead. They are also Mother Earth's children. Like us, they can be imprinted, and like us, they can be entered, they can be read, and they can give up useful information. They too have a spiritual life, and we can learn to contact it. These mysteries stimulate, in some of us, a burning rage to *know*. It is part of our exploration of spirit. Mingling with the sacred stones of England had already taught me that this might be a long apprenticeship.

In this spirit Violette and I drove up to 7'300 feet, then hiked upwards for an hour to reach the Pierre Creuse — "hollow stone" — one thousand feet higher on a modest crest she called the Torumänggini, a shoulder of the Einig Alichij. The lonely stone was indeed holed and hollow; it was gnarled like an old tree.

Our approach here was to test the frequencies related to cultures and to spiritual practice. In other words, did this unique stone have a religious significance?

First of all, was it a sacred site of some kind? To test this concept we used the 6.9 frequency, with negative polarity. Working simultaneously but not side by side, we both received positive responses. Was it Christian or non-Christian? The wavelength 3.5 told us it was non-Christian. Lack of response on 5.1 said it had nothing to do with Jesus Christ. In fact, the 4.1 frequency told us it was Celtic.

And that is how it went. Violette's little red notebook contained hundreds of wavelengths she tested regularly, wavelengths discovered by Schneider, by other colleagues with whom she had worked, all originally found by trial-and-error. Philosophers like to use the word "empirical", meaning "based on observation and experience". The frequencies we were using on this windswept mountainside had been validated through testing on archaeological and anthropological sites known to have certain histories and qualities.

Thus we found the Pierre Creuse had been a place of Celtic ritual using fire, sometimes involving sacrifices (6.3 negative polarity). There was no underground water (7.2 and 9.2), the Romans had not been here (8.4), there was a fault line (8.6) running north and south, the Sun (2.0) had a role in the rituals but not the Moon (1.8), and it was not a place of "illumination" (8.0).

To my eyes the stone looked clearly to be of volcanic origin. It resembled lava. The frequency for basalt, the volcanic stone, is 4.6, and both of us got positive "hits". Testing this stone for sulphur (8.8) was equally successful. Our antennae did not react when we tested for other kinds of rock, such as feldspar, magnetite, and the limestone so common in the Alps. We took a small sample of this rock back to the chalet and tested it again during the evening. We feel secure in our judgement it was volcanic.

We also used the Hartmann antenna here, finding that the force lines were tightened up to a one-meter interval for a radius of seven meters out from the stone. Our pendulums were in agreement that the Bovis vibratory rate was a modestly high 9'000. The geiger counter presented no deviation from the base rate found at the chalet in the morning.

Taken all together, these various measurements told us that this unusual standing stone, geologically different from its surroundings, had been recognized and used by Celtic peoples as a place of ritual sacrifice. Violette and I have followed the same method — each of us testing for the same qualities, but at a little distance from one another — in subsequent work together on numerous other sites in and around Switzerland, Nearly all of the time we are in complete agreement.

After picnicking downslope out of the wind, we climbed up into a little bowl called the Heruhubel. There was a very pleasant feeling here, and our instruments quickly gave us some reasons. The Lecher told us it had been a place of worship, that the imprint of "eloquence" clung to the site, and that there was an aura of positiveness for life (4.5, positive polarity). With Bovis vibrations in the 11'000 to 12'000 range we had reason to sense a certain benevolence.

That evening Violette allowed me to copy extensively from her little red notebook. This enabled me to begin getting experience testing about a hundred different wavelengths with the Lecher. It made sense to my mind to divide them into groups: earth energies, spiritual, minerals and metals, fluids, colors, cultures, gods and planets, and "qualities". To illustrate the latter basket of frequencies, be advised that chilly fieldworkers with a sense of humor have discovered there is a wavelength for cold feet! Yes, it is 3.1, with negative polarity (makes sense!). This basket has values for qualities such as wisdom, eloquence, benediction, disorganization, sound and resonance, radioactivity, and many others.

What neither of us knew was that some very relevant scientific research was just getting started at Princeton University in New Jersey. Research on the influence of the human mind on machines, especially electronic equipment, was going on at the Princeton Engineering Anomalies Research laboratories. It took a sharp turn after Roger Nelson, a doctor in psychology, devised a pocket-size version of a contraption known as a Random Event Generator. This gadget could detect and register significant deviations, beyond the normal range, of the mental/emotional climate of a place. Nelson took his REG to meetings and events which would produce out-of-the-ordinary sensations, and he began to compile a mass of data.

At a native American healing ceremony in Wyoming he found the machine had been definitely affected. It was as if "there were some lingering memory of the thoughts of all the people who'd lived and died there"[2].

Meditators can produce similar measurable effects on the atmosphere around them, he found. He accompanied a group who traveled to the Egyptian pyramids and other sacred sites to chant and meditate, and his machine registered significant effects through all of it. But there was more:

"...when he put together all the data of the twenty-seven sacred sites he'd visited, while simply walking around them with no more than a respectful silence, the results were even more astounding. The spirit of the place itself appeared to register effects every bit as large as the meditating group."

When the group performed in the same manner at sites which were merely interesting, not sacred, or during some event like a birthday party, the effect on the machine was small. "Clearly, some resonance reverberated at the sites, possibly even a vortex of coherent memory," editor-researcher Lynne McTaggart comments[3].

Writing these lines more than a decade after Violette and I began to work together, and more than a decade after Nelson's findings, and several years after McTaggart described them, it is fascinating to realize that our instinctive work was going to have its scientific confirmation. What I knew then was what happened when I dowsed. Schneider's adaptation of Lecher's antenna provided a rationale which Violette had been exploring, which now I would also explore. We were engaged in scientific research at a level which establishment science usually brushed off as inconsequential. Yet a scientific parallel for our methods was under development.

In blissful ignorance of all that, we began to plan some more ambitious dowsing trips together, a nice relief from my solitary itineraries and field work. Violette was enthusiastic about Ireland but fall was already in the air and spring seemed more promising for the Emerald Isle and the humidity that kept it that color. An organized tour of spiritual sites in Provence was on offer, and we snapped up that one. Meanwhile, she knew about several potentially fascinating sites to investigate in the regions of France and Germany immediately north of the Swiss city of Basel. Within a few weeks the tour in Provence fell through — we were the only ones to sign up for it! — and we opted to head immediately across our northern border.

We were going to explore a riddle, a theory whose protagonist wove together tantalizing threads of geography, anthropology and astronomy. We wanted to find out if our dowsing could bring out the missing "fifth dimension". Along the way we would pause to dig into the energies of several churches and a mountaintop monastery.

1   Blanche Merz, *Hauts Lieux Cosmo-Telluriques en Suisse*. Geneva: Georg, 2000. 289p + iv p., glosssary, biblioography. ISBN 2-8257-0709-0. Originally published in 1998 as *Orte der Kraft in der Schweiz*, Aarau: AT Verlag, 1998.
     My quotation (my translation) is from pages 240-41.
2   Lynne McTaggart, *The Field, the quest for the secret force of the universe*. London: HarperCollins, 2001. Page 206 of xx+268p., notes, bibliography, index. ISBN 0-7225 3764 6.
     McTaggart is founder-editor of the monthly newsletter "What Doctors Don't Tell You," as well as the book of the same title. *The Field* presents the result of seven years of travel and research into the scientific basis for homeopathic and spiritual healing.
3   *Idem*, p.207.

Chapter Twenty-One

SUN, MOON AND MOSAICS

A year earlier an archaeologist had presented a paper describing a phenomenon that he called the "Belchen Triangle". It appeared that the names of a group of mountain peaks could be correlated with prehistoric religious practices, which were in turn related to seasonal astronomical phenomena[1]. Violette sniffed some interesting research to be performed with our Lecher antennae and the Bovis biometrical method. The concept of leys immediately sprang to mind when I saw the map she had drawn.

Peaks in southern Germany's Black Forest seemed to be linked with others in the Vosges mountains, across the Rhine river in northern France, and with still others in the Swiss Jura mountains south of Basel. For those unfamiliar with the geography of that area, it is useful to know that Basel sits astride the Rhine exactly where the frontiers of France and Germany meet those of Switzerland. When I am traveling north and reach Basel, it is a question of "turn left for France, turn right for Germany". As the river flows northward out of Basel it becomes the boundary between those two countries.

In early October 1992 I drove up to Bern to collect Violette. After a light lunch in her apartment we drove north an hour to cross the border at Stein am Rhein, and then we wound another hour through lovely, heavily-forested river valleys to reach Schönau. Here we were in the heart of the Schwarzwald, the Black Forest. Schönau is a small town which, though attractive, was not much of a tourist center. That meant lower prices, but its real importance to us was that it lay at the foot of the Belchen.

This was the first of the mountaintops we wanted to visit, the eastern anchor point of the "triangle" we proposed to analyze. In fact, there were three overlapping landform triangles and a total of seven peaks in this system straddling the Rhine and international boundaries.

"Belchen" bears the name of the Celtic sun god known variously as Bel, Belen, Belten, and Beltane, and is associated with both the spring equinox and May Day, the first of May. There are Belchens in both Germany and Switzerland. Across the Rhine in France the word Belchen translates as Ballon, and there are three Ballons in those mountains: Ballon d'Alsace, Grand Ballon and Petit Ballon. We hoped to take readings on all of them.

The last two peaks are named Blauen, once again in both Germany and Switzerland. "Blauen" is derived directly from the word "blau", meaning "blue". These two peaks are linked with ancient Moon cult ceremonies, and we sought to verify this and to fit them into the triangular system.

In the Lecher system of frequencies, the Sun responds to the wavelength of 2.0 and the Moon answers to 1.8. I had to take Violette's word for this, as for all the empirically-established frequencies we would work with.

After taking possession of a pleasant room in Haus Kaiser, a modest *pension* on a side street, we drove up to the summit of Belchen. It was shrouded in fog, visibility zero, and the big old restaurant was closed, so we turned around and headed down again. On the way we found a café whose hot chocolate and cheesecake restored our morale at tea time. Hope that the weather would be better in the morning dominated our supper in the Gasthof Adler. We lingered at table to sketch out the finer details of our itinerary, for we planned to interrupt our Belchen-Ballon-Blauen observations with a visit to the mountaintop monastery-convent of Sainte Odile. According to Violette its popularity as a major tourist attraction concealed some geomantic treasures we could try to measure, confirm or deny, as the case may be. En route there would be some additional points of interest to examine.

In the morning we found our prayers gradually being answered, shreds of damp fog slowly melting away. After a twenty-minute hike from the parking area we were the first people on the spacious summit and could go about our dowsing analyses with little interruption. Visibility was good enough though far from sparkling. As we faced west we could easily sight on Ballon d'Alsace, thirty-six miles away across the broad Rhine valley. Altitudes were roughly comparable: 4'642 feet where we stood and 4'101 across the way. These are gently-rounded grassy domes, not the craggy, dizzying Alps that inform my daily life.

Working independently, we quickly confirmed that a sun energy line did indeed link this Belchen to Ballon d'Alsace. This was quite clear. The two mountains are jointly aligned with sunrise on the equinox days of spring and fall.

The German Blauen stood only a bit more than three miles away in the southwest, half-left as we stood and 3'822 feet high. We strolled some distance away from the Belchen-Ballon influence and set our Lecher antennas to 1.8, the Moon frequency. They wobbled and nodded emphatically when we aimed them at the Blauen. Clouds to the south prevented us from sighting across to the Swiss Blauen. These three summits do not quite make a perfect alignment, to qualify as a full-fledged ley, but the two Blauens align perfectly with the city of Basel, which lies between them. That's a ley, and as we confirmed much later, a Moon alignment.

Our antennae also told us that this Belchen summit was a site of early Celtic religious ceremonies. It was a place for recharging energies, with a vibrational rate of 10'000 Bovis. Christian and Roman wavelengths did not respond, but a frequency which came up strongly was that of Jupiter the god. He is not in the panoply of Celtic gods, so possibly the Romans did appropriate this sacred site from the Celts. That happened everywhere in western Europe that the two cultures collided, and it happened again when Christianity drove out its competitors, taking over centers of high energy.

We drove back down to Schönau to take a few photographs and to fill out our picnic supplies. The mountain road westward was easy, winding through picturesque hamlets in deep valleys, lots of photogenic Black Forest rustic architecture, very similar to traditional Swiss farmhouse design. This makes sense because the hills of the Black Forest are a continuation of the Jura mountain range which forms Switzerland's northwestern frontier.

Emerging onto the Rhine plain, we crossed the river west of Mullheim and zigzagged to get to Ottmarsheim and its curious octagonal church. We picnicked in the car before swinging our dowsing bags over our shoulders and entering the eleventh-century edifice created by Benedictine monks. This eight-sided church is perfectly aligned between the German Blauen in the east and Ballon d'Alsace in the west. The three points form another ley within the triangular system.

Scaffolding attested to the damage wrought by a catastrophic fire the previous year. St. Ottmarsheim's central dome tower was damaged and the upper reaches could not be visited. Below, however, we quickly discovered ourselves to be on an authentic power point. Flames could wound the structure but they had no effect on the underlying spirituality of the site.

The church was built perfectly centered on a double intersection of Hartmann lines and the diagonal Curry lines. All the relevant wavelengths were in accord. The Moon line coming from Blauen in the east was part of the Hartmann system and ran right down the center of the building in the direction of Ballon d'Alsace. There were two altars on the east end of this line, with Bovis values of 16'000 to 16'500. Right in the center, at the major crossing-point of all those force lines, my pendulum registered 18'000 and 19'000 Bovis. Violette got similar values. I will not bore the reader with reciting all the frequencies we tested. Ten of the nineteen I tried gave me hits, confirming what Violette was getting. There was much evidence of underground water, particularly outside the eastern end. This should not be surprising in view of the location on flat land barely a mile west of the Rhine river.

St. Ottmarsheim and its rare carologinien architecture registered everything to do with sacred energy, priests, protection, benediction. It had been a Celtic and Roman site long before the Benedictines appropriated it. Its spectacular alignment showed it to be a geomantic zone of the first order.

It was a deeply satisfying place simply *to be*, and we could easily understand why successive cultures down through the millenia had used this place on which to express their spirituality.

Heading northward now, we paused at Guebwiller which is on the main road winding tortuously up to Grand Ballon. On the way we detoured toward a hotel underneath a knob called the Belchenthal. ("Thal" is a dialect variation of "Tal", which means valley in German.) This valley is reputed to be very floral, but the October colors were subdued and the hotel proved to be closed. No matter, it was only a spur-of-the-moment idea and we turned around.

Back down on the valley floor we cruised northward until we found Eguisheim in the rolling uplands west of Colmar. Eguisheim is surrounded by vineyards, an absolute riot of color at this season, and the region seemed to be in full ferment. This town is wildly romantic and picturesque in its traditional architectural garb, steep roofs with ornate gables, wood-and-stucco walls, bay windows. We found a good hotel quickly and then set out down the main street to buy some wine before the shops closed. There was a sense of excitement in the air, for the wine harvest was in full swing and a strong aroma of fermenting grapes permeated the atmosphere. Many vintners here had retail outlets open to the main street, but most were so busy with getting in the day's harvest of grapes that we had trouble finding someone who had time to sell us a few bottles, much less engage in the leisurely wine-tasting we had in mind.

When dowsers take hotel rooms one of the first things they do is to check out the energy lines. And in the Auberge Alsacien we found a mixed bag: one of the beds was in clear neutral territory, assuring a good night's sleep to its occupant. The other one was afflicted, especially by underground water. Dilemma! The hotel was full, so we could not request another room, on whatever pretext acceptable to the geobiologically uninitated. So we had to flip a coin, and I lost. Before bedding down, however, there was the evening meal to be enjoyed. And enjoy it we did, for the nearby Hostellerie du Pape fed us exceedingly well. My *roulade* of salmon in dill sauce was divine, the veal kidneys in mustard sauce which followed put me in seventh heaven. A good thing too, for the rest of the night was less than heavenly. Digestion was happy, but the energies of the bed's placement had me tossing and turning all night. Violette was chirpy and very well-rested over in her neutral corner, and while I grumped and groaned into the morning routine, she had the good taste not to crow about winning the coin toss.

The next morning we made a quick photographic hike around Eguisheim, trying to capture morning light on the gingerbready architecture before graying skies cast their pall on the landscape. Onward then to Colmar, a treasure trove of purely Alsatian architecture, streets full of ornate, sculpted houses, and a canal quarter called Little Venice[2]. Our first objective in Colmar was the former convent of Issenheim, now a museum housing the famed Retable d'Issenheim. When tour buses disgorge, one shuffles and elbows slowly through the throngs, and if we hadn't had other destinations in mind for the day we would have retired to a café for a warm drink. The elements of the Retable[2] are displayed in a long room; they are disassembled and shown in a kind of progression, one panel after another, like the cars in a railroad train.

Aside from the artistic beauty of the various panels of the Retable, this was for us another exercise in studying the vibrations emitted by works of art. Our work in front of the Delaunay paintings in Bern proved to have been only a warm-up for what now confronted us. First we stood in front of a sarcophagus measuring Bovis 4'500 (negative polarity), but already my legs began feeling the collapse of energy as we moved slowly toward the painting of the Crucifixion. It was the most horrible Crucifixion I had ever seen. It registered Bovis 2'500 (negative again), and I know Violette had something similar but we didn't stop then and there to compare notes. We pendled in turn, taking care to shield each other from the gaze of the numerous ecclesiastics and security guards in the hall.

Then you walk around the wide display of panels to see Grünewald's painting of the Ascension on the back side of that Crucifixion. Immediately there is a shift, a buoyancy of the energies. It was amazing to this non-Christian to see her pendulum measure 9'000 on the Bovis meter, and then when we came next to the Nativity the vibrational rate soared to 11'000. What is going on here that can so strongly override individual religious feelings or the lack of same? I took it as proof of my ability to detach, stand aside and let the semi-meditational measuring method work by itself.

One more surprise awaited us. The panel on the reverse side of the Nativity displays The Temptation of St. Anthony. Immediately my energies collapsed in front of this painting, the Bovis reading falling to a scant 2'000 (negative polarity once again). Let me emphasize that these low readings are not a reflection on the artist but on his treatment of his subject. Artists, especially painters of religious subjects, have a message to convey. It is easy for me to believe that an artist with an esoteric bent or a psychological motivation could deliberately set about to create high or low vibrations in order to influence the emotions of the viewer.

Colmar still had two splendid medieval churches to offer us, so we gave them each a quick tour, and both had harmonious vibrations. The Collégiale St-Martin was rebuilt in the thirteenth century on the site of a roman church. The entry to the nave registered 10'000 Bovis, and in the transept there was a wonderful series of pulsations ranging from 15'000 to 20'000. We could have lingered here and in the Dominican Church, but we had a room reserved at the cloister on Mount St- Odile. The town of Sélestat and its ancient manuscripts and old stones lay ahead, but we had no idea what was really in store for us.

Sélestat's cathedral, St-Georges, was very harmonious, with Bovis readings pulsing from 16'000 to 20'000 throughout the transept-choir-altar system. However, we didn't feel compelled to spend a lot of time there. We had come to see the Bibliothèque Humaniste, just a few steps down the street. This famous Humanist Library developed in the middle of the fifteenth century around the two thousand volumes collected by the famed scholar Beatus Rhenanus. His university and the nearby Latin school made Sélestat a center of humanist learning, and his book collection is the best remnant available of that era. We marveled over the works of Vitruvius, the correspondence of Erasmus, the twelfth-century "Miracles of Sainte Foy", and a Merovingian manuscript of the late seventh-century, one of the oldest manuscript books I have ever been privileged to see. Spiritual vibrations did not overwhelm us here; instead we were made reverent by immersion in a power point of knowledge, evidence that the upper Rhine valley had been at the time of the Renaissance a beacon of European intellect.

Turning right a few steps from the door put us in the Rue du Sel, "Salt Street", and we were quickly in front of the Eglise de Sainte-Foy, only fifty yards or so from St. Georges. Ste. Foy is really a handsome twelfth-century pile, two magnificent towers flanking the main door, and a tall octagonal tower rising above the crossing. The neighboring Vosges mountains provided the granite and red sandstone used to execute this romanesque design, over the ruins of an ancient Benedictine priory.

Once inside, however, our initial impression was depressing. The nave was filled with rickety wooden chairs, the kind you can almost blow over, and there was a vile woven mat covering much of the floor. It was dirty and breaking up into thousands of little cocos bristles. We stood inside the door, gazing around, and then I spied a mosaic peeking out from under that frightful mat.

Quickly, by lifting corners of the mat, we discovered not one but four mosaics. These symbolic designs were about two feet square, arranged to form the corners of a rectangle just inside the door, and they framed a labyrinth in black and white stone. This in itself was startling, because such labyrinths are usually associated with great cathedrals, most notably Chartres. And these four mosaics bore the names of rivers: Tigris, Euphrates, Ganges, and Geon.

Geon? We didn't know this name. What did it designate? The Tigris and the Euphrates are well-known for irrigating Mesopotamia, now Iraq, when it was the cradle of agriculture, possibly even the biblical Garden of Eden. The Ganges was clearly a sacred river, but to the Hindus, not the Christian Church.

"Water!" I hissed at Violette.

We whipped out our Lecher antennae and quickly confirmed that these four mosaics precisely signaled the passage of an underground stream. So our Geon was surely a river, but where?

The coconut fiber mat was too heavy and too dirty, so we could not see all these treasures at once. We did hold it up long enough to run the pendulum over the center of the labyrinth, harvesting a gratifying 18'000 on the Bovis scale.

By now, of course, Sainte Foy of Sélestat had turned into an Ali Baba's cavern of treasures. We made diagrams and notes, then moved down the main aisle toward the transept, our eyes peeled like those of hawks. We were not disappointed. The north window of the transept showed a man with red hair and beard enthroned in a celestial blue firmament, heavenly bodies spinning about his head. This was almost certainly Jesus, his bare feet resting on a green-and-blue cushion. He held the Earth in his left hand with the Sun shining over his left shoulder and the Moon above his right shoulder. From that distance it appeared that the whole background was stars, and the circular border seemed populated by more planets than one could imagine.

Only when we were home and I could study my freshly-developed photographs was it clear that the background of what seemed to be stars was more like a sea of blue flowers with white centers. You could read it either way. On my photos what had seemed to be a circle of planets revealed themselves to be a series of amorphous shapes, vaguely organic piles of matter. Around the outside of the window six circular medallions emerged, each decorated with strange shapes that could be taken as floral but also as organisms. Each of the six contained a few spiral seashell shapes. Never before in any church or cathedral had I ever seen a major window executed in themes that were not derived from Bible stories. The effect was all the more pronounced when we lowered our eyes to the floor.

There at our feet lay another dozen mosaics, and these presented the twelve symbols of the zodiac. They were the same size and format as the four rivers at the other end of the nave, and they were distributed equidistantly in two lines along the north-south axis of the transept. What's more, care had been taken to respect the division of these signs by reference to earth, air, fire and water. The signs linked to the element earth are Taurus, Virgo, and Capricorn. The air signs are Gemini, Libra and Aquarius. Leo, Sagittarius and Aries are the dynamic fire signs, while the element water is represented by Cancer, Scorpio and Pisces.

Thus, beneath the impassive gaze of Jesus, the mosaics were arranged at equal intervals but in groups of four. Once again we had to pick up the edges of another disgraceful coco fiber carpet to see them all. Aquarius the water-carrier and the ram of Aries lay at his feet, grouped with the Piscean fish and Taurus the bull. The center quartet, entirely covered by the mat, were Gemini's twins, Cancer's crab, the lion of Leo, and Virgo with her sheaf of harvested grain. The last four, under the south window, were the scales of Libra, Scorpio's scorpion, the archer Sagittarius and Capricorn the goat.

And that south window had us scratching our heads. Once again this rosette seemed to have nothing to do with a biblical tale. We saw instead a young woman in some kind of oriental costume with, quite unbiblical, her bare, creamy, and braceleted forearms spread in benediction. She was blonde and wore a crown and red slippers. Her fetching robe of turquoise and cream, bordered with rich gold embroidery, was secured at the breast with a large emerald brooch. All around her was a sea of red flowers with white centers. Seven white doves flew toward her from the inner edge of the rosette, and between them were more amorphous forms echoing those around Jesus. Around her window emerged seven medaillons (not six, as for Jesus) filled with white and gold flowers.

Who was this? Speculation on this point had to wait for a leisurely moment.

Stepping up from the transept and its signs of the zodiac, we entered the choir to be greeted by more mosaics symbolizing the four apostles, identified there as Marcus, Matheus, Johannes and Lucas.

With all these wondrous sights to digest we had almost forgotten our usual dowsing routines. Rapidly getting down to business, we found the lines of the global network were tightened up in the center third of the transept, very close together, reinforced by equally clustered Curry lines. It was a very harmonious mesh, and in the center of that force field, directly beneath the octagonal tower, the pendulum marked 19'000. Up in the choir among the four apostles it rose higher, breaking rhythm at 21'000.

Everywhere in the church the Hartmann lines were regular and intersected within the pillars, as did the diagonal Curry system. These two systems intersected in the center of the labyrinth too.

Using our calibrated antennae, we got very powerful responses for water. It ran beneath the long axis of the church, the whole length from east to west, and it ran north-south through the transept, along the line of a fault in the earth's crust. Thus Sélestat had a crucifix of underground water echoing the shape of the edifice.

Appropriate wavelengths attested to probable use of the site for Celtic ceremony, and we got reactions for both the sun and the moon frequencies. I picked up the Moon directly under the Jesus rosette containing that satellite, and Violette found the sun line running through the nave. And, as usual, there were a lot of frequencies we tried which did not respond. The method always requires testing an abundance of possible qualities in order to fish out those which are valid to the site.

Down the street we found a bookstore stocking many fine editions, art books, architecture, cultural treasures and the like. Here we hoped to get some detailed information about this treasure of a church we had just visited. To our consternation the proprietor, clearly a learned man who understood perfectly what we sought, said there was nothing available. No guide to the church, no picture book edited by the vestry, no scholarly monograph. He could not even educate us about the river Geon[4]. Total silence. We left Sélestat with the clear impression that the Catholic Church found this unique church to be an embarrassment. Cover everything with nasty cocos mats, and the less said the better!

From Sélestat our route led toward Mount Sainte Odile, the northernmost point on our circuit. From there we would turn south again to visit the Ballons and, with luck, the Swiss Blauen, so as to complete our survey of the intriguing triangle.

Once again on the open road, we had leisure to ponder Sélestat's puzzles.

Our astrological church is named after Sainte Foy. Later research revealed her to be a girl from the village of Conques in southwestern France and who was martyred at the age of twelve in the year 303. The Benedictines who founded the church in Sélestat came from Conques, where there is also a church named after Sainte Foy. We did not yet know this bit of history, however. All we had to go on at the time was the window, which depicts a full-figured fairskinned queen, not a pubescent girl.

Violette had read something about the life of Ste. Odile, in whose cloister we had reservations for two nights. She was born blind in the seventh century and repudiated by her father, the third Duke of Alsace, who wanted to kill her. She was hidden away in an abbey, where a miracle restored her sight. She consecrated her life to God and, after some melodramatic episodes her father repented and gave her his château atop the Hohenbourg to transform into a convent. Her life was one of assistance to the poor, the sick, and the unfortunate. There is nothing in what we know of Ste. Odile's life that suggests the exotic oriental queen of the window, although the red flowers and the seven doves might fit in somewhere.

Food for thought was in plentiful supply as we turned toward the mountains at Barr and wound up to the top of Mont Ste. Odile. Like the Jura, and the Appalachians of North America, the Vosges mountains are basically long ranges of rounded hogbacks, rising to 2500 feet at our destination. The eleventh-century chapel is the only part of the original convent and cloister to have survived a terrible fire in the sixteenth-century. Thus we found ourselves in a complex reconstructed for the most part in the nineteenth century. This modern convent is a favorite for pilgrimages, and we found ourselves surrounded by happy groups of the faithful. People strolled about to the various holy sites, and no one could be impervious to the panoramic view from this promontory high above the plain.

We parked my red Toyota station wagon under a cross just below the windows of the reception. Our reservation entitled us to a two-bedded room with minimal but adequate furnishings and the usual crucifix above the beds. Meals were served in a large refectory. Supper was bland and tasteless, although sufficiently filling and probably wholesome. Creature comfort was spartan, reminding us that we had entered a monastic environment.

Dowsing of our room showed we were in a neutral zone, our beds unperturbed by geopathic phenomena of any kind. This was a holy place, however, and the pendulum advised us we would sleep in an atmosphere of 9'000 Bovis. One sleeps lightly when the vibrational rate is that high, and so did we. Lightly and short, six hours maximum.

The next morning we worked with Lecher and Bovis in the chapels and on the ramparts lined with old lime trees. Quickly we discovered that Hartmann's "global" network was non-existent up here; it was a vast neutral zone. And there was no above-normal radioactivity anywhere. Our antenna were enthusiastic about fourteen varied wavelengths denoting spiritual qualities, half of which confirmed the site to have been a place of worship in pre-Christian times. There were typically high vibrations in the main church of the convent, soaring by half again to 23'000 at Sainte Odile's sepulchre.

Of the four chapels clustered in and around the convent, we especially liked the Chapel of the Angels, sitting on the rampart close to the edge of the precipice. Inside it was a dream in blue and gold, an unexpected splendor. Two streams of water flowed beneath, under a corner farthest from the cliff, and the point where they crossed yielded an elevating 17'000 Bovis.

After lunch we scurried down the stone trail to the holy well, trying to be ahead of the crowds. Here we took samples of the water to be dowsed off-site, because there were too many people right on our heels. At the well we measured 9'000 Bovis but the waters themselves vibrated 15'000 to 16'000.

Safely away from the steady stream of pilgrims it was possible to "read" the water and the surroundings of the well for numerous qualities. Although this part of the Vosges mountains is granitic and crystalline, we got a reading for basalt, which means volcanic lava. The Lecher signaled a fault zone, thus we could understand a lava intrusion in the granite. And that intrusion could possibly explain why the Hartmann network was absent on the mountaintop, harking back to my experience on California's Mt. Lassen.

The water also told us it was good for rheumatism. Legend surrounding Sainte Odile says that she used these waters to heal a case of blindness, and many pilgrims come because of that. We could not test the sample for "healthy eyes" simply because Violette did not know the appropriate frequency.

After visiting the well we planned to lope out into the forest and find the pagan wall which winds along the hogback. I went to fetch my hiking boots in the car. To my astonishment I could not open any of the doors. Thieves had tried to break into the car, probably to steal it, and they had wrecked the three locks with a screwdriver or similar tool. This had happened between 09h30 and 14h30, in broad daylight, right under the windows of the cloister office! Suddenly all our plans were thrown into a cocked hat.

We had to wait for a mechanic to come up from the valley. I watched him struggle to open the door with the usual jimmying gadgets. He had a real battle, which made me appreciate that my new Toyota was almost burglar-proof.

After more than a quarter-hour he got the door open. We agreed he would drive it down the mountain and change the locks, which he thought would be available in nearby Strasbourg. We'd have the car back the next morning.

With what remained of the afternoon we spent two hours in the forest, trying in vain to find the Druids' Grotto. In our wanderings we began to feel vaguely uneasy, and then we came to a vast ragged rectangle where the forest had been logged off — or so it appeared at first glance. Violette recalled there had been a plane crash in the Vosges some time in the recent past. The sense of this disaster still hung in the atmosphere of the dark forest, partly the odor of charred wood and metal, partly the heavy energy of death, partly something else we could not seize. Our Lecher antennae quickly diagnosed death (4.5 negative) as opposed to life (4.5 positive). Confirmation of the catastrophe came to us that evening back at the cloister. Something had gone horribly wrong with the landing approach of a passenger plane heading into Strasbourg early in the year. Fog over these mountains, as on this day? In any case, eighty-seven lives were lost, and then we understood that other heavy energy we hadn't been able to grasp. It was the grief of eighty-seven families.

My red Toyota rolled back to us the next morning, unrepaired. The locks were not quickly available. We had planned to be en route south toward the three Ballons this afternoon, but there was urgent paperwork demanding priority. We would lose most of this day and would have to stay over an extra night in order to complete our research on the Mont. At the cloister the management was able to extend our stay, even moving us to another room, this time with bath, a welcome development indeed. Thus our morning required a descent to the valley, where we found the Gendarmerie in the village of Rosheim. A fine young man drew up the police report which would ease my path through the paperwork of the inevitable insurance claim. We lunched very well at Le Petit Auberge, occasionally peering out the window at the unlocked car, and considering this matter of the failed car theft.

It was well-known at the time that cars were being stolen in Western Europe for resale in Eastern Europe. Three years earlier the Berlin Wall had crumbled and with it the so-called Iron Curtain. Busloads of former East Germans were coming to my mountain as tourists, tasting the outside world for the first time in thirty years. The dark side of this political victory was an increase in crime. After crossing the Rhine en route to Ottmarsheim we had followed a small car with Polish license plates and holding four young men. It was easy to imagine their purpose was not tourism -- which requires money -- but to steal cars. We wondered if they had been the ones who tried to spirit my new red Toyota and its four-wheel drive off to snowy Russia, where it would bring a big price.

Graying skies solidified during the day, cloaking the mountains in fog and light rain. We had hard choices to make: we could not do everything on our agenda for this junket, and the weather was breaking down. Another trip would be necessary. We were farther north than the three Ballons, and our original program called for visiting them on the southward-homeward leg. Now this began to look very much in doubt. The vile weather and poor visibility over the mountaintops was not helpful; it really dictated staying down in the valley for the afternoon as long as there was something constructive to do. Which there was, in the realm of country churches.

We dowsed two such that afternoon, finding one that honored Ste. Odile. Her image reigned over the corner of St. Pierre and St. Paul that was the power point of the edifice. We were getting vibrational rates of 14'500 to 18'500 in the choir and sanctuary area. Then we had a superfluous half-hour of walking in the rain until we found the ruins of St. Jacques. If the priests had been dowsers perhaps it would not have been allowed to collapse, for spiritual power persists. The central axis was rich with good wavelengths: a Curry line, a sun line, underground water, cosmic energy, benediction, amd a line associated with sacred Roman ways. So there was history here too, plus good vibrations, from 16'000 to 18'000 in spite of being in ruins, in spite of the rain. Man's works may come and go, but the imprint lingers long after. And if we walking antennas can measure that imprint, then we have been touched by it, soggy or not!

I believe we *are* touched by all this work, whether we sense it or not as a tangible effect. Spending time in places of high vibration rubs off on the human aura. You don't need to agree with the religious or philosophical reasons for the existence of the site, you don't need the ritual intervention of priests, you need only to be attuned to the fact of yourself as a spiritual being. We are spirit, inhabiting human bodies. Being spirit, we are moved by contact with the spiritual life of other beings, no matter how distant in time their work may have been.

Spiritual does not mean perennially solemn. Being humans, we became slaphappy with the discomfort of working in the rain, keeping our gear dry, and trying to get some decent photographs. We were glad not to be on the socked-in mountain, to which we returned in time for the evening meal and our packing. Up early the next morning, we were breakfasted and out of the cloister by nine o'clock. It was foggy and cold for our hike to the Druids' Grotto, which we now knew how to find, and the "Heidenmaur", the Heathen or Pagan Wall.

This "grotto" was really a cluster of huge boulders that had been manipulated into forming two dolmens. You could almost stand up in the big one, with five feet four inches of headroom. You could only crouch in the smaller one, with only four feet of clearance. This little complex was adjacent to the ancient wall, which we knew was supposed to wind around the mountain for more than six miles. Typical of this rain forest environment, there were enormous clusters of mushrooms all around, including the colorful *Amanita muscaria*, red with white pimples. So photogenic, so poisonous!

Well then, was this really a holy place for the Druids or were the guidebooks simply peddling fairy stories? Our tools told us the stories were true. It was clearly a dolmen, and a whole series of Lecher frequencies confirmed the ceremonial and druidic identification of the site[5]. It also triggered the relatively rare frequencies for feminine, "goddess" energy and for one of the Earth's sacred places. The vibrational rate was uniformly 9'000 all around the complex. Violette and I disagreed on the rate inside: I measured 12'500 and she got 15'000. Divergence of this degree was rare in our work together, but both measurements are elevated.

There were other geomantic indications as well: underground water, a fault line, and both Sun and Moon energy. Dating such sites is always a delicate matter, for it involves interrogating our tools for "yes" or "no" and waiting for a change, a movement. You can do this with a pendulum or with a dowsing wand. We came to the conclusion this site had been used in a ceremonial way from about five thousand years ago until about five hundred years before Jesus Christ. It dated from the time of the Celts.

This was Saturday and there were hikers about, in spite of the fog and cold. Two groups of them stopped to chat, and to learn. The French are very open to all these matters of earth mysteries and dowsing, and these people asked intelligent questions and accepted our answers as reasonable.

Immense blocks formed the Heathen Wall[6]. Its construction reminded us of pictures we had seen of Incan stonework in Peru. In some sections the wall was almost ten feet high and five to six feet thick. It is claimed to be the longest in Europe, and it is certainly the most mysterious. It could possibly represent an ancient desire to honor and protect the mountaintop, which implies that it was a sacred place long before Ste. Odile created her convent. Our Lecher antennae rejected the notion of a fortification, as well as a whole series of "sacred" frequencies we threw at them. They agreed only that this wall was megalithic, which meant very old. We disagreed slightly on the age of this wall. Violette said it preceded Jesus Christ by 2'800 years, whereas I got "only" 2'600. The vibratory rate along the sides and on top of the wall was the same favorable 9'000 we found at the cloister.

In terms of polarity, these stones were laid in the same way that cathedrals were built. The outer surface of the wall showed negative polarity, echoing the cathedral masons' habit of turning the negative side down and toward the outside. Atop the wall polarity was positive, reflecting the center, the interior of the construction, echoing the polarity of the inside walls of cathedrals. Ancient knowledge of the same type that later informed Christian builders appears to have been applied here. However, this effect seems to have been the only one sought by the wall-builders. There was no unusual configuration of the Hartmann and Curry networks, and we did not find that the wall followed a fault line. However, we did not track it for six miles.

We had to stop. Thanks to the would-be car thieves we were running out of time. We felt as if we had only scratched the surface of what Sainte Odile's mountain might tell us. We found later that our work dovetailed nicely with that of other investigators; I could cite especially the work of Adolphe Landspurg and his army of Alsatian colleagues[7]. If I had fallen upon his books before our trip, instead of much later, we would have found additional wonders to study.

We lunched in a good village restaurant, the loaded but unlocked car well-hidden. En route southward we paused three times to seek the Ballon-Belchen-Blauen Sun and Moon lines on the valley floor. Success every time, Sun or Moon registering neatly according to whichever alignment. Just north of the town of Cernay, on the French Route Nationale 83, we cruised slowly, our psychic senses swiveling like radars trying to pick up any kind of a blip. We wanted to intercept the Sun line linking Ballon d'Alsace and the German Belchen, but it wasn't easy in the car. We parked on the shoulder where we thought the straight line on the map should pass. Not quite. It took a bit of prowling up and down the roadside, antennae deployed, then we got the wiggle. A clear hit on the appropriate wavelength.

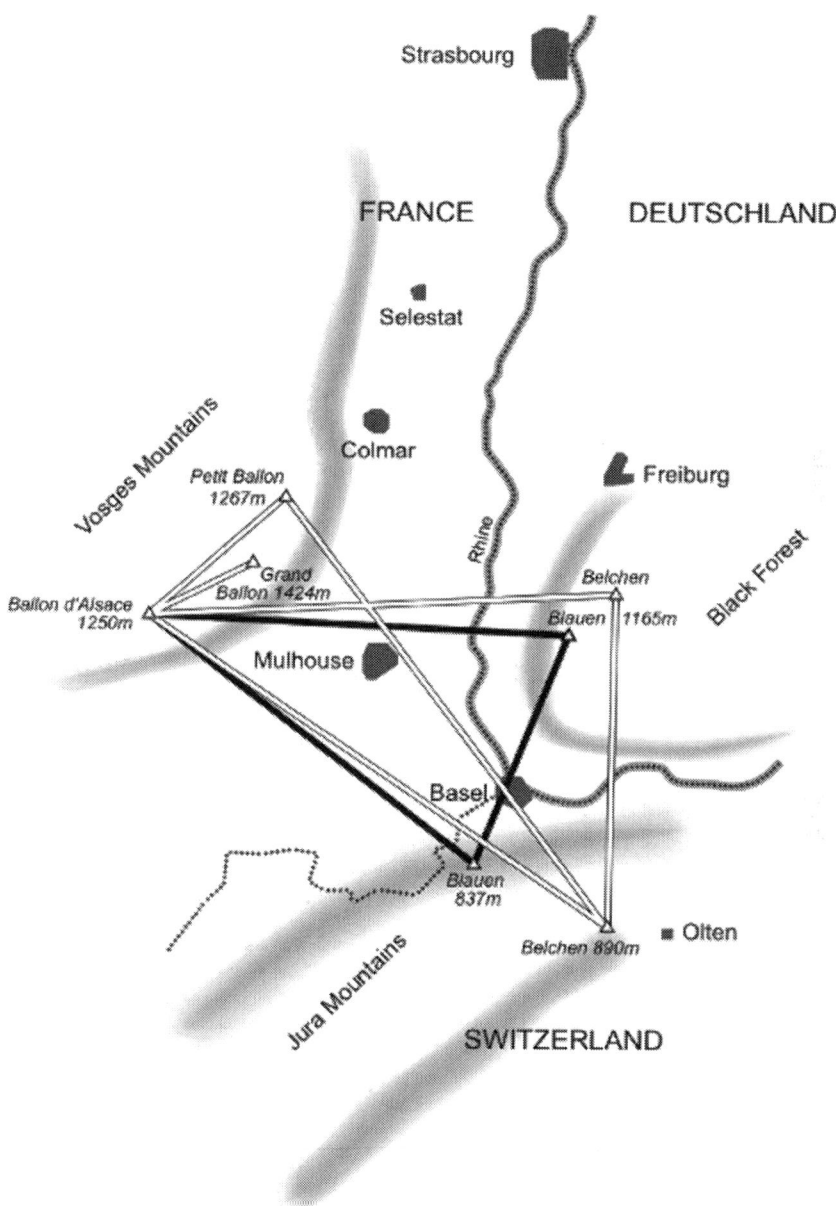

BELCHEN-BLAUEN ENERGY TRIANGLES

The pastry shop in Cernay gave us tea and a dessert, then we began to walk the town, radar deployed once again. In front of the church we got another hit. This time we had picked up the Sun line connecting Grand Ballon and the Swiss Belchen. It was very clear, the right frequency on the right spot on the map.

There was one more alignment we wanted to touch, a Moon line connecting Ballon d'Alsace and the Swiss Blauen. This had to be somewhere near Altkirch but we found it just north of the town, in the village of Aspach, with clean hits on 1.8.

Not far out of Altkirch, closer to the Swiss border, we found a fine country inn which could offer a garage for the red wagon. We ate copiously, drank gaily, and slept like logs.

When morning dawned brightly we thought it might be possible to go up the Swiss Blauen. It was so close we could almost taste it. But we had to abandon that plan when the skies resumed their dance of black cloud-white cloud. It was going to rain, and Blauen would require a hike.

In any event, we knew by now that we would be coming back in the spring. The idea of leaving this fascinating piece of triangular research unfinished was intolerable.

At the end of that month of October we met again for the IRG seminar on Feng Shui. An architect gave a well-constructed daylong presentation, leaving me feeling I could give a conference on the subject from my sheaf of notes. Then at the beginning of December came the final wrap-up seminar of the two-year series. In the afternoon session Violette presented our research on the Belchen Triangle, what we had verified so far and what we still had to accomplish, and I joined her in presenting our fun with the mosaics of Sélestat.

Six months later we went back to the Triangle. We left Violette's apartment early one sunny morning in June, 1993, and we went directly to the Swiss Blauen, southwest of Basel. This is another one of those long, rounded hogbacks and its summits are gentle swellings you could easily miss.

From the Challpass we walked uphill half an hour to reach the official summit at 2'864 feet. We were in a beautiful forest surrounded with birdsong. Violette identified a dozen different species solely by their song, whereas I could only recognize the blackbird and the chickadee, with whom I dialogue in my garden. There was also an eagle sailing over, which was a fine omen. But this summit was a big disappointment. Its Bovis vibration was only 7'500 and our Lecher antennae were very unimpressed. They did not react to the wavelengths we threw at them.

Undiscouraged, we continued our promenade along this wooded crest, almost a plateau. This was turning out to be a very hot day and we were happy to be in the shade. Our trail dipped into a swale and there stood an ancient cross, the Metzerlenchrüz, formed out of a knotty tree trunk and an equally knotty cross-branch. Great vibes here — 14'000 to 14'500 — this was planted on a double crossing-point of both the Hartmann and Curry networks, but it was not yet the power point that theory told us had to be on this mountain. So we plodded on, enjoying the June heat in our T-shirts, the birdsong, and the sylvan paradise in general. The ridge was now virtually level at 2'690 feet altitude for quite a long distance and ultimately we came to a sign identifying the Hofstettenspitz ("spitz" means point or peak). Instinct drew me to an uprooted tree, its roots having carried lots of stone into the open air, and close by in the underbrush we found a "blind spring", without water. Violette is very keen on blind springs, and that told her we had arrived. So did the pendulum, which registered 18'000 Bovis for me. So we circulated around the area, Lechers deployed, testing frequencies one after the other.

Within a few minutes it was clear, we had found the power point. Our antennae wiggled for the Moon line frequency, which was omnipresent in a large circle. There was also lots of Celtic imprint of a non-religious nature. Success required a toast, but lacking champagne we had to settle for our thirst-quenching water bottles and our picnic. It was that time of day already.

We'd found the place, but we couldn't see the relevant peaks of the Triangle because of the underbrush. We had to weave through trees and underbrush to reach the north edge of the crest area, and then we could see our mountaintops. Ballon d'Alsace was clearly visible to the northwest, giving us Sun line reactions. Our Moon energy squirted north-northeast, over the city of Basel and directly toward the German Blauen. It was a perfect ley, Basel right on the line connecting the two Blauen peaks. We could not make out details of the city from this distance and relatively low altitude, but we could see clearly where it was. This was the same line we had dowsed from atop the Black Forest Belchen our first day in the field last October, and we could just make out that peak and its neighboring Blauen.

That evening we hove into the country inn south of Altkirch where we had been so well cared-for in October. This time it was summer and we could dine on the terrace, unworried about the security of the red Toyota. Allow me to cite an excellent gazpacho, a fine little salad built around succulent bits of guinea-hen, and a splendid carp, all washed down with a spicy Alsatian Gewürztraminer. This was living; it was excellent to be alive, spoiling our tastebuds. Spiritually we were at peace too, for our bodies had bathed in strong energies up on Blauen.

Enjoying our supper, we kept one eye on the sky, for it had been a very hot day. Angry clouds were gathering, then flashing and rumbling. Protected by a generous awning, we had the thunderstorm for dessert, praying we would not have it for breakfast too. One doesn't want to be on mountaintops when lightning strikes, and we were headed for the Ballons.

Morning offered us clearing skies and summery warmth. We headed back north again, across the rolling plain between Mulhouse and Belfort, then into the foothills and up a road that became progessively more tortuous as we gained altitude, Nine hairpin turns guarded the final approach to the parking area below Ballon d'Alsace. Then came a half-hour stroll up to the gentle, almost flat summit, during which we measured agreeable Bovis vibrations of 10'000 to 11'000 permeating these high pastures. We gained the grassy, treeless summit about ten-thirty and came first to a great monument to Joan of Arc, waving the flag triumphantly as her horse reared. This was interesting but it was not in our line of inquiry. Farther on there was an observation platform with a panoramic table of the landmarks.

According to the triangular scheme, Ballon d'Alsace was a key point from which alignments fanned out in harmony with all the equinoxes and solstices. Finding the precise points required quite a bit of concentrated dowsing with our Lecher antennae. In fact, we found there were three principal power points: next to the observation platform, onward about one hundred yards, and then a group of fallen stones about fifty yards farther on.

The first one yielded 14'000 Bovis, the second one 13'000, and the last one 18'000. These points responded to a double handful of wavelengths, including both the Sun and the Moon. Violette's work clearly showed one of these spots to be a Moon place and the other a Sun site, thus confirming Ballon d'Alsace as the hinge of both triangles. These latter frequencies each corresponded to different alignments. I used a compass to double-check the azimuths toward various of the Belchen and Blauen peaks, with topographical map at hand.

Our results clearly confirmed the hypothesis offered by Dr. d'Aujourd'hui. The alignments were clear, and our antennae found the imprints of ancient religious practices down through the ages.

From where we stood on this Ballon, he said the sun should be seen to rise on the morning of the summer solstice from behind Petit Ballon, seventeen miles away at 4157 feet altitude, on a northeasterly line. Also, at a flatter angle, closer to east-northeast, one would see sunrise coming up over Grand Ballon (4672 feet, the tallest of the three) on Beltane, the first of May. Then, almost true east, the sun of the spring and fall equinoxes would rise from behind Belchen of the Black Forest. Looking now fifty miles southeast, and assuming crystal clear weather, one would see the sun come up from behind the Swiss Belchenflue (3605 feet) on the morning of the winter solstice. Our antennae confirmed these sun lines.

Up here on Ballon d'Alsace we got the same reaction for the god Jupiter as atop Belchen on the other side of the Rhine. The Romans had liked this site, but so had the Germanic tribes and the Celts. Each culture had left its imprint for rituals of all kinds, including fire ceremonies and the burning of sacrificial foods. So spake Lecher.

We found the Moon frequency linking Ballon d'Alsace to the two Blauens, as well as linking them mutually over the center of Basel. The "blue" triangle became quite clear, except that we could not deduce what it meant. Aside from exchanging Moon energy, what function did the two Blauens perform, if any? The Blauen ley runs thirty degrees off of true north-south, and we don't know what that means either.

The longest line in the larger system is a Sun line linking Petit Ballon and the Swiss Belchen, passing en route through the cities of Mulhouse and Basel. This is clearly another ley, and it is the third side of the Sun triangle. Best of all, it intersects the Blauen-Blauen ley in the oldest part of Basel. The twelfth-century cathedral, built on a bluff above the Rhine, stands within two hundreds yards of the precise point where the center line of two leys intersects. If one applies the measure proposed for the Michael-Mary line in England, that it should be considered as a band of energetic influence up to half a kilometer wide, then this intersection would easily encompass the cathedral and other historical buildings. This was a true geomantic zone, widely considered to have been a site sacred to the Celts as well.

Equally striking to us, our antennae reacted to the Sun and Moon frequencies at the right places. That is, when facing the Belchens, they gave us the Sun frequency, as well as that of the dominant male god Jupiter. When facing the Blauens they gave us the Moon frequency, and they also reflected the rather rare wavelength of 28.25, feminine, "goddess" energy.

This was a great morning's work, and our spirits soared. Hunger spoke, and we went to the nearby fallen stones for our picnic. These small boulders seemed to be the rudiments of what must have been a rough temple. Certainly the Bovis method thought highly of these stones, awarding 18'000 vibrations, the highest reading I got on this summit. Violette's reading came in at 17'500, so we felt comfortable with these results. Our antennae rejected a whole host of spiritual wavelengths we threw at them, but they did confirm pre-Christian ceremonies. Our ritual was lunch, which we thought appropriate for a place were food sacrifices seem to have occurred.

Clouds were gathering when we finished our picnic and headed back to the car. It took an hour by car to reach Grand Ballon, having to go down one mountain, down a valley, and then up again. Then a thirty-five minute walk up another hogback to the nearly flat summit at 4671 feet. Those clouds were darkening, taking on the anvil shape forecasting summer thunderstorms, and we could see this was the last work of the day. Going on to Petit Ballon would not be possible.

We did not immediately find anything like a power point until we spied a pile of stones — one big rock to which a lot of smaller ones seemed to cling. Here we found the vibratory memory of ancient worship, priestly activity, more sacrifices (non-human). It was a multiple crossing-point of the Hartmann and Curry energy networks. Not much remained of it, but we were clearly on the site of an ancient temple. My pendulum registered 19'000 Bovis, hence the spiritual impact was clear.

We were about fifty miles northwest of the Swiss Belchen and could not detect its hogback hump. I worked with maps and compass in order to establish the azimuth, and then unleashed my Lecher. Yes, it reacted to the Sun line frequency.

Ballon d'Alsace stood in the southwest, reflecting back the Sun frequency obtained there, when aiming here. Logical.

There was a flash of lightning as we headed for the car, and raindrops began pelting down as we scuttled safely inside. Driving back to our hotel was wet work, rewarded by another good dinner. It rained most of the night and continued into the morning. We had planned to ascend the Swiss Belchen, but it was out of the question in these conditions. There is a country road winding up its slopes, to within easy hiking distance, but we had had enough of walking and working in the rain. The main north-south superhighway passes through that mountain in one of Switzerland's longest tunnels, and that was as close as we got to the summit.

We had accomplished the essential part of our investigation: the Belchen-Blauen triangles were real. Invisible energies animated in a coherent way the sterile lines which could be drawn on a map.

We could not visit the Basel cathedral on this trip and were obliged to complete our research independently. It was years later before I got there one brisk winter day, hoping to learn something about the energies of the intersection of our two mountain-based leys. It proved to be a bit frustrating. Dowsing conditions were not optimum, with mobs of Christmas shoppers choking the narrow streets. Inside there were clusters of tourists herded by docents. The *déambulatoire* was partially closed off because of work on access to the crypt. And bleachers had been constructed in the choir to accommodate the singers of a holiday concert. They were assembling for practice, starting vocal warmups, and an assiduous factotum kept thwarting my efforts to penetrate the transept. With all this going on I felt lucky to obtain wildly fluctuating Bovis readings, between 15'000 and 25'000. I see such values, obtained under stress, as appetizers for the main course which could not be consumed that day.

And yet, those leys lifted me up when I strolled the available portions of the *déambulatoire*. Along the south wall, nearest the Swiss Belchen, farthest from the civic turmoil, I felt a delicious sense of lightness, of weightlessness.

Violette gained admission to the crypt during her own visit, preceding mine. Able to work in total tranquillity, she found the Moon line of the Blauens and, a few yards away, the Sun line linking Petit Ballon and Swiss Belchen.

On a later occasion Violette encountered Dr. d'Aujourd'hui at a meeting and told him of our expeditions to verify the theory he had published. She said he seemed amused. Scientists who claim the mainstream are never enthusiastic when the esoteric validates their theories.

[1]   Dr. Rolf d'Aujourd'hui, "Archaeo-Geometrie: Beziehung zwischen astronomischen Fixpunten und praehistorischen Fundstellen in Belchendreieck der Region Basel."
Lecture presented by the Cantonal Archaeologist of Basel to the General Meeting of the Gesellschaft für Forschung auf Biophysikalischen Grenzgebieten, September 1991. (Translates as "Association for Research in Biophysical Frontier Areas".)

[2]   Alsace has a special culture all its own, tributary to its war-torn history. Alsace was part of the Holy Roman Empire from the 10th until the 17th centuries. French influence became dominant in the 16th century and it became a protectorate and then was fully incorporated into France by King Louis XIV. French culture spread although the popular language was German. As a result of the Franco-Prussian War of 1870-71 Alsace was taken over by the Germans. France regained control in 1919 as a result of World War I. Hitler's Germany took it back in 1940, and at the end of World War Two in 1945 it again became French. Alsace consists of the two *Départements* bordering the Rhine River: Upper Rhine and Lower Rhine. Alsace-Lorraine is a region comprising Alsace and the Département of the Moselle, immediately to the west. Numerous transits and brief sojourns in this beautiful region have taught me that the population is delighted to be French but they are proud of their German culture as well, especially their own private dialect of that language.

[3]   In its simplest expression a "retable" is a shelf above an altar used for candles, the crucifix and other ritual objects. Sometimes they are decorated with painted panels which can be quite elaborate, even with shutters opening like a book to reveal additional painted scenes and sculpture. The Retable of Issenheim was created in the early 16th century by the painter Mathias Grunewald for the convent of Issenheim and was transported later to Colmar where it is shown in separate sections in the convent of Unterlinden.

[4]   Trying to answer this question I first approached an anthropologist and an antiquarian among my acquaintances. No help. Finally I dug into the biblical sources on my shelves, and there one finds plenty of verification that the Geon, or sometimes Gihon, is indeed a river. There is disagreement on where it flows. *La Bible de Jerusalem*, authority in Protestant Switzerland, calls it the Gihon and says it flows through Kush. This is in Genesis II, 11-14. Cush or Kush is said to be Ethiopia, which would make this river the Nile. Other researchers refute this, saying the Cush is in Arabia, or even in the Kassites east of Mesopotamia.

The Geon/Gihon is mentioned in the Apocalypse of St. Paul, found in the apocrypha but not in official versions of the Christian New Testament. The M.R. James translation (Oxford: Clarendon Press, 1924) verse 23, cites four rivers: "in the land of promise.....the river of honey is called Phison, and the river of milk Euphrates, and the river of oil Geon, and the river of wine Tigris." Willis Barnstone, in *The Other Bible* (Harper, 1984), spells it Gihon in his version of that Apocalypse.

None of my sources speak of the Ganges. James and Barnstone agree on Phison, the Jerusalem Bible says Pishon. Charles W. Laymon in his *Commentary on the Bible* (Abingdon Press, 1971) is dogmatic: "Proposed identification of Pishon (the Indus or a river in Arabia) and of Gihon (the Nile of "Nubian Nile") lack cogent support," he maintains. He suggests the Pishon and the Geon were simply other regional streams that drained into the Garden of Eden. The short river we call the Jordan is also evoked, without enthusiasm.

My own opinion is that the Benedictine monks who built this church knew what they wanted. When they laid mosaic tiles reading Ganges they meant Ganges. Alternative literature on the life of Jesus places him in India for a large portion of the so-called "missing years" of the New Testament. Supporting citations from my bookshelves are too copious for this footnote. And I think they meant the Nile, the world's longest river, also known to Jesus during his extensive travels between the ages of twelve and thirty.

5   A dolmen in its simplest expression is two boulders roofed by a third one, the latter being flattish in aspect. The effect is to create a kind of shelter, a tent of rock. Dolmens were created for ritual purposes, sometimes to serve as tombs. In our dowsing of dolmens we used the 8.6 wavelength, a response to positive polarity indicating a place of ceremony and a response to negative polarity indicating a sepulchre.

6   This, of course, is not what the builders called it. For the medieval Christians who brought their type of spirituality to Mont Sainte-Odile, anyone earlier than the Romans was heathen and the Romans were pagan. This was a kind of racial discrimination, directed also at those of the Celtic people who had not converted. Because they did not know Jesus Christ, they were obviously heathen or pagan, meaning uncivilized and probably savage. But we know of ancient peoples unfortunately described as savage who still enjoyed a level of culture and civility that we might envy in these violent "Christian" centuries.

7   Adolphe Landspurg, *Les Hauts-Lieux d'Energie d'Alsace, des Vosges et de la Forêt Noire*. Mulhouse: Editions duRhin, 1992. 376p., bibliography. ISBN 2-86-339083-X.
Adolphe Landspurg, *Alsace Terre de Sourciers*. Mulhouse: Editions du Rhin, 1990. 325p., bibliography. ISBN 2-86-339064-X.

Chapter Twenty-Two

PICNICS

Home again from Alsace, I spent most of a week taking care of the home and garden essentials, with an evening of rock-climbing thrown in for good measure. Then it was time to head for Cluny for my first visit in two years.

Paul had uncovered some old Roman roads, one of their outposts, and a pre-Christian burial mound, so our first morning in the field was amply furnished. He had discovered a network of roads hidden by the passage of time, not known to contemporary mapmakers. A small stone outpost, a mini-fortress in effect, stood on a dominating hilltop at the intersection of a cluster of these roads. Paul thought he had found six of them, which my Lecher speedily confirmed, even adding a few more. In fact, it seemed to be picking up some footpaths too, one of which led into the forest behind the outpost. Less than one hundred yards into the woods is a tumulus (or barrow). The Lecher and Bovis quickly confirmed it to be a burial mound. Seven thousand years old, said the Lecher, whereas the Roman guard post dated only to 240 BC +/-.

After lunch that first day we went up to the knoll to run the Lecher over the power points. Quickly it confirmed them, although a lot of the ancillary frequencies did not respond. One that did respond was 6.3 negative, indicating sacrifices, right on the negative power point at the top of the hill.

Saturday's public market in Cluny kept us busy admiring and selecting country-fresh vegetables, fruits, eggs, cheeses and other table treats. It was hot and muggy, inducing us to laze around under the trees until four o'clock. Then we went out to do some more prospecting of Roman roads. We did find one, plus a crossroads shrine. Our path led to a known Roman bridge connecting two meadows, and it was possible to date that to 200 BC.

Sheets and sheets of heat lightning, accompanied by ominous rumblings, provided the show for our late supper under the trees. It rained during the night, and in the morning fog shrouded our mountaintop destination for the day. Indecision crept in — do we go or not? In mid-morning we got our answer as skies began to clear. We hastened to gather gear and to get our food ready.

Paul and Margaret had asked me to come on this particular weekend because there was going to be a big Sunday picnic on Mont St-Romain. A friend, another eccentric like us, proposed to gather about fifty people up on the generous, rounded summit to celebrate the summer solstice, which fell on the next day, Monday. This site was believed to have been a Roman "oppidum" -- a fortified town. Granted it was a fine hilltop for the purpose, but when we got there it was hard to spy any ruins.

There was to be a treasure hunt, and we three agreed to "plant the treasure". As soon as we had our fill of sausages and potato salad Paul and I left discreetly to investigate a small amphitheater he remembered. This would be where we would hide the "treasure". Hidden in a grove of trees there was a stone circle, and in the center there were three or four rows of stone benches rimming a circular pit. At last, some vestiges!

"The archaeologists say this was Roman," Paul said.

"Let's verify that," I suggested, unsheathing the Lecher antenna.

After trying my series of wavelengths that identify cultures, seeing/feeling what wobbled, what didn't, I had news for him.

"Probably the Romans took advantage of what was here," I said with an ill-concealed grin, "but this was Celtic first."

We continued busily dowsing the site with both the Lecher and Paul's copy of the Hartmann lobe antenna, when suddenly we realized we had company. In fact, we found ourselves being asked questions. Picnickers and treasure hunters had gradually infiltrated the grove, were watching us at work, began to sit on the circles of stone benches, and they wanted to *know*.

Thus I began to give an impromptu lecture, *une conférence* in French, before an audience of about twenty friendly, cordial strangers who asked intelligent, perceptive questions. With Paul assisting, I explained the Hartmann network, power points and polarity, vibrational rates and the lot, and our listeners were enchanting to work with. Paul said I did it very well, pitched just right to the audience. But my praise is for the audience — they were wonderful. This was a mind-expanding moment for me, even more rewarding than my first experience of its kind in the forest on Mont Ste-Odile. Once again I had found the French to be particularly open to what might be called the "occult sciences".

At home that evening Paul demonstrated his exploration of the human aura using the lobe antenna as finder. It worked, quite evidently. He found the edge of my aura about two feet out from my body.

After supper in the garden I went alone to measure the knoll energies at sunset on the eve of the solstice. This became a mystical experience. As the sun hovered just above the horizon I began to get readings similar to an early sunrise two years previously, but in reverse order. As I stood on the central power point, the pendulum gave me 12'000 Bovis. I let the sun sink into the western hills and then, with just its upper rim glowing, I measured again — it hit 14'500. A few minutes later, with the sun now quite gone, the vibrational rate had fallen back to 12'500. All this time my neck hairs prickled.

Now, with dusk falling, I moved to the center of the contiguous set of circles, onto the negative point which had dowsed for sacrifices. Standing in a semi-meditative state, I began to feel acutely uncomfortable. The Bovis rate had collapsed to 3'000 and I felt uneasy, as if I were being watched. I felt malevolent eyes boring into my back. A chill joined that prickle in the neck. Time to get out of there! I went back down the hill to rejoin Paul and Margaret.

"Before I say anything," I told Paul, "please check my aura again with your antenna." He murmured assent.

To our joint surprise, he found the edge of my aura about six feet out from the body. Then I related my experience up there with the sunset energies.

"This was a very spiritual moment," I told them. "First it was elating, on the beneficial spot. And then it was bad on the other spot, beginnng to be frightening."

"The antenna shows what effect all that had on your aura," he confirmed.

We concluded that my aura may have expanded somewhat in response to the sunset energies, but that it expanded further as a form of defense when an intangible threat manifested, when I *felt* the threat. In other words, the aura might spontaneously form a shield against psychic attack.

Elated but very tired, and more than a little pensive, I said goodnight and went upstairs. It was good I took my rest, because Monday's discoveries were boggling.

Three days earlier, while following Roman roads, we had seen a kind of a circle in a field about half a kilometer north of the knoll. It was time to check it out. This was basically a cow pasture, unoccupied at the moment, sloping rather than level. Halfway downslope our dowsing revealed the arc of an invisible inner circle about twenty feet in diameter and about five feet thick. We began to find flat stones, just visible in the grass and arranged in vaguely curving lines. Paul counted fifteen of them.

My testing with the Lecher was inconclusive, nothing seemed to fit. Prowling through the little notebook under my own subheading of "qualities" I found a frequency Violette had given me, one I had never used. My notes said "sound, resonance, acoustic sources, Roman/Greek theatres". Without further ado I set the Lecher's cursor to 7.4. Paul and I watched in amazement as the antenna began to react very positively while I slowly rotated.

"Paul, this is a Roman theatre!" I exclaimed. Immediately the field took on another aspect in our eyes. Yes, it was sloping gently downwards in kind of a bowl shape. Yes, those flat stones could be lines of seats fitting the curve of the bowl. At my suggestion Paul went down to the bottom and I ran up to the top. Slowly orienting himself on what might have been the stage, he began to declaim. That is, he recited some Shakespeare aloud, with dramatic emphasis but without raising his voice to a yell.

"It's perfect up here, Paul," I called. "We've found an ancient theater."

An open-air theater, rows climbing the hill, actors and chorus below, exploiting the really fine acoustics.

Forest began across the fence at the top of the bowl. We prowled around inside the woods and found a tumulus, another burial mound. Bovis 1'000, as befits death. But tumuli seem to be everywhere in that part of France, and this one was anticlimactic to our theatrical discovery. After dating it to 4675 BC, we returned to the house and Margaret's great vegetable curry, our last meal together this trip. Then they were off to the airport and I was off to my Alps.

A few weeks earlier, at a sort of metaphysical evening on the lakeshore, I had met a young woman who I will call Juliette. We were there to listen to the lady who had given me a clairvoyant reading some years earlier. Juliette said she had begun helping people regress to pick up pastlife information. I'd been wanting to try this ever since that evening conference in Molly's big attic room, so after returning from my trips to Alsace and France I called for an appointment.

Juliette had a small room set aside in the family home, on the fringe of one of the lakeshore cities. This meditation space was ornamented with wall hangings, the usual Buddha and other sacred objects, a few crystals, light new age-y music and incense wafting lazily through the atmosphere. She did not use hypnosis, as do most regression therapists, but relied on creating a trance-like mood with her voice. Her words aimed at guiding me to meet my "Higher Self". It took a long time, a very long time, for this method to open me up. If I had not been (by this time) a longterm meditator I think nothing at all would have come of it. It is not clear to me that I ever met my Higher Self during this hour.

Images formed slowly. Finally I saw a spare old man staring at me from a sun-drenched, freshly-cut cornfield. He wore what seemed to be an old corduroy work suit, if there ever was such a thing, with cap, and gray stubble covered his deeply-lined face. Possibly he symbolized something from a past life, even a past life itself, but I could not link him to the notion of "Higher Self". Right after the old man came a swarm of blue-and-green bees against a dark background.

Then I saw myself in France, standing in a sunny field similar to the old man's cornfield, a vast plain. My name was Doris and I saw myself from the rear, with a thick braid of long blonde hair hanging down my back, wearing a loose dress like a caftan, down to mid-calf. I seemed to be looking into the distance. The number "1839" flashed in luminous figures, without any strong sense that it applied to the me that was Doris.

Juliette tried to lead me through a portal, and after a bit I saw a purple door which led to a tunnel. Purple became a dominant theme for a while, until the scene showed a clear cleavage between light and dark --- left was light and right was dark. Against this background I saw myself as much shorter, dark-haired, a bride in a white gown, on the arm of my new husband. He started out to be a vaguely French type, black-haired, with a square Hitler mustache, but he turned away as if I had spurned him. Certainly his appearance turned me off. My groom mutated into a tall, blond, good-looking man with a strong jaw and a generous mouth smiling at me adoringly. This was more like it! If we're going to daydream, let's do it right! But quickly I was nude, almost Rubenslike, suckling my new-born baby, handing it to this new husband, who then handed our child back to me, saying "merci."

Doris returned to the scene, moving slowly through a hot, dull, empty village with a very ordinary fountain. She was alone, and I got the sense she was a "serveuse", a waitress. One of those past lives that was basically dreary. Then the effort to meet my Higher Self limped: I was distracted from the purple doors by the old man in the field.

Space flowed into blue/green, and I saw a purple form outlined in gold, shaped like shoulders and a head. This gold-rimmed purple shape reminded me of the evolving forms that came frequently in meditation. The left side went dark, until another snapshot emerged: I was wearing a tightly-molded dress with a long waist and a flared skirt. I had time to note that my hair was dark gray and flat, then it all clicked off.

Juliette called herself a "facilitator", but none of this imagery had come easily. There was nothing "facile" about it. It was all like pulling teeth, stumbling uncertainly down a stony path. She thought I needed to work on this material and integrate it, which task I began on the way home. Overall I was disappointed in this effort. I could accept these scenes as snatches from past lives, but I found it all a bit chaotic. The experience left me hungry for better definition, a sharper sense of what and when.

The hiking and climbing season had already begun with a series of "warm-up" expeditions. I'd been to Juliette on a Monday, following a long Sunday hike that had all my joints complaining. Thermal baths helped sooth and smooth the physical body, and the following Sunday brought that "sharper sense of what and when" in a different context. A dozen of us attacked the Petite Dent-de-Morcles, a jagged pinnacle that punctuates the panorama as seen from my home. This was very difficult because the rock was occasionally crumbly, disintegrating under one's foot, thus requiring exquisite care in moving upwards. It was challenging, hard, satisfying to conquer but nothing I ever wanted to do again.

For the next two months there was a lot of mountaineering. I guided two teenage grandchildren onto the heights, separately, and had the satisfaction of seeing them take to rock like ducks take to water. "Granny Michèle" was allowed to open doors as her grandmother had opened them for her. My daughter Carol came as summer slid into September, and we enjoyed a variety of hikes and excursions. One of the best was our "vibrational pilgrimage" to the standing stones at Yverdon and the perenially mystic atmosphere of the Abbey at Romainmôtier, where five years earlier I had chanted with Pierre's dowsing group.

On that first expedition I had had only the Hartmann antenna with which to glean information. Now I could bring the Bovis and Lecher techniques to bear on these inspiring sites. The stones told the Lecher they were Celtic, which is not a surprise or new information. The taller menhirs vibrated to 9'000 and 10'000 Bovis, but many of the smaller ones yielded only a normal rate. One can suspect they may not have been restored to the precise position they would prefer.

We bathed in beauty at Romainmôtier. My own vibrations turned somersaults on the steps descending into the nave, a vertiginous perspective worth 15'000 on the scale. I've noticed on other occasions that this entry point can be awe-inspiring, simply from the sense of stepping into a softly buzzing vibrational field. It was slightly higher in the transept, 16'000. We did a little chanting for our own sakes in the focal center, at a moment when we had the Abbey to ourselves. It was divine, a sacred moment.

The vibrational structure increased but also became unstable as we penetrated deeper into the church. Where the waters cross behind the altar in the sanctuary the pendulum settled hesitantly on 21'000, but for a moment it seemed on the brink of zooming toward 40'000. I felt happily "otherworldly" all the time in there, and I know that Carol was moved by her first experience of medieval stone power.

The weekend after Carol's departure found me on the Gastlosen range for two days of climbing with Alpine Club companions. We celebrated my seventieth birthday atop the Rüdigerspitze, after a lot of interesting rope work. There were no candles on my sandwiches, but there was plenty of dirt under my fingernails after a hairy series of rappels down steep muddy slopes.

That put a glorious, but grimy, end to my alpine season. Within a short time I was packing my valises for a long autumn ramble to New England, to Canada (for a reunion with Molly and her new family), to California and to Arizona. Entering my eighth decade required what would be two months of visiting with family and friends on both coasts, plus explorations into territories new to me.

PART FOUR
Another World Opens

Chapter Twenty-Three

VOICES

One day in California in the late 1980s I was browsing in a metaphysical-esoteric bookshop, and I asked the clerk to point me to shelves focusing on dowsing and earth energies. She directed me to a shelf and said to look on its left end. No wonder I had trouble finding these titles: there wasn't much there.

Among the handful of books on my subjects were two about a place in Arizona called Sedona, of which I had never heard. There was also a foldout map of sites around Sedona called "vortexes". We didn't then use that term in Europe, but I understood it to mean "power points" as we know them. The books didn't speak to me but I selected the foldout map for later reference.

This place called Sedona seemed to be loaded with power points, worthy of my attention on some future trip. The notion got filed away in the mental cabinet, and the map went into a file box in my "California gear". The notion and the map slumbered for several years.

In early 1993 I prepared another issue of my annual "Midwinter Missive", which I send out early in the year in the same spirit as some people send holiday greeting cards. While looking over the mailing list it was evident I hadn't heard from Marina in several years, so I sent a copy of the letter to her usual address. About a month later it came back, marked "Moved - address unknown".

Finding "lost" friends is always a challenge. In this case I was not ready to give up easily, for Marina had been a factor in opening the way for me. She had served as a catalyst in my spiritual development, sending me the books and pushing the button that started me on the meditational path. Thus I wrote to a former colleague who had known us both in New York, and after some weeks there came a reply. Yes, she had found Marina in one of our professional directories, and there was a new address: Sedona, Arizona.

Coincidence? Until this moment in my life I still could allow a coincidence to creep in from time to time, but I knew this was not one. It was time to act. My letter to her new address brought a rapid reply: "you must come!"

Thus in November of that year I drove my rental car eastward out of Southern California and up through the Cajon Pass to the high desert. I began to breath comfortably again, both physically and spiritually. The vast

Mojave Desert speaks to me in mysterious ways. I love the long vistas across the stony, cactus-studded plateaus, the myriad dry streambeds leading up to peaks of fractured stone and rubble, the sage brush, the lava beds, and the saguaro "Joshua" trees, their arms raised to the cosmos. The air is clearer, the sky bluer, and the horizon seems full of promise.

Make no mistake, this desert is a harsh place that can kill the careless adventurer. In a well-fueled automobile on a splendid highway, carrying adequate drinking water and picnic supplies, it is a lark. To venture off-road, as an explorer, one must be equipped for survival.

The land slopes gently downward again to the Colorado River and the sprawling town of Needles, where one crosses to Arizona. I stopped often to make photographs and then to picnic. The long climb from the river's near-sea level altitude arrowed through stark desert until Kingman. There the road bends hard-right to the east, after which desert gives way subtly and slowly to steppes where the bushes are man-high, the mountains beginning to be covered with foliage. Somewhere around Ash Fork I began to feel like a different person, lighter, happier, filling with serenity. Then one is in the pine forest country of Williams and Flagstaff, around 7'000 feet, and my spirits soared with the altitude.

This was the second Monday of November and dusk was gathering as I descended Oak Creek Canyon from Flagstaff. There were raccoons near the creek!

Sedona sprawls on both sides of the highway, under a backdrop of red rock mountains already fading to purple as night fell. I found Marina's home easily enough and she received me warmly.

"Before we do anything else, I want you to see something," she said, leading me out onto her garden deck. She pointed uphill to a mountain mass behind the town.

"Look," she said.

I looked. The mountain was glowing.

I looked around some more. No moon. No city lights. It was dark all around us, yet that mountain was glowing. Sedona's first mystery!

Sleep was sound and refreshing, but not long. Opening the curtain, I could watch the piton of Chimney Rock as the early morning sun painted it red. After breakfast we strolled up the lane to the national forest area on the apron of Capitol Butte, the mass which had been illuminated the night before.

It was fantastic how the color of the rocks kept shifting in the morning light. There was steady, constant sunlight pouring out of a blue, blue sky, but the Butte and Chimney Rock kept mutating within a warm segment of the spectrum. I could perceive no visible geological explanation for the nighttime glow.

Shortly after my arrival Marina told me that we had a luncheon date for the next day.

"A friend and I have a standing date for lunch on Mondays, but today we both had problems," she said. "So she proposed tomorrow instead, and I told her you would be with us, and she said that would be fine with her. Is that all right with you?"

"Yes, of course," I replied.

At midday we drove down to Shugrue's restaurant on the highway. We were directed to a table tucked away in a corner, and there I was introduced to Marina's friend.

I found myself across the table from a strong-looking lady with brownish hair and eyeglasses which gave her a slightly owlish look. It took only a few minutes of conversation to discover a very forthright personality, a powerful, take-charge type. Her name was Eileen and she was a writer, a very successful novelist. That much Marina had told me in the car.

And there was immediate rapport between the two of us. So much so that I realized later that Marina had been almost relegated to the role of spectator at a verbal tennis match.

Eileen quickly interested herself in what I did. So we talked about my flourishing career as an alpinist, but also my work as an energy dowser, my years of meditation, my interest in stones. Eileen was not just an author, it turned out. She was also a metaphysician, a doctor of homeopathy, an astrologer, an expert on stones, crystals, herbs and floral essences, and she was part Cherokee.

More facets of this amazing individual began to emerge as we talked. She seemed to have psychic powers. She saw me -- clairvoyantly, that is -- moving from my present home for at least part of the year. She insisted that I was farther along the spiritual path than I believed, that I didn't need my dowsing rods and antennae for surveying spiritual energies.

And another arrow in her quiver proved to be the most mysterious of all: she's a shaman. At the time I did not really have much of a grasp on what that meant. Future developments took care of that gap in my knowledge.

All this was happening over the luncheon table, but I cannot tell you what was on the plate before me. Something vaguely saladic, vegetablic, proteinic, edible but unmemorable. We had been chatting for an hour, discovering some of those little ways in which two personalities fit together, finding a rapport. And then Eileen spoke quite earnestly.

"You really ought to go to Secret Canyon," she said.

"Secret Canyon?"

"Yes, and leave your dowsing tools at home. Just go with your body. See what you feel."

"What's in Secret Canyon?" I asked.

"I'm not going to tell you what you might find. That's for you to discover."

I protested that I could not dowse without my gear, but she was adamant. "If you will come out to my place in a couple of days, we'll walk the land and you will see. You can do it all with your hands."

"Walking the land", I came to understand, is a concept from her native American heritage. I found all of this intriguing and agreed that I would go to Secret Canyon.

Marina also found Eileen's proposal intriguing, and she was quite willing to indulge my growing impatience to explore Secret Canyon. Thus we drove out a few miles northwest of Sedona to the area where canyons slice down through the Mogollon Rim[1]. We pulled off the highway onto a red clay Forest Service road and then parked. Marina led me onto a broad, sandy trail winding through brush and trees at the mouth of a canyon. This was an essentially level trail, rising only very slightly and rhythmed by dips into dry stream beds and rises over little swells, as on a quiet sea. The path was easy compared to my usual alpine excursions. My stride was rapid, echoing my eagerness to probe the mystery of the canyon.

Marina began to complain about the fast pace. "My knees are not so good any more," she said.

"Why is that? Arthritis?" I asked.

"No, it's from levitation," she explained. "I'm a siddha, you know."

Oh yes, now I remembered she had told me that in the beginning. Back in my days in Transcendental Meditation my mentors had proposed "siddha" training but I had declined. They were siddhas and they went downstairs to a special room where, I understood, they levitated and practiced other powers called "siddhis". Certainly levitation was part of the bait offered to nibbling meditators. Not having snapped at the bait — for reasons covered in Chapter Six — I was not given answers about the phenomena I had been experiencing.

So Marina had gone that far, and now she was paying the price in an incapacity to walk a relatively easy trail that was not perfectly level, much less hike it fast.

I went on ahead, opening a gap of a couple of hundred yards between us, but soon I suspected we were not in Secret Canyon. We had not started at an official trailhead with signs and arrows. This was terra incognita, not Secret Canyon. I raced back to find Marina and we agreed to go home. Later consultation of a map proved the error: we had been in Long Canyon, not the elusive secret one.

Wisps of lacy cloud floated high overhead the next morning. A young man named Steve was digging up Marina's septic tank, and she was staying home to supervise this operation.

My mood was paradoxical, my first intention to get an early start toward Secret Canyon held back by an unwillingness to hurry. Steve, between shovelfuls of red clay, discoursed on UFOs, on biblical coding, on the Ark of the Covenant as an electrical transformer. This echo from Alfred DeGrazia's theories held me for a few minutes but my destination was pulling me toward it[2]. After some wrong turns in the village I found the Forest Service office and got a small directional map.

Secret Canyon appeared to be parallel to Long Canyon, so I retraced our route up Dry Creek Road and then 3.4 miles up a hardpan Forest Service road. Logs defined the small sandy parking lot, and a jeep was parked there. The little map seemed to be showing about three miles of trail before reaching a fork where the true Secret Canyon would begin. This looked like another essentially level trail, rising only very slowly. One hour to that fork, I estimated.

Then, a few yards up the trail, I stopped and did something I had never done before. I asked permission. Steve had mentioned an alternative entry to the canyon, through a tunnel, but "you have to ask permission," he had said. I didn't know how to find that tunnel, and I don't like long tunnels anyway, but something in me said that asking permission was the thing to do here.

So I stopped and silently asked permission, with my palms turned up facing the sky. Then I waited for a sign, not really expecting a voice from the sky, or even a voice in my head.

What happened was that after a moment my hands became energized, especially the left hand. There was a sensation of tingling heat. Up ahead a bird chirped, then flew out.

"So that's how permission is given?" I mused. This was definitely a new experience.

I began my hike into Secret Canyon, scanning the brushy sidehills that steadily rose to become canyon walls deeper in, with a high wall seeming to bar the way far ahead. That's the fork, I thought.

My admiration of the landscape gave way to another sensation. There seemed to be the murmur of voices in the distance ahead of me. That is to say, I heard these voices while walking, but they stopped when I stopped.

"Curious," I thought. If there were hikers far ahead, why would they stop talking when I stopped walking? I must be hearing a noise generated by my footsteps.

So I resumed walking, paying close attention to the sound of my footsteps.

And I heard the voices. Now I began to perceive them as the casual chatter of a group of people in the forest far ahead, and the image formed in my mind of elderly native Americans, men and women busy gathering nuts, acorns, herbs, roots and berries.

"What nonsense!" I told myself, stopping once again. And the voices stopped. Clearly my backpack was rubbing against my T-shirt in an unusual way, creating the illusion of voices. So I shifted the pack a bit, adjusted the straps slightly, made sure it was not slipping and rubbing as I walked.

Again I resumed my penetration of Secret Canyon and again I heard the voices. There was no noise from my backpack, just the conversation of the elderly gatherers in a distant grove. Or was it really quite close? I stopped again, and they stopped again.

"Well now, what's going on?" Yes, there was a jeep in the parking lot, there must be hikers or campers up ahead. But a puff of breeze on my back put the lie to that notion. People ahead of me were downwind from me. If they were far enough ahead of me that I couldn't see them, then I could not possibly hear them unless they were shouting directly at me.

I resumed walking, hearing the voices, at ease with the notion of the elderly gatherers, even though I knew they were probably an illusion.

This canyon had a nice feeling about it, over and above the eerie sensation of hearing people who weren't there. There were pleasant "vibes". The trail led up the canyon toward that mountain wall, capped with strange-looking rocks which almost seemed alive. The side wall had become high as well, and there were rocks which seemed to be observing me. One wondered if there were camouflaged windows and doors in those heights, like the wartime fortresses hidden in cliffs at home in Switzerland.

Low oaks and scrub pine began to dominate the undergrowth as I approached the inevitable fork toward the left. At one point my eye was intrigued by several pebbles and small stones. Their pale brown was almost salmon in color, and they seemed good representatives of the place. After asking permission, I picked up three of them, along with a small piece of wood shaped in a vague "y". This piece of wood and one of the pebbles ultimately went into my medicine bag as gifts from Mother Earth.

That left fork of the canyon began to fill with taller trees and the walls were visible only through gaps in the gray and green of the trunks and foliage. When I could see the rimrocks they always seemed mysterious.

About four miles in, after nearly ninety minutes of hiking, I found myself in a friendly grove with a sense of good vibrations. Below the trail ran a stream bed with some pools rimmed by a natural bench of rocks, facing a red wall. There had not been water in the lower canyon, but here there were remnants from the last cloudburst. This spot invited me to clamber down and eat my picnic. It felt almost like a temple.

And these recesses of Secret Canyon were also the perfect place to measure the vibrational state. Before packing up to leave I took out my pendulum and the Bovis biometer. In this delightful setting of rocks, trees and water they gave me a reading of 16'000. Cathedral strength! Some yards away, up on the trail, they measured 12'500. Later, on my way out of the canyon I got a reading of 10'000, at the threshold of spirituality. So Secret Canyon conceals some real power points.

Going deeper into the canyon began to look unwise, for clouds were coagulating overhead. Those lacy wisps of the early morning had taken on mass, form and the darkness that suggests rain. My rental car did not have four-wheel drive and that Forest Service road looked as if it would become a slippery clay surface when wet. Not running but certainly walking fast, I left Secret Canyon in a bit more than an hour and ahead of the rain.

Far ahead of the rain, it seemed. No reason to run for cover. The afternoon was far from over and other canyons were right next door. These major canyons are roughly parallel and can be compared to the fingers on a hand.

Thus I passed the mouth of Long Canyon and went on toward Boynton Canyon and its "vortex" about which I had heard so much. Those dark skies had not yet dumped their load of water.

This turned into a small dowsing ramble. The vortex is supposed to be not far from the parking lot — another typical sand-and-logs Forest Service space — and somewhere on the lower flanks of a little crest at right. This crest slopes down at the end of the northern wall of Boynton Canyon, and there are a series of red rock spires descending the ridge. It's a small scramble through brush and around rocks to get onto the crest.

Up there is where I found the most evidence of telluric energies. My dowsing gear had not gone into Secret Canyon — as Eileen had requested — but it was all in the car.

In fact, coming after the energetic high of Secret Canyon, the Boynton vortex did not show me much. (Future visits proved to be more productive.) I worked with pendulum and the Lecher antenna, and they gave me some negative resonance on the lower part of the crest. The Lecher picked up some electrical energy here and there.

Upcrest from the spire my Bovis measurement gave 7500 units, above average but not impressive. Downcrest from the spire I read from 2000 to 4000, really unhealthy. That first spire looked eminently climbable, but I do not do sandstone and its fine film of red grit without a partner, a rope and adherent shoes.

There was a man seated with his back against the spire, and he looked almost ecstatic.

"What are you getting?" I asked him.

"I'm very happy here," he told me, his eyes half-shut.

It turned out he was a dealer in crystals and stones, traveling a lot, and he found this Boynton spire a fine antidote to road fatigue. But he was clearly uninterested in a real conversation. The sky was finally dropping a light sprinkle, so I headed for home.

During the evening Marina and I talked about my experiences in Secret Canyon, which she found very significant. She handed me a small book entitled *Soul Recovery and Extraction*[3], written by my new friend Eileen.

"This will tell you what she does, what shamanism is all about," my hostess explained.

Avidly curious at this point, I plunged into this exposition of a set of concepts that were wholly new to me. Once "in" the book it was hard to put down. This Arizona adventure was expanding my horizons with the speed of light.

"Shamanism," Eileen wrote, "is the ability of an individual to move into an altered state and travel the inner dimensions of what we call nonphysical reality. This technique is as old as humans have been here on earth. It is practiced around the world, and in the last decade [referring to the 1980s] has been reintroduced to Western civilization — although among indigenous cultures, it has continued to be practiced as a healing tool without interruption."

Soul recovery, as she explains it, "is about regaining the fragments of one's soul energy that have been trapped, lost or stolen, either by another person or through a traumatic incident that has occurred in one's life."

And "extraction" is a shamanic tool for dissolving blockages in our auras or in our physical bodies inside this shroud of electromagnetic energy.

These two terms, soul recovery and extraction, were totally new concepts to me. So were the voices I had heard earlier in the day. As I read into the night, finally putting down this new kind of "thriller" in favor of needed sleep, I felt myself passing through some kind of threshold. The sense of being on a distinct path blossomed.

---

[1]   The Mogollon Rim is a giant escarpment running roughly east and west for about two hundred miles across northern Arizona. It forms the southern edge of the Colorado Plateau, and erosion of this edge has created a series of great canyons behind Sedona. From the Rim the land drops abruptly, the altitude difference between Flagstaff , on the Plateau, and Sedona being nearly three thousand feet.

[2]   Alfred de Grazia, *God's Fire: Moses and the Management of Exodus*. Princeton: Metron Publications, 1983. xi+322 p., notes, index, illustrations, tables. ISBN 0-940268-03-5.

    Fifth voume in the author's Quantavolution Series (ten titles announced).

[3]   Ai Gvhdi Waya, *Soul Recovery and Extraction*. Cottonwood, AZ 86326: Blue Turtle Publishing, 1992, 1993. 86p. ISBN 0-9634662-3-2.

The author and her new friend Molly

The author at her favorite menhir at Avebury

273

Stonehenge

Scissors arches in Wells Cathedral

Sedona's sweeping panoramas

Cathedral Rocks, a major Sedona power point

Tom, UFO researcher
and author, and my
daughter Carol

Kay at the Boynton vortex

Chapter Twenty-Four

THE PANTHER

Late the next morning we drove down toward Cottonwood, pausing at a virtually anonymous intersection lost in the desert to pick up Eileen and her mother Ruth. They guided us to a small restaurant next to the bridge over the Verde River. We settled ourselves at table and ordered from the interesting menu. Eileen sat facing me.

"Well, did you ever get to Secret Canyon?" she asked.

"Oh yes, I sure did."

"So, did anything happen?"

Not an innocent question, that. She knew something would happen, otherwise she wouldn't have suggested that I go there.

"I heard voices."

A small, secret smile stole over her face.

"Uh-huh. Tell me about it."

So I related the story of my hearing the voices, of pausing, observing the sounds of my boots and my backpack, studying the wind, and always hearing the quiet voices downwind when I resumed walking.

"My impression was that I was hearing a group of indigenous people gathering nuts and berries and acorns and other things to eat."

"Uh-huh." Still that knowing little smile, but she didn't offer any comment.

I produced one of the stones I'd picked up in the grove and placed it in her hand.

"Something I picked up for you."

She held it for a moment, then said "it's strong. Thank you."

And the conversation turned in other directions until the end of our pleasant meal. Her mother Ruth was an absolute delight. Also, she made deerskin pouches, of which I needed several. When we had paid our bill Eileen said "now let's go out to the ranch."

Marina drove us back up toward Sedona, then turned off onto a side road into a land of sand, stone and sagebrush. A dirt track wound through some hills and led us, bumpily, down into a canyon. Ultimately we were on a flat alongside a creek, flanked on the other side by steep walls of lava-like rock.

Now it was time for my lesson in "walking the land". Except that there was no lesson, and we didn't do it together. Eileen more or less turned me loose to find my way through the invisible lines of earth energies, which I usually surveyed with my dowsing rods.

My hands did indeed begin to pick up vibrations as I moved slowly through the orchard. It was something other than the Hartmann grid but I couldn't say what. I was following an energy line with my hands deployed and really felt as if this technique was indeed working. My line was leading me in the direction of a corral and suddenly, when I smelled horse, the energy connection stopped dead as if a switch had been thrown.

What happened? Then I saw the horse I had smelled, and a light bulb went on in my head. I'm allergic — to cat hair, to long-haired dogs, and to horsehair. It's as simple as that.

Then I turned away from the corral, moving toward the berry patch, and my sense of the energy returned the farther I got from the horse. Something new had been learned!

Eileen proposed we go into her mother's "medicine room" for another experiment. It smelled like she had a program, but I was entirely willing to try anything and everything. We went into Ruth's double-wide trailer and into the small medicine room, with a table full of stones, crystals, and other artifacts, and a bearskin rug on the floor.

Eileen explained what she wanted me to do here. The three of them stood around, observing, while I did a standing meditation holding Ruth's "medicine piece". This kind of artifact is a native American necklace from which hangs a collection of minerals, objects of bone and wood, feathers, whatever suits the wearer, whatever is perceived to help the wearer on her path. Simply looking at a medicine piece convinces one of its ritual significance.

Eileen had asked me to hold it in my left hand and then do brief meditations at each of the four compass points. I was to start at the south and revolve clockwise.

"Let's see what you get," she said.

Eyes closed, breath control, and into a semi-meditative state. I knew instinctively where north and south were, so I faced south. Nothing happened. West was equally unproductive. North likewise. Then I quarter-turned to the east and the colors came.

"She's swaying," someone whispered. Yes, I was rocking a bit.

There was a wonderful evolution of indigos and emeralds, masses of color slowly swirling and reforming on the screen in the front of my head. I stayed a while with this pleasant variation of cerevision.

In answer to the questioning expressions around me, I explained how nice it was when I turned east. Once again there was no commentary. Eileen now proposed we go into her writing studio in the main cottage.

In the house she led us down a hall and into a light-filled room like a veranda, windows on the ends and a wall of windows on the broad facade overlooking the creek. Blue was the dominant color of the space, reflecting up from the carpet. There was a sense of great peace. I was jealous of this delightful place to work.

Eileen produced a sculpted wooden doll and led me to a chair near the door. I recognized the doll as a Hopi Kachina but didn't know which one it was. Most of the Kachinas are fairly grotesque but this one was very sober, graceful, almost Madonna-like.

"This is the Corn Maiden," she said. "Meditate with her in your left hand. You can touch her with the right hand too if you want, but she should be held in the left. While you're doing that I'll be showing Marina my new computer."

Thus I settled into meditative mode, cradling the Corn Maiden in my left palm, my right hand resting on my thigh. After a bit I realized that, although meditation is good to do any time, nothing special was happening in this one. And I was learning to look for the special in Eileen's suggestions. Everything had a purpose.

So I placed my right hand on top of the Corn Maiden, and soon something did indeed begin to happen.

Gradually, slowly, steadily, she sent heat up my left arm, through the shoulders and shoulder blades, warming the chest, all the thorax. My heart became very warm. I sensed my heart area as a great white flower slowly opening and spreading its petals wide. Like a lotus. It was incredible. My heart chakra was opening, my whole upper body infused with the energy of this blossoming.

I was still bathing in this marvelous energy field when Eileen came over.

"How's it going?" she asked.

I explained what had been happening.

"That's what she's supposed to do," she commented. "She has been ritually programmed to open the heart chakra."

Those two had finishing playing with the new computer, and Eileen put the Corn Maiden away in her special place.

"Let's go over to my hogan and do a meditation," she proposed.

No argument from either of us, this seemed like a great idea.

Eileen's hogan is an eight-sided room constructed in the garden, right behind Ruth's trailer home. A hogan is a traditional Navajo structure, usually a circular, domed and earth-covered house. Eileen's engineer husband David had built her hogan, and perhaps that is why it is octagonal instead of round. I didn't ask. The hogan's walls were lined with pictures of animals but there was no furniture except for a kind of commode against one wall. Its surface was covered with objects I didn't have time to observe closely.

Marina and I settled on the animal pelt rug and Eileen suggested I hold her personal medicine piece during the meditation. In the left hand, of course.

She picked up a drum and began circling around us, beating the drum with a strong, steady rhythm. The drumming resonated with my personal vibrations, it was stimulating, even exciting. But I was physically uncomfortable, my seventy-year-old back and hips not happy with sitting on the floor. This meditation did not get off the ground for me, the power of her medicine piece not communicating with the rest of me.

She stopped drumming, asked how we were doing, digested the fact it was not going well. At least, not for me.

"Let's go back to the house and have some tea," she said, hanging up the drum.

This was mid-November, we were in the bottom of a canyon in northern Arizona, the afternoon was maturing, and evening chill was warning of its arrival. In these circumstances our cup of herbal tea was doubly welcome. It was a pleasurable moment of companionship, after which our hostess suggested we go back to the hogan for another try. Yes, indeed, I was happy about the possibility of doing another meditation.

Back in the octagonal space Eileen pointed to the mass of objects littering the commode.

"Pick out anything you like to help you this time."

Quickly my eyes and then my hand settled on a big amethyst crystal point.

Again we settled onto the floor and Eileen began to drum, slowly circling us as she beat out the resonance. Bit by bit colors invaded the psychic screen in the front of the head: my cerevision was coming into play.

Then I heard a panther cough.

It was really more of a harsh, coughed, stifled screech, but I heard it. Then a bear growled (yes!), a fox barked, an eagle screamed, a crow chawked. There was an endless babble of animal and bird jabberings and squawkings. I could no longer identify all the creatures I was hearing, but there was a whole zoo roaring and warbling. It was wild, eerie, magical.

The sound of a rattle entered the chorus, a very scratchy kind of rattle. Eileen had her two hands full with the drumming; she could not possibly have been shaking a rattle too. Then a second drum began to beat, in counterpoint to hers. Yes, there were now two drums filling the room with resonance, filling my senses with their pulsating rhythm, reorganizing my consciousness.

She stopped, hung up the drum, sat down facing us.

"Well?"

"I heard a panther cough."

She smiled that secret little smile. I went on to describe everything I had heard, the animals, the birds, the scratchy rattle, the second drum.

She stood up and gestured around the room, at the pictures on the wall. She pointed to the sketch of a leopard basking on a tree branch.

"There's your panther." She strode rapidly around the hogan, pointing out one picture after another of her collection of drawings, sketches, photographs, newspaper and magazine illustrations. "There are your bear, your fox, your birds."

What she was telling me, in fact, was that I had traveled in another dimension, where the creatures whose images lined the walls came alive in my ears and brain and consciousness. This was entering a magical dimension. Eileen had cleverly hacked open my sensory apparatus. It was incredible, another reality.

She sat down again and looked me in the eye.

"You could be a shaman," she announced. "You are shaman material."

Bombshell.

I was dumbfounded, unable to muster words to deal with this new situation.

"Let's go have another tea," she proposed.

While we were conversing over another herbal brew Eileen gave me permission to go back to the hogan with my dowsing gear. I took the Lecher antenna and my Bovis meter. The pendulum made its telltale agitation above 18'000 on the Bovis biometer — up in high spiritual territory. The Lecher reacted positively to all the cosmic frequencies, as well as those for female ritual and the Earth Goddess. Eileen was pleased to hear these observations.

It was evening when Marina and I drove out of the canyon. We went down to Cottonwood for pasta and conversation with "Ecclesiastes", the publisher of a small alternative bulletin.

That night in bed my reading of *Soul Recovery and Extraction* took on a new dimension. I began trying to fit myself into the schema she was describing.

Since Tuesday's lunch Eileen had taken me as a mystic unsure of her powers and led me into deeper understanding of my potentialities. The afternoon's auditory phenomena had bowled me over, especially coming on top of the voices in Secret Canyon. She had generously used her shamanic powers of perception and diagnosis to show me what I have and what I might become.

Best of all, I thought as I snuggled down under the covers, she had also opened my heart chakra. That sensation glowed within me as sleep took over.

Chapter Twenty-Five

THE LIZARD IS GREEN

Those medicine pieces — Ruth's and Eileen's — impressed me deeply. Stones and crystals, pieces of animal bone and skin, small artifacts of all kinds were fashioned into pendants hanging from beadwork necklaces. Their general composition of natural objects resonated within me, there was a kind of atavistic attraction. There was nothing in my known genealogy to suggest a native American ancestor, but I could easily believe in a karmic connection. The pull was too strong to be ignored.

Before the day at the ranch was over I asked Eileen if she would tell me how to obtain one. She had hesitated a moment before answering; I could see her thinking. Yes, it's a ceremonial object; did she judge me worthy to have one? At least that is how I interpreted her hesitation.

Then she told us about Chloe the artist/artisan and how to find her. The directions were very complicated and we needed to telephone ahead. That evening Marina arranged our appointment for the next day. She wanted a piece of jewelry for herself, not necessarily a tribal medicine piece.

Before we said our goodbyes Eileen had told me "if you are still here on Saturday, let's have lunch together again." I liked this idea, but I had planned to leave on Saturday to return to Pasadena. I replied to Eileen that I would try to work out the family matter in Pasadena, and if this was possible I would be delighted to have that luncheon meeting.

The next day, Friday, Marina and I drove south toward Phoenix, then east into another group of mountains. We found Chloe in a forest service cabin in the bottom of a canyon, after fording one stream in the car and parking just before the next stream.

This vivacious redhead works intuitively, one could say clairvoyantly. After consulting a long time with Marina, to create a truly beautiful piece of silver jewelry with stones, she turned to me. She listened to my ideas about what I should have in my medicine piece, but then she told me of stones she thought were important for me.

"You will need these for working with the animal and plant spirits in the forest," she observed, pointing to pieces of forest agate, amber, apatite, Botswana agate, spectrolite, kunzite, a small Tibetan bell, and a grouse feather.

The notion of working with the forest spirits had not yet crossed my mind, but immediately I knew she was right. I would indeed begin performing rituals — I had no idea what rituals — and they would occur in my mountains, their canyons and rocks and forests and high pastures. These pictures zoomed into my consciousness. Mother Earth would get whatever little inventive boost I could dream up.

Chloe's inventory was mind-boggling. A huge cabinet containing dozens and dozens of drawers occupied one wall of the cabin, and she pulled out packets of everything she had proposed plus those items I had requested. Then she left me to make my selections while she bargained with Marina. I used my pendulum to select the pieces which meshed best with my personal vibrations. The crystals, stones and objects I chose in that way make up — with slight later modifications — the medicine piece I wear now for ceremonial occasions, including rituals out in the mountains.

This was a long day for Marina and me. We were gone more than ten hours, in all kinds of weather, many hours at the wheel. Back in Sedona I telephoned my mother to firm up what was expected of me and learned that I need only be there Sunday evening for a small family dinner party. Staying over an extra day looked just do-able, just. Then I called Eileen to organize our date for the morrow.

For bedtime reading, I finished her book on "Soul Recovery and Extraction." There was no hesitation in my mind about wanting such an experience. The idea of getting back lost soul pieces spoke emphatically in me. I was sure there were a lot out there, imprisoned in other dimensions. Marina had obviously foreseen what effect those pages would have on me.

Eileen and Ruth met me at Shugrue's promptly at noon the next day. Marina had stayed at home, wiped out from the previous day and happy not to be needed as a chaperone. After we had ordered our meals my two companions pulled out a series of gifts. There were three small "give-aways", wrapped in red cotton cloth in the native American tradition, and a bundle of sage for smudging. All this took me very much by surprise. I felt honored, and that is also part of the native American tradition.

Ruth left the table after we had finished eating, and I seized this occasion to ask Eileen if she would be willing to do a shamanic soul journey for me.

"I'm sorry to disappoint you, but no, I won't do it. At this point I take on life-and-death cases only. Go to one of the facilitators I have trained. They are listed in the back of the book."

No use masking my disappointment. It was real. Her refusal had not been uncordial, simply realistic from her point of view. And I would have to follow through with one of her associates.

When Ruth returned to the table they told me that they had some gifts for Marina too, so they would follow me back to the house.

About half an hour later, once they had arrived and had presented Marina with their gifts, Eileen produced a large brown paper shopping bag and set it on the floor near me.

"Would you be willing to do another exercise?" she asked.

"Sure, what's this one?"

She pulled a package from the depths of the shopping bag and set it on the table in front of me. It was about the size of a fat paperback book, wrapped in plain paper, with string.

"I want you to tell me what's in this package," she said.

"How can I do that?" I protested. "I'm not psychic."

"Oh yes, you are." she insisted. "Everyone is. You only have to open to it."

"What do I do?"

"Simply let your left hand hang just above the package. Don't touch it, just collect the vibrations. And tell me what's inside. Go into that little meditative state and read the vibrations."

Holy smoke, I thought, this is all going too fast for me.

So I closed my eyes, took a couple of Apache breaths as Eileen had taught me that previous afternoon at the ranch, and began to concentrate on the package under my hand. It wasn't easy, nothing was coming.

"Hurry up," Eileen said. "You're too slow."

I muttered a small protest and searched for impressions. Something finally began to come.

Here I must make a confession. Eileen produced three packages, all similar, and in each case I struggled to identify the contents. Each time I described a chunk of something, stone or wood or metal, and each time I was wrong. Inside the wrapping was some other kind of object, usually wood or stone but not at all as I had described it. I had seen something else, and Eileen withheld comment.

And I have absolutely no recall of those first three objects.

Then she pulled out package number four.

"Be quicker this time," she urged.

Indeed; I was starting to get the hang of this procedure.

I opened to the packet's vibrations. And a picture began forming.

"Come on," Eileen implored.

The cerevision field was all orange-red and beginning to flicker into form.

"I see fire," I said. "I see flames."

"Anything else?"

"Yes, there's an object, no, it's a creature. A salamander? No, it's a lizard."

"What color?" she asked.

"Green," I replied.

Briskly she set about opening the package. It was a hand-size chunk of grey rock, vaguely rhomboidal in form.

"You see!" I exclaimed. "I'm not psychic. I haven't properly identified a single one of these things."

"Oh yes, you have," she insisted. "This rock is used in a fire ceremony in which a green lizard has a role."

My jaw gaped.

"In each case," she went on, "you have correctly identified the symbolic or the ritual nature of the object. Stone or wood or whatever, you got to the core of it. You didn't see the matter, but you saw the spirit."

Useless to fish for words. I was speechless, but also feeling a slow sense of exultation creep up my spine.

"Now," she said, stuffing the packages back into her shopping bag, "if you ladies can be down at the ranch at seven o'clock I'll do a soul journey for Michèle."

This abrupt about-face took me by surprise. What had happened? Had there been discussion between Ruth and Eileen during the half hour after I left them? Had this psychic exercise played a role? Whatever, I hastened to agree, and Marina said she would come along too.

The two of us did a little shopping, then had an early supper. By six-thirty we were heading south on the highway. It had begun to rain, and Marina asked me to drive. She didn't like to negotiate the dirt road into Eileen's canyon when it would be wet and potentially slick.

We went into Ruth's little medicine room for the journey ritual. The atmosphere of stones and crystals, rattles and feathers, wall hangings, tanned animal skins for the leather pouches she made, and that female buffalo pelt rug — it certainly seemed the right place for such a ceremony.

Everyone who even vaguely needed to do so went to the toilet. Ruth unplugged the telephone. Marina sat crowded into the corner by the door.

"Stay in your body!" Eileen commanded her. "I know you!"

Marina murmured amused assent.

Eileen then explained that she and I would lie down side-by-side on the buffalo skin rug. She placed two bowls of water on the floor nearby, one for washing her hands between operations and the other for disposing of the goo she might pull from my body during the "extraction" phase. Entering her altered state she would ask her Guides and mine for permission to journey and would then go where they led her.

After the journey proper she would blow returned soul pieces first into my heart chakra and then into my crown chakra. Then she would scan my body for the extraction phase, once again taking instruction from the Guides.

When she was finished she would ask for the lights to go on and would expect Ruth and Marina to leave the room. I could not yet ask questions. She would write down everything she had done as fast as she could, so as not to lose any of it, and only after that would we talk. The whole event would take roughly twenty minutes until she called for the lights.

Eileen lay down beside me, on my right, and took my hand. Ruth turned out the lights and picked up the drum. She pounded a steady, strong rhythm, not missing a beat. The drum's hypnotic resonance filled the darkness, to the exclusion of all other sensations. It went on and on, boom, boom, boom, boom, for many minutes.

Then, suddenly, I could feel Eileen stirring beside me. There was sensation as she blew into my heart chakra, and she lifted my torso gently so that the top of my head was accessible to her mouth. Then she seemed to be moving around me, touching me a little bit here and there, finally holding my feet for several minutes before calling for the lights to go on.

The drumming stopped and the light came on. Ruth and Marina left the room. Eileen seized her notepad and scribbled feverishly.

Finally the shaman looked up and began to tell me what had happened, referring constantly to her notepad.

"I flew through a huge cloud of skulls, white bone parts, distorted faces screaming, distortions of anger, hatred, pain, devil, Satan," she said. "It was a black cloud and I felt like Luke Skywalker hurtling through an asteroid belt. As we got clear of it, I saw you down below, in a house, lying on your right side."

She went on: "First my teacher and I netted this cloud. My teacher said that these were the fears that you had brought with you into this lifetime from a former lifetime. My teacher took these netted fears away, so they would never bother you again."

She saw me then as a five-year-old child, asleep on my bed, wearing a blue pinafore over a white, puffed-sleeve blouse, and I was clutching my blanket.

"I felt this terrible, threatening presence behind me," Eileen continued. "I turned and saw this outline of a man, just a dark shape of him, and knew he was a discarnate soul. When he started toward us I told him to stop, but he refused, saying he owned Michèle. The discarnate refused to leave her alone, so we took him to the Dark World, where spirits like him must go."

"I asked the little Michèle if she'd like to return to her older counterpart, and she said yes instantly."

This scene instantly brought to my mind a bedroom that was quite boxy, proportioned like a cube, and rather dark with only high clerestory windows on two sides. There was a dark mustard paisley wallpaper. I have no idea if this was the way my bedroom really was when I was a tiny child; I have no recall of that at all. This was what Eileen's story inspired in me.

There was definitely evil nearby at that time, if not actually in my bedroom. One morning my parents opened the newspaper to discover that our next-door neighbor was a kingpin criminal, at the head of a major bootlegging ring. These were the 1920s, and Prohibition was the law of the land. They had two savage police dogs who snarled at me through the lattice fence, beside the little boy of the family, who seemed mean and taunting to me and was not a desirable playmate. This was a fearful environment for the little me, and it took me more than a decade to conquer my fear of dogs.

Eileen had only begun to spin the story of her journey into the recesses of my soul. The next piece she brought back came as a delightful surprise. She said it was from a past life.

"I saw you in your twenties, with shining black hair all rolled up on top of your head. You were young, beautiful, and dancing the flamenco in a city square. There was a large, white adobe-like building behind you — a city building of some sort. On the right there was a tall wooden pole, like a May Pole, with bright, colorful ribbons that were six to ten feet long, hanging from the spokes of a wheel atop the pole and waving in the breeze. These ribbons and the spokes were decorated with colorful flowers."

Eileen continued reading from her hasty notes.

"There was a crowd of people around you, mostly men dressed in black or embroidered clothing. You were sinuous, dancing with such grace. I didn't hear the music. You wore a bright yellow dress that was skintight, revealing your beautiful body, and below your knees it flared out into a skirt to your ankles. The men were watching you, slavering, their eyes bright with desire, wanting you, wanting to capture your lovely, carefree spirit."

"So I asked this Michèle if she wanted to come back, but she said no, she loved what she was doing," she said. "What this means is that a piece of your soul was trapped in this time when you were so happy. It split off in order to stay there, not wanting to face the unhappier times which she knew, unconsciously, lay ahead for you."

"When I told her that Michèle was climbing mountains at 70, she instantly brightened and said she would come back because she loved living life and loved adventure," she concluded.

Wow, what a picture that is! The May pole Eileen described is found throughout Europe, especially in England and the north of the continent, as I learned in later research. In contrast, the dress and the plaza scene are clearly Andalusian, but similar poles are sometimes found in Spain too. This vivacious soul piece really perked me up after the rather lugubrious event in my childhood bedroom.

Eileen was far from finished. There was one more soul piece.

"On the way back with this second piece I had a huge old manuscript book shoved in my face. Two tall, thin monks handed me this book. They were dressed in black wool, their faces buried in deep hoods and I couldn't see their features. It was a huge manuscript, and I don't know whether it was a Bible — my sense is that it was not."

Here she began to make a sketch of what she had seen. "This book was bound in leather, old and shiny from use. The paper was yellow, dog-eared, chipped papyrus-type material. It was eight to twelve inches thick! It was huge. There was hammered gold all around the rectangular shape of the front cover. In the center was a maltese-type cross. In the center of the cross was a red ruby-like stone, not very well faceted, but shiny. On each of the four points of the cross were much smaller stones like emeralds, also not faceted well but still polished and shining."

"They told me to give this book to you. You had been a monk 600 years earlier in France. They were giving you the book because you had earned the right to have the knowledge it contained."

"My sense of it, after coming out of the journey," she commented, "was that in the center of France there once stood an abbey where you spent a lifetime. I believe there is another building now on this site, it's no longer a religious center."

"You need to go find this place, but wait at least three months after the integration of this book soul-piece. By being at that power point you will physically trigger the memories stored in your subconscious. The knowledge will spill out and be available to you consciously," she concluded.

"Do you have any idea where in France it is," I asked.

"Not really," she replied. "When I asked the monks they pulled out a map of France and pointed a finger in the center. I didn't receive a place name."

Already I could see a quest in my future — the quest to identify the old parchment book, and the quest to find a place where an abbey once stood. Talk about your needle in a haystack. And what a contrast in past lives between a sexy flamenco dancer and a monk!

Those faceless monks triggered recall of the vision I had while doing TM, about two years into meditation. In that film clip I stood at the side of a road as two monks hooded like the Grim Reaper and carrying torches on long poles filed slowly past toward a burning building. (See Chapter Nine.) Flames rose high above the trees as the thatched roof burned in the fading light of a long summer evening. At the time I had wondered if that scene was surging up out of karmic memory. My paternal family traces back to the Huguenots, religious protestants who were viciously persecuted in sixteenth and seventeenth-century France. My ancestors fled to England to escape ending up with their heads on pikes. The burning building, the monks with torches, my subconscious did not invent this out of whole cloth. Of that I felt sure. And here we were again, bringing home a soul piece involving shadowy monks. Not only had we been persecuted by Catholic monks, but at another time I had also been one of them. We weave strange patterns throughout our karmic voyage.

Eileen's notes on the extraction she had performed were equally interesting but not at all as long and detailed.

She opened both my knees and removed tar-like goo. For the right knee she had needed to make two cuts into two different levels of the aura. "It was pretty badly clogged up," she said.

This was certainly well-targeted work. My knees have suffered more than any other part of my body from my adventures as an alpinist. Like most other hikers and climbers I find it easy to ascend but sometimes painful to come downhill. The knees take a beating, and for several years I had been pulling on elastic braces before starting a long descent. And the right knee was unquestionably the worst of the two.

She'd found fat around the top of my heart and aorta, which was removed. She'd found one of my hips very hot, and this is also sometimes a problem region. She'd found both wrists hot and had removed goo. And she had observed the fact of my hysterectomy.

While she was doing these jobs her "helpers" were cleaning up my eyes and my throat (ancient tonsillectomy). She'd found a red lesion at the top entry to my stomach, certainly a reflection of my decades-long battle with ulcers. They had only melted away a couple of years earlier but I could believe there was residual trauma, and she had found it.

Then Eileen told me about the important act of welcoming back one's soul pieces.

"Tell them you welcome them home, that you love them and you want them to stay. Say `please don't leave me again — I need you,' " she instructed me. "And ask what gift they bring you."

She explained that this ritual should go on daily for at least a month to insure that the pieces did not get discouraged and leave again. Twice a day, morning and night while in bed, is a good rhythm.

Then we stood up and left the medicine room. Eileen had me carry the bowl of water into which she had thrown all the goo removed from my body during the extraction process. In the kitchen she instructed me to pour it all down the sink and say a little goodbye prayer over my goo.

It was over. Eileen was obviously tired and did not linger over the goodbyes, except to say I would be protected during the long day I would spend at the wheel on the morrow. We pulled on our rain jackets and left the trailer, got into the car and drove back up that tortuous road.

Chapter Twenty-Six

LIFE WITH NEW CIRCUITRY

It was raining as I loaded the car. It was raining much of this mid-November day, when it wasn't snowing or blowing. Vile weather for the 500-mile drive to Pasadena.

Marina had suggested asking the four Archangels — Michael, Gabriel, Raphael and Uriel — to ride on the fenders of the rental Pontiac. Not a bad idea. Despite my abhorrence of organized religion I no longer had any difficulty believing in the supernatural world in general and in these angels in particular. So I requested their protection, asking them to "ride shotgun".

My spirit floated lightly over the freeways, even when crossing the endless 4'000-foot pass south of Camp Verde in a snowstorm. No snow tires, no four-wheel drive, but the five of us sailed along safely. I couldn't see my invisible companions, but between them and my Guides we met with no mishap. At one point west of Phoenix I had to stop the car during a violent rainstorm whipped by gale-force winds. If my archangels had been humans they would have drowned out there. After crossing the Colorado River at Blythe it turned dry but remained blustery.

My heart sang, and so did my voice sometimes, especially thanking my soul pieces for coming home. I felt so fine, so carefree, so detached from trouble. I hoped my Guardian Angels out there on the fenders enjoyed the concert — alternately recordings on my portable CD player and my joy singing aloud. There *was* a difference in me!

Mingled with this happiness was an intense inner dialogue with my mother. There was so much to ask her about my childhood. Rehearsing our eventual chat alternated with song and the joy of arrowing through the turbulent elements.

The sun was but a memory when I pulled into Pasadena. Mother made me welcome but could not resist pointing out I was just barely in time for our guests. True. There was just time for a quick shower to wash off the road ions, and then a couple of my favorite cousins arrived. We all went out to dinner, Chinese or Indian, memory does not serve, and enjoyed one another highly.

When they asked what I had been doing in Arizona I replied "two hikes and a lot of metaphysics." No one rose to the bait. There used to be advertising for a soap that warned about body odor: "even your best friends won't tell you." Being on the spiritual path is somewhat similar. Family and friends don't want to hear about it. There's a reaction of unrecognized fear deep inside, almost as if you were exposing them to leprosy.

That evening I telephoned Marina to advise her of my safe arrival, to thank her once again for her marvelous hospitality. She asked for my forward address, so as to send some articles. This cordial, loving conversation turned out to be the last time we have spoken to one another. The reason for that manifested some days later.

It was an uphill struggle having a meaningful talk with my mother the next morning. The intense dialogue imagined on the highway did not happen. Instead I took pains to dwell on her strengths, then slid into a discussion of psychic work, trying to winkle out of her more tidbits on what I knew of her father's mystical side. But she couldn't be steered in that direction. At 95 Grace still had her wits, but her Gemini nature zipped from one topic to another like a grasshopper. Patience was the only tactic available to me.

The next morning was time to telephone Eileen for the regular soul journey follow-up, and there was a dream to talk about. My fine sleep had ended with a dream about trying to escape the low-key menace of three male intruders. There was not much trouble relating that to the return of the first soul piece.

Our marathon talk focused on changes. She pointed out I will feel changes, not all of them good. She repeated an alert she had given me in the medicine room after her shamanic journey for me. My aura is now vibrating differently, she said. In a sense, I had been rewired. This could turn away some old friends but it could also attract new ones. People will be reacting to a new me. And I must call her again one moon month after the soul journey to confirm the settling-in of the pieces that have come home. She would do the next journey three months hence.

"You're going on the last, big adventure of your life," she told me. "It will last as long as you live, from the impressions I received. What an adventure! I'm dying to know what's in that book, but that is for you to discover — it's your treasure chest you've earned, my dear."

I should have curbed for a few more hours my impatience to talk to Eileen. Following our chat something new came up, totally relevant.

After lunch I questioned Mother again about the burglar we had surprised when returning home one afternoon when I was four years old. When we came in the front door he was in the hall to the bedrooms, with a fur coat draped over his arm. Mother, gutsy little thing that she was, went after him, yelling. She said he brushed past us and fled through the front door. I remember a tallish man with red hair creeping out from under a cap.

We talked about this a moment, then I asked if there was anything else.

"Yes," she said, "when you were nine months old a man tried to enter the bedroom."

At that time we lived in my parents' first home together, a tiny place with one bedroom. One evening they heard me whimper, and Mother went in to find the window shade swelled out as if someone were trying to push into the room. Soon she prepared for bed and went to bed, leaving my father in the living-room.

She heard steps on the walk outside their ground-floor flat, then the shade billowed again and a man started to climb into the room. She called my father. The police came. They found fingerprints on the sill and footprints in the soil under the window. I slept through it all, more deeply and longer than usual, to the point Mother wondered if I had not been chloroformed or otherwise drugged.

To these events of infancy one could add a phenomenon experienced during the frequent illnesses of my first ten years. During episodes of feverishness a fuzzy, bloblike darkness, the size of a beach ball, would materialize beside the left side of my bed. It got so I could expect it and would not be surprised to see it. This apparition was clearly not benevolent, but there was no terror in seeing it. More like a low level of apprehensiveness.

Needless to say, I put these confirmations into my first letter to Eileen a few days later. To my mind the malevolence she encountered while retrieving the first soul piece needed no further elucidation. She, however, had a deeper interpretation.

"I was *very* clear that the discarnate was exactly that, not a living person," she wrote me. "By his presence he *drew* these other incidents into your life."

"A discarnate is extremely territorial about his/her `human property'," she explained. "In order for a discarnate to stay earthbound they must continually `suck' energy off the aura of a living person. In this case, you. That is why they become territorial, because to lose their `gas station' is to be forced off this third dimensional plane of existence, and they don't want to go."

"They will literally `fight' other discarnates for the right to suck off you," she added.

With all of this rolling around in my spirit, there was no shortage of things to think about as I drove northward a few days later. As usual, I said my goodbyes to Mother and got out of the Los Angeles basin before my sinuses and bronchi began to react too badly. One day ahead of wheeze, you might say.

Driving up the coast highway began to liberate me from the grip of the air pollution. Salt air always has a tonic effect on me but so does the high altitude at which I live. To find a livable spot on Mother Earth which combines sea air *and* truly high altitude feels like an impossible quest. In the meantime, living on a mountain above a salt mine, as I do, seems the best compromise.

After soul recovery work it is supposed to be best to have a day or two in which to really "space out" and let the effects soak in peacefully. In planning my itinerary I had had no idea of what was going to occur in Sedona. There was no breathing space in the schedule until I got back up north. Finding the freedom to enjoy that total "letting go" had to be put on hold, although I could see a window of time a week hence. The hard race across the desert in foul weather had been demanding, living under a pall of smog had not helped one bit, and now I was driving again. Soul was screaming silently for respite, and the best I could do was to quit the main expressway at San Luis Obispo and slip over to the dramatic State Highway One. First there was a metaphysical meeting with a sea gull on a state beach parking place. Of course, what she really wanted was crumbs and crusts from a picnic, but she stayed close, stalking me, following me around like a little dog. *Was this what Eileen meant by new friends coming into my life because of my altered vibrations?*

Then I was on the road to Big Sur, winding along the cliffs high above the ocean. *That* was refreshing. The sea was like glass, the sun yielding to clouds about halfway up these one hundred miles-plus of pure magic. The whales were not out this day and the sea otters were not basking and bobbing in the kelp beds of their official refuge, but spying the intriguing rustic hideaways tucked away in coves and canyons stimulated moments of enchanted daydreaming. This long drive above the sea ultimately provided some of the needed therapy. Spirit began to relax as the miles slipped away.

At Nepenthe I paused to stretch my legs and back, and the gift shop yielded an unexpected treasure. In amongst the crazy mixture of books, postcards, posters and touristy kitsch I found a dog-eared folder containing two Tibetan *thankas* at knockdown prices[1]. The one that pleased me most came home to the Alps with me.

At Santa Cruz I found the key left for me by Anna the acupuncturist. She'd given me bed and breakfast on the way south; this time she was absent but allowed me to borrow her wonderful "tree-house" bedroom. It was up one flight with windows on all sides, the gentle swaying of leaf-heavy branches creating a romantic bower. If every night on the road could be so blessed! Anna's treehouse was an ideal space in which to pursue the work of welcoming and integrating into my circuitry the beleaguered child, the flamenco dancer, and the ancient book with the stone-studded cover.

The next day I picnicked beside an estuary south of San Francisco and then later closed my weary eyes for ten minutes at the Vista Point off the north end of the Golden Gate Bridge. That evening over supper my frequent hosts, Joyce and Clark, listened to my tale of Sedona with evident interest, accepting. From the time I dowsed their living room with only a pendulum they had begun to expect the unexpected from me. We had broken out of the traditional mold thirty years earlier, exploring Unitarianism together, yet it was clear they now sometimes raised their eyebrows at my endless river of new eccentricities. But tolerantly. Their younger son had already stretched the matrix. He had fulfilled his youthful ambition to be a minister by becoming one in the spiritual movement founded by Paramahansa Yogananda. In fact, I expected him to provide my safety valve. It took only a phone call to arrange that. Six days later I was at the Ananda Expanding Light village in the Sierra Nevada foothills, warmly welcomed by the dynamic man I had last seen playing Little League baseball with my son.

Wayne introduced me to a rhythm of yoga and meditation which provided a perfect antidote to the stress of the road. On arrival late in the day, I took a cup of herbal tea, then was able to slip into the softly vibrating meditation room during a break. Ten or twelve people stretched, shifted into new positions and chanted as Wayne played a harmonium, then we all slipped into a long meditation. The atmosphere was totally conducive: a vast stretch of blue carpet, ceiling rising to a peak, windows giving onto forest views, and other people also moving into communion with their souls. This was what I had been looking for, this was what I needed.

After the evening's vegetarian meal, Wayne led me to the cottage he shared with his beautiful dark-haired wife (absent at the time). We began talking our way through a generation of life changes on both sides. He was, of course, interested in my spiritual life, and he was fascinated by the Sedona story. Before our heavy lids forced a halt to this marathon reunion, just short of midnight, he predicted that I was already capable of healing others. Well, that would be fulfilling, I agreed, if it should declare itself unambiguously.

The next day was the American Thanksgiving Day. It began at 08h00 with a long, wonderful program of readings, chants and meditations in the Crystal Hermitage occupied by Expanding Light's founder Sri Kriyananda (J. Donald Walters), a direct disciple of Yogananda.

It was cold and frosty this last Thursday of November, all the little pools iced up. Indeed, down at coastal altitudes it had been cold enough to turn Joyce and Clark's birdbath into a skating rink for sparrows. Up in the deep forests of the lower Sierras one could feel the snows would not be long in coming. Expanding Light's guesthouse offered modern comfort, but I had been cold in my bed.

We were possibly thirty in the Crystal Hermitage, mostly residents of the Village but a few visitors like me. Wayne led the service with a reading, a prayer, then chanting to the accompaniment of the harmonium. After this spiritual warmup we dove into a twenty-minute meditation, followed by listening to a taped discourse of Yogananda. Then came the main meditation, forty-five minutes, for which the first session had simply been the hors d'oeuvre.

Slowly plunging into the depths of spirit, surrounded by the vibrations of dozens of others, I found myself swaying gently, forward and backward. Then came vertiginous sensations, losing physical contact, almost levitating. My cerevision bloomed and faded, bloomed and faded. There were jagged crystalline forms, there was a brief explosion of "sun". At the 09h30 break I told Wayne my physical body could not do the third meditation of twenty-five minutes, my seventy-year-old joints did not tolerate long periods of sitting on the floor, even when well-carpeted. The same problem had arisen during the first meditation in Eileen's hogan. Wayne guided me into the adjoining library, where I amused myself fully until the séance was finished.

After the meditation space had emptied, Wayne allowed me to go back in and measure the vibrations. I had found them overwhelming even before applying the Bovis method. They went wild before finally settling down to give a reading of 34'000 angstroms. The power of the long group meditation, in a space devoted to spiritual life, had been enormous. Never underestimate the power of the collective human spirit!

Brunch at 10h30 was more than welcome. My metabolism leaped with joy at a big plate of eggs and pancakes. Afterward Wayne drove me around to visit retreat sites located at some distance from the main village in its secluded valley. We visited the temple of the Seclusion Retreat and once again the vibrations created by meditators were palpable. I measured 27'000 Bovis there.

It is worth observing that this temple, and the Crystal Hermitage earlier in the day, gave evidence of greater spiritual power than any of the wonderful cathedrals I had visited. When we returned to the Village I participated in a class teaching the Hong Sau technique, which echoes some of the methods I had been using. We did not do a real meditation in this class, but the vibrations in the Expanding Light temple reached 26'000 anyway. As mentioned earlier, my experience is that all these values can fluctuate widely during the course of a day. Even so, high readings in all three temples created within this Yogananda-inspired community testify to the power of spiritual living.

What do vegetarians eat on Thanksgiving Day in place of the traditional turkey? At Ananda Village our "turkey" was fashioned from a nut loaf shaped vaguely like the noble bird and just as delicious.

Earlier I had tested the temple for its vibrational rate. Late in the day it was empty for awhile and I could deploy my Hartmann antenna. I found only two widely-spaced H-lines in that huge room. Seeing me at work, Wayne asked me to dowse his home, so up we went. There the Hartmann network was present but spaced-out here and there. Bovis values were normal but they soared to 10'000 at his wife's meditation bench.

The next morning I was up and ready, despite the cold, for the seven o'clock Hatha yoga and meditation call. We did more than an hour of yoga then two meditations of ten and thirty minutes.

After breakfast and goodbyes, it was time to leave this haven of peace and spiritual highs. Being there, however briefly, had served my soul's purpose very well. Spirit was refreshed, invigorated, content, and at ease.

The day's itinerary was complicated: shopping in Nevada City, visiting friends for lunch in a hilly, horsy community south of Placerville, then to Santa Rosa for supper with Carol, with whom I could not stay because of a severe allergy to cats, including hers. Late that evening I rolled into my cat-free home-away-from-home with Joyce and Clark. They were still up and eager to hear everything. They wanted a complete report on my trip and, of course, their son. I could tell them that Ananada Village was just what the doctor ordered, that their son was pursuing his destiny as a minister to hungry souls with evident love and success, and I would likely return for another sojourn, with a glad heart.

Eileen had predicted old friends would shun me and new friends would be drawn in by my altered state. Even so, it was a bit of a shock to read the terse note among the pile of forwarded mail waiting for me on this return to the Bay Area. It had gone to Switzerland and come back in record time. In it my recent hostess Marina, thrice a catalyst in my life, suggested she would prefer not to receive me again. I could not imagine why, for we had gotten on well and parted the best of friends. She must have written her sixteen words only hours after the affectionate phone call to Pasadena. Sadness. A puzzle. Sudden short circuit? Whatever, remembering Eileen's prediction, I had to accept with one of her favorite expressions: "it is what it is."

Two more weeks remained before I would be home: one of them to round out my visits in northern California and the other with my friend Kay tasting the splendors of the Chesapeake Bay region. Then I would be home in my Alps for mid-December.

My son Neil and I had been obliged to postpone an earlier hike because of rain, but on December 1 we went up Mount St. Helena at the head of the Napa Valley. Climbing up to the 4'343-foot peak of this extinct volcano was an easy matter, allowing us abundant conversation. It was windy and bitter cold on the summit, the sky filling up, glowering, clearly raining in the north. Beneath that cloud cover, however, visibility was superb. We could see the snow-capped Sierras far to the east, yet turning to the west we spotted the glint of sunlight on the waters of Bodega Bay, thus spanning two hundred miles with the leap of an eyeball. Mt. Tamalpais and Mt. Diablo raised their distinctive profiles in the south, there were ponds, reservoirs and the famous Geysers to the north and northwest. The view was therefore splendid, but the cold drove us off the top after we had eaten our sandwiches.

Before leaving California I visited David, my favorite acupuncturist, for one last needling. After several of his treatments during this trip he was content with the state of my meridians and ready to accede to my request to do some "spiritual gate opening." That work had me floating for three-quarters of an hour, with lots of purple and gold cerevision. Points he had stimulated continued to cool and rekindle several times — this felt like an important step in fine-tuning my electrical network, readying it for whatever lay ahead. After Sedona I perceived the future stretching ahead in full color. The geography was unclear, but rainbows arched over it.

[1] A "thanka" (derived from thang-ka) is a devotional painting of Tibetan buddhism, usually very complex in composition, containing many personages, deities, symbols and icons. They are always colorful. Some contain mandalas and thus become objects of meditation. Magical powers are frequently imputed. It takes a specialist to decipher the spiritual meaning.

Chapter Twenty-Seven

CHANNELING ENERGY

Meditation began to demand more of my time. Spirit began calling me more often to sit and dive into its embrace, after the spiritual openings stimulated in Sedona and Ananda Village. During the last days of that long trip the door to inner space kept opening before me and commanding my attention. All the engaging phenomena were back: cerevision with its technicolor shows, visions, lovely quiet spaces, time warps and lots of vibrational effects. Before leaving California I was experiencing strong vibrations in my right hand.

Another example of Eileen's admonition about my new vibrational status came as I flew eastward across the North American continent. On this flight I was wearing my new medicine piece, which arrived in the mail while I was still in California. Chloe had done a marvelous job. Despite hesitancy about wearing it in public, I felt it might help protect me in the air.

Next to me sat a trim, attractive young woman who proved to be from Taiwan. Late in the flight she asked if I was a Buddhist, and I replied that I was not, despite considerable empathy for that spiritual persuasion.

"Why do you ask me that?" I added.

She pointed to my bracelet of small round amethysts, saying it was a signal.

"Are you a Buddhist?" I asked.

"Yes." She showed me her own bracelet of small round fluorites, which closely resemble amethyst but are paler, with wisps of green. "We wear twenty-one stones," she added.

Quickly I counted the stones in my bracelet. "Twenty-two!" I announced.

We shared a giggle over that.

Then she gestured discreetly to the book in my lap, *The Way of the Shaman*[1], which I was reading in order to enlarge my understanding of this pasture into which Eileen had led me.

"Are you a shaman?" she asked.

"No," I replied, "but I seem to be on that path."

This led her to explain that the Chinese character for shaman was pronounced "shama" or "saman". And she was going to buy the book I was reading. In later reading I learned that the version "saman" is the Asian root term. It seems to come from the Tungusic culture, derived from the Turkish-Mongolian group of languages[2]. My companion was also intrigued by my medicine piece, like so many others before I stopped wearing it in public. A brief explanation was thus necessary.

At home again in mid-December the frequency of meditation increased as counterpoint to the demands of the season. Abundant snows were falling and I was often piloting the snowblower up and down the sixty-five yard drive. This meant that unpacking my bags after nine weeks on the road, then getting things washed and put away took an eternity. Although important mail had been forwarded, there were still mountains of it to be sorted, including the inevitable bills requiring attention.

Despite all these distractions, the frequency of meditation increased. An imperious need welled up, requiring that I meditate two and often three times a day. Most of the time I wore the new medicine piece during these meditations. Although it is essentially a ceremonial object, I sensed that something sacred was happening. Wearing the neck-piece seemed to help me go deeper. It warmed my heart but also my bronchi, a lovely bonus during the cold alpine winter.

My daily journal relates what was going on, and I will summarize from its lines about the three meditation sessions on that final day of 1993. One of the gifts Eileen had given me on the fateful day of the green lizard was a little ceramic piece I called "Mother Earth/Father Sun", and I often used it as a meditational tool.

In the morning my thoughts were sometimes roving but the etheric layers were feeling, they were stirring and stirring. Intensity mounted in the mid-day session. Cerevision came, then I felt Mother Earth alive and moving in my left hand, while the right hand was acquiring great energy. This sensation was more than just tingling but nothing like an uncontrollable palsy — I could have shut it off at any time. A slight increase of heat gradually augmented the effect. Aural vibrations leaped in response to an outside noise. Then I slipped away, into a space I don't remember, except that vibration and light were central. In the evening, before going to the year-end party, energy confirmed its invasion of my hands, starting again with the right hand. After about fifteen minutes the vibrations moved into my head, especially around the ears.

New Year's Eve with a handful of friends was merry but "safe and sane." It snowed all night while I slept, and then after breakfast it was best to clear away the lovely powder before it turned mushy. In mid-morning I opened the spiritual chapter of 1994.

"Energy came in quickly," my journal reports. "My meditations are full of power. It went quickly into my hands, eventually working up into my neck and head." The clock struck ten-thirty, "sending me deeper, and I lost the thread of time."

"I continue to wonder at the utility of all this energy, how to employ it," I wrote.

The next day my first meditation "knocked me for a loop; power came quickly into my hands and soon into my head." Then my cerevision showed me "a green-gold sun, source of that energy." Afterward I had to rest in my bed for half an hour.

A few evenings later I received another installment in Eileen's lesson about losing some friends, gaining others. At the Alpine Club meeting a young hiking companion stared at me from across the large room, then made a bee-line for me.

"Michèle, what's happened to you!" she exclaimed. Whatever it was, she *saw* something that was different, something I could not see in the mirror. She was deeply interested to hear about my Sedona adventure, and a certain *complicité* developed between us, persisting to this day.

Before leaving on my long autumnal safari I had read a book review which intrigued me powerfully. It was about the channelings of a deep-trance medium who communicated with a group of entities who called themselves the Council of Nine. One could think of them as universal beings, existing outside of time and space. They served as a kind of "board of governors" for the universe — they emphasized that they were not "God" — nor did they take human form except when it was necessary to visit this planet. *The Only Planet of Choice* arrived in the mail as I was experiencing the input of all that energy, and it was fantastic[3]. Immediately I had to fight the desire to simply sit and read — no, devour — a new version of who we are and why we are here.

The Only Planet of Choice was the most penetrating statement of cosmic intent I had ever read, up to that time. As the seasons rolled on and other books rolled in, I began to find that *TOPC* was a pioneer in a new generation of thought about human history and spirituality. One could say it was on the cutting edge of an explosion of books channeled from "out there". My own selection of readings in this spectrum, which will be referenced as you read along in future chapters, constitute for me more of a "bible" than the Christian tome which their spokesman "Tom" calls "your word book."

In brief, I read in *TOPC* that we come to this planet to learn how to balance the physical and the spiritual. The concept of multiple incarnations, and not necessarily on this planet, is implicit throughout. The soul we call Jesus is described as having come thrice, as Moses, as Buddha, and as Jesus. Close reading reveals that the Council of Nine (who are "principles" rather than "people") seems to have underestimated how much this planet's density would affect us, so that we and our habitat are badly out of kilter with one another.

It is dangerous for me to try to define "God", even after having consumed this book. Let me make a feeble attempt: God comes through as a kind of collective concept, a universal intelligence expressed through each and all of us. God is love, and love is God, and each of us is a spark of that totality.

The Only Planet of Choice presents a singular view of Earth's history, how and why it was populated, what's going right and what's going wrong. And it told me what to do with that energy flooding into my body through my hands.

On page 275 of *TOPC* Tom says "we would wish each day, at your time of choosing, for you to be with us for eighteen minutes of your time, to bring about the ending of conflict......the elimination of the destruction of the environment, everywhere, and the acceleration of the return to a state of wellbeing......and you will also include the intention of permitting nations, and each group of entity-souls, to be allowed to be who they are, without being enforced by a nation that would wish to control them."

From earlier passages it was clear that we emanate a personal light, and that our meditations could be a vehicle for expressing that light and energy.

"Enlightenment is constant reaching, constant searching, constant consideration of whatever needs to be removed or modified or purified, but with total acceptance of yourself.....since you are part of divinity, anything you desire you may accomplish, if it is for the betterment of the Universe," Tom explained[4].

When the energy flow began in December I had wondered "where does this get me?" It was a question I had planned to ask Eileen. Reading the above passages made that question unnecessary.

It was not lost on me that within a matter of days I had been given a gift of energy and then an explanation of how it could be used. There was really nothing more to ask. It was time to do, and I needed no further encouragement to start informing my meditational life with this work.

My first efforts in this direction were to request expanding light and joy for a number of people who I knew to be suffering physically and/or emotionally. The second time I added to that by asking that all the "peoples of all civilizations" be liberated from domination by nations and religions. I felt as if I were probing for an effective way to operate and hadn't yet quite found it.

Quickly I realized that after all these years of basically turning inward through meditation, suddenly I was turning outward. Yet it was still meditation, I was very much in an altered state. "Targeted" meditation is what I began to call this method of inner work.

After these initial trials, and with my inner meditations becoming more and more powerful, with strong vibrations in head and torso, I asked the

Council of Nine for guidance. Assuming they are not omniscient, I reviewed tendencies and developments in my life related to service, and then the metaphysical marker points, the "highs". I asked them to help me know and recognize what I should be doing. The next morning I meditated toward the Nine and found myself going straight to Tibet, where I visualized "Chinese out", "Tibetans in", no genocide, no violence.

That day produced another high spot, another marker point. Agnès, a reflexoloigst who entered the Soroptimist Club shortly after I did, had moved on to expand her therapeutic capacities. She now worked also with sound, light and color. With all that was bubbling up in my psyche I thought it would be a good idea to insure a certain amount of harmony, and her techniques sounded like they were worth trying. I was not wrong.

She asked me to choose a color from a light panel. I chose magenta, and she draped me in magenta silk. She then began to massage my aura with scented hands -- *I could feel it.* While this was going on she saw two Guides attached to me. They both appeared to be North American Indians, a woman seen very clearly and a man who seemed to be hovering indistinctly in the background. She then switched to stroking a huge gong so that the waves of sound reverberated gently over me, followed by ringing bowls and then a wooden tube filled with tiny sea shells. I saw the female Guide in two forms, first as a very broad-faced Apache woman with a pitted, scarred face, oily brown skin and an aggressive expression. Surprised, taken aback, I then saw another woman, who I seemed to recognize. She had graying short hair, wide and high cheekbones, cream-beige skin, a pleasant face, and she wore a deerskin dress. This woman was the one that Agnès had seen, but they were both there as Guides. It was clearly up to me to get acquainted, find out who they were, how they could help me, and if there was something I could do for them.

The next morning I meditated early on the gray-haired woman, who gave me her name. (Sorry, we don't share these names with others, they are part of an intensely private relationship. I will call her "M".) She helped me project love toward the Council of Nine and then we radiated "North Korea -- no bombs" for a while. Ultimately my inner vision shifted to a white pueblo-type building. Was M showing me that? Have I got her name right?

That day I rendezvoused with my dowsing chum Violette in the Vallée de Conches, a long, level valley deep in the Alps and noted for its fine cross-country ski trails. We planned a week together, skiing the broad trails paralleling the headwaters of the Rhône River. The first morning in our hotel room I meditated again on the theme of "North Korea -- no bombs", receiving a brief vision of the Nine coming to the major capitals. World Peace unfolded like a set of wide stairs which ebbed and flowed, back and forth. This was a spontaneous effect, but what it symbolized certainly reflected my own thinking.

Aside from one or two chronic but not debilitating weaknesses, my general health and energies had been at a high level for some years. It had never occurred to me that this story needed to dwell on such matters. However, this passage of my life appeared to be a major turning point. With everything else that was going on I had also decided to see if homeopathy could do a better job of maintaining my vigor and dealing with my allergies than the modern pharmaceuticals which usually bothered me and which on one occasion had nearly killed me.

One of these allergies, discovered only in my late fifties, was to milk products, specifically the lactose in milk. This had nearly killed me as an infant, when my mother's milk dried up. In those days such allergies were not understood by medical science. In desperation to save her starving baby, my mother had used a milk powder substitute scoffed at by the pediatrician. Thus I was bottle-fed adulterated milk, gradually weaned over to ordinary milk, and had subsequently developed all the allergies that are now known to stem from what is called lactose-intolerance.

One morning at the breakfast table with my husband I felt nausea when drinking my daily glass of milk. After several days of this reaction, I realized that I should not drink milk. From then on I avoided it. No more nausea until the same effect developed with the cottage cheese I spread on my morning toast. Another milk product to be abandoned. All that had occurred ten years or more before Violette and I went on our skiing holiday. At the breakfast buffet in our hotel I was tempted by the *muesli*, because my usual porridge was not available. Thus, for three mornings in a row, I moistened this cereal mix with milk from the handy pitcher. On the ski trails all went well for the first kilometer or so, then I began to feel poorly. When my growing discomfort turned to nausea, and my face took on a sickly green hue, we stopped for a herbal tea. This helped a lot, along with an enzyme tablet, but I had lost my strength and could not continue. Violette continued down the trail, and I returned to the hotel to lie down. The next day I was fine again, but I now knew that lactose was dangerous for me. This was something else to place before my new homeopathic doctor. Ultimately he provided me with a homeopathic remedy which blocked the allergic reaction when I found myself in gustatory circumstances I could not control. In this period I first began to have difficulties digesting *pasta* in its multitudinous forms. Trying to be vegetarian, for purely philosophical reasons, was not going very well either. All this was not very spiritual, but it was certainly accompanying my quiet revolution.

Meditation continued during that holiday, with daily "targeted" work. I was striving to send healing energy to Tibet, to Northern Ireland, or to North Korea on a daily basis. In mid-February came great news: North Korea was backing down from its aggressive, saber-rattling stance and would also permit international inspection teams to examine its nuclear sites.

"How many others, influenced by the Council of Nine, have been directing meditations toward such trouble zones?" I asked my journal. I had only been trying to project love and encouragement over the spiritual airwaves for a few weeks, but surely others had been at it longer. The news anchored my intention to continue this work.

It was only mid-winter, I had been home from America barely two months, and it seemed as if new phenomena were exploding into consciousness with dizzying rapidity.

In addition to developing this new "world healing" form of meditation I found myself deeply involved in a whole series of activities, such as:

- Finding that big stone-studded book became a major project and led to several days of research in big-city libraries before embarking on a physical journey to France to look for it;

- Eileen did soul recovery journeys for me at three-month intervals, and we began to talk about my next visit to Sedona;

- After twelve years of learning, my time to teach seemed to be approaching, and I acquired my first student;

- I began to become a healer of people as well as the planet;

- I subscribed to the very metaphysical *Sedona Journal of Emergence*, that led to ordering a book by a Sedona writer, that led to a surprising discovery, and that led to enriching the next trip out there with the presence of some people from my village;

- A mystical hiking companion entered my life;

- I abandoned standard "allopathic" medical care and began to consult with a homeopathic doctor;

- And, as if that were not enough, two kinds of supernatural phenomena entered my life, one auditory and the other visual.

That's a lot for just one calendar year, and I will try to organize it so that you, my handful of cherished readers, can make sense of it.

My attention was riveted on the inner structure of life, not the outer world. Nothing else mattered.

"My present ability to concentrate on administration work is nil," I wrote in my daily journal. *"Heart and mind focus on meditation, on my first student coming for the weekend, on Eileen's various techniques, on knowing, on seeing, on that big old book waiting to be identified, on myriad questions about my own meditations. Some books insist that phenomena are to be tolerated until they disappear, others suggest they have a role. TM says they are nothing, Eileen says they are everything. After twelve years what I have are primarily phenomena. It happens often enough that I get lost in energy fields. Progress or not?"* I asked.

In mid-February Eileen performed another soul journey for me. She had told me in November to contact her after three months, which was the minimum interval required for the client to integrate what the shaman brought back. On the telephone she told me she journeyed only when she felt ripe for it and not otherwise. I didn't need to be there, most of her work was done at distance. Her journey for me could happen during the coming four or five days, that's all she could say.

"How will I know?" I asked.

"You'll know, " she answered cryptically.

Two days later I had to get up at three in the morning to answer a call of nature, then couldn't get back to sleep. Began reading at four o'clock, back to sleep at five o'clock, up again, then down in a short final nap, during which I lived a very vivid dream.

In this dream I went down to the laundry room in the basement, and water began to rise. I took refuge on the ledge of a high window and through it I saw a number of valises and soft-sided folding travel bags hanging from the balconies of a neighboring chalet; I understood they were airing after a trip. Then the water receded and I was able to escape. My friend Kay drove me downtown to a travel agency, which proved to be closed, with brown paper blocking the windows. Turning away from that door I encountered a small woman struggling with a heavy suitcase. I helped her carry it into a neighboring shop.

Could a dream be more explicit? This was all about travel, and as I came awake for the day I understood that Eileen must have journeyed for me during the night (allowing for an eight-hour time difference). "You'll know!" she had said, and now I knew. I also knew that a powerful psychic communication had occurred, and it was no surprise when her fax message arrived during the afternoon.

This time her journey was all about pain, the Guides seeming to consider I'm ready for some of the heavy stuff. In the first piece I was a baby, crying incessantly and no one coming to the rescue. In the next one my brother and I were waylaid on a dark street by a group of bigger boys and girls, and we got some pummeling before escaping. This seemed to symbolize the bullying and torments we had both experienced in early adolescence. And the third piece had me in a hospital operating room surrounded by doctors and nurses, with soul pieces floating in the air. This was all too realistic, for immediately I felt myself back in surgery twenty-three years earlier, everyone dressed in green scrub clothes, about to carve into my thigh to find out what was wrong deep inside. This had been a particularly traumatic episode in my life, with lasting physiological consequences, and Eileen had brought it back for me to exorcise.

That day I had no head for the text I was writing. Spirit was only in that soul journey, pondering the pieces. There was pain to purge in the process of welcoming them back as one must do. Meditation demanded, and I responded three times again that day. The next morning my ulcer — silent for more than a year after I had changed my way of eating — suddenly flared while I lay in bed welcoming back those pieces. The ulcer could, of course, have been a reflection of my first homeopathic treatment begun the same day of the dream and Eileen's report.

That afternoon my student arrived for the weekend. Danielle had been the first person here to "see" the difference in me, and we had begun to talk about meditation one day on the cross-country ski trails. She was not a stranger to inner seeking but had not found a technique. Thus I led her through a series of breathing exercises, letting her try them out before settling on one method to use for our meditation together. I explained the use of mantras and proposed she use Om Mani Padme Hum, still my favorite. Then we ended this afternoon with a long and strong meditation together. In the evening, as the logs in the fireplace began to become embers, we tried it again. Apparently my approach was correct, for she was pleased and grateful.

It was clear Danielle was ready to move ahead, so in the morning I introduced her to the spiral chakra technique. She took to it instantly the first time, found what I'd taught her "delicious". We skied up to Solalex, lunched with friends at the Refuge, and had another good meditation before I put her on the bus down the mountain.

The next morning I was back with the Council of Nine, projecting healing energy to my three target areas: Tibet/China, North Korea and Northern Ireland.

Two days later there was a note from Danielle. She was very pleased about her meditation now. The spiral chakra sent her off to work in great form, and hatha yoga restored her body at the end of the office day. Thus my first effort at teaching appeared to have been a success. But six weeks later at a club meeting she admitted there were a few "hics" creeping into her meditations. She felt there were times the mantra did not seem to hold well despite what she thought was strong focusing. I explained that all meditants, even the most experienced, have "dry spells". In such moments it sometimes helps to vary the technique just a bit, tinker with the breathing method or work with another mantra. And sometimes it seems to be just us on an "off" day, or perhaps something with the moon in our personal astrology. However, I shared with her a new mantra which I had just invented, searching for a phrase in French which would respect the power of the "m" sound.

"Try 'Om, amour au monde'," I proposed. This translates as "Om, love to the world" but in French it has a strong resonance.

Eileen's prediction that new people would be attracted to me continued to be coming true. Sometimes it was simply an appreciative smile in a public place.

(If any of these had been a flirtatious male of good aspect I would have done more than simply smiling back!) After a concert in a nearby village the lead violinist, with whom I had barely exchanged half a dozen words in the past, made a bee line for me and entered a long and warm conversation. This magnetism, which I still could not see in the mirror, pulled in the cellist. He thought I must be a fellow musician. And then along came the virtuoso of the viola, who spoke at length about his beautiful old instrument. They could not have recognized me as a "regular" because I always sat well back in the audience, buried in the mass of people at a spot where I felt the parabolic sound landed after bouncing off the ceiling. Suddenly I seemed to stand out instead of fading into the scenery.

One day a Mr. W. telephoned from a local hotel, citing our mutual friendship with a lady who was one of my favorites among my late husband's Dutch cousins. Another of our Dutch cousins, living an hour away in another alpine village, had given him my number.

"Yes, of course, come ahead and we'll have tea," I responded, adding the necessary directions.

At the door I was surprised to meet Matthew, who I knew very well from my cousin's home but whose full name I had never known. He was a musician and often used the music room as a good place in which to practice. He hadn't expected to be received by me, and I hadn't expected to see him at my door. But there was another reason for this serendipity. His new wife, who I'd never met, was at his side, and they were fun. Moreover, she had a story to tell, so tea extended into a light supper.

Susanna had had a near-death experience. She was home alone, recovering from a brain infection, and there she was out of her body, looking down at her body, lying corpse-like. With her silver cord trailing, she floated off toward the God-light and surrounding beings in a place she loved being. Then she realized she had to come back. Reentering her body was a hard jolt, and her full recovery was long, complicated by temporary paralysis. This recital was the springboard for a full evening of exchanging metaphysical experiences. Susanna appeared to be rather psychic.

After they had left I reflected on how perfectly amazing it was that such encounters kept piling up.

"My life is constantly refreshed and enriched by sharing this mystical domain of life," I wrote that evening before sleep.

Meanwhile, my meditations for the Council of Nine were going very well. When I needed extra energy for the work all I had to do was ask, and soon it began flowing upward through the chakras. Cerevision slipped in frequently, sometimes leading to a real color show.

One evening in early spring I was trying to knit, mend, darn the hole in the ozone layer over the South Pole. The ozone holes were becoming a preoccupation around the globe, and from my second reading of *TOPC* it seemed clear this was a project I should attempt. My effort to create a good image of the hole over this Pole did not go well. Something was not jelling, and I needed help. Undaunted I asked the Council of Nine plus my two native American guides for help.

Soon I received an image of the top half of the planet, and it rose up slowly, blue and cloud-strewn. It didn't stay long enough for me to work with it, but it seemed like a hint.

"Well, they're trying to help," I noted in my journal.

The next morning I went right to work again trying to reweave the ozone hole, this time the one over the North Pole. And it worked. My meditative artistry seemed ragged but I threw loops across the hole and wove them across one another before finally lashing the edges of this impromptu net to the edges of the hole. There was a sense of succeeding, which held until the mental monkey began leaping from thought branch to thought branch. That told me my job was finished for this session.

A few days later I went back up there for another whack at it. My imaging grew strong enough, and held well enough, that I could extend the task to wrapping the globe with energies of love, peace and harmony. From there I spent half an hour going after the trouble spots: Africa, Moslem fundamentalism, Israelis versus Palestinians, support for the Tibetans and the Dalai Lama, opening the hearts of the Chinese leadership, the same for the two Kims of North Korea, Latin America, and North America.

That evening the new magnetism was working again in those little ways that were beginning to light up my heart. Supping with friends in a restaurant, before the Alpine Club meeting, a nice-looking man, serene and agreeable in his expression, not handsome, not homely, glanced my way with a smile. He lit up, and that lit me up. He was with other people and nothing came of it, but that tiny exchange warmed me.

Ten days later a small article at the bottom of a newspaper page sent me through the roof. It reported that the air pollution monitor aboard the space shuttle was finding "surprisingly high levels of carbon monoxide" above the Northern Hemisphere. Previously their readings had shown the atmosphere's pollution concentrated over the Southern Hemisphere.

Now the south was clean but the north was more polluted than expected. "We didn't expect it to be as dirty as it appears to be," a scientist observed[5].

"Is that why I got the message to shift my focus from south to north?" I asked my journal. Carbon monoxide was not reputed to be the biggest contributor to the formation of ozone holes, but even so....... No longer willing to believe in coincidences, I had to credit psychic guidance.

[1]   Michael Harner, *The Way of the Shaman,* 10th anniversary ed. New York: Harper, 1980, 1990. xxiv+171 p., appendices, notes, bibliography, index. ISBN 0-06-250373-1

Harner is a pioneer of the modern "shamanic renaissance".

[2]   Mircea Eliade, *Shamanism: Archaic Techniques of Ecstasy.* Princeton Univ. Press, 1964 (originally published in French by Librarie Payot, Paris, 1951). xxiii+610 p., bibliography, index. ISBN 0-691-01779-4.

This is the classic, global survey of the subject.

[3]   Phyllis V. Schlemmer and Palden Jenkins, *The Only Planet of Choice, essential briefings from deep space.* Wellow (Bath): Gateway Books, 1993. xv+398 p., index. ISBN 1-85860-004-9.

Schlemmer is a deep-trance channel, surrendering control of her physical body to the Council of Nine while receiving text from one of their number, who calls himself "Tom" but confesses to several important Egyptian incarnations. This book is a compilation of material received over twenty-two years, which has been winnowed with the aid of the historian Palden Jenkins. He provides bridging passages between relevant channeled passages, as well as deep historical end-notes.

The second edition, edited by Mary Bennett in 1994, was compressed for the purpose of foreign-language translations. Jenkins' notes are compressed into an appendix, some material is trimmed here and there, and a chapter channeled in May of that year is added. *TOPC* has been published in German as *Planet der Wandlung.*

[4]   *Ibid,* p. 343.

[5]   Associated Press in the *International Herald-Tribune,* April 16, 1994.

Chapter Twenty-Eight

BOOKS

That big stone-studded book never strayed far from my consciousness. Finding it was a major goal. Its content, its subject matter was a mystery, but the monks had said it was intended for me. They had indicated, in a general way, that it came from the center of France. This was a clue but not very precise. France is a big country, almost as large as Arizona and New Mexico together but with ten times their combined populations, thus its "center" covers a lot of territory. Think of a target with a diameter of two hundred miles, studded with towns and cities, containing hundreds of religious structures and an untold number that have been deconsecrated.

One approach would be simply to leap into the car and tootle across the border, head for the geographic center of our neighboring republic, switch on all the "feeling" tools at my command, and hope for the best. In short, follow my nose. However, with all the ancient books lurking in libraries, museums and churches, a certain amount of research seemed in order. This Virgo needed to *prepare* her voyage. And even if I found the book would I be allowed to touch it, to read it? In fact, *could* I read it? Those old books — the pre-Gutenberg volumes — were written by hand and usually in Latin.

In late March I started the detective work in Geneva. During his lifetime Martin Bodmer amassed a marvelous collection of early books and pre-Gutenberg manuscripts, carefully guarded and displayed at the Fondation Bodmer in the suburban town of Cologny. The director kindly gave me a quarter-hour of his time. He said that decorated books like the one I sought abound in the pre-printing era, the stones usually only semi-precious, or less, and rough. Which is how Eileen had seen them. Whatever, the foundation over which he presided possessed nothing that would fit our description. He added that one of the biggest collections, the library of Cluny, had been dispersed throughout France when that great Abbey was destroyed in the Revolution. None of that was in Cologny, which I had not expected in any case.

The next morning found me in the Manuscript Room of the Bibliothèque Publique et Universitaire de Genève, the university library. The director of that space told me right away that my book was not there, and he confirmed they had none of the old Cluny collection. Once again I was not surprised. I devoted the morning to a long search in the catalogue of manuscript holdings in French regional libraries. This resource is composed of numerous volumes, and they revealed very little of promise. There also exists, according to the main catalogue, a multi-volume compendium of monastic archives possessed by the abbeys and priories of France.

Three volumes of this resource were available for my scrutiny. Rather quickly I saw that large ancient bindings with stones on the covers were not terribly common. The catalogues illustrated some of the most impressive specimens, and there was nothing remotely ressembling our description. Catalogue listings frequently provided the physical dimensions of the binding, making it possible to filter out many items on that basis alone. And I did not waste time on listings that were not in central France. I learned a lot that morning even though the book was far from being found.

Paul, over in the back country of Cluny, had done some map-dowsing for my book's location and came up with strong feelings about Paray-le-Monial. I had not dowsed the map for that location, because Paray was too far east of the exact center, but I had been *wishing* it could be there. Paray sang in my heart. Also, it was on the way to the center.

The road for France beckoned in late April. My student Danielle offered me lodging for the first night out. Harmony reigned in her flat in an old building in Lausanne facing the lake and France. Almost instantly I found myself surrounded with wonderful vibrations, resonating immediately with my physical body. No wonder she had spiritual inclinations! We meditated together, after I had introduced her to the Council of Nine's concept of healing the planet by projecting the energy of love. She found this to be a powerful technique and was amazed at the energy she could take in and send out.

Her space cried out for dowsing, and I quickly found we had been meditating next to a Curry line which crossed the living room. The Bovis vibrational rate began at 8'500 — very healthy — as one entered that main room, and it zoomed up to 11'000 on that Curry line. Danielle had a wonderful environment for pursuing her inner quest.

The next day I reached Paray-le-Monial in three hours of easy, unhurried driving, traffic much lighter than I had expected on a Sunday. Paray's vibes were muted that afternoon and I felt no temptation to make measurements. There were too many people visiting the basilica, and the sunless skies did not allow any play of colors through the windows.

The information office was open, but the woman on duty discouraged me on the prospect of finding old manuscript books in the region. There weren't any in Paray-le-Monial, she said. This was daunting news, considering that the town had once been home to twenty religious institutions.

For this foray I had reserved a room in a bed-and-breakfast on a working farm about five miles out of town. My hosts Guy and Michèle proved to be charming, my room was just right -- the bed in a neutral zone, no underground water, and about 7'000 Bovis -- and the calm was total. He was no stranger to the pendulum, thus soon we were discussing geobiology.

Later, as I leafed through their looseleaf notebooks full of tourist information, one of those unexpected "clicks" occurred. A Himalayan Buddhist temple and monastery named Kagyu Ling glowed up at me from the color brochure. The proportions of the buildings, the roof line, the immense stupa in front, the spectrum of prayer flags, called to me in a magnetic way. Would the rather loose itinerary offer a chance to go there?

It rained all night, and Monday morning was damp and grey. Worse, my first sources in Paray -- the library and the tourist office -- were closed. Most of the town seemed to be slumbering, typically French on Mondays. What to do now? Some decisions are made instantly as if pre-ordained. It was as if I had been guided to stay in that farmhouse B&B in order to learn about the existence of the Temple of a Thousand Buddhas. Without further head-scratching I turned onto the road leading northward to Autun, and on which I would first come to Kagyu Ling.

After my late start, it was lunchtime before I spied the spire of the gleaming square-based stupa in front of the pagoda-like roofs of the Temple. A gravel drive led up the slight knoll to a place to leave my car. All was very quiet, not a soul was stirring, the office and the bookstore were closed. Exploring in a rather anonymous building behind the Temple I found a door marked "Restaurant" and poked my head in. A young woman asked if I wanted to eat. Yes, please. She asked me to wait five minutes for the cook to return. I busied myself at the salad buffet, and then the cook appeared. He became quite cordial, after looking me over, and gave me a plateful of vegetarian fare, which is kind to me when traveling. After I had found a table he brought me half an avocado. Life was becoming very agreeable.

And then it turned mystic as well. I went back to the kitchen window to pay the cook for my meal and we got into conversation. His curiosity was direct, and I told him I was searching for a book. What kind? He was searching too. My description rang a bell with him, and he told me about his quest. We were searching for similar things, coming from different starting points. Jean-François also sought a book perceived in another dimension. He had dreamed his, now he coveted the physicial object.

He studied Eileen's sketch of the big book and then told me the colored stones and the hammered gold suggest the book deals with the vegetal and mineral worlds....which corresponds to what I had been intuiting. He saw it as answering the physical description of a work by Nicolas Flamel, a fourteenth-century alchemist and "electrician" of Paris. I'd heard that name before, but what floored me was the notion of Flamel as an "electrician". Before electricity became a domestic commonplace a century ago, electricity for most people meant lightning. Only for dowsers did it have a second meaning, which was seldom expressed. I'm certain that my ancient colleagues of centuries ago felt the dowsing response in a way that we would now call "electric".

We had the definite sense that we were intended to meet, to learn from one another, to share our intuitions. To me it felt amazing that I was guided to the farmhouse so as to fall upon knowledge of Kagyu Ling, so as to meet Jean-François...but also, as it turned out, to meet Sarah.

After lunch I wandered over to the Temple and climbed the stairs to a reception room from which one could admire the huge ceremonial room below, with its massive statue of Buddha and its bright colors. Buddhist temples are high in color, warm and gay, anything except sober!

As I looked around, a small European woman in monastic red robes offered to provide guidance and information. This was how I met Sarah, and our subsequent conversation went on for *hours*. It seemed we had much to tell one another.

She told me about her eight years at the monastery. Among other duties she had been a kind of servant to Kalou Rimpotché, the lama who had founded this Temple. He had died, and she had met the little boy who was his reincarnation, but now she had been told she would be sent to the United States where her command of English was needed at another monastery. She had many fears about the US and was unhappy about the idea of leaving France. To ease her mind I told her about the spiritual upsurge in North America, the centers such as Ananda Village being established far from the publicized violence, the numerous centers of activity such as the Himalayan Institute, the "counter-culture" focal points such as Sedona, Santa Cruz, Sebastopol, Virginia Beach. Everywhere east and west, in fact. She said this information relieved her anxiety. In turn I told her of my meditations for the Council of Nine, how I was targeting the Tibetans and the Dalai Lama, how I was attracted to some aspects of Buddhism, how I was working with all this new energy.

The power of the Temple rippled through my outer layers, and meditation called to me. I found a quiet corner on the balcony under a large full-figure portrait of the Dalai Lama, facing a huge green statue of the goddess Tara, symbol of feminine energy and wisdom. As I moved inward I could sense the Dalai Lama's gaze on me, expressed as a feeling of gentle pressure on the side of my head. This was remarkable and most agreeable.

When I had finished meditating Sarah asked me to use some of my healing energy on her. What? I had not yet employed the gift on a human, but an instant of reflection told me this responsibility came with it. It appeared that she suffered from chronic pleurisy and was taking medication from a doctor. Indeed, she looked worn, drawn, lined. I stood behind her, placing my hands where she directed them on her chest, and concentrating on the flow. This might have been five minutes, probably not ten. I could feel the energy moving through, and she told me that it was hot and beneficial. She was grateful.

It was after six o'clock when I drove away from Kagyu Ling, its temple, its exuberant stupa. I had been there close to six hours without sensing the passage of time.

That evening the long table at "Les Bruyères" was full and merry. We were six guests, and our hosts sat down afterward to chat and chuckle over the wine. They were passionate about their "agriculture biologique" and what they served of it was delicious and abundant. Although my spirits were already bubbling inside from the events of the day, this atmosphere zinged with another facet of the jewel that life can be. Half a dozen strangers became friends through the alchemy of good food and a warm human environment.

The next day brought me no nearer to my goal. In retrospect I ponder what prompted me to go to Nevers, for it was a mistake. It was an error of judgment. What made me think I would find "the book" there? Sweet memories of a romantic fling on the Côte d'Azur, a quarter of a century earlier with a man whose family came from Nevers, may have fogged my intuition. On this day the old provincial city, once famous for its splendid *faience*, was just plain dreary. There seemed to be a pall hanging over the streets. I attributed this to the recent suicide of a famous son, of which newsprint and airwaves had made much.

Its cathedral, St-Cyr, bathes in a moderate vibrational soup. Stained-glass windows had just been installed to replace those blasted in a World War II bombing, half a century earlier. Colored light streaming into the choir raised the Bovis rate to 19'000, by far the highest in the edifice.

Across town the cadaver of St. Bernadette, whose visions turned Lourdes into a place of pilgrimage, reposes in a convent. Tour buses clog the approaches. One queues up for the chance to view the sainted lady in her eternal sleep. Jean-François had reported strong vibrations emanating from the saint. To me she looked like a mannequin in a wax museum. The shuffling crowd afforded no chance to test the vibrational rate, but the effect on me was nil. I would guess about 1'000 Bovis, which opinion would have sent me straight to the burning stake during the time of the Inquisition. (Maybe it did!)

There was nothing at Nevers to suggest my book was there.

At Autun, however, my hopes soared for a while. Autun pleased me as much as Nevers had displeased. There is a different feeling in the air, a sense of culture, a friendliness that manifested with each encounter. The town is happily alive with good vibrations. To get there one sails past Kagyu Ling and continues northward another twenty minutes or so as the land gradually rises.

Perhaps the city's position on the lower slopes of large mountains confers good Feng Shui.

In the City Hall a man offered directions with friendliness. In the Municipal Library an assistant allowed me to use their private toilet. She was helpful and friendly, apologetic that the noon hour was going to block my perusal of the catalogs and an interview with the *Conservatrice*, but she came all the way down the steps to point me toward a good Vietnamese restaurant.

My research in the university library at Geneva had turned up a major collection of ancient books in the library at Autun. After lunch the *Conservatrice* (the Curator) accorded me some pleasant conversation. She wanted to know how I came to be searching for such a specific ancient binding and, with total frankness, I told her it came via the vision of a shaman. She didn't bat an eye (bravo once again, les Francais!) but she felt the ornate cover could be of the Carolingian era, earlier by several centuries than we had thought. It wasn't in her collection, she was sorry to say. She gave me a few tips for further bibliographic research, and she allowed me a few minutes to wander reverently through her treasure trove, a vaulted room with eighty thousand ancient books in its stacks.

Reference books in the reading room were not encouraging on Nicolas Flamel either. His alchemy and his books are doubted, but another point of view suggests the doubt is a smokescreen invented by the Renaissance-era alchemists themselves, so as to avoid the burnable suspicion of sorcery.

Autun's Cathédral St-Lazare is massive in the roman style. It rears skyward with a certain somber sobriety from thick, powerful pillars, in contrast to the lightness and soaring elegance of Sens, Bourges or Vézelay. Paul and I had visited Autun several years earlier, and it attracted me again, with tools I hadn't then had. The choir was inaccessible this day, under repair, with the sound of sawing. Bovis values rose gradually as I moved up the nave toward the transept, reaching 19'000 in spite of the noise level.

Nature was bursting out all over on this late April afternoon. As I drove southward the meadows were lush, and there were lots of gleaming white Charollais calves, sturdy on their legs now but still hugging their mothers.

It wasn't too late as I drew abreast of Kagyu Ling, so I turned in. A temple service was underway, giving me the perfect springboard for a meditation under that living portrait of the Dalai Lama. Afterward I checked the vibrational rate of that image: 31'000 Bovis. Around the corner of the balcony hung a portrait of the Kalou Rimpotché, even more alive, beaming as if enjoying a good joke. The founding lama gave me a Bovis reading of 55'000. Kagyu Ling was reinforcing the lesson of Ananda Village: the high vibrational values that percolate in these colorful Buddhist temples can exceed what one finds in those magnificent and powerful Gothic cathedrals.

Sarah was on duty again up there.

"I'm feeling a lot better since your treatment," she told me. "I've stopped taking the medicine the doctor gave me."

There and then I scolded her. "Don't do that," I warned. "Take your medicine. What I bring you may not last. I'm not a doctor."

Did I really and truly have such healing power? Sarah seemed to have no doubts. She asked for more, so I went to the portrait of the Dalai Lama and "charged" my hands in front of him. Then I gave her another, longer, deeper treatment. She claimed to feel the heat coming through me.

Two months later she sent me a snapshot that showed her playing with the little reincarnated Rimpotché. At first I could not believe it was her, for the lines of illness, the haggardness, had left her face. She looked ten years younger.

Returning to Paray-le-Monial the next morning I found the stars still against me. The library was closed for the day. I did not expect to find the book in a small public library, but I had hoped to obtain helpful information about the evolution of the numerous religious communities in Paray during earlier times. Which ones had disappeared, their buildings mutated into other use? Eileen had received the notion that the book would be found in a building that had once been church-oriented but no longer was. This trip, admittedly short, was running out of time. Interesting things were happening but the essential was slippery, like a blob of quicksilver.

The basilica swarmed with a large group of teenagers and teachers who seemed bent on demonstrating that spirit moves in waves. They manipulated a long cloth so as to evoke a kind of oceanic rising and falling, all to the tune of a guitar. By thus distracting the priest they enabled me to sneak into the choir and unleash my pendulum, where 20'000 angstroms registered in several spots.

That appeared to be the sum of my metaphysical research for this day. Back in the streets of Paray I surrendered to every-day preoccupations, like gassing up Tanya Toyota, buying a phone card, finding lunch, and getting my hair washed and set. On the way to the car park I stumbled on a book in a shop window.

No, it flared at me. It was about Nicolas Flamel. It proved to be fiction, with little hard fact on first leafing-through, slender booty, but I bought it. One does not ignore such synchronicities. There might just be something relevant buried deep in those pages.

At that point I had to admit the clock had run out on my quest, for this season at any rate. I'd picked up some clues, but there had been no breakthrough, no clear discovery. The Toyota and I turned eastward for Cluny, where Paul and Margaret expected me for afternoon tea and an overnight visit.

He had discovered more Roman influences in the region, and we spent a few hours dowsing them before going on to Gourdon. This ancient chapel was undergoing artistic resurrection. A woman worked high on a scaffolding trying to restore what could be uncovered of the old frescoes. Many frescoes were glowing softly in the new light created by cleaning of the beige/rose sandstone walls and columns. Our dowsing picked up two intersections of underground water, and there were excellent vibratory rates. Obviously sympathetic to our work, the artist talked long and enthusiastically with us. With a twinkle in her eye, she suggested we test the energies of St-Quentin.

We found this twelfth-century chapel on a rockbound promontory at the end of a long ridge, deep in the countryside, reached via an unpaved track branching off a farm road. St-Quentin's architectural simplicity conceals a veritable beehive of energy. Our upraised palms tingled strongly as we moved slowly up the aisle. The energy was physically palpable. We found Hartmann's telluric lines jammed together and interacting with a staggering concentration of water points. Water was vivacious on the crest of that hill, reminding me of the surprising situation at Vézelay. We meditated behind the altar, where the Bovis reading exploded to 27'000. Totally unprepossessing, St-Quentin was an energetic powerhouse.

There was more. Granite boulders, geologically out of place, ringed the hilltop and the chapel inside a diameter of about two hundred meters. Oaks bloomed roundly within the boulder clusters. The stones appeared to have been rolled into place — rolled uphill, if you please — creating islands of rocks with pleasant flats and glades between. The Lecher antenna resonated to a Celtic frequency all over the hilltop. Lines of rocks stretched down two slopes, reinforcing our sense of being on an important pre-Christian spiritual site. Medieval Christian clerics had the good sense to feel and harness those energies.

Back in the house on the hill above the vineyards I introduced my friends to *The Only Planet of Choice*. We ended the day with hours of readings and enthusiastic discussion. Before I left the next morning Paul joined me in the energy meditation proposed by the Council of Nine, finding it similar to his personal form of prayer.

Great caution governs my attitude to hitchhikers, and that was my reflex as I sailed past a man on the roadside on the far side of Cluny. About two hundreds yards down the highway something clicked in my being. "Don't be an idiot" rang in my head. I turned the car, circling back, and picked him up. That late-functioning instinct was not wrong, and I was glad to have listened and obeyed. Jean was a Canadian living with friends on the heights above Montreux, right on my way. He proved to be an amiable and appropriate companion for the otherwise boring three-hour drive ahead.

He had worked with a geobiologist, had read Blanche's books, and had just passed the weekend in a spiritual community. We had a *lot* to talk about and the trip passed quickly. At Montreux I dropped him on the highway and never saw him again, but Spirit had provided for my diversion and possibly even my safety. Learning to recognize the signals that come in is a slow apprenticeship.

When I got home there was, of course, a big pile of mail. In it was my first copy of the *Sedona Journal of Emergence*, which I had first seen when there six months earlier. I read many of the articles with interest, especially one by a man who investigated reports of UFOs and extraterrestrials. In the back pages I found his books listed for sale and ordered one.

Several weeks later that book was in my post office box. When I returned home and began to open the mail, I opened this book first[1]. And a lightning bolt hit me.

There, staring at me, was a photograph of a young man I had known. The last time I had seen Jacky he had mentioned leaving for Sedona, and I never saw him again because he was killed in a snow avalanche after returning to Europe. The author of *The Quest* had dedicated his book to my friend, a kind of "in memoriam" page of recollections. It was appropriate, for our mutual friend's life had been one long quest, and he had made an impression on the people he met out in Sedona. That did not surprise me, for the first time Jacky and I met we spent hours talking metaphysics, meditation, crystals, earth energies, the whole apple cart. Each of us had felt a kind of spiritual loneliness, like being the only one up here on the mountain with such interests — these deep, absorbing, dominating interests — and it was a delight for me to discover there were two of us, when he was here. He lived and worked as a ski guide in France and he traveled a lot during the off-season. He'd gone to Sedona several months after our meeting, and the avalanche took him a few months later. Not being an intimate of the family I had learned of his death third-hand and long afterward. It had been a shock.

Receiving this book gave me the photo of Jacky that I didn't have. *The Quest's* stories of people who had moved to Sedona on their own personal quests told me a lot about the place, and it stimulated me to contact his father. Jacques is well-known up here, I knew him slightly, and the book gave me an idea. A letter to Tom, the book's author, set the wheels in motion. I knew already that I would be returning to Sedona in the fall of this year, 1994, and it occurred to me that Tom and I could guide Jacques to the various sites his son had frequented and had found powerful. Tom agreed enthusiastically to participate in this project.

Meanwhile, I picked up a copy of another book: *Autobiography of a Yogi*[2].

Its author, Paramahansa Yogananda, was the patron saint and inspiration for the founders of the Expanding Light community where I had found refreshing retreat in the prior autumn. His teachings underlay their spiritual life and I decided to delve into that philosophy. In Sedona my own path, which had been evolving as a kind of aimless wandering through the inner landscape, received a sudden, unexpected sense of direction. At home I began to read about shamanism, trying to understand the full nature of what Eileen had seen in me. It seemed only reasonable to explore also the yogic world which had so quickly smoothed the wrinkles in my road-worn psyche. Another visit to Ananda Village should not be excluded.

Yogananda's story proved to be fascinating. In it he described the advanced meditational technique called *kriya yoga* and a whole series of its presumed beneficial effects. It appeared to increase the flow of oxygen to the brain, to help the adept burn away karma, to prevent the decay of tissues, to transmute cells into energy, even to dematerialize and rematerialize the body at will. My ancient skepticism could not swallow all of this with the first spoonful, but it was impossible to ignore the happiness that seemed to permeate everyone at Expanding Light. The source of that inner joy must come from their Master's teachings. Reading his story was clearly the first step to understanding. Would *kriya yoga* benefit my inner work? It was not long before I wanted to find out.

My basic urge, however, was to understand what a shaman did. Before meeting Eileen my sense of the world of medicine men, witch doctors and shamans was a poorly-defined stew. Her little book did a lot to straighten me out, but I am a glutton for information, requiring more, always more. In the pursuit of this bluebird I followed her suggestions.

"If you understand only the words *intention* and *trust*, you understand the key to shamanic healing," states Sandra Ingerman[3]. "Shamans are just the instruments through which the power of the universe works....asking the spirits for help and trusting that they will be there is the basis of the shaman's responsibilities."

She explains that it is her soul that enters non-ordinary reality and does the traveling in the shamanic journey. She described in detail how she prepared to journey and what she did while "out there". Except for the technique of actually getting into that non-ordinary reality, which is clearly the core of a shaman's training and which she glossed over, the whole process sounded logical and straightforward. Her narrative also made clear the necessity for training, discipline and, sometimes, a certain amount of courage. Ingerman's account enabled me to feel very comfortable with the idea of this ceremony. It became easier to imagine myself doing shamanic work, assuming I could learn how to enter the necessary state. There I was skeptical, in spite of all my profound experiences in meditation.

Before Ingerman there was Harner. Michael Harner appears to be the prime mover of what might be called a shamanic renaissance in North America and which was germinating about the same time in Europe. An anthropologist, Harner discovered shamanism in the Amazon in 1961, learned it there, and ultimately began to propagate it through teaching. "The Way of the Shaman" describes some of the "nuts and bolts" of shamanic work, although like Ingerman he does not reveal precisely how to enter the necessary altered state of consciousness[4].

Harner points out that the shaman "sees" in this altered state, which is not the same as trance.

"This may be called 'visualizing,' 'imaging', or as expressed by Australian aborigines, using 'the strong eye'. Although such seeing is done in an altered state of consciousness, it would be an unempirical prejudgment inimical to achieving firsthand understanding to dismiss such visions as hallucinations," he pointed out[5].

These readings satisfied my need to know what shamanism was, how it worked, and what it accomplished. In their own styles, Ingerman and Harner echoed Eileen's exposition. All three had distinctly personal approaches, their experiences varied widely, but the central core resonated to the same tune. My simplistic notion at this point was that I understood enough to make a decision about following that path. Maybe.

Finding "the book" still tickled my mind. At the end of the summer it was possible to visit the university library in Lausanne, whose 800'000 volumes are split into two collections, one in the center of the city and one in the new campus on the fringe of the city agglomeration. The curator at Autun had suggested that I delve into the books of a certain Yves Devaux, a bibliographer of ancient books. On the telephone a very helpful lady had informed me that the Cantonal and University holdings included five or six of his books divided between the two collections.

In the course of an afternoon, traveling from one site to the other, I examined five of Devaux's volumes on the ancient and decorative bindings of books of medieval France. There was nothing remotely resembling our book, neither described nor illustrated. Nor did the works of two other bibliographers offer any clues. It was even possible to scan some of the splendid bindings and covers in the Bibliothèque Nationale de France in Paris, but there was nothing with colored gemstones on the cover. Two big works on Spanish bindings produced the same result. Subsequent searching in the computerized catalog of the Bibliothèque Nationale de France proved to be frustrating. Medieval books were there, in profusion. They even had one by Nicolas Flamel, about sulphur, but I could not see the cover without going to Paris, and that was not the part of France indicated by the monks.

There remained the book that had sprung before me in Paray-le-Monial[6]. Translated, the title reads "The Fabulous Secret of the Alchemist, Nicolas Flamel, Prophet or Imposter." It is fictional autobiography, written as if from beyond the tomb. In it Flamel reveals that he did achieve the alchemists' dream of creating gold from base materials (on the night of 25 April 1382, to be exact), but more than that, he created an elixir of longevity, a veritable "fountain of youth". For five hundred years he and his wife Pernelle moved from country to country so as not to arouse suspicions about their age. Much of the book is devoted to Flamel's supposed philosophical debates with learned people down through the centuries. Was longevity the prize the monks said I had earned?

It also occurred to me that the vision Eileen received might have been a symbol for a body of knowledge. That wasn't her impression, but intuitive touring combined with bibliographic research were not hitting the target.

Meanwhile, interesting things were manifesting in other domains.

[1]   Tom Dongo, *The Quest*. Sedona; Hummingbird Publishing, 1993. 144p, illustrated. ISBN 0-9622748-2-8.

[2]   Paramahansa Yogananda, *Autobiography of a Yogi*. Los Angeles: Self-Realization Fellowship, 1946, 12th ed. 1993. xv+592p, index, illus. ISBN 0-87612-079-6.

[3]   Sandra Ingerman, *Soul Retrieval, mending the fragmented self*. New York: HarperCollins, 1991. xii+221p., index, bibliography, notes. ISBN 0-06-250406-1. Quote is on page 63.

[4]   Michael Harner, *The Way of the Shaman*. New York: HarperCollins, 1980, 1990. xxiv+171p., index, bibliography, notes. ISBN 0-06-250373-1

[5]   *Ibid*, p. 50.

[6]   Gilbert Prouteau, *Le Fabuleux Secret de l'Alchimiste, Nicolas Flamel Prophète ou Imposteur*. Etrépilly (France): De Bartillat, 1994. 282p., bibliographie. ISBN 2-84100-020-6.

Chapter Twenty-Nine

SON ET LUMIERE

Reading in bed, close to sleep, I had slipped into a kind of pre-dream scene. A female voice called something, just a couple of syllables. Three nights later, slipping into another scene while still holding my book, I heard voices in my left ear. The next night there was a strange noise in my right ear: it was vaguely pneumatic/mechanical, something like a vacuumed-up inhalation with an electromagnetic tone. Our vocabulary is inadequate to describe this.

They left me in peace for two weeks, then as I was falling asleep over my book there were two clicks in my right ear. Five minutes later there was a kind of "aah-h-h" in that ear.

A week later I was at Cluny and we were "digesting" a late lunch in that glass veranda. Paul was napping in the chair opposite, and somnolence was stalking me when a feminine voice quietly said "Michèle" in my right ear. This whispered greeting repeated itself every few months.

Such auditory phenomena were something new in my life. So much had happened in a handful of months — healing energy pouring through my hands, the Council of Nine showing me which polar region to heal, meeting two of my spiritual Guides, attracting a student and repelling an old friend — that these new arrivals could not be thought of as surprising except in their form. "What next?" sums up the inner reflection. Having learned years earlier the value of recording my dreams, I now checked the bedside drawer for its supply of three-by-five file cards. "Night signals" became the new topic.

These sounds and phrases came mostly as my bedtime reading was leading me from full wakefulness into that threshold world before sleep takes control. Occasionally they came to me in the daytime at a moment when my work-related reading slowly became hypnotic. Thus one morning about ten o'clock, as I was studying, a feminine voice began speaking to me about a story that had nothing to do with what I was reading. She was explaining something.

In bed, lying flat, the lights out for the night, a voice said "....must be Jerry it's already going slowly."

Ten nights later someone named Edward was ending a dialogue very emphatically with "...and here I'm getting you out of this axis here."

A week later a close friend's voice was in conversation with me, once again in that hypnagogic state.

Was I slipping in and out of parallel realities? Or had my slender psychic capacities begun to bloom to the point that I was tuning into real conversations happening somewhere else? Could it be that humanity's babble was accessible simply by dialing to other frequencies on the cosmic radio?

There were solitary, isolated noises, like the rustling of heavy paper, a whistling that rose and fell like a sine wave, the sound of wooden blocks knocking together, a motor going past (which didn't), chirping and chattering like birds in a nest (or baby mice in the mattress), a grinding sound that was not mechanical, the ring of a telephone (which didn't, but which woke me at three o'clock in the morning), a distant roaring of water, a tug on my nightdress at the waist, my grandfather's clock striking when it wasn't any kind of an hour or half hour, furniture being moved around, another ring followed by a knock on the door, a noise like an internal bodily valve or sphincter squirting fluid, an animal braying in my left ear, a few minutes later "tink, tink" in my right ear and then the sound of someone clearing her throat. Isolated clicks, pops, slams, rings, and grunts also animated slumber time. The ring of a telephone that hadn't rung got me up more than once in the middle of the night. One time a yellow tennis ball smacked me in the chest, from two feet away.

Late one night about three months into this phenomenon I was sitting up with my book and slipped into a dream — without any "night signal". When I popped out of it the main question was "Grandfather Hardy, was he really here?" This was the first time I could recall experiencing my theosophist forebear (see Chapter Seven) in another dimension. This mini-event was not exactly auditory but came among a series of signals and was just as mysterious. It needs to be mentioned because of its relevance to something nine years farther down the path.

In all this the snippets of conversation were the most fascinating:

"...what would you have gotten from this status?"

"...if you see Jim..."

"...I'm your lawyer."

"...is that an aircraft?", heard while reading about the early Mayans

"...wasn't it Faulensee?" (a place passed on the route to Grindelwald)

"...Il faut trouver, dire.......nonante-cinq" (in the voice of a woman who was walking with a man)

"What was the pleasure......in taking her (somewhere)?"

"You are? Oh, come on!"

"What? What?" then two blocks of wood clopped together

"did you hear?" said by a bicyclist, and someone else answered "Yes, I heard."

"It's a long time....to see animals" said my mother

Conversation including "oui, oui!"

"Thanks, she has stolen the news from Thanksgiving dinner.......Ed, come here, three hundred thousand guerillas..."

"Je m'appelle Greg Fanton" ending a long conversation I was listening to; I've never heard of anyone by that name

"...my fingers to the phone", said a well-dressed, handsome woman

I had just been reading an observation on discarnate beings when someone said "as we heard you" into my right ear.

"I'll get out." "No, don't get out."

"C'est du fourbier!" (uttered by the voice of a woman I know well, this word "fourbier" does not exist, even in the 24-volume dictionary)

Where did all this stuff come from? What did it mean? Eileen's answer was terse and clear: it was probably a kind of clairaudience (the sound equivalent of clairvoyance). She surmised I was picking it all off the astral dimension, not far from my notion of being tuned into cosmic radio. It was just another sign that my mystical qualities were evolving.

My "night signals" went on for about two years and then gradually faded out. When it all started I had not been doing anything to protect my aura from intrusion. During those two years I began creating a auric shield and as my practice of this art became fairly well developed the auditory assault faded away. As I became stronger in protecting myself, that stuff could no longer penetrate.

Late that summer there materialized, before my eyes and possibly no one else's, what I have termed the "mysterious glow".

On Monday, September 5, I rose briefly from my bed about 02h30. After pulling the flush trigger I went into the guest room and looked out the window at my mountains. It was New Moon and I was hoping perhaps to see the aura over the peaks and crests. I'd seen it a couple of times but not lately (my psychic talents are quite modest). All the houses behind and to the side of me were dark, there are none in front, there were no street lights on our lanes, and the only illumination came from the stars. I didn't see any alpine aura but my eyes were attracted by something else: a soft illumination in the meadow across the highway.

As my eyes adjusted I began to see that this gentle white glow was basically circular, brightening the grass in front of the big solitary tree. Nothing else seemed to be happening, it (the glow) was simply *there*. I had lived in the chalet for twenty-three years at the time and I had never before seen anything like that. This glowing circle appeared to be about ten meters in diameter, the tree being about more than one hundred meters distant and the forest edge still fifty to seventy-five meters farther away. The meadows undulate and slope gently, and they are cut for hay in the summer, but at the forest edge the land falls steeply into a thickly-wooded canyon system.

This phenomenon reminded me of the phosphorescent glow one used to see in the surf when the grunion were running[1]. Studying that glow, I began to feel a real prickle on the back of my neck and immediately projected a protective bubble.

I made a mental note to check in the morning for a carpet of white wildflowers.

Then, in order to get back to sleep, I picked up my bedside book, *Secrets of the Soil*[2]. Here we go again, you jolly little coincidences! The next pages told about floral essence expert Machaelle Wright, who works with the energies called *elementals*, nature spirits, the *devas*. Twenty minutes later I got up again and went back to the window in the other bedroom. Yes, still there. There was also the suggestion of the same kind of light against some of the trees that form a backdrop to the field.

At midday I went out to dowse the area with the Lecher antenna. As one might expect, there was positive energy within the drip line of the tree (which is actually a composition of five trunks). In front of that drip line, where the glow rested, the antenna gave me negative energy. It also reacted to the wave length for "sound and resonance", which one doesn't encounter very often. There were no whitish wildflowers.

Machaelle Wright describes a simple kinesiological method of contacting her "invisible companions"[3]. I tried it. It told me that, yes, elementals were at work in the meadow and they were benign. (My later efforts to use this method were inconclusive. I can think of three possible reasons to explain this: 1) I'm not very good at the technique, 2) the elementals were simply playing with me, or 3) the technique itself is pure malarkey.)

Even so, I was edgy about venturing into the meadow at night. First I tried photography. One night I made a long series of time exposures, varying lengths, from the upstairs balcony. Results: zero. There was a bit of artificial light in the region: a light over a door of the house nearest the circle, but that light was on the side of the building away from the meadow.

The circle of light was visible again a month later, two days before New Moon. I saw it at four-fifteen in the morning. Later, at eleven o'clock that evening, I was driving up the mountain from the valley and noticed a street light about one hundred meters higher in altitude than the meadow. But, at about three hundred yards lateral distance, it was not casting illumination of any kind on the meadow. The Glow never appeared before midnight, and the meadow was dark. I stopped the car even with the big tree, but there was nothing. My Glow could not be blamed on that street light.

When I went to bed the night of New Moon there was nothing to be seen in the meadow, despite that distant street light. There it was again, when I arose at three-fifteen, but it had rotated slightly with reference to the tree.

I pulled on warm clothing and went out to the balcony with tripod and camera again, this time using faster film: Kodak Ektar ASA 1000. Normally I used ASA 200. And this time I did get one photo. It isn't very well aimed, because I was working in almost total darkness, but the glow can be discerned in front of the tree. It took twenty exposures during two different periods, but that glow stands documented. Unfortunately it doesn't reproduce well, beyond simple paper copies.

A few nights later I went out to the field at eleven-thirty; it was a starry night with no moon. It was too early for the circle to light up. To my surprise, there was a line of newly-installed, strong street lights up the hill, at about half a kilometer distance. They did cast a very faint light all over the meadows, casting my shadow on the grass. But no circle.

After those first sightings the seasons rolled on, winter snows covered the meadows for months, then the snowline began its springtime hesitation waltz, bouncing up-and-down like a yo-yo, finally leaving for the summer. Dark-of-the-moon had transited a number of tmes, usually in rain, sometimes under a cloud cover which promoted the twenty-three night lights of Villars (one hundred meters higher and one mile away as the crow flies) into a kind of skyshine that simulates weak moonlight.

More than once I went back to that window in the wee small hours. There was nothing to do except wait for a New Moon in clear weather. Patience had to be the order of the night.

And finally, there it was again! Clouds, rain, snow higher up --- the exact dark-of-the-moon was blotted out until two nights beyond the date, early in the morning of September 26, 1995. It had not been there when I went to bed, which was the usual case, but at three o'clock it was visible. The circular glow was not strong, not photographable, just faintly discernable. Twenty-four hours later it was there again, but very faintly. One had to be really focused; it didn't leap out and smack me in the eyes as it had the first time a year earlier. The next morning, about half an hour past midnight, it wasn't there. My observations had been that the glow typically appeared about two or three o'clock; it wouldn't be visible in the hours before midnight, even with a total absence of manmade light in the environs.

During two years the Glow came, around New Moon in the season of the fall equinox, in dark, starry nights. The incidence of man-created illumination never seemed to be relevant. It was visible in all a double handful of times, and then I never saw it again. The notion that it was some kind of a message for me ccould not be avoided. Intuition went to work in a subterranean way, and several years down the path I got a glimmer of what the glow might have been trying to tell me.

[1] The grunion are a small silver-sided fish (Leuresthes tenuis) of the California coastline. They swarm inshore to the beaches at full moon in order to spawn. and could be seen glittering in the surf. People used to talk about the grunion when I was a youngster in the 1930s, newspaper columnists would joke about the "grunion are running", but I have no idea if these fish still "run" toward Californian shores.

[2] Peter Tompkins and Christopher Bird, *Secrets of the Soil*. London and New York: Arkana, Penguin, 1989, xxiv+444p., six appendices, bibliography, index. ISBN 014-01-9311-1.

Both authors were separately prolific; this was their second book together, succeeding *The Secret Life of Plants* (Arkana/Penguin, 1973, 1974). Both of these books are landmark compilations of important "fringe" research and are strongly recommended to anyone who is an earth person.

[3] *idem*, p 305.

Chapter Thirty

BACK TO THE RED ROCKS

Sedona's Red Rocks are sandstone but they were like magnetite for me. Their power of attraction leaped oceans and continents. The desire to return there itched within me constantly, both before and after my return from the interesting but somewhat frustrating trip to France in search of the book. If my days had a backbone, programming the next trip and its stages were the vertebrae. None of us had e-mail in those days; everything had to be arranged by letter mail, taking one week each way, and telephone for the last-minute fine tuning.

It was agreed with Eileen that on arrival in Arizona I would stay the first few days in the cottage formerly occupied by her grandmother (who had gone to an elder-care facility). She would squeeze out bits and pieces of time to work with me. Then I would move for two weeks to a motel with kitchenette. My list of things to do and see was long. Jacques decided definitely to meet me out there, with his companion. Tom expressed delight and set aside time to work with us.

There wasn't going to be time to immerse myself in the Red Rock energies as much as I would like. This Arizona segment of the itinerary would consume nearly three weeks, enclosed by quality time with my California family. During these planning stages it was, of course, impossible to foresee the difficulties with which destiny had seeded the program. One went blithely ahead.

Those few days in 1993 had shown me there was a fertile field for energy dowsing, which tempted me mightily. I had seen that dowser-authors were well-represented on the bookshop shelves and so asked Eileen for a recommendation. She proposed, and I brought home in my luggage a slender volume by Nicholas Mann[1]. It detailed the fruit of his geomantic explorations and brought some intriguing concepts to my attention. Mann had found a series of leys and a set of chakra systems imprinted on the land. His maps laid it all out and had me almost drooling with anticipation.

In the spring Eileen journeyed for me again. She brought back two soul pieces from past lives: in one I was an anguished monk in France, in the other I had been an eighteenth-century doctor. And there was a third piece, which I will let her describe:

"I saw you — about the age you are now — maybe five years ago, falling off the side of a mountain — not a long fall — but a sharp fall that caused you bumps, bruises and some mild injuries. You were more scared than anything else. It was a beautiful summer day and I saw the Alps," she wrote in her fax report.

She had nailed an actual event, without knowing about this piece of my personal history. It was easy to identify this soul piece with the toboggan-like slide I had had down the snowfield, ripping my trousers and the flesh under my hip. She was off by two years, for it had been seven years earlier, a few weeks after my husband's death. There could be no more eloquent example of shamanic power to penetrate the heart of client traumas. And she saw me capable of learning to do the same thing? Amazing!

As always, the Alps beckoned all summer long. I was on the mountains many times with my Alpine Club companions, and there were a number of wonderful adventures with a new friend. My friends Gerry and Beverly had asked if I would be willing to show their son some of the local trails when he came to visit. Of course I would. At the end of June they invited me to supper to meet him. Pushing forty, André turned out to be athletic, trim and handsome. Several days later we went for an easy hike with his father Gerry, down into the canyon and back up on the other side, and it became clear we would get along well.

Thus a week later the two of us embarked on a more ambitious trek. We took the steep trail that rises three thousand feet to the Cabane de Plan-Névé, during which we made a major discovery: we were both meditators, both following a spiritual path. After lunch up there we mounted the glacial moraine to an intermediate crag, admired the view, and then found some not-too-uncomfortable rocks on which to sit and meditate together. The next morning we climbed up the chimney leading to the Col des Chamois, where I had led Molly half a dozen years earlier. One descends the other side to the glacier which becomes an easy downhill stroll, and on that path to the Col des Essets we found a comfortable hollow which was perfect for meditation.

I could not believe my luck, for André was strong and easy on the trail, a crosscountry marathoner to boot, and he was a natural alpinist who had never done anything like this kind of mountaineering before. Our weekend proved to be the beginning of a long, amiable partnership. A week later we hiked up to the Col des Pauvres together, stopping for cheese at the goat farm. In between times he came down to the chalet often for late-afternoon meditations. Another weekend we ascended the Grande Dent-de-Morcles, accompanied by Daniel from Zürich, a young friend of André's family.

On that itinerary I like to start early enough to reach the refuge on the saddle below the peak before noon. Here, at La Tourche, it is possible to dump a lot of the weight of our packs into baskets available to overnighters. With just picnics, water and rainjackets we were off rapidly and made the 9'740-foot summit by mid-afternoon.

It was a glorious day, but the sky was massing its battalions of cumuli in all tones from yellow-white to gunmetal gray. The last part of the climb zigzags up a steep ravine of spectacular rock walls, and at the very top there is a little chimney where it's nice to have the rope for the last five meters. With two strong young men in tow, I had no trouble finding someone to carry that rope.

On the summit André and I settled for a twenty-minute meditation. which brought me a lovely cerevision of Sedona-like red walls. Those colors faded gradually into my familiar enjoyable waves of amethyst-and-gold circles. Daniel alerted us to the deteriorating sky, so we bolted our picnic and got off the summit, down that chimney, down the ravine, ahead of any potential storm. Before starting that descent I measured Bovis 17'000. These peaks usually score high! The storm was not breaking just yet. There was time to photograph tiny blue flowers in crevices, as well as each other against a backdrop of tormented rock strata in the wilderness of rocky spires. That upper region, above the highest grass and well into the crags and towers, is an enchanting, exotic desert. It could be the Atlas Mountains of Morocco. The elevated vibrational level kept all three of us highly energized. That threatened storm never broke on our heads.

After overnight in the refuge we climbed up to the Col des Martinets, then traversed the narrow, dangerous trail under the Perris Blancs. Mother Nature began to put on the rest of her great weekend show.

First we saw a mother raven leading her brood of three fledglings around the crags, with much cawing and wheeling.Not long after came a splendid, soughing flight of birds curving dramatically in front of us, a singing harp of feathers, a soul sound. The flight turned in one tilting plane, like swallows, but they weren't swallows. They were alpine swifts (Apus melba), *martinets* in French, thus explaining the name of the Col, the pass. They like to nest in cliffs and they feed on insects while in flight, again like swallows.

This trail led to the Col des Pauvres which André and I had already visited, and there we sat to picnic in the lunar landscape of boulders and grassy hollows. André and I started to meditate again, but this time the sky had the last word. Light rain brought out the rain jackets but did not prevent another pause for cheeses from the goat farm[2].

One morning my heart and spirit sought to create a ritual of thanks and healing at a secret place in the mountains. In meditation I asked my Guides and the Council of Nine for suggestions and inspiration. In the afternoon I knew what to do. Another young friend had arrived from Canada — Pia, daughter of dear friend Elisabeth, she who brought acupuncturists into my life — and with André we headed for the spectacular Vallon de Nant under the base walls of the Grand Muveran.

With one eye on the ominous skies, we found an isolated glade in the upper forest, just before the valley widens into treeless pasture. We were well off the jeep trail we had been following, screened from the outside world, high above the roaring river. Great trees, ferns and mushrooms surrounded us. And there was more: a compound Hartmann and Curry grid crossing-point boasting 13'000 vibes on the Bovis scale. Mother Earth clearly blessed our proposed ceremony. After hanging my medicine piece around my neck, I laid out crystals, and we smudged with Arizona sage. Finally we anointed our heart and crown chakras with a special powdery substance Eileen had given me. I led a ritual of gratitude and appreciation to the mountains, the trees, the meadows and Father Sky, each participating according to his or her heart. It was simple, improvised, but satisfying and moving for all three. We sat to meditate. My heart was full of joy for the gift of spiritual companions with whom to create and relish such moments.

On the way down we explored the rain forest among the huge blocs from an ancient rockfall. We spied a troop of chamois grazing the slopes high above us. Those glowering clouds finally opened, and we drove home under sprinkles.

Summer sped toward maturity, bringing arm loads of fresh vegetables from my garden. Rutabaga, fennel, carrots, onions, radishes, potatoes, zucchini and slender green beans made the short trip from earth to the kitchen. The deer came out, the doe still reddish from the mating season, her youngster dressed in brindle. No longer reckless with lust, the buck was nowhere to be seen this day but did appear briefly two weeks later, still red. I started to see the "mysterious glow" described in the previous chapter. There were still alpine treks as the season wound down. The telephone rang itself off the hook the day of my seventy-first birthday. From that point of the year, the fall equinox, there is a subtle shift of the way morning light slants over the passes in the eastern mountains. Wistfulness wiggles into my heart and has to be allowed its moment. In early October it was time to pack my bags and start closing the house. On the twelfth of the month I began the long safari to North America.

Kay met me at Washington and gave me two days and nights of rest before the next leg to San Francisco. Joyce and Clark had the guest room ready for me in California, warmly. Even though Switzerland had long since become my permanent home, presumably "for the duration", there is deep pleasure in reuniting with old friends and family in familiar surroundings. Happy times with my daughter, my son, and my seven-year-old granddaughter followed. After a week in the north I began repacking my bags and loading my rental car for the trek south and east.

An urgent telephone call moved these preparations into overdrive. When I arrived in San Francisco for Sunday lunch with my cousin David and his

Jane, they asked me to return a call from his sister Alice in Southern California. She reported my mother was having trouble and I was urgently needed. Several months earlier Mother had fallen and been briefly hospitalized. Now she had been found in distress in her apartment in the Birch Grove senior residence. Maids had found her sleeping on the sofa, apparently never having gone to her bed the night before. She couldn't walk, a wheelchair was being mobilized, as were "helpers".

"I'm on my way instantly," I told Alice, "but can't be there in less than thirty hours."

Sleeping that night in Santa Cruz, I telephoned my Mother.

"I feel weak as a kitten," she told me. Nurses were popping in, food was being brought in. I called the Birch Grove manager to tell her I would be there tomorrow. Her expressions of relief were eloquent. They were not geared up to provide care — residents had to be independent, autonomous.

Monday morning I crossed the Hecker Pass, bought sandwiches in Gilroy, crossed the Pacheco Pass and then roared down Interstate 5. Three times I interrupted this sprint to stretch my legs and nibble on my provisions. At five o'clock I was in Pasadena.

Mother was in poor shape. There was no strength at all in her legs and she could not get to her feet without strong assistance. Two ladies who were untrained, uncredentialed "aides" from the neighborhood, not on any official payroll, were helping her. It was a rickety situation.

Her lucidity was relative — sometimes briefly on, sometimes living an illusion of earlier times when she was fully fit. Getting her to the toilet was a major enterprise. It took a long and strenuous effort to get her on her feet and leaning on a "walker", gently pulling and supporting. The whole operation — the round trip from bed to toilet and back to bed — took an hour. My back began to send signals of distress, and I observed that Mother had two incipient bed sores.

Once again, however, I uttered to myself the now legendary phrase: "I can do this." I needed time to think, to consult, to organize. After a shower to wash away road sweat and nursing sweat, I fell into bed at midnight. I was deep in a dream, possibly even out of body, when Mother's bedside bell roused me. At first I thought someone in the dream was ringing a Tibetan meditation bell. Coming up from such a depth gave me a headache that lasted through the morning. This was another toilet call, another hour of exertion, before diving back into sleep.

That first day started with a telephone call to my sister on the East Coast. She had been coming about twice a year, her daughter (who lived an hour away) about weekly. She had all the legal powers because she was the nearest of the two of us. She began to organize her emergency arrival. Later in the day I met with the financial manager, for it was obvious that my Mother, who at the age of 96 still clung stubbornly to a whole mass of administrative paperwork, needed to be relieved immediately. The tax accountant, who had been chewing her fingernails waiting for documents, expressed vast relief that the family was taking over.

In all of this I could see echoes, lessons for me. My own independence, rooted in a strong genetic characteristic, could suddenly dissolve at some indeterminate time in the future. It was possibly not too early to start setting up my own safety net. How disagreeable are these intimations of our own mortality!

My cousin and her husband pushed me to take Mother to the hospital. A second heavy night convinced me they were right. Mother's breathing was very labored as she dozed in the wheel chair. Long telephone powwows with the hospital got me to her cardiologist, then back to the hospital. Neither Mother nor anyone else in the family could remember the name of the doctor who had treated her in the summer, but they were unanimous in liking him. I charged the hospital with finding him, and then Birch Grove prepared to transport her in one of their vans. The two "aides" were marvelous in convincing Mother to allow herself to be taken to the hospital.

Meanwhile I began to learn what had really been happening. She had sprained an ankle in that fall four months earlier. She had fallen again in the Birch Grove dining room three days ago; a security man and a table waiter had brought her home to her bed. It was questionnable how much she had eaten since then, in fact it began to look as if she had been too sedentary since the sprain and was on the edge of malnutrition. This is a classic example of how we begin to fall apart, isn't it?

At the hospital a very efficient and likeable young doctor organized a whole battery of tests. And they found the doctor everyone liked. Henri — he was a European — and I hit it off well and spoke in French when we wanted to be utterly frank. After several powwows with me in the corridor, out of everyone's earshot, Henri charmed Mother into accepting our joint decision: she must go to a nursing home until she could get back on her feet again. Within a few hours she was comfortably installed in a "skilled nursing center", eating a delicious supper. I sat with her while she ate, and she seemed almost happy.

The next day taught me that I had not yet lost management skills. In a series of conversations with my sister, with the financial manager, the accountant, and a lawyer they recommended, we organized a meeting for all of them. I would not be present. I had no legal authority beyond what I had already done — even the instructions I had given the nursing center would have to be countersigned by my sister. Moreover, my lungs and bronches could not stand more than four days of Southern California air, and that limit was dead ahead. I would go to Arizona as planned and would be back to help at the end of that trip.

Thus the next telephone call was to Eileen in Arizona. I would be arriving one day later than planned but I would be there.

At the nursing center they were getting Mother up for tiny strolls, firmly assisted by trained young nurses wearing heavy back braces. Otherwise, she was fighting the system.

"I want to go home," she complained to me.

With a deep sigh of the heart, I said something I hope my daughter never has to say to me.

"Mother, stand up."

She just stared at me. How I hated myself at that moment!

"If you can stand up, if you can walk, you can go home. These people here will help you get back on your feet, but most of it is up to you."

I told her of my sister's imminent arrival, of the business meeting set up for the following Monday, but I'm not sure it registered. She seemed to look at me blankly, as if I were talking Chinese.

It's still hot in the southern desert in late October, hot and dry. My lungs and bronches exulted in the clear, clean desert air. The little hacking cough that had started in Pasadena began to lift, dissolve, and there was only a hint of it as I traversed the smog of Phoenix. It took nine hours to reach Cottonwood. I stocked up on food at the big Smith Market, then sat down to an agreeable meal at the Sizzler across the street. It was after eight-thirty when I wound down the canyon to the Nauman ranch and knocked on their door. Eileen installed me in the guest house and I began to unwind. Good vibes surrounded me as I settled into the north-headed bed and under a "Sioux star" blanket.

The next morning we sat in Eileen's kitchen and began to catch up. I told her the complete story of the "book quest". Mention of the name Nicolas Flamel gave her chills. It was a clairvoyant "hit". I must dig deeper, she said.

"If all else fails," she proposed, "you should try to get into the Vatican Library."

Well, yes, but people with much more theocratic clout than I have cannot get into the deep reserves of ancient knowledge the Catholic Church has squirreled away in Rome. To me that suggestion was a non-starter.

Eileen had some friendly advice for me as we drove up 89-A into Sedona. First she cautioned me on observing strictly the leisurely pace of vehicles on the local roads. The highway police were not tolerant toward out-of-state drivers. Then she got into more interesting matters.

"You need to start putting up some protection around yourself," she counseled. "You don't realize your own power, you don't understand how your spiritual energy attracts predators."

Then she named a particular bookstore. "I don't want you ever to go in there. A sorcerer hangs out there, and after taking one look at you he will be putting hooks into you, sucking your energy."

My notions of how to create an energetic shield were rather sketchy, but I understood this was a job for my "inner teacher". Eileen was not going to tell me how to do it, just that it needed doing. She had refused the role of teacher, and I had already seen that her method was to propose activities that would lead to a lesson or an "aha". In short, empowering the inner teacher.

We had a great lunch at "La Méditerranée", specializing in Lebanese food, which goes very well within me. Thus fueled, we headed up Schnebly Hill Road and parked off the road. We dropped downslope for a little exercise in "walking the land", off the beaten trails, shunning the big medicine wheel that everyone visits.

"You lead," she said, "follow your nose and let's see what we find."

After a moment of sensing, trying to feel where the psychic wind was blowing, I struck off on a track that led roughly toward the south. There was no trail other than an occasional bit of deer droppings. We weaved through waist-high brush, keeping more or less the same altitude. This wasn't dowsing as I usually practiced it, for there was no known target and the only instrument was my body. Specifically, the instinct that inhabits it. A few scrub pines announced a possible change of influence, and we came to a dry stream bed. It was bare rock and right in the middle lay a small medicine wheel.

In its simplest expression a medicine wheel is a circle of stones with spokes radiating in the four cardinal directions. In native American usage "medicine" refers more to power, especially spiritual power, than to a healing function. My "medicine piece" necklace is a kind of power tool that helps me connect with spiritual dimensions. Stonehenge could be thought of as a medicine wheel, although its builders probably would not have called it that. Medicine wheels are very often created in a process of structured prayer, and there is a body of ritual lore surrounding them.

The circle of stones we found was simple, laid on the naked stream bed and not heavy enough to withstand heavy rains, a real "gully-washer". Our circle was about three feet in diameter, without the internal spokes. My feeling was that this incomplete wheel was more the work of tourists rather than native Americans, but that did not deprive it of some small magical power. It had been created with intent, and the circle, any circle, is a basic element of sacred geometry. It had attracted my senses there, not in some other direction.

We scrambled up the stream's bank and, continuing our tack, moved toward an area with more and larger trees. It became apparent that the trees themselves were forming a circle. Eileen asked me to stop and observe. Yes, there were several of these natural circles of vegetation, forming a line, one could almost say a ley. Eileen proposed that I dowse the largest of these tree circles.

It was protected by a belt of dense brush and thorn, almost inaccessible, but we found a way in. Using the Lecher, I found it registered strongly on the frequencies for life and vitality, feminine energy and the Earth goddess, and some Celtic influence. The latter reading did not surprise Eileen. Researchers in "alternative archaeology" consider there is clear evidence the Celts were in North America long before Columbus. This reaction of the Lecher antenna made me think of David Hatcher Childress and his wide-ranging explorations[3].

That was our first field trip together. Quickly I learned they would always be short, just a few hours, slipped into her demanding schedule of writing, healing, researching, teaching. This night there was turkey for dinner, in my honor, she said. Normally I prepared my own meals in the guest house across the garden.

Two days later we had another time slot together. Eileen answered questions for me all the way into Sedona and over lunch at Shugrue's. There was a lot to talk about: the energy that had come into my hands and which I was using for the world, how to use it with human patients, the things that happened when I went looking for the big book, and the phenomena which had begun crowding into my life. High on that list were the "night signals" and the "mysterious glow". This is when she explained that I was probably picking those sounds off the "astral", a dimension neighboring our reality where there is a lot of traffic. It was a form of clairaudience, a sign that my psychic capacities were struggling to blossom. She was less explicit about the illuminated circle in the meadow. She didn't know, it was something for me to learn in time. In retrospect I think she did have an idea but wanted me to "get it" alone.

There was also the question of shamanism. For months I had hemmed and hawed to myself about it. Training with Eileen would require frequent trips to Arizona during a year or two, and I did not see how that could be possible. My physical energies could not handle the drain imposed by frequent overseas flights — this is where my seventy-one years weighed the heaviest — and financially they would be too much of a challenge. She'd told me the training was hard and the work itself could be dangerous, but these were lesser considerations. The path attracted me, but I was not ready to start walking it at that time and told her so.

"I respect your decision," she said. I think she sniffed the future.

Bell Rock is probably the most powerful pile of red sandstone in Sedona, maybe in all of Arizona. In our world of earth-centered mysticism I learned she is known as "Grandmother Bell", revered by the native Americans long before white Europeans overran the country.

We turned south on Highway 179 and soon the bell-like form rose in a gap between the Courthouse Rocks on the east and a jumble of red rocks called the Seven Warriors. We had barely parked the car before the first lesson arrived. This was about asking permission. In the native American world one is attentive to the presence of "portals". Most of the time a pair of trees framing the path constitute a doorway; sometimes it will be boulders. Crossing a fence also qualifies. One must ask permission and then wait for the response. I had done that for the first time in my life when entering Secret Canyon the previous year.

Now we asked permission before crossing through the barbed-wire fence which separates the skirts of Bell Rock from the highway. In fact, I went through the fence without asking and almost immediately tripped over a root and nearly fell.

"See?" Eileen said. "Go back and do it right."

Back I went, and asked. Soon I felt a gentle tug as if a cord attached to my solar plexus was being pulled through the doorway. That's how I knew permission had been granted, and I passed through the fence.

Grandmother's energies are palpable, although I didn't feel them until we started to approach her slowly. We examined some splendid formations. The first one, a very sheltering womb-like concavity, is a place for meditation, and Eileen urged me to come often and meditate there. Standing about fifteen feet in front of the cleft I began to feel a kind of feminine flow which became an invitation, an attraction to come closer, to enter.

About fifty yards farther on around the hem of Grandmother Bell's skirts we came to a kind of a rock nose. Eileen proposed waiting, feeling. Soon I began to sense a kind of pressure, a push, almost an aggression. The protuberance was hurling masculine energy at me. Remarkable!

Gradually we moved from Grandmother's ground-level qualities to the circles and cairns humans have imposed on the successively rising platforms of her aprons. Some of them were positive to life, as confirmed by the Lecher antenna, and some were negative. This was especially true of those which were fire circles. On one occasion I walked across a circle unconsciously, which brought me a scolding — and a warning of dire consequences had it been a sorcerer's trap.

Some of the cairns bothered me. This was pure feeling. I didn't like their configurations, and we avoided them.

Eileen tells me over and over again that I already know everything about how to feel. She said I simply have to suppress the left brain, stop thinking, let feeling dominate. That means shifting one's consciousness from the left hemisphere to the right. There are meditative breathing techniques to achieve this. The shift had certainly begun to work for me these days on Schnebly Hill and Bell Rock.

That evening Eileen performed a fourth Soul Recovery journey for me. This would be the last one in the series which opened my spirit to the path that lay before me. I knew only that I was on a spiritual path, but I could not see all the contours. Her clairvoyance saw more of the possibilities than I did, but she kept them to herself. She had ignited my Inner Teacher and the rest was up to me.

That fourth journey went very fast. She returned to me three pieces of my soul, and performed a series of repairs on closed chakras, knees and elbows that were clogged.

In the first piece she "saw a soldier in a bullet-shaped helmet, wearing chain mail, in a pouring rain, leaning against the front wheel of a heavy cart to push it up and over a little hill. I could hear the horses snorting, the mud was ankle-deep. You slipped and fell. The rear wheel rolled over you, snapping your left shoulder blade, breaking your back. You died in the cold rain and mud."

When I got home the enyclopedia told me that shape of helmet was used in France in the eleventh century.

That was dramatic, and historic, a past life. The next one was also dramatic but totally symbolic. "I saw a beautiful, slender woman in her twenties, her blonde hair down to her hips, in a wooden cage that was suspended in a huge old oak tree above a swamp," she told me. "You were screaming to get out, frantically trying to shake the thick wood that held you prisoner."

For the third piece she drew a picture of a crown she had seen. "The feeling of `prince' was around it. It was being given to you as a gift you had earned. You might have been this prince. I got the feeling it was England."

That night I began the process of receiving, welcoming and integrating these fragments of my soul. The girl in the cage held my attention: what kind of a lifetime had provoked such desperate symbolism? A woman in a loveless marriage, an inhabitant of a harem, a prostitute in jail?

The next morning we chatted before the wood fire which dissolved the canyon chill on this first day of November. Eileen was entering a demanding period of her tightly-structured writer-healer schedule, and I was going to move to a motel. A lot of serious dowsing awaited me, inspired by Nicholas Mann's geomantic research, and also I would be meeting Tom, then Jacques, and bringing them together.

From my knoll-top motel in Cottonwood one could see the Red Rocks of Sedona nearly twenty miles to the north. That's where I headed, after taking care of the usual unloading, unpacking, and also stocking the kitchenette shelves with a few food essentials. The afternoon gave me space and time to get better acquainted with Sedona. Dowsing would begin the next day.

One of the most important power points in the Sedona region has to be the so-called Airport "vortex"[4]. Nicholas Mann identified two landscape temple systems, the "basic" system and an extended version he calls the "realised" system[5]. The Airport vortex is the crown chakra of his basic system and it is the solar plexus chakra of his realised system. In spite of threatening skies, heavy cloud, wind, cold, I could think of no better starting place.

The Airport lies on a large mesa, a tabletop affording magnificent views in all directions. To the northeast squats a twin butte, not flat-topped, and in the notch between the two sits a smaller pair of knolls. It is here that one finds the vortex energy. After several visits, I am convinced that these energies surge willy-nilly over a long strip of this rough terrain. Most visitors, I suspect, do not find the true vortex, if indeed it can be pinned down.

On this my first visit I followed a clear trail into the most obvious notch. The area was overrun with people hiking up the smaller of the two central buttes. No one was going in the other direction, which I followed. In rather short order I came upon a medicine circle occupying a flat clearing. It tested 11'500 to 12'500 on the Bovis scale — nice but not spectacular considering the reputation enjoyed by this vortex. Strong gusts of wind made it impossible to handle the Lecher antenna reliably.

As I pondered the situation, a tall, lean woman came striding around a bush and asked "I say, may I ask you a question?"

"Yes, of course."

"Is this the Airport Vortex?"

"Yes, well possibly," I replied.

We began talking and the onrush of mutual interests proved staggering. Standing there in the blustery wind, with a modest circle of stones at our feet, I learned that she was a healer with her hands, a teacher of yoga and meditation, beginning to channel against her will, part of a group that had Native American spiritual guides, she lived in Richmond on the western fringe of London, and she knew my step-granddaughter, also a yoga teacher in the same town where I visited frequently.

Chimes, bells, whistles, sirens, a gong bonging cavernously. There came a mental image of a flame-wrapped dirigible crashing to earth, not emblazoned with advertising painted on its sides but the word "coincidences". In point of fact, while I was thinking it, Pamela said it first: "there are no coincidences." We were clearly intended to meet, and our friendship continues, nourished by meetings whenever I get to England.

I explained my reticence to identify this particular point as the notorious Airport vortex. We began to explore together. We followed a footpath that skirts the mesa in the direction of Cathedral Rock to the southwest, and we met a series of bulbous rock formations that emanated palpable energy. Pamela chose to meditate right there, while I went on exploring.

Soon I came upon another stone circle with the points of a triangle touching its inner perimeter, all in hand-size stones. I did the "quarter-turn" cardinal points meditation there, then took a Bovis reading: 20'000. Something good was happening here. I looked around, which I should have done first. This small stone design was surrounded by more circles. First there was an informal circle created by Nature in heavier rocks rooted in the red soil, then outside that was a rather circular tree distribution. I had not seen anything resembling a natural portal, but it smelled as if I had blundered through one anyway. I retreated back up the trail, beyond the trees, then asked permission before going back in. After the familiar tug came I made a liberal offering of cornmeal before entering.

Nothing of further interest manifested as the trail began to bend around the mesa, and I returned to Pamela. With the weather spoiling, we gave up for the day and made a date to meet the next afternoon at her motel in uptown Sedona.

That day was indeed vile, the skies so menacing that we did not go wandering in nature. The wind was blowing cold and colder, encouraging us to stay there in the spacious motel room. Her husband was out on the golf course, as he had been the previous day, and we were free to talk. We talked about books, we talked about spiritual guides (hers was a native American who had been a medicine colleague of Black Elk), we talked the afternoon away, never getting it all said.

Loaning her my medicine piece, I taught her the cardinal points meditation which Eileen and her mother had given me. She held the medicine piece in her left hand, and I instructed her in Apache breathing — in through the nose, audibly out through the mouth, three times. Starting at south, she meditated, then turned to the right. As with me, nothing happened until she got to East, where she sank to her knees. When she stood up her eyes were teary. She had had an important vision involving people and symbols meaningful in her life.

Our parting that day was warm, and we knew we would see one another again. What a delight to have found another spiritual companion!

The next morning I telephoned to say goodbye and to suggest another book. This was Eileen's new novel *Hangar 13*, which I had read recently[6]. This little paperback is a marvelous primer on shamanism, disguised as a romance novel. It explores the dangers of that spiritual work under the sugar coating of an innocently erotic love story. Not a dirty word or thought in Eileen's stories, but they *steam*.

Sedona's fall weather was clearing nicely, the clouds pushed by a chilly breeze. That afternoon I returned to Bell Rock. This time I did not forget about asking permission. Meditation in her "womb" was a cold affair, not very comfortable, and ultimately I had to put on gloves. Grandmother Bell's energy was throbbing at me as I approached the fence but seemed less intense once I was in the sheltered cleft. That was only an illusion, for my meditation was full of shifting lights, pulling me into a strong vibrational state. The Bovis rate was high and fluctuating wildly in the woman-sized fissure; readings ranged from 10'000 to 20'000 and back down again.

Tom Dongo, the author of *The Quest*, proposed we get acquainted over breakfast at a coffee shop in Cottonwood. That's my idea of how to get the day off to a good start, for I am clearly a morning person. I found myself across the table from a tall, lean, dark-haired and soft-spoken man still in his forties. This was no expansive extrovert but a quiet man who thought before he spoke. He was easy-going and quite likeable.

Tom's investigations into UFO incidents have led to the creation of a huge library of photographs, his own and those he has been able to collect from others who have had encounters. After chomping though our eggs and pancakes we cleared some space on the table and looked through a short file he'd brought along. The waitress, who knew Tom and his work, occasionally looked over our shoulders. There were lots of flying saucer-type objects, some of them hovering above Sedona scenery, and a lot that were just mysterious lights. Some of these lights appear as very coherent beams next to people who are known psychics.

My last roll of film from Switzerland had just been developed in Sedona, and I was able to show him the sole photograph of the "mysterious glow" in the meadow opposite my home. He found its mysterious nature entirely convincing, agreeing with me that a distant street light could not have produced such a spot glow. We agreed to breakfast again in three or four days, by which time I hoped to have news of Jacques' arrival. We talked, of course, about our mutual friend Jacky, the son of Jacques. Tom said a group of about eight people had gathered around Jacky during the few months he was in Sedona. He gave me the telephone number of Susan, of whom I had heard from Jacky's sister Line.

It was midday before I passed Bell Rock, approaching from the south, and continued on to the Chapel of the Holy Cross. My objective was to hike toward the lower chakras of the alignment Nicholas Mann had described as his "realised" chakra system. Finding the start of the trail near the Chapel was fiendishly difficult and cost me a lot of time. Vibrational forces assailed me, made me wobbly as I traversed under the Twin Buttes, which hold the sacral (second) chakra. Cairns marked the trail, winding through low brush and scrub pines. The Buttes end in a pair of slender towers called the Madonna spires. Dead ahead lies the massive bulk of Lee Mountain, defended by sheer cliffs. The base or root chakra nests in this rugged mountain, and there was no question of my approaching it without an experienced climbing companion and a rope.

A narrow passage divided the Buttes and Lee Mountain's lower cliffs, and here I found a wonderful, shady meditation spot under the spires. This point was on the seam between the circles which bound the root and sacral chakras, and my twenty-minute meditation was powerful, bathed in 28'000 and 29'000 Bovis. The gap opens on the east to an interior valley which remains wild. As I sat there with my back to the mass of Lee Mountain it was impossible not to think of flying saucers. Close by on my right hand loomed a domelike structure of red sandstone that looks like a space ship, with a line of indentations suggesting porthole-like windows. Success thus crowned this first attempt to explore and confirm Mann's chakra ley. The high vibrational rate provided evidence enough.

Grandmother Bell received me warmly the next day for my third visit. A strong energetic reaction greeted me at the fence, and the fissure's gentle feminine flow registered 12'000 Bovis. Meditation there was difficult with the sun in my eyes, telling me that getting there in the morning might be better. Climbing up the layers of red rock I met a couple of ladies who paused to comment on the lovely energy. We enjoyed a friendly, but anonymous, moment under Grandmother's benign gaze, not knowing we would soon meet again.

Most of the cairns and stone circles that we had seen earlier up on Grandmother's apron had been dispersed or knocked down, probably by the Forest Service. All the twigs had been removed from an infinity design. Farther around on the north side I found a naturel alignment which included two large squarish boulders. Their energetic vibration was in the range of 2'500 to 3'000, not at all propitious. In the distance, possibly half a mile, a red kiva-like dome rose beyond a sparsely-wooded, grassy plateau. Eileen had mentioned that there was an inter-dimensional portal somewhere on this side of Bell Rock. Could it lie in that direction? It was a temptation to investigate, but the Airport vortex was pulling at me from this considerable distance, and the kiva dome was not. Indeed, those low vibrations at the two boulders might be organized to discourage wanderers in that direction. Blanche Merz has described this phenomenon installed energetically in thresholds to power points inside Egyptian sacred sites and Gothic cathedrals in France.

From Grandmother's lap the configuration of the distant Airport vortex area becomes clear. The two knobs between the Mesa and the hill on its east are very distinct, as are the three notches which define this system. With my program for the evening pointing me in that direction, I allowed myself to be drawn toward the Airport. November evenings come down like thunder in that part of the world, and I did not have time to do more by daylight.

My hesitations about that little circle of stones in the right-hand notch, where I had first paused, were well-founded. Wending around the westerly of the two knobs I reached the central notch. Quite a lot was happening there. A deep cleft, an impasssable ravine, dropped steeply away toward the canyon below and energy was waving up through it onto the slopes of the knobs. People were gathering for a sunset meditation, atop the knobs and on their slopes.

A heavily-used trail led eastward. On a wide spot under that eastern knob lay a very nice medicine-wheel, fully developed and several times larger than the little circle where Pam and I had met. It was made of melon-sized stones and had the normal four spokes and central hub. The hub invited me in for a moment of meditation, after which I measured 35'000 Bovis. The steepness of the slope, above and below, grew dangerous and there were few trailside boulders on which to sit. Most were occupied but I found a place for a ten-minute meditation. Moving back to the notch, I sat on the top edge of the cleft. Energy swirled around me, and after a brief meditation I unlimbered the pendulum again. It changed direction and rhythm at 32'000 on the scale, so I knew this cleft and the trail eastward concentrated the power of Sedona's best-known vortex. The high measurement at the medicine wheel showed that what rose out of the ravine spread like a mushroom, which explained why people sat all over the knob slopes for their sunset space-out. The variation between the two measurements was simply an indication that the energy was dynamic and constantly fluctuating.

It's a splendid spot on which to pause and receive an infusion of fresh soul power. From the notch one sees clearly the landscape chakras in both directions. To the southeast the line of sight carries across the Twin Buttes onto Lee Mountain, the two lower chakras. Here under the Airport one bathes in the power of the solar plexus chakra, where the emotions generated in the sacral (second) chakra merge with action, the pursuit of physical goals.

Turning in the opposite direction, Sugar Loaf looms above a residential neighborhood. Nicholas Mann said the heart chakra lodged there, and I planned to go there. Beyond it, still following the northwesterly line, the throat chakra lies high atop Capitol Butte, in the mass of the summit area (somewhere high above Devils' Bridge). Lacking a mountaineering partner, I would not go there.

Bell Rock, not a part of this chakra ley, stands out clearly as a symmetrical center point between Courthouse Rocks and the Seven Warriors mass to the west. She's like the center of a "W", in effect. Grandmother Bell sits on her own ley, reaching halfway around the world. A ley corridor connecting Bell Rock with the Airport notch vortex grazes a modest hilltop before diving into the Mogollon Rim just east of Secret Canyon.

Nicholas Mann reports that this line, 77°49' north of west, when extended on a "great circle" arc around our planet, intersects with Kailash, the sacred mountain of Tibet[7]. Mount Kailash is a magnet for Tibetan Buddhist pilgrims, who circle the mountain while prostrating themselves every inch of the way. This can take months, or even years if it is accomplished in segments. The monumental nature of this devotion can be appreciated in knowing that occidental trekkers need three days to walk around it upright.

From the Airport Vortex I went to supper, and then began to search for the location of a channeling session I had learned about.

So-called "channeling" is a phenomenon of modern metaphysics. It can be seen as an outgrowth of the early twentieth century seances presided over by a "spirit medium". My mother once told me of being invited to accompany a friend to one of these meetings in about 1922. As the seance unfolded in a darkened room the medium began to deliver messages and observations. She greeted the "newcomer" (my mother) who, she said, would soon be married. My mother found that interesting and accurate, for she was at that time engaged to be married to my father. Which event, in the fullness of time, allowed me to issue forth. Mother did not credit the medium with predicting my birth.

Channeling, then, is the transmission of information from the spirit world, from "out there", through a human medium. Nowadays the medium is called a channeler. Channeling does not have to be limited to oral transmission. It had become apparent to me that when I received and transmitted healing energy to trouble spots on the planet I was, in effect, channeling energy rather than words.

I had read many transcriptions of channeling sessions, but I had not yet witnessed the phenomenon taking place.

Finding the Sunday Salon proved to be difficult. The Center for Sedona was dark when I arrived slightly before the announced hour to hear "Sananda". So I went hunting and stumbled on another hall advertising another spiritual entity. That seemed like the wrong alley, so I returned to the Center and this time it was lit up. Surprise! The two ladies I had met at Bell Rock earlier in the afternoon proved to be the stars of the evening. One of them presented some information about floral essences, using photographic slides, leading me to wonder again if I had come to the wrong place. Then the younger woman stood up and introduced herself as Shumala. She began to channel the entity who calls itself "Sananda", allegedly a spiritual splinter of Jesus.

The whole thing was surprising. I was expecting the lady to sit down and close her eyes in the darkened room. This did not happen. She remained standing, never closed her eyes, and the lights did not go down. She stared straight ahead and delivered Sananda's spiritual sermon as if she were reading it off the back wall. And soon I knew that, after all the confusion and the unusual (to me) form of delivery, I *was* in the right place.

Her Sananda radiated a tremendous energy. I made no notes and don't recall a single word, but I could definitely feel a lot going on. Energy was bubbling all around my head and stimulating my crown chakra.

Question time gave me an opening. I asked about the presence of an interdimensional portal at Bell Rock. Sananda/Shumala answered that the door to the other world will affect passing hikers only in the sense of a greater sensitivity which may manifest much later. Um, well, okay I guess. Then I asked about the apparent fluctuations of energy rhythms in the Sedona region. Sananda's response dwelt especially on the sound tone specific to each site. It seemed as if the answer was "yes, they fluctuate", but the explanation trailed off into fuzziness.

Outside after the seance I spoke at length with a lady I shall call Berenice. She confirmed she had felt the same energy swirling around her crown chakra. Thus we were in agreement that a strong energetic influence had been circulating in the room during the channeling. Berenice told me she kept returning to Sedona at increasingly frequent intervals, to the point she wanted to move there from the East Coast. That was becoming a familiar refrain during my days in the Red Rock country.

Whatever the relevance of Sananda's answers to my questions, there was a welcome and unexpected after-effect of bathing in all that power: my spiritual practice received a boost. The next morning, and for some days thereafter, "getting in" was unusually rapid, and vibrations swirled vigorously in the brain.

November's sky menaced to erupt, so I concocted for the next day a series of activities that would allow me to zip in and out of shelter. Climbing Sugarloaf stood high on the list. Winding through residential streets to find the trailhead took longer than the brief walk up this knoll which marks the heart chakra in Mann's landscape temple. My route followed the east flank to the north end, then I turned back toward the south to gain the top in eighteen minutes. This pretty little hill, despite being marred by bulldozer carvings and picnickers' trash, clearly fulfills the role of a heart chakra. As Mann points out, in geomantic tradition the heart of a ley is always a small knoll lying between larger mountains, and that is precisely what prevails here[8].

Its alignment with the three lower chakras is exact. From Sugarloaf one sights through the notch of the Airport vortex to the gap in the Twin Buttes and beyond to the top of Lee Mountain. In the other direction you can sight through a summit notch of Capitol Butte to the pinnacle that dominates the Devil's Bridge on the other side[9]. That spire is accessible only as a major rock climb beyond my capacities and had to be bypassed. From Sugarloaf one must rely on a topographic map to confirm the continuing alignment with the "grassy knolls" and Isis Rock that closes the pattern.

Sugarloaf has one other qualification: it respects the distance between chakras. In the "realised system" the seven topographical chakra points stretch equidistantly over the slightly more than fifteen miles of the ley alignment. Variations are measurable in a handful of yards.

Despite a heavy breeze it was possible to obtain some measurements. Bovis readings fluctuated here on the heart chakra, but three of the five held at 18'000 vibrations and the other two were only slightly lower. Such a level represents great harmony, which one wants in a heart chakra, as compared to the raw power surging through the solar plexus chakra at the Airport vortex.

Gusty winds whipped the Lecher wand quite a bit, with the result that not many Lecher frequencies could be read reliably. In order to work I placed myself in the lee of a tree. I have high confidence in three wave lengths confirmed up there: life energy, green (the color associated with the heart chakra), and the sun. Our closest star is most often associated with the solar plexus chakra, but I have been told that Rudolf Steiner, the clairvoyant founder of Anthroposophism, associated the sun with the color green. The antenna failed to respond for the wave length of a Curry line and for that of a ritual site.

Difficult weather kept me off the trails for several days, during which I participated in an evening of dream analysis, had a session with a clairvoyant who contacted my Guides, breakfasted again with Tom, and played at being a tourist. Old Cottonwood was fun, the old mining town of Jerome left me amazed at what souvenirs tourists are supposed to buy, and I roamed with interest through the ruins of the pre-Columbian knolltop pueblo of Tuzigoot. When the skies cleared I headed for the "grassy knolls" which Nicholas Mann labeled the brow chakra or "third eye" of his landscape alignment.

It was a short but nasty climb, lots of ordinary brush to wade through and thorny clumps to be evaded, requiring a zigzag course. Mann had described two medicine wheels on the southerly of the two knolls, but when I explored the small summit four of them greeted me. True, one just below the sun-facing crest is disaffected and delapidated, fading away, but the other three are alive and well. I had stumbled into a dowser's paradise and spent about three hours up there, testing, measuring, meditating, and physically repairing the three good wheels.

Three functioning medicine wheels on one hilltop suggested to me that the tribal people of the region came regularly to this relatively untouristic site. Appreciated within the context of a larger landscape temple of great mountains all around, one *could* visualize this knoll as being a central point, a spiritual focus. Capitol Butte's mass screens it from Sedona's creeping urbanism, and in the other direction the canyons of the Mogollon Rim absorb the more intrepid of the tourists. The white man's world pays little attention to this knoll, particularly because it is not comfortable to climb. It is, however, the "third eye" of the chakra system, a place for receiving visions.

Before reaching the two medicine wheels cited by Mann I came to a much newer one, created since he wrote. Two concentric wheels surrounded a central hub, which was constructed of twelve rocks and whose path of access led from the east. The whole covered a diameter of nearly twenty feet. Inside the hub the Bovis reading was 10'000 angstroms, while on the outer circle the cardinal points registered (clockwise from the eastern entrance) 11'000, 9'000, 9'000, and 8'000.

Strong wind, frequently gusty, made using the Lecher difficult. I had to exercise patience and do my work in the calm between gusts. The wave length for indigo, the color of the brow chakra, responded cleanly, as did several frequencies denoting places of worship. To my surprise, "Celtic" came up, and so did the frequency for an earth chakra. The latter is most unusual, limited in its appearances around the planet, but its presence here reinforced my growing notion that the indigenous people knew more about the site than we had divined.

Moving about thirty yards farther north I came to Mann's two wheels, both about five meters in diameter. They were aligned north-south and were just barely touching. The Hartmann grid was alive here and a Curry line passed at the point of contact between the two circles. With the Lecher I found both Sun and Moon responding at that point of contact, then splitting. Sun owned the northern wheel, while Moon inhabited the southern one.

Few other frequencies answered my call, chief among them non-Christian ritual sites, perfectly coherent with the tribal influences. The Earth chakra wave length was quite weak here, suggesting a reason why indigenous sensitives had constructed another wheel nearby where it was stronger. The big surprise here was a very positive reaction to the frequency for Druid priests. We really do not know all the movements of the numerous European explorations that preceded Columbus to North America. I am willing to be skeptical about Celts and Druids having come this far west, into arid territories so opposed to the green, lush, humid regions with which these peoples are traditionally associated. My confidence in the Lecher reading leads me to reflect that the wave length really reflects a higher influence. It may signal a global archetype that encompasses various spiritual threads including Celtics and Druids, among others.

As this scenario began to take form I found it puzzling that it was not confirmed by Bovis readings in these two wheels. They were unexceptional here, uniformly 7'000 around the Sun circle and ranging from 7'5'00 to 9'500 in the Moon wheel. The first wheel I'd visited had higher vibrational rates and that unusual Earth chakra signal. Possibly the energy has shifted a little bit and the sensitives who built the new wheel caught that and ran with it. These energy leys are not sharp, knife-edge lines but corridors, sometimes hundreds of yards wide when a major landscape formation is involved. Within them, however, the power can wiggle around, like the serpent it emulates.

Gusty wind was a problem on this otherwise fine day. I had not been able to keep sage lit and smoking. Exquisite care was necessary to sandwich antenna and pendulum readings in between the gusts, and I'd repeated numerous readings that had been blown askew.

Numerous short meditations punctuated my hours with these sacred symbols of stone. Peering through the short junipers crowning the knoll I could sight on Isis Rock and then turn around to link it directly with the pinnacle on Capitol Butte, above Devil's Bridge. It all felt connected.

Long Canyon and Isis Rock, the crown chakra, invited me and I hurried to get there as the afternoon collapsed into dusk. I started the hike into Isis, but night was coming down rapidly and I soon realized that by the time I reached the pinnacle I would barely be able to see it. The trail into Long Canyon is indeed long. It hurt to abandon Isis, especially because the tyranny of my travel schedule was beginning to compress the remaining daylight hours in the Red Rock country. It was unlikely I could come back to her during this trip. My eyes had probably been bigger than my feet in attempting to retrace and verify Nicholas Mann's intriguing chakra system, but all the connections had been made. Telluric power surged through the system, and I had found it measureable in four locations.

The time ahead promised to be more people-oriented, instead of just me wandering the wilds alone in search of energy. Tom had put me in touch with Susan, who was one of the group around Jacky four years earlier. Contacted by telephone, she had invited me to participate in a "psychic development class" she would be giving this very evening. Thus, driving out of the canyon country and back into Sedona proper, I supped in a Thai restaurant after changing from my hiking clothes in the ladies' room. Then I had a difficult time finding the home where Susan was to give her class. Stupidly I had left the address next to the telephone down in Cottonwood, so I had to try to recall it by remote viewing. This was not a total success. What I "saw" was a few doors down the street from being right but it got me close enough. Susan, being psychic, came outside to hail me. She was shorter than me (as usual), curvier than me, with long brown hair neatly arranged around an oval face. Her bright alertness made it easy to like her.

We were four in Paddy's home. Susan described Jacky and his death so the others would understand the significance of this first encounter. Then she went into the class proper. She began talking, and it took me a while to catch on that she was channeling information from another level. She spoke staring into space across the room, as if there were someone there. It was interesting to watch her occasionally grope, or stammer, or back-track, or say "thank you" when she received a clarification permitting her to rephrase something more accurately.

For the next hour, preceded and followed by brief meditations, she brought through some fascinating information about the "countries of the soul". She thought there are eight of them, of which we heard mostly about the redemptive, the cathartic, and the joyful. She said she was channeling the "Council of Five". They told her that none of us present were in the redemptive country -- we'd already been there.

Afterward we went to Paddy's table for a delicious cheesecake. Then Susan pulled out a deck of Egyptian divining cards (similar to the Tarot) and dealt with a question from each of us. I sketched briefly Mother's situation and how we interrelate. Susan came up with five cards that suggested my little Gemini was really almost gone. She was just barely there, close to passage. Susan's cards clearly showed the dynamics between Mother and I, with a transfer of authority marking our joint evolution. This conformed to my estimate of what was happening, but neither I nor the cards saw Mother's amazing resilience.

Jacques telephoned from Phoenix and we agreed to meet in Oak Creek Village. Susan had invited me for a late-morning visit to her apartment there, and getting to Oak Creek was easy to describe over the telephone. Then I would guide him and his companion to Cottonwood, where I had reserved a room for them in my motel.

Susan received me warmly and we talked for an hour-and-a-half. She described how Jacky had been catalytic in her metaphysical development, that he had powerful psychic energy. He had rented a cabin beyond West Sedona, and there he held regular spiritual working sessions with the group of friends who quickly formed around him. One day he proposed to hypnotize her and regress her back to an earlier session, as he had done previously, with the idea she would be able to see what was invisible to them in normal space. What happened instead was, as she told me, his energy catapulted her out of body. It was an awesome experience, both blindingly beautiful but also with notes of sadness from the entities she met. She traveled far and loved being "out there", communicating with very high entities, finally agreeing with her new-found Council of Five that she would come back into body and resume her incarnational contract.

Returning proved to be difficult. She'd been gone about five minutes and then came back partially but still half "out there", suffering from the vibrational shift, the dimensional cleavage. Jacky and their friend struggled to bring her back, they feared to lose her. She seemed to be almost beyond reach, beyond return. Once vaguely back she kept flipping out again. They got her to her feet and out of the cabin, walked her around in nature, helping her in every way to become regrounded.

This was a major turning point in Susan's spiritual life, moving up and down through several vibrational levels. She felt that this experience was instrumental in getting her started channeling[10].

Jacky's father Jacques and his companion Madeleine loved Sedona. They arrived in mid-afternoon and I led them to the Airport Mesa for an initial panoramic view. Then we headed back to Cottonwood and got them installed. Over supper I was able to answer their questions about the golfing possibilities, and I briefed them on the meetings scheduled for the next two days with Tom and Susan. Jacques said his son had roamed the world during his off-season as ski teacher and guide. He had visited famous spiritual centers such as India and Egypt, had trekked through Nepal, wandered the South Pacific, always seeking. In the last months of his life, after returning from Sedona, Jacky reported he had finally "found what he was looking for" in the Red Rock country. Jacques wanted to see, to feel, to understand better just what that was.

The next morning, Saturday, we all met for breakfast at Shugrue's: Tom, Susan, Jacques and Madeleine. Meeting his son's friends was a joyous occasion for Jacques — there was an undercurrent of deep emotion. This happy occasion became a moveable feast, for we went down to Susan's place in Oak Creek to continued the animated talk, her recollections of Jacky, looking over old photographs, and enjoying a warm soup for lunch. It was a cold, stormy mid-November day. Ultimately I led my two guests to some sites for late-day photography, taking advantage of the marvelous play of light and shadow over the red cliffs as the storm clouds dissipated.

The next day Tom guided the three of us out to a site beyond Boynton Canyon. We hiked toward Bear Mountain and then halfway up to a point where scrub trees and red dirt met the cliff face. Here a lonely spire of rock jutted up about twenty feet. This, Tom told us, was Jacky's favorite meditation spot, atop the spire. Yes, of course it was a power point. The pendulum told me it marked 15'000 on the Bovis scale. The chill wind following yesterday's storm made it difficult to control the Lecher antenna. The only reading in which I have confidence was on the frequency for Celtic and Druids, but there could certainly be other positive signals on a calm day.

This spire, adjacent the opening to Fay Canyon, appears to be closely aligned on Chimney Rock and the Airport vortex. If there is a ley, and I do not claim it on so little evidence, its other end is buried in the mass of Lee Mountain east of the summit. We picnicked here, and Jacques did a lot of photography.

Then Tom led us into Red Canyon to see the pictographs. More miles of bumping over dirt roads full of ruts and potholes brought us to Loy Butte. It's a ten-minute walk to the cliff-dwelling ruins, which were in a pitiful state and not at all spectacular. That evenng my guests and I whipped up a ratatouille in my motel kitchenette and the three of us enjoyed early supper and probably our last conversation together.

They were planning to play as much golf as the area could offer, now that the skies were turning sunny again. My sojourn was down to its last thirty-six hours, and on this evening I planned to witness another channeling. Apppparently up to their eyeballs in metaphysics at this point, they declined the invitation to accompany me.

Robert Shapiro's channeling took place at the Community Hall in Sedona, and by this time I knew exactly where to go. Shapiro receives several entities, chief among them a certain "Zoosh". After observing this performance I believe that Shapiro is a true channel, going deeper than either Susan or Shumala.

I am less convinced by Zoosh. This entity is a joker, and I wonder how much of what he says is real and how much is a gigantic practical joke.[11]

Zoosh dwelt much on the "shadow government", as he calls it. When I raised the question of a possible connection with the Trilateral Commission, he called it a "good question" but talked all around the point. He seemed to be saying that the political philosophies had a lot in common but not necessarily the people. Later, when I asked how old this shadow government was, he repeated "good question" — only used when answering me. Did he sniff the old journalist? Finally he dated it at about 1895 but only beginning to operate about the time of World War I. Membership in the secret government appears to be hereditary. He said this was its age on a "benevolent time line", whatever that is. On a "negative" time line he placed it at about 10'000 years ago.

Early in his remarks Zoosh asked how many people present had been hearing noises, bumps, sounds, etc., in the night. Lots of hands shot up! He explained that this phenomenon was related to building awareness, but his point was unclear. Anyway, I'm not alone with my "night signals".

Robert Shapiro seems to undergo a personality transformation when he channels Zoosh. He is a kind of shambling bear of a man, rather reserved and quiet. When Zoosh comes in there are sweeping gestures, smiles, little jokes, all the marks of an extrovert; he's almost a thespian, declaiming, with lots of inflection. Shapiro has a lot of nervous mannerisms while in his trance. He drinks frequently from a bottle of mineral water which he keeps on the floor at his left hand. He touches the recording gear. He reaches for a bit of paper, a kind of fetish, which he keeps on the table at his right.

After the session I found Shapiro in a back corridor and was able to ask him several questions privately. He told me that he isn't conscious of what is coming out while he channels and depends on the eventual transcript to know what emerged. When I told him about the "night signals" he told me that he and his wife also heard these noises in the night. He didn't know Zoosh had mentioned them until I told him.

The next day was a round of last-minute errands and purchases, interspersed with packing. Jacques and Madeleine went off to play golf. I bought a handful of Tom's books from him. Late in the afternoon I squeezed in a goodbye visit to Grandmother Bell, on my way to accept Susan's invitation for dessert and a final chat.

Crossing the deserts to the Los Angeles basin is more than five hundred miles, and it is a full day's drive. Up in the Flagstaff-Williams high country there was snow on the north slopes, in the woods and covering the San Francisco peaks, which exceed 12'000 feet. It was beautiful, sunny, but chilly. I prefer this high plateau-high desert route to the southern desert itinerary. It simply agrees better with my feelings about this world. As early as Pisgah Crater — well across the Colorado River and east of Barstow — one could see snowcapped Mount San Gorgonio, from eighty miles out. Then the western sky reddened dramatically under the fringe of clouds, creating a splendid and very long sunset, then sudden darkness. In just over eight hours on the highway I was back in Pasadena, in the soup.

There I remained for three days, visiting my mother, and helping my sister. She had come to the conclusion that Mother would never be able to leave the nursing home, which meant her apartment had to be emptied. By the time of my arrival her furniture and belongings were ready to go into storage. I talked to the doctor, the attorney, the financial manager and the accountant.

Mother seemed cheerful but muzzy-minded. Her short-term memory was quite topsy-turvy She looked well, ate well, but could not stand without assistance. She made little jokes about being in her second childhood. Her mind did not parse memories well. She mixed places, had trouble with time. In other words, decline had set in with a vengeance. She was 96 years old, and meaningful life appeared to be over.

On the trip north I had ample time to reflect on the happy times of the past, and the pleasures of the table we had shared during my trips to California. Physically I was not yet an orphan. Psychically it had already come to pass.

1   Nicholas R. Mann, *Sedona - Sacred Earth, ancient lore, modern myths, a guide to the Red Rock country*. Prescott: Zivah, 1989, 1991. vi+101p., index, bibliography, maps, illus. ISBN 0-9622707-3-3. (Copiously illustrated.)
The 1991 edition went out of print by 2000, but when I met Nicholas in 2002 he was striving to bring out a new printing.

2   I have mentioned this place twice but hasten to point out that, as of this writing, cheese-making has been interrupted on this *alpage*. Best to enquire ahead.

3   David Hatcher Childress, *Lost Cities of North and Central America*. Stelle, IL: Adventures Unlimited Press, 1992. 588p., bibliography. ISBN 0-932813-09-7. There are at least five titles in Childress's "Lost Cities" series, and three more in his "anti-gravity" series. His explorations have clearly shown that establishment archaeology and anthropology are deliberately avoiding a great deal of evidence that would upset their theories of history.

4   In Europe we speak of power points but in the Red Rock country I learned quickly that Westerners identify them as vortexes. It's convenient to have more words available, and I will use both terms interchangeably.

5   *Ibid,* per maps on pages 71 and 84.

6   Lindsay McKenna, *Hangar 13*. New York: Silhouette, 1994. ISBN 0-373-27027-5.
Eileen writes all her fiction under the above pen name.

7   *Ibid.,* p. 32

8   *Ibid,* p. 85.

9   Capitol Butte is also known variously as Thunder Mountain, Old Grayback, and Gray Mountain, but I shall stick to the first name I learned for it. Devil's Bridge is sometimes called Rainbow Bridge, but I will stay with what the maps say.

10   Jacky maintained copious, detailed journals, and when I returned to Switzerland his sister Line loaned me a copy. This experience was noted there, in voluminous detail and with all their anguish about bringing Susan back to this dimension.

11   In a telephone conversation the next day Eileen agreed with me that Zoosh comes across as an example of "Coyote", who for the native Americans is the preeminent trickster among the animal spirits.

Chapter Thirty-One

A YOGIC PATH

During the year I had read Paramahansa Yogananda's book with much pleasure and interest[1]. His enthusiasm for the Kriya Yoga technique of deep meditation was infectious and I became entranced with the idea of learning it. I wanted to discuss this subject with Wayne, all the more so because I had learned that Kriya would be taught at the Sierra retreat center before my departure for the East. It appeared to be the backbone of spiritual practice for everyone up there. It appeared to be why they were such a happy crowd.

My trip north had been easy, interrupted with visits to friends and to my cousin David in San Francisco. Up in Marin and Sonoma Counties there was a mixture of partying and low-level chaos in the families around me. Gaiety would inform one day, tension would reign the next day, up and down in yo-yo style. Bad news poured in from all sides. I learned that a cherished old friend was dying and did not want visitors, another had had a stroke, and letters told me that two others had died. Several people with whom I had dates fell ill — in one of these cases I received a premonitory message about the individual during my morning meditation. A key that had been left for me in a hiding place was simply not there. Against this background I went again up to Expanding Light in the Sierras.

The Anandans' late-day program of yoga and meditation provides a wonderful way to work off all kinds of weariness, and once again my arrival was just in time for this soothing ritual. Nearly an hour of meditation reinforced me for the procedural obstacles lying ahead. In Yogananda's autobiography he taught the Kriya Yoga technique to people who needed or wanted it, on the spot and in less than an hour. Rather quickly I discovered it was not going to be that easy in the organization his disciples had created. Months of study and meditational preparation were required. It was necessary to dissolve my notion of receiving the teaching then and there. Yogananda's followers have become more rigid than he when it comes to the advancement of other souls, verifying my ancient reluctance to embrace metaphysical organizations. Whatever, Great Spirit did not want it to happen for me at this time and place, and I soon learned why.

The happy people around me radiated good will and benevolence, serving to soften my disappointment. And encouragement took a very positive form as a new development leaked out: the Kriya teaching was now going to be offered at the Ananda retreat center in the mountains behind Assisi. This Italian location was eminently practical for me, accessible from home at the wheel of my own car.

My healing work up to that time counted two humans (Sarah and a Swiss friend) and an immense amount of meditation travel to trouble spots around the globe. My third human patient fell, almost into my hands, when she tripped going down a step and collapsed onto the floor of the Expanding Light dining room. This was Fern, a gregarious 85-year-old spiritual pilgrim from Oregon, and she hurt her leg and knee. At bedtime I gave her a light treatment with gentle massage using borrowed Tiger Balm and some healing energy which channeled in. For the night I gave her some Arnica from my small homeopathic kit.

The next morning at breakfast Fern came down with her companion and stopped in front of my table. With a broad grin she swung her knee gaily back and forth like a chorus girl, all smiles and rarin' to go. My treatment worked! God, or Great Spirit, or whoever, is channeling healing energy through me. "It is an honor," I wrote in my journal.

Later that day I had a very long discussion with Haridas, an elder of the community who had a reputation as a counselor. He listened to the recital of my path and how its multitudinous strands were unfolding. He advised me that Kriya would enhance what I was doing, and he did so convincingly. Then at lunch Wayne and Vairagi (a lady from the Assisi center) agreed that Kriya would be more valuable to me for perfecting my healing work than years of training courses with any of the well-known experts who were springing up like mushrooms. This was easy for me to believe, for I'd heard tales both good and bad about these people. Choosing the right one sounded to be something of a gamble.

Wayne and his dark-haired Naomi invited me to a long meditation and supper in their home in the pines. Part of the Kriya teaching deals with the sounds attributed to each of the seven major chakras, and my new friends now engaged in educating me on the subject. It was her feeling that my chronic tinnitus related to the industrious bee-hive sound of the root chakra. Its persistence suggested that my kundalini was being awakened[2].

Naomi and I had become amiably acquainted around the table when we had Joyce and Clark's house to ourselves, one evening at the beginning of my trip. We'd engaged in a long, wide-ranging exploration of each other's spiritual paths, resumed the next morning while I was packing for the south. She was a fount of knowledge and spiritual wisdom, and it was easy to see why Wayne had become attracted to her. This information about my tinnitus echoed something Eileen had said while we drove toward one of our sacred sites. There is nothing more reassuring than a "double check".

At home again in mid-December, reentry into my habitual pattern of life did not come quickly. Fortunately I had found a doctor who did acupuncture, and she did a good job of readjusting the flow through my meridians to the nine-hour time change.

My social friends were beginning to see me as a mystic....one of them used the term over the luncheon table. One could say it's about time they caught on, but I don't wear my soul as an outer garment. They were interested to know all about Sedona, what kind of a place it is, and I trotted out my standard dichotomy.

Two kinds of people co-exist under the vibrations of the Red Rocks. First there is the well-heeled, chic and touristy part of the population, who tour the scenic spots in the colorful jeeps that make a business of doing just that. They keep the boutiques in business, dine in the best restaurants and occasionally wind up building expensive homes in the scrub pines and sagebrush.

Such people are usually the clients of the second category, who are psychics, clairvoyants, astrologers, yogis, channelers, shamans, masseurs, Rolfers, crystal healers and alternative therapists of every stripe, UFO specialists, and a variety of shop and boutique proprietors. Both groups like to hike the hills and the canyons, although the denizens of the metaphysical community often have less time for that than their clients.

The visitors stay in the expensive hotels of Sedona. The metaphysicians hang out or work there, but inexpensive housing is scarce and most often they live in cheaper areas such as Cottonwood, Clarkdale, Page Springs, Cornville and Camp Verde.

Echoes of Sedona trickled in. There was a card from Pam Grant, and then Jacques called to reminiscence about the rest of their trip in America's Southwest: the Grand Canyon, Las Vegas and lots of golf. A few weeks into the New Year we relived the Red Rocks with an evening of photos. He and his companion Madeleine came to the chalet for a raclette supper, together with his daughter Line. She proposed to make a copy of Jacky's Sedona journal for me, and that happened (contents cited in the previous chapter). A week later Madeleine and Jacques invited me for supper and an evening viewing the videofilms she'd shot in Sedona, a wonderful souvenir of his visit to that land which had meant so much to his son. A few weeks later we celebrated his 75th birthday with a big surprise party she organized.

Meditation was moving into new, delightful pastures, going deeper, staying there longer. More and more time was going into these twice daily sessions. In the morning I preceded them with my usual exercise program, and in the evening I did hatha yoga asanas as preparation. One morning in midwinter everything moved to another dimension. High frequency vibrations blossomed in my head. They were moderately noticeable in the morning and very important in the evening, possibly signs of rising Kundalini. My skull felt like a large vibrating pleasure center. It was stupendous. Both times I felt rather spaced-out, almost vertiginous, when coming out. In the morning I had been sending energy to raise consciousness and stimulate spiritual awakening, around the globe. In the evening I had been using a breathing technique called "Hong Sau", taught by the Anandans but very similar to a method I had been using already.

Not long afterward this state of cerebral vibration came again, gradually becoming a frequent phenomenon. It was taking very little Hong Sau to send me traveling.

The Ananda preparation program, called "Fourteen Steps" and contained in a fat looseleaf notebook, includes a lot of yoga postures which it is recommended to try. Try them I did, and quite a few of them I could do without much strain. Some of them echoed what I had already been doing, some of them were frankly hard. Others put too much strain in my leg-lower back region and I decided not to push very far in that direction.

Going to Ananda Assisi in March began to look like a possibility, but there was also an enticing alternative: an American healer would be giving a workshop in Bavaria. Which one of these directions would be the most beneficial?

One morning I asked vaguely for guidance and did receive a message. It was spoken softly in my right ear: "Il faut un temps tampon", which I have interpreted to mean there needed to be a quiet period, an interval in which a kind of consolidation could occur.

That was the warning. The reality came when an ancient back injury flared up. Everything else went on hold while I devoted a week to volcanic mud packs, followed by massage, and then basking in the nearby thermal baths. My physiotherapist asserts that yoga postures are not made for occidentals.

As I emerged from this mini-crisis my attention turned to the "why" of it. There seemed to have been no clear physical trigger, no excessive shoveling of snow or the like. There remained the metaphysical side to consider. Were my Guides, the Council of Nine and Great Spirit cooperating to prevent me from going to Ananda Assisi? I could not be blind to that possibility. The conflict of choice between Italy and Bavaria had been settled by a circumstance which prevented both.

My own Spirit returned to meditation with fresh zest after several days when it simply would not jell. After a few days I could sense the current passing again. Kundalini moved sweetly up my spine when I asked for fresh power at the conclusion of a long transmission of loving, healing energy to the eastern Mediterranean countries surrounding Israel, and Israel herself.

My back passed the acid test of tennis, although I took the precaution of having one last thermal soak and then a hot mud pack afterward. Suppleness had come home and physiotherapy could end.

As if on signal there were letters from Assisi. It sounded more and more as if they were looking for all kinds of ways to get me to do more preparation. I wondered why thirteen years of meditation was not enough. In any event, I would have to go there in order to see and, more important it seemed, be seen. If we were all happy with one another, the next possibilities for the Kriya initiation would be August or December, my choice. A few days later I could once again touch my toes, so I prepared to travel.

Late in the afternoon on the last day of April the red Toyota and I were on the road again, through the St. Bernard tunnel and down into northern Italy. A wonderful supper in a market town off the beaten path fortified me for the next day's long slog down the Po Valley through May Day traffic, and then down the Adriatic coast. This *autostrada* is endlessly boring, except for the snowy peaks that I gradually left behind, and the flooded rice fields of the lower Piemont. From Rimini the highway followed the sea, passing Cattolica and Pesaro, an itinerary unrelieved by beauty until the turnoff at Fano. From there I followed the ancient "Via Flaminia" into the mountains[3]. It became a "sporty" drive full of scenic pleasures as one wound through the valleys, over the passes and along the ridge lines.

My eyes were alert for buildings that looked like the pictures in the brochure, but what caught my eye first was a small sign reproducing what I see in cerevision. Circular colors rippling outward toward amethyst. Passing it at cruising speed, I had a mental double-take. "That looks familiar!" I thought. Turning around at the next wide spot in the road and coming back, I saw that the other face of the sign identified the establishment. It was positioned for people coming from the direction of Assisi, and in my usual fashion, I had done it differently. I had reached Il Refugio.

My first evening at Ananda Assisi was disappointing. My principal goal was to see the spiritual leader Kirtani, but she was absent and I would have to wait three days to speak with her. The vegetarian supper was good enough, but these Anandans observe monastic silence at the first and last meals of the day. This was not what I needed after six hundred miles at the wheel with only my thoughts for company. Some kind of interpersonal rub would have helped compensate for the lack of protein on my plate. Most of the material in the shop was in Italian or German. There were some anglophones, but they were all young. *Everyone* was young except me and a white-haired man who disappeared after the silent supper.

Assisi beckoned. It was only ten miles downhill to the west, and I went there twice in the next two days. First I went to the Church of Santa Clara, where my Kagyu Ling friend Sarah believed she had been a nun in the twelfth century. Santa Chiara's remains repose in a crypt below the transept. With misgivings, I allowed myself to be carried along in a mob of people lined up to commune with the wax effigy atop her tomb. My aura resisted an energetic disaster area, and I fled back up to the main floor. Moving as close to the transept as permissable, just above the crypt, the pendulum gave me Bovis 1'000, negative polarity. Clearly, adding this experience to Bernadette in Nevers, I do not have the devout gift which creates successful pilgrims. This reading was such a shocker that I repeated it several times just to be sure.

The next morning six of us went back to Assisi -— three inhabitants of the center, two likeable Italian girls and me. First we walked the path into the hermitage of St. Francis, where one visits chapels and grottos. In contrast to my experience at the crypt, this time my pendulum gave me readings of 12'000, 15'000 and then 17'000. And one could feel the spiritual beauty of this wooded retreat where St. Francis came to meditate and pray with his disciples.

Having decided to avoid the tourist-beseiged town center and its major Basilica of St. Francis, we followed another country road down to the convent of St. Damian. This thirteenth-century ensemble exerted a certain quiet appeal. In the masonry of an anteroom two large lozenge-like eyes, supporting a mural, exerted a distinct force. Their visual impact clearly induced a wave-related vibration within me, about 12'000 on the Bovis scale, once up to 13'000.

Conversation was permitted at lunchtime in Il Refugio, which allowed me to get further acquainted with my companions of the morning, Julia, Jim, Prita, and the Italian visitors Claudia and Sandra. Open and friendly, Claudia spoke English, so she interpreted between me and the dark-haired Sandra, who turned out to conceal a bubbling personality. Things were looking up.

After lunch I found myself engaged in conversation with Boris, one of the permanent staff, and rather quickly we got onto the subject of phenomena. He proposed that my tinnitus sounds are wonderful, great to experience, that my colorful targets seen in cerevision are fine, and that these are signs of advanced progress. He told me these were attributes that other meditators might envy. Dive into those sounds, he counseled, follow them as deeply as I can. These ideas took me by surprise.

Meditation times were essentially first thing in the morning and last thing of the afternoon, and I took full advantage of these possibilities. There was an hour of yoga before the late-day meditation, and Jutta led that in a slow, harmonious fashion. We focused on a handful of positions, emphasizing the flow of energies up the spine and through the seven major chakras. This was lovely, dreamy body work, and it showed me how to adapt yoga to my aging body. I was having trouble with my right hip after the long automobile trip, and I was having trouble finding an adequate seat for the meditations. There was no possibility of holding my body in the traditional lotus position for more than a minute. Pain and strain prevented me from holding any floor posture. More than ever before I needed the perfect chair for ensuring meditation, and I tried all three kinds of chairs available without finding it. Ultimately I discovered how to "upholster" with pillows a folding chair so that my bones didn't hurt, I could sit straight at the right height, and spirit could flow freely.

My techniques began to take wing in the small meditation chapel, under the kindly gazes of Paramahansa Yogananda, his own masters, and Jesus. On this third morning my meditation was one of the most vibrant and glowing I have ever had. Kundalini rose sweetly but firmly, fairly rapidly, cleanly, in a way I had never felt before. My head and upper body bathed in vibrations, the crown chakra flipping open. Cosmic connection was "on".

My interview with the spiritual leader occurred the next day, and this meeting went very well. Kirtani seemed to need very little time reading my energy to form her decision. She told me that I could take the Kriya Yoga initiation the next time it was offered, which meant I could choose to come back in either August or December. With a serene, clear skin and flowing prematurely white hair, she radiated the essence of feminine spiritual power. I felt myself in touch with heart-centered divinity. Our conversation under the trees was very long and comprehensive. She made me feel that everything I had done, been doing, trying to do, was starting to crystallize. There was one last detail: it would be necessary to accept discipleship within the energy of Paramahansa Yogananda.

Despite my stubborn motivation to learn Kriya Yoga, my decision to accept this discipleship did not flow smoothly and naturally. I hesitated. The old reluctance to surrender an iota of my independence flared like an amber "caution" light. It took hours of discussion with a handful of new friends for me to come to terms with myself.

By this time I had met a great many of the permanent residents of the community. They were about twenty-five or thirty, most of them with some kind of a job within the organization. They were happy people. Half a century earlier Paramahansa Yogananda had urged his disciples to subtract themselves from the hurly-burly of twentieth-century society and to create their spiritual communities in remote, natural environments. Ananda Village in California's Sierra Nevada mountains was one such. On this saddle of the Umbrian mountains, at 2690 feet of altitude, Ananda Assisi was in a process of continual growth and development. Il Refugio had been created out of an old stone-and-timber hotel. Five minutes away on the other side of the road Il Retiro occupied a long stone hunters' lodge. A number of cottages were springing up like mushrooms, some for the disciples and some for long-term visitors. A double handful of Ananda centers in Italian cities sent a continuous stream of meditants for retreats and teaching programs. The permanent staff taught, counseled, cooked, cleaned and constructed. Marriages happened and babies were born. They all did Kriya Yoga twice a day, blissfully, and they were largely a very happy group of people, a harmonious tribe in effect.

Prita, Paula, Van, Boris, Helmut and others helped me to comprehend that I would give up nothing. Their attitude was "everything to gain, nothing to lose".

Meanwhile, my meditations were soaring in this rarefied atmosphere. The next morning Prita and I chanted and meditated together in the small temple. My inner space took a long time to jell, but then it began to expand, to fill, to fly. I stayed on (and in) much longer than usual, reluctant to give up such a good thing. At breakfast I was drunk with Great Spirit's energy and was on cosmic roller skates all morning. I began to understand why there was a rule of silence at meals after the morning and evening meditations. People leaving the temple were frequently still in another space and did not want to break that lovely spell while eating.

In between times I was strolling the countryside, climbing the little hill behind Il Refugio, and doing lots of dowsing. I analyzed the yoga room (a multitude of good frequencies despite underground water) and a whole clutch of personal bedrooms. No one of the staff did this kind of work and I enjoyed a certain small popularity. My own room revealed very high vibrations, 12'000 and 13'000, including the bed and pillow. This explained why my sleep had been so shallow during the week. One afternoon a big bus pulled up and disgorged twenty-five Czech meditators. Some of them spoke English but most of them needed translation help during meditation classes. They exuded bubbling good nature and it was fun to get acquainted.

Sunday morning's meditation incorporated all these new people and then ended with my initiation. This was a very brief but moving little ceremony, followed by a huge outpouring of love. Most of my new friends welcomed me with embraces and so did some of the Czechs. After breakfast we moved across the road to Il Retiro for the "Sunday service", which was a kind of ceremony of Light. Candlelight played a central role. About three-quarters of the way through this non-Christian ceremony something big welled up in me, and the tears began streaming gently. No religious service had ever affected me in such a way, never before had I been seized deep in my being, my emotions overwhelmed. The love that kept pouring out from the people around me certainly stimulated such a reaction, and it was augmented by the chanting with its Om climaxes. These created giant energy projections similar in concept to what I had been doing all alone. This simple but beautiful ceremony moved me, unquestionably.

After breakfast the next morning perhaps forty Anandans and Czechs formed a large "circle of joy" around me. They sang a farewell song and sent me vast waves of OM energy to conclude. They'd done the same thing for me the last time I had departed the California center, but this was several times larger. Truly I felt blessed as I pivoted slowly around to receive the loving energy of this happy mob. What an uplifting experience! It took an hour or so of puttering and loading the car before I could come down off this high enough to drive away.

Driving up the Adriatic Coast and the Po Valley was a long, hot and hard slog, complete with missed turns on the Autostrada and all the backtracking that implies. I was home the following afternoon, suffering from a major pollen attack that moved in as I descended the Swiss side of the St. Bernard pass. Pollen was everywhere and everyone had hayfever. Homeopathy brought relief.

At home my writer's head began composing a letter to Kirtani, suggesting they make an effort to improve the protein content of the diet at Il Refugio. My path so far had impressed on me that there could be spiritual as well as physiological advantages to vegetarianism. I ate vegetarian frequently, sometimes for several days at a time, but not excluding eggs, cheese, and nuts. At Ananda Assisi I had gradually become ravenous, never satisfied. At that time their diet was preponderantly carbohydrate with a small fraction of vegetables. It was evident to me my body was not getting what it required. One week of that brand of vegetarianism was ample. I wanted to propose also that they develop a large vegetable garden, for they had abundant space. That letter never got written, but when I returned some months later there was an ice chest in the car, loaded with soy sausages, cheese and hard-boiled eggs.

I did not realize at the time that major dietary changes would force themselves on me a few years down the road.

The summer began with some pleasant mid-altitude hikes in good company but nothing very challenging. My dear friend Kay came for two weeks in July, and we had a marvelous time catching up. More than a quarter-century earlier she had been my closest friend during the New York experience (forty months, and out of there!). A few days here and there on the tag ends of my trips had left us eager for a longer time together, and now we had it. Kay and I were sisters in spiritual rebellion, although our inner explorations followed different chromatic scales. Our paths were not parallel but they converged from time to time. She was happy to join me in meditation.

Ten days after Kay's departure Mother Nature reminded me that her realm is not intrinsically benevolent. Her Alps can be dangerous, especially if wrong decisions are made. We were six leaving the Cabane Plan-Névé at seven o'clock on the first Sunday in August. We trudged up the small glacier without needing our crampons and then climbed the delightful corridor of the Pacheu. My first outing with the Alpine Club had been a romp up this sporty wall and it remained one of my favorite passages. On this day we were on the rock before eight o'clock and up top half an hour later. Nice. Then scrunching down the snowfield on the north side, facing Les Diablerets in the middle distance. At the bottom we expected to follow an easy trail that passed through a narrows called the Pas de Derbon before climbing uphill to find a notch called the Brotzet. That wasn't what happened.

Our leader didn't know the way, but half of us did not know that. Her fiancé's father, a superb alpinist noted for being a free spirit, peeled off and steeply upward to our left long before we reached the Pas de Derbon. Her man Ed followed him.

"This doesn't look right to me," I said. "Where are they going? Is *that* the way to the Derbon?"

Our *chef de course* Irene insisted we must follow, that the men knew the way. So follow we did, upward onto the savage slope named in the ancient dialect Luis Tsernou. Above we could see the free spirit moving along the ridge. Halfway up our leaders turned to follow the sidehill laterally. This wall was steep, full of narrow ledges, rubble and scree, inhospitable, nothing but vague animal trails. We had no climbing gear, for this was supposed to be an ordinary hike. My misgivings mounted as we progressed with difficulty along this trackless track. We steadied ourselves with our hands while our feet groped for each few meters of solid footing. This was absolutely mad, total folly, and I knew it.

"I have half a mind to turn back and go down to the bottom. This cannot be the way to the Derbon," I said to Pascal and Marie-Jo, who were near me.

"It's down there," I pointed, remembering the topographic map I had studied. "There was no reason to climb up here. We're supposed to be down there."

We paused to consider the problem, then decided reluctantly that going back would be as scabrous as going forward, and it would not be a good idea to split the group. What we were doing was delicate, unforeseen and difficult, but I was certainly not going to try to backtrack alone.

We came to a large boulder, a big jagged bloc, hanging over our tiny ledge trail. Meeting an overhang without climbing gear was really bad news. Ed, far ahead, had gotten past it. Marie-Jo got around it. It was my turn next, and I hesitated, studying the hand grips before venturing forward. "Go ahead, Michèle," urged Irene.

Moving forward I found holds for both my hands and moved my feet forward onto the small patches of dirt and scree. About halfway around the boulder, my feet slipped on the scrabble of loose stone. They shot out from under me and suddenly I was on my backside, sitting on scree that slid under my weight. Heels and hands were resisting gravity but my slide was inexorable. The edge of the precipice was only about six feet beyond my outstretched heels, which struggled vainly to dig in.

My memory of all this plays in slow motion. I was sliding and would fall, probably to my death, and I was totally calm and unafraid. My life was not flashing before my eyes although my hands and feet were not arresting the slide.

"Michèle!" Irene screamed.

My slide stopped with a jerk, short of the edge. With split-second instinctive reaction, Irene had grabbed one of the straps of my backpack. Her reflexive action had saved my life. There was no doubt of that. She could not hold me for long, but Pascal quickly seized the other strap. Together they hauled me up to the overhang, eased me past it and helped me to my feet. I found secure footing and handholds.

"Don't move!" they commanded. Then she called uphill toward Ed and his father.

"Does anyone have a rope?" she yelled.

Yes, it turned out someone up above did have a rope after all, and one end of it began snaking downhill toward us.

"Don't move," my rescuers reminded me. I faced the wall and held on, Pascal remaining at my side with words and touches of encouragement. "Don't be afraid."

I wasn't afraid at all, I was angry, in a towering rage but fully aware that my life had just been saved. The rope end eventually came within my grasp and I tied it around my waist.

"Go around the rock now, onto the trail," came the counsel in my ears.

There was a second boulder to be turned before reaching our silly little lizard trail. But there was a nice chimney stretching up between the big rocks.

"No, I'm climbing the chimney," I said.

And so I did, apparently to everyone's amazement. Once reunited on the crest, we continued on until there was a level spot to rest and picnic. I had some miscellaneous scratches and gouges on my hands, a couple of bad cuts on the forearm. We got me patched up and continued our hike down the Brotzet, over the Col des Essets and down to Pont de Nant.

Once at the car park I suggested we settle our emotional day with a fondue supper together. It was a relaxing, restorative way to evacuate the stress of the near-catastrophe. The molten cheese and plenty of wine did wonders. Once home again I took a long tub soak with magnesium salts before collapsing into bed. The next day Dr. G. sewed up the worst of the cuts and gave me a tetanus booster shot.

Life resumed in the normal pattern: all the usual householding activities, harvesting vegetables and berries from my garden, lunching with some friends and taking tea with others. Everyone wanted to hear about my misadventure. The reaction finally set in on the third day.

"Rock bottom, that's where I am this morning," I wrote in my journal. "There is no ambition, no drive, no dynamism. I am a dragging, shuffling automaton."

Meditation was not helpful because the drama on the mountain kept on replaying. My hiking companions had unaccountably asked me to write the traditional "récit de course" for the Club bulletin. Doing this helped me organize my thoughts, but spirit was still disorganized. The story could not be told in a few spare, witty phrases as was so often my style for these reports. I set the scene by indirection to avoid pointing fingers of blame — letting people draw their own conclusions. Shock waves rippled through the membership after the story appeared. It was discussed at length in two meetings of the governing committee, which ultimately adopted a tame little rule requiring that each "chef de course" must obligatorily know the itinerary in detail.

My handful of small wounds began healing, some faster than others. My homeopathic doctor prescribed phosphorus and this began rapidly to do some good, smoothing energies and helping restore emotional order. Meditations were not holding focus until I began working regularly to charge up my chakras. Agnès, the reflexologist who had expanded her skills, did a long massage of my aura. She found it somewhat lopsided, with a tear on the right side which she sealed up. This work on the subtle levels felt quite restorative, as if Agnès had tweaked some waves that reached into the cellular level. Rather quickly after this treatment my meditational energies floated back into focus.

That evening Kay telephoned from the US, full of concern for me and full of her vacation plans at the beach in Delaware. My mind lit up at the idea of being at the beach, sloshing through the surf, gamboling in the waves. I wondered aloud if she could fit me into that schedule somehow. Within twenty-four hours Kay reported back that she could extend her stay for an extra week, and my travel agent found she could get me flights in harmony with that program. It was meant to be. Spirit soared, and I began bubbling inside. The spur-of-the-moment decision buoyed me up considerably, completing the regeneration of my energies. This told me much about the karmic depth of the tie with my old friend.

In meditation I was working partly with Ananda techniques, partly with those I had found tried and true. Sometimes it was twice daily, sometimes only once. Sometimes I traveled to my mother just to leave a sheet of healing energy for her guides to distribute as needed. She sounded all right on the telephone until you asked a few questions. Then the confusion was evident. One day she told me she was 89, so I spent a little time gently convincing her she was really 97. She spoke about doing daily activities which she no longer did, such as taking out the trash. It was clear that she was fuzzy on days, dates, years, and everything of the contemporary world. At least she remembered who I was — for the moment.

Eric pulled up in front of the house, just back from a hike and having heard from the Club president that "we almost lost Michèle". Eric was a powerhouse of alpinism, a locomotive on the trails, a leader of strong character and, unknown to many, a very spiritual man whose path touched mine here and there. He knew our mountains like the back of his hand and was part of the rescue column. Rather than explain what happened, I gave him a copy of the piece I had written for the bulletin.

He became almost livid as he read, crying "wrong!" and "fault!". He couldn't believe we had been on the Luis Tsernou, which he compared to a set of tilted tiles. It was no place to be, ever.

The next day my back went out, for the second time of the year. It took a week of physiotherapy, mud packs, thermal baths, and an analgesic I didn't like taking. The most dramatic relief came via my friend Nini. She had become an adept of the healing method called Reiki, and she proposed to treat me at distance (about twenty miles air line). One morning I sat down with the newspaper while she worked from her home. Soon I became drowsy, stopped reading, and sat in a stupor for five minutes. When I snapped out of that slump the pain was gone, my back was free.

Ten days later I landed at Dulles Airport and took the shuttle bus out to Bethesda. Kay had hidden a key for me and there was fish in the freezer. After a shower and a comforting meal my jet-lagged carcass fell into bed without discussion. Before midnight she arrived from Rehoboth Beach. The next day both of us were tired, wiped out. There were some banal chores to do before we could get back into the car. A young tree waited to be planted and seemed to be suffering from not being in the ground. Kay had started a hole but could not penetrate the hard clay. I took the pick and gave it a swing. My back let out a silent yelp. I went to my knees and swung again. No yelp. Thus I punched through the Maryland hardpan, on my knees, and we got the hole dug and the tree planted.

There was one other thing to do before we turned her car toward the eastern shore. Kay had found a psychic/clairvoyant lady who had brought her fascinating and helpful insights. I wanted a generous helping of the same. On the telephone it was arranged that I would have a long interview with Susan one day after we returned from the beach.

We slept through it, but rain dominated the early hours of our first morning at Rehoboth. A profound blackness receded toward the east, apparently the final fringe of a hurricane named Luis. We don't say "coincidence", we use the word "synchronicity". The day promised to be gloriously sunny. Sand and surf beckoned. It made me feel like a little girl again, lacking only the toy shovel and pail. I walked and ran up the morning beach, scampering through and over wet sand and the curling fringes of surf as they crawled up out of the deep. Soul leaped and bubbled. That first day was full of practical matters such as getting in groceries, sunbathing and swimming, but my early morning jog set a pattern for the days to come.

Every morning Inner Teacher took Inner Puppy for an enthusiastic pre-breakfast romp up and down the beach. Brisk breeze blowing off the sea stiffened flags, but it felt good at the water's edge. It was a golden hour. My inner joy must have radiated, for the handful of early risers were spontanously friendly. The little lady in a white fishnet pullover atop her black bikini exclaimed "isn't it glorious!" to launch a few minutes of gay, animated chat. Surf fishermen, usually a dour lot, said "good morning" as if they meant it. A two-year-old offered me her pink plastic crab, which I dutifully admired while chatting with her young mother. The wind didn't blow the sky away, just a lot of inhibiting ionization.

Most mornings I was out early while my chum slept in. In this respect we are diametrically opposed: she loves to sleep late, while for me it is physiologically impossible. My eyelids spring up soon after the sun.

We installed umbrella and backrests on the broad beach. The breeze abated and the sun was warm. We read in the shade, then we ran, we swam in the surf, we ran and walked some more. What a delight! Warmed by the Gulf Stream, the water was much less cold than the Pacific surf of my youth. We bucked the surf, which was rough and tumble. I tried body-surfing but the waves crested too close to shore and simply rolled me into the sand.

Quickly I made a habit of the early morning turn up and down the long beach. This active promenade through the surf became my morning meditation. The usual pattern did not invite me "in", resulting in the longest break for several years. Jogging and striding replaced the usual breathing exercises; communion with sand and sea took the place of a mantra. The endless ebb and flow of the waters *was* a mantra. I felt no compulsion to do anything that was "usual".

Dipping into *The Only Planet of Choice* for the second or third reading kept my mind focused on the spiritual world. Kay had been reading *Joy's Way* at my suggestion, and this nourished lively discussion. One evening there was a long exploration of what happened on the mountain. She diagnosed me as depressed and dwelt at great length on what it all might mean. One of my morning strolls was indeed very difficult when existential matters forced their way through my psychic seawall along the sand. I was unhappy, depressed, uncertain, having difficulty digesting the emotions that continued to well up. Basically, though, we were vacationing from everything, and the healing I sought gradually settled in.

Our days were composed of time on the beach, walking, swimming occasionally, and eating well. One afternoon little fishes kept jumping around me as I swam. It was simultaneously fun and disquieting, because they did not answer me verbally, just kept on leaping. We lunched on sun-drenched terraces and dined out every night except one, when we brought lobsters home, gorging on them with fresh corn and broccoli, all washed down with a very nice Pouilly-Fuissé '92. One of my favorite mottoes says "living well is the best revenge".

Mid-September was the end of the season for this beach town and the restaurant resources dwindled almost daily. Two days before our departure a cold north wind brought temperatures down by twenty degrees. This did not stop the walking but it cooled any remaining ardor for immersion in the ocean.

Autumn was thus announcing itself as we drove across the Delaware flatlands that must surely have reminded the seventeenth-century Dutch settlers of the land they'd left behind. Rain began again as we crossed the Chesapeake Bay Bridge and it rained all night. My week at the beach was over.

Late the next afternoon Kay drove me into Washington for my appointment with Susan. Psychics look like everyone else, and Susan was no exception. She was blonde, trim but not thin, inhabiting what appeared to be a garden apartment of which I did not see any of the garden. She worked through what she saw, but she used stones and dowsing irons to help frame her vision.

She began by commenting on her perception of my high energy, high frequency. She placed a chunk of green selenite — a new mineral for me — in my left palm. It felt immediately warm, reminding me of the Corn Maiden kachina. Susan said the stone helped her to observe its movement through my energy system. Then she began to speak of past lives she was seeing, lives which she believed to have deep significance.

First she saw a tribal chieftain of northern Europe in the sixth to eighth century CE. The man was, she said, "a peerless leader, intelligent, well-balanced, brimming with strength and vitality." He was also capable of great cruelty, slaughtering priestesses and sacking a sacred site in the Macedonian mountains — far from home. These actions created a huge karmic debt. There followed an eleventh-century incarnation as a warrior-monk devoted to adoration of the Virgin Mary. The third lifetime she saw was that of an ugly, crippled black woman of central Africa, an outcast from her tribe, who birthed a deformed baby in the bush, watching her child die in suffering and isolation.

Susan sensed that my Higher Soul has been using the accident on the mountain and the ensuing back failure to get my attention. She said that I must "study, learn, practice, write, use music, and heal." She emphasized that Higher Soul, after going through a series of "pay-back" incarnations, seemed now to be trying to pull all the strands together. It has packed this current lifetime with qualities, actions, events, and changes in an apparent attempt to "tie it all up" this time.

"Does that mean I may now be living my final incarnation on Planet Earth?" I asked her.

"That's how it looks to me."

"Why does Higher Soul need to grab my attention? Aren't meditation and total outlook enough?"

"Look within for that answer," she replied. "You are missing something, allowing distraction to prevent you from doing more. Because the message came during a mountain adventure they want you to do less of that now."

It was true that in eight years of widowhood my boots had trod the trails relentlessly, visiting and revisiting the peaks that surround my villages. Roaming the heights had been an obsession. But Susan's report bothered me. Couldn't Higher Soul see that my alpine activity was already slacking off considerably? My perception of the matter was that I was already shifting focus. Alpine goals no longer itched within me. Mountain trails continued to provide spiritual refreshment and walking them kept my physical being well-tuned, but they no longer claimed priority on my energies. During the season just finishing I had hiked much less than usual, the near-fatal excursion having been the only full weekend out. Higher Soul might possibly claim that I had chosen not to go to Assisi in August because of this alpine excursion, but there are often overriding practical reasons of which entities outside this dimension seem to be blissfully unaware. August is a bad time to travel, extremely hot all over Italy, and the Anandan facilities would be overwhelmed with people who could only go there in vacation time. One of the joys of being "senior" is the liberty of off-season travel. Thus I would travel south in December. Meanwhile, I was drafting a long article entitled "Investigations Inside the Invisible", and there were like-minded companions with whom to broaden my horizons. My mystical agenda was already leaving alpine trails in their own dust.

It is stimulating to be able to compare experiences with spiritual friends, and with that in mind three of us had been meeting about twice a year for a convivial supper. Liliane and Yves had been fascinated by the meanders of my spiritual path, the dowsing trips, my rambles in Red Rock country, and they in turn always seemed to be going to spiritual destinations which intrigued me. Dark-haired, with serene oval features, Liliane was a professional astrologer well-keyed to karmic interpretations, and her generosity and warmth had often been of good counsel to me in recent years. Lean and craggy, Yves ran a family business, with heavy responsibilities, and had found that meditation was a great help in managing stress. They made a good team. We sated our reciprocal curiosity around the fondue pot in midwinter and midsummer. We talked about going some place together, but we had never been able to mesh the holes in our schedules. Finally those holes merged in late October, and we leaped to exploit the lingering Indian summer before it collapsed into November damp and darkness. They proposed we might just have time for a sprint into nearby France to see some of the wonders I had been telling them about.

Bourg-en-Bresse is famous for its chickens, so that's what we had for lunch on the first day out. Thus restored, we paused at the church of Brou. It is architecturally marvelous but spiritually empty. Built in the sixteenth century, it is no longer in consecration but simply touristic. There is much fine sculpture but no magic as I have learned to sense it. Brou did not "sing" for us that day.

Paray-le-Monial was another matter, as the damp afternoon slipped into dusk. My appreciation of the fine vibrations was higher than ever, and my companions shared these sensations. Paray was truly singing for us, even without the play of sunlight through the windows or sunset on the golden stone of the facade. Bovis readings fluctuated, as always, but hit a high of 28'000 in the center of the transept.

At the farmhouse Guy and Michèle deployed their own brand of magic. They gave us a warm welcome and a copious supper, and my companions were happy.

We met Paul at the isolated hilltop chapel of St-Quentin, where he and I had felt such powerful energies in the hands on our first visit. The four of us spent about two hours palpating and testing the energies, more outside than in. We roamed at length through the non-conforming, anomalistic boulders amid their splendid oaks. These rocks are granite, rounded like great bowling balls, sprouting from the meadow grass like a collection of breasts, and they had to have been transported several kilometers to the top of this spur. I have a photo of Yves standing trancelike atop a boulder.

Inside the chapel, behind the altar, the pendulum gave me a vibrational rate of 28'000. On the outside of this wall two big blocs registered 25'000 and 26'000. Such high readings suggest a spiritual history exceeding the modest aspect of the chapel. The Lecher gave me two different confirmations of Celtic influence here, coupled with a strong 28.25, the rare sign of a dominant female ritual. Thus one can theorize the hilltop was a place of Celtic ceremony long before the arrival of Christianity. They thought enough of the energy here to bring great boulders a long distance to create some kind of a temple. Did the mammary-like boulders celebrate female fecundity? The Christians, as they have always done, merely took over an existing holy site.

Moving on, we visited the Merovingian cemetery near St-Ythaire[4]. Here was another example of the Hartmann network having been extremely deformed. A central cross is surrounded by 108 tightly-spaced concentric circles of energy. The inner ninety rings showed negative polarity, and the outer eighteen were positive. This kind of energy is a total puzzle to me, especially since the cross itself registered only 2'000 on the Bovis scale. Intuition — or maybe just a wild guess — suggests some kind of a huge void deep in the earth, possibly even a raging torrent with a whirlpool. The Lecher antenna did not help me with this at all.

By this time we were more than ready for Saturday lunch, so we drove southward to Paul's house on the hill near Cluny. Margaret honored my guests with a major effort, for she was battling a case of the flu. In turn, we honored her roast leg of lamb, which followed champagne inside. The season for meals under the trees had long since been washed away; small drizzles and showers promised a wet afternoon.

Toward the end of the afternoon, during a lull in the precipitations, we wandered up onto the knoll to "see" the invisible circles. Once again the central nest of circles yielded a good Bovis rate: 12'000. And once again the neighboring nest stood in stark contrast: only 1'500. We noticed that the slump pit under the trees was not collecting water, and Paul confirmed that it never did, always remaining dry. That, of course, suggests some kind of a natural drain just under the surface. Digging was tempting only in the mind. It could be back-breaking work because of the nearness of sub-surface stone, and — as previously explained — the risk of invasion by archaeological officaldom created a kind of Pandora's box situation.

My pendulum was reacting to some kind of anomalies in the pit, and it "felt" magnetic. The presence of magnetite in the subsurface became a working hypothesis. We needed a good clairvoyant on the team.

We left our rural bed-and-breakfast in time to meet Paul the next morning at St. Bonnet-en-Joux, from whence he guided us to the Butte de Suin. This marvelous promontory offers a good panorama over the rolling countryside, but there was more. Paul told us it was a holy place for the Druids and Celts, for the Romans and now the Christians. The Lecher confirmed all this rapidly, but it wasn't necessary for the Christian part. A statue of the Virgin took care of that. This hilltop had a lot of boulders but they did not have the mammillary aspect of those that decorate St-Quentin. They seemed instead to be remnants of dolmens. After working through a long list of Lecher frequencies confirming the sacredness of the site, one unpleasant wave length stood out. It took a bit of surveying to find the exact locus of this offensive frequency. It was somewhat downhill, a place where the Celts performed ritual sacrifice. A large rock group gave only 1'500 vibrations, and one of these boulders, flatter than the others, yielded only 500. That was clearly where animals were slaughtered. All that took place before the Romans came. Still farther downhill one finds vestiges of a Roman villa hidden in a cornfield, and it was possible to pick up a few shards of pottery and tiles.

After a pleasing lunch at St. Bonnet (light, delicious, reasonably-priced) we left Paul's car in front of the basilica at Paray-le-Monial and pointed ourselves toward Kagyu Ling. Sarah was no longer there to greet the tourists but her colleague Jill could tell me that she was happily installed in a Tibetan center in New England. There were a lot of tourists milling around, admiring the portraits and photographs up on the gallery overlooking the Temple floor. We went up there first to smile with the happy portrait of the founding lama, Kalou Rinpoché (Bovis 57-58'000), and then we asked permission to meditate downstairs on the main floor of the Temple.

There, seated at the rear of the temple and well within the auras of the great Buddha and the equally imposing green goddess Tara, we spaced out. We were at the back of the area where the monks meditate, not infringing on the collective aura, but we were still soaking up some of the vibrational structure with which they had impregnated their temple. The tourist hubbub on the gallery above faded from our consciousness. We bathed in a deep sea, lapped by waves from the depths of our souls for nearly half an hour. When finally we emerged, one by one, peace pervaded us. Using the Bovis I measured 117'000 angstroms around us, the highest value I've ever recorded in any temple, church or cathedral.

We drove back to Paray in a benign state, found Paul's vehicle and said our goodbyes. After our final night at the farmhouse, we returned to Paray in the morning for a final prowl through the basilica. Its atmosphere was both light and thick, if that makes sense. After a moment of meditation in the center of the transept I measured 36'000 Bovis, a new high for Paray-le-Monial (in my limited experience). The range of vibrational fluctuations in such a spiritually intense edifice is of course broad, and we probably caught it on a crest.

Before going into the town of Cluny we visited a "chateau" that was more of a fortified farmhouse. Our goal here was to taste the wine, on Paul's recommendation, and we liked it enough to collect a few bottles for home, along with some of the wildly flavorful goat cheese.

After lunch in Cluny we visited the vestiges of the great Abbaye. Using the Lecher antenna I tried to pick up the hint of ancient Celtic/Druidic influences preceding the Christian takeover of the site. The antenna gave me only a feeble sign in the courtyard which had once been the transept. The weakness of the signal suggests that, if the Celts had used the site, it could have been fifty or a hundred feet away, or more, lost in twentieth-century urbanism. We didn't have time for extended research on this esoteric point, for Liliane and Yves persuaded me we should seize the opportunity to visit the Curé d'Ars. I had to go along with this proposition, because it was their car and they had me outvoted. My tepid experiences with Sainte Bernadette at Nevers and Santa Chiara in Assisi had used up my tolerance for waxified mummies. One more sainted cadaver was simply going to delay getting home.

We drove south from Macon in the direction of Lyon. After about twenty-five miles, roughly two-thirds of the way to Lyon, one arrives at the modest city of Villefranche-sur-Saône. A left turn into the countryside leads quickly to the village of Ars-sur-Formans, become a center of pilgrimage. Jean-Baptiste Marie-Vianney was the catholic priest here until his death in 1859 and was canonized a saint early in the twentieth-century. Why? Apparently because he developed a reputation for helping people with their souls, to the point people came from long distance to consult him, even other clergy. He was said to have supernatural knowledge and appears to have been a clairvoyant, able to see when parishioners in the confession booth were lying. Thus he turned struggling souls onto a virtuous path. There is now a small basilica built onto and dominating his old parish church, and there he rests.

My usual skepticism before sainted cadavers melted away as I tested the emanations from the glass coffin. He really does radiate: 23'000 Bovis up close, 20 to 26'000 seated at the near end of a pew, 17'000 at the far end. I could feel it, Yves and Liliane felt it most strongly, and it was evident that tens of thousands of pilgrims felt it too. The village of Ars had developed a considerable touristic infrastructure. Their ancient curé, who had been an indifferent student at school and in the seminary, had brought a powerful soul to his vocation, so strongly that it lingered on more than a century after his death.

We were away from Ars at six o'clock on this next-to-last evening of October, 1995, and reached their home overlooking Montreux in less than three hours. Our talk during the drive home reflected the ups and downs of these adventures together, and a light supper of fruit and cheese fueled me for the half-hour trip to my alpine nest. My mind was already churning over the next trip, to Assisi in mid-December, and the multitude of tasks to be accomplished before then.

High on that list was finishing my "Investigations Inside the Invisible". Sharing some of my mystic adventures had become an imperative. I needed to communicate and thereby, with luck, discover kindred souls among my friends and acquaintances. My intent had been to relate the highlights of my irregular path and to do so in an amusing, light-hearted way. "Beyond the Fringe" was my subtitle. In the weeks following our return from Burgundy I finally finished writing this article. It printed out at fourteen pages, including deep endnotes, five photographs and four cartoons (keep it light, Michèle, keep it light). Everything in it has been told in greater detail in this book. When I first started drafting those pages my estimate of the print run was "about fifteen". In the end I found forty likely names on my mailing list, and that's how many I mailed out. The response was underwhelming: aside from a few polite remarks, one couple asked to spend an evening with me to talk about it. So much for the rage to communicate!

While this work neared its end in late November I took a couple of afternoons off to take part in a "Congress of Light" in Lausanne. A workshop on the healing method called Reiki attracted my attention, for I was open to learning new tricks in my budding career as an energy channeler. The two ladies who animated this workshop had light, airy voices which were feeble competition for the drumming going on in the workshop next door. They did manage to explain the technique, short of actually teaching it. My journal says "I didn't learn much, for it became quite clear that their Reiki and my hand energy are the same thing." In fact, that was a valuable lesson, for it spared me the temptation of ever taking training in the three levels of that excellent technique. My inner teacher was doing the job just fine and we didn't need to give it an oriental name.

One of the organizers of the congress gave a program involving perfumes. We selected them by color and vibratory sense, testing them in meditation. It was interesting but not fascinating. Perfumes are already an airy subject, but the presentation itself was gossamer, insubstantial. The next afternoon a man who makes floral elixirs demonstrated that it was possible to bring substance to the evanescent. He explained the first step in creating floral essences: placing the chosen blossoms in distilled water and leaving their glass bowl to work in the sun next to the plant. Then he offered to let us test the drops of three different essences of his creation, one at a time. I took the first two in the mouth and both gave me sensations in the upper chakras. California poppy stimulated the crown chakra, while passiflora worked in the brow chakra-medulla oblongata axis. Sage, received in the palm of my hand, did nothing for me. Could that have been because I frequently drank sage tea at that time?

The evening program was supposed to explore the chakras in relation to the planes of light. Neither of the two men who spoke provided any insights on this intriguing subject. Both wandered around in their own egoistic gardens instead of communicating. I came away with nothing, absolutely nothing, and begrudged the evening taking me home and to bed later than I like. This "Congress of Light" seemed like a good idea, and the number of people who attended proves that it was timely. But good ideas are one thing and meticulous execution is another. A significant population was becoming attracted to anything "alternative" and so were the lazy and the verbose.

Clear, sunny skies blessed my mid-December departure for Assisi. Claudia had invited me to spend the night in her apartment near Bologna, which was an easy day's drive. It was clear and sunny crossing the Alps, via the St-Bernard tunnel, but Aosta buried in its deep valley had a coating of snow. As one emerges from the foothills the broad expanses of cornfields reminded me of California's Sacramento Valley. It was ice-in-the-ditches time, sun shone through the morning fog, and one could imagine a cock pheasant thundering out of the rubble of stalks. Rice fields stretched infinitely through the wintry mists as I rolled down the broad, flat Po Valley. In the afternoon the sky began to cover. First there was mist, becoming heavy before Modena, and then steady rain at Bologna, turning cold. I found the hotel parking lot where Claudia promised to meet me, and she was right on time. She guided me to her village of Budrio via back roads so as to avoid losing one another in the rush hour traffic.

After aperitifs in her apartment, and talking much about our time together at Assisi in May, we went to supper in the Trattoria dei Cannone (the Grenadiers or artillerymen). That was the best lasagna I've ever had. In the morning Claudia showed me her paintings. She was working in acrylics then, mostly abstract expressionist, but there were also watercolors. She needed a couple for a collective exposition, and I thought one was ready and two more close to ready. She invited me to stay with her again on the way north, with yet another trattoria on the agenda. (Artists and spiritual workers have healthy appetites.)

But the big news of the morning was wet, white and thick: snow, the first of the season. Getting to the Autostrada was terribly slow because no other car was equipped with four-wheel drive and all-season tires like my red Toyota. Snow faded into sleet, then wind-whipped rain blasted the Adriatic coast. These conditions required unrelenting concentration. Crossing the Appenines westward was not hard despite "winter wonderland" conditions west of the Furlo tunnel.

Il Refugio was free of snow despite its altitude. The Anandans greeted me warmly: Prita, Jim, Dan, Beate, all the kitchen crew, Van, all the guys building the new temple, in fact everyone except the double handful bedded with influenza. Kirtani flung herself around me warmly. It felt very much like coming home.

The next afternoon I drove Dan to Perugia. He needed to shop for a Christmas present for the person whose name he had drawn, and we thought a red sweater would be fine for her. We found that easily. My goal was to sniff the old Etruscan city. It proved to be splendid visually but not very warm in ambiance. However, hilltop Perugia had done one thing absolutely superbly: a series of escalators from the lower parking plaza up to the city center. These "scala mobili" passed through tunnels and corridors of the old walls and fortifications, traversing the city's sub-basement. It was a very original way to leave twentieth-century decor behind and enter an urban landscape that stimulated visual memories of ancient times. I found this much of it exciting to the senses. I don't need to return to Perugia, but the entry through its root structure lives in memory.

That evening, Thursday, Kirtani met with a group of us who would take the Kriya training and initiation on Saturday. She proposed that Friday be a time of withdrawal, reflection, and quiet attunement. In the morning I withdrew to Assisi for a visit to the Basilica of San Franciso, which seemed to me an appropriately contemplative activity. A nativity scene to end all nativity scenes sprawled gracefully up the lawn in front of the facade, occupying perhaps half an acre. Scene decorators were still at work sticking palm fronds around the manger, while dozens of costumed mannequins stood in various poses of biblical times like shepherds and water-carriers. Inside the basilica a television crew was setting up its trolleys and cameras and klieg lights, effectively blocking the transept to the public. Well, the form of the vault and the windows and the famous murals all did their part, enabling a reading of Bovis 14'000 to 15'000 in spite of the high-tech clutter. Japanese Franciscan friars wandered about, and one of them occupied the offering booth. Another Japanese crouched over the piano keyboard, struggling to tune it through the hubbub.

Down in the crypt I sensed bad vibrations right away. In front of the tomb of St. Francis my pendulum refused to go farther than 2'000 Bovis, in two locations. This was a sharp contrast to the wonderful atmosphere of his hermitage, which we had visited in May. There the spirit of meditation and natural beauty was vibrantly alive, a more fitting tribute to the man than a cold stone box. My visit to the saint's basilica had not quite fulfilled my mission of "quiet attunement", but the afternoon permitted total loafing.

The rhythm of life here appealed to me. One sensed there was a general happiness and satisfaction in the daily routine of deep meditations and work for the community. I allowed imagination to play with the idea of living here, of joining the community. It could be a beautiful life. My little fantasy conveniently avoided the nature of the vegetarian fare here, which was not providing me with the protein I needed. There was always salad and usually a real vegetable or two, but the fare was heavily potatoes, rice, pasta and fresh homemade bread. I had brought some extra food: cheese, hardboiled eggs, soy sausages. The latter caused raised eyebrows when I sought permission to grill them in the kitchen, and I was obliged to emphasize that they were NOT of animal origin.

On the surface all was serene, although I knew there was some stress. One couple was returning to Oregon and would divorce. Lots of people were down with influenza: Paula, Boris, Arjuna, Jutta, Vairagi and another handful I didn't know so well. It was clearly a localized epidemic, prompting me to dose myself with extra zinc, echinacea and homeopathy.

Kriya training for our class of eight began at seven o'clock in the morning with a long meditation. I still hadn't found the magic formula for sitting comfortably; spiritual concentration battled continually with physical strain and pain.

You will not find a lesson in Kriya Yoga in these lines. We all took a vow not to divulge nor teach the technique, and I honor my word. I can say that the technique itself does not add much to my existing longterm practice of stimulating chakras and kundalini. Anandans do call upon music and chanting to enhance meditative techniques, whether Kriya or not. Indeed, I found the Om-ing to be a real high. During Hatha Yoga I held back on everything that might overstrain my joints. It went rather well, but I must never overdo those postures. We worked with Shivani for more than half a day, and all this was only the warmup. It was a day of semi-fasting, nourishing ourselves on fruits, nuts and bouillon. At five in the evening Kirtani took over for the actual instruction and initiation into this rarefied method of approaching Nirvana. It's very technical and needs a lot of practice to get right. This was a three-hour affair, by candlelight, all of us in white to the limit of our traveling resources, and quite a few of the staff joined in because of the beauty of the ceremony and to benefit from a review of the technique.

The next day was review and practice, review and practice. Shivani, Kirtani and her husband Mark spent much time adjusting our breathing techniques. At the end of a Kriya meditation there is a final technique for bringing forth light. You close off all other sources of sensory input and let the momentum of your meditation open a panorama of light. During this period I "closed the circuit" and saw the brightest light I have ever experienced (except for a bolt of lightning). My "working" day closed with a long private session with the brown-haired, warm Shivani, going over some of my questions. When we were finished I had been active for twelve hours, fueled by very little food, and I lost "drive". Half a dozen years later I realized that I cannot do this kind of a schedule: hypoglycemic since childhood, I had always had a big appetite and had not yet learned that people like me should never try to fast. The lesson fell upon me with severity one day in Peru, but that is getting ahead of the story.

On this occasion I had no stamina, nor taste, for the Sunday evening Advent service and instead did a long meditation in my room before starting to pack for the morrow's departure. There was a fine conversation with Prita, who was the same age as my daughter, and then Paula came out of seclusion. She looked pale and wan from her bout with the flu, and we took supper together. She and her Van had been a great support to me. Their apparent love and attachment for me, starting in May, was touching and gratifying.

For my trip north I chose to take a different route that might allow me to pass some pottery yards in the ceramic center of Deruta. As it turned out I found nothing to my taste, because everything was gaudy majolica whereas I was seeking earthy, unpainted terra cotta. What *was* to my taste was a very satisfying vegetarian lunch in Citta di Castillo: a vegetable flan to begin, then ravioli stuffed with spinach and ricotta, closing with grilled zucchini and eggplant. If I could eat like that, it might be possible to go along with the vegetarian notion most of the time.

After lunch the road led upward into fairly savage mountains and over a snow-clogged pass at 2600 feet of altitude, such conditions prevailing for a long segment of the route. Budrio came into view at 17h30, well after dark. Claudia informed me that snow conditions had worsened after my departure five days earlier. The main road had finally been closed for twelve hours, but I was out just ahead of that. Winter travel can be full of surprises, which is why we alpine people drive cars with four-wheel traction and special tires. After my shower and a joint meditation, my vivacious companion guided me to the Trattoria "i Canaletti" for a dinner of Bolognese specialties. From the road you saw nothing to suggest a fine restaurant. You drive on a dirt track to the back of the long building, entering a well-lit, long dining room. There was no touristy decor. There were probably no foreigners at all, except me. What unrolled before our eyes, onto our plates, and into our gullets was an indescribable parade of delicacies.

Getting home again was easy. Rain and fog gave way to blue skies in the upper Po Valley, affording splendid vistas of the snowy Alps. Crossing them posed no problems and I was in home territory early enough to shop for food.

The winter season opened before me with a new feature on the landscape: Kriya Yoga. It became the mainstay of my meditational life as the future prepared to unfold.

[1] Autobiography of a Yogi.

[2] "Kundalini" is identified as spiritual energy lodged in the base of the spine. It is frequently symbolized as a tiny serpent coiled up inside the coccyx, waiting for the stimulation that will unlock it and allow it to rise up the spinal column. In brief, this movement can bring powerful illumination coupled with high energy. Its rise also has the capacity, sometimes, of surging out of control and overwhelming the nervous system in general and specifically the brain. Controlling Kundalini's rise is a goal for many spiritual practitioners.

[3] The Via Flaminia was the ancient road from Rome to Ariminum (now Rimini), built by the general and statesman Gaius Flaminius in 220 BC

[4] The Merovingians were the Frankish kings who reigned in western Europe from the late fifth century CE until Pepin the Short deposed the last of the line in 751. The Franks originally moved out of present-day northwestern Germany and extended southward to cover, at various times, what is now Belgium and then most of present-day France.

Chapter Thirty-Two

STUMBLING THROUGH
AN ENERGETIC JUNGLE

After returning home from Italy my meditational life focused entirely on the Kriya Yoga method. That's how it began in December and how it continued as the festive season carried us into 1996. During the long months of preparation for Kriya I had gradually set aside the energy work for the world which had dominated my practice for more than a year.

During my years of meditation I had experimented with numerous methods of breathing and was familiar with the respiratory slowdown that occurs as the body accustoms itself to new ways of managing the oxygen intake that is vital to life. One of these methods, alternate nostril breathing, had been taught me in TM and I continued to use it ever since. Over time my respiratory cycle during meditation normally slowed to between two and four times a minute[1]. Also, I had been working for years with my chakras, moving the kundalini energy. These exercises, already part of my life, proved to be part of the daily "limbering-up" for the Kriya techniques. In these respects I was more than ready for the yogic studies that preceded initiation into Yogananda's specialty.

These studies also included some information on *mudras*, which are defined as postures especially designed to increase awareness of the flow of energy through the body, to awaken subtle energies which can stimulate deeper meditation. Mudras can be full body postures or sometimes a small manipulation of another body part, such as hand or tongue. One of these *mudras* is identified and received only during the final initiation, and I have mentioned it near the close of the preceding chapter. Let me call it simply the "light" mudra, because its Sanskrit name is part of the secret I am honor-bound not to teach. I will speak of it because I had been seeing lights and colors in the spiritual eye for a good ten years. Kriya's special light, available at the conclusion of the full ritual, came to me not as a new concept but as another form of phenomena with which I was familiar.

I threw myself into Yogananda's technique with the enthusiasm that had pushed me toward it ever since reading his autobiography. All went reasonably well for quite a few weeks, although doubts began to creep in from time to time. In late January my technique was improving, becoming smoother, and I began to see this special light at the end of the breathing ritual. It didn't come with the same blast of brilliance I'd seen on the final day at Il Refugio, but it was starting to dribble in.

Something else was also dribbling in, sometimes quite strongly. I was missing my energetic work for the world, under guidance of the Council of Nine.

"At the moment I am rebelling against meditation," I scribbled in my journal one day at the end of January.

The next morning I did a full-scale, global "everything" meditation with the Council of Nine, and it felt really good. A few days later I was working at knitting/mending/meshing together the ozone holes over the two Poles, first the North then the South. There followed the suspicion that my concentration on yoga techniques and then Kriya had taken me too far from this satisfying, useful sort of psychic exercise.

Once set into motion, this line of thought could not be stopped. Much as I had sought the Kriya method, it was not bringing me any particular satisfaction. I seemed to get more of a sense of cosmic contact through my energy projections for the planet. I recognized this reaction was a peculiarity all my own, out of phase with the sensations affirmed by all my Anandan friends and teachers. My meditational rhythm found its own adjustment. I continued to emphasize the Kriya breath technique but went to the Council of Nine every second or third day. The thinking about meditation and Ananda went on continually. Much as I had sought Kriya, and much as I found it an interesting technique, I had to admit it was not bringing me much. A greater sense of cosmic contact entered my consciousness when I projected loving, healing energy to targets suggested by the Council of Nine. However, considerable time and effort had been invested in this teaching and I was not ready to give up on it.

Another insight slipped in. Eileen's warning not to give power away came back to mind. What did this mean, one's "power"? Your energy, drive to move forward, independence, sense of personal responsibility are all facets of power. This does not mean power over others, only your own inner force, the underlying force which directs our lives. It does not mean the power to lift a one-hundred pound sack of cement, it means the power to find your path through the current incarnation. Learning new tools, receiving instruction, involves dancing a fine line between remaining in control and accepting the authority of a teacher. Which is one reason for seeking the counsel of one's own Inner Teacher.

In the process of learning a new tool, was I unwittingly giving away some of my power to the Kriya mystique, to Yogananda? What exactly was I accomplishing as I sat there breathing, channeling my breath in the specific Kriya fashion? Fourteen years earlier I had certainly given away power to TM until I recognized that the Maharishi's program was flawed. I had slipped away from his organization and found my own path, which evolved in line with my needs. More recently I had found a unique way to work for the planet, following suggestions of the Council of Nine. This could also be construed as giving away power, but to me it felt more like an investment in a better world than a gift to a guru, and it brought a great sense of satisfaction. Kriya Yoga was supposed to lead toward greater self-realization by awakening energy in the spine and brain, opening a kind of high-speed superhighway to enlightenment. In a helpful spirit, a friend wrote to describe Kriya as a "jet" to deeper, faster stillness of mind, place, and light.

It took me a long time to work my way through this philosophical underbrush. Enlightenment is enticing, no doubt about it, until you try to define it. Then it spreads out to encompass a vast spectrum of cosmic appreciations, total understanding, illuminations, flashes of joy, awe, and bliss. It seemed to me that elusive bird of enlightenment had already dropped some of its feathers on me. Kriya Yoga was reputed to lead to bliss, one of the cardinal goals of the disciples I met. Did I want bliss? If so, then I already had it. Bliss best describes what I felt whenever the evolving swirls of color I call cerevision lit up my inner screen. It was cerebral orgasm. I'd experienced that intermittently for years, but Kriya Yoga did not seem to be leading me toward the bliss of *nirvana* that I heard Anandans talk about.

Nonetheless, there were occasional dividends from this new tool. One day, while mentally chanting "Om" at the top of a Kriya, I saw a whirling propeller in the spiritual eye. This little whirligig was small, with a dark center against a bright orange-beige field, and the edges of the blades were accented in a dark line, spinning through a vertical plane. That was the first time I had ever seen a chakra.

Still following Kriya twice a day, most days, and gradually increasing the number of kriya breaths I did, I telephoned to Ananda Assisi for a "checking" and found myself in a long chat with Vairagi. My practical problems came out but not all the philosophical turmoil. Vairagi felt that perhaps I needed to loosen up, perhaps shorten the breath, not to make work of it. She opined that my practice sounded quite "dry", and I agreed. I went a bit further even, using the word "drudgery". This took her aback — I could hear the incomprehension in her voice. She recommended more intensely asking Paramahansa Yogananda and his antecedent gurus to help.

When I realized that I could not do this, I gave up the idea of writing Eileen for a deeper explanation of the notion of personal power. Suddenly I *knew*. I was unwilling to surrender my power. My Inner Teacher refused to let me take that step. I value my hard-won power too much to efface it, to drown it — and myself — in Yogananda's teachings. This realization carried with it a bit of a shock. What I had previously experienced and developed was too strong to be surrendered.

Going as deeply within as I could, I sought clarification, asking spirit to choose the variety of meditation I should follow, whether with Council of Nine ideas, or with Kriya, or with my earlier practices. The whole matter floated in the air for some minutes, then my hands received a heavy input of energy. That was a sign I could understand. My healing energy was an expression of power, and I had received it in meditation. A shaman in Arizona had gently opened some windows and allowed me to glimpse new inner horizons. Beyond that she refused to go, other than introducing me to my power and pointing out I needed to protect it. She didn't tell me how to do that. Inner Teacher taught me. It was up to me to navigate my path.

In this spirit, I decided to continue seeking benefit from the practice of Kriya Yoga. Loosening up, as suggested by Vairagi, informed my approach as I slowly increased the number of Kriya breaths I did during a session. Once in a while that special light came, sometimes moving into the color evolutions that characterized my cerevision. There is a "dead" quarter-hour after one has finished doing Kriyas and is supposed to be letting the nervous system settle itself. One time I used that period to revive an old practice of bringing energy up through the feet, allowing/encouraging it to float upward at its own speed. After a moment coalescing in the pelvis and focusing in the coccyx, it began to drift upwards. And suddenly I found myself with the crown chakra open and pulsing. Like old times, almost better!

In this season of mid-1996 my family was engaged in a kind of death watch. My mother had pneumonia and we expected she would leave, and then she decided to stay. C.P. transited in June; he had been the husband of a cherished cousin, and was of great help to Mother and me. My dearest cousin Shirley, a real sister to me, a companion since childhood, left us in July. In November it was the turn of a Californian sister-in-law. And in December declining health finally blew away my favorite male cousin David. Habitual meditation allowed me to reach out to all of them via the transmission of loving, healing energy. Inner Teacher helped me with this work, in which the energy must be sent not to the patient but to her or his spiritual Guides. They apply what arrives when and as they see fit. This was not Kriya work, underlining for me the fact that I had been given other tools for performing service to the planet and its people.

Twice in conventional meditation I received "visits". One morning my work with the Council of Nine took an unprogrammed turn. An old friend came in, so strongly that it appeared to me that he may be one of my Guides. He'd been a fast friend, even rather protective, when I'd lived in New York, and he been on the other side for nearly twenty years. Suddenly it seemed as if I had a new guardian angel. His image was luminous, sitting in a window in the upper right of the screen.

Then one early morning, still in sleep, I dreamed of a woman who got into the car with me, rather clumsy in her movements, but quite friendly. Two days later she arrived in a meditation, to be with me as another new Guide. She had a luminous face, which I first described as "rather Italianate", white skin but not fair, smooth skin, large nose, not a pretty person, but glowing in a special way, dark hair in rolls over the ears in the nineteenth-century fashion. The next morning I realized that "Italianate" was off the mark. She looks like a bleached-out Plains Indian -- that was the nose and facial shape exactly. Yet she was dressed in the high-necked, leg-of-mutton sleeved style of white women of the period. She stayed on, occupying a chair at my right, below the old friend glowing in his window.

These manifestations reinforced for me the notion that my Kriya Yoga was a deviation from my true path. The good things that I had previously experienced in meditation had almost been chased away by the long preparation and initiation into Kriya. A quotation from the Pleiadians sums up neatly where my thinking was headed:

"If you go into a meditative state, you will receive a picture of your identity and reality and the next step of your assignment day by day. Meditation is a state of communication; it is not a way to go somewhere to get lost. Meditation is a way to get informed and to go to a place that nourishes you[2]."

A few weeks later, in the fall of 1996, I went down to the lakeshore for an evening meditation and get-together with a charismatic lady who proposed a unique kind of seminar.

Christine was young, dark-haired, pretty, not yet thirty I guessed, but she transmitted a lot of energy. For the coming weekend she proposed to teach the art of channeling. Her ideas about channeling struck me as somewhat imprecise and perhaps misdirected, for everything I had witnessed so far paled before the superb work of Phyllis Schlemmer for the Council of Nine. I expected that this seminar would not even flirt with the edges of Schlemmer's accomplishment, but I was intensely curious about the phenomenon. Also, working alone on my mountaintop made me hungry for the company of like-spirited people, and the Congress of Light a year earlier had not really filled that void in my life.

Our group meditation was too short but very effective. I was diving deeply, receiving through the crown, really getting down, when Christine stopped it after twenty minutes. She initiated a hand-holding circle. In such an exercise you receive energy from the left, move it through your body and send it to your neighbor through your right hand. I was on her right and received a lot of energy in my left hand, from her right hand. I ran it through me and sent it toward my neighbor, where I hit a wall. My right arm and shoulder suffered with the connection to the young man on my right. Energy blocked on his side? Negativity there? Finally he moved it through and the flow made the circuit. However, he did not show up for the weekend seminar. Afterward the six of us took teas and munched on raisins while Christine described her own spiritual path leading up to this teaching program. I found it a bit incoherent, but that did not lead me to back away from the seminar. Gold is where you find it, and I was prepared to dig for specks, not receive a shower of coins.

On Saturday morning, after some preliminary talk about our objectives, Christine led us into a heart exercise set to appropriate music by a New Age composer. We were about fourteen people, mostly female, prancing around in the huge salon of a big old house Christine had rented two streets inland from the lake. Our routine was very active, and very long, and I found it progressively entrancing, bewitching, a marvelous preparation for the guided meditation which followed. But I found that too much guided and could not follow her very soft voice. My third eye colors took over, then a series of fleeting images, the last of which focused on a real-life scene from years earlier. Nothing unusual so far, as we broke for lunch.

At table we began to get acquainted with one another. I found empathy with the slender Hedy, quiet and reflective, just as I enjoyed the blonde Nadine, more of an extrovert. A spark of rapport emerged with the husky Ulysse and his animated companion, the brunette Fleur.

Serious work began that afternoon. Christine had us dance a long time, to digest our lunches, then we settled down for an afternoon of learning to "see". We paired off -- I found myself working with Hedy -- and we took turns with affirmations. First, "I decide". Then "I see, I hear, I feel the Guide (clearly)." Each of us worked for three-quarters of an hour, with the intent of receiving an entity or a message. I perceived an energy, palpable only through its radiations, which were visible and audible. During our debriefing Christine said she had seen that energy form.

The next morning we got directly into channeling. Our first exercise was hard for me, I could not rise above the background noise. Hedy and I retired to the front hall to get some peace. She led off, following a mental path into my brow chakra, seeing me leading a column of hikers in the mountains. Her very accurate vision included the image of Jean's dog and the two young sons of Henri and Anne-Marie. This was very validating. She saw me lead my group into a large temple where I was received by a bishop-like figure. I was supposed to be receiving echoes of her vision through my third eye, but they were meager. Then it was my turn. I followed a path to a mountain chalet, into the chalet where Hedy was cooking a meal for her husband. I got the layout of the rooms wrong and the eggs wrong but my other descriptions were accurate, both of him and his ultimate departure from her life. My feeling was that she did much better than me. In my view she'd hit well and I had received poorly.

The "real" channeling began after we had returned from lunch in a nearby restaurant. To start with I was paired with Nadine, who could not get anywhere. While she was trying I began to receive an entity named "Ruth", coming in between my brow and crown chakras. I held this vision in reserve until it was my turn to work. It was not at all easy to separate the "real" from the mental which tries to remain in control. Nadine was pleased but I was dissatisfied. My performance was not strong, in my opinion, just barely adequate. Later, back with Hedy again, I brought in a rambling message from my old guardian angel friend who had materialized as a Guide. I was still not content with all this. The mind tries to take over -- restraining it is a battle (just as in meditation). These results confirmed my early judgment that channelers are born, not made.

Everything came to a climax at the end of the second day, when Christine performed what she called an initiation. This was basically a blessing and a channeled message for each of us, coming from her contact among the Ascended Masters (who I will not name). We were divided into two groups of about seven people, and in the second group she chose me to come forward first. She explained that the messages would probably be illustrated with hand gestures she called mudras (which we have already met at Assisi). Then she went into what seemed to be a light trance, connected to her Ascended Master and began to deliver a message, accompanied by slow, stately mudras.

"Beloved daughter, shaman, medicine woman, for a long time you have sought the summit of your consciousness, now I give you the power of healing," were the first words she brought through. Then, with her hands broadly shaping a kind of basin at the bottom of my abdomen, she added "I give you the source of your compassion and the courage to show it."

Frankly speaking, this blew my mind. I had not been expecting anything of this nature. Christine said the basin-like mudra was a new one in her repertoire. Afterward, in the big room, the others who had been in the same session came over to embrace me. Although they had all received messages, they were impressed with what had been given me. Fleur and Ulysse came over for a hug and to tell me "we've been saying this weekend: if there is a shaman here it's you." This surprised me. Metaphysical people in general seemed to be talking more and more about shamanism without necessarily knowing very much about the subject. "Shaman" was in danger of becoming a buzzword. Christine came along to say that it was possible her Master referred to me as a shaman because I have already been one (in another lifetime).

I supped quietly at a restaurant in town, then drove home late, full of thought. The next day I tried to call Eileen but was obliged to leave a message. The day after that Fleur called to propose I accompany them the following weekend to a Kriya Yoga seminar in France. By that time I knew that several spiritual offshoots from Paramahansa Yogananda were quarreling over the right to propagate his teachings. Traveling with Ulysse and Fleur sounded like great fun, and the idea of comparing another Kriya teaching to the one I had received was tempting. However, this little junket would have required a four-day absence and that I could not do.

Fleur had more information to pass along, which emerged as my intuition told me to prolong the conversation. In effect, she and Ulysse had pegged me for a shaman from the very beginning of the seminar; they had lunched with Christine and she had agreed. What had they seen in me that prompted such an idea? They all saw it as a past-life calling. So, I asked, how spontaneous had this channeling been? Fleur counseled trust: she herself had received factual confirmation of material which Christine had channeled for her.

After some long introspection I decided to attend Christine's next channeling workshop two weeks later. Hedy told me she found the message brought through for her to be very stimulating and she planned to continue the experiment as well.

Late in the week I tried to do a shamanic voyage, using drumming tapes I had bought after meeting Eileen three years earlier. In contrast to earlier attempts with those tapes, this time I got a rapid notion of the shaman's "hole" I needed to use to descend deep into Mother Earth. It was a famous cavern to which my grandmother had taken me when I was eight years old. It was difficult to concentrate down there. I did not enter an altered state and I cut off the attempt after fifteen minutes.

The next day Eileen returned my call. She told me that the rule of thumb on calls to shamanism was to wait until it happens twice or even three times. When the time is ripe, the teacher will appear. In other words, wait. If it is real, confirmation will come.

The seminar, however inconclusive, had piqued my interest. More and more I devoted my usual meditation time to trying to move into channeling mode. One morning in the second week something began to happen. A being arrived in visualization; it was my old friend and new guardian angel Guide, whose name was Jim. He addressed me by name and said he could not speak French but would allow me to translate when working with francophone people. This was very "conscious" channeling, not at all deep, but I felt that the mental thread was hardly present. Jim's words came spontaneously, although there was no message.

During this period my spiritual practice was a mix of deep meditation, often enriched with visions, unsuccessful attempts at channeling, and one session of Kriya Yoga. It was not quite a year since my initiation into the technique, and already I was finding it irrelevant to where Spirit seemed to be leading me. One could say that the powerful message about shamanism capsized my kriya canoe and it was sinking.

We were only seven for the second channeling weekend, six of us women from the first workshop and a young man named Frédéric. Fleur and Ulysse didn't participate. Christine talked for an hour before starting us on the heart chakra dance which I had found to be such a good warmer-upper. Then she called for meditation. I saw myself on a path, everything very orange-gold like the sun, and I met a spirit who took me by the hand. It led me to the edge of a circular pit like a bomb crater or the top of a funnel, everything now orange-red.

Right there I blocked and needed some time before getting back into the flow.

At lunch in a restaurant Christine proposed we observe the people around the room and focus on the one who repels us the most. These would be our "negative mirrors", worth pondering. This little business was clearly a warmup for the afternoon's exercise, dubbed "I see into you". We paired off again, this time with the challenge to see into the eyes of our partner and discover how what we find there mirrors ourselves. Frédéric and I chose to work together, seated in a corner next to the fireplace. Soon it became apparent that we saw the same things in each other. In that respect we were sister souls. His visions into me were trenchant and lapidary, echoing in advance what I was seeing in him. Later, in channeling, neither of us could get down. I had a very strong, high-vibration threshold but could never get beyond it. Then came a vision of a man running to a fire (the flames not seen), which ended in blocking against a big dark building-like rectangle of a cloud. Frédéric spoke of blocking also. The other Michèle in the group told me later that she had a similar blockage — a dark bar — at the same time. Christine cut the session short, referring vaguely to the way energies were circulating. Then, as we sat in a circle for the final summing-up, there was a commotion in the fireplace that Frédéric and I had just left. Nothing was initially visible but there was movement/activity in the hearth, noise, a ruckus. Christine spoke of the chimney sweep at work (at that hour on a Saturday?), while I had the notion of birds fighting at the top of the chimney. A few twigs and bits of char seemed to be falling to the hearth. We went on with our discussion for a while longer, but Christine was visibly nervous and soon she closed our day about half an hour early.

This time I had taken a room in a hostelry on the town square, which allowed me to be first on the doorstep for the Sunday morning session. A major surprise awaited us. Christine's assistant met us at the door to announce there would be no teaching this day. She referred vaguely to circumstances arising during the night that put the future of the center in jeopardy. It was all very mysterious. I invited everyone to come up to my mountain home for the day, and two of them -- Anne and the other Michèle (a head shorter and twenty-five years younger than me) -- did join me.

We spent hours massaging the question, gradually developing some insights.

Pooling our observations from the preceding afternoon's happenings, we came to believe there was a clear case of psychic warfare via black magic. My companions knew bits and pieces of Christine's history and previous associates. There was a struggle over ownership of an aromatherapy business, jealousy, shadowy figures in the background. After turning the situation in a dozen directions, we decided to meditate on it. This ended with Michèle channeling aloud. She brought through a message for me relevant to my trip to the orange-red crater. Then emerged information about the workshop center. Michèle's guide said the house was under Buddha's protection, that it would not be harmed if the Light was maintained. I was taping Michèle's effort, and there was interference on the tape.

This brought to mind my meditative vision of the man — short, blocky, blond hair cut close, white shirt — running because of a fire. Later came the commotion in the fireplace. What had I seen? What form did this phenomenon possess: poltergeist, demon, what? My personal shield, created daily, was functioning; I was probably not a target and was not harmed. But I began to think I should have recognized what was happening and attacked with some kind of shamanic combativity. Once again I felt the lack of appropriate tools.

The next morning I had planned to do a long Kriya Yoga meditation, but another kind of work imposed itself. My Guides and the Council of Nine proposed that I surround Christine's school with healing white light, first inside then outside, for "the highest use" of everyone involved. Had it not been for the sponsorship of this task I would not have gotten involved, for fear of performing unwitting sorcery. As it was, my white light around the house grew rapidly thick, broad and bright, as if Spirit wanted it so. Inside was much more difficult: it took several passes to brighten the passage back to the initiation room, and the big room was very stubborn. At first it would not lighten, but when I came back again, insisting gradually, it began to fill with the white light. Then I surrounded and filled the house with gold light. Having spent three days doing spiritual work there, it seemed to me that cleaning up after myself was certainly permissable. Our departure had been abrupt but we had expected to return. Such was not allowed and there were, I was certain, spiritual traces of all of us in that space. Black magic can wander around looking for targets and I did not want to leave any trail back to me.

Later that day I wrote to Christine, referring to psychic attack and the need for a purification ritual in which I would be willing to participate. She never replied, and I never did uncover the whole story.

Some mornings I continued trying to channel but I never got past the stage of emitting spontaneous lines such as "it doesn't matter," "let it go" or "crystals are everywhere". In meditation I spiraled down into that orange-red crater, in search of the message Michèle had said was there. What ultimately came was very surprising: a vision of a silk jersey dress I had bought twenty-four years earlier to wear while selling my husband's paintings during an exposition we held at that time in Lausanne. Colors of lilac, sky blue and turquoise animated designs that echoed the symbology of western native American art, especially that of Navajo rugs. This meditation revealed that dress as part of my "medicine woman" garb. Buying it had occurred instantaneously, instinctively, without a moment's hesitation, And I still had it.

That evening I tried to dive through the bottom of that crater, using a drumming tape for support. It didn't happen, but it felt like "almost" — lots of consciousness shifts. The more I raised the volume on the drumming the closer I seemed to get to traveling. This felt like an approach with potential. The whole enterprise was an exploration, wandering into "terra incognita". I decided to count on my Guides to make it happen when it should and to prevent it until that threshold would be reached. Let it happen spontaneously, don't force it. Eileen had said a teacher would appear at the appropriate time. To be some kind of a medicine woman without doing soul retrieval might suit my possibilities better, but I did not know if that was a valid approach. To work on the surface, not deal with either the Lower World or the Upper World, was that a realistic option?

Snow and ice dominated this end of November and I was often busy clearing snow with the machine, with spiritual matters taking a back seat to material needs. Ultimately I telephoned Nadine. We had worked together briefly during the first channeling workshop and had discovered sympathetic responses. She had learned of a psychic-clairvoyant who was offering a weekend workshop in the immediate future. With my endorsement she met him, Stéphane, for coffee and reported back that he exuded good energy. Like me, he did not believe one can learn channeling in a class setting. His seminar was scheduled for mid-December and we agreed to attend jointly.

Meanwhile Martina, another participant in the ill-fated workshop, called. She related a powerful dream she had the night following the psychic attack.

In her dream she was sitting in the big room, trying to channel. From successive spots in the room she saw, first, black-suited men with black felt hats standing outside the garden door, second, a dead chicken in front of the bookcase, and then her own sweater draped over a chair and turning into a big black bird which bit her in the left arm each time she reached for the sweater. She told this dream to Christine's companion, who confirmed these elements had been part of their traumatic night at the center.

Family matters surged to the fore at this time. My mother was holding on, as confused as ever about dates, events, visitors, plus little flights of fantasy.

At least she still picked up the telephone. Her close contemporary, my sister-in-law Elise, living in the mountain village of Grindelwald, suddenly had a breakdown. A Dutch friend found her confused and disoriented on the telephone, asked another friend to double-check. When he confirmed her suspicions, she, Sjaanse, took the night train from Utrecht to Berne, Interlaken and Grindelwald, and the next morning she found Elise in a poor state — weak, hungry, and suffering from a fractured collarbone. She had fallen some days earlier — it took us a long time to learn exactly when. In conference with our nephew in Geneva, I agreed to go to Grindelwald to help in the transition from one volunteer caretaker to the next. Elise was obstinate about avoiding anything smacking of hospitalization. Thus began a long process which in later family conclaves we described as the "heroic" times. Fortunately the timing of all this did not require that I abandon the seminar with Stèphane.

In meditation I was working extensively with my chakras and with hand sensitivity to their radiation. For the Council of Nine I journeyed often in meditation to Tibet and once to Easter Island, where I had had a vision of its disappearance. The other Michèle and I tried magnetism on each other, sensing each other's chakras from short distances. She had a massage table and we took turns being healer or patient. I could feel and affect her chakras from eight to twelve inches above the body, and she felt my power strongly. In turn, I could feel the heat from her hands as she balanced my chakras from a foot above them. This was all very encouraging — I could firmly believe in my burgeoning power.

Everything seemed to be accelerating. The following night, immediately before sleeping and in the dark with my eyes already closed, I saw a face. It flickered on and off a couple of times, the wrinkled face of an old American Indian chief. I asked for his name, and the reply came back "Red Cloud".

Mind immediately sailed back to Pamela in London. During our long get-acquainted chat in Sedona she had said her group had native American guides. Could Red Cloud be one of them? As sleep closed in I promised myself to call her and also to meditate with this new arrival.

The next afternoon, on the eve of Stéphane's weekend seminar, Liliane read my progressed astrological transits and scored a real bull's-eye. She found an "opening" since mid-October, suggesting spiritual activities would become more and more dominating. Both Uranus and Pluto had moved into positions favoring this opening, which was clearly underway.

Stéphane had rented a conference room in a center above the town of Morges. Nadine and I were the only "outsiders", and the oldest; the other half-dozen seemed to be familiar with our host. Stéphane's theme was "The Messengers of Paradise", aimed at stimulating contact with angels and guides. Our lanky, craggy leader was not yet thirty. Everyone was young, Nadine closer to them in age than to me, while I seemed to be a total surprise and mystery to all of them. I offered myself as "grandmother". Stéphane led us through a series of exercises, often set to music. Saturday's most significant experiment involved purification of our *nadis*. These are nerve channels I had met while studying for the Kriya Yoga initiation. They run beside the spinal column, interweaving with the chakras. One inhales with the *ida nadi* and exhales with the *pingala nadi*. Our purification ritual, executed in pairs, was basically a matter of moving energy. Paul-André's light touch enabled me to receive the clear, bright colors of blue and light green. My touch, however, caused him to experience electricity as lines of sparks running through his body. That made me stop and think. Paul-André made it clear he thought I had a lot of power.

Truth sometimes spurts out of the blue, and it happened again during one of the morning exercises. Stéphane came over and said to me: "vous êtes chaman!" ("you are a shaman"!) and then put his fingers to his lips in mock secrecy. We didn't communicate further about this, other than via a few conspiratorial glances.

Cousins of my husband lived nearby, and that evening I paid Georges and Germaine a brief visit. Germaine admitted to being stressed out. Thus, full of my burgeoning talent and straining to unleash it on the world, I gave her an energy treatment to reinforce her chakras and her aura. She had so much power of her own — being a longtime Reiki practitioner — that my hands seemed to be surfing over fire. Yet, she said that I had great force and that I really made her body bubble and rumble. As my hands cruised above her body I found a hot spot on the lower right abdomen, just to the right of the bladder. Then she told me it was a suspected polyp and she would see her doctor in a few days to discuss their healing strategy. This experience, my fire meeting the fire of an experienced healer, remains firmly embedded in memory. It was a kind of landmark, a real confirmation.

Stéphane used a lot of music to accompany some of our exercises. We did a very profound "Om" chant to appropriate music. This was a marvelous moment, for the group's power became magnified. It was too short for my taste; I could have built that into flight.

Stéphane exhibited strong clairvoyant qualities. At lunch he asked if I used the Bach flower remedy "Rescue", while my fingers were touching the flacon in my pocket, out of his sight. The conversation turned to tribal cultures, and I mentioned having several native American guides. Immediately he described the face of the gray-haired "M" — who Agnès had brought to me — without my having made any specific reference to her.

Georges and Germaine had proposed I drop in for a cup of tea after the end of the seminar, before getting out onto the highway for the trip home.

This time I saw that she had an ankle wrapped in an elastic bandage. I hadn't seen it the preceding evening. She'd suffered a sprain, it was slow to heal and quite swollen. I took the foot in my hand and held/pressed/heated it for quite a long time, trying to reduce the swelling. She said I succeeded.

The new week began with preparations for going to Grindelwald, although my personal batteries were flat because of so much spiritual work. I was learning another lesson about "running energy". The energy I had used for Germaine did not come *from* me, it came *through* me, but the conduit that is my physical system still sustains wear and tear. I needed a long nap that Monday afternoon.

What do dowsers do when winter chill and a white landscape inhibit their investigations? They go skiing together. Because her home in Bern was on my way to Grindelwald, Violette proposed I stay overnight with her. The next morning she would accompany me to that mountain valley where we could have a morning ski over the local crosscountry trails. It seemed a fine plan and I agreed quickly. November's early snows had melted and now, one week before Christmas, the holiday snows were late in coming. Over here we had none below eight thousand feet — giving fits to the ski-lift operators and to all my village neighbors who survived the winter by selling snow-related services. It was said to be better over in Grindelwald, in the shadow of the famed Eiger north wall.

Skies were blue and sunny when Violette and I drove south toward the Oberland, the Alps glorious under heavy snow. In seventy-five minutes we were in the valley below the village of Grindelwald. Frigid fog came and went, putting an edge on the deep cold as we tackled the trail between Grund and the Untergletscher. We found the snow thin, icy and slick, not at all ideal for our idea of sport. After a couple of turns around the four-kilometer circuit we went up to the village for a convivial lunch at the Weisse Kreuz. Then I put her on the train for Bern and hied myself up to Chalet Bärghof to look after my beloved Elise.

---

[1] The normal adult respiratory rate is ten to fifteen times per minutes. My own normal rate seems to be about six to eight times. To explain this difference I offer three possible contributing factors: living at altitude (4'000 feet) for many years, hiking and climbing at much higher altitudes without strain, and using breath control techniques in daily meditation for a good many years.

[2] Barbara Marciniak, *Bringers of the Dawn, teaching from the Pleiadians*. Rochester, VT: Bear & Co., 1992. Channelings edited by Tera Thomas. xxvii+243p. ISBN 0-939680-98-X. Quoted from page 141.

Chapter Thirty-Three

HEALING OVER THE AGES

Elise was clearly at low ebb. My quick scanning of her chakras confirmed appearances; they were weak, very faint. "Can she really snap back?" I wondered to myself. Her attitude, on the other hand, was positive. She accepted that the price of remaining in her beloved apartment would be to accept having constant help.

Here she was surrounded with her overloaded bookshelves, the lifeblood of a polylingual intellectual, family pictures on all the walls, and her mountains. She could see the dramatic, stark Finsteraarhorn from her bed, and from the glassed-in veranda the Bernese call a *Lauber* one could study the Eiger in all its menacing detail. For aging alpinists — and she'd scaled her share of peaks — such views are treasures to be savored daily. She confided to me that her vision had declined so much that she could no longer read or write. She hoped to die before going completely blind. And she wanted to die right here, in her own bed.

While the afternoon was still fresh I sat for a council of war with Sjaanse, whose great heart had propelled her to the rescue on that night train. Numerous practical and household problems needed quick solution. Rob, a kind of informally "adopted son", was due to arrive before supper as Sjaanse would be returning to her family in the Netherlands in two days. My sister-in-law — who had become a close sister to me, which is how I shall refer to her — had grown up in that country and had until recently traveled there for long visits twice a year. She had a vast army of friends and cousins who offered regular hospitality.

We needed someone to wash and dress her every morning, get her ready for each day. She already knew who she wanted: a trusted friend named Christine (not the same Christine who had given the channeling seminar, of course). I telephoned to Frau G., the local woman who functioned as coordinator of social services and made a date to see her the following morning. Then I went down to the village to buy underwear and a pair of warmer slacks for our patient. She had not been looking after herself in recent months, and the clothing inventory was less than superb.

Elise had a little respiratory crisis while Sjaanse, Rob and I were munching our supper of sauerkraut and sausages. That cleared up rapidly, but her situation was clearly preoccupying.

Energy came into my hands with unusual strength the next morning when — still in my hotel room — I proposed to the Council of Nine to transmit some power to Elise. This went well, and everything on her behalf was crowned with success later in the day. Her own energy seemed to pick up. She was cheerful, positive and lucid. Her physical strength was not remarkable but the old indomitable spirit began to return. My meeting with Frau G. went well even though she told me that Christine was fully booked for home-care assignments. An hour later she telephoned me to say that it was all right, Christine could come and would start the next morning. I raced around to the bank and succeeded in arranging for Christine and myself to become signatories on Elise's household account. (This required two visits to the bank, one to Christine, and a chat with my sister, but it all got organized.)

Rob had arrived, Sjaanse was leaving, and everyone understood I would come for longer stays after the New Year. I left Grindelwald late in the day content in the knowledge that much had been accomplished in a short time, that our beloved Elise was comfortable and being looked after correctly.

One of my neighbors became my next "patient". She had lost her husband after a short illness and was not managing her transition to widowhood. The day after returning from Grindelwald I paid her a social call. She ventilated a string of problems, none of them foreign to any woman who has had to relearn life as a widow. She was nervous, tired, wrestling with legal snarls, and generally down in the dumps.

My offer to perk up her energy centers met with a certain skepticism. This was something new, quite unconventional. I explained without insisting, and she decided to give it a try. She stretched out on her sofa and I began a session of chakra-balancing. Hers were not very strong except for the root and the heart, but that was already a good start. Bit by bit I warmed them all, still trying to learn what my technique should be. Then I smoothed two layers of her aura. Her initial skepticism turned to wonder as her heat built up under my hands. At the end she was very enthusiastic and said she felt as if she had just stepped out of a warm bath. That evening she left a message of gratitude on my answering-machine, and the next afternoon she knocked at my door, bearing a bag of home-baked cookies and still more thanks. Her attitude had shifted toward the positive — the underlying attitude, not the superficial — and it was reflected in her voice. She had had her best sleep in months. Her son recognized the change over the telephone and declared that what had happened was her "salvation."

This was fabulous. I thanked Great Spirit, my Guides, and the Council of Nine for making me a party to such a salutary transformation. What a blessing to be the instrument of such a healing! Two months later she asked me to do more, and I began to refine my technique for relieving pain and anxiety and for balancing and charging the chakras and aura. Her initial skepticism in December had melted and she was opening to the liberation of her own energies. She felt strongly almost all the hands-off-the-body part of my work, joking that the waves of energy were going to hypnotize her.

In the first few months of 1997 I returned to Grindelwald four times — twice for consecutive three-day weekends in January, then for longer sojourns in February and March. Elise was weak but she was easier in spirit, not physically stronger but much cheerier. Christine's warm and loving presence got her off to a good start in the mornings and then Rob was taking exceedingly fine care of his "honorary mother". During my first visit of the New Year we managed to organize the rotation of care-givers for the next period. Our niece Marcelle and her husband Jan would come from Geneva for a week, then Sjaanse would come back from the Netherlands, then I would arrive to stay for ten days. This risked becoming a jigsaw puzzle, but there was a lot of good will in evidence.

At this time I learned another lesson about the transfer of healing energy: it can happen involuntarily. Drowsy after lunch one day, I sat on the sofa next to my sister Elise and allowed my eyelids freedom to droop, surfing the upper surface of sleep. I was drifting in and out in a bizarre way, slowly realizing groggily that I was somehow being changed. Her vital force was so needy that it was pumping from me, draining me. I had to get up, drink a big glass of water, go outside into the cold winter air, move around a bit. Elise's aura had reached out and begun to gobble from me, illustrating perfectly the phenomenon of energy vampirism. The following weekend, just holding her hand, my energy seemed to be drawing illness from her. It was necessary to "snap" it out of my hand frequently to avoid having it clog and bog down within me. I kept on learning!

Our nephew André came from Geneva to collect me for that second three-day weekend. His sister Marcelle and her Jan arrived and settled in, allowing Rob to return to the Netherlands after a solid month of devotion. He'd brought Elise up to an unanticipated level of recuperation. She spent most of the day on the sofa, alternately alive and interested in talking, then slipping away into rest. But she shuffled around the apartment once in a while and he had taken her down to the village one day, by taxi, to visit the bank, do an errand, have a coffee. That had exhausted her, but we knew that her willpower was working overtime.

Everything was better by the time I arrived in February for a long stay. This time I moved into the apartment instead of being in the nearby hotel. After supper the first evening there was time for Sjaanse and me to really get acquainted, to discover shared values and views on life. The next morning I took her to the station for the eleven-hour train ride back to Utrecht.

Many happy moments marked those ten days in close contact with Elise. We reminisced about everything, my husband (her brother), family, hikes we'd done together, the mountains in general. She liked some of my favorite dishes and even asked for a second portion once or twice. Sometimes I walked down to the village and back up, trudging through fresh snow, my back (which was "out" again) enjoying the movement. I set up a desk on that sun-drenched *Lauber*, using Elise's ancient Royal typewriter to pound out letters. That wonderful veranda set me to dreaming about ways to improve my chalet.

Organizing my sister's life for the long term became a priority. She was beginning to thrive, relative to the recent past, but it was also obvious that she could no longer manage life alone. We could not go on endlessly counting on family, all of whom were aging, and friends from Holland. She herself understood this perfectly, and slowly she began to accept the notion of a paid companion as the only way she could stay home. I spoke to the knowledgeable ladies of the social services, but there was no one available in Grindelwald. They advised advertising in "Glückspost" a tabloid weekly that was almost a scandal sheet, but its classified advertising was a major resource and everyone used it or consulted it when they needed someone or something. Thus I drafted a brief insertion and asked Christine to look it over. She made tactful corrections in my German and then offered to receive and filter the responses. This was an unexpected piece of help, meaning that we could possibly begin interviewing live-in care-givers after I returned in March. It was clear that this was going to be my responsibility because Elise accepted my counsel. Marcelle pointed out that I could make her see logic when no one else could. Although all of us were "senior", for Elise the others were still the younger generation, the "children", whereas I was credible because I'd been her eldest brother's wife and guided him through his last years. To make it tougher, I overheard her tell André on the telephone that "with Michèle here, nothing can go wrong." It was clear that when a distasteful matter had to be solved, the task fell to me.

In fact, very little had gone wrong, except for my aching back. Fortunately it liked the physiotherapist in the village. She moved my back muscles around as if they were jelly, digging into all the little nooks and crannies.

Soon I would be able to touch my toes again.

Marcelle and Jan arrived for their second week of devoted duty, and I sped home. Rolling down the autoroute past Bern and then across the plateau to my Rhône Valley, my mind raced back and forth over the problem we faced. I found it very stressful to contemplate the interviewing, negotiating, training, organizing, and then controlling the situation at distance.

During all this time I had continued meditation, of course, although it was not always easy to find a peaceful, duty-free moment in the morning or late afternoon, which were my preferred times. Recharging my chakras needed doing at regular intervals. Mostly I seemed to travel wherever the Council of Nine wanted to send me, dispensing healing energy around the planet. From time to time Red Cloud checked in, simply appearing while I said hello to my Guides. Pam called from England to catch up on the news. When I told her about Red Cloud, she advised me to accept him, clarifying that when he appears wearing his war bonnet that means he is coming as a teacher. It turned out that Pam talks with him through a trance medium. A few days later she reported that her medium agreed that I should welcome him without skepticism. We talked about my traveling to England to meet him through that lady, but I could not see the future clearly enough to start planning such a trip. Meanwhile, it came as a shock one morning to realize that I was hardly ever doing Kriya. Yogananda's prized technique had not survived the reawakening in my spirit of the shamanic current, kindled during those seminars. My spiritual life seemed to be roaring ahead on another track.

At home after ten days of Grindelwald, my own village offered shocking news: Eric had been killed in a snow avalanche while leading a group of skiers down from the Wildstrubel. Hélène had lost her rock of a man; my closest neighbors had lost father and grandfather. It was hard to absorb the fact we would no longer enjoy his strength of character, his determined attitude which concealed a deeply spiritual nature. The church was overflowing the day we buried him. Pastor Jean outdid himself in painting the contrast between the indefatigable "force of nature" and the deep spirituality which lay concealed beneath that power. It was impossible for me not to think of Jacky, who had passed over in a similar way. Discovering the mystic souls of both these men had illuminated my path, teaching me that I was not the only one on our mountain.

Christine called from Grindelwald to report she had received many responses to our advertisement, had compiled a "short list" of four names, and had asked the most promising of the lot to come for an interview during the ensuing week. The next day, Saturday the first of March, I was back in the Bernese Oberland, and she reported there were more responses and yet another good candidate.

My Elise was stronger: we managed little afternoon strolls around the chalet and the immediate neighborhood, soaking up March's sunshine. There were moments of merriment, for her sense of humor returned along with her strength. She found being 97 simply "absurd." One day as I was tying her shoes for the afternoon ramble she observed that one of our favorite television detectives had diagnosed a murder by noticing that the shoes were tied backward, hence done by someone facing the victim. Thereupon I presented her with my backside, took her foot between my legs and tied the shoe as if she had done it. "You are not being murdered," I told her. One evening as I helped her to bed she recited an old rhyme: "Won't you walk a little faster, said the whiting to the snail -- there's a tortoise right behind me and he's treading on my tail." Right after this she complained that the new mattress we had installed for her was uncomfortable because it did not have the customary depression for her rump. I proposed she make a new depression, which led to a discussion of birds nesting in sand (her father had been a famous bird photographer). So I suggested she emulate those birds but also the sea tortoises of the Mexican coast and dig a deep pit. We were beginning to laugh a lot, like old times together.

In midweek we devoted an afternoon to interviewing two fine ladies. Our nephew André came from Geneva to participate, and his aunt took an active part in the discussions. Frau K. was brisk but warm, and she had worked recently in the neighborhood. Elise took to her immediately and she was engaged. We needed two of them, for alternate weeks, and so there was no reluctance to engage the second candidate, Frau R., when she proved to be equally agreeable.

All three of us heaved a big sigh of relief. At bedtime Elise said she felt as if she had crossed a high alpine pass. The next day Frau R. backed out, so Christine scrambled to telephone some of candidates. I was totally amazed at the response to our advertising in what seemed to me a real tabloid scandal sheet. Within a few days Elise and I had interviewed two more ladies, and after some prolonged hesitations and negotiations, it was finally settled. Frau B. and Frau K. would divide the week, each of them resident around the clock.

Catastrophe struck the day before my scheduled departure. There was a loud crash in the bathroom and I was instantly at her side. She'd hurt her back and was in great pain. Gentle palpation quickly located the rib she had broken.

"Only" a rib! Shivers of worry had run down my spine at the sound of her fall, for the consequences of a broken hip — the classic oldsters' fracture — were so often fatal. There had been examples in both our families. As she had prepared to sit down in the bathroom to start dressing, Elise's backside missed the little round stool. It skidded out from under her and she fell heavily against the radiator. The doctor came, confirmed what we already knew, and strapped up her rib cage securely.

Bep arrived to take over the care of her old friend, and on the seventeenth day I headed for home. The ladies we had interviewed began their rotation at the end of the month. I kept in touch by telephone, as did the rest of the family. Elise's life took on the superficial aspect of stability for about a year.

The gift of healing had come into my hands four years earlier, but this case had required much more than transferring cosmic energy for a few minutes. It had demanded and received my willing, total commitment of heart and physical presence. My sister-in-law's plight had dominated my life for a full three months, now it was time to move on.

In early April I began planning a trip to England. Pam offered active help. Over and over again it was shown that our meeting three years earlier at the Airport vortex at Sedona had been one of perfect synchronicity, that the usual words "chance" or "coincidence" had no relevance. Now, she offered to set up appointments with the medium who received Red Cloud. And almost immediately she had need of me. She had fallen when a London bus braked suddenly, and she was suffering from stiffnesses and multiple bruises and contusions.

This was another first for me: healing at distance. I chose an early morning time, taking advantage of the one-hour time differential between here and there to catch her still asleep in bed. It took me some minutes to get into an adequate meditational state, then I asked my guides to help me journey to London. This worked, and the treatment I gave lasted twenty minutes. Having projected myself to her bedside, I gave her a light full-body massage, then balanced her chakras via energy transmittal. Visualizing her standing up, I used my hands to drain what I conceived of as "dross", then put her back in bed. The energy I needed came slowly at first but once it came it held strongly, right through the whole visualization.

She telephoned later in the morning and reported she was feeling "marvelously better". She gave me more information on her injuries and I went back for a shorter treatment that evening. It turned out she had a swelling on one leg and another on a temple. So I spent ten minutes on those two sites, musing later about my failure to "see" them when I had journeyed in the morning.

Red Cloud was usually present when I entered meditation in the mornings, along with my little group of guides and helpers, but he wasn't communicating verbally with me. All this changed when I got to London in mid-May. Pam, I was learning, did things with a certain foresight and generosity. In this case she organized two afternoon sessions for me with Red Cloud. He spoke through Margaret, a small, fair-skinned, fine-boned lady of uncertain age. Margaret took pains to prepare her clients for the channeling session. She led me slowly up through the seven usual chakras and then up to the eighth and ninth levels. Then she went into trance, a process that took a few minutes and which was characterized by occasional strong, loud exhalations. Finally the voice changed, deepened, and someone else was speaking.

"Peace with you. I am Red Cloud, welcome. It is a great joy to be with and speaking to you. Of course, you are fully aware that it is no coincidence that you sit in this temple of light with me today." Red Cloud spoke with great changes of pace, sometimes rapidly, sometimes slowly, deliberately. There was a lot of dramatic emphasis on certain words and phrases; there were often noticeable pauses between statements. Mostly he seemed to weigh his words and phrases carefully. His enunciation didn't sound anything like the Margaret I had been speaking with and listening to for half an hour. "I would like to ask you if you have any questions at this point that you would like me to answer for you," he added.

"I have three pages of questions," I replied.

"We will do our very best," he said drily.

"Messages have been coming to me that I am or shall be a shaman, others say that I was a shaman in an earlier life. I am seeking guidance as to what I should do or not do in this situation."

"Very well. It is truth, it is reality," he said. "You have indeed had a significant past life as a shaman. It is your destiny. You expressed a desire many, many years ago to be of spiritual service. This is how you can best fulfill this destiny. Think of yourself today as the sum total of all those many past incarnations which you have experienced, and they have been many." This response continued for long minutes, and it was relevant, caring, and helpful.

All of this was captured on Pam's battered old cassette recorder with a microphone set on a footstool in front of Margaret. I had proposed to bring my own recorder but Pam had advised against it.

"It could blow up," she said. "It has happened with other people's little machines. They can't handle the frequency when Red Cloud comes in." I understood that immediately: my own energy had rendered my video cassette player useless one very electric winter night, despite my standing on a rubber mat. Pam's old machine could handle Red Cloud, newer gear could not.

My willingness to believe in this channeling process did not blind me to the possibility that what emerged as Red Cloud's persona might in fact be all conceived in the medium's conscious and subconscious mind. Experience to date had convinced me that the process was real, but in this situation I thought it prudent to be doubly sure. From time to time I inserted questions involving facts that Margaret could not possibly know, and in this way I became satisfied that this conversation across the veil was mostly real. For example, at one point I asked the following question:

"In the past I have received information on various past lives through meditations and through several clairvoyants," and here I gave a list of names. "Have these revelations been truth?"

"The teacher who you refer to as Eileen," Red Cloud replied, ".... this is your source of truth. I hope that too is the answer you required."

"It is a very helpful answer," I agreed.

Red Cloud then expanded this reply with a warning.

"You know, and you must have realized already, there are many who say this or say that, and it can become quite confusing to know which is truth, which is reality. It is vital to be able to recognize the wolves and the lambs, and the lambs from the wolves. I think you will know what I am saying."

Having listened to three quite different channelings during my last visit to Sedona, and having recently participated in a workshop aimed at teaching it as a technique instead of the gift it surely is, I treasured the spontaneity and the lucidity of these answers. Even so, there were moments when the medium Margaret seemed to lose contact, rambling off into other fields for a minute or two, and then she would reconnect. Several of these instances leaped out again clearly during the long hours I spent transcribing my handful of cassettes from the two afternoons. When Red Cloud returned it was quite evident. Every once in a while he referred to her as his "instrument". In these pages I do not intend to quote at great length from the twenty-two pages of single-spaced manuscript resulting from the two afternoons we conversed. On both occasions Margaret channeled for nearly an hour-and-a-half, with relatively few moments of seeming to be disconnected. Much later I gave copies of the transcript to Pam for comparison with her many sessions with Margaret and Red Cloud. She reported he had given me several kinds of information she had never heard before.

"It is no surprise to you if I tell you that you have indeed been a shaman in a Sioux life," he told me during the second afternoon.

"A shaman, what does that word mean? A holy man, for you were a man. There were female shamans too, but in that life you were male. A holy man. A man, skilled in the ways of medicine, and herbs, a healer, with great power, and, of course, you were highly mediumistic. If a member of the tribe would come to you, as they did, you would go into a trance state, as my instrument does. You would intercede with the spirit friends on the other side of life on behalf of your patient. You were everything to the tribe: doctor, teacher, eloquent, everything."

He said that was my significant native American lifetime, which occurred during the nineteenth-century. We were both part of the Oglala band of the Sioux, and so was Margaret[1]. He did evoke, very briefly, an earlier lifetime as a Mayan.

Red Cloud taught me a wonderful meditation, a trip into what he called "the mineral kingdom", accessed through the ninth chakra. We went there twice, and I have subsequently led small groups of fellow meditators through this "itinerary", and they love it.

Red Cloud reassured me about some of the accidents and blind alleys I have met on this long spiritual path. He spoke of my "blueprint of life", but also of how I was accompanied and guided by the entities who I consider to be my spiritual guides and helpers.

"Nothing that you have done is without purpose, and particularly over the past few months. Nothing that you do will be a time-wasting exercise. When we wish you to cease doing something, we will find a way, dear one, to let you know. We are great lateral thinkers, you know. If we don't get there one way, then we will come in another direction. We close doors sometimes as well as open them. Oh yes, always look upon the closing of a door as the beginning of something beautiful and new. Never try to back up on a closed door. There is only one way that you can go, it is forward and upwards."

Without dwelling on specifics, Red Cloud made it clear that my path was one of healing others, through multiple methods. He said they would never require anything of me that was beyond my capacities, but that the future was going to be full. My age was irrelevant, he told me, forget about it. But he did make an important point about creating and maintaining my psychic shield, reinforcing one of Eileen's first lessons to me.

"Do not worry," he told me. "you have much to do, much to do. You will have the energy provided and the time in which to do it.........We will never ask you to do anything for which you are not more than adequately prepared."

He made it clear that my work would take numerous forms, including healing with my hands, doing that at distance, crystals, herbs and shamanic techniques.

"But there are millions of different ways of healing. Words are the greatest healers of all. Color. Crystals. Reflexology. Aromatherapy. All these so-called "new age" therapies are as old as time itself. And you have used these means of healing."

With respect to working at distance, he had this to add: "No healing that is sent or given, is pointless."

Nor had my time in Kriya Yoga been pointless.

"The period when you practiced the yogic system was a plateau of rest," he told me. "It has not been a waste of time. Plateaus of rest come when one must consolidate, must absorb."

Fleur and Ulysse had brought back from France a brochure for me, describing a weeklong seminar devoted to shamanic ritual, with sweat lodges and teaching by native Americans. They had, of course, thought this was exactly right for me. I told Red Cloud about it.

"Will this week of exercises be beneficial in my training?" I asked him.

"Yes indeed it will.... you must go," he urged.

My three hours of conversation with this powerful spirit were rich with all kinds of information, in addition to several "journeys" which had in themselves been learning experiences.

Red Cloud brought home to me forcefully the fact that healing work had informed my life in several incarnations, even as far back as Atlantis. Between his revelations and what past life information Eileen had brought me, it was clear that I had worked with every technique, from ancient forms of healing to the early methods of "modern" medicine and back again to tribal work. I'd been a healer down through the ages. The current had started to flow late in this lifetime but it seemed destined to go on for years to come. At first this was merely amazing, but soon enough it became stimulating.

So much to learn, so much to do!

[1]   Red Cloud, born 1822 among the Oglala Sioux, was one of the few warrior chiefs who defeated the American army. He was instrumental in closing the Bozeman trail to the western Montana gold fields during the period 1864-1868 and withheld his signature to the peace treaty until he could see the forts evacuated and destroyed. The United States did not observe the treaty very long, but Red Cloud kept his word and refused to resume warfare despite great provocation. He died in 1909.

Chapter Thirty-Four

LEARNING AND TEACHING

Around the campfire I met an old grandmother and a grandfather who remained half in shadow. She had long gray hair, wore a mauve-lilac blouse with v-neck and a necklace with silver crescent moons, teeth, claws and other animal artifacts. He seemed to be the corduroy-suited old man I'd seen in a stubble field four years earlier when trying to regress through Juliette. The grandmother gave me a bulky package wrapped with red twine, American Indian-style, which I didn't open right away, nor did she open my wrapped gift. When we parted I stood up and held open my hands, and a *chanunpa* (ceremonial pipe) appeared in them — her gift. Wonderful! We seemed to be camped on a plateau above a lake in the Alpstein massif of northeastern Switzerland.

All this came to me while Billy, an Apache from New Mexico, guided us through a meditation to close the first morning of the seminar in France. Our host Pierre had introduced our teachers the preceding evening in the opening session. Billy's sidekick Donald, a Sioux from northeastern Montana, opened the teachings this Sunday morning with an illuminating comparison of the Tibetan and Sioux philosophies of sickness and health. Then he'd drummed a strong beat while Billy led us into that first meditation.

That afternoon all fifty of us began rebuilding an old sweat lodge in a meadow rimmed on two sides by forest. Some of the men reseated those of the vertical poles which were still sturdy and others were in the forest cutting new saplings flexible enough to be bent into the traditional dome shape. As fast as the men supplied us with flexible poles and laterals, we women began lashing the structure together with stout cord. The fire pit had to be dug out anew and then we covered the lodge with tarpaulins and old blankets. Those who preferred sedentary jobs began the task of creating masses of prayer "ties" to be hung in the lodge. Eventually all of us worked to tie these tiny packets of tobacco in red, blue, yellow and white cotton cloth, for each of us needed to dedicate our own prayers.

When everything was ready our teachers built and lit the fire to heat the stones for the first of what would ultimately be four sweat lodges. Everything was running late — they grinned about "Indian time" — and it was nine o'clock before we straggled up to the dining room to eat our supper while the stones roasted.

Our seminar took place on the grounds of an eighteenth-century manor house that had been converted to modern life as a conference center. Although buried deep in the countryside, it was not far from some of the famous chateaux of the Loire Valley. We were lodged in comfortable rooms created in a long building that had once been princely stables. Dining room and kitchens adjoined, and off that stood a large modern space that could equally serve as banquet hall, ballroom or, as was the present case, the scene of a workshop for fifty people seated around the fringes. A wall of high windows made it agreeably luminous.

During our alpine winters I often enjoyed a sauna — nice and hot — but this was my first sweat lodge. There was a sense of coming home which had not occurred in sauna. We crawled in, uttering the ritual greeting "mitakuye oyasin" — "all my relations". Our semi-naked bodies — swimsuits, t-shirts, simple loose shifts worked best — were too crowded for comfort and the earth on which we sat began to become mud. It was a true ceremony, with drumming, chanting, moments of silent prayer, but especially the arrival of incandescent rocks sliding in on a hayfork, tumbling into the pit, sloshed with water and anointed with herbs to create a fragrant steam. The extreme heat opened our pores, allowing the beginnings of physical purification, and discomfort gradually lost importance as spirit began to weave its tapestries. I was enchanted, carried back into shadowy atavistic memories. At intervals of about fifteen minutes Donald would call for more stones, and seven or eight brightly hot rocks would slide under the door-flap. A splash of water, a brush of herbs, and billows of new steam would spread upward to engulf us. Our sweat began at about half an hour before midnight and went on for at least an hour. This ceremony led to deep introspection, traveling through multiple layers of self, and it could also ignite emotions. One woman had to leave halfway through, for an old trauma had surfaced and left her sobbing on the ground outside the lodge. When we had exhausted the steam from the fourth set of stones we assembled outside in a circle under the stars, wrapped in towels. Donald and Billy prepared a pipe and slowly passed it around the circle so that each of us could dedicate a puff of the smoke.

Everyone was groggy but happy the next morning. Donald lectured us on power animals, sorcery, and spiritual hygiene, then before lunch Billy led a new kind of meditation. He sang us into a power animal journey, with Donald drumming a rapid beat. This developed a fantastic vibrational field all around me, entering via the ears. I didn't meet any animals. At the end I had a quick vision of a clearing with trees, with some shapes at the bottom which could have been animals. This snapshot was like a color negative, transparent, orange going red.

Late in the afternoon they launched another journey. Donald led us this time, reinforced by strong drumming. I started in my meadow, where the "mysterious glow" had formed in front of the five-trunked tree. The glow slowly opened to allow my descent into the world beneath the tree roots. A stag appeared briefly, then a bear, and finally a large green lizard led me deeper into the lower world. Scenes flipped in and out like snapshots I could not recall, until Donald brought us up. That green lizard really got my attention, for it echoed what I had seen when identifying packages for Eileen four years earlier in 1993.

When this little trip was finished they divided us into half a dozen groups according to the families of creatures we had met. I found myself in a cluster of reptilians. Rosa had a salamander, Françoise had a large lizard similar to mine, Robert found turtles, Fred met a snake face-on, and Gilles also had seen a serpent. It was very interesting to me that all six of us had been friendly together more than with other people, and here we were fellow reptilians. It was, of course, not a coincidence.

Working together rebuilding the sweat lodge had proved to be a good way to explore relationships with new people. Meals were served at large round tables, where we passed serving dishes to one another, and this proved to be very sociable. The people in my "reptile" group were mostly those with whom I had developed budding friendships. Of my handful of new friends only the black-haired lady who called herself "Fireass" was not a "reptile". She was an intellectual, a former schoolteacher given to philosophy and poetry, married to a sober professional man, a suburbanite with teen-aged children, all of which seemed to deny her self-imposed nickname. Or perhaps they explained why she needed it. She and I quickly began to enjoy our conversational jousts.

That afternoon Billy asked me to head the fire crew for the evening's sweat lodge. Why me? It was simply a matter of language, but also Billy had seen me observing closely when he constructed the first fire. English-speakers were a rare commodity in this mass of Frenchmen, and for each sweat they needed someone who could understand Donald's orders for new stones during the ceremony. Billy showed me on a paper napkin at lunch how to lay the logs and then how the stones nested within and atop the burning wood. Yves and the blonde lioness Muriel were the rest of my crew. Thus late in the day I laid the base of logs and the stones, then the three of us built up a large "teepee" of firewood.

When our stones were getting incandescent and everyone was assembled, I became "doorkeeper". This involved relaying the call for a certain number of stones to the tall rangy Yves, who forked them up one at a time. Muriel brushed them clean just before they slid through the portal, and she helped me there too. We had to renew the lodge's supply of water and put the drum near our fire to tighten up during the few minutes it took to bring in stones. It appears this lodge was a great success. We were profusely and repeatedly thanked for our work when the sweat was over at about one-thirty in the morning.

Once again everyone was tired and slow at breakfast time, but a break in the sweat lodge schedule would allow everyone to sleep long the coming night.

At lunch I received an illumination: here is the book I seek. What Eileen brought me was a symbolic book, not a physical one. Here I was sitting in the center of France, where the "book" was supposed to be findable, surrounded by new friends. The wisdom and knowledge it contained was coming through in many ways. The rough-cut stones of its cover are the fire stones I laid and which became incandescent. It all seemed to fit together.

There were other aspects to this large communion to reinforce my deep intuition. We were half a hundred, including our teachers, and roughly half of those seemed to be what I privately think of as "groupies." They were people who had participated in a lot of Pierre's seminars. They followed him like a guru. And the other half, it suddenly hit me, were deeply attracted to the native American Indian ambiance. They gobbled up the "red road" as if starving, as did I. Gradually I saw that this half were, in terms of incarnations, former native Americans who were trying out being French this time. They took to the teachings as if coming home.

In this part of the group I found my tribe and, to my surprise, a sense almost of leadership. My "light" was switched on that week, one could almost speak of charisma, although I am cautious with that term. I was the only one who was not French, a fact which offered me an unanticipated role. I could serve as go-between, as interpreter between my tribes-people and our teachers, who spoke no French. And because Billy and Donald conveyed their teachings only in American English, it was part of Pierre's role as organizer to translate everything they said, all day long. Two or three of the "groupies" spoke enough English to spell him, and they did it very well for short periods. But from time to time Pierre or his relievers would block on a piece of American slang or regional usage. I found myself blurting out the needed interpretation in French about twice a day on average. The first time it startled Pierre. The second time he was less surprised. The next day he turned automatically to me for translation of the troublesome word or phrase. I think only my chum Fireass knew enough non-academic English to have possibly done this, but it was not in her personality to intervene as I had. I dwell on this matter because it seems to be relevant to something that happened later.

We had a free evening in order to catch up on our sleep, then there were two more late evening sweat lodges. After the last one, our fourth in five nights, our teachers served a "sacred" meal which focused on red berries, blue cornmeal and overcooked beef helped by some pine nuts. We ate this off paper plates, after two o'clock in the morning, standing around the embers of the fire.

Morning sessions started late and continued into early afternoon, giving the kitchen staff conniption fits. Donald and Billy presented a long series of topics. Donald's lecture on the use of plants became a discourse on mushrooms and, especially, peyote. We learned a lot about peyote and its ritual use but there was no intention of giving us any — too dangerous. He also gave a long lesson on the care of the dead. Billy led us through a guided meditation in which we were supposed to receive an animal as we focused on each of the seven major chakras. This was rather interesting, inasmuch as the green lizard came again, this time in my brow chakra. Otherwise I received the animals which often informed my meditations at home, especially deer, bear, eagle. The one real surprise was the black labrador dog who had shared family life more than thirty years earlier. She came in my second chakra, which was very appropriate because she was such a loving, emotionally satisfying creature.

Earth energies became a major topic, starting with using the hands to diagnose illness in a way resembling my own. There was a lot about prophecies of earth changes and how these may be precipitated by America's reckless propagation of extra-low frequency waves through the earth and the oceans. Donald suggested Mother Earth was regenerating herself through increasing catastrophes of all kinds, leading ultimately to a major reduction of the human population. He cited resurgent diseases and hidden pollution as factors in this process. This discussion resonated strongly with just about everyone.

This was mid-July, which can be very hot throughout France. There had been frequent rain in the days preceding the workshop; I'd driven through a lot of water on the two-day trip from home. As if by magic it cleared for the beginning of our week of spending so much time out-of-doors. The days were mostly hot and sometimes heavy. Thus we were grateful for the big shade trees near the sweat lodge one afternoon when Donald's wife Laura, of the Cheyenne nation, held a private class with all the female participants. We sat in a large circle in relative comfort while she outlined the role and responsibilities of women in traditional tribal life. The woman is the undisputed owner of the family tepee and everything related to her responsibilities of home and food, she told us. The man holds the weapons and tools he needs to defend and feed his family. Women could be pipe carriers as well as men.

We were all rather ragged on the final morning, for the sweat lodge and sacred meal had kept us up until after three o'clock. After some initial discussions we were invited to perform a mass healing for one of Pierre's friends in the group. She was alleged to be suffering from an ailment which had surfaced overnight. Pierre did not divulge her symptoms. Billy and Donald beat their big drum while the slender, good-looking blonde Madeleine lay down in the center of the big room. We all gathered around in a dense circle with the task of projecting healing energy to her through our hands.

From my position near her right foot, but aiming at her torso, my hands began to pull wads of dark negativity from her body. Soon, though, little chunks of blackness were hurtling at me and I was kept busy catching and shaking them out. I kept on blocking these dregs as they came at me horizontally instead of up from her. What I didn't catch and hurl to the floor simply bounced off my aura. Every morning before leaving my room I devoted a significant moment to rebuilding the shield around my energy field, and now that work was paying off. Out of the corner of my eye I noticed that Rosa seemed to be vibrating physically and my friend Fireass looked rather grim and determined. Comparing notes afterward we could not agree that our patient had a real physical ailment. It was hard for me to accept that my hands were magnetizing all those dark blobs out of Madeleine. Where was all that coming from?

On this final morning, before the healing, Donald invited questions. This was my chance to try to discover why so little truly shamanic material had been presented. The word "shaman" had not even been defined. I asked if this art was part of Sioux tradition, and he replied "not especially." He defined himself as a warrior, not a healer (in the sense of "medicine man"). That rather explained things. Shamanism as such was never part of the teaching program, I realized, only part of Pierre's publicity. I liked one of Donald's final statements, however.

"We do ceremonies," he said, "so as to train ourselves in the correct behaviors of life."

The week's program ended with a traditional Red Road "give-away". We had all contributed to the purchase of gifts for our teachers. And they had gifts for us. Billy had a big supply of sage smudging bundles, which he distributed to everyone. Donald passed around the big circle with little red meditation bundles for everyone plus a variety of special gifts. He gave me a glorious long feather from the Brazilian golden macaw, blue on one side and gold on the other, along with his thanks for my help.

Breaking up was painful. In a relatively short time I had become quite attached to my little clan including Fireass, Rosa, Françoise, Yves, Muriel, Jean-Paul, Danuta, Evelyne, Isabelle and Fred, and others whose names I failed to note.

That night I was back at the farmhouse B&B, bathing in Michèle and Guy's warm hospitality. En route the next morning, I paused long at the basilica in Paray-le-Monial. The edifice speaks volumes to me, suggesting a possible past life in that community. Paray's columns and vault ribs appear to have been imprinted in memory long ago.

Three weeks later my clairvoyant healer colleague Perchette gave me a jolt. I'd just gone to her for a visit and a routine tune-up of my chakras, but she made a stunning diagnosis.

"You've been attacked by a sorceror!" she exclaimed. Shock colored her voice. "What has happened?"

Catching on instantly, I told her about the so-called healing ritual during the last day of the workshop, about the chunks of dark matter zooming at me. She nodded. Then I laid out the photographs I had taken during the week. Her pendulum sailed over them, stopping three times. She picked out three people – Madeleine, her husband, and a young woman who was close to them -- as the perpetrators of what she termed "typical French black magic." I gave her a thumbnail account of how the week had evolved, already understanding the trio's role within the "groupies", how they could have perceived my personal radiance as a threat to their status. Perchette confirmed my growing suspicion that the "healing" ceremony had been fabricated as a framework for transmitting dark energy.

"They were jealous of you," she observed, "and they tried to demolish you."

"My auric shield blocked that black stuff," I pointed out. I had not felt any ill effects, but Perchette's out-of-the-blue diagnosis could not be ignored.

"A little bit of it got through anyway," — which was clearly true, because she had seen it — "but I'm going to clean it up."

She proceeded to perform an exorcism ritual, applying to my chakras salt blessed by a famous priest. She did this three times, muttering an incantation as she worked. That I hadn't been more affected could be credited to the protective measures which had become an integral part of my morning routine. I uttered a silent thank-you to Eileen for her words of warning as we had driven through Sedona three years earlier. The more you follow a spiritual path the more you need to protect your energetic structure from attack. A well-maintained auric shield becomes as necessary as brushing the teeth.

Gregory, an English clairvoyant with whom I sat a month later confirmed that one frequently encountered black magic in France. "But it was worse ten years ago," he observed. This gentleman knew nothing about me when I sat down, but his ignorance evaporated as he read my aura and the chakras. He saw an Indian medicine man dancing and rattling; he compared this motion to the activity of my hands when channeling energy for healing; he saw shamanism as a basic trait. On the subject of trance mediums he agreed with my notion that they can surf in and out during a channeling.

"They all do," he said, adding that he had once seen the spirit entity leave the auric field although the medium went right on babbling.

He saw a condor soaring over the Andes, sometimes blocking out the sun. "It might be a power animal," he ventured. This notion was bemusing, because I'd never been to South America and had no plan to go there. His vision stirred something vague, indefinable, but I did not "see" the condor. He went on to propose that the giant bird's blotting out of the sun could symbolize the "three days of darkness" foreseen in a variety of prophecies about the years leading up to 2012.

Brooding about such matters did not linger long in spirit. Too much else was bubbling within me. Immersion in native American thought, interacting with my little clan during that week in France had allowed a yeasty idea to rise: possibly I could teach, possibly I could give little seminars. After fifteen years on a clear spiritual path it was not impossible that I had something to communicate. I parked this notion "on the back burner" to simmer quietly while I planned something more immediate: another trip to the American West, especially Sedona. First, however, an inner voice was urging me to express what I had recently lived by constructing a medicine wheel.

The day after the fall equinox, two days after my seventy-fourth birthday, I hiked up to the high pastures of Anzeindaz. The sky seems to expand up there above six thousand feet. Once again my sensation of the "back of beyond" began to itch. Two miles and another five hundred feet higher took me to a remote spot above the Pas de Cheville, at the foot of Les Diablerets.

Before leaving home I had done a deep meditation, calling on Red Cloud to guide me again through the "mineral kingdom" and later to inform my building project. When I raised the shutter after the meditation, there was a fine four-point buck deer staring at me across the meadow. What a great omen!

Two large stones thoughtfully deposited by an ancient avalanche served as the north and south poles of my medicine wheel. To them I added thirty-eight big stones scrounged and lugged from nearby rockfalls, then chanting them into place. My completed wheel was about fifty feet in diameter and had eight spokes. To consecrate it I dabbed each stone with a point of the precious powdery "grandmother's milk" that Eileen had given me. After a brief dedicatory meditation it was time to scurry ahead of the weather. Wind was rising and gray threatened to close the big sky. My pendulum played the last act: the stone wheel radiated 10'000 on the Bovis scale. I could not imagine what effect twenty or thirty feet of winter snow might have on my new sacred site.

Mid-October saw me on North American soil. A few days with Kay on the East Coast brought us up-to-date and helped with jet lag, then it was California and the usual warm welcome from Joyce and Clark. Carol was only forty minutes north, and we managed to squeeze in a lot of good food and some interesting adventures with herbal teachers. In one sprawling garden south of Santa Rosa I learned how to take seed, and this added fuel to my project of converting part of the vegetable garden to medicinal herbs. These were good times with family and good friends but I do not dwell on them for the telling would not serve to advance this story.

"Why does your face seem so familiar?" my mother asked. We had a lot of inconclusive talk about the "why" of it. In forty-eight hours I visited her four times and then headed east toward Arizona.

The desert was, as always, vast and grandiose. The play of light and shadow over the huge panorama fascinates me. Also it relaxes me. I had left Pasadena too late and had to overnight at spare, utilitarian Needles. My spirits began to rise steadily the next morning after the Colorado crossing, but the great change doesn't hit me until well east of Kingman. At Ash Fork, to be precise. That's where happiness begins. At Ash Fork I have finally escaped from the heaviness that plagues me in Southern California. It's partly a result of regaining the altitude at which I thrive but also simply coming back into the wonderful energies that seem to inform most of northern Arizona.

Working with Eileen stood at the top of my agenda for the two weeks I'd scheduled in Sedona and Cottonwood. She lived an impossible whirl of writing, teaching and healing, and I knew in advance whatever time she gave to me would be limited but of high quality. Two couples of my own friends were also going to converge on me in Cottonwood, and now I had local friends such as Tom and Susan to see again.

Over lunch Eileen and I talked about the shamanistic messages that had been coming in during the past year.

"It's clear, the work of a shaman lies on your path. I saw it, and now you have all the confirmation anyone could want. Consider yourself an apprentice shaman and simply let it flow as it comes," she said.

All the teaching could come from within, she pointed out. That was how she was trained — entirely on the inner planes — and she herself was not offering classes at this time.

"It could take years," she added, repeating that was how it happened with her. I'd shown inner resistance to start with, but as that dissolved the learning would go forward.

The following week she proposed we do a hike in a particular canyon she felt drawn to explore. We met at the bridge over Dry Creek and began rambling down the wide streambed.

"There's something here that's pulling on me," she said. "Maybe a cave."

Quickly, however, this walk turned into a tutorial on plants and trees. I had brought to our luncheon several floral essences I'd made during the summer, my first effort in this domain. She'd liked their energy. She began to explain how to deduce a plant's therapeutic value by studying its appearance and other physical aspects. Stem color, leaf shape, compactness as opposed to wild proliferation were some of the clues.

Far down the canyon, beyond a bend, we saw a cliff and this made her antennae wiggle. High up on the wall we spied a vertical cleft, and one hundred yards farther on there was a bluff of protruding rock. The symbolism of female then male was obvious. On the opposite side of the wide, sandy streambed, close to us, grew a young cedar. It was a symmetrical pyramid of fresh sage green, isolated, and it seemed to pin the third angle of a power triangle. Eileen felt we were at or near a dimensional portal. It would be inactive at this time of day, she said, probably up and running only at night.

My dowsing tools agreed that something was indeed going on. My pendulum gyrated over the Bovis scale in an anarchical fashion I'd never seen before. It ran up and down the scale, from zero to twenty thousand vibrations, all with positive polarity but completely unstable. The Lecher antenna gave positive reactions to the frequencies for an earth chakra, for a focal point of feminine energy and for both life and death. "Sacred site" it certainly was. Eileen was running out of time and proposed coming back in two days to continue the work.

On this second visit we went first to a magnificent red cedar to prepare a floral essence from a bowl of twigs holding pollen and seed pods. After setting this to "cook" in a cleft of the big tree, we went down to the portal area. Eileen selected stones from in front of the female and male cliff faces and from the little pyramidal cedar and set them with small cuttings in a bowl of water under the tree to "cook" as an elixir. She'd brought a floral blend helpful to meditation and had laced it with Datura, a hallucogenic plant that grows in the dry wash. We both took a few drops and set ourselves to meditate on opposite banks.

These things develop slowly in me, but soon I was feeling Kundalini rising. It was a light golden color as it moved up my spine, and it opened the heart chakra from behind. There was a growing sensation of being pulled over backwards, possibly out of body, but that does not quite happen with me.

Meanwhile, Eileen journeyed. When she came back in she said we were at a Pleiadian star gate. It was protected, she reported, by a "big, white, primitive polar bear who is nervous."

"That's astonishing!" I exclaimed. Then I explained how I had bought a soapstone sculpture of a polar bear three weeks earlier in California. It was wounded in the neck and I had not accepted delivery until the sculptor made substantial repairs to camouflage the damage. I could have refused it but did not because the piece spoke volumes to me, injured or not. My polar bear had every reason to be "nervous"! Resonance between the two polar bears seemed undeniable; it could not be "coincidence". Our limited conversations so far had offered no space for mention of the soapstone bear; Eileen hadn't known about it. The notion of the sculpted bear as some kind of precursor of the spirit bear rattled around in my head inconclusively.

Tom had greeted me warmly on my arrival in Sedona. We met for breakfast soon thereafter and we met several times for lunch during the ensuing two weeks. Twice we drove into the mountains behind the old mining town of Jerome, hiking up a rough jeep trail to the crest and wandering at length along it. The views toward Sedona and the photographic possibilities were splendid. The natural world seemed determined to entertain us. There were a couple of hare. A yellow butterfly hovered around, greeting me wthout fear. A young tarantula crossed our path and posed patiently while we photographed it. It was early November yet some flowers were blooming in the nearly eighty-degree warmth, and not far away there was a big bush of mistletoe.

Bell Rock called to me insistently, I went to visit her soon after arriving in the area. Grandmother and I had a nice chat, and my second visit was blessed with a soaring, circling black hawk. For the third visit I brought along my hiking companion André, who had driven across the continent with his lady friend, en route west. I gave them the quick two-day tour which started with hiking to the headwall of Boynton Canyon, then a meditation on a knoll of the Airport Vortex, and Bell Rock for the second day. By that time the blonde willowy Pia and her mustachioed George had arrived from Vancouver for an overnight. All these people would leave me the next day in order to pursue their itineraries, but that evening the five of us created our own "harmonic convergence" around the festive table. It was also a kind of reunion for Pia and André, who had met while helping me perform a Mother Earth ceremony in the Alps three years earlier. My healing hands were called on to work on all of them except George, who claimed the only painfree back in the group.

Susan had a lot of counsel for me, some of it her own and some of it channeled. By now I knew how to recognize when she was reading from her "tape in the air". We talked a lot about herbs, crystals and Hildegarde von Bingen, the medieval healer. A few mornings later Susan called to suggest I contact a certain Marilyn, an artist. This lady did not understand what Susan had in mind until I mentioned earth energies and dowsing. That got her attention. "How soon can you come?" she insisted. Our first meeting was an instant success.

Marilyn was a very successful portrait painter who was now trying to paint energy and spirits, following advice from her guides/angels. Her canvases were covered with astounding vortexes of light and energy, mysterious spirits with net-like "dreamcatcher" holes opening to other dimensions, portals in gardens and landscapes.

My dowsing fascinated her, especially when I unfolded the Bovis biometer. Most of her paintings registered in the 10'000 to 12'000 range, but one of them went up to 14'000. That was a splendid, riveting portrait of Albert Einstein, done in forty-five minutes, she said, while she felt herself to be "out of body." Our non-stop exchange raged on for three hours, until both of us realized it was time to feed our physical bodies. Before I left for a dinner date in uptown Sedona, Marilyn asked me to come again while she would be painting and simply "contribute energy".

Two mornings later I sat in her studio doing nothing , as I saw it, but radiating energy, as she sensed it. She was embarking on a new canvas, a Tibetan landscape to be sold for the benefit of relief activities in that country. She squirted big blobs of acrylic colors out of their tubes and then began to paint with gusto. She used lots of paint applied in broad strokes and blobs using brushes I would have chosen for painting a window frame. She modeled form with color, rather carefully, but without any preliminary sketching. I gazed with wonder at this performance, accustomed as I was to the careful, controlled, introspective style of my late husband. After about an hour I went into meditation, concentrating on Tibetan scenes in a photomontage I used as a "mandala" for sending healing energy to the oppressed people of that mountain domain. Eventually she set aside the Tibetan picture and went to work finishing up two "works in progress". Both of them dealt with the theme of dimensional portals. It was amazing to see the boldness with which she effaced something she didn't like and began to recreate a different play of shadow and lively color. Marilyn claimed my energy had made her productive, but I can believe it was more a matter of the Sagittarian extrovert needing and responding to an audience. Half a workday passed before she laid down her brushes, concentration flagging. The whole experience was vitalizing for me, in one sense, but my body was beginning to fidget. I had been painting right along with her, executing each brush stroke through her.

Susan had suggested I might have some interesting experiences at the "Conference of Light" to be held during my last weekend in Sedona. If for no other reason, I went to the first morning session so as to compare this event with the "Congress of Light" I had attended two years earlier in Lausanne. The Sedona production was marginally superior. A presentation on crystals was interesting. A talk on vortexes didn't happen because the speaker didn't show up. Then came "The Touch That Heals", which proved to be why my guides had told me the night before not to miss it. Dr. Bill is a passionate advocate of lymphatic manipulation. He made the subject come alive, so much so that I prolonged my sojourn by a couple of days in order to receive private instruction from him. The knowledge and technique acquired in that intensive training have been helpful in my healing work.

Beyond that, my day at the Conference of Light convinced me that I could give seminars too. I had asked Eileen how to go about getting healing clients without turning it into a business.

"Give lectures," she recommended.

Home again from America in late December, I offered to give a conference to my Soroptimist Club and was quickly put on the program. Six weeks later, in February 1998, I stood before a friendly audience of thirty colleagues. I knew in advance that a small handful would be totally with me and another fraction would find everything I had to say unacceptable. Throwing caution to the wind, I told them how joining their ranks sixteen years earlier had marked the beginning of my conscious spiritual path, after a period of directionless searching. I took them from my stumbling beginnings with meditation and earth energies up to the opening of shamanic horizons. To my relief most of them loved it. Afterwards a group clustered around me to ask questions, and I knew then that I had to teach. I learned to my surprise that a number of these friends had toyed with the idea of dipping into "alternative" spirituality — meditation and yoga primarily — but they were all fearful of getting caught in the web of a sect. They'd heard too much about manipulative gurus. What I offered them was "safe" because they knew me well and could trust me. This realization humbled me; it made me understand how much responsibility I bore.

My first seminar took place in midsummer. I weaved meditation, psychic protection, and earth energies into a two-day program for small groups. My living-room was not overly generous, just right for four students and me. It was an intimate way of teaching that suits my character, and it worked.

My students wanted first of all to be trained in meditation, but those of them who ran small businesses or otherwise dealt with the public on a daily basis locked eagerly onto the concept of psychic protection. None of them understood what earth energies had to do with meditation. But after I had taken them into the field and had them try to dowse they "got it". My reasoning is simple: where in your living space you sit to meditate is going to have an effect on how well you meditate. They had to develop a basic sensitivity to the energies swirling around them. None of the meditational techniques which I had learned over the years paid an iota of attention to this facet of spiritual life.

That first morning Lidorly, Rolande, Béatrice and Ghislaine sat around the coffee table while I launched into the basics of meditation, starting with breathing. Smoothing, calming one's respiration is an indispensable step in preparing body and mind, I explained, demonstrating five techniques. Then I presented the concept of the object on which one meditates, whether a mantra, a mandala or a physical object. During my conference I had told the story of the little blue whale who had informed my very first meditation, and there it was on the table in front of them. I had asked them all to bring a small object to which they were attached, and we went right into the first meditation. At the end of the first hour we all meditated for ten minutes, using the alternate-nostril breathing technique and then focusing on a favorite object. (One of them chose the little blue whale.) And it worked. After this meditation, and all the others which followed, we did a quick debriefing in which they described what they had experienced. This allowed me to help them immediately, and you can't do that when you have filled a hall with one hundred people.

For the second half of the morning I introduced the concepts of energy, auras, chakras, and the resonance of mantras. This is going pretty fast, but a small group can move ahead rapidly. I used a flipchart to diagram auras and energy centers, and to immerse them quickly in vibrational resonance I played part of a favorite recording[1]. To conclude the morning we meditated again, using a different breathing technique to lead them into concentration on a mantra instead of an object. When we broke for lunch my neophytes had meditated twice and were bubbling with enthusiasm.

The rest of the two-day program rolled along at the same pace. They were paying me for initiation and information, and they got it. They all made copious notes, to the point I sometimes had to slow my presentation while they scribbled furiously. The rest of that first day introduced them to protecting their auras against psychic intrusion, and then we piled into the car and drove over to the Vallon de Nant. This spectacular alpine valley, a kind of miniature Yosemite, brims with telluric energies. The Hartmann grid ripples across the hummocky meadows, and there are small wooded knolls with some spiral hotspots. Each of them had a chance to prowl across the meadows with Hartmann lobe antenna deployed, and when it began to wiggle for them the nature of earth energies came alive.

For psychic protection I taught them first how to "pop a bubble", to surround themselves with light, to visualize their bubble, to turn it into a veritable shield, and finally to expand it to meet its neighbors. Later I outlined a number of small techniques, such as painting pentagrams in the air, and we spent a solid hour on the use of stones, crystals and floral essences for protection.

Meditation was, however, the main course in this broad menu, and we kept at it. We closed the weekend with Brugh Joy's "spiral meditation", during which I led them in repeating the Om Mani Padme Hum mantra at each point on the spiral. This blockbuster carries one deep into an altered state, and when you emerge from the return spiral it is wise to take a few minutes to open the eyes slowly. The return to our material dimension is best achieved gently. I did not want my neophytes groggy. In two days they had meditated seven times, experimenting with a spectrum of different techniques, and after the spiral there is nothing more to be said. I sent my students home with a big kit of tools from which to select what worked best in the home environment. Two of this first quartet were still meditating with me eight years later.

Teaching in this way was also a learning experience for me. I had prepared a four-page syllabus of what I wanted to present, how and in what order. The first half-hour of teaching taught me that such schedules are made to be broken, programs must be allowed to mutate. My four friends asked the kinds of questions that forced forward leaps on my outline. This was not upsetting, for the logic of my outline was only one kind of logic. Their questions, echoes of preoccupations, sprang from a different logic. In the end nearly everything got covered and during the final afternoon a question about resonance inspired me to invent a new exercise: opening the chakras against a background of Gregorian chant.

This little seminar had a ripple effect, and two months later I had Mariette, Arlette and Line around the coffee table. A last-minute cancellation had reduced us to three, but it still worked. In order to reinforce the importance of a protective shield I had told the story of the psychic attack in France. Later in the program it was appropriate to mention briefly my energy projections for the world, and Line pointed out that this was white magic. Arlette quickly compared it to what happened in France. "That was black magic," she observed. Suddenly they put it all together: the difference between black magic and white magic became clear.

"We can move energy around," I concluded, "but our *intention* is of primary importance. Intention is everything!"

After that my spiritual buffet did not tempt any more Soroptimists, but new people materialized. In January 1999 my very first student Patricia came back for more, and a couple from Lausanne joined her around the coffee table for what proved to be the last of the series. These three seminars had each been successful, but in order to continue I would have had to do a lot of advertising and otherwise "go commercial". My sense of vocation as a teacher did not extend that far. It proved possible to start a monthly meditation circle, with the first seven new meditators as a nucleus plus two more Soroptimists who were already in the spiritual bath. This was highly satisfying to me, and it was enough.

This little fling at teaching was not a revolution. My meditative life continued to carry me to the far corners of the planet, trying to assuage conflicts as they rose, adding new targets to the existing round of seemingly insoluble problems. Sometimes a political breakthrough would lead me to think that, just perhaps, my small efforts combined with those of thousands of other meditators did indeed make a difference. We were an anonymous team, but I believe we existed and still do. "Ordinary" meditation, going within for the sake of my soul's ease, punctuated all this "travel".

Healing clients wandered in from time to time, carried to my doorstep by word of mouth. Perchette occasionally sent me cases that fell outside of her domain. One afternoon in the spring of 1999 a young newlywed telephoned with a frightening problem of irritation all around the area of her private parts and neighboring orifices. Leery of treading on medical toes, I questioned her about obvious medical reasons for this situation before accepting to receive her the following week. After hanging up the receiver, inspiration suddenly flowered. I picked up my wellworn copy of *The Encyclopedia of Natural Medicine*[2] and it fell open, as if by magic, to the chapter dealing with "candidiasis". In it I read all about yeast infections and their associated problems and knew I had struck gold. I called back my new client and asked her to keep a journal of everything she ate and drank during the coming week. My trusty encyclopedia had convinced me that she suffered from an overgrowth of *candida albicans* and that we could cure her with a change of diet. Such proved to be the case. She brought her husband and we went over the nature of the problem in relation to her food journal and to possible other causes. For antibiotics and hormones are major contributors to the syndrome, and she'd been on them too. In terms of sugars and yeasts, her food intake was a disaster. The physical symptoms were undermining their new married life, thus their motivation to correct the situation was strong. I'd insisted she bring him along, because without his total cooperation there could be no lasting cure for her. Allopathic medicine treats chronic yeast infections in a limited fashion, with yeast-killers that only suppress symptoms temporarily. My client agreed to a drastic change of diet: eliminating everything containing sugar and yeast. And she had to get off the contraceptive pill.

It is a daunting challenge for most people to suddenly stop consuming bread, pasta, pizza, milk products, sweets and sweeteners, many fruits, juices, mushrooms, beer and wine. They did it. It worked as the vaginal lozenges never had. Her symptoms began to fade within a few days, and three weeks later she called with a joyous message.

"I'm clean!" she gloated.

The following year they produced a bouncing baby girl, and my client has lived ever since with her diet close to hand, for the moments when too much sugar or yeast, or antibiotics or hormones threaten a relapse.

In this way my gift of channeling healing energy through my hands was sometimes set aside in favor of counseling. And sometimes people who came with unreasonable expectations got sent to the medical doctor. I do not pretend to practice medicine.

Several months after this episode I read about a French shaman who was giving classes in my part of Switzerland. Curiosity could not be restrained. His internet site described a seminar at a farm in the forest in October. I signed up.

It began with a long, deep meditation during which the shaman Loup ("wolf" in French) created a drumbeat that rose and fell with the songs he sang. Drumming has a powerful effect on me, and I suspect most people on this path react in a similar way, sensing a vibrational crescendo within themselves. I became aware that Loup was observing me a lot. What did he see? When all this had calmed down we were asked to introduce ourselves and explain our purpose. My brief digest apparently did not satisfy him, and I felt his gaze upon me often during that first morning. Ultimately Loup donned a wolfhead mask, sang, chanted, howled, rattled, shuffled about and went into a deep trance in which he wobbled, weaved and flopped about so much it was obvious why he needed an assistant. The slender, delicate young Marie had the knack of preventing him from falling with just the slightest push of a finger. Their dance — his semi-conscious floundering and her almost mystical gestures — was fascinating to observe. He was uttering a kind of barbaric language, apparently handed-down from a primitive culture through his shamanic grandfather and great-grandmother.

Fall chill was changing the structure of the air when we went into the forest after lunch. Surrounded by ferns, rotting logs, small boulders and towering evergreens, we practiced a kind of energy "pulling" exercise, and Loup taught us some of his songs.

The next morning began with another intense drumming session, punctuated with singing of the songs we had learned. This drumming got through to me in a big way, for I began to hear a second drum (as had happened years earlier in Eileen's hogan). For an instant, my senses received three drums, but Loup coughed and the spell was broken. The drumming resumed, rose again, but my extra drums did not return. Instead I received a nice man, standing in an open square. He had a mass of white hair and was a bit rosy-checked. He seemed to have something for me — a message? — but dissolved before delivering it.

Loup went into a slow dancing trance in his wolf mask, Marie steering him away from obstacles with her little arrows of energy. This was a moment during which he gave those of us who were new to his group an initiation, an injection of energy that he called "chana". This was like getting a fresh jolt of the energy which came to me starting six years earlier after the first visit to Sedona. Loup said the Tibetans transmitted a similar power but had another name for it. One could as well have said "prana" or "chi", I felt.

Rain gear over warm layers was necessary for our second afternoon in the forest. One could almost smell the snow which was forecast for the coming twenty-four hours. After a long, wet meditation sitting on logs and mossy boulders we did some energy-raising exercises. This was pure Kundalini but Loup did not call it that. We paired off to do visualizations in the crown chakra. Jan, paired with me, said she saw me as a strong Sioux warrior/medicine man. Considering that I had not said anything about this phase of my mystical path, her vision struck me powerfully. She'd seen what Perchette, Red Cloud and others were seeing. Loup also? Such a past life was beginning to acquire substantial credibility.

After our chilly hours in the heart of Mother Nature it was comforting to be back in the farmhouse, where Loup initiated a long drumming, rattling and singing meditation. Rather quickly I felt close to trance and my feet wanted to move, to dance my way into that trance. The farmer lived downstairs, so we could not all clump around dancing, but my feet never stopped wiggling and imagining themselves shuffling around the floor, rattle in hand.

Four months later I returned for another weekend with Loup. His methods were interesting, quite different from what I had learned of Eileen's, but clearly shamanic. Heavy midwinter snows had melted and there was not much on the ground in Loup's forest in early February. Mittens were essential but snowshoes not. We followed his usual format that began with lots of good drumming to move our spirits into deeper dimensions. We learned about opening energy channels, receiving healing power, and then applying it. Loup introduced a symbol which we had to memorize so as to be able to call it up when needed. This was an object, a cousin to the hourglass, a cousin to the Tibetan "thunderbolt" which a friend had brought me from the Himalayas. It did not exist as a physical object (although it could have been carved, and probably has been somewhere in the world). We memorized a sketch, and slowly learned to turn the idea into reality, so that we could hold it in a hand and apply its power to a healing. It came to me powerfully, feeling like a solid object in my hands which I could enlarge, shrink and multiply. Late in the day I could create a large version occupying my spine. We practiced on one another, opening and closing the energy flow through ourselves and into our partner-patient.

This was a very meaty seminar. Loup obviously had a valid system to communicate, and I liked the ambiance in which he dressed it. I found his concepts impressive and knew that what I had learned could be useful. He offered a continuing program pointing to full shamanism, and it was tempting. Two reasons held me back: first, what I was learning from Eileen, albeit more slowly, resonated strongly within my being, and second, I had a dramatically different program for this year 2000. (The next chapter is about that.)

About an hour after I got home from this weekend Molly was on the telephone from America. She asked me to consider healing her at distance. Her energies were down but mostly she suffered from pain in her neck -- it appeared she had a herniated cervical disk. Could I help? Her plight was a trumpet call, blaring with synchronicity. Hours ago I had learned new techniques, and here she was testing them.

I asked her to fax me a sketch of her bedroom, indicating all furniture, windows, doors, pictures. Her floor plan came across the wires that evening, and the next morning I was there in spirit.

Once I had projected myself into her bedroom in New Jersey I tried to find a comfortable position. Sitting on the edge of the bed was not good. So I created an upholstered stool and sat on that. The technique Loup had taught, powered by the symbol, was a winner. The symbol flared in my hands and it filled my spinal column. I was able to channel healing energy in a very clear (to me) manner. Her message seven hours later made it clear her pain had been relieved, but the effect was not lasting.

I went to her the next three mornings, massaging, applying my new power tool to her neck, and charging her chakras. In fact, I built fire in those energy centers and planted some guardian animals.

After my four "visits" Molly telephoned to report her neck was "significantly better" and she did not need any more treatment.

"What else did you do?" she demanded.

"What do you mean?" I asked.

"My energies are overflowing. I feel dynamic, charged-up."

So I explained about firing up her chakras, and I told her about learning to work with her new guardian animals. These results from working at long distance were, in a sense, beyond a marvel. Somehow I did not expect either my Guides nor Loup to be surprised.

Five days later my mother achieved her passage to the other side. At her time of departure I had been leading a group meditation of my former students. Five of us were meditating on our chakras when Mother slipped away. Carol called the next morning to pass on the news. Mother had been slightly ill earlier in the week, but that morning her vital forces had been all right at seven, eight and nine o'clock. At ten o'clock she was gone, having cleverly stolen away while no one was looking.

"That's the way to go!" I applauded silently, not wiping away the tears that welled up.

She had lived to within a few months of being one hundred and two. At seventy-six and still going strong, I gave a moment of thought to my own mortality. Life was full of projects, and my next objective -- a trip to Peru -- was supposed to unfold in two months.

[1]   Christophe Martin de Montagu, *OM*. Lausanne: Editions "Ciel et Terre", 1996. Compact disc, series "Eveil de conscience et guérison énergétique", vol. 5.

[2]   Michael Murray and Joseph Pizzorno, *The Encyclopedia of Natural Medicine*. London: Macdonald, Maxwell Macmillan, 1990. 622p., glossary, references, index. ISBN 0-356-17218-X.

The authors are naturopathic doctors, Murray being on the faculty of Bastyr College, of which Pizzorno is a co-founder. This volume presents natural medicine as a deeply scientific discipline, witnessed by 59 pages of scientific references in fine print. Each of the seventy-three chapters deals with a common kind of medical problem whose remedies are natural (diet, vitamins, minerals, etc.) as opposed to pharmaceutical (e.g., penicillin, cortisone, etc.)

Chapter Thirty-Five

BENEATH THE CONDOR'S WING

Machu Picchu's magic pumped me full of incredible energy. High altitude seems to empower me spiritually and my physical body feels light and dynamic, in its element. Among the stones of the old Inka city I was almost permanently in a state of exaltation. Awareness of having been there before, in some other lifetime, flooded my senses. It was another homecoming.

We spent three days in and around the stones, performing one ritual after another. It was April, 2000, and "we" were a merry band of Danes with whom I made the trip, and our spiritual guide and leader, the Peruvian anthropologist Juan Nunez del Prado. Machu Picchu was certainly the centerpiece of our ten-day program, but we were touring — and interacting mystically with — the heart and soul of the Andes.

How I got there is, of course, a story in itself. The trip was the high spot of a process that began at almost the same time that I was taking the first shamanic seminar with Loup.

Seventeen years after first starting to use a personal computer I got connected to the internet and entered the world of e-mail and websites. Eileen had been urging me to do this, so as to facilitate our own communications. She had gone further, creating an interactive website, the "Athena Medicine Garden". Everything metaphysical and health-oriented we had talked about together was discussed there. I began participating in the give-and-take of the on-line discussions while Eileen went on vacation. Going to Peru, she said.

I had never entertained the notion of going to Peru, but her announcement to all her "Athenians" provoked an inner reaction that took me by surprise. Suddenly I wanted to go to Peru too, and I didn't understand why.

"I was thinking of you down there -- I believe this is for you," she messaged me after returning. She related her experiences in a nine-part series of articles on the Medicine Garden, and by the time I had read the first three chapters of "Walking the Inka Path"[1] there was no question in my mind. I had to go.

While on Machu Picchu Eileen had received a psychic instruction to pick up a particular rather nondescript gray stone. Home again in Arizona, in the company of friends, the stone got passed around from hand to hand.

They were amazed to see it change color in certain hands. Eileen made a gem elixir from that stone, and I was one of the first to order it.

During the weeks I took the condor stone elixir, following its creator's instructions, my dream life expanded in spectacular fashion. There were close to twenty dreams that were brilliant, bizarre and well outside the usual pattern of dream subjects. Spiritual practices were enhanced, and there was also a physical symptom that came and went, came and went, and finally went.

Of all the extraordinary dreams that came, the one in the big, rectangular temple-like space took the prize. It was a healing room and I was the healer. Alcoves punctuated the walls of this large space, and they were linked to the chakras of my patient. My table and I were the sole occupants of this space, along with my patient, who was not really material but an abstract concept. Indeed, I was almost abstract, evanescent myself, simply a denser manifestation of energy as the temple's field developed. Healing energy carried over into wakefulness in the form of increased body heat. Healing popped up in other dreams, but this one was the most emphatic. It proved to be premonitory.

Another time I dreamed of participating with another woman in an initiation. The man who performed this ritual laid his hands on and around the sides of the head. He wore a kind of wooly cap. This was fully predictive, or — in mystical jargon — precognitive.

My desire to meditate increased and, along with it, the Kundalini energy flowing up the spine. One evening, as I led a group of my former students in a program of meditations, Kundalini rose in silvery wave after wave, my hands were vibrating with this power, and everyone in the circle became highly charged. They all felt the energy moving into their hands.

In the past I had experienced episodes of neuralgic pain in the legs, especially in the underside of the left thigh. The condor reawakened these old symptoms; they ebbed and flowed throughout the month, finally abating. Four months later the neuralgia returned on the day of my arrival in Peru. I took a dropperful of the stone elixir and the pains gradually faded away over the next twenty-four hours, never to return.

Such were some of the high spots of my experimental results with the condor stone elixir. My typed-up notes fill six single-spaced pages, which I will not inflict on you.

Getting to Peru happened under the auspices of Elizabeth B. Jenkins, whose book on working with Juan proved to be the first step in the process[2]. It was required reading for all participants, and it was a fascinating tour in itself. Elizabeth told me I could go with a European group, which turned out to be entirely Danish. Thus on the second Sunday in April, 2000, I went to the assigned gate at Schipol Airport in Amsterdam, for the flight to Lima. My Danes were nowhere in sight, and I went in search of a bottle of water. When I returned to the line I saw a new group lounging behind a pillar. They were mostly blond and all had backpacks. Patiently I sought and finally met the eye of one who looked like the photo of Anita. I raised a finger in salute, she raised a finger in return, and I strolled over to my new companions. Anita and her husband Jens Peter were our leaders for the trip and made the introductions. Quickly I received warm hugs from them, then Susanne, who would be my room-mate, Annette, Kirsten, Jeanett, Henrik, Torben, Randi, Margit and her husband Peder.

In great gaiety we boarded our aircraft and took off for Aruba and Lima. We were not able to sit together but managed to meet for chats near the galley or the toilets. There was an hour off the plane at Aruba, then we landed at Lima in the early evening, twelve hours after leaving Amsterdam. Much delay ensued over missing baggage, but we finally got to our hotel in time for ten o'clock bedtime. Susanne and I proved to be compatible despite a nearly forty-year age difference; Anita had intuited this arrangement beautifully. Had she known that I was the widow of an artist? With long blonde hair, Susanne is an artist and teacher of art, with a calm, introspective nature, and we found immediate rapport. Our one-hour flight to Cusco was supposed to lift off at six o'clock in the morning, thus a dozen sleepy Europeans left their hotel at four-twenty a.m.

My doctor and I had discussed the brutal change of altitude on this flight, boarding at sea level and disembarking at nearly eleven thousand feet. He suggested a product called Diamox, which I took for the first time just as we left our hotel rooms for the airport. At first I did not understand my strange symptoms — not vertigo but rather "fuzzy-wuzzy". It was as if my energy envelope, my aura, were all jangled, the etheric layers tangled and dispersed. It felt like there were several of me, and all of them were operating on the wrong vibratory frequency. Kirsten, who turned out to be a Reiki master, fixed me up while we sat in the airport. She restored order to my chakras with talented hands and quickly I began to feel myself again. Reading the Diamox information sheet told me that my reaction had been an exaggeration of a known side-effect. I did not take this "remedy" again.

Cusco hotels serve their new arrivals with a cup or two of coca tea, and this takes care of all altitude problems. It certainly took care of mine. All of us bought little bags of coca leaves from the corner grocer near our hotel and I learned to chew a few of them regularly, as does the indigenous population. The uninformed raise their eyebrows skeptically, muttering "cocaine", but that reaction stems from ignorance. Coca leaves contain fourten alkaloids, of which cocaine is only one. It can only be separated and turned into a narcotic by a series of chemical distillations; only then is it harmful. In their natural state, chemically intact, integrated, coca leaves are rich in vitamins and minerals that help the Andean people endure life at high altitude. They contain more proteins, more calcium and iron, and almost as much phosphorus as corn, rice, wheat and the other major cereals. Coca leaves contain strong quantities of vitamins A, C, E and the B group. There is also magnesium, zinc and copper. They are nutritious, and no one gets "stoned". From our experienced leaders Jens Peter and Anita we learned to keep headaches and other early symptoms of altitude sickness at bay by stuffing a few of these super-nutritious leaves into our mouths from time to time.

Our group had decided to arrive in Cusco five days ahead of our initiatory tour under the guidance of Juan Nunez del Prado. At first Juan did not understand why we wanted to be there so early, but when he started to work with us on the sixth day he discovered we were well-rested, thoroughly acclimated and very harmoniously integrated. We had had time to explore in twos and threes but also to do some group excursions, beginning to experience Inkan energies ahead of our initiation.

Candidates for this tour were asked to take a preliminary weekend seminar with Juan, in order to learn the basics of the energy work we would do.

My companions had all taken this seminar with him in Denmark at various times ahead of departure, for Juan journeyed to Europe twice a year. One month ahead of the trip I found him in Amsterdam, teaching a roomful of sixty people. Juan's personal warmth was a powerful teaching tool. His warm eyes twinkled above the greying beard, his tan features exuded friendliness. The basic exercises and principles he taught in those two days had shown me this trip was going to be a powerful experience.

The first thing Juan teaches is how to find your *qosqo*, an energy point on the abdomen. He taught us to explore with a fingertip the space between the umbilicus and the sternum. Somewhere along that invisible line is a spot that is more sensitive than the rest. You have found your qosqo and are ready to learn how to open it and pull in energy. In Amsterdam we started doing this in front of one another, but in Peru we often worked to connect our qosqos with a distant source of energy, like a mountain peak or the sun.

Then Juan explained the concepts of *sami* and *hucha*, light energy and heavy energy. This concept of Andean philosophy says that things are not good or bad, positive or negative, but light or heavy. Ultimately Juan had us digesting energy in a process called *hucha mikquy*, meaning "eating hucha". The point of the exercise is to suck in the energies around you via your qosqo and then sort them. You send the heavy energy, the hucha, down through your legs and back into Mother Earth, *Pachamama*. Then you send the sami up through your upper body and into the crown chakra. Pachamama feeds on hucha, recycling it, and she sends us sami in exchange. Soon you learn to clean the energetic space around you, even to clean the energy fields of people near you. It is not hard to do once you get the hang of it. Like many spiritual practices, the purity of your intention is highly important.

In Cusco we began our acclimatization with coca tea in the patio of our modest Hotel Ninos. Lima had been overcast and muggy at about 71°; Cusco was bright and sunny, a very pleasant 68° in spite of the altitude and the fact April corresponds to October in the northern hemisphere. We basked in the sun, sipping our tea, waiting for our rooms to be ready. After settling into our room Susanne and I collected Annette and dropped down to the central square, the Plaza des Armas. We joined some of the others in an upstairs coffee shop called Trotamundos, used the internet connection to send e-mails, and then went in search of a vegetarian meal. That we found and enjoyed via highly-spiced Asiatic cooking at Al Grano.

After lunching so well the three of us wandered the back streets and came across a pair of big old wooden doors festooned with hand-lettered signs announcing a variety of excursions and esoteric services. I peered into that dim cave, spied humanity and led my companions up the stone steps. One of the placards proposed "San Pedro cleansing", and that intrigued me. I knew that San Pedro was a hallucogenic cactus but the cleansing bit mystified me. Inside I squinted in the dim light, then saw the proprietress sitting behind a kind of desk. Encouraged by seeing warm, beige-brown features emerging from a mass of curly, wavy brown hair, I posed my question about San Pedro.

She looked at me intently, passed behind me to a pot serving as a doorstop, plucked out a baby cactus, and handed it to me. That was the first surprise. We began to talk about healing techniques, comparing notes, quickly discovered a community of interests and talents, and soon we were in each other's arms. I recognized Doris as she had recognized me, not only as a fellow healer but as a sister. She was as small as I am tall, not resembling me in any physical way, but we were soul sisters. My companions were, of course, struck dumb by the rapidity of this development. Later Doris confided that she gave me the cactus as if in a trance, never having intended to give it to anyone.

My first day in Peru and already there was a karmic reunion! Doris and I began to talk about how to work together, making a date for the next afternoon.

That next day began for me with some healing work. Kirsten, who had restored my aura to good form, had suffered a smashed ankle earlier in the year. Metal was removed surgically shortly before our trip, but she had no flex, there was swelling, and she limped. This first treatment was one of channeling energy into the mangled joint, and I rubbed in an herbal ointment. She felt something happening, and it seemed like we gained a millimeter of flex. As a group we visited the ancient Inka sun temple, the Qorikancha, now within the walls of the church of San Domingo. We knew that Juan would have energy work for us here so we amused ourselves with meditating and connecting to the energies in a temple space dedicated to the moon and the stars. There were power points in the main courtyard, and I made a mental note to start carrying dowsing gear in my daypack.

In the late afternoon, after a little jetlag nap, I kept my date with Doris. She padlocked the big wooden doors and then led me up the steep streets and above the city. We were going to Sacsayhuaman, the ancient fortress, and it was fascinating to see how the city really nestled right up under the brow of the hill without letting you see the massive fortifications. On the way up we met a couple of Q'ero tribesmen, just then arriving at Cusco after the four or five-day walk from their village. Doris had been expecting the elder of the two and his load of woven goods. We sat on the grass with them in this late afternoon light, chewing coca leaves in the ceremonial way. You choose three perfect leaves, arrange them into a fanlike *kintu* and then dedicate them to an Apu before offering them to your partner to chew[3]. "Apus" are mountain spirits, each peak having its own character. Eventually our companions unrolled their wares and we bargained a little bit, with Doris interpreting.

Up at Sacsayhuaman we ascended the dramatic zigzag rampants by a stairway. In the center of the main circle Doris taught me a power meditation exclusive to women. Then we went down again, found our Q'ero friends and took delivery of the two mantas I had chosen. It was getting dark as we reached the Plaza de Armas, where I was to link up with some of my Danish pals to have supper. Before separating Doris and I made a date for the following evening at her shop. One of the specialities she advertised on her placards was coca leaf readings, a form of clairvoyance. To do a reading for me she would work in tandem with a colleague, also named Doris. "Until tomorrow night then!"

The next morning another of my companions needed help. Meditating on the power points in the Qorikancha had provoked a strong emotional and physical reaction, shaking up her condition of early menopause. The temple's energy had sent her into deep discomfort. This situation seemed to call for homeopathy. My traveling kit of remedies was necessarily limited in scope, with few options for this kind of problem, but the Sepia I chose appeased the physical symptoms and appeared to restore her emotions to good cheer relatively quickly.

That evening at eight-thirty I knocked on the wooden doors — they were closed but a faint gleam escaped through some cracks. Indeed, by candlelight, I met the other Doris, a sweet lady who works very hard to support her five children. She proved to be a powerful clairvoyant too. This became clear within a few minutes.

She spread a big bag of coca leaves on the table, mixed them, picked up one or two and let them fall, fiddled with them, arranging little designs. The leaves were a support for her clairvoyance, in the same way that some use cards, coffee grounds, stones, or crystal balls. Doris used coca leaves. Much of what she told me was deeply personal, down to "the last five per cent" as I told my Danes later, but she came up with so much known truth that the rest seems automatically validated.

What did come up, you may well ask? Well, shamanism. She identified me clearly with the shamanistic world but went a little further.

"You have transcended shamanism, gone beyond it," she said in Spanish, with Doris number one translating into English the whole evening. She identified me as a healer for people and for the planet, which certainly fit the work I had been doing. She said I was twice a hermit, once an Egyptian princess. This last I took with a large grain of salt, because so many women have been told they were Egyptian princesses they would occupy more generations of royalty than actually existed. The Dorises combined, both reading the leaves, also told me that I would probably not enjoy a durable relationship with a new male companion. After thirteen years of widowhood that was an unwelcome forecast. They told me that Spirit doesn't want me to be distracted from my spiritual work; "they" don't want my intensity to be diluted. Unfortunately I had already heard the same thing from an excellent astrologer.

During the winter months before this spring trip I had spent several days on our snowcovered mountains, dowsing unsuccessfully for the bodies of two teenage snowboarders lost during a stormy day. Doris number two had a lot of trouble understanding the configuration of that mountain. The little relief map I created of coca leaves didn't help much. She saw the boys moving ahead of a snow avalanche and said they would be found in fifteen to thirty days, near a lake but not in it. In fact, they were ultimately found thirty-three days later when ten feet of snow began to melt, and they *had* been caught in an avalanche. The site was not really close to the only lake of the area, but it was adjoining what is in summer a hillside swamp.

My experience this evening was sufficiently vivid and convincing that half a dozen of my Viking companions had readings the next three nights. Only one was disappointed, but she admitted she had been told the truth about herself.

Our group became welded together rather rapidly. The blonde Anita and her brown-haired Jens Peter, both psychologists, guided us around Cusco just enough to facilitate our little explorations in twos and threes. We prowled the crafts arcades and stalls, the little silversmiths, tried out all the internet cafés to check and send e-mail, visited the sprawling public market, organized rendezvous for coffee at Trotamundos or for lunch.

On our fourth day Jens Peter and Anita led us over the mountains (via public bus) to Pisac in the Sacred Valley. Another bus took us up the mountain to the temple ruins, where eagle-eyed guards prevented our penetration into the intriguing Sun Temple. The best part of this site was the female temple up behind and to the left of the Sun Temple. I meditated with my back to the wall opposite the entrance, my arms outstretched, each hand in a niche. Lots of orange light swam through my closed eyes. Using my Lecher antenna as proxy for a Bovis biometer[4], I measured the vibrational frequency of Pisac at 30'000 angstroms, right up there with the best of the Gothic cathedrals.

Anita came to join Randi, the elfin physiotherapist, Henrik the rugged forester, and me to form a meditational square, with her mesa[5] on the ground between us. This was a long, powerful session, the energy pulling me toward the center despite frequent re-rooting — ever drawn forward and down, almost falling. I saw a dull orange field with a small turquoise heart which melted into a sequence of dark stone Andean faces, ancestors the color of basalt. I did my Great Spirit invocation silently, then aloud for the four of us. They told me it was deeply moving, in the context of this high-altitude temple (more than ten thousand feet).

My dowsing at Pisac produced a positive reaction to the frequencies for cosmic energy and for Atlantis. The latter did not surprise me because of the colorful, close-fitting knit caps the Q'eros wear, with earflaps and a pompom on top. They resemble closely the caps worn by the peasants on the island of Madeira, an overnight sail from Portugal.

That night it was evident that Kirsten needed help with her bad ankle, which suffered a lot up there on the mountain. I gave ankle and foot a long massage with an ordinary cream, then switched to a soothing salve around the bone and scar, finishing up with a painkiller ointment. We gained another millimeter of flex. Then I did an energy balancing reinforced with stones and crystals on the seven chakras, and recharged her aura. She became blissfully somnolent. I gave her Arnica 30c for the night and Ruta graveolens 30c for the morning. Symphytum (comfrey) would have been the remedy of choice for her ankle, but it wasn't in my travel kit. The next day Kirsten was much improved, much happier.

Our initiation tour with Juan was to begin formally the following evening, so during the day we moved crosstown to the Hotel Libertador, our "official" hotel. Late in the day I strolled across town to Doris' cubbyhole shop, also meeting one of her daughters, herself a budding healer. We enjoyed lots of warm, animated talk, and Doris began a little campaign to have me prolong my stay in Cusco after the ten days with Juan and my Danes. She proposed I move to her apartment when my gang left for Lima and the flight home. The idea was bewitching, it resonated strongly within me, but my cautious nature began grappling with the ifs, ands or buts. Peru's input was overwhelming.

Juan launched Hatun Karpay, the "Great Initiation" he had received from his own Q'ero master, with an evening conference in the hotel. He called Hatun Karpay a fourth-level initiation, and we would receive in ten days what had taken him ten years to accomplish. "Fourth-level" did not refer to a hierarchy but to a level of consciousness as well as a sense of geographic scope.

"These levels are universal and can be achieved through any kind of spiritual work, not only through the Andean Path," he explains[6]. In his view, the Europeans and North Americans who are attracted to Peru for this initiation have usually already advanced through the earlier levels. There is also the geographical concept of "levels", in which family, community and state are levels rippling outward, the fourth level being global. He told us that in carrying Inkan energetic practices back to our countries we would be, in fact, working at the fourth level.

Our initiation began the next morning at the cathedral on the Plaza des Armas. The Catholic cathedral? Yes, as Juan explained, it is important to understand how the Peruvians have melded together the old and the new. Before the arrival of the Conquistadors in the mid-sixteenth century, a temple to the Inka god Wiraqocha occupied the site. It thus remains a place of powerful spiritual significance. We entered to observe morning Mass, which was in fact being given by a priest with a distinct Indian cast of features, and one of the hymns was sung in Quechua. Juan drew our attention to a famous statue of the Black Christ and then to an equally famous painting of the White Virgin. The former yielded 22'000 on the Bovis scale and the painting revved up to 28'000, to my surprise.

"This temple is an energetic opening to the spiritual world, the world of refined energies," he told the first Hatun Karpay group brought to Peru by Elizabeth Jenkins[7]. He gave us the same message. Thus the high vibrational rates, I reasoned, would equally reflect centuries of Inkan spiritual energy underlying the Christian additions.

Our private bus carried us up and out of Cusco, past Sacsayhuaman, and finally stopped on a hillside above the ruins of Q'enko. We plunged down a little slope, up another and followed Juan and his son Ivan through a eucalyptus grove into an area of bushes and rocks. Some really huge boulders clustered around a slightly smaller one, about six feet high, with a flat top and which we discovered to be an altar stone. We were at Illia Pata, the "Platform of Light".

Juan began the rituals by energizing his mesa on the altar stone, then told us to open our qosqos, our abdominal energy centers. He passed among us, applying his charged mesa to our qosqos, sucking out our heavy energy, our hucha.

Then he led us a to a small clearing between rocks and bushes where we learned how to create a "despacho", a message to the gods. Each of us chose three coca leaves and formed them into a fanlike kintu, dedicated it to an Apu, and then handed it to Juan, who placed our kintus in a circular pattern on a large sheet of blank paper. In the center he placed a variety of small offerings: grains and seeds, beans, corn, flowers, fruit, candy and other goodies. Juan said this despacho needed wind to carry our awareness out to the Apus. It was perfectly still, not a leaf stirring. When the despacho was almost completed I whispered softly to the wind to come. And, to my great surprise, it came, softly, then building up into a gentle breeze. Anita heard me and muttered "I'm beginning to get ideas about you!"

This tiny event threw me for a loop, symbolically, because I had embarked on the trip with a certain amount of trepidation, not knowing how much I might get from it. Eileen had set an impossibly high target with her fantastic visions and experiences six months earlier. It was hard for me to believe I could experience anything comparable, in line with my sense that I had only a tiny fraction of her power.

Then we moved back to the rocks for a major ritual, practicing "ayni" or energy exchange with Juan. This ritual is a cornerstone of Andean spiritual practice, for ayni means reciprocity, the only true dogma in the Inkan religion. Ayni Karpay is the exchange of personal power, and that is what we would do.

Frequently I hang back and let others go first but something impelled me today to charge ahead. When Juan got up on the flat altar rock, the "Platform of Light", I scrambled right on up. We were to start by filling our bubbles with a thought, a situation or an experience which was of highest significance to us, then place our hands on his head and transmit that energy to him. Then we would reverse roles and he would transit traditional power to us.

Meeting my newfound soul sister Doris was an obvious "high", so I sent that joy through to Juan, and I know he got it. Then he gave me back some traditional power, and I was so moved that instead of immediately getting down from the altar rock I gave him back some more happy energy. He was surprised but pleased, from the look on his face.

As I climbed down from the Illia Pata stone onto the grassy area where my companions were waiting, a powerful wave of emotion swept over me. I was literally overcome and had to lie down on the bosom of Mother Earth, arms outspread, face to the sun, and let it wash over me. Pachamama heated my back like a fango. Tears of joy flowed and kept on flowing for twenty minutes. Rarely, if ever, have I had such a strong reaction to any spiritual practice. And colors came. When I covered my eyes the red-orange turned yellow, then melded into a light green princess face. This was probably the Green Nusta' about whom Juan told us later in the week.

After this experience I forgot my worries that important things might not happen to me in Peru.

When everyone had enjoyed the ayni ritual Juan led us into another small clearing to create a second despacho. We gathered small sticks in the eucalyptus grove, then Juan and his son Ivan built a little fire on a small rock shelf. Here we burned the first despacho, whose poster-paper base had been folded around it to make a square packet and then tied with silver string. Once it was throughly burned and the fire extinguished, we returned to our bus for a short cross-country jaunt.

We strolled across fields to a large rocky mound, up some carved steps and saw the narrow slit of the Serpent Cave, Amaru Machay. Down some steps, through a short passage, and we were in a small room with an altar stone under a small chimney hole to the sky. We had to climb up and crowd ourselves like sardines on the big stone, which was not quite level. Juan's instructions were complex: we were to review our lives and give up our hucha to the walls of the cave, then we were to go back to the union of our parents and discover the moment of our conception. What a program! The interesting thing is that it works: it came to me that I was conceived on New Year's morning of 1923. This was a detail of my life that I had never considered, but it is of course the true beginning, and today's rituals were also about beginnings.

Back in Cusco, we surrounded a restorative lunch at Puchar on the corner opposite the Plaza des Armas. Fed and watered, we piled back into the bus for the trip out to the lake of Huascar, who is commemorated as the last Inka.

We scrambled down a weedy, bushy bank to the lakeshore and deployed ourselves gingerly on rocks and dry spots around Juan. There was only a fringe of dry land between the steep bank and the reeds which fill the shallow borders of the lake. As instructed, we called silently to Huascar Inka, trying to absorb the energy of the lake. Then we dedicated the second despacho made at Illia Pata and Juan launched it on the water. Our fragile little vessel-message slowly drifted through a channel in the reeds to the open water.

As the despacho sailed out of sight Juan began to initiate us one by one with his mesa on our crowns. After that each of us received three symbols of our Hatun Karpay initiation: a shell representing the lower world (*ukku pacha*), a small metal cross representing the upper world (*hanaq pacha*), and a little brown tile standing for the middle, material world in which we dwell (*kay pacha*). The little brown tile, into which symbols are engraved, is a replica of the one given Juan by his Q'ero shaman-teacher Don Benito Qoriwaman. I could not help but be reminded of the three levels through which shamans travel although, as rereading the description in Eileen's book verifies, the concept of the lower world is not quite the same in both systems. For the Andeans ukku pacha is filled with hucha, heavy energy. In the life of the shaman the lower world is the home of Mother Earth, containing some important dark corners but also a full spectrum of colorful, beautiful scenery[8].

Finishing up the ceremony, Juan said "you are a marvelous bunch!"

To which I replied, daring to speak for all of us, "we've been working and playing together for four days. We've become welded together and we all love one another."

Juan beamed. Earlier he and Elizabeth Jenkins could not understand why this weird group of Europeans wanted to be in Peru days ahead of schedule. Now he knew.

Back in Cusco we had to pack for Machu Picchu, cramming everything for three days into our smaller bags. The larger ones were to be stored in the hotel. Everyone ran off on little errands, changing money, checking e-mail, buying more water and snack food. High altitude burns energy: we were always thirsty and hungry. It was too late to find Doris in her cubbyhole, but I slipped a note under the wooden doors.

Early the next morning our driver Eddie pointed the bus north toward Pisaq, Ollantaytambo, and Yucay in the Sacred Valley. On the morrow we would head for Machu Picchu by train, for only rails penetrate that deeply into the narrow, sinuous gorge of the Urubamba. Eddie drove us much higher on Pisaq's mountain than the public bus had gone. Juan took us first to an intricate network of crop terraces fed by irrigation. The ancient Inkas required that the water used to grow food be energetically charged and they had a unique way of achieving that. Water flowed straight downhill in a steep stone ditch which was punctuated with seven stone "tubs". These were basically a pair of enclosed seats facing one another. We were going to imitate the meditative force of the priests who had charged the water from their seats in the "bathtubs". Randi and I took the top tub. We charged the water with our strong intention, facing one another across the narrow conduit. The pair next below added to our initial charge, and sooner than I could have imagined Juan came up from the bottom tub to tell us the work was accomplished. Our energy had transited.

Inkan energy work focuses on what they call *kausay*, which in one sense can be considered to be the living, vital force of the cosmos. It is the same thing as *chi* in the Asiatic world, and for me it is the same as the spiritual power one can learn to experience in many of the early cathedrals of Europe. For the Inkans it goes beyond the purely energetic, to become a way of life closely linked to the ayni we had learned to give and receive. It refers to living in harmony with one's neighbors and one's environment. Many, if not all, of the rituals we learned from Juan were ways of tapping into this bio-electro-magnetic force and using it for a specific purpose. This was what we did while sitting in Pisaq's irrigation tubs: we contacted the energy with our minds, then each other, then the water jointly, and then we gave it a gentle shove downhill. Sacred sites around the world pose the challenge of learning how the power of the place can be absorbed and applied. Every time we visit a power point there is something to be understood and then transmitted.

Pisaq's sacred area covers a vast chunk of the mountain, and the trails over which we entered and left the landscape temple had portals and tunnels to be traversed with sense and respect. On the way we paused on a broad ledge to connect ourselves with its system of five rock niches and then five Apus on the mountains across the deep valley. Up on the temple's top level we executed a series of rituals, blending our own energies with those of the site and our companions. My Bovis biometer technique confirmed that the vibrational rates of these sites were very high, usually in the 17'000 to 22'000 range. These Bovis readings can certainly be considered measures of chi, of kausay.

Driving down the valley we saw our first condor. It was soaring high above the fields to our right, clearly on the lookout for edible small creatures.

After lunch in a garden restaurant at Calca, where a kittenish young anteater amused us by playing around our feet, Eddie drove us to Ollantaytambo. This ancient Inka town lies at the end of the Sacred Valley, where the vegetation of irrigated fields ends and the Urubamba enters its narrow gorge. Above the town rises an impressive fortress-structure guarding the narrows. The complex is incomplete, the Spanish attack having come before the work was done. Manco Inka turned back the Conquistadores' cavalry here, but when they returned with a much larger force he had to retreat into the jungle.

Steep stone steps led us to an exposed promontory next to the unfinished temple. Here the Wind Spirit is said to roar down from a glacier seated between two distant peaks, creating the "Windgate". On the edge of the precipice Juan opened our throat centers with his mesa. For others before us the Wind Spirit had raged, blasted, blown in fierce gusts. For us this afternoon it was a real pussycat, just a gentle breeze, opening our throat chakras with a feather instead of a scalpel.

The road stops here at Ollantaytambo; only the railroad penetrates the river valley walled by steep, densely-wooded mountains. Eddie drove us back to our overnight stop in Yucay, and in the morning he returned us here to catch the train that links Cusco and Aguas Calientes. The latter town, carved from jungle in a bend of the river below the sacred ruins, is the "pueblo" of Machu Picchu.

Before supper at Yucay there were Pisco Sours in the bar, and in the dining room many of us chose lama steak, which was delicious. One night in Cusco four of us had discovered a great Chilean red wine, Cousino Macul, and now Torben and I had the pleasure of offering our table neighbors a bottle of this nectar. Torben is instantly recognizable as a Viking descendant, with his husky build and extremely blond complexion. Younger than my son, with wife and daughters at home in Jutland, he became a gallant companion, looking out for the "old lady" of the group. Before bedtime I gave Kirsten another of the ongoing series of ankle treatments, using the soothing salve and a painkiller ointment, touching up the chakras lightly as well. She was surviving, with pain, walking with two telescopic ski poles.

There was a long wait on the station platform at Ollantaytambo the next morning. Even the local women selling bananas, corn on the cob, and souvenirs finally gave up and sat down aross the tracks. Once aboard, we snacked and picnicked as this narrow-gauge "backpacker's special" wound down the river gorge to the tune of occasional toots of the steam whistle. At Machu Picchu station in Aguas Calientes we left our luggage in the care of hotel staff and went directly for lunch at Inka Pizza near the plaza.

This funky little jungle town occupies a wide place in a bend of the river which changes its name from Urubamba to Vilcanota to Willka'nusta. Sugar-loaf peaks soar abruptly on all sides, swathed in heavy vegetation. It is warmer here, at 6'500 feet altitude compared to Cusco's 10'800 feet. Pleasant in April, not at all sweltering.

Juan led us through a dozen rituals during our first afternoon among the ruins of Machu Picchu, a thousand feet above the village. As soon as we had piled out of the buses that climb the dirt road up the mountain we stood to connect our qosqos with "Flowering Beauty", the Apu Mamita Putukusi. Towering just across the gorge, she is the only female Apu of all those surrounding Machu Picchu. We went to the Sun Temple, whose stairway has another seven baths for seven pairs of priests. Susanne and I shared one of them, doing our connection ritual. Together we brought in the four elements — wind, water, fire and earth — still in the tub.

Machu Picchu is staggering. The power of the stones grabbed me, held me in its atavistic embrace, told me I had come home again. Ritual after ritual connected us more and more tightly to the energy of the ancient city. Juan did not allow time to pause and space out in this breakneck afternoon, there was so much to do. There are temples to the Sun, the Condor, to Mother Earth. There are the Mirrors, the Three Windows, Intihuatana, and the fabulous great slab we lovingly call the Pachamama stone. Standing across the plaza from her, we connect to the earth energy, then we send it across to her, then we go over to receive her energy in return. It sometimes comes in the form of visions and colors. There is a low bench-like stage against Pachamama's wall; you clamber up on this stone walkway and lean full body against Pachamama, plastered against her maternal warmth. It quickly becomes addictive: the Pachamama stone is a place we all visited often during the next two afternoons, which we had free to explore Machu Picchu according to our own impulses.

The Mirrors are two low basins, not a yard in diameter, one round and one not quite round but not yet egg-shaped. Archaeology calls them "The Mortars", which makes no sense for they are too shallow and too small for grain-pounding. Juan explained that their bottoms still bore traces of black paint before an archaeologist "cleaned them up". With black bottoms and filled with water they became mirrors, reflecting the heavens so that Inkan astronomers could study the stars. Eileen's psychic work in that room seven months earlier demonstrated that all the niches — the Inkans loved to build groups of niches into their walls — related to planets and astronomical phenomena. They serve as shelves, but we can theorize that these niches probably held objects symbolizing planets and stars.

We finished our day at the Wiraqocha stone high above and outside the city's ruins. When the guards are not looking you can lie on this slab, pick up the energy of this Inka god, and possibly soar. Today we could not.

What we could do was to complete a cycle of seeding, germination and flowering. Juan explained that at the Lake of Huascar we became Inka seeds. At Pisaq and Ollantaytambo we were exposed to the water and wind elements needed for germination. On arrival up here we set the stage by greeting Mamita Putukusi, "Flowering Beauty". We were ready to exercise "Phutuy". Juan instructed us to grow a stalk within our bodies and let its flowers sprout through the crown of the head. For a while I thought what would emerge would be lupines or peonies, now preparing to bloom in my alpine garden. No, to my surprise I grew a calla lily, then two, three, finally a bouquet of four. Where within me did these calla lilies come from? I hadn't seen any for years. The secrets of the heart!

We bussed down the mountain road of endless switchbacks, walked the railroad tracks to the Pueblo Hotel, unpacked, showered, and assembled in the lounge for the walk back to our restaurant. Stepping along the railroad ties Juan and I got into an intense conversation, a logical outgrowth of a chat that had begun the previous day in the parking lot at Ollantaytambo. We lagged behind and finally got to table upstairs at India Feliz, still talking, the proprietress Cannie waiting patiently to take our order. I brought up the subject of shamanism, explaining what the two Dorises had told me over the coca leaves, and sought his opinion. He agreed with them.

"You *have* transcended shamanism," he said, with emphasis. When I insisted on something more specific, he said "it's a lower form of energy than what you do." This marathon dialogue touched on energy work, Eileen, the necessity of reading C.C. Jung's *Psychology and Religion*, and the possibility of bringing a Swiss group for Hatun Karpay the following year. The tour was not half done and already I knew I had to return.

Yesterday there had been neuralgia in my thigh, and I took Condor Stone drops. I took them perhaps three times in twenty-four hours. The neuralgia had gone. Condor allows me to proceed.

And proceed we did. Juan had us out of the hotel at seven-fifteen the next morning, and an hour later we had bussed up the mountain, traversed Machu Picchu and were on the trail down to the Pachamama cave. You climb almost halfway up the steep, striking Huayna Picchu (the peak in the background of most postcard views of the ruins), then turn left and plunge down a jungle trail. After a brief steep descent, it's a wide, fine trail lined on both sides with dense forest and foliage. I wouldn't venture off that trail without a machete, a spear, a broad-brimmed hat and leather pants. On this day all you needed was a T-shirt, your ever-present water bottle, and a tube of sun screen — there are lots of open spaces in this jungle.

The jungle has its mystic facet. As we descended deeper into the valley Randi, who was walking just behind me — no one else visible in front or behind us — and I spoke about the absence of wild life. We heard some parrots but couldn't see them. The trail was levelling out fast when, about a hundred yards from our destination I found myself engaged, in a kind of reverie that almost became a daymare, in a struggle with a huge anaconda snake. Impressive jungle, impressionable me!

So I stopped and described to Randi what I had just felt/dreamed.

"Well, I've been having a snake in my mind too, but nothing as big or fearful as yours," is approximately how she replied. We'll be coming back to these words.

Down in the cave and its group of niches we were deep in Pachamama's womb. We did a series of rituals here, principally connecting with the nature princesses, the Nust'as. This was concentrated work and when picnic time came we were ready, gobbling our bag lunches on Pachamama's terrace. We had a visitor, the only other person who came down the trail that morning. He was a husky blond, crewcut type named Dane. 'Tis said that for lightworkers there are no coincidences. We chatted while I munched my lunch, dangling my legs over the wall of the terrace. I didn't know that he would reappear.

After picnicking we moved to a neighboring cave, the Cave of the Inka. Here we did more energy work, leaning into more of those ever-present niches, each of these holding a melon-shaped stone. Meteorites, we learned. Some are cold, some are warm to the touch, some vibrate, but they all radiate differing qualities. You move from niche to niche in a kind of fog. I felt qualities here but didn't scribble much. My notes about our work here are skimpy. You get so caught up in the work you forget the material, left-brain act of writing. In the end we connected back to Huascar, the Inka god we met on the first day at the lake, asking him to help recapitulate the chaotic energies we'd been plugged into.

We were back up on Machu Picchu's crest by mid-afternoon, with time for personal experiments. Randi and I tried spreading our spiritual wings in the Condor Temple, for inspiration blooms beneath the massive, savage rock formations which suggest the bird and its wings. We climbed above it, stood in tall niches above the Condor's back, worked to connect/project ourselves onto a free flight around the Apus. Much too ambitious, we learned. Those niches offered much less sense of liftoff than what I would experience several days later at Tambo Machay. After another visit to the Sun Temple and the cave beneath it, I felt that was enough for the day. Several of us had talked about soaking in the thermal baths at the top of Aguas Calientes, and I decided to take an early bus down.

Just after I left the complex via the little labyrinth corridor that connects with the outside world, there came a tall, thin American woman and her university-age daughter. From one of the southern states, her accent told me. She wanted to know how far it was, was it worth while, did they have time, all those questions. I led them back in and, with a few eloquent waves of the hand, showed them how to get around the site quickly.

But this lady had some kind of a bee in her bonnet. She saw me as a mystic and pushed for more information about what I was doing there. Explaining Hatun Karpay really wasn't what I wanted to do, so I waffled a bit.

"I'm a healer," I said, trotting out the short answer.

"Ah knew it!" she cried triumphantly. "Can you heal me?"

When this kind of thing happens you have to recognize that, once again, the meeting was not a coincidence. We never exchanged names or addresses, but this lady needed something and a few quick questions convinced me she was not a sick woman.

So I did a very fast off-the-body energy charging with my hands, finishing hands-on at the crown chakra, and her slow "*ahhhhhs*" told me this was right. The tall woman was happy, even relieved, and her daughter, who had been watching with a Mona Lisa smile, didn't want any. We said goodbye and I ran down and climbed into the waiting bus.

There were only two seats left when I got on, and guess who came along to take the empty one next to me? That's right, the blond guy, Dane.

It turned out that Dane had been taking a lot of film with one of those new-fangled digital camcorders.

"You wanna see some footage of a coral snake I met on the trail?"

"Sure, how much do you have?"

"Oh, I got about five minutes of him moving." He was busy running the film back to the right spot on the little foldout screen.

Yes, there was a five-foot coral snake, looking very venomous, slowly writhing along and across the trail. I suppose he took his time before deciding not to attack the cameraman. It was great footage. I was impressed.

"Where on the trail did you meet this snake?"

"Oh, it was about a hundred yards up from where I met you guys."

Tilt. Gulp. That coral snake must have been watching Randi and me sashay down the trail while both of us were having snake dreams. Talk about the psychic power of the serpent! Real *amaru* energy!

Threading my way through the bazaars of Aguas Calientes, where the buses unload, I ran into Juan. Very quickly we found ourselves in another deep conversation. He made a point of encouraging me in the perception of my power as a healer, as a medicine woman.

"You are very powerful," he said forcefully.

It had taken a long time to develop self-confidence in this respect, so Juan's encouragement was welcome.

Back at the hotel I went to visit Annette, who had felt ill and turned back before we got very far on the jungle trail. A few questions and a little bit of observation convinced me she had a case of influenza, probably the 24-48 hour variety. I gave her enough homeopathy (a German combination remedy in this case) for the night and the morning. Be confident, Michèle!

Susanne, Jeanett, also an artist, and I hiked up the long village street and into the canyon where we found the thermal baths. The medium-sized pool looked and smelled quite sulphurous as we slipped into it. It was deliciously warm, soothing to tired muscles, but it felt strange to be standing on a gravel bed. My toes wondered about all those microorganisms that live deep in the earth and deep under the sea. Aguas Calientes clearly came by its name honestly, but none of us felt like having a long lingering soak.

Most touristic images of Machu Picchu have in the immediate background a steep, pointy, sugarloaf of a mountain. This is not the mountain Machu Picchu, which is rather bulky and undramatic and which overlooks its namesake city from the south. This is Huayna Picchu, the "young peak", on the north. Ceremony on its summit was the centerpiece of our third day among the ruins.

After we piled out of the buses Juan led us directly to the Pachamama slab at the northern end of the city. Opening my qosqo from across the plaza I discovered a veritable blowtorch at my disposal. Pachamama reeled me in like a fish she had caught. What an evolution overnight!

The trail up Huayna Picchu is steep and rocky, but very well made. I can understand that some people might feel a little anxious about all that "air" next to their feet, but it is really a very safe and generous trail. Pachamama has looked after her aging daughters by causing little half-steps to be created here and there. This is an eleven hundred-foot ascension, a regulation one-hour climb for trained alpinists, and that's how long it took. My Danes handled this altitude and hiking exceedingly smartly, considering they are sea level people.

After landing on a little balcony we crawled through a tube-tunnel, about ten yards long and rising slightly. After emerging from this passage another fifteen feet upward brought us onto the summit and its panoramic view on the surrounding huge mountains. Juan took us one at a time to a large slightly-tilted flat rock on which we were to lie. We would receive the forceful masculine energy of all those male Apus. I have read accounts of this ceremony as a kind of battleground in which these warrior spirits come at one aggressively, but such was not my experience. As Juan held his mesa firmly against my qosqo I began to feel the Apu power settle softly over me like a light blanket, in a delicious way. There was nothing aggressive about it, to my spiritual senses.

Juan had told us ahead of time we should simply get up when we'd had enough. Therefore, when it was my turn, it was no surprise to hear him say "when you feel you've had enough, get up." But I didn't quickly budge from that nearly flat altar rock, replying "I'm greedy". Of course, I did get up very soon, for others were waiting.

This ritual was wonderfully empowering. It remains as one of the high spots of my trip to Peru. My feeling is that the Apu force remains with me, or at least it did for many weeks thereafter. There is as yet no scientific measure for such inner appreciations, but the healing work I did later in Cusco was marked by enormous power transiting through me. And it remained. Twenty-four days after Huayna Picchu the cosmos poured this stronger energy into one of my "regulars", a man with a lot of inner tension. Aside from charging up his chakras and smoothing his aura, both usual operations, I was able to relax him as never before and then make some progress in loosening his hard ankle.

Back down in Machu Picchu I accompanied Juan, Jens Peter and Henrik up to the main temple on the crest of the citadel. Here I ate my picnic while all of us admired the stone compass star. I wandered alone across the crest, climbing the seventy-eight steps up to the Intiwatana stone on the highest platform.

The ceremonial stone on this pyramidal promontory mystifies everyone, with its three-foot rectangular block standing on end atop a large five-sided slab. Some think it had astronomical functions. The first twentieth-century archaeologist who laid eyes on it, the American Hiram Bingham in 1915, called it "the hitching post of the Sun". Others point out it appears to be an abstract version of Huayna Picchu when they are visually aligned. There are numerous such "echo" shapes and alignments on Machu Picchu, and this latter theory makes sense to me.

Whatever, I thought it valuable to probe the structure's vibrational frequencies. There were a lot of people around and I would have preferred to dowse in private, but that wasn't going to be possible, so I whipped out my antenna and pendulum and went to work. Eventually a few people expressed interest in my unusual manipulations and, as so often happens, such questioners are open and honestly interested, or they know someone "who does that", etc. In other words, don't fret Michèle, just get on with it.

Here I worked only with the Lecher antenna. It gave me positive responses for: a ritual site of important ceremony (5.3); a place where acoustical resonance is important (like the Roman theater in the Burgundy countryside) but which frequency Violette had found to be prevalent at power sites in Mexico (7.4); another frequency she found in Mexico and which I had not yet tested in Europe (14.8); and two frequencies which reflect the influence of Atlantis. These I had already found at Pisaq, and here they were again.

After working under the Sun Temple and in the Condor Temple, both sites registering 30'000 vibrations on the Bovis scale, I went to the Pachamama slab for one last embrace. Susanne, Randi and Torben were there, speculating about the location of a flat stone inside the citadel which, Juan had told Annette, yielded almost as much as Huayna Picchu. One of them had seen a promising slab near the Mirrors, so the four of us headed there. Yes, in a long corridor we found a fine low, flat slab, very suitable for reclining. We decided to replicate the ceremony, using our own mesas. Rather brash of us, perhaps. To my consternation the three of them unanimously asked me to officiate.

Thus they lay down, one after the other, and I used my medicine bag (not yet converted to a mesa) to channel Apu power into their qosqos. And it worked. That's what they said. Torben even told me he got more than he'd received up on the summit. To finish off the ceremony, I lay down on the rock and Susanne funneled soft energy into my qosqo with her mesa. This was our goodbye to Machu Picchu, for the next day we would travel back to Cusco.

In the morning, after we had checked out of the hotel and deposited our luggage, Juan led us about five hundred yards up the railroad tracks to a convenient spot on the rocky shore of the tumultuous Willka'nusta, also known as the Urubamba, or the Vilcanota if you are resolutely modern.

Standing next to the roiling waters, Juan explained that the energy of the green Nust'a, one of the princesses we had met earlier, fills the river gorge to a height of nearly one hundred feet. The earth energy grids which I try to read are three-dimensional, which made it easy for me to imagine this thick channel of wet energy. We opened our qosqos to absorb the power flowing from the headwaters of the Urubamba, near Lake Titicaca, down to the Amazon.

Curiously, I found myself yawning continually, and then I realized that each yawn was expelling heavy energy, hucha. And my qosqo began to glow warmer and warmer with each succeeding yawn. I saw amethyst, a frequent visitor, flooding my inner screen.

This yawning phenomenon gives me a hunch: what if every time in life that we yawn our systems are simply trying to expel heavy energy? I have not found a scientific explanation for yawning beyond "an involuntary intake of breath", but might we not suppose the physiological reason is subordinate to the spiritual reason? Or that they are somehow joined?

Beside this powerful river my pendulum registered 35'000 Bovis, the highest value I recorded in Peru. This is in the same general range of vibrational rates found in the best of the Gothic cathedrals and in temples inspired by Buddhist principles. Meditation and music can raise the ambient vibrational rate in such structures. Waterfalls raise the frequency, and here alongside the Willka'nusta it was deep water rushing through a narrow canyon.

We got off the late afternoon train at Ollantaytambo, transferring to our private bus with Eddie at the wheel. We drove up the Sacred Valley as the day waned, all very uneventful until our bus rounded a hill and we gasped at the sight of Cusco. The city was luminous, bathed in golden light, a dazzling magical sight dressed in its evening illumination, everything brilliant, the Plaza des Armas and its great churches all golden. This fabulous sight lasted less than a minute, for we lost it when the bus went behind another hill before dropping down into the city.

There was a note from Doris waiting for me at the hotel. She confirmed that she would not be traveling and would like me to stay on as her house guest. Ivan had offered to take care of changing my flight reservations accordingly, so we quickly set those wheels in motion.

Back up at eleven thousand feet the first sleep was light and short. I felt tired and heavy-limbed the next morning in the field, which I attribute to not chewing or drinking coca. Down at Aguas Calientes we hadn't needed that help. My vitality returned as soon as I resumed consuming coca.

Tambo Machay is all about death.

This little valley is not far out of Cusco, not far beyond Sacsayhuaman. There are two temples, as different from one another as day and night, as life and death. And that is their role, to initiate us into the passage from one to the other.

The temple on the left is composed of four levels of Inka stonework that becomes more highly refined as it rises, the whole structure possibly seventy-five feet wide. The top level is a wall containing four tall niches and, at the right as seen from below, a low dark stone vaguely chair-like in form. The wall supporting this level is the tallest and its stonework presents a flowing, wavy aspect, even kind of dreamy. A channel of water flows laterally across in front of this wall and becomes a little waterfall emptying onto the second level, where it divides into two spouts that emerge from the bottom wall and spill into a small semicircular pool. This temple is a place of life, the life that we prepare to surrender.

The temple on the right stands across the little streambed and is hardly a structure at all, maybe a ruin that has been filled in. It's a rough, squarish butte about thirty feet wide and maybe twenty feet high but rising out of several tiers of casual stone work. This temple is the place of death.

Juan instructed us to meditate in each niche, working from left to right. We prepare our own crossing from life to death by absorbing the energy of the living temple and using it to construct a bridge of energy to the other side. Each of these niches represents one of the four winds. After the fourth niche we were to sit in the stone chair and die.

That's right, die. Die and float over the valley and its stream to the ruin of death.

First, though, we had to build bridges from the niches. A very strange phenomenon began to develop within me. At each successive niche I had a greater and greater sensation that levitation was going to happen. I was only supposed to build a bridge, not sail over so soon, and I plunged my roots deeper into the stone floor. In the fourth niche the feeling was so strong that my toes kept involuntarily lifting off the stone, my body pulling out and up, my head bumping the ceiling of the niche. No, I did not levitate, and I did not leave my body. The illusion was powerful, but my roots held.

It was interesting to note the Andean family sitting on a bit of grass on the flat top of the death ruin. They were observing us casually, as if on a picnic. But they got up and left soon after all of us began to build our bridges to their side. Incoming mail must have become a bit perturbing. What we were doing was essentially a Q'ero ritual, and they did not look at all like people of that tribe.

After negotiating the four niches you go to the chair-like stone to die. Dying with these four winds was easy — I have nearly died at least three times in my adult life, once by blood-poisoning, once by nearly drowning, once by nearly sliding over a cliff. And it is easy for me to believe that in an earlier century I died by fire, either as a heretic at the stake or by my house being burned when my Huguenot ancestors fled France in the sixteenth century. In Chapter Nine I described a similar event received as a vision in meditation. Red Cloud had told me I would ultimately die very quietly when my work is done, hands folded and closing my eyes. This is how I died on the stone. It was easy and peaceful, slipping into a tranquil giving-up of life, floating across the valley to the temple of the other world. I think of it also as training for the real thing.

Then I followed the others who had died before me, stepping down to the flowing water of the lower worlds to wash hands and face on each of the three levels. Tambo Machay had produced a powerful effect in me. Rinsing in its energized waters did not wash away the power but seemed to smooth its edges.

Looking up at the walls I had just left, it appeared to me that the wavy lines created by the seams of the upper supporting wall could be compared to the thirty meters of energy hovering above the Willka'nusta. Juan agreed with me.

We started the next day with a series of energy connections in Qorikancha, the "qosqo of Qosqo", the Temple of the Sun which we had visited our second day in Cusco. I found myself making the connections more and more easily; all these felt like something moving. We meditated in the inner rooms then went to the balcony overlooking the garden. Juan told us the Inka religion welcomed fifty-two varieties of solar worship, being very inclusive in contrast to the Mediterranean religions. The Egyptian, Judaic, Christian and Moslem beliefs, he pointed out, have been exclusive and aggressive since the time of Akhenaton. On this balcony there are fifty-two stones, one for each cult.

Our bus was waiting when we emerged from Qorikancha and soon we were rolling southward out of the city toward Tipon. We had a special cargo aboard: six Q'ero Indians in their spectacularly colorful garb. They were four men, one of them a high priest, and two women, and we learned that the women are only now being included in these rituals with foreigners. The Q'eros are said to be the true descendants of the Inkas, and they are the torchbearers of the old philosophy, religion, history and mythology. Juan's father, the anthropologist Oscar Nunez del Prado, discovered the tribe in 1955 and was instrumental in liberating them from serfdom in 1959. Juan had followed the same academic tradition until meeting and becoming the student of the Q'ero Don Benito Qoriman.

Tipon is above all a water temple. It occupies a wide vale in the mountainside, with half a dozen broad and very deep terraces ascending the bowl. They are retained by stone walls, appearing to be sculpted from the soil.

Juan explained that this site was conceived for growing the potato seed that would be used to feed the entire Inka nation. Water control was critical to this effort, and the whole site is planned around the flow of water to the growing beds in the broad terraces. Earlier, in the baths at Pisaq and Machu Picchu, we had worked to charge the descending current. This time we aimed at connecting with the spirits of the water.

The Q'eros led us in "Unu", a ritual union with those spirits. We all crowded around while they prepared a first despacho. Then we moved along a major wall to connect at each of three niches, an exercise that most people would certainly imagine to be nothing at all. However, the cumulative effect of all the rituals we had been doing cannot be denied. At the first niche, the widest of the three, I saw amethyst. At the next slot I saw indigo. At the last one I saw blue and green. Moving around to a small room within a larger one, we meditated at two more niches. In the first I saw green and in the second, red-brown. I couldn't help thinking that we had descended a chain of chakras, color by color, although the Andeans don't follow that Hindu concept.

In that smaller room the Q'eros had laid out blankets on which they were preparing two more despachos. These were to be *despachos completos*, because they were filled with food and drink for Pachamama. There were two because the four men made one of them and the two women made the other, and there were definite qualitive differences. I sat opposite the older of the two women, surely an elder of some kind judging from her presence and the lines in her face. It felt as if, bit by bit and despite a total language barrier, I connected with her too. There was a little wave of sympathy in the airlanes. After all, I'm the elder of our group, and by more than twenty years.

Preparation of these two despachos was a long exercise. Both of them received a sunburst of coca leaves to start with, of course, then some confetti, and both were laced with dribbles of wine and pisco, a local firewater. After that the divergence was marked. The men sprinkled in white flour, slices of white fruit, seeds, pasta, white and yellow corn (representing gold and silver, we were told), and grains. For their despacho, the women artfully arranged shards of fruit, red potatoes, a feather, little candies and sweets, a "Wiraqocha candy baby" doll, yellow rice, vicuna fur, wild rabbit pieces, and the foetus of a guinea pig. (Some days later, in the sprawling Cusco public market, I wandered into a shop whose walls were lined with ritual items. The staggering display of dried animal foetuses and other body parts was, for me, mind-expanding. I accept that others might be horrified and disgusted).

With the despachos fully designed, folded and tied, the Q'eros performed a ritual in which they cleansed us with short lengths of colored string. The women worked on we women and the male priests worked on our male companions. The strings were touched to our heads, breasts, hands and feet, and finally our faces.

Tipon's water flows into two parallel flowing ditches, then is channeled into four little falls. Before the split we meditated again, women connecting to the lefthand conduit, symbolizing silver, and the men connecting to the righthand stream, symbolizing gold. Below the four falls we connected the whole water system with our crown centers, letting it all flow down to the base of the spine. On the way to the car park we paused at another one of those baths composed of facing stone seats, with a water spout between them. Juan told us those seats were identified with the reigning Inka and his queen, the Qoya. At the spout point I saw a perfect amethyst in an indigo setting. The Q'eros also performed this ritual of the bath, and then we all piled into the bus.

For us these Q'eros were spiritual people, following the old ways, carriers of the teachings and the spiritual heritage of the Inkas. We felt bonded to them through shared ceremony and values. Thus it was a bit of a shock to learn that the tribal peoples' position in Peruvian society is not very high[9]. Juan had chosen our country restaurant in function of its willingness to serve the Q'eros at the same table with "whites". Our meal was very good and the proprietor warm and welcoming as he served *all* of us.

That evening Juan and his son Ivan opened our "invisible belts" in a unique ceremony that employs a set of five stones called *khuyas*. Three belts circle the body, resembling horizontal meridians and connecting the energy centers: base of the spine (black, water), the qosqo (red, earth), the heart (gold, fire and the sun). Above the belts are two points to be opened independently: the throat (silver, the wind), and the point between the eyebrows (purple, the upper world). Juan and Ivan murmured prayers as they worked on us. It is a very special routine, and the perception of being "opened" in this fashion is as fine and subtle as connecting one's qosqo to the spirit of a place.

The next morning Eddie drove us southward again, passing the turnoff to Tipon, and continuing on in the direction of Lake Titicaca. This is a main highway but is not paved after the first thirty miles or so. After two-and-a-half hours, passing Andahuaylillas, Urcos and Tinta, having driven possibly eighty miles, we left the main road and drove into the humble village of Raqchi. Well off the highway but still on the flat, Raqchi is the site of a temple which was devoted to choosing Inka rulers. Our ceremonies here would terminate our Hatun Karpay initiation.

A huge wall of stone and adobe dominates the Temple of Wiraqocha, the eighth Inka. What remains of the wall stands about fifty feet high and perhaps one hundred feet long. Erosion of the adobe and some crude efforts at destruction have left vestiges in segments linked so as to provide portals at regular intervals. The wall is about three feet thick. A peaked roof, which looks like an afterthought, seems designed to prevent further erosion of the adobe. Additionally, there are windows penetrating the wall at regular intervals.

Beyond this great wall we walked into a vast area of ruined temples. Twelve of them are arranged in two rows of six, everything perfectly aligned. In Inka times, after a ruler had died, the next Inka was chosen from among the twelve royal families. The selection process began with each family's candidate occupying and literally taking energetic control of their temple. We would imitate this entirely metaphysical process.

We walked the length of the central avenue, each of us gradually moving into a temple. I had my eye on the one at the far end, on my right hand. All these temples are large, really large, the size of two generous houses, and they are divided in half by a high central wall containing six niches on each side. In spite of the advanced state of decay there are sufficient remnants to visualize each structure. It seemed to me they must have had peaked roofs.

Our task here was not simply to occupy our temple but to take charge of its energies. In other words, encompass the whole thing with one's personal bubble, your aura. You stand in one half but you have to take psychic control of both halves.

To do this you open your energy bubble and gradually expand it until you cover the allotted real estate, that's all. Nothing could be simpler! (Joke.) Our daily round of rituals had amounted to a carefully-designed program meant to train us to do just that.

From healthy doubt I went to confidence as I discovered there was no problem in expanding my bubble to encompass both halves of the temple. Take a few deep breaths, close the eyes in order to see your bubble, then slowly puff it up with steady exhaling and deep concentration. Then open the eyes and direct the bubble to reach out, expand, crawl over walls, and gradually swallow the whole structure. I held my bubble steady, appreciating with delight its size and vibratory power as it settled around the adobe walls of My Temple. I did indeed surround the structure.

Finally, we began a procession back to the center, each of us pulling the energy of her/his temple, towing it like a wagonload of power. We met in the center to consolidate the experience. Then we strolled back to the towering wall for the next step.

We formed two parallel lines of seven each (counting our two mentors), my roommate Susanne opposite me. Then we began to weave energy, facing one another at the windows to exchange qosqo energy. After each window we crossed through the next portal, so that we changed sides of the wall. As Susanne and I faced one another, opening our qosqos, meditating a good moment, then crisscrossing, I realized we were weaving a pattern like human DNA. And because one side of the wall symbolized gold and the other side silver, we were also weaving metallic strands of energy. One is continually astounded by the power of the Inka vision.

Farther on we paused at a set of five fountains gushing three and two in an "L" shape. These were spouts emerging from a waist-high wall bordering a field. After connecting, we splashed some of the water on our faces and little touches down the body. This was a purification ritual before moving into the temple of the culminating ceremony.

Once again, almost all of this site was in ruins, with only the stones outlining the foundations still in place. There were two squares and two circles of stone on the ground, arranged in another "L", all enclosed in a larger rectangle. We women were to choose two of our number and the men were to do the same, selecting priests and priestesses for the final empowerment. The men chose the red-haired Peder and Henrik, and the women turned to me and then to Susanne. The male squares were closest, so Peder occupied the first one. Henrik went to him for the ritual laying-on of hands, then he took possession of the second square. Susanne and I followed, receiving the exchange of personal power from Peder and Henrik in succession. She went first, then entered the first circle, giving me the power before I took my place in the last circle.

One by one our companions came to Peder, to Henrik, to Susanne, and then to me for the ritual consecration, a true laying-on of hands. I placed my medicine bag/mesa at my feet and prayed to Great Spirit for the strength to do this well. Initiates came to me last, and after each one I requested a renewal of the energy flowing through me. It was a source of both pride and humility to be giving the final infusion of energy to each of my friends. And it flowed. Henrik is the greatest conduit of the group, and he trembled, vibrating visibly. So did Anita. I rested my hands on their heads for a long moment, until I sensed it was enough, then rested my palms an instant on their shoulders, then swiped slowly down the upper arms, and off.

After the last one I picked up my mesa and joined the group surrounding our pile of mesas. Juan asked Torben to crown us with "old energy" from his mesa, then Margit crowned us with a bag of new energy. As a final touch Juan presented the contents of this bag of new energy — tiles inspired by Don Benito — and Ivan distributed them. And it was over.

Back in the village we found a mob of kids lined up at the bus door, for it was known we had brought gifts of school material. My fifty pencils went out one at a time, Juan controlling the line in front of me. Kirsten gave ballpoint pens. Others gave pads of paper, pencil sharpeners, erasers and the like. This village is not on the touristic circuit, it is very poor, and Juan's groups are almost the only foreigners who come through.

We picnicked about a kilometer out of the village, on the grass under a spreading tree, gobbling the hotel's box lunches and our own private snack supplies. Surplus food, and there was some, was given to roadside stragglers, mostly kids.

Our gala farewell dinner was across the street from our hotel in a very touristy restaurant, with all the personnel in Inka costume, a native singer, and a harpist. Susanne made a nice speech in English (for Juan and me), then presented Henrik with our joint gift for his fortieth birthday — an Inkan cross which he had coveted. I circulated a plate of Peruvian turquoises which I had found in a cubbyhole stone-and-silver shop in Procuradores street. Very tired, wiped out, I said goodnight early and went up to bed. All of us had packing to do, for tomorrow was departure day.

My Danes had to leave at six-thirty to get to the airport, so I arose with Susanne and went down to say goodbye to my Viking family. Embraces and tears all around, an emptiness as I waved them around the corner. Hatun Karpay was finished, but for me Peru was not.

[1]   Unfortunately this series is no longer available on <www.medicinegarden.com>, which has suffered server crashes and important mutations over the years.

[2]   Elizabeth B. Jenkins, INITIATION, a Woman's Spiritual Adventure in the Heart of the Andes. New York: Penguin Putnam Berkley, 1997. 273p. ISBN 0-425-16476-4.

[3]   This was my introduction to the mountain spirits, called Apus, with whom we would learn to work under Juan's direction. The Apus are the peaks, the upper mass, and they bear human names, such as Apu Mama Simona or Apu Don Manuel Pinta.

[4]   Such improvisations do work — it is once again a matter of the convention between dowser and instrument, calibrations being adjusted within the meditational state.

[5]   For Andean initiates, a "mesa" is a square package containing power objects wrapped in a woven manta. This corresponds to the native American medicine bag or bundle. My own medicine bag became converted to a mesa, using one of the mantas I had bought from the Q'eros. All of our group began to create their own mesas.

[6]   Jenkins, Initiation, p. 119.

[7]   Ibid., pp. 129-130.

[8]   Soul Recovery and Extraction, p. 34.

[9]   To the outsider this may seem a bit mysterious. Lonely Planet tells us that "About 45% of Peru's population is Indian (*indigenas* is an appropriate term; *indios* is insulting.) Most are Quechua-speaking and are mainly found in the highlands......About 37% is mestizo (mixed blood), 15% is white and the remaining 3% is black, Asian or other groups." (Lonely Planet, Peru, p.36. 4th ed., 2000. ISBN 0-86442-710-7.) One has to be Peruvian to understand the subtleties of discrimination when 85% of the population are varieties of non-white. Lima excepted, it was my impression to be swimming in a sea of humanity ranging from beige to red-brown in color. This was certainly true in Cusco, where the majority of people with whom we dealt were various shades of tan.

Chapter Thirty-Six

ANDES and FJORDS

Apu Pikola loomed green and seemingly climbable from my bedroom window in Larapa. She hypnotized me as I studied a possible itinerary, skirting the scar of a old landside and a weak flank that looked equally capable of slipping away. Doris occupied a double apartment in a relatively modern building in this southern suburb of Cusco, and she had prepared a nice room for me. The picture window received morning sun, the bed was comfortable and warm enough, there was a tiny closet, and there was a bathroom directly across the hall.

After my Danes departed, I'd wandered at midday over to her cubbyhole boutique/office in Teqsecocha street, between the top of Procuradores and the little pizzeria which served nice trout. In mid-afternoon we took one of the inexpensive taxis which circle the Plaza des Armas, stopping to collect my luggage from the hotel and then following the highway in the direction of the airport, Tipon and Raqchi. Doris instructed the cabbie to turn off after the big gasoline station and a new university called the Andina, and we bumped uphill, then turned into a wide lane built on one side with recently constructed two-storey dwellings. Once off the main road the streets were unpaved and did not seem to have names. Later I learned they had numbers, but these were not posted anywhere, the system remaining impenetrable to my northern mind.

Thus began the last segment of my trip to Peru, a nine-day extension as the houseguest of my soul sister. This sojourn had nothing to do with Hatun Karpay. It was mostly "hanging out", with private ceremony mixed in occasionally. We were a big household in two apartments whose doors faced one another across the top of the stairs. On one side there were two bedrooms for Doris's daughters and above them her own little penthouse bedroom. The other side was home to the ritual room, sometimes very busy, and two bedrooms: mine, and that of Indra, a young European who had been knocking about Latin America for a dozen years, eking out a living giving massages and doing ear-candling. She aspired to become a yoga teacher. We got along quite well.

These apartments were well-built, relatively new, fairly modern, with nice big windows both front and back. In common with many houses in that part of the world, they had no central heating and no hot water. What did people do to keep warm in June-July-August, when Cusco's mornings could freeze and snow was not unheard-of? They dressed warmly, that seemed to be the answer. And because late April in Cusco can be compared to late October in Europe, I was already happy in the antique poncho Doris had found for me when I said "please get me one like that". Ponchos, pullovers and mantas were part of her boutique offerings. Earlier I'd bought another, bigger and warmer, in one of the bazaars, and most nights I piled both of them atop the bed which already had a pair of blankets.

We boiled water continually, for the cold water that flows through Cusco's pipes is not to be trusted. Every kitchen operation required a supply of sterile water, so there was nearly always a big pot simmering on a gas burner. We did wash and shower with that contaminated water — that's what soap is for — but I used bottled water to brush my teeth. Taking a shower was possible, with care.

I said there was no hot water, but that is not quite correct. There was indeed hot water in Doris' shower, via a crazy contraption with an industrial switch on the wall and the need to exercise exquisite care to avoid electrocution. We all used it, we all survived. Yes, I got a shock the first time, never again. Pain is a great teacher.

For me such details were irrelevant. This was a valuable time of cooling out after one of the most intense metaphysical experiences of my life. Spirit needed and wanted it this way. Separating from both Peru and my Danish family at the same moment would have been too much at once. Staying in Cusco a while, in the company of spiritual friends, allowed winding down in a harmonious way.

The center of the city was easily accessible by taxi and minibus, and I went there almost daily, sometimes with Doris, sometimes alone. There was a lot of personal business to handle, which took me daily to one or another of the cybercafés to spend an hour writing e-mail. Internet access shops abounded, were very popular with the younger cusquenos, and had the virtue of being cheap for we northerners. Several times I went to the sprawling public market, learning to haggle in my flimsy Spanish for fresh vegetables for our household. Herbal teas from the jungle and from the high mountains were widely available. Doris gave me a little list of ritual items we needed, which is how I found the shop selling dried foetus's and other animal parts.

Just being in Cusco felt good, satisfying a deep soul need. One midday I simply sat in the Plaza de Armas, wrapped in my poncho, listening to water splashing in the big central fountain, feeling the sun on one side of my face and the first autumn breeze on the other.

Hatun Karpay had augmented my personal power, my healing power. Subtle transformation had occurred. This was not something I could see in the mirror or feel in my body. It was something I could know only through the reactions of the people around me, including a handful of healing patients. In Peru I did a lot of energy healing, first for my Viking colleagues, later for Doris and some of her friends. These treatments were powerful, and I am cautious about letting ego into this statement.

The other Doris, the clairvoyant coca leaf reader, came to the apartment to give me a second reading, but before she worked on me I worked on her. She needed a lot, and a lot of energy came through for her. Four of her chakras were flat, and I used stones to magnify the charge I transmitted. She was an ideal patient, feeling everything and able to describe it. She received as heat what flowed through my hands at every level up to and including one foot above the body. With her clairvoyance she could see the energies flaring around me. What she described blew my mind, for the silvery light and flashing energy weren't just limited to my hands, as I had always thought. They were all around me.

Doris and her eldest daughter Debora were feeling unwell and I did some massaging and light energy work. The second day they decided a sorceror had attacked them, motivated by a dispute over a property in the Sacred Valley. They found their inner way to quick recovery once the problem was diagnosed. Don't ask me how.

We had planned to take a quickie trip together, but a group of clients with cash made a date for Doris' services. We chatted away the evening while she carefully carved up a big San Pedro cactus to make the "big drink". *Trichocereus pachanol* is the Latin name, and it is reputed to contain up to two per cent of mescaline. That's the same alkaloid contained in peyote, the hallucogenic mushroom that grows on another cactus. Ayahuasca, the Brazilian vine, relies upon a different set of alkaloids to produce its colorful visions and dreams. Peeled and sliced, Doris's cactus cooked for hours and hours to produce a bilious green soup. With it she did a San Pedro "cure" for a young German man who didn't like me. He seemed almost afraid, looked at me wall-eyed as if hallucinating (which is, of course, a reason for the green drink). Perhaps he saw the red Indian chief some clairvoyants had seen, or the Inca and the Maya the two Dorises had seen with the aid of coca leaves.

Then one day came my turn for what Doris called the "green Mass". Three young people from Lima would be arriving the next day. More cactus had to be sliced up and cooked. In honor of these occasions I baptized the ritual room "Catedral San Pedro".

"Huachuma", which is the indigenous name for San Pedro, acted very slowly on me. Several glasses of the vile stuff went down the hatch over a period of hours. Doris and Indra surrounded me with music, massage, aromas, jokes. They were expecting me, almost eagerly it seemed, to vomit like most people do. That didn't happen. I tried to explain that my inner body had unusual resistance: sleeping pills didn't work, marijuana did nothing for me, and alcohol was a waste of time. I would get bored and tired long before getting drunk, with the result that my hard-drinking postwar generation expected me to put the rest of them to bed after a big party.

Some power objects from my medicine bag, piled on the little altar, began to wiggle and to take on life. Since, for me, they *were* alive, it was fitting to see them finally move without human intervention. The anticipated hallucogenic "high" came slowly. One could compare it to drunkenness without the staggering, wobbling or slurring of speech. It was mostly visual. In the mid-afternoon Doris, getting bored with waiting for me to produce a lot of exciting visions, proposed a walk up the hill toward Apu Pikola. Feet and legs moved well and I began to enjoy how colors seemed heightened as we strolled upslope, on trails skirting cornfields and bordered by bushes and eucalyptus-like trees. My hands, fingers, feet and toes tingled in a prickly way, symptoms which I observed but did not find disagreeable.

Our little hike was a fuzzy, shimmering affair. Colors became very intense: each tree leaf was showing me its aura. Huachuma brought me no big hallucogenic reaction, no powerful insights. In the end, lying on a bank in the late afternoon sun, my emotions overflowed into slowly trickling tears. And that was it for me. Back in the apartment I "normalized" over a supper of Indra's rice topped with my ratatouille.

For the next days before my departure Doris gave me a small glass of diluted San Pedro every morning. It might as well have been a vitamin cocktail, for I felt energetic and in a very pleasant mood.

While Doris worked with her Peruvian clients I did a major healing on Indra, who had suffered surgical damage in infancy and who had taken a lot of falls on her coccyx. This called for my full bag of tricks: massage, crystals, and channeling energy into the chakras and the aura. She was purring by the time I finished. It was appropriate to thank Great Spirit and our Guides, and I did, fervently. We went into town together to do e-mail and a spot of food shopping, and when we returned to Larapa it was time to prepare supper for Doris and her three clients. She had worked ten hours with them and they were very happy with their trips.

My pleasant sojourn in Peru was coming to an end. The next morning was time to pack my two valises and my backpack, then I had time to wander through the neighborhood and make some photographs. Doris and Indra were both in Cusco, and soon after they returned I received Maria for a healing. She was a friend of Doris' and I had given her a "first-aid" treatment the evening the other Doris had come.

Once again I had to "pull out all the stops", for this lady had problems that I did not like. There was clearly inflammation in the lower right abdomen, and her right kidney was tender when touched. She'd already had kidney stones once. She liked my treatment, saying I had pulled long strings of pain out of her right side. Regardless, suspicious of appendicitis and more kidney problems, I urged her to see a doctor without delay. Later I told Doris of my concern and asked her to push Maria toward a good internist.

That evening we three went into the city for dinner. Guinea pig, called "cuy", is something of a traditional meal for Andeans, and I wanted to try it. It had to be ordered ahead, and this Doris had done. It was nice meat, similar to rabbit but smaller and sweeter. I would eat it again with pleasure.

At my bedtime Doris and Indra sat long with me. This was our last real talk, for my taxi for the airport would arrive early in the morning. Indra did some Reiki on my chakras to prepare me for travel. Doris evoked the contrast between our lives, invoking the polar opposites of permanence and impermanence. Permanence, she said, was the essence of my well-organized Swiss life, whereas impermanence was the essence of her volatile, disorganized, madcap lifestyle. She complimented me on dealing well with impermanence. In return I reminded her that she had said in the beginning that we were opposites, whereas I maintained that we were complementary. Being together in this sisterly fashion made us both whole.

Flight time the next morning was before eight o'clock, meaning that at Lima I had much of the day to kill before the evening flight back to Amsterdam. After checking my baggage for the day with the help of a pair of taxi shills, I allowed their driver Carlos to take me into Miraflores, Lima's upscale quarter. After some time on the internet I took another cab down to Costa Verde on the beach. They served wonderful food at high prices. Doris had proposed it and I recognized quickly she was having fun with me, sending me to one of the most expensive places. No matter, this meal was restorative as well as delicious.

When first contemplating this trip I had been apprehensive about how I would manage to eat properly for my body's peculiar needs. It isn't easy to live with, simultaneously, lacto-intolerance, gluten-allergy, hypoglycemia, a body that does best on food "combining" and prefers to be fed according to its blood group, and a clutch of allergies ranging from sulfites and MSG to penicillin and most other antibiotics. However, I managed. Of all the foodstuffs I packed into my luggage only three proved useful: Scottish oat biscuits, Turkish dried apricots, and thin slices of dried beef vacuum-packed by my Swiss butcher. While prowling Cusco with my Danes it had been possible for me to eat tasty and digestible food in a variety of restaurants large and small, humble and upscale. Juan's choice of hotels and restaurants had been easy on me, and now so was Doris' little joke on the beach.

After finishing the afternoon on the internet in Miraflores, I took a position on the sidewalk on the Diagonal opposite the Parque Central. Carlos had agreed to pick me up for the trip to the airport, and at the appointed hour there he was. My flight left on time. Four hours later it landed on the dry-looking isle of Aruba to collect Netherlanders finishing their vacations, and we touched down at Amsterdam/Schipol late the next afternoon. Florence, one of the regulars on the Medicine Garden, had proposed an acupressure/shiatsu routine to ease the jet lag transition. I tried this and it worked! The system she gave me is: as the plane begins its descent, about ten to fifteen minutes before touchdown, massage your left earlobe with fingers of the left hand while finding and massaging a meridian point under the left breast with a finger of the right hand. There is a tender spot along the line of the crease, and that's it.

This little routine produced the easiest eastbound resetting of the body clock I had ever experienced.

A major planetary alignment hovered over this day, and it certainly brought me minor chaos. Stupidity at check-in almost caused me to miss my flight to Geneva, and once there they had lost one of my bags. This was day three, and it got me home in mid-afternoon. The missing bag arrived shortly before midnight. Three days from Cusco to my alpine lair, and it's almost impossible to shave that.

Re-entry was bumpy after four weeks of absence, all the more so because I was no longer the same person. Spirit, still in Peru, balked at the mountains of routine "catchup" facing me. On the third morning home meditation brought me a message: "send healing to Doris". I asked Spirit and my Guides to confirm via my hands, which immediately filled with emphatically strong power. Which I transmitted, of course. Healing power seemed to have magnified. I dreamed of preparing despachos. I started e-mailing my Danes. One of my clients has a bad ankle, reminiscent of Kirsten's problem. I had worked on his ankle previously but this time there seemed to be much more power transiting through my hands and he felt much better. Michael called to say they had found the boys' bodies in a gulley which had been under ten feet of snow -- at a spot marked on the map as swampy.

Messages from several directions advised that my sister-in-law Elise was failing and becoming comatose in a nursing home. With an architect I worked on a little plan to open a dark corner with a pair of windows. One of my neighbors died too young. With my hair stylist we discussed new ways to handle my hair now, because in Cusco I unpinned the perennial "French twist" and let the tresses fall to my shoulders. Everyone here liked it. Much gardening demanded my attention, as did my finances. The computer received the visit of a technician. The following lines from my journal, written two weeks after my return, tell truth:

"Not much of this interests me deeply, although furnishing and remodeling do have creative appeal. What really interests me intensely is spiritual work: expanding my healing practice, doing more Hatun Karpay, being in Peru again, seeing my Peruvians, seeing my Danish family again."

And that is what happened in the next few months. Violette invited me to her alpine balcony deep in the Valais, from whence we did several days of wonderful hiking. Several Danes spoke of coming to visit but only Torben, and later Susanne actually did so. Torben's train was at Aigle three hours after my return from Jeizinen. We hiked several days, spent hours and hours talking about Peru and our spiritual worlds. Both of us wanted to return to Peru. He wanted to work more with Doris. He and Randi had absorbed San Pedro in an all-night session just before leaving Cusco, and he felt like the resulting inner work was incomplete. With Juan I had dreamed up the notion of taking a Swiss group to Peru, but over and above any such program I felt a deep need to spend more time at Machu Picchu.

A month later it was my turn to be in Denmark, for the group decided to hold a reunion at the beginning of September and one week later Juan would be giving a seminar. Kirsten's home outside Aarhus managed to squeeze us all in for nearly forty-eight hours of being together. It was a joyous time, for everyone managed to come, and our hugs were strong and affectionate. Our weekend began on a Friday night and after a communal supper we did Inkan ceremony in the garden. This brought me a vision of six priests in skin robes; they carried poles topped with antlers, advancing toward us. We took a field trip the next day, doing ritual on a series of sacred sites along the eastern Jutland shore. At home we made a despacho and burned it in the garden. On Sunday morning we strolled through a drizzle, consciously taking in hucha and disposing of it, then sucking the negative energy from a standing stone. and we worked as a group to clear it. We closed our happy weekend with a group meditation.

That evening I worked long and lovingly on Kirsten's ankle, which still pained her and was freshly swollen. A salve rich with yarrow helped remove the pain. After a light, brief massage I placed stones on the major chakras and went into "off the body" mode, for a lot of energy was channeling for her. She felt everything, saw colors, felt the energy flow, experienced waves of release, and she felt the Guides the moment I asked them to move in. It is deeply satisfying to be able to perform such work.

My tour of Denmark began the next day by exploring Aarhus while Kirsten went to her high-tech job. This little city's energy vitalized me. The streets bustled with activity, the shopkeepers were kind to a foreigner, and it was unusually easy to find wearables that look good on me. I took an afternoon train to Silkeborg, where Randi met me at the station. We had a gay, happy time, shopping for our supper, preparing it together, laughing a lot (including snakes on the jungle trail), exchanging confidences. Kirsten arrived at ten-thirty, after a workshop, to collect me for the trip home. First though, she had to treat Randi's cat. Animals of all sizes talk to her, tell her what ails them, and she helps them heal.

Kirsten worked on me the next morning. Her methods resemble mine, but the sequence differs. I felt movement in my aura with the first pass of her hands. This grew into an intense experience, ultimately very emotional for me. She used vials of floral and gem essences as well as stones on certain chakras. After a full quarter-hour she began to sense the presence of my father, who manifested as a spark of bright light. This was totally unexpected and she didn't know that we had been estranged at the time of his untimely death. All this time energy was circulating in a refined, subtle flow. That spark of my father was radiating good humour and forgiveness, she said.

But before he arrived she saw me as a tall native American medicine man wearing the usual feather bonnet. This keeps coming up! She saw that he/me was at the end of life, standing on a promontory with a vast view over our country, and I was there to die quietly, peacefully. People came to collect my body and prepare it for its final voyage. They put my corpse in a canoe filled with flowers, then placed it in a river. My spirit canoe sailed downstream until it was seized by a whirlpool and sucked into the depths.

I didn't want this treatment to end, so much was coming out, so much was breaking up. Few therapists have worked on me in a spiritual way, and none had ever brought me as much as had Kirsten.

That afternoon she put me on the train for Holstebro, where Torben and his four-year-old met me at the station. His own Kirsten was very welcoming and soon we were developing a sunny friendship. The next morning Torben commanded that we meditate together, so we sat in a triangle for twenty minutes. My father came into consciousness and we worked on this light-hearted reconciliation that Kirsten had engineered. Then they took me out to a nature reserve called Sir Lungbjorg. It's a park, a forest, and one climbs the observation tower atop a peaklet — one of the Danish "Alps" perhaps one hundred feet high. The September air was fresh but drizzly, filling the forest lanes and glades with the scent of pine.

Kirsten left us to meet with clients, leaving Torben to drive me out to the west coast. The North Sea rumbles and chews along the endless beaches, having eaten away more than fifty yards of coastline since the end of World War Two. German blockhouses that once sat on bluffs have fallen into the sea, forlorn lumps of concrete lapped by the fringes of curling surf. We hiked long up the beach in the bracing sea breeze, then back following the crest of the rolling dunes. Sea grass, wild cereals, carpets of moss and lichen, and lilac-purple heather cover the ups and downs of this sandy wonderland. The big red Huben berries, bigger than cherry tomatoes, are rich in vitamin C and very edible. We drove north, then turned inland along a fjord, a vast complex of lagoons and canals leading ultimately to the town of Struer. At the Marine Club Torben and I wolfed down a copious seafood platter, washed down with a very nice Alsatian Pinot Gris.

Imagine my surprise when, the next morning, Kirsten pulled out the report of a geobiologist, at base a geologist, who had surveyed their home for earth energies. He'd dowsed and drawn the Hartmann, Curry and underground water lines, and it was a shocker. I could not turn my back on the mess he had outlined, but my only tools on this trip were my hands and a pendulum with Bovis biometer. Packing for this trip had been done in catastrophic haste, following three days of hiking in Italy. All my dowsing gear was at home. I could not totally verify the crowding of force lines the man had sketched, but I could not deny that there was heavy affliction here and there. The energies coming through my hands confirmed there was a lot going on, and the occasional pain in my left hand suggested it was heavy. The pendulum registered several points of very low vibration. The girls, Christina and Michaela, had to contort themselves in their beds in search of relative sleeping comfort. My gut reaction was "build a new house!"

Torben had reserved me a window seat on the afternoon train to Copenhagen. It was a peaceful, scenic four-hour ride down the length of Jutland and then across country and a long bridge to Zealand. My delightful Peru room-mate, the long-haired blonde Susanne, met me at the station for the short walk to her flat in an old building right in the center. She began to treat me like a queen, spoiling me in a dozen little ways, and I had to remind her that my physical decline was not yet on the horizon.

We had only two days together, Friday and Saturday. The first one we spent walking all over Copenhagen: shopping, crosstown to her studio, then bussing back to ramble through the great Fredericksborg Park. Like most art teachers, Susanne is also a working artist. With a group of other painters she shared a long attic space in a big building. It was fascinating to see that her method focused on trying to paint energy, like Marilyn in Sedona but more abstract. Two different styles but similar inner dynamics. Susanne worked in primary colors, blending them into large swaths of warm oranges and summery light greens. The Park, however, was a cool palette: all green lawns punctuating groves of tall, dark trees. She led me to a place where she did ritual and immediately I felt the warmth. She'd instinctively found a telluric hot spot. Imbued with our recent Peruvian work, we opened our "bubbles" so as to separate the energies flowing into our qosqos. We sent the hucha down to Pachamama and the sami upward, reaching out with our qosqos to a distant tree. Before leaving our hot spot we raised an energy column to cover the entire park, a powerful experience.

The next morning her friend John straightened me out on a bit of Danish history affecting my family. My favorite grandmother's[1] own grandparents had emigrated in 1848 -- a time of insurrection and revolution over much of Europe -- from what we assumed was northern Germany. Thus we'd thought they were German. No, John corrected me, their native Schleswig-Holstein was Danish for seven centuries before Bismarck conquered it for Germany. My great-great-grandparents had fled to Wisconsin during the first of two German-Danish wars, and they had fled from Denmark, not Germany.

"What was the family name?" John asked.

"Abel," I replied, spelling it out.

"That's Danish," he clarified. "If they were German it would have been spelled Ebel."

No wonder I felt so happy and at home with my Danes! Thinking back to a favorite photoportrait of my grandmother I suddenly saw "Dane" written all over her face.

"You look Danish and you have a Danish mentality," Susanne pointed out.

Annette picked us up for the drive to Roskilde and then onward. At Roskilde we discharged my luggage and took aboard Jeanett, who would be my next hostess. We drove through the rolling green countryside northward to an Iron Age experimental center called Lerje. Deep inside this rural complex was a village of huts where families tried out primitive living during their vacations. They went about their daily lives in the rough, drab clothing of the time while we tourists gawked from behind a fence.

We drifted past the village to a dirty pond identified as a "sacrifical bog", allowing thoughts of body-sucking mud to pass through our minds. Wiraqocha rewarded our search by leading us to a tiny clearing on the shore of a lake. My companions had assembled the necessary big square of paper and a large variety of small things: leaves, flowers, tiny sweets, shells and small edibles. They asked me to create the despacho, a real honor. When it was finished and tied I used it as a mesa to sweep their bodies, in the same way that native American ritual smudges participants with sage. Susanne swept me, then I leaned far out over the water and set our message sailing. It was time for our picnic on a hilltop in the gentle September sun.

Back in Roskilde we made a meditation circle in the garden, and there was lots of metaphysical talk over supper, after which Annette and Susanne drove back to the city.

Sunday was sunny and a bit breezy, cumuli riding the airways. Roskilde lies at the head of a long, narrow fjord whose twists and turns had helped the city defend itself against medieval invaders. These Danish fjords are not walled by big mountain masses as in Norway, they echo the country's flatness and one can stroll along their shores. As we rambled beside the waters Jeanett reminded me of an event in Cusco that I had forgotten, even failed to note in my journal. In the hotel lobby she had seen a huge Inkan standing behind the sofa. Without actually seeing him, I had gone over and outlined his energy. Juan and Torben were there. Juan said the Inka wanted to pass through Jeanett's bubble. After she permitted that, the Inka became normal size, and she feels his presence whenever she asks him to be there.

Juan came to Europe twice a year to give seminars. What he called "Level II" of Inkan energy work was to be held at a summer hotel on a finger of land pointing into the Samso Baelt which separates the peninsula of Jylland (Jutland) from the big island of Sjaelland (Zealand)[2].

Jeanett put me on the train to Hoje Taestrup, where I finally found the bus to that finger of land. The grumpy driver hadn't liked the fact I could not speak enough Danish to understand the fare he demanded, and he was in no mood to drop me at Willemoes. It wasn't a regular stop, and we zoomed straight on quite a few miles more to the ferry terminal at Sjaelland's Odde. Ultimately I was able to negotiate a taxi to come out from Willemoes and take me there. Our seminar was lodged in a simple gray one-storey wooden hotel. When I stepped out of my cab and into the courtyard the first person I saw was Juan, reading at a picnic table next to the main door. This was a joyful meeting and we had a couple of private conversations during the next few days, for we had rooms across the hall from one another. Our hotel had some conference rooms, a kitchen, and a lot of small bedrooms not much bigger than third-class staterooms on a ship.

Our seminar started that evening with a three-hour session, built around powerful sami-hucha-ayni exercises. This was review for me but new for most of the participants that Anita and Jens Peter had gathered. Few of the thirty-three seminar participants had taken the Hatun Karpay with Juan. Thus the next two days were full of concepts with which I was already familiar, spiced by exercises new to me. Dividing us into three groups, he spent most of the first day on the energy belts which circle the body. We had received this initiation-ritual one evening in Cusco; this time I had abundant time to observe, comprehend, take notes, and learn.

There was an unexpected gift for me: a new friend, another Susanne. She was brunette instead of blonde, a dowser, a shaman, in appearance could be the daughter of one of my Guides who I "see" daily, and she also created amazing, beautiful jewelry. Susanne and I found ourselves working together regularly, by choice. This friendship blossomed quickly; it is hindered by geography, but it does not dissolve with distance.

The next day he had us working with the concepts of birth, death, and play. This day we dealt with birth by repeating the Serpent Cave ritual our Peruvian group had done after Illia Pata. Exiting life recapitulated the ritual at Tambo Machay: raise sami, release fear, die, perceive life after death. For play, Juan unleased his sense of fun. He designed a spiral ritual, a dance, executed with the attitude of children at play. We formed a complex pattern of four lines radiating like arms from a hub. First we spiraled to the right, clockwise, to mounting hilarity as the end people spun off involuntarily. Then we reformed and spiraled to the left, which broke down much faster, with even greater gales of laughter. Back in the classroom Juan explained that this exercise showed it was easiest to go with the flow. Spinning clockwise we were rotating with the earth, with Pachamama; spinning counter-clockwise we were trying to "break the wave", which doesn't work.

His amused grin when I raised my hand prompted me to exclaim "you're reading my mind!" Benignly, he urged me to go on. I pointed out that these polarity differences would be reversed in Peru, in the southern hemisphere -- "in the toilet bowl too!" More hilarity.

Before the final ritual Juan closed his teaching by explaining that geographic scope determines our level as teachers of Andean energy work. *Paqos* of one valley work at the first level, those covering several valleys occupy the second level, while teaching an entire region classifies the *paqo* as third level. Foreigners like ourselves who had taken the Hatun Karpay initiation worked at the fourth level because we had the capacity to span the religions of the world. We could find the transcendance in each, tolerate them all, and teach the Inka path everywhere. We could function all over the world, in any tradition, transcending the limitations of any religion. We could find the sami in a cathedral, in a synagogue, a mosque, a Buddhist temple, anywhere. He'd made this point in Peru, now he reinforced it.

To close, we formed a large circle in the yard. With our arms we raised a *saiwa*, an energy column twenty meters high, each of us directing the top of our personal column to a target of our choice. I directed my power as a long, arcing arrow aimed at a friend at home, Hella, slowly dying of cancer. Then we brought it all down so that our energy bubbles joined and mingled.

There was an hour of goodbyes, packing our bags, people leaving, lots of hugs and picture-taking. Anita drove me to the ferry terminal at Sjaelland's Odde, and soon I was crossing the waters where the Samso Baelt meets the Kattegat. Kirsten was at the port of Aarhus to meet me, took me to her home and fed me a wonderful hamburger from Scottish red cattle. The next morning I gave her ankle another long treatment. It was still far from fully flexible, even though progress had been made, and I could understand that pain returned. I put generous portions of the yarrow and other salves which had helped into little pots and left them for her continuing use. At midday we were off for the long drive to the airport north of the city, and that evening I was home.

Returning to Peru became a dominant preoccupation as soon as my bags were unpacked. My target date was April 2001, only seven months away, but I was quite uncertain who would be with me. My effort to form a group from here seemed stalled; I would soon have to confirm our numbers to Juan, but it was not coming together. Meanwhile, California and Arizona were calling loudly. I had not been out there in three years. It looked as if those bags might be repacked in the near future.

1   See Chapter Thirteen
2   This is an over-simplification, but think of Denmark as a lopsided "U" filled with water.

Chapter Thirty-Seven

VIBRANT LIFE AND VIBRANT DEATH

It was fun to be in Sedona again, especially because some of my favorite people joined me there. On this third trip of the year I did not want a complicated itinerary. Arriving first in San Francisco, I spent a week in the north to enjoy the daily company of my small family -- daughter, son, granddaughter, and the nearest surviving cousin. There was time for lunch with close friends Joyce and Clark. Neil and I hiked the hills around Santa Rosa in the rain, hanging our umbrellas under a big oak to keep dry while we picnicked. In mid-November it was time to set out for the two-day trip to my Arizona heartland, with Carol sharing the driving and the anticipation.

Kay flew west to test the desert sands for once, in spite of her distinct preference for salt water. After a week together, Carol and I went to Phoenix where Kay was basking poolside. They'd never met, a good reason for passing thirty-six hours together before putting Carol on her homeward flight. Kay took over the room adjoining mine at the motel on the hill. One after the other, they received their baptisms in Red Rock energies.

My daughter and I headed straight for Bell Rock our first morning in Arizona. After picnicking on Grandmother Bell's aprons we walked completely around the mountain. I think Carol was already agog with the energies before we'd gotten very far on this circumnavigation. In the evening we went around to some of the book-and-psychic centers to observe another breed of energies: the two-leggeds. Book browsers and crystal shoppers roamed slowly through the aisles, while astrologers and clairvoyants seemed to be hanging around expectantly between appointments with tourists. All in all, a rich harvest, and we passed some amusing moments sparring verbally with several of the last category, trying to decide who was real and who was a charlatan.

Under the Airport Mesa we visited the principal vortex, whose energies were up and running. Carol was tuning in quickly to the power swirling around us, and on that day I did not need dowsing gear. My hands were prickling over every hot spot. We followed a long trail eastward and marveled at the southern panorama, which slowly expanded as we left behind the bulk of the Mesa.

Thanksgiving Day was sunny and bright blue, the temperatures soft and soothing. We spent the morning hiking to the end of Boynton Canyon, on the trail early and plunging ahead with buoyancy. The depths of the canyon offered staggering beauty in the morning light -- the reds were fully alive and vibrating.

Deep in the left fork we came to a clearing inhabited by cairns and little circles created from sticks and stones. There were a spiral wheel of yucca leaves, two portals marked by cairns, and a medicine circle. My pendulum indicated negative energies. Our guard was up, neither of us felt tempted to enter this weird area which smacked too much of sorcery and the wrong kind of witchcraft. We skirted the trap and continued on toward the headwall, encountering patches of old snow and the trail frozen hard in the shadiest places. On the way in we had not found a trail into the right fork, but coming out we spied a vaguely visible path that appeared to be a viable passage through the brush. We followed that for a while, finding a barrel cactus in permanent shade, rather an oddity. Time was marching on, and we were inscribed for a mid-afternoon sitting at Murphy's Grill. We abandoned the right fork in favor of showers and a change of clothes before dining. Carol insisted on turkey but I preferred salmon trout stuffed with crab. Both of us were pleased.

My painter friend Marilyn was not at home. She was in hospital, with a bad leukemia, receiving aggressive chemotherapy, and her immune system was consequently collapsing. Her close friend told me that survival seemed questionable. She said Marilyn had received my e-mail from Switzerland and was anxious to see me. Marilyn had told her all about the time I had contributed energy to her painting, she added. It was agreed I would call her at the hospital the next day. That night Carol and I experimented with asking questions of Spirit through the pendulum. We wrote out a lot of questions and Carol asked them aloud while I tuned to the other side to be an antenna for the answers. Most of our questions concerned ourselves, but there were a couple about Marilyn. The pendulum indicated clearly that her soul desired transition.

Marilyn's voice was strong on the telephone the next morning. So was her will, tempered with a hard dose of reality.

"Soul seems to want out," she said, and I could hear her smiling. "I'm ready to work on either side of the veil."

Emboldened by her composure, I told her about Spirit's answer through the pendulum. She thanked me for being frank and open. She was grateful for that interpretation.

"There was a kind of premonition while I was walking the streets of Paris in September," she confided. I remembered that she loved Paris and would go there whenever possible, even for a day or two.

We talked about the forward projects of the soul, and it was agreed I would go up to Flagstaff hospital for a visit after taking Carol to Phoenix airport.

Red Rock energy informed the next days. On a ledge halfway up Grandmother Bell we meditated to link her energies with the Airport vortex, clearly visible four miles northwest. Carol may have succeeded in this effort better than I did. Instead of the Airport vortex, my spirit sought to transfer some of Grandmother's power to Marilyn.

We tried to approach Cathedral Rock via the Loop road leading down into Oak Creek Canyon from the west. It became clear this would be a long challenging hike, hampered by thick brush before a steep climb into the saddle. Prudence dictated trying from the other side, and we had no time. The cathedral-like geology grew more spectacular with each passing minute as the late afternoon light continued to play through the red spectrum. My eyes picked out where the vortex should be: a heart shape of foliage topped by an eccentric nose of gray rock just under the saddle. Getting there moved up a notch on my mental agenda. We meditated briefly, focusing consciousness in the heart of the mass, and when we opened our eyes the sinking sun was painting everything deep red. Inner joy overflowed.

Relentlessly bluebird weather helped us walk a lot of this red land. One sunny morning we hiked up into the pine-studded Soldier Pass region, gaping at the huge smooth-walled sinkhole, admiring the seven descending pools. There were moments when the cliffs and spires seemed to vibrate visually, auras shimmering, other times when there was a green light where the red and ochre met. That afternoon we rambled through and over the domes and slabs in the Schnebly Hill area. On these excursions we always found a place to settle for meditation, someplace suggestive of connecting the energies of one site to another.

Relatively few of Sedona's tourists come to work with the terrestrial energies as we do. There are other worthy, even fascinating attractions, and so we visited the cliffhouse called Montezuma's Castle, the ruins of the Sinaguan pueblo of Tuzigoot, the old mining town of Jerome, the "Mexican village" collection of boutiques called Tlaquepaque, and several centers of arts and crafts. Soon after our arrival we lunched with Eileen, exchanging ideas, information and questions. Quiet joy filled my heart to observe that my daughter and my spiritual mentor got along so well. We joined Tom for lunch at our favorite Chinese restaurant, learning from him that Susan and her husband had moved to New Mexico. Marilyn's plight needed to be reported, but I had no luck finding Susan telephonically.

Ten days after arriving in Arizona, we drove south to link up with Kay. We found her in a resort hotel north of Phoenix, where she had organized enough space for the three of us for two nights. Number one on my touristic agenda for Phoenix was the famous Heard Museum. It is easy to lose yourself spiritually in this beautifully organized tour through the world of native American life, history, culture and arts. We spent five hours there, lunching in the patio and then going back for further immersion. We wandered on into Scottsdale and its art galleries, ultimately dining Japanese.

Carol needed to be at the Phoenix "Sky Harbor" in the late morning the next day, and we met that target. Jammed phone lines had complicated my efforts to reach Marilyn in her hospital room. On the interstate highway north there is a panoramic rest stop with telephone, and from there I finally got through. The person who answered said Marilyn was having a bad day, and then Marilyn came on, weakly. She said she really wanted to talk with me but.....and her voice trailed off. Kay, quite understanding, had accepted my idea to keep zooming directly up to Flagstaff and its Medical Center as long as we were already on the fast road, but the voice that took over the telephone suggested a postponement of my visit. I promised to call again in a day or two.

That afternoon we went to Bell Rock, climbing part of the way up Grandmother's layered aprons. Kay was enraptured by the colors and the overall grandeur. She began to understand the magnetism of the region. The next morning we met Tom for breakfast and he opened up a new album from his vast collection of photos. These are all about UFOs, extraterrestrials, and energies that register on photographic negatives but are invisible to the human eye. My friend from the east had trouble understanding why all this was not out in the open, widely publicized. She was incredulous, her scientific mind rebelling at the evidence. The waitresses had no such trouble. They all know Tom and his photos, and being people of the region, they are believers.

We went to the Airport Vortex in the afternoon. I led my friend into the notch between the two knobs. Few people go that way and we were undisturbed. There is some power on the knobs and a strong point about seventy-five yards out to the east, but my earlier work had demonstrated that the real vortex sweeps up the main draw to the saddle between the knobs. We meditated on a rock bench, allowing the vibrations to envelop us. They weave around one slowly. I felt it first in the fingers, then slowly they covered me, being most intense around the head. I had the floating impression of a spirit, vaporlike, then cloudlike, a kind of ectoplasm, passing in front of us. Colors kept moving through my cerevision field — no red or other deep tones but pastel golds, green, blue. Kay had a strong session. She felt the energy and talked about it afterward. She gave me a big hug — now she understood why I came to Sedona.

Eileen met us for lunch the next day. She had much enjoyed Carol, now she switched on her clairvoyance for Kay. Her manner became tough and direct, bringing my chum a wakeup call. She saw the mass of chronic darkness in Kay's bronchial region, then probed orally for the stress events that preceded a virus pneumonia of thirty-three years earlier. There was a long, powerful exchange, Eileen pushing Kay to be consequent with herself.

"If, as you say, you want to know your Guides, you have to meditate daily for at least twenty minutes. Otherwise they won't bother," she emphasized.

It was obvious she liked Kay, and in her forthright way she pushed my dear friend to "put up or shut up spiritually."

The two of us went to Boynton Canyon and I led my friend, who was not an alpinist, cautiously up the little climb over slippery sandstone to the ridge of the spire. The vibes were up there and we settled for a short meditation as the sun began to sink. I led her through "rooting" and a light breathing exercise, then we went "inside". The energies were soft and caressing. Kay felt her head open and the top lift off. In other words, her crown chakra opened on the first visit to this vortex.

The next morning, Sunday, she was up early and meditating alone on the edge of her bed, taking up Eileen's challenge. After breakfast we returned to the Airport Vortex, sitting opposite our previous site by about ten yards — and it was strong but less so than two days earlier. Kay's chakras did not respond this time.

At breakfast time I had called Marilyn, who sounded stronger and urged me to visit during the midday. So from the Airport Vortex we went straight to Flagstaff Medical Center. Before seeing Marilyn I was required to wash in a small intermediate chamber, then don gloves and a mask.

She brought forth smiles, although one look told me how far from health she had fallen. She was cheerful, positive, but suffering intermittent pain. She asked if my hands could bring her some relief. I'd been instructed not to touch her, because her immune system was all but destroyed. She pooh-poohed all that as ridiculous under the circumstances. When cramps hit her again in the pelvic region I did ask for energy for her, and it did come through. For about ten minutes I channeled healing energy through my gloved hands at the bottom of the abdomen. She felt the transmission as heat and it did dissolve the pain. She felt immediate relief; the cramps were gone. I became quite red in the face, went outside to do a little wash, and went right back in, regloved. Marilyn was free of pain for about twenty minutes, then it returned. (Discussing this later with Eileen, I expressed doubt about whether I should have worked. Eileen was lucid: "you gave her twenty minutes without pain, that's better than nothing.")

Marilyn felt much stronger than in midweek, thinking now that it could turn either way. Reciting the inventory of her ailing organs, she admitted there were "lots of parts to repair". The doctors planned to do a marrow biopsy to see if she was going into remission.

Kay had only one more day with me, and we used that to visit again the Boynton vortex, and later she had a session with one of the local clairvoyants.

Seated comfortably on a dead tree trunk on the little sandstone crest, my chum enjoyed another opening. This time the second and third chakras spun open, and she came out of our twenty-minute session smiling, happy, sensing her Guides were ready to manifest. For me, sitting nearby, it was simply nice vibes and nice colors. Working with the pendulum, I found Bovis rates of 16'500 to 18'500 in three spots on that crest.

Kay's airport shuttle left the next morning, and then I made two key phone calls. The first one was to my Soroptimist Club, gathered together for their Christmas party, and all excited to have my message. What none of us knew at the time was that Hella had transited a few hours earlier that day. My second call was to Marilyn, passing along the address for Susan that Tom had discovered. Marilyn was having a mediocre day and repeated the address to someone else who wrote it down. A few days later I called again and got a surprise. The hospital said she had been discharged the previous day!

Calling her home, I learned from her close friend that it wasn't quite like that. The doctors hadn't done that biopsy. Like a true Spiritual Warrior, Marilyn had taken matters into her own hands. She invited her closest friends and family into that hospital room, said goodbye, and then pulled out the life-sustaining tubes herself. The friend said it was "beautiful and moving". Marilyn faded away and crossed over in a matter of minutes.

That two dying people with whom I had worked in a spiritual way passed over in the space of three days could not leave me unmoved. No tears, but lots of remembering the strong moments with those two.

In our next luncheon together, alone this time, Eileen reminded me that fifty per cent of a shaman's work is with the dead and dying. "Get used to it," was the unspoken message.

We talked a lot about Peru, especially Machu Picchu and the power slab on Huayna Picchu, and how we were going to get there again. She had a project to gather a group of us, representing a spectrum of metaphysical talents, to spend time solving problems on Machu Picchu. I still had my notion of taking a Swiss group in the spring, although one by one my prospective participants were dropping out.

She was pleased, gave a "thumbs up", when I related Kay's progress after taking up the meditational challenge. We made a date for coffee at the little ranch in the canyon before my departure, which was getting close.

Well to the west of Sedona and Cottonwood lies a deep, wild cleft in the landscape named Sycamore Canyon. I'd heard about it but never been there. On my third visit to Arizona in 1997 I had the good fortune to meet Rhonda and Curt. Everyday life occupations aside, many people of the Red Rock region might be called "mystics of the land", with their own spiritual practices, their own private rituals. Rhonda and Curt were such, their special ceremony being a weekly meditation at a remote pass overlooking Sycamore Canyon.

Invited to join them, I had jumped at the chance on that earlier occasion and now accepted with enthusiasm when they repeated the invitation. Late in the afternoon I met them at a point on the highway leading up to Sedona. We hid my car behind tall bushes and began the rough ten-mile jeep ride over a desert track toward the distant hills. After half an hour the land began to rise gently and we took to our feet. Another half an hour of swinging through the knee-high brush brought us to the rock dome where my hosts had chosen to be married, with thirty witnesses.

This is a real power point. The Lecher confirmed it is on a ley, and the Bovis registered a vibratory rate of 12'000. Just above us rose the crest and its three short knobs of red sandstone, and it was with keen anticipation that I unlimbered the rest of my tools. There proved to be a compound crossing-point of the Hartmann and Curry grids on the middle one of our three knobs, as well as a ley passing through. Clambering up onto the highest of the knobs, we could see into the depths of the dusk-shrouded canyon. The Bovis read 17'000, and the Lecher told me our knob hosted both Moon/female and Sun/male force lines. This power point was both electric and magnetic, but it was not an earth chakra. It had enough going for it without that honor!

Curt beat on his drum, we smudged one another with white sage, then settled into a tight circle, chanting our way into this sunset meditation. Deeply connected to spirit, I was continually conscious of a sound like the rumble of distant thunder. The cloudy sky, however, held nothing remotely stormlike. Something plucked, with a tiny noise, at my collar. Twice something passed in front of me, but this was felt, not seen through my closed eyes. My companions remarked later on the heightened vibrational level of this joint meditation. Yes, the perpetual ringing in my ears had reached a much higher level of decibels.

We picked our way carefully downslope for the next half-hour in the dying light, avoiding bushes and stones with eyes dilated like cats. By the time we reached Curt's vehicle I was pulling the flashlight from my pocket. Back at their home higher on the apron of Mingus Mountain than my motel, Rhonda offered me a fresh look at her herbal preparations. Homeopath, therapist, counselor, she is an expert herbalist with a thriving business in essences and ointments. At the time she was working on a book, which has since appeared and provided me with many pleasurable and informative moments of research[1]. I opted for a handful of salves, and then we went to Murphy's for supper. At table they prevailed on me to give a mini-tutorial on the Bovis biometer, from Bovis through Simoneton to Merz, with a nod to the Hartmann and Curry networks.

There remained one challenge before leaving the Arizona sun for eastern blizzards: Cathedral Rocks. Carol and I had balked at the thicket-ridden approach from the west, learning later that there is a vortex on that side but across the creek. This time I went down Highway 179 from the "T" under the Sedona Post Office, for I wanted to climb up into the rocks. Well before Bell Rock there is a turnoff to the right which leads to a parking area. From there I hiked half a mile to the base and then clambered several hundred feet up the smooth sandstone until I was in the saddle between the spires. As I climbed my hands began to tingle about one hundred feet below the saddle, suggesting the thrill of an energy adventure.

And yes, it glows up there! The early afternoon light turned the rocks into a magical garden of red stone. My journal says "awesome, an exultation, an exaltation!" Alone up there for a long time, I felt a huge, expanding joy. It is *the* power point, without question. Before sitting to meditate I took Bovis readings. The pendulum gave me 28,000 for the gray pyramid we had seen from below, but along the saddle itself it spiraled at 43,000 in two places and then 48,000 on the northwest end of the ledge, where the path narrows to nothingness.

Here I chose to meditate. My watch said it was only a handful of minutes, but there was a sensation of expanded time. This gave me a wolfish appetite, and fortunately there was a picnic in my pack. Then came a long series of testing Lecher frequencies: everything pointed to a site used primarily by women. There were positive reactions for feminine power, for goddess energy, for the Moon. It felt maternal, mothering up there. I could imagine indigenous women bringing their babies up into this powerful vertical cleft in the giant towers of stone. The antenna confirmed everything cosmic, spiritual, magnetic, and life-affirming. Best of all, it registered a big hit when I tested for an earth chakra. Such are not everywhere.

I did not want to leave the Cathedral Rocks. They cradled spirit in a loving way that spelled "home". I'd felt this in Machu Picchu, at Bell Rock, and here it was again. I remembered my first visit to the vortex at the entry to Boynton Canyon, and the man meditating against the spire. "I'm very happy here," he'd told me. I was very happy, serenely content, up here in the bosom of the maternal Cathedral Rocks, and I lingered nearly two hours.

From there I went to Bell Rock for a goodbye visit. All too soon it was time to pack up for the long series of flights home. Heavy storms were battering the Midwest and the East, suggesting it was high time to get going. It had been beautiful, T-shirt weather well into December, now winter was presenting itself. Cloudy skies and cold informed the drive down to Phoenix; it became windy, and there was a sandstorm over the city. I flew off to Memphis, not yet snowbound, changed planes for Amsterdam, changed again to get to Geneva, and slept in my alpine home on the thirteenth of December.

The next day I visited Perchette. She said I looked great and she found my chakras to be wide open and humming nicely. Thank you, Sedona! We talked about my plan to lead a group to Peru in the spring, which was not coming together at all well. She read a series of "angel" cards for me: they suggest great openings ahead. Perchette proposed I go to Peru alone, without the encumbrance of a group to be shepherded from point to point. Perhaps my guides and guardian angels were sending me a message with the lack of interest in my prospectus, she pointed out. In her outer office she introduced me to a group of waiting patients, presenting me as a "great shaman". As usual!

The next day it snowed. Winter had reached the Alps. The "indoor season" was beginning, a fine time for making decisions.

[1]   Rhonda Pallasdowney, *The complete book of flower essences, 48 Natural and Beautiful Ways to Heal Yourself and Your Life.* Novato, CA: New World Library, 2002. xxii+456p., notes, glossary, bibliography, index, appendix. ISBN 1-57731-141-8.

Chapter Thirty-Eight

REKINDLING INKAN ENERGY

That year 2000 ended with a joyous reunion, for my room-mate Susanne arrived eight days after my return from Arizona. This was programmed ahead, of course, and it made for a very merry Christmas and a happy New Year. She brought her companion and they stayed through the holidays. We meditated, did healings, made despachos and they skied. After their departure we began meditating at long distance once a week, adding others of the Danish group as time went on.

There was a sour note in all this music, but it had nothing to do with them. Another couple decided not to go to Peru with me, and with that my idea of escorting a group was definitely dead in the water. It was necessary to give Juan the bad news at the turn of the year. He was not upset with me, fortunately, although disappointed. When we had first cooked up the plan in Cusco he'd been pleased with the idea of receiving a first group from the land of C. G. Jung, the great Swiss psychologist. One of Jung's books had convinced him to take up the challenge of teaching Inka spiritual work to foreigners.

My determination to return to Peru was not diminished. The idea of going alone did not please me, but the trip was going to happen. I began to take the Condor drops at bedtime, and the reaction was instantaneous and powerful. The first time I dreamed about shamanism most of the night. A man was encouraging me, drumming with me. Was this my father? This was my incredulous impression. The presence of my high-Episcopalian, mystic-scoffing father was provocative. Recalling that Kirsten had brought him to me as a fun-loving spirit opened the door to believing. The next significant dream focused on animals, all kinds of animals in tones of sunny brown, gold, sepia, touches of red, dots of black. Nothing could be more significant, for shamans work closely with animals, especially on the spiritual plane.

My sister-in-law Elise left for the other side, in her sleep, and at 101 years of age. Several of her close friends received little messages, such as the fresh odor of flowers and forest, for example. During her final hour I was busy piloting the snowblower, but something impelled me to look at my watch at what proved to be the precise moment. She'd departed, but she couldn't signal through the noise of my machine. Memories of our alpine rambles together flooded in when I received the news by telephone. The next day I reserved my flight to Peru, planning to be there more than three weeks in April. I began studying Spanish. With an architect I began planning the creation of a meditation room to be added onto the chalet, astride a powerful Curry line that runs down the hall. And, best of all, my mountains-and-meditation friend André agreed to go to Peru with me. Arriving from different directions, we agreed to meet in Lima.

The flight from Amsterdam crossed the Atlantic on the first of April. My hotel arranged a taxi to meet me that evening at Lima Internacional, which is how Alfonso became my trustworthy driver. Eileen had urged me to visit the Museo d'Oro, the Gold Museum, and Alfonso took me there on my first day in Lima and later to the South American Explorers Club. Never had I seen so much gold in one place, all of it fashioned into a spectrum of jewelry, sacred animals, decorative and wearable objects of all kinds which had been hidden from the Spanish invaders. In addition to the gold, there were masses of turquoise, emeralds like golf balls, monster lapis lazuli, rough amethyst, and more quartz than the eye can take in. There was so much, an incredible amount and variety, yet one must keep in mind that the Conquistadores made off with every piece of gold they could find. Alfonso returned to fetch me after two hours, driving me across town to the South American Explorers Club. On the second day I asked him to take me out to Pachacamaq, the oldest group of Inkan and pre-Inkan temples, located on the seacoast south of Lima. What remains of the temples and pyramids is an austere desert of semi-melted structures. Alfonso accompanied me on the four-kilometer circuit in the boiling sun, and he watched with interest while I did ceremony and meditated on a long balcony of weathered adobe armchairs.

André arrived well after midnight, and Alfonso was there before eight in the morning to drive us to the Aeropuerto Internacional. I won't go into the details of how hard it was to arrange our tickets to Cusco, simply that it took weeks of nail-biting. Finally, they were waiting for me at the hotel, thanks to Juan's son Ivan.

Cusco glowed in the sun that April day, and we were quickly sitting in the café at our Hotel Ninos, sipping coca tea. That took care of our initial light-headedness due to the abrupt increase in altitude, and a good lunch at Puchar opposite the Plaza de Armas finished the job of restoring energies. It was a joy to be there again, and André was overwhelmed with the flood of new sights, sounds and smells. Quickly he became enchanted with the idea of taking the four-day Inka trail trek that ends at Machu Picchu. During our first few days in Cusco we spent time organizing that adventure for him, our rail tickets for Aguas Calientes and our hotel room there. At the Cusco house of the Explorers Club we sought and received advice and maps. Those were the mundane details. Communication with Doris was — always is —

a challenge, there being no telephone in the apartment, and I used e-mail there within Cusco to organize the first contact. She knew we were coming and had tried, without signaling ahead, to meet us at the Ninos but we had already gone to supper. She had moved her boutique from Teqseqocha to I didn't know where. It took several days to effect our reunion.

To introduce André to Inkan energies I led him to the Qorikancha. Tour groups were everywhere, but we found a quiet corner in the Sun Temple where I taught him how to open his qosqo and to filter the energies he pulled in. We practiced projecting energy at one another and worked a bit with the surviving walls of fitted stones.

All this was preamble to visiting a handful of my favorite sites outside the city. One day we hired one of the cabs that circle around the Plaza de Armas and went first to Tambo Machay, where one prepares to die. The four niches retained their power: it was just like the previous year, my body swaying and almost falling out of the niche but also tryng to lift off. These sensations are remarkable.

We found Illia Pata with some difficulty. I did not remember the barbed-wire fence, but a young horse tender named Martin helped us go around the knoll and come in behind that barrier. Up on the Altar of Light we performed ayni, the ritual exchange of good energies. When André and I had done each other, I beckoned to Martin and gave him some of that energy. He really liked that. Across the road and down the hill is Q'enko, a cluster of rocks laced with clefts, tunnels and caves. Outside the tunnel entrance sat a young Quechua offering small beaded jewelry items. Looking again, I recognized Alejandro whom I'd met the previous year with Doris, buying a manta from him. Later he had been part of the Quechua group with whom we did ceremony at Tipon. My Spanish was worse than his, so our brief chat was primitive but full of smiles.

At the Explorers Club someone had suggested that we mystics might enjoy meeting Leona. Ultimately a taxi struggled up the dirt track to the hillside home she rented on the edge of the city. She had two suggestions for us. First, we must absolutely meet "Puma", who did coca leaf readings. And second, would we like to do a day of San Pedro out in the country? I could have passed on this one, but André was eager to have the adventure, so we made the date. Telephone contact with Puma was achieved rapidly.

The next day was noteworthy in four ways: 1) Puma came and gave both of us coca leaf readings; 2) Jens Peter arrived at the head of a Danish party who would do Hatun Karpay with Juan; 3) we walked up to Sacsayhuaman; and 4) we went out to Larapa to visit Doris.

Fredy "Puma" Quispe Singona, of a family of Chavin paqos, proved to be quite a young man. Sitting in the sunny courtyard, he spread the leaves on a little white table and read them for me first. Suffice it to say there were echoes of what the two Dorises had told me last year, a prediction of some further spiritual openings, and a warning about my liver and kidneys. These words of caution I took seriously, for there were antecedents he could not know about. Penicillin poisoning had damaged my kidneys more than twenty years earlier. It had taken long years of patience to restore order and now we lived in peace with one another, most of the time but not always. Years of digestive disorders had made me solicitous of my liver's happiness, to which herbal remedies seemed to contribute.

André said Puma saw so much truth that he, André, was crying from the start. Puma confirmed what I already knew, that André has much spiritual power, that it is not "how" to access it but "when". My own experience confirms that most of us have untapped spiritual capacities. The "when" of it needs to be stimulated with quite a bit of "how".

I said that Puma was young, about 20, very sweet and loving, but when he is working he matures, looks like a wise older man.

Right after that seventeen Danes surged through the heavy street door into the patio, with Jens Peter in the lead. Four or five of the women came over to greet me warmly, for these were friends made at the seminar in Sjaellands Odde barely seven months earlier. And Ivan was there too, embracing me, at last giving me the chance to thank him for his work with airline tickets. Then Doris called and we made a date for the mid-afternoon.

André and I grabbed a quick lunch and started the climb up steep city streets, passing the Church of San Christobal, and after a hairpin turn, we were on the old stone road which climbs further to approach the ancient structure of Sacsayhuaman. It seems to have functioned as a fortress but was also a kind of administrative center before the Spanish arrived.

The big blocks inspire wonderment. André marveled at the way the huge stones were cut and fitted. So many of the joints are unusual: Y's, L's, angles, a few curves. One ponders at the reasons, groping for the significance. After seeing how the stones at Tambo Machay echoed the waves of the energy above the river at Aguas Calientes, I tend to think the fitting of the stones must be related to perceptions of energy flow. Inkan spiritual practice is all about the flow of energy, leaving me to imagine that the stonecutters wove that intelligence into their work. We met an English couple who were speculating on the age of the stonework. Thus I dowsed with the pendulum and came up with 1175-1185 C.E. as the time of construction. History, which relies on suspect documentation and a packet of mythology, says it was built in the fifteenth century, during the reign of the warrior king Pachacuteq[1]. Archaeology, which places major development of the Cusco area in the 1100s, supports my version[2]. Either way, those huge stones were placed without the benefit of modern technology.

Not wanting to be late getting to Larapa, we did not spend long hours at Sacsayhuaman. We rambled down, gambled on the cleanliness of freshly-squeezed carrot juice at a stand opposite the church, and ultimately cabbed out to the suburbs. The driver dropped us at the wrong place and we spent an anxious half-hour trying to find the right street uphill. I found a place to telephone, and soon we spied Doris coming downhill about three hundred yards from where we stood.

She greeted me with great warmth and love, remarking that she sees me as a mirror of herself — not physically, of course, for there we couldn't be more different, the short brown-haired pepperpot and the tall gray-haired deliberator — but on the spiritual plane. She scrutinized André appraisingly and told me later, while he was out of the room, "he's beautiful!" She meant spiritually as well as the handsome man he was.

We passed two hours of mystical conviviality, seated on the floor of the ritual room, my "Catedral San Pedro". It was a luminous moment, beyond just a happy reunion. Doris was by turns ebullient and meditative. We drank Maca, we shared joints (which do nothing for me but I never spoil a party), and we talked, talked, talked. André was enchanted by my soul sister, who tries to pull the cosmos down to meet the earth. It became time to go as the sun waned, evening shadows sliding over Apu Pikol out the big window. Doris, daughter Debbie and son-in-law Mohan hopped on a bus headed for Urubamba. We taxied back to the Plaza de Armas, walked up to Ninos for showers and meditation, then supper down in Teqseqocha.

Before leaving for Aguas Calientes and Machu Picchu we spent a day in the deep country with Leona. We drove far out to the southeast, following the Vilcanota upstream, passing the turns for Tipon and Raqchi. Well beyond the crossroads town of Urqos we came to a lake, which I believe was Pomacanchi. A dirt road turned halfway around it to reach a set of ruins, lying between lake and mountain.

We set up our ritual site against one of the walls. This had not been a large structure, more along the lines of a big farmhouse. Roofless, the walls were fragmented and overgrown with weeds, vines, and cactus. In front a swampy area led to the shallow waters of the lake. A few red flowers bloomed here and there, the whole scene suggesting a kind of rotting Garden of Eden. Green mountains swelled upward at our backs as we looked across lake and highway to more green mountains on the east. Cloud cover obstructed the view, depriving us of the chance to see the tip of twenty-thousand foot Apu Ausangate about twenty miles away. Ausangate is the highest peak of the Cusco region, only slightly higher than Apu Salcantay, the giant of the Machu Picchu region.

Leona poured each of us a big cup of the green drink. Her San Pedro was not at all like Doris's concoction. Leona's *huachuma* was filtered, smooth, sweetened with apple and not at all disgusting. An hour later we had a second cup. And that was quite enough to put everyone in a pleasantly altered state. "Think with the heart, feel with the head," she counseled.

We were five in number, the others being a bleached-blonde of indeterminate age from North Carolina and a tall, thin Bangladeshi from London.

This time I got moderately high as the day wore on, a different altered state from the first time, with a more vivid awareness. No one became wildly expansive, as you see sometimes with heavy drinkers. There was a happy mood, although nearly everyone seemed to slip from time to time into an introspective mood. We felt heightened sensitivity to each other's feelings. Rama, always talkative, was a bottomless pit, drinking up all the leftover San Pedro. The blonde Coralie spent the day cleansing the air around her with a condor feather. André expanded, talking to the rocks, relating to the little lizards as if they were his children. As for me, at the end of the afternoon I had a good cry. Apparently that was what needed to come out of me, all the huachuma could do for me.

Well, it did one other thing for me: it made me ravenously hungry. There was nothing left to eat except a few cookies which I devoured rapidly. Leona had wanted us to make it a fasting day, for maximum effect from the cactus. That I could not do, which I told her at the beginning. I carried a small picnic, but it wasn't enough. The day in the field was about two hours too long. As we piled into the minibus I was already feeling weak. Hypoglycemia hammered me on the slow sixty-mile drive back to Cusco. My blood sugar collapsed and my blood pressure with it. André kept me conscious with continuous massage of my hands and wrists, watching my respiration and commanding me to take another deep breath, and another, and another. When we finally arrived at Leona's house on the ridge we found nothing in the larder except a can of chicken soup. While the soup was heating on the cooker Leona's friend Lorraine brought out her oregano ointment and herbal tea. Oregano under the nose was a powerful stimulant, and the tea helped too. Combined, they had a very tonic effect. Thus was crisis averted. I survived, and an hour later I was wolfing down a plate of trout and vegetables at Pucara.

Up in our Hotel Ninos we got busy frantically packing for the morrow. Somehow I found the energy to achieve the task before collapsing into my bed for a fitful night's rest. Five o'clock in the morning came too soon. André carried our four valises down the long staircase and left them inside the big door. Well before six o'clock he was on his way to the trekking office. One of the cheerful, helpful ladies in the office gave me breakfast while I waited for her nephew, the chosen taximan. Miguel proved to be just the man I needed. He helped me all the way with the double load of luggage. He stood in line with me, intervened with the guards, and carried three of the four bags onto the train. On the spot I made a date for him to meet us when our evening train would bring us back ten days hence.

Settling in at Aguas Calientes required patience. The promised porter did not meet me at trainside and finally a village man volunteered to help "la Senora". There are moments in life when it pays to have nearly white hair and a puzzled expression. Half an hour later I was sitting in a kind of treetops room overlooking rooftops, focused on the town square, and with its back against the jungle. Margarita, the proprietress of Gringo Bill's Hostal, had put me at the top of her rambling cluster of rustic structures which climbed the hill like a confused earthworm. Two walls of windows gave a light airy sense, providing charm which the functional, adequate furniture lacked. This is, after all, backpacker territory at the end of civilization. There is no road coming here; the town is accessible only by rail and helicopter. The buses which carry tourists up the dozen or more switchbacks to Machu Picchu arrived here on railroad flatcars; there are no other vehicles. Aguas Calientes is pedestrian.

An adequate trout and avocado lunch at an internet café on the railroad quai braced me for a frustrating hour at the keyboard. Aguas Calientes has few phone lines, and trying to turn pages on the internet is worse than digging a grave with a spoon. Up in my jungly penthouse I retired to my bed. My body soaked up sleep like a dried-out sponge, surfacing from time to time then blissfully falling back into the arms of Morpheus. Two hours of repair restored energy, and I attacked all the housekeeping challenges: unpacking, requisitioning light bulbs, a new table lamp, another pillow and blanket. With the chores done it was time to walk and learn the town. Cannie at Indio Feliz greeted me warmly, delighted to see me return. When Juan had led our group into her restaurant the previous year she had greeted me with unusual warmth, as if I were a longlost cousin. Another Peruvian soul sister?

It is tempting to skim over health matters, as if such messy details did not exist. In fact, this trip was more difficult for me than the previous one, which Juan had engineered around top hotels and restaurants so as to keep his group healthy. My problems began in Cusco, and I do not know which restaurant to blame. My fifth day of diarrhea made the train trip to Aguas Calientes especially trying. Once installed there I hoped everything would come right, for I was running out of homeopathic options.

My plan was to visit Machu Picchu every day. The digestive tube was not very cooperative, so it was ten-thirty before I got on the bus the next morning. The first half-hour on the mountain was not pleasant, for sanitary facilities are scarce up there. Finally things settled down, allowing me to pursue my program.

My sense of ritual prompted me to walk quickly the whole length of the ruins every morning so as to start my day at the Pachamama slab, our affectionate term for the "Temple of Balance". It lies at the far side of a small plaza flanked by two open rooms, the only buildings of Machu Picchu which have roofs. After traversing the chain of grassy plazas which divide the city into two halves, then passing an empty, wild area, one arrives at the open end of this courtyard. There we stop to open our qosqos, throwing our energy about twenty yards across the space to make our connection to the great stone. On this day I had the uncanny feeling that Pachamama recognized me. She began pulling on the invisible cord that linked us with such intensity I almost fell flat on my face. Keeping my balance, I moved directly to the stone and climbed up on the high step. After the first embrace I pulled back about an inch and saw a big black bird, a condor, in the stone, then a black butterfly, then the condor again. When I leaned back onto her smooth bosom she opened a vast field of amethyst/purple centered on my brow chakra. Pulling away again, for a moment, then leaning in for the third time I saw a flash of fire before the amethyst cloud enveloped me.

That day I explored the lower half of Machu Picchu, wandering from room to room, working my way from Pachamama back toward the entrance, frequently interrogating the Lecher antenna and my pendulum. In a grassy plaza between sets of rooms, there was a steep staircase climbing a small knoll.

Curious, I climbed the very steep steps, finding that the staircase narrowed so that at the top one person could just barely pass. Beyond this stricture several rooms flanked a small courtyard, a high stone wall blocking all view toward (and from) the western higher levels of the city, and on the east a wall opening framed a massive shaped stone. There were two ample shelves for sitting (?), one above the other, and the stone's upper profile echoed the eastern mountains behind it. To the south some steps led onto a set of terraces overlooking the whole eastern sector, but there was no egress. One could access these grassy benches only from the rooms above. It was obvious that this knoll-top apartment was very private. The only possible entrance was via the steep staircase, easily defendable at its summit by one guard. There was no visibility into this space from any direction, not even from the much higher Sacred Plaza in the upper sections across the way. During subsequent days I did a lot of dowsing and meditating on this knoll, seeking to learn its function. It is "conjunto" 15 on the extremely useful Wright map[3]

Redescending the staircase, I turned a corner and found a kind of shrine beneath that set of inaccessible terraces. This is a large alcove formed by three tall stone walls, the back wall reaching high toward the bottom terrace. There are three niches in that back wall, and below it are two generous benches about ten feet long. There had been a lot of niches in the principal room of the complex on the knoll. I wanted to know what they meant, so I began by asking in this alcove. I tried to tune into the spirit of the place and simply posed my question, one niche at a time. The one on the left gave me a vision of what resembled a dry lake bed, gray and cracked by drought. The center niche showed me a dark circle dancing around, and for some reason it made me think of a rogue planet. The third niche presented a scene of lacy green lines tracing irregularly over a gray background. On intuition, I asked the pendulum if all this had something to do with water. YES. Moving my left hand slowly into each niche, I could feel the energy increasing the deeper I penetrated.

Along came an official guide, escorting a couple of tourists and their child. The guide, Nilo, proved to be quite pleasant and was willing to talk with me for a moment. He agreed with me that the complex on the knoll was important but he didn't know its ancient function. Another question had been bothering me: there is a Sun Temple in the upper section, but there did not seem to be a Moon Temple. Did he know of such on Machu Picchu? No, he did not.

That evening Margarita served me a big bowl of rice, with a big chunk of dense cheese on the side. Very tired, I went early to bed. Sleep was long and refreshing, and I awoke to a sense of inner stability. Strength flowed back and that haunting sense of impending disaster melted in the morning sun. Margarita did me another fine service: she spoke to the head of the bus service and negotiated a student discount for me, for I would be using the bus every day. The young people who inspected tickets at the bus door raised their eyebrows the first time I presented my student tickets. Students are not usually white-haired. In my halting Spanish I explained that I was doing doctoral research on the relationship of earth energies to sacred sites. They liked that.

The next day, Good Friday, I revisited a whole series of plazas and temples, Pachamama to start with, of course, but also the Condor Temple and the equally unique Sun Temple, which is partly square and partly round. There is an intriguing cave beneath the Sun Temple, but my instruments revealed it had something to do with death. Nilo had said it was a mortuary. The Lecher denied any link to the Moon and the pendulum responded affirmatively when I asked if it was a tomb for the royal family. It appeared that Nilo was right: no Moon Temple on Machu Picchu, but I was having trouble believing that. It did not make sense. The Incas were strongly oriented to nature in all her aspects.

Far down the trail below Huayna Picchu, almost to the river, is a cavern that many call a Moon Temple, but which Juan called the Pachamama cave.

My experience there with the Hatun Karpay group did not suggest anything to do with the Moon. In that cavern we interacted with the Nust'as, the nature princesses.

This day was unique in another respect: it was the very first time that the locals, the people of Aguas Calientes, enjoyed reduced rates to enter their sacred city. They came in large numbers to stroll, to see, and to rest on the lawns, soaking up the ambient energy.

André's trekking group was due to arrive on Saturday, and at midday I found them and him lounging under the only tree of the central plaza on the mountain. They had just come down through Intipunku, the Sun Gate up on the ridge of the mountain Machu Picchu, which looms above the city on the south. He'd had a wonderful time, but planned to stay with his companions until they broke up officially down in the village. I told him how to find our hotel. Then I started my day's explorations by greeting Pachamama. After she pulled on my qosqo I plastered myself three times against her slab, reaping numerous visions of faces evolving one into the other, within the stone.

My path led directly to that isolated, well-guarded knoll labeled "15" on the WWE map. This place has been built up around and on a huge rock. I can easily believe a lot of earth was carried up those steep steps to create a flat space for construction. The puzzle called for slow, systematic analysis. I wrote down a list of nearly sixty Lecher frequencies, culled from the sublists on gods, planets, qualities and spirituality. Testing these wave lengths took a good piece of the afternoon, but gradually a pattern began to emerge. This complex was a refuge for women, a temple where they retired for spiritual work together, especially during their "moon time". North American tribes often had a tepee or other shelter set aside where women retreated during their menses. This sequestered knoll appeared to serve the same purpose for the Inka women of Machu Picchu.

The frequencies which responded "yes" touched on silence, meditation, wisdom, protection, maternity. spiritual life, women's worship, resonance, magnetism, electricity, equilibrium between earth and cosmos, earth goddess, a holy place. Four wave lengths agreed on the spiritual qualities of the site, and seven wave lengths identifying Venus all responded in the affirmative. Then I began to question the pendulum. It confirmed this to be a place of women, of their own meditation, their own ceremonies, their own songs, a place of seclusion, a place honoring fertility. But the pendulum denied that babies were born or baptized here. It also said the place was not a harem, and that men were not allowed here. The strongest gyrations of all came when I asked if it was a place for our "moon time", a Moon Temple, a temple of Pachamama.

Thus the Lecher had forced out a pattern and the pendulum confirmed it. *This* was Machu Picchu's Moon Temple It had taken painstaking work to "winkle out" such a conclusion, to accumulate such a weight of evidence. It filled me with elation.

Clouds had gathered, and as drizzle set in I began trying to identify the functions of all the niches in the biggest room. This windowless room measured twelve paces by seven, and these were full strides. There was a total of eighteen niches to examine. In the front wall two doors separated three segments of wall, each with a niche resonating to Venus. The two side walls each had four niches exhibiting symmetry of use to their opposite: the two niches closest to the doors reacted to "household objects" and the two closest to the back wall were connected to the Moon. That back wall held seven niches, of which the center three resonated to Venus again, echoing the front wall. The two on each end had all held objects relating to healing.

The opposite room, smaller, had three windows in its back wall looking down on the terraces and beyond, the Condor Temple.

It would have been fascinating to try to refine all this a little deeper, but that drizzle had become rain. My gear and I were getting wet, and it was a problem to keep my notebook from getting soaked. Thus I closed my backpack, pulled a hood over my head, and struck out for the gate and the bus plaza. Further work would have to wait for the morrow. On the way down the stairs I met the tail end of Juan's latest Danish group leaving the Mirrors and heading for the Pachamama stone. Jens Peter was bringing up the rear, and we had a happy hug.

That evening André and I shared experiences over a royal supper at Indio Feliz. He was elated by his four-day hike over the mountains, and I was bubbling over with my discovery of the true Moon Temple. He wanted to spend Sunday resting after four days of hiking, but I was hot to continue my work on the knoll. Also, his enthusiastic talk about the splendors of the Inka Trail inspired me to consider hiking up to Intipunku, the Sun Gate. Easter morning dawned sunny, not a cloud in the sky, encouraging me to head first for Intipunku. I took an early bus and headed straight for that trail, which starts before you enter the city ruins. On one of the upper terraces I met François and Pierrette, Canadians with whom I had breakfasted several times at Gringo Bill's, and we agreed to meet again when I came down.

Walking up to the Sun Gate took me a bit over an hour, including stops to chat with people coming down. Before starting to hike my "eyeball" estimate of the climb had been about three hundred feet. That was quite wrong. It was double that, for when I arrived at the Sun Gate's notch in the ridge the view to Huayna Picchu was quite level. The average altitude of Machu Picchu is about eight thousand feet, more than a thousand feet above Aguas Calientes. Huayna Picchu on the north is 8,700 feet, and Machu Picchu mountain, on the south, is not quite 10,100 feet (still less than Cusco).

Thus I had hiked up six to seven hundred feet, up a stone-paved trail, and it felt good. I had wanted to get some vertical work into my legs, for we were planning to climb Huayna Picchu in a few days, and this was just what they needed. My hour on this gently-rising trail was well-rewarded when I turned around and looked at what I had left behind

Intipunku is the point at which trekkers get their first glimpse of Machu Picchu. After days on the trail, they stride around a curve, enter the notch, and suddenly the vista opens and there is Machu Picchu spread out at their feet. Huayna Picchu's sugar loaf rises behind the city, and beyond that rolls a magnificent panorama of the Andes.

Down in the city again I met my friends at the lone tree of the grass plaza. After a moment to picnic a bit, I led Pierrette and François up to my Moon Temple. They seemed impressed but did not linger. From then on I was left to work intensely and in peace, for that steep, narrowing stone staircase up to the knoll seems to intimidate tourists. No one interrupted me.

The Moon Temple had not given up all its secrets the previous day. Now the Lecher antenna told me that the Moon's influence was everywhere in this complex of rooms. That was not really a surprise. What did blow me away was the omnipresence of both the Hartmann and the Curry networks. They were solid, not distinguishable as lines and grids. I'd only seen that once before. It was all solid energy, reminiscent of the courtyard of Qorikancha. That was the hub of the *ceques*, the leys that radiate from Cusco. Was Machu Picchu the hub of another set of leys? I asked the pendulum and it said "yes".

Vibrational rates in this Temple confirmed lots of power, consistent with the remarkable Hartmann-Curry juxtaposition. The great stone shrine registered 39'000 Bovis and the big room with its eighteen niches -- which I call the "quiet" room -- measured 34'000 angstroms. That smaller room registered 17'000 Bovis, and the others showed between 9'000 and 14'000. Observation of what remains of the construction suggests the quiet room had an upper storey. And so, it seemed, did the room opposite, whose windows overlook the terraces. There are now no roofs at Machu Picchu, except for the two shelters flanking the Pachamama stone. However, the surviving end walls all suggest steeply-pitched roofs which would have easily accommodated standing space.

With all the feminine energy on this knoll it would have been a gross error not to search for the *nust'as*, the nature princesses. Finding an unknown frequency involves using the Lecher and the pendulum together, as Eileen and I had done at Woodhenge. This time the technique did not work. I asked for wave lengths for the nust'as and got no response at all. Thus I began posing questions to the pendulum.

Can you give me a vibrational frequency for a nust'a? No.

Because I am inadequate as a conduit? No.
Because they transcend vibrations? Yes.
Because they transcend our physics? Yes.
Are nust'as associated with the niches? No.

Following this line of interrogation I learned that three of the five nust'as were here. The red, green and silver nust'as were present in both the quiet room and at the stone. The black and gold nust'as were not here.

Feeling a bit drained by the intensity of these energies, I lay down on the sunny top bench of the stone. It was warm and restful. Spirit drifted. There were hints of cloud when I sat up again, but rain was not yet threatening. I hadn't been to Pachamama for my morning greeting, and the skies seemed to be saying I had time for that. Once again I marveled at observing that the Inkas liked to carve the top of sacred stones to resemble the profile of distant mountains. Pachamama echoed the Andes in the east, but she did not give me much this afternoon. A reproach for having missed my morning visit?

We dined in company with François and Pierrette, up the steep main street in a restaurant that looked nice. Appearances proved to be deceiving, for this place's food was mediocre and its service abysmally slow. Fortunately the company was good.

Aguas Calientes is three thousand feet lower than Cusco, and when the sun is out the village is pleasant and summery with jungle heat and humidity. In the evening it is cool and at night I was always glad to snuggle under several blankets. No sooner had I done so this night than the rain began to drum on the roof.

It was imperative to firm up our ticketing and reservations for the train trip back to Cusco. With only four days remaining, we tackled the problem at the little ticket office. It took a full hour of waiting — and the replacement of a drunken agent by a sober one — to get our seats reserved together. We had not yet devoted much time to Aguas Calientes itself, and today, which was drizzly and unpromising, began to seem the day for that. Climbing Huayna Picchu was on our agenda for the next day, so it would do neither of us any harm to have a lazy day around the pueblo. The Hot Springs had to be bathed in, the mineral shop required thorough scrutiny, and there was a kind of esoteric boutique which should not be neglected. We went there first.

We were greeted quietly by an Andean lady with deep eyes and a soft smile. It became clear that she kept the shop for her husband, who was evidently a silversmith, surely a passionate collector and, it became clear, a man of shamanic persuasion. Shops in Aguas Calientes do not present the polished facades and interiors of urban boutiques. This is the jungle, and structures are cobbled together with a creativity and resourcefulness that would drive a Boston building inspector out of his mind. Around us shelves bulged with books, drums, cassettes, gourds, a gong, brass bowls, rattles, beadwork, rawhide objects and leather bags. Sitting Bull looked down on us from a place high on the back wall, next to a tall thin San Pedro growing slowly in a big pot. In the center was a display of hand-wrought silver jewelry.

We browsed. I asked questions in my rudimentary Spanish. André listened with delight to the shaman's musical recording. The sweet lady, who said her name was Rosa, went to a secret recess and withdrew a package which she unwrapped for my inspection, revealing condor feathers. Exactly what I wanted! Her craftsman husband had tipped each quill with a spiral of silver wire and a lightly designed insignia. She left me to enjoy these treasures, and it was clear from her demeanor that not everyone who entered the shop was shown the feathers. Not all of them were perfect nor undamaged -- condors do not lose feathers in ideal circumstances. I asked the pendulum to choose, and it allowed me to consider only one from the dozen or more. Not the most perfect, but nice, with a certain character, appropriate to my own vibrations. Rosa cut a long strip from soft cardboard, folded it into an envelope, and wrapped my feather with exquisite care. André decided the music disc was a necessary enhancement to his life, so we left Rosa with thanks, smiles and small parcels.

On our way up the steep concrete street we came across a gentle man sitting in front of a vague structure, slowly carving animals and totems from soapstone. There were condors, jaguars, serpents, llamas of all sizes, and a variety of totem poles resembling, in this gray stone, the tall wooden totem poles of the tribes of British Columbia. Stone carvings and mouldings of animals abound in the bazaars of Cusco, but these exhibited a special authenticity reflecting the care and precision of this quiet craftsman. My choice fell on a coiled snake above which gaped an angry jaguar mouth, with a condor perched on its head.

At the top of the town is a proper shop with display windows full of stones and crystals. Here I chose a large handful of amethysts, rose quartz and Peruvian blue opals, many of them cut and polished into surprising shapes. I love bringing such gifts to friends and students. This is yet another shop animated by the calm strength of one of those gentle souls who seem to gather at the foot of Machu Picchu.

After a mediocre lunch on the railroad quay, we walked up the tracks paralleling the Urubamba, coming to the big rock where Susanne, Annette and I had meditated the previous year. The river was higher this year, dirtier, and occasionally smelly. It looked like a tan sewer. I wondered if the river's guardian spirits were affected by the stink, and if so, how long before they would invite a purgative flood.

That evening we wanted to dine at Indio Feliz, but Cannie had a full house — including Juan's group — and could not seat us. Up the street we found an excellent supper at Candamo, another of those places with a roof and some walls but a large openness to the passing world. Back at Indio Feliz we climbed the stairs to find Juan, Jens Peter and their group of Danes. They were leaving the next day and I wanted to say goodbye, for quite a few of them had been at the seminar on the sandy peninsula of Sjaellandesodde. Moreover, this was also a wedding party, for up on Machu Picchu this day Juan had performed the marriage ceremony of two of my new friends. Gaiety filled the room.

Juan greeted me with great warmth, introducing me to the group as "our jewel". This startled the life out of me, but I reminded myself that Peru is also a land of latin gallantry. There was no mistaking, however, the intense warmth and love swelling toward me from that group. Jens Peter wanted a hug, saying he thinks of me as his grandmother, and I had to remind him I was old enough to be his mother but not his grandmother. Juan was warm and friendly with André, urging him to meditate, to pray and to "nurture the life form".

I told him then of our plan to mount Huayna Picchu the next morning, and of my hope that I would be capable of performing the transmittal of Apu energy for André. Juan agreed immediately that I could do it, saying "you are extremely powerful". Once again he took my breath away.

He was, however, absolutely right. We enjoyed a real blockbuster the next day. It was a glowing sunny day, no sign of yesterday's mists and drizzles. We took an early bus and paused as usual to greet Pachamama, and this was the day she repeated last year's performance. My qosqo turned into a blowtorch and when she reeled me in to her slab there was no nonsense of hovering delicately an inch off the stone. She pulled me to her so firmly that my forehead knocked against her granite bosom. I saw glimpses of landforms, mostly greenish, as if seen from a satellite in orbit. I remember one peninsula shaped like Cape Cod but turned the other way, and green. Then she bathed me in amethyst.

It's a steep climb up Huayna Picchu, a real alpine staircase, and my old body just kept powering upwards. Something was pulling me up. On top, after a few moments to catch my breath, I moved onto the ceremonial slab and began connecting my mesa to the rock and to the Andean Apus in a circle around us. There were a number of young hikers lounging around the summit, but it was evident that they had no idea of what power could be tapped up there.

When it felt right, I invited André to stretch out on the slab. With my mesa applied to his qosqo and my free hand reaching heavenward like an antenna, I channeled the Apus' power to him. He got a really good charge — his body vibrated visibly — and he loved it. Then I asked him to channel for me. I knew he could because he had the power latent in him and was just starting to let it out. And he did it well. I got a good shot in the qosqo and then just lay there to float and bathe in it for a while.

On my feet again I saw a young woman sitting nearby in lotus position and seeming to meditate. André told me later she had been watching us with one eye open, but she was the only one up there who had paid attention, who understood there was something to be had. I beckoned her to join us. Her French was better than her English, so we managed communication without much trouble. She was a beautiful raven-haired young woman with a voluptuous figure, so it came as no surprise when she admitted to being an actress. Her name was Luz and her Spanish film company was on location near Urubamba. She had a day free, had hopped on the first train and had come up here alone. She asked about the ritual we had performed, so I explained briefly the concept of the Apus' energy.

"Would you do that for me?" she asked.

I hesitated; one does not perform energy work indiscriminately. Luz was obviously no stranger to meditation, but what weighed most with me was the fact she had made a singular effort to arrive on this peak. I agreed, cautioning her that I could not control nor predict what might come.

She stretched out on the slab and, calling on the Apus to bring to Luz what she needed, I applied my mesa. After a moment her body began to tremble and her fingertips vibrated on the granite as the energy poured through her body. Once the flow was established I removed the mesa and let her receive as the Apus intended.

Luz was radiant when she sat up. Full of gratitude, she embraced me warmly, then began asking what she could give me in return. She began to strip off her nice mineral jewelry to give me, but I stopped her.

"If you want to give me something, send me a videocassette of your film," I suggested. We agreed on that.

Before finally tearing ourselves away from this magnetic, hospitable peak, I used the Bovis technique to measure its power. The pendulum kept on swinging until it hovered and then gyrated over forty thousand, more than six times the normal rate.

The three of us hiked down together in a fine, sociable mood. At the Pachamama stone Luz embraced us and said goodbye, for she needed to catch the afternoon train back to Urubamba. Up on my Moon Temple André and I shared some dried apricots, a tin of sardines and a power bar, unwilling to leave the city in order to lunch outside the main gate. Then we moved down to the room of the "Mirrors". It was here that Juan had performed the wedding ceremony, for the circle and its nearly egg-shaped companion, not identical, symbolize the Inkan concept of *yanantin*, the coming together of dissimilar persons or energies. The site seemed to open something in André, for he began to receive vague clairvoyant images. There had been some kind of overarching wooden structure here, he sensed, and sound had an important role. He couldn't get more, but my Lecher antenna reacted strongly to the frequency for sound and open-air acoustical phenomena. We moved on to the nearby Condor Temple, then headed to the labyrinthine gate and the buses. Suddenly we were both wiped out from the day's bursts of power. In Aguas Calientes we showered, browsed one or two shops, then sat to a restorative dinner at Indio Feliz. Cannie hovered over us in a motherly way.

The next morning I was walking briskly up to my favorite internet café when Rosa came swinging down the street with a letter in her hand. She asked me to wait for her in the shop, *por favor*, just a moment or two. I continued uphill but rather quickly my way was blocked by a young man who was dashing down the street. It was Puma! He embraced me and, with excuses, cut off my questions.

"I've got to catch the bus to Machu Picchu. We're doing ceremony up there today," he explained. With a friendly wave he was gone, not giving me time to ask "who is we?"

At Rosa's "Arte Sipan" I pushed aside the sandwich board that was serving to block the doorway. Inside I picked up a book and waited, then waited some more as that moment or two stretched. Eventually Rosa returned and sat with me. We discussed the book, which linked Sacsayhuaman to Atlantis, and finally I asked her:

"Digame por que esta momento?"

To my great surprise she then asked if I would come and do ritual with her husband. Apparently he requested this, without having met me. We settled on ten o'clock the next morning, and I proposed to bring André. Fine. I was jealous of the little time remaining to work on the mountain, but this kind of a proposition was intriguing too.

André was unwell. He thought it was a digestive upset, and he planned to sleep and rest the whole day. Thus I took the midday bus up to Machu Picchu, grabbing a grilled sausage at the lunch terrace. At the Pachamama slab I met two Australians with whom we were chatting at the breakfast table in Gringo Bill's. So there was a long talk about UFOs with Nicole and Juliana before I got to work.

Curious about the energy patterns on this mountain I roamed around testing the wave length for the Curry network. Like the Hartmann, it appeared to be omnipresent. There was no network, just a vast sea of energy. Machu Picchu was clearly a hub, but tracing the force lines which might be radiating outward presented an impossible challenge. Nearly vertical jungle-clad sugar loaves and mountains rose everywhere, like a sea of teeth, to say nothing of the fanged creatures slithering around. A dowser-alpinist would need to be escorted by a squad of machete-wielding bushwhackers.

On the way to the Moon Temple I stumbled across a big room with three long, hip-high stones embedded in the earth floor. This was number seven on the Wright map. Two of the stones were huge and the third had a vaguely amphibian shape, like a boat or a whale. These stones are twice as large as shown on the map. There were no windows here but twenty niches. Could I afford the time to analyze this complex too? I decided to give it a lick and a promise. The Lecher declined to confirm a long list of spiritual qualities but it did respond to the wave lengths for priests, benedictions, ritual, and illumination. The pendulum told me it was a residence and place of meditation for those priests.

Moving on to my Moon Temple, I worked on identifying the function of the two smaller rooms. The kitchen seems to have occupied a space immediately at the top of the great staircase, on the right. It had had a roof. My tools told me that four of its niches were for food and three for utensils, with an alcove for food storage. On the opposite side, where steps lead down to the terraces, an unroofed space appeared to have been a washroom.

To end the afternoon I meditated at the great stone. Eileen had given me an "Uluru" meditation, which she received at Ayers Rock in Australia, and I had been saving it for a special time[1]. That was now. I made offerings of corn meal and Perchette's sacred salt, then received permission to enter the rather complex meditation. Above the crown chakra I saw green and black intertwined, then an orange-gold door opened before me. Brilliant golden light shone beyond the door, but just inside it there were fluid, sylph-like figures, very light, graceful, evolving, circling around. Beyond them all was gold. And I went "out". When my focus returned, after some minutes, I knew it was time to go. That vision of a golden world remained, inviting me to return.

André was not yet feeling like dining. His Peruvian "bug", whatever it was, did not want to leave. Margarita had given me access to the kitchen, where I was able to prepare him a bowl of soup. Up the street at Indio Feliz I dined alone, but Cannie came over to sit and converse with me. We shared as kindred souls who had known one another a very long time.

One more full day remained available for the village and Machu Picchu. André was on his feet again and we kept our date with Herbert, the shaman of "Arte Sipan/Andean Cosmology". This was a happy experience. Herbert spoke of traveling here and there for New Moon ceremonies. I didn't learn if he "journeys", the essence of shamanism, but soon he led us through an hour of fine home-made music. Call it tribal music, moving into a spiritual plane.

There were drums, rattles and other sound-makers for the three of us. Soon we were deeply absorbed in chanting, singing, drumming, rubbing

Tibetan bowls, striking bells and stroking a gong, and listening to Herbert's didgeridoo, maracas, rain sticks, and his ceramic bird whistle. This is a remarkable Andean instrument, said to be two thousand years old. It enables a skilled whistler to imitate a veritable aviary, and Herbert took us to the heart of the jungle to commune with the birds. An hour of this kind of intuitive musical invention brought us to a kind of plateau, where inner rhythms have been stimulated and rearranged, and where the chakras are vibrating harmoniously. We were deep in the natural world and came back slowly, somewhat reluctantly.

About an hour later an unreasoning command of spirit propelled me back up to Machu Picchu for one last communion. My body was tired, and André had the wisdom to take an easy afternoon which possibly I should have done too. Even so, I took the bus up, and ordered some wieners at the cafeteria. Lucky to find a seat, I munched. After a moment a familiar-looking blonde lady came over to say hello. We'd met at Juan's seminar at Sjaellandsodde. In fact, at a nearby table there was a large group of Danes, ten or twelve, many familiar faces from that seminar. They had come independently, were not working with Juan, and quickly I found myself surrounded by warmth and cordiality. They related to me in the loving way of kin. One lady said I reminded her of an aunt; to my eyes a younger woman reminded me of how I had looked in my twenties. The lone male of the group squatted next to my chair and began talking about how he saw me as an American Indian on horseback, scanning the lands seized by the white man. This phenomenon occurs so often that I am obliged to give it credibility, but it always takes me by surprise.

They were intrigued by my story of the Moon Temple and accompanied me there. Once on the site, they told me they had meditated on that great altar stone just before descending for lunch. I explained my findings in detail, then we created a large meditation circle to end the visit with ceremony.

André and I dined quietly for the last time in Aguas Calientes. He was coming back to his strength, while I was desperately tired. During the night I coughed a bit and in the morning my voice was weak. One could joke about "jungle rot". It was time to fill our valises. Margarita recommended a simple place for our lunch. It was full of locals, excellent, and very inexpensive. Afterward we sunned in the central square and she joined us for friendly talk. In mid-afternoon we dragged our luggage over the rough path to the station, waiting a long time for our train to allow loading and then depart. It was a comfortable trip back to Cusco. The city lights glowed like gold as the train rolled around the last mountain. Miguel was there at the station to meet us, as promised. Peru is so poor on the material plane, but it is rich with wonderful people who are helpful and reliable to tourists of whom they have every right to be jealous.

In Cusco we began the tedious business of confirming flight reservations, changing money, replenishing our stock of bottled water, and just plain lazing about. We sat in the sun in the Plaza de Armas, besieged by gangs of children who were drawn to André like flies to honey. We allowed the tourist police to chase them away, having learned the hard way there are Peruvian microbes against which our northern physiologies have meagre defenses. I spent one whole afternoon sleeping during which I became aware of the recurrence of a dream.

Something very important was happening in my subconscious. With each cough, during the dream state, I was aware of sending waves of energy up and over Huayna Picchu, blue energy which came back to me. A benevolent Guide stood there, encouraging me. Much larger than life, he was dressed in hiking clothes, day pack, brimmed hat, and he smiled benignly at me. I do not quite understand the triggering action of my coughing, but those waves of blue energy were marvelous as they swept over and through me. This dream came three times in twenty-four hours: the night we returned to Cusco, during that long Saturday afternoon nap and again that night.

Cusco was still my home for three days after André's departure on Monday morning. I walked him down the street until we found a cab to take him to the airport. Then it was time to spend serious time at the Telser communications center and its battery of computers. I'd promised e-mail reports, which I titled "Picchugrams", for Eileen's Medicine Garden. It had been impossible to get reliable connections in Aguas Calientes and I'd given up the effort after losing one long piece to the caprices of the fragile telephone lines. E-mail reunited me with Doris, who had moved her office to a corner of a travel agency on Plateros. I found her there, along with son Daniel and younger daughter Gracia, and all hugged and kissed me warmly. Doris reminded me that I am family. She invited me out to Larapa the next day, which would be my last in Cusco. I taxied out there after doing a writing stint on the computers at Telser. This was a family day, warm and cozy.

Elder daughter Debora was pregnant, and they asked me to determine the sex of her foetus. This was a job for my trusty ebony pendulum, and soon there was a clear answer: a boy. Doris then commandeered the pendulum to do it her way. Same answer[5].

Lunch with all of us at table together was joy. Solicitous of my health, Doris insisted that I nap on her bed under the benign protection of Apu Pikola. The rest of the afternoon was simply spent catching up, enjoying the opportunity to be sisterly.

That night I packed my bags and paid my bill at Ninos. The faithful Miguel came at nine o'clock in the morning to drive me to the airport. Alfonso was not at Lima to meet me but La Castellana had sent a replacement.

Knowing that I would need rest, I'd asked Claudia to give me a room for the afternoon only. In the patio I asked for a bowl of their creole soup, and the breakfast lady -- pleased to see me return -- presented her cheek for a kiss when she served it. Then I napped until time to leave. At five-thirty Alfonso was there, with a warm smile, to drive me out to Jorge Chavez Aéropuerto for my evening flight.

Thus I left Peru with good memories of having been well-taken care of whenever I had the foresight and the time to organize things ahead. One pays, but one pays everywhere and not always with such a sense of satisfaction. I cannot speak for people who travel as tourists with nothing on the agenda except diversion and following a guide from curiosity to curiosity. Speaking as a spiritual explorer, my cup was full.

[1] Peter Frost, *Exploring Cusco*. Lima: Nuevas Imagenes, 5th ed. 1999. 280p., index, glossary, bibliography. ISBN 9972-9015-6-4.
   "In truth we have no clearcut Inca history," says Frost. He cites several reasons for that: the Incas had no written languages; the Spanish conquerors arrived at the end of a civil war, producing conflicting versions of the truth; the Conquistadores spoke very little Quechua and relied on native interpreters, who had a survival-based need to tell their new masters what they wanted to hear. Page 54.

[2] *Ibid*, p.58.

[3] Wright Water Engineers, *Archaeologic Map of Machu Picchu.*, 2000. Prepared by Machu Picchu Paleohydrological Survey, Wright Water Engineers Inc., 2490 West 26th Avenue, Denver, Colorado 80211, or visit: <www.wrightwater.com> This remarkable folding map shows everything on Machu Picchu: every wall, every opening, every flight of steps, every walkway, and most major stone slabs lying on the ground,

[4] "Uluru" is the Aboriginal name for the huge red extrusion known as Ayers Rock, in the center of the Australian desert.

[5] As it turned out, we were both right.

Danes at the Pachamama slab

Juan preparing a Despacho

Juan charging me
with Apu energy
on Huayna Picchu

My soul sister Doris

Rosa and Herbert

With André at Gringo Bill's

Making a Despacho
at home

Eileen sitting in the
Devil's Den dolmen

Chapter Thirty-Nine

JOURNEYS

Whatever bells and whistles may be added to it in a given culture, the journey is the essence of a shaman's work. Great Spirit seemed determined to drive home this lesson, to emphasize this facet of what was coming. The next two years were full of travel to Denmark, to the Netherlands and to England. These journeys were not in themselves shamanic, but they were totally devoted to metaphysical work, with a growing movement toward shamanic practice.

It took most of two weeks to restore my energies after returning from Peru. Eastbound jet lag always bothers me considerably, but this time a skilled acupuncturist made short work of that syndrome the day after my reentry. Chinese, he also gave me some of his native herbs to knock out the residue of cough/cold or whatever it was I brought home from Aguas Calientes. My doctor gave me a well-chosen homeopathic remedy to clean up the situation.

Spirit wanted to bask a while in the afterglow of three weeks in Cusco and Machu Picchu, but the demands of the material world were incessant. Work had already started on the remodeling contracted before my departure, and I needed all the vitality that could be summoned up. From time to time I had to clear certain areas. Cartons of household goods and office papers began to line the staircases. Aside from completely revising the kitchen, my major objective was to create a meditation room straddling an energy line which ran down the hallway and crossed the studio on an ordinarily unexploitable tack. It was satisfying to see this addition gradually begin to take shape on the sunset side of the chalet. With all this going on it was a relief to do some hiking on the weekends, but there were no major alpine exploits on my agenda for this summer. Nearing seventy-seven years of age, I was struggling to learn to bite off no more than I could chew.

On the equinox, the day after that birthday, I flew off to Denmark for another reunion with my Danes. We had become a spiritual family in Peru. Being together was a way of returning to the sacred sites which had nourished us, which had expanded our spiritual practices to encompass the Andean cosmology, which had formed us into fourth-level paqos. Being with my Danes took me back to my beloved Machu Picchu without days and days of travel. Reentry from Peru had been somewhat less spiritually traumatic than after the first trip, but only somewhat. A tiny ache of homesickness lodged somewhere between the fourth and fifth chakras.

After two flights I stepped onto the tarmac at Aalborg in the far north of the Jutland peninsula. Margit stood just inside the door so I could not miss her. Smoothly and efficiently she drove me across the green countryside in a southwesterly direction; down one of those bucolic roads we passed quickly Peder's business enterprise. In another half hour we were at their remodeled farmhouse at Gedsted, from which you can just see one of the inner sounds of the vast Limfjorden system of inland waterways.

Torben was waiting for us, ready with a big embrace. Henrik and Jens-Peter arrived soon after, but the carload coming from Copenhagen ran out of gas, could not find the road and arrived after we had reluctantly begun a late supper. Susanne, John, Annette and Jeanett eventually pulled in, tired and hungry and more than ready to share the roast beef, vegetables, fish-and-veggie stew and succulent apple pie which Margit had prepared. Before the night was over we had settled into ceremony, creating a despacho and then burning it outside under the stars. In this way we connected with the Peruvian roots all of us had discovered.

We lived in rain for our principal day in the field and ended it soaked to the skin. We started by tramping across a barnyard and through grassy, soggy fields to reach a tumulus, a burial mound. Somehow we all managed to crowd into a tiny anteroom with very low energy (Bovis 4'000). Then onward to Borup Hede, a heath area, a moor. Between rain showers we formed an energy circle around a big spreading tree. If this was Andean, I mused, it was also a link to the Druids. In the town of Vyborg we parked next to the small Norman cathedral, the Domkirche. We found Anita waiting for us, having arrived separately from Jens-Peter for reasons connected to the new member of the family, baby Freya.

The twelfth-century builders really knew what they were doing. They had obviously designed this church to exploit three positive Curry lines. One force line ran the full length from nave to abside, the second one crossed at right angles to energize the transept, and the third line of force crossed through the choir. An underground stream ran diagonally through transept and choir. In terms of vibratory rates the results were splendid: 18'000 at the Curry crossing in the transept and a resounding 35'000 in the choir. It's a pleasant, harmonious small cathedral with marvelous murals and a huge seven-stemmed candelabra, dating from 1494. You can climb the tower, and I did that with Henryk for a long view over the flat countryside.

On the shore of Lovns Bredning, a big bay within the Limfjord, we picnicked in the cars because of the rain. When that had abated we trudged up the stony beach, following Margit to a big sandy bluff called Ulbjerg Klint (meaning "cliff"). We did some Inkan energy work, facing the bluff. Farther up the shore we connected our energies to a big rock reminiscent of Uluru in form but not in size nor color. I felt a deep, serene connection, non-specific but promising, which led me to call it a "dreaming stone". This afternoon finished under hot showers, after hanging rainjackets and backpacks to dry in Peder's furnace room.

After a late, leisurely supper, basking in the warmth of being together, we made another despacho and reserved its dispatch for the morrow. This one we dedicated to the troubled world, for all of us were sobered by the destruction, only eleven days earlier, of the twin towers in New York.

Sunday became just as fine a day as Saturday had been miserable. We devoted the morning to a series of rituals in the ruins of the Vitskol Kloster. Only low brick walls and pillar bases remained of this twelfth-century abbey. We roamed the corridors of the ruin, my Lecher antenna reporting magnetism, water, and pre-Christian religion. Henryk led us through a spiraling, dancing routine that turned hilarious. Jens-Peter opened our root chakras with his mesa on our tailbones — he was becoming an expert at this. Half a dozen of my colleagues allowed me to open their crown chakras, with some powerful reactions. We were a bit like children at play in this surprisingly pleasant environment. We explored the Kloster herb garden which turned out to be a chain of gardens, planted according to the part of the body served. There were lots of familiar floral faces.

Back at Gedsted we burned the waiting "world" despacho under bright sun, then had a final communal meal. Nearly everyone left in the early afternoon, leaving four of us: Margit, Peder, Henryk and me. We went off in search of another tumulus Henryk had found on the map. This was a long, low burial chamber adjoining a poultry farm on a muddy road. It was a double chamber, with tiny entrances north and south. The three of them crawled in on hands and knees, but it was too cramped for me. Henryk described the north room as serene, heavy, feminine, and he called the south room "confused". From the outside I measured 3'500 Bovis for the north and 5'000 for the south.

Then we drove slowly down a muddy track and across a wooden bridge — the brook below, the Simested °A, simply reeked of good trout fishing. Up, over and beyond we came to a ridge where seventeen small mounds formed a ley aligned along an east-west Hartmann line. The energy here was quite variable, but Hartmann knots marked each of these mounds. Henryk was very sensitive to everything here, a walking dowsing rod. There and then I taught him the Bovis method, urging him to trust his antenna-like perceptions.

My flight home from Aalborg was Monday afternoon, allowing Margit and I to have a private morning together, to compare metaphysical notes, to map our affinities. The aircraft — an old DeHavilland overwing propeller plane — took off on time that afternoon, climbed high above the sound, circled, and came right back to land at the airport. It appeared a baggage hatch had been improperly closed, but nothing was lost. In this jet age, such antiques still flew!

Getting home was easy, but being there was anything but tranquil. There were more than three hundred new messages in the computer's "inbox", mostly about the aftermath of "September 11", there was weak water pressure in the kitchen, the plumber had left a royal mess in the laundry room, and there was a bat in the house. Yes, a bat. When I lit up the studio a dark object began zooming back and forth, skimming my head. It took me a moment to diagnose what was happening, then I turned off the lights, opened the balcony door, and invited my panicky guest to find its way out. It did. Carpenters and plumbers had worked with doors wide open, as they are apt to do when there is no finicky housewife keeping track of things.

One month later I was on my way to Geneva airport again. This time the destination was the Netherlands. Eileen was coming to Europe for the first time, having been invited to give a seminar during the last weekend of October. Sponsored by a society of homeopathic practitioners, the seminar would focus on Eileen's particular techniques for the use of remedies derived from plants. When I asked her if a non-homeopath could participate, she asked me to come and serve as a metaphysicial "resource person". I needed no further encouragement. Rob agreed generously to meet me at Amsterdam/ Schipol and drive me to Waalwijk, a small city in the south of the country. In the conference hotel we met Eileen and her Dave for what proved to be a long supper animated with much talk.

More than one hundred Dutch homeopaths jammed the conference room the next morning for "Plant Talk". She introduced me as a shaman and as someone to whom they could address all their metaphysical questions, for she was sure her presentation would provoke them. She explained that the organizers Jan and Ger had asked her to present in two days the teaching for which she usually took five days. She started by introducing her own native American Eastern Cherokee upbringing and philosophy, her way of life, all illustrated in color on the giant screen that loomed behind her. Then she moved on to the concept of the Doctrine of Signatures, our chakras, numerology, and then the flowers, their colors, their parts. It was all very well-received. At the first coffee break I asked the young woman sitting next to me how she found it.

"It's exactly what I wanted!" she replied enthusiastically.

It was very educational for me too. I'd been teaching myself homeopathy and plant lore, based on my daily exposition to the varied menu of information that came across Eileen's Medicine Garden website.

She dwelt long on the controversial Doctrine of Signatures, which examines a plant or other organic substance (or something inorganic such as a mineral) to deduce from its appearance how it can be used. Classical homeopathy is not enthusiastic about this method, preferring the more scientific method of "proving" a new remedy. She pointed out that tribal and indigenous cultures around the world choose remedies on the basis of "signatures" — how the various aspects of the plant suggest their use and relate to the patient's symptoms.

Floral parts include stems, petals, stamens, anthers, pistils, shapes, leaves and a host of other botanical qualities, in addition to color and not forgetting the nature of its roots and the soil it grows in. She wove all of this skillfully into the homeopath's perception of his patient's human qualities, problems and symptoms. She introduced the native American concept she called "flower girl". This is basically a superposition of plant structure over the human body: the flower itself is related to the head, its stamens to the hemispheres of the brain, the leaves related to arms and shoulders, the stem related to the chest, abdomen and the lower limbs, and the roots related to feet and toes. Onto this vision she grafted our chakras, their colors and meaning. Everyone had received a thick sheaf of material she titled "Plant Talk Template", and during the weekend she struggled to cover it all. Five days crammed into two, and I have only skimmed the surface in these lines.

Meanwhile, during all the breaks I was in constant conversation striving to answer the questions she had known would come. Dreams, reincarnation, the host of phenomena that can crop up in meditation, how long had I known Eileen, could her system be applied to stones, what was Sedona like — such questions kept me busy between sessions. It was great fun for me and gave me the opportunity to meet a lot of people and make a few new friends.

In the evening Eileen offered a separate, optional program: "meeting your Guide". This had nothing to do with "Plant Talk" but a majority of the participants subscribed for it. She presented a standard ritual trip down the tree trunk and its roots, into the tunnel that leads to the Lower World, and calling for one's Guide to come. It was nearly a twin of what I had done once or twice in the past, notably during the weeklong seminar in France four years earlier.

Eileen gave this ritual added piquancy by talking first about shamanism. She explained that a shaman is a catalyst, a conduit, a medium between Spirit and the patient. The shaman moves at will into a state of non-ordinary reality and goes with her Guides into one of three levels called the Light World, the Real World, and the Dark (or Lower) World. The spirit Guides do most of the work, but the shaman is essential as a bridge between the spiritual worlds and the patient.

"We become what you need us to become, for you to heal," she explained.

Shamans have a place of safety deep inside Mother Earth where they go to rest and to be healed, and it is off-limits to the "Dark Side". Non-shamans can also go there simply to meet their Guides, and that was what she now proposed to this crowd of homeopathic practitioners.

I participated, of course. When she began to talk us down, I went through a squirrel hole in a big tree I like, down the trunk head first, through a root, into and down a long tunnel. When I emerged into a fascinating landscape, I sat up and looked around, calling for my Guide to appear. Even before I had finished asking a big bird flapped in for a landing, coming from my right side (which is preferred). It was an eagle. I asked for her name and she gave it. I asked if there was anything I could do to further my development.

"Meditate," she answered.

"How often should I come here?" I asked.

"Every ten days," the eagle replied

"Is there anything I can do for you?" I asked.

"Smooth my feathers."

I did so carefully, softly, then thanked her for coming.

Eileen was signaling us that it was time to come back, so I moved back up my tunnel, miniaturized myself to squeeze into the tree root, and thus moved upward toward the squirrel hole. I thanked the tree and asked to come again. Then I popped out of the tree and joined the roomful of travelers.

Afterward a handful of people asked my counsel on various features of what they had just experienced. I ended the evening in the bar chatting with two ladies who were curious about meditation and how to do it.

"Plant Talk" turned into a marathon the next day. Eileen had tons of material to present and she chose to wind it around an exposition of poppies, whose varieties present a multitude of applications as homeopathic remedies. There were, in short, a myriad of signatures to consider. In the afternoon she moved into the animal kingdom, dwelling at length on the qualities of the sepia cuttlefish -- sepia is a popular homeopathic remedy -- but also birds, snakes, and mammals. At the end of the day she asked me to step to the microphone to describe my proving of the Condor Stone essence, "in five words or less." I got away with about two hundred words and was just getting wound up when she tugged on my sleeve.

The whole day was a high. I had talk and questions from a lot of people, and when it was all over there were dozens of hugs. While sitting at the bar to "wet my whistle" a man came over to thank me for being there, for contributing my energy to the event. I was astonished, but pleasantly, of course. That's how I met Peter of Waalwijk, where I have since paused for overnights with him and his delightful wife Jeannette. Eileen, Dave and I finished the weekend with a merry meal at table with the organizers Jan and Ger.

These two days of Plant Talk were so successful they soon decided to produce a second installment the following year. Before that journey of return to the Netherlands, however, I went again to Denmark.

My Danish family was not planning another reunion, at least not so soon, but Juan was making his annual early spring trip to Europe. He would be giving another seminar in Denmark in early March of 2002. Susanne received me warmly in Copenhagen on the last day of February. The next afternoon Annette picked us up for the drive west out of the metropolis and then north. We were going to a country place outside Nykoebing. I'd been up that way to go to Sjaellandsodde eighteen months earlier, but instead of veering left toward the extremity of the peninsula we kept to the right. Our goal was a big house, a hostel called Anneberg.

Juan called this seminar "Level III", basing it on teachings from his three shaman teachers: Don Melchor Desa, Don Andreas Espinosa and Don Benito Qoriman. This being a kind of sequel to the Hatun Karpay work, but including quite a few people who had not taken the initiation in Peru, Juan sketched those concepts broadly rather than plunging into great detail. For that I refer you to the splendid book of Joan Parisi Wilcox, who has worked with Juan intensively and has spent considerable time researching Andean energy practices[1].

The Andean energy concepts we had been learning, Juan pointed out, are really globally known. He cited the teachings of Sri Aurobindo in India. Aurobindo taught that you can use kundalini to empower the self by bringing up earth energy but only after performing internal cleansing with cosmic energy. In this way Aurobindo tried to bring Nirvana down to use in daily life. This echoes and parallels the Andean teachings of Juan's three shamans. He proposed that a natural law must underlie the fact that so many masters have worked in the same way around the world in the twentieth century.

"They were all pioneers, 'surfing' over universal energy. They were breaking dams, letting energy flow, unblocking hucha," he told us.

After lunch on the first day we went out to the park around the hostel's broad lawns, a big tree, a pond. We were all bundled up against the wind and cold, for snow was imminent. Our objective was to grow our personal trees, working with the sami of two male energies — wind and sun — and two female energies — water and earth. We grounded ourselves in the earth, sucked up the pond water, and sent down our roots. Then we grew branches and leaves in the thin spring sun and the chilling breeze. It began to snow as we completed this exercise and scurried back into the hostel.

Juan's presentations this weekend were multiple and dense; it would take one chapter of this book alone to cover everything he gave us. This was a big group, about thirty or so, and eight of us had been to Peru together. And my second Susanne, the shaman, was there too, adding to my joy. There was lots of merriment, for Juan's group exercises often spiral into hilarity.

On the last afternoon he instructed us in the creation of a great serpent, an anaconda. He chose me to lead, to be the head of the "amaru" that wound through the large rooms of the main floor. My job was to pull sami from the cosmos and hucha from the earth and then send them through the back of my qosqo to the person behind, who was holding my shoulders. Each person was to receive both sami and hucha from in front and send it back. Meanwhile I shuffled through the rooms — to the considerable amusement of the kitchen crew — leading my wobbly snake, pulling in energy from above and below and pumping it backward as hard as I could. At the halfway point I began to receive a lot of blue and sent that back too. My instructions from Juan were to start coiling our serpent into a tight spiral, and this I did as we completed the circuit of the rooms. We wound up tighter and tighter until we were simply swaying in an oceanic mass, someone's shoes making the sound of a boat rubbing against a creaking pier. It was a powerful group effort which worked wonderfully well, for the sami and hucha reached the tail of our amaru.

To conclude Juan led us through a set of three exercises to pull up our kundalini power. We activated our energy belts and then made a deep connection with Pachamama, Mother Earth. To illustrate the final phase he drew on the blackboard an anaconda rising from the earth and clinging to a human backbone. As soon as he drew it I felt it move up my backbone, and later Randi and Susanne confirmed they had identical reactions. As we moved through the ritual my sense of the serpent was strong, comfortable, benign. It was not fearful at all but empowering. This ritual echoes the legendary arrival of the giant cobra to lie against the back of Siddhartha Gautama, the moment of enlightenment under the Bodhi Tree when the young prince became the Buddha.

There is another facet of this experience worth evoking. Two weeks earlier, while meditating with my monthly meditation circle, I went down into my place of safety deep inside Mother Earth. In the tunnel a serpent came to greet me. It was very long, like an anaconda or python, but was friendly, benevolent, guiding me, not in any way menacing. My attitude toward snakes has always been quite cautious and reserved, but this one immediately led me to feel comfortable. He was almost jolly. After Anneberg I realized that he had come to prepare me for his manifestation as the Amaru, just as long but much thicker.

Three months later I was on the road again, this time driving my new red Subaru to the Netherlands. One can drive from my home to Waalwijk in a day if one has iron endurance, but I choose to make these northbound trips in easier stages. I paused overnight at Marlenheim in Alsace, finding the winery recommended by friends, and laid in a supply of their delicious "vin mousseux", which is not allowed to be called champagne because it is not produced in said region. On the second afternoon I was in Waalwijk. This was going to be a longer, more complex seminar. Jan and Ger had invited Eileen to give the other three days of her weeklong Plant Talk. Sixty homeopaths showed up for three days in the middle of a workweek, which tells you how much they appreciated what she was presenting.

Over the winter and spring there had been a lot of electronic mail contact with some of people at the first seminar, especially the man named Peter who had thanked me for bringing my energy. He'd become a lively participant in the Medicine Garden. At the hotel I found a bouquet of red roses from Peter, and after supper he came to take me to his duplex painting studio and private gallery. Up in the gallery my eyes popped out. Peter has sold a lot of art, but around these walls I saw the best of his work, the ones he keeps for himself. The most compelling (to me) of his canvases were heavily-textured, dense, almost like flat sculpture. A warm, sometimes hot palette enhanced a definite mystic approach. I felt the inner fire of Mother Earth, a chaotic rapport between earth and sky, a question of mood as much as form. There was not exactly a *"Wind that blew the Sky away"* as had hypnotized me sixty-odd years earlier. If there were volcanoes in Peter's mind, he did not express them as such. Instead one sensed an intimate propinquity to the igneous extrusions that punch holes in Pachamama's crust. Humanity was miniscule, sometimes vaguely present in little phantom brush strokes but completely absent from a powerful black-and-red crucifix.

The next day he fetched me for lunch at his home. His wife Jeannette and I got along well from the start, for she is a librarian, a profession in which I felt totally at home. When Peter took me back to the hotel we found Eileen and her Dave at table. The moment she heard about Peter's paintings, it became imperative that all four of us go back to the upstairs gallery. She was enthusiastic about the depth of Peter's metaphysical approach. And I had more time to soak up his work. His Phoenix reminded me of the Condor Temple at Machu Picchu.

That night Eileen and I had work to do organizing the evening programs. She planned to spend one evening focused on the Condor Stone essence, for which I was to present my experience, my "proving" of the essence in greater detail. The second evening we would present a medicine wheel ceremony, for which I would be the drummer, using my double-faced drum. Rehearsal was necessary, for she had to be sure I mastered the exact beat she wanted. This evening I broke out a bottle of the Alsatian bubbly, for which Eileen expressed immediate approval. We talked and talked and drank and talked. She said that it was now time to really get into my shamanic training, but it would happen the native American way, without formalism. "On the job", in other words.

It would be fastidious to outline the next three days of Plant Talk teaching. Allow me to sketch a few of the highlights and skim the rest. She presented a powerful, dense, fascinating section on soil types and the kinds of people who grow on them. When she began to describe "sandy soil types" the Dutch homeopaths began to react with questions and debate. This intensified when she moved on to root types, for she told them they were "bulbs". The seminar became very animated at this point, until they began to understand how she meant that, how it applied to them and to their own diagnostic procedures. There were long sections on applying her template to various animal species, and there were, of course, more floral examples.

For the first evening program Eileen began with slides and text on Peru and Machu Picchu, leading into the story of how the Condor Stone appeared at her feet. We had evoked this essence very briefly at the end of the first seminar, and since then a number of the Dutch participants had been "proving" it for themselves. She asked me to present a quarter-hour about my Condor-induced dreams and kundalini experiences. Which I did. Then she asked the Dutch provers to share their experiences, and no one budged, no one raised a hand. Four or five of them did tell their stories the next morning, however. There had been some strong reactions, some very emotional effects. Tears alternated with blockages as their stories emerged.

None of them was prepared for the power of the following evening's "medicine wheel" healing ceremony. We were both attired in native American regalia, Eileen in a beautiful deerskin dress, and with our gear laid out on another skin. She placed the Pipe she carries next to the other objects she would need, such as the feathers and rattle I'd also brought. After I established a slow beat, she had the sixty file in and form a big ring in the conference room. She walked the circle twice, singing her sacred song and rattling. On her signal I stepped it up to a hard and fast beat. She picked up my condor and goose feathers and, with the rattle, began her healing circuit of the medicine wheel[2].

Using the feathers to open auras, flick out toxins, and then the rattle to seal the incisions, she worked her way around the room. She cleansed me first, so that they could see how she would treat them. All the psychic "gunk" went onto the floor, like Andean hucha. She made the circuit of the room in about twenty minutes, a real psychic tour de force, while I concentrated on maintaining the strong beat she needed to maintain her altered state. She'd told me ahead of time that twenty minutes was about as long as a drummer could hold the required beat, and this limitation applied to more profound shamanic rituals, such as soul recovery journeys. The practitioner had to move fast without losing concentration within a deeply meditative state.

When she had completed her circuit of the sixty she took the drum from me and used it to blast chakras, mostly the lower four, one person at a time.

Then I resumed drumming at a quieter rhythm while she brought the Pipe briefly to each participant. Then it was all over, and she signaled for them to file out. Emptying the room went slowly, as we had to help several people who were unsteady on their pins. One lady was out on her feet and both of us guided her slowly, sat her down in a chair near the door and used healing techniques (hands and the Pipe) to bring her around. Many were deeply affected, crying softly. Then she asked them to come back in quietly with their notepads and write their experiences.

We packed up and moved upstairs, together with a bucket of ice Eileen had promoted. I fetched the remaining bottle of Alsatian dew from the car, which kept the two of us busy talking for a couple of hours.

In the morning we began the seminar with a recapitulation of the ceremony, numerous people coming to the microphone to relate their experiences. Emotion filled the hall. Ultimately I had a busy day listening to emotional stories, helping, reassuring, and being part of further episodes of ongoing catharsis. One man told me about receiving the goodbye message of love from his late father. A lady broke down in my arms while visioning her daughter among "her people" — a tribe of Indians. The woman who had been out on her feet told me about bringing up and releasing deep reservoirs of old anger. Numerous people consulted with me or thanked me for my role. Apparently the drum had a powerful effect on many.

After finishing her elaboration of roots and how they link with character, Eileen explored the application of her Plant Talk template to the animal world — wolves, birds, skunks, snakes, and one last flower, the complex *Hyoscyamus niger* (henbane).

The essence of this flower can help to heal a fractured psyche, she proposed.

"Dark-center flowers can deal with the darkness in us," she explained. Henbane "is bold, arrogant and enjoys your discomfort. It changes colors, having a red corolla when young. It is diabolical, its center looking like a black tarantula." She supported this analysis with a detailed examination of the flower's parts, bringing the full power of the template to bear on the plant's potential.

Then it was over, with much milling around during extended goodbyes. We dined with the organizers Ger and Jan, and there was talk of some kind of a sequel to Plant Talk. A substantial number of the participants were eager for more of Eileen's kind of teaching. We discussed this a lot the next day on the road to Switzerland. Dave and Eileen were coming home with me for a short week of alpine botanical photography. With Eileen trading places with me at the wheel we made it back to my mountain fastness in a bit more than twelve hours, including a stop at Marlenheim for more provisions. It was a very hot day at the beginning of summer. We followed my preferred route southward: Eindhoven, Maastricht, Liège and the eastern edge of Belgium (the Ardennes), skimming Luxembourg, into France near Metz, then eastward into Alsace, finally southward to Basel and into Switzerland.

Eileen was goggle-eyed at the floral beauty exploding in front of her camera. During the next days we visited the alpine botanical garden at Pont de Nant and that spectacular valley and its riverbanks three times, the rain forest flank of the Chamossaire, and the private botanical garden created by William Aviolat at St-Triphon. It was a delight to have these close friends in my home for the first time, after four sojourns in their Red Rock country.

Two months later Eileen was back for a longer stay. There was indeed going to be a sequel to Plant Talk, but it would be a week-long seminar on the natural world from the native American perspective. It would take place in September in the north of the Netherlands. Before that she wanted to continue her floral photography, with a book in mind, and she had to do final editing on the manuscript of a novel.

These two weeks encompassed much ritual and meditative work together, during which she offered me some initiatory teachings. We were out in search of floral exuberance nearly every day. My new meditation room, completed the preceding fall, began to prove its energetic power. I'd applied sacred geometry to its proportions and Fibonacci ratios[3] to its fenestration, all of which reinforced the strong telluric current running straight through the room in the direction of the Dents-du-Midi across the valley. These ten thousand-foot peaks, seven of them rising from a common base, may be the most powerful energy transmitters of Switzerland. Certainly they gave Eileen a major mystique experience when Agnes and Mariette of my meditation group came one evening. Eileen connected with spirits she hadn't seen in years and was very tearful when she explained to us what had happened. She proposed a pilgrimage to the mountain, thus Agnes and Mariette returned two days later.

Eileen taught us the art of creating prayer bundles, using squares of red, yellow, blue and black cloth tied with red yarn. The four of us took our bundles — filled with trail mix, corn meal, tobacco and a few tiny pebbles — across the valley to that dramatic mountain mass. We walked along its northern flanks until we found a forest grove ideal for meditation and ritual.

There we climbed into the grove and, separating, found our individual trees for hanging our bundles and then meditation with them and the prayers they carried for us.

Wildflowers that Eileen had photographed in June had now evolved, some had disappeared and late-bloomers had shown up in the mountain meadows. We revisited the botanical gardens of June and ventured into other areas. This work was totally serious, focused on an eventual book, and she spent hours in the evenings loading hundreds of digital photos into her laptop computer.

At the end of August we drove north together, with my drum and other ritual objects wedged carefully among the baggage. It took us two long days to reach Steenwijk just south of the limits of Friesland. En route Eileen proposed training shamans in my new meditation room, whose energies had proven to be so appropriate for spiritual work. We roughed out the details for a seminar as we drove along. She had already trained shamans in seminars in New Zealand and now thought it was high time to work in Europe. I couldn't have agreed more, for it was now twenty years since I'd begun meditation and nine years since I'd heard the voices in Secret Canyon. With all the supporting events that had been piling in over the years, I was eager to move forward.

Steenwijk proved to be our shopping-and-restaurant town, but the Natural World seminar was to take place in a hamlet called Witte Paarden ("white horses" in Dutch). Ingrid, a homeopath who had participated in the Plant Talk seminars at Waalwijk, offered her teaching room for the sessions. She and Anneke had a modern farmhouse with a big herb garden and a separate teaching room big enough for our needs. The site was ideal, surrounded by green fields to the horizons. Ingrid prepared herbal remedies and gave classes in that room, and Eileen was delighted with its vibrations. She was even more delighted when she saw the lava rocks Jan had accumulated for the sweat lodge fires and then the red willow saplings which were to be cut to build the lodge. We had one day of rest between the road and the teaching, and at the end of that day we collected Dave at the railroad station in Steenwijk. He had flown over from Arizona expressly to create the sweat lodge and tend the fires.

Eileen had developed a cold in Switzerland and during the trip I'd begun to give her healing treatments at bedtime. She liked the lightness of the energy that channeled in for her. I worked both with hands on and hands off, and my Peruvian mesa was a help dissolving congestion in her chest. Even so, her voice was weak and husky for her first day of teaching.

We were nearly thirty in the seminar room for that opening session on Sunday, the first of September. Most participants were Dutch homeopaths from the Plant Talk seminars, but three people came from England and two from Austria. It would be incorrect of me to detail everything that Eileen taught. The subjects she covered included death, dying, rebirth, the meanings inherent to the four directions, and the symbolism of animals, stones, trees, plants, flowers. She taught the making of prayer bundles and how to use them; how to use feathers, rattles and crystals in healing; grounding one's self; and a lot about talking to plants, flowers, trees and rocks. There was an initiation with blue cornmeal, a journey to the Lower World to meet one's Guide — which could be anything, an animal of any kind from insect to elephant, a former human, a spirit. Such spirits were alive on another dimension but could join us on this one. We were going to get intimate with the inanimate too.

"Rocks and trees like to work with humans," she explained. "They are pure love, all heart, but they have no brain, no mobility. All things are messengers: flies, spiders, birds, creatures that appear out of nowhere," she added. We have to learn to be aware and to notice the symbols that present themselves.

On the third morning she taught the philosophy and practice of the sweat lodge. While she was giving that lesson she asked me to go outside to do a Pipe Ceremony for the red willow saplings we were going to cut. By eleven o'clock we were outside working under Dave's direction. He organized crews to cut the saplings, to prepare the site of the lodge and to dig holes for the saplings and for the fire pit. I chose to work with Pamela cutting willow saplings, for this was the part of the job I had not done in my earlier experience with sweat lodges. There was a handful of cutters in action, so she and I tackled the center section, chopping and sawing until we had it all down. Then we helped with the bending and lashing of our green poles into the dome-like skeleton of the principal lodge. We created two of them, a big one for the group's use and a "six-seater" for Ingrid and Anneke to use with a few friends.

By two o'clock Dave's fire to heat the stones was blazing, by three o'clock our lodges were completed, and at four o'clock Eileen began the first sweat with seventeen of us crowded together. She asked me to sit at the back, opposite the east-facing door, in order to "anchor the West". Dave brought in incandescent stones for the four rounds at Eileen's request. She poured water over them to create great billows of steam filling the lodge, then anointed them with fragrant herbs. She drummed, chanted, sang. We sweated, prayed, let our consciousnesses roam through the multiple dimensions inspired by the heat that overwhelmed the physical senses. I have a lot of trouble sitting on the ground, getting stiff rather soon, and sweat lodges are no exception. They bring me physical suffering before spirit takes command and lets me flow through time. It was finished after somewhat more than an hour. We crawled out, chanting "mitakuye oyasin" as we exited into the balmy September air. I lay for a bit, drinking a lot of water, then turned my attention to the others. Some were just lying on the ground in a state of beatitude, some were working through deep emotions, some needed comforting. Some had received visions. Eileen had been visited by a group of Druids.

The other half of the group got their sweat the next afternoon. Once again I anchored the West. Francine asked to be on my right and I asked Jeannette to honor me on the left; she's strong and served as a good guardian. This sweat was hotter than the previous day, but that was fine with me. I received a healing in the back, most welcome, and also in the abdomen. Afterward I stretched out for a few minutes, on my back under the big sky. Then people needed help. Eileen directed me to a lady who needed to finish sobbing out her grief before letting out two great shrieking primal screams. Then I shifted to another who was crying her heart out, all the frustration of the past welling up and out. I crouched next to her, cuddling, soothing, and when she complained of headaches I managed to extract what appeared to be dark worms from her forehead and temples. Eileen came along and removed more of those psychic critters. Then we all headed for the showers.

After the first day's teachings Ingrid and Anneke agreed to show me the interesting stones of the regions. In the elevator of our hotel there was a tiny picture of something that looked like a dolmen, and I wanted to see that. In this case I let my agenda get in the way of receiving messages. My friends first took me to a grove of trees not more than one hundred yards from the hotel. After we passed through some oaks and were in the grove, they showed me two big flat stones, which they said were known as the "Cow and Calf". I didn't get it. My mind was on a dolmen, and I insisted on seeing that. So they took me to the "hunnebad" stones, which proved to be a set of stones organized into a kind of a long dolmen, a low tunnel of stone slabs about ten yards long through which one could crawl. The vibrations were very disappointing. And then I learned the story: German soldiers had dismantled the historical stone structure during World War II to make room for a military landing strip. After the war the Netherlands government restored the stones, after a fashion.

After the second sweat lodge Eileen, Dave and I dined on the plaza in Steenwijk. Sitting in the open air we wolfed down perfect lamb filets (a steak for Dave), good veggies, and pitchers of water to recharge our tissues. On the way back to our hotel we had to pass the grove where I had been earlier in the week. It was on our left as we approached, and suddenly I "saw" the opening.

"That's a portal!" I exclaimed, quickly braking the Subaru and pulling off the road. We piled out of the car, and Eileen became as excited as I was.

Two big spreading oaks, flanked by smaller trunks, formed a gateway. It was so obvious I couldn't believe I had missed it earlier. We paused halfway to those oaks and asked permission, and after it came we passed into the grove. Quickly I found that the "cow" stone promoted a sense of weightlessness. I hadn't felt that the first time, but many stone sites gain energetic intensity after sunset. That was only the beginning. As we moved deeper into this forest Eileen saw the Druids who had come to her during the sweat. This time they were bearing gifts. Dave and I could not see them, but Eileen's clairvoyance was fully switched on. They told her there had once been a stone circle in these woods, twelve stones around a central menhir, all leveled by eleventh-century French troops bent on eradicating "heathen" sacred sites. The "cow" stone, now lying flat, had been the center point. The Druids had a request: they asked that we/Eileen restore the energetic configuration of the former stone circle, and she agreed to try. How this could be accomplished she didn't immediately tell Dave and I. But we knew her spirit was working on it.

In the hotel we ran some loads of laundry and the two of us prowled around the gardens, finding a powerful energy line running across the lawn. Along came two of our seminarists, Sylvia and Deirdre, and we led them to the grove. Eileen was sure they had both been Druids here. Sylvia walked toward the portal and began to get impressions.

"I see them!" she whispered.

"Talk to them," Eileen urged.

Sylvia had trouble with that. She was seeing, and she was receiving a message that echoed what Eileen had received earlier, but Sylvia couldn't get any deeper.

It's a wonder any of us slept that night, but I have recorded no special dreams!

What we now called the Druid Grove dominated the next morning's session.

Many of our participants knew bits and pieces of the medieval history of the region, and they brought possible modifications to what the Druids told Eileen. It might have been the eighth century, and the troops were not necessarily French but certainly Christian. Regardless, everyone was enthusiastic about restoring the energy of the site, if that could be done. At eleven o'clock we piled into cars and drove the few miles to the grove, the country lanes describing three sides of a square, for the air line between seminar room and grove was probably not more than a mile.

Eileen intuited where the circle had been, and she knew where the stones had stood. She used pairs of humans as proxies for stones and began to construct a living circle, placing Deirdre and Sylvia as the center stone. She placed my pipe on the ground to run the energy through the center and put me there as its guardian. I could feel the energy pouring through it as the ceremony progressed.

She began a Pipe Ceremony and then enlarged it to energize each of the new "stones", smoking all around each of them. This ritual stirred atavisms in many of our people; they were deeply moved, tears streaming down their cheeks. I could feel the spirits moving around us and admit to a few tears of my own.

Back at Witte Paarden we were greeted by a flock of crows wheeling overhead, one of the good signs. "Look!" someone exclaimed, pointing back toward the east, where the grove lay hidden in the landscape about a mile away. A small white cloud had appeared directly above it. The cloud took the form of an eagle, and then it mutated into the white dove of peace. All of us saw that. We'd lived a spiritual manifestation that had not been on Eileen's teaching syllabus.

That afternoon we learned how to talk to plants and rocks, which is easier than talking to phantom Druids. Several flowers declined to communicate with me but a red anthurium was chatty. It told me that the famous Brazilian healer "Joao" had problems keeping administration from getting in the way of his sacred work. This seemed to be a warning.

Eileen then talked about shamanism, saying that many of our group had demonstrated the potential to move in that direction. She would receive applications, she would not necessarily accept everyone who applied, there would be lessons and exercises via e-mail, and the core teaching would took place one year later at my home in the Alps. To close the seminar we moved out to the garden for a medicine wheel healing, with Paul and I drumming.

The next morning I took Eileen and Dave to the train station, returning to the hotel to close my bags and check out. The trip south could not start without a farewell visit to the Druid Grove. No, I didn't see any Druids, "seeing" is not my gift, but I sensed a warm welcome. It felt good all around me. There was a strong vibratory field: I found myself absolutely wading knee-deep through a surf of energy. My legs seemed to be pushing through a thickened atmosphere. It was a heaviness below, reminiscent of Andean hucha, and above there was lightness, like sami. When I reached the center I whirled around, spinning nine times. Don't ask me why. Instinct told me to do it. Before leaving I remembered to unlimber the pendulum: at 32'000 Bovis the Grove's energy was up and running. Cathedral strength already. (Subsequently we learned that various of the seminarists who lived not too far away returned in the following days to perform their own ceremonies.)

On my way out I paused to embrace the portal oaks. The group of trunks on the left whispered "love" in my ear, and when I went to hug the righthand cluster they said "energy". After that adventure I had to sit quietly in the car for a few minutes before I dared face the material world on the main north-south highway.

It was only a bit more than two hours down to Waalwijk, where Peter and Jeannette welcomed me with open arms. As a special treat Ada was there. She had been in the Plant Talk seminars but had traveled to New Zealand to follow shamanic training there. These lovely people spoiled me, sending me southward the next morning in a relaxed, happy frame of mind. Overnight I paused at Amnéville in its forest, for the wonderful zoo is a powerful magnet. Seeing the antlered people, the buffalo, the bears, all the big cats, especially the jaguars in their small jungle compound, flushes the roaring of the road from my ears and refreshes spirit.

The day after my return home André came for our first meditation since we'd been together in Peru eighteen months earlier. He was visiting his parents here on the mountain, and we began to plan hikes and climbs. Ultimately we squeezed in several all-day rambles over familiar territory and one delicious afternoon climbing rock. It was getting late in the season for more ambitious adventures, and his sojourn here was over all too soon.

Meanwhile, Eileen and I discussed via e-mail possible dates for the shamanic training, finally settling on October 2003. She announced it to our Natural World participants and the applications began to come in. My meditation room could accommodate six students with ease, eight in a pinch. When she had accepted six students, she thought it might stop there.

"Don't be hasty," I urged. "There is more enthusiasm than you realize. I'll bet you are going to have enough students for two or three weeks."

And so it turned out. In November 2002, two months after we hugged everyone goodbye at Witte Paarden, there were twenty candidates signed up for the following autumn. I organized their hotel space and spent a lot of miscellaneous time getting the chalet ready for the invasion. My good friend Hélène agreed to be "guard dog" for three weeks, insulating us from outside disturbance.

Eileen began sending out exercises and articles designed to loosen up her students' psychic muscles. The most important of those exercises was working with plants. We were to start visiting with plants as we had done on the last afternoon of the seminar, but now we would sketch, color, label the parts, and finally, with the plant's permission, we would enter through the roots and rise up the interior of the stem until we reached the flowering part. This applied to herbs, vegetables, flowers, bushes and trees. We would ask questions, especially how the plant could help us to heal. We did this continually, posting our journeys and their results on a private website Eileen had created to serve as a classroom. It was not at all easy but gradually everyone got into the swing of it. And, of course, we were learning how to enter another dimension and travel through it.

Some of these journeys were quite entertaining. After roaming inside *Clivia miniata*, the Kaffir Lily, I wrote:

"It's very feminine, concerned with second chakra issues, overflowing with love. An emotional bath. I felt a contrast between the frivolous nature of the blossom and the long flatness of the leaves, almost glued together for security. Clivia is gay, she wants to be frivolous but wants protection too. Inside her I felt this urge to be extravagant and extroverted. They prefer to be in a family, several bulbs planted together make a big clump with blade leaves spreading outward, protectively."

Iris germanica, Flag Iris, was quite a different story. When I asked to work with her, she said "I'd love it" in a bored tone without warmth, making me think of a high fashion model allowing yet one more photographer to snap her image (oh, yawn, how boring my dear!)

My initial admiration for this raving beauty began turning to caution. She seemed to be on a kind of a "head trip". As I climbed up inside, she seemed closed in on herself, introspective. I sensed a stunted personality, even though the shades of lilac and purple around me were ravishing. It was spacey up there, not grounded. No sense of heart, and she was not connected to the soil, stands too far above it. Her dead blossoms, having become beige, curl up like a crinkled foetus. As for a therapeutic use, she remained silent, leading me to suspect this iris could be used homeopathically to treat autistic conditions.

Golden Rain, the flowering tree named *Cytise*, turned out to be an old grump. "This tree is not happy," I wrote, "does not like the fast-growing pine planted near it. Golden Rain leans away from his neighbor. The tree is angry, crabby and grumpy, possibly it can be used to treat such conditions. It is really intolerant of evergreens, is petulant on the subject." Eileen proposed it could be used to treat prejudice.

Buddleia is one of my favorite bushes in the garden, but you have to wait until late August and September to see its showy blossoms. It grows to eight or nine feet and the willowy branches begin to bend with the weight of the big purple cones. *Buddleia davidii* then becomes home to dozens of butterflies who appear to be so drunkenly attached to the flowers that they allow humans to approach within a few inches. It's a photographer's delight.

"The butterflies carouse recklessly," I reported. "The bush is a butterfly social club and a place of feeding frenzy. It is a place of uninhibited joy, of reckless abandonment to pleasure. One could theorize that Buddleia people love a lot of company, very extroverted. Its essence might work on depression, but one must be wary of the component of recklessness. There is no symmetry to the root development, and the branches seem to twist in every direction."

Over the winter Eileen and I began to plan another trip. She was invited to a "think tank" homeopathic conference in England at the beginning of June. Also she wanted to have a quickie seminar with as many of the shamanic students as could get to Witte Paarden. We settled on a plan that brought her here first to finish up her botanical photography, then off to England. I would drive north and we would meet in the Netherlands, after which we would cross to England for a couple of weeks of what I like to call "mystics at play".

In the spring of 2003 I created a course of teaching meditation by e-mail, for many of the Dutch group had never learned that art. To me it was clearly an important tool in any shaman's kit, and Eileen agreed with that. There were five lessons, which I sent out every week or two. Questions came back, leading to a certain amount of "online" counseling.

Eileen arrived for the last week of May. We revisited some of the botanical gardens and sites for further photography. While she prowled around snapping flowers I sat quietly and journeyed into them. We managed to burn up her week doing things that pleased us, a combination of metaphysical work and living well. After taking her to the airport I had five days of writing, gardening, journeying into plants, packing and preparing my house to be left alone for a few weeks. Then I headed north. After overnighting with cousins in the center of Holland, I found my way to a hideaway in the deep countryside. Lique and her artist husband Erwin lived at the end of a dirt road, in a paradise of green fields bounded by forests. She was one of the group and would be coming to Switzerland in the fall for our seminars. They had offered me a guest house about one hundred yards across the meadows. It was big and rambling, meant as a center for campers who would come in the summer, but it served me handsomely. At day's end I found Eileen in Witte Paarden.

We started the seminar on a Sunday. Eileen wanted to see how everyone was coming along. Over the winter she had done a soul journey for each of them, and they were learning to journey inside the plant world. We devoted the morning to a debriefing, each of them relating what changes she/he was experiencing. And changes there were! Some of them looked different, some of them "came on" differently. One was more feminine, one was more solid and certain in her thinking, several simply exhibited a new radiance. It was remarkable. In the afternoon Eileen went deeper into the technique of crystal healing, which had been cut short by our work in the Druid Grove. Then she allotted me an hour to work with my online students and lead them in a group meditation.

We were finishing up a successful effort at "going within" when Eileen entered and dropped a bombshell. No one had taken the initiative to prepare the sweat lodge and the fire pit, therefore there could be no sweat. It was on the agenda, but nothing had been done. Eileen then lectured them on the native American way of everyone just pitching in and getting things done without a boss.

They were stunned. There were a few minutes of awkward babble, and I could see there had also been a failure of communication. I broke in.

"If you will get organized to prepare everything, I will build the fire and tend it," I told them. "For those of you who can stay over, we can have a sweat tomorrow." Eileen, indispensable, agreed.

At five-thirty we moved into action and divided up into small crews. Some chopped and split wood for my fire. Three went to work cleaning out the two fire pits — one outside for heating the stones and the other in the center of the lodge, where the stones would ultimately glow. Several others began to stretch the plastic covers over the sapling frame of the lodge. In an hour it was ready for the next day.

During the morning session, which was mostly discussion of some aspects of shamanic work, they voted unanimously to have the sweat at three o'clock.

At twelve-thirty I got my team busy twisting newspaper and reducing kindling to smaller pieces. That's another thing my wonderful grandmother taught me: how to build a fire. Working furiously we got the fire laid correctly in its own pit and I arranged the stones on top. Then Eileen took them all into session again while I lit and tended my fire. Winds were blowing in every direction, a good sign from the spiritual sense but rather challenging for fire safety. I had to keep the perimeter damp — sparks kept trying to spread into the grass — and I used the dug soil to build a firebreak, rimmed by burned-out fire stones. Eternal vigilance was necessary. By three o'clock our stones were incandescent, deep inside ash.

Ingeborg and Els, who helped prepare the fire, had volunteered to be my assistants tending it, but as it turned out their sacrifice was unnecessary. Jos said he did not feel well enough for a sweat, and he offered to handle the fire alone. This meant we three could also sweat. Eileen placed me next to the door, opposite her, so that I could help Jos bring in hot stones for each of the four rounds.

This was my best sweat ever, for I had room to move my legs a bit and my back suffered less. I recognized one of Eileen's songs and was able to sing along behind her. The drum was awesome, deep and full. In one of the early rounds I felt a small, furry thing under my hand — I imagined something like a gopher or a small squirrel. Many other things happened during the sweat that I did not sense. For some, the top of the lodge lifted off and several were in the stars with Eileen. They saw Druids and Tibetan monks, heard monks chanting Gregorian, and there were visions of a big golden circle of light, jaguars, a white horse, and dragonflies. Jos saw two of those circling above the outside fire. The day before a big dragonfly chose to die on the bumper of my car parked outside the seminar room. Eileen held it a moment, it was clearly dead, then laid it carefully on the car. We turned our attention elsewhere, then when we looked again the dragonfly had vanished. This event allowed Eileen to point out that dragonflies are shamanic symbols, along with butterflies and jaguars.

The debriefing was rollicking, so many had experienced so much that was wild and wonderful. Eileen had seen the tiny animal I had only felt. "It was a baby hedgehog," she said. That corresponded with what I had sensed. It does not seem to be my privilege to have visions of the cosmos and to hear heavenly hosts, but in my heart I honored my baby hedgehog. I have a fondness for these country creatures and would love to have one resident in the garden. In meditation the next morning, Tuesday, I went down to my private retreat and called the hedgehog to me. He gave me his name and then became instantly adult in size. During that meditation I went into a country space, poplar and birch trees and a green area in front of a steep grassy hill, and there was the suggestion of a white horse, plus a man in a red polo shirt. We had quite a conversation and he said we would meet again in England. "Is that hill Silbury Hill?" I asked. "No", he replied.

Late that afternoon Ingrid joined me in a visit to the Druid Grove. I had a mission: to plant one of three stones given me by Claude, a very clairvoyant man who has unearthed and set erect buried menhirs on a round hill near my home. In front of the portal Ingrid and I met an energy barrier, but "they" pulled us in. Then a fallen sapling barred the way. You don't step over such obstacles when in a sacred place. With my hands and sacred intent I opened a slit and spread a kind of window through which we stepped. There was lots of energy in the glade, and Ingrid saw the Druids. I held up Claude's stone and told them about it, asking guidance to plant it. Then I slowly rotated, scanning the energy with one hand, seeking the right line, my hand tingling when I hit it. I turned again for a double-check. Then I moved ninety degrees away and scanned from another direction until I got an intersection. The spot was under a tree. I looked at Ingrid, who was watching the Druids, and she nodded. Right! There I buried Claude's stone, then stepped back to salute the Druids. Ingrid said they were gesturing thanks and laid a gift, wrapped in red, at my feet. I picked up this etheric package, and we said goodbye, leaving the Grove.

We left our Dutch friends the next morning, Wednesday, for the port of Hoek van Holland. It's fun to travel with a fellow hypoglycemic! No need to apologize for always being hungry and having a big appetite. We had a marvelous early supper after our car ferry put out to sea. The crossing was smooth and easy, disembarking rapid, and the Time Zone change gave us an extra hour to find our bed-and-breakfast buried in the deep countryside of East Anglia. Highfields Farm was not easy to find, but we were welcomed nicely. Our room was cramped but well-appointed, and the bathroom gleamed. So close to the summer solstice the sun was high deep into the evening, inviting us. We took the hint and walked abut two miles up a farm lane between wheat fields, wildflowers, brambles, bushes and old trees. Country air cleared our souls and brought us the scents of a blooming land.

It took one more day on the road to bring us to the heart of Wessex, specifically to our hostelry in the town of Radstock. We had chosen this location because it seemed to be more or less centrally-located between our destinations of Glastonbury, Wells, Avebury and Stonehenge. We had ten days in which to dip our toes into new energies and were itching to get started. After installing our belongings in our room we drove off to Glastonbury. There wasn't enough of the day left to do very much, but we strolled the streets, poked our heads into boutiques, stone shops and bookstores. The verdict was easy: we had found "Sedona East". Instead of Red Rocks there were the ruins of the famed Abbey, the Tor to be climbed, and the Chalice Well and Garden to be enjoyed. Back in Radstock Paul and Verena served us a superb supper which fueled our enthusiasm for what lay ahead.

One of the first things that happened in Glastonbury the next morning was that I met my hedgehog. We walked into a shop that had a little bit of everything and there he was, smiling at me. He had grown once again. From a baby cuddled under my palm, then become adult, now he was as big as a basketball. Not alive, not even a stuffed carcass, some kind of imitation pelt filled with who-knows-what. No matter, we connected and he came home with me.

We were supposed to connect also with Arizona friends, and that happened in laid-back Glastonbury. Rosemary and Ani guided us to a good place for lunch and we met them again later in the day. Inside the Abbey park Eileen and I went to work trying to unlock whatever secrets lay hidden there. There are fragments of ancient towers and walls, and the footprints of the ancient pillars holding up the vaulted roof are still present as stone outlines[4]. I found the vibrations of what I believed to be an undiscovered crypt in the grassy transept. I was working with a tree that helped me figure out the complicated arithmetic of some ancient steps when Eileen came over.

She'd just met the ghost of an angry abbott in red robes. He was buried at the back of the abside, behind the altar. He wanted all the tourists, all the faithful, to go away, get off the grounds of his beloved Abbey. He'd been drawn and quartered, which would make anyone grumpy, but we were disappointed in his lack of Christian tolerance toward the tourists, at least some of whom were surely reverent as they trod the Abbey lawns.

After my little dowsing task was complete and jotted down a magnetic pull drew me to that abside. More than that, the story of the abbott had stirred in me a critical attitude that demanded expression. I stood in front of those ruins and criticized the ghost abbott for not following his faith in Jesus, for not accepting the promised Resurrection that he had preached. "How could you crab at the pious believers who come to your church in reverence?" I scolded. In sum, I gave him a solid talking-to before trying to guide him toward the Light and to meet his Jesus. Apparently it worked. Eileen came back to the area and said he was gone. A big tree told me I had done well. I was astonished at both my own brashness and at its result.

New dimensions do not open every day. This moment with the ghost abbott was a real mind-expander, but there was more dead ahead. Ani had told us about a new crop circle on Windmill Hill near Avebury, with rough directions how to find it. We set out early the next day on the long drive eastward, pausing only to photograph the White Horse of Cherwell. Ani's directions were good — we found Windmill Hill easily enough — but somehow we missed seeing the "gate slightly ajar". We drove up the hill, parked, walked into a small forest and around the hill, over its evocation of ancient fortifications and back into the car. It was a sunny day in mid-June, getting hot. We drove down the road, seeing nothing except a couple of jackrabbits bounding past a huge manure heap. At the bottom of the hill we turned right into another farm lane and then we saw the cereal sculpture. It lay below the road we had just left, a full five hundred yards away across fields, fences and hedges. We parked, hiked along a bridle trail, scrooched through barbed wire and found our way into the lower edge of the field, following a tram line along the bottom[5]. The formation stretched far above us, and we saw it would be impossible to reach without tramping through the farmer's maturing barley, effectively trashing it. Thus, perspiring in the midday sun, we drove back up that dirt track and quickly spotted the slightly open gate. It was directly opposite where the bounding hares had scampered across our path. They had given us the sign and we had failed to recognize it! I have a mental image of two hare snickering behind that manure pile. "Pay attention, dummies!" On the gate was a cardboard box for contributions, which we honored, before following an easy hard-packed tram line into the circle.

We prowled through it in wonderment. Bit by bit we understood the outer perimeter of twelve arcs was all scallops. There was an inner ring and a central area, both defined by more scallops and both baffling to understand on the ground. We meditated for a while in the center, feeling a great calm.

Throwing out ideas willy-nilly, we groped for an explanation. I asked if it was planetary; Eileen spoke of the eccentric orbit of Venus. The Lecher came out of my bag, quickly responding affirmatively to all six frequencies available for Venus as well as those for Goddess and feminine energy. I spent an hour walking the perimeter, trying to sketch the form into being. Were these forms heavy-bodied birds? Was I seeing the outline of the three-lobed hypothalamus? Was the central section a replica of the coronavirus? We puzzled over the design during a late lunch outside the Avebury cafeteria. It was clear we would have to search the Internet to get our answer.

Then it was time to introduce Eileen to the wonderful stones of Avebury, here in the heart of England's concentration of earth energies. We strolled into the meadows lined with menhirs, touched, meditated, photographed. These moments among the stones are heart-filling for me, and of course my companion was quickly filled with a similar joy. In the shade of my favorite "Aries" stone I planted one of the stones given me by Claude, thus linking Avebury with the resurrected menhirs on our mountain. Eileen and I roamed the stones until the heat began to wear us down, then we retreated into a grove of four grandmother beech trees to cool off while meditating within their embroidery of exposed roots.

The inner complexities of the Windmill Hill formation sprang suddenly to life when seen from above. Back in our B&B, and thanks to Paul's generosity with his computer, we discovered the aerial photographs which had been posted on the Internet[6]. The outer circle created a giant braid, the inner section resembled a kind of a crown, and one could also see four hearts. None of this had been visible while tramping the inner paths through the waist-high crop. The circle had been created during a rainy night, and we had seen clearly that its artists left no muddy footprints. It measured more than one hundred yards in diameter, which explained why it took so long to walk around and through its avenues, stopping from time to time to sketch.

Could the stars and planets be telling us about their worlds in the only language available? Our enthusiastic brainstorming over supper allowed a wild idea to bubble up: that the circular designs are the energetic signatures of heavenly bodies and extra-terrestrial civilizations. America's space program had sent into outer space a satellite decorated with signs, symbols, and two human images. And what had come back? Crop circles, which became more and more complex with each succeeding summer season.

Several days later we returned to Windmill Hill under cloudy, cooler skies. We had learned how to work together to measure vibratory rates, Eileen's psychic ability providing a double-check to what my pendulum told us. To our surprise there was nothing resembling symmetry. At the top, nearest the gate, the pendulum gave us 35'000, but otherwise the outer perimeter yielded rates in the 16'000 to 19'000 range. Values in the inner ring varied widely but were always lower, between 8'500 and 13'000. We theorized an interplay between the rich telluric energies of the region, themselves variable from spot to spot, with some kind of unknown cosmic intelligence.

Say "megalithic monument" to most people and they will reply "you mean Stonehenge?". Those noble sarsens have captured the public mind. Nothing else exists. I discovered the fallacy of this point of view in my first visit to Wessex, years earlier. Yes, Stonehenge is unquestionably important, but lesser-known Avebury is far and away the major site in terms of energy.

Stonehenge is isolated energetically from the powerful intertwining of the Michael and Mary lines. It does, however, occupy a central position on a shorter ley that runs for thirty-one miles from some minor sites north of Avebury, through Silbury Hill, thence to Stonehenge and southward through Old Sarum and Salisbury[1]. With some perserverance you can extend this line to Bournemouth on the sea and across the Channel to the French Cotentin Peninsula and to the sacred Mount St-Michel in the gulf of St. Malo. The twelfth-century abbey crowning this tiny granite island very probably occupies an ancient Druidic site. Would there have been a connection at some time with northern neighbors? I leave it to your imagination. Miller and Broadhurst say that the axis of Glastonbury Abbey, which is on the Michael line, points straight across country to Stonehenge[8]. Extending that line brings one to Canterbury, more than one hundred fifty miles from Glastonbury. Canterbury is now Britain's ecclesiastic center, its religious equivalent of Rome, but it appears to have been a site of pilgrimage since prehistoric times. Thus Stonehenge could have been some kind of a hub.

We entered with the crowds and slowly wound around the stones in the counterclockwise (feminine) fashion imposed by authority. Sitting on a bench and just tuning in, we tried to filter out the endless stream of humanity. Eileen connected with a rather disinterested and huge spirit, who was clearly bored with all the visitors. It showed her spirals of energy and told her that they were stronger morning and evening and strongest of all during the night, when the meadow was closed to the public. That made a lot of sense to us. Even so, my Bovis measurements registered high energy when I projected into the center. Where we sat, at the southeast, the method yielded 32'000 angstroms, and there I planted Claude's third stone, connecting Stonehenge to his resurrected menhirs. A bit farther along, the Heel Stone is the sunrise point for the summer solstice, and on its little bridge the reading soared up to 54'000. The solstice would be only five days later.

Woodhenge, only two miles away, inspired more effort. It's a completely different picture. Eileen met a group of Druidesses, quite gay and happy to greet her. As usual, I did not see them, but I have no doubt of their presence.

They described a set of labyrinthine itineraries among the stumps which we did not attempt. Using the Lecher antenna we began to examine the site's ancient uses, with the priestesses confirming most of what we got. In sum, this was a place of teaching, where the mystery schools were studied. There was a strong shamanic tradition here, and there are links to Saturn, Pluto and the Moon. It was not a place where life as such was celebrated but a place of sacrifice; it was an entrance to the Dark World and not to the Light World. We did not try to enter either.

We devoted another day to three sites south of Avebury. At Silbury Hill we were limited to standing and staring at the conical mound. The visitor's fence is a good hundred yards away from the hill, frustrating us as at Stonehenge, and we would have loved to clamber over the fence and go to it. When we arrived there was a police car in the parking lot, and a kind of a constable was standing around. He seemed determined that we should understand we couldn't go there. We tried to penetrate the mound telepathically but got nowhere. It links visually Windmill Hill, a neolithic assembly point far older than Avebury, and nearby West Kennett Long Barrow. Silbury Hill itself is alleged to be as old as the Egyptian pyramids. The short ley of which it is the center is like a spoke radiating a few degrees off the Avebury-Stonehenge line on which it also lies. Thus Silbury Hill is clearly an energetic hub. We felt ourselves to be under intense scrutiny, to the point that I did not pull out the dowsing gear. Later, at a distance but within sight of the mound, my pendulum gave me readings of 49'000 and 51'000 angstroms. Silbury only looks motionless; it dances.

West Kennett Long Barrow is barely a mile away and easy to reach. This is England's longest burial mound, measuring three hundred forty feet from end to end. Huge slabs greet the visitor, and turning behind them you find the entrance. On the left and right are a set of four small, dark rooms flanking a forty-foot corridor, and that ends in a slightly larger space where lots of people have lit candles and done ceremony. The energy in that inner chamber rocked us back and forth. We dubbed it a "place of balance", and it vibrated at 30'000 Bovis. This portion had been a place of initiation, Eileen opined, and the Lecher antenna agreed. It pointed to a staggering array of earth goddess, astronomical and shamanic connections. Sections of the back wall are bricked up, limiting public access to about one-eighth of the barrow. About fifty skeletons, mostly fragmented, came to light when the barrow was excavated in 1956. Why is the rest blocked off?

Archaeology dates the barrow's construction to about 5'500 years ago, using a special limestone quarried at Frome, twenty-five miles away. It is said the mound was used for 1'300 years and then filled in with rubble. At some point it became a mortuary. Julian Cope reports a theory about observing planetary movements[9]. It is tempting to say there are unsolved mysteries here, which may or may not be the case. The barrow is on both the Michael and Mary lines, and there must be a reason which we have not yet penetrated.

We'd been hoping to find a dolmen, and eventually Eileen's scanning of our Ordnance Survey map found one in this same general area. Labeled the "Devil's Den", it appeared to be just west of Marlborough. It took us a long time to find the right country lane, for there were no directional signs. After a couple of false starts we reached a parking area near a horse farm and began walking a public trail westward. Eventually we spotted big rocks in a hollow at our left, and it was necessary to leave the main trail and walk a wide spiral through fields before we got into the appropriate bean field. There it was, a huge stone — about three to four yards on each of its sides and about a yard thick — balanced precariously on a couple of substantial boulders, themselves supported by smaller stones. There was shooting in trees bordering a farm on the southern rise; it worried Eileen but I put it down to hunters, having been married to one.

This structure appeared outrageously and satisfyingly pagan. One could understand why local clergy probably attributed it to the Devil. Eileen clambered up into the shelter, up on one of the supporting stones, and I lost sight of her top half. After some minutes she climbed down again, grinning, and told me to put my head into the hollow I would find up there.

Inside the dolmen I hoisted myself up onto a precarious ledge and found the hollow in the underside of the giant table. It was like the mould for a helmet resembling a bishop's mitre. Cautiously I moved my head up into the helmet hole. It must have been created deliberately, for it was a reasonable fit for a human head. A cavernous, cosmic void kind of sound filled my ears. The rushing sounds of the cosmos began to engulf me, and there was a faint whistling. This was a very spacey sensation, wearing a ten-ton granite hat with sound effects. A thread of cold air, no bigger than a flea, teased my crown chakra. Climbing down, standing again on terra firma, I was just a bit wobbly.

"I think this is a teleportation tool," Eileen said, "but I booted it. The spirit of the place asked where I wanted to go, and I didn't catch on fast enough and answered stupidly. He lost interest in me immediately."

Shotgun blasts continued from the hill, and Eileen expressed skepticism about my "hunters". I tried to reassure her that buckshot doesn't carry much more than thirty-five yards and we were much farther away from those trees that masked the shooters from our view.

The Lecher antenna gave us a coherent set of responses. Among its forest of "no's", it confirmed Druidic ceremonies, both the Michael and Mary lines, both masculine and feminine energy, and, to our great interest, the Pleiades. Could you get there from here, wearing the granite helmet?

With buckshot rattling the bean plants rather close by, I tested the vibrational rates. Just outside the dolmen the pendulum indicated a fairly routine 17'000, but up inside was a different story: a cosmic 67'000. Aha!

By that time I had to agree with Eileen that perhaps someone was indeed shooting at us. Pellets were falling like hailstones on the broad leaves a few yards away. We were not trampling bean plants and we had every right to be there, for the dolmen was protected by English Heritage. Apparently that cut no ice with the invisible farmer on the hill. His shotgun had a range far exceeding my thirty-five yards, and he was pointing it high enough to carry from his woodsy hiding-place to the bean plants just short of the dolmen. One could theorize that he and the dolmen had a feud going, for the plants close around the structure were definitely stunted in comparison to the rest of the field.

Subsequent reading also explained the pinpoint of cold air on my crown chakra. "...it used to be an article of faith that if water was poured at night into any of the hollows of the roof-stone, it would always be found drained to the last drop in the morning by some demon[10]."

Up in Avebury one of the numerous friendly folk we met while browsing among the menhirs told us that our assailant had a bad reputation with English Heritage, continually removing the directional signs they installed. In one of the shops we met Brian, the local antiquarian and a fellow pagan full of useful tidbits of information. After we told him about our visits to Windmill Hill he gave us directions to a new formation under the White Horse[11] within sight of Alton Barnes. The big field sweeping up to Milk Hill adorned by the White Horse seems to receive an important cereal design every growing season.

It's a long hike to this slope, uphill and downdale, at least a mile over rough trails skirting the wheat fields. The very idea of hoaxers lugging heavy rollers and other big garden tools to this site in the middle of a short midsummer night, and still having time to execute a complicated design, is preposterous. It had to come from above. This formation was easier for us to comprehend than the one on Windmill Hill. The external design offered a six-pointed star and four circular patterns rippled concentrically inward -- six triangles, six leaves, etc. This was all about things in sixes, which in numerology can suggest the idea of completeness. Darkening skies suggested we had better not linger, so we made a few measurements and then scurried away ahead of the storm. Bovis values were modest, averaging about 8'000, and I attribute that to the rapid shift in barometric pressure. The Lecher was more generous with ideas. It gave positive readings for Life, a Light World entry, feminine energy, the Mary line, shamanism, Neptune the mystical, and the Pleiadian constellation.

The summer solstice was upon us; our Wessex romp was drawing to a close. We visited Glastonbury over and over again, working in the Abbey, meditating in the fairies' grove on the slopes of the Tor, roaming the Chalice Gardens and journeying with some of the plants. Summer warmth was lovely there during the afternoon of the Solstice, when numbers of people gathered for peaceful meditation around the pools. Or nearly peaceful. Two men insisted on carrying on a very banal conversation, totally inconsiderate of more than a dozen people sitting around them in meditation. Why did I not follow my impulse to get up and give them a "shut your traps or get out of here"? Because I knew that would send my adrenalin into orbit, just the opposite of my purpose in being there.

Wells, within sight of the Tor, is my favorite among all the Christian cathedrals. The giant scissors arches and their "eyes" are unique symbols in stone of the All That Is. It had taken a lot of insistence to bring my companion there, but it proved to be the right day. Waves of energy greeted us on the walkway in front of the main doors, and inside a chorus of beautiful female voices, a truly angelic host, was giving a concert in front of the transept. That, coupled with the tremendous vibrational force, brought tears to our eyes. Conditions were not appropriate for much dowsing, but several pendulum readings yielded 25'000 Bovis in the nave and the transept. In the garden we established that the Michael and Mary lines were both present. Eileen, not at all a Christian, received a message from Jesus to the effect that "this is Mary's house". Meaning his mother. There are some graves in the garden, which began to put an idea into our heads. We tested that idea with the pendulum, getting nothing.

So we went back into the transept and were able to stand on the precise power point to ask a critical question: "Is Mary the mother of Jesus buried here?" The next day, in the Mary Chapel of the Abbey at Glastonbury, we asked a parallel question: "Is Mary the Magdalen buried here?". Allow me to emphasize that neither Eileen nor I consider outselves to be Christian, that both of us are extremely skeptical about the veracity of much that is in the Gospels, and that these questions also fly in the face of all the unorthodox legends about the post-crucifixion period.

In both cases the answer was "yes", unequivocally, and with my spirit standing aside, neutral, my physical eyes closed while Eileen watched the pendulum move. In the Mary Chapel my tools provided a mass of additional information: Druids, a "mystery school", the Michael line, teleportation, and the constellations Draco and the Pleiades, with a big hit on the latter's star Alcyone. Our work attracted a handful of spectators. One of them proved to be a local dowser who showed us exactly where, in his opinion, had stood the original church which Joseph of Arimathea built of "mud and wattles".

That particular morning's work ran huge amounts of energy, really draining me, and at a given moment we had to surrender and head to the "Who'd a Thought It?" pub for a solid lunch.

After a day of lounging, packing and writing our e-mail "postcards", it was time to drive Eileen to Heathrow airport for her afternoon flight. Over lunch we tried to review the planning for October's seminars on my mountain, but our spirits were too full of the wonderful mystical adventures we had been living. After that parting I embarked on a series of visits in West Sussex, in Richmond with Pam, and in the Midlands. Doug and his mother Alaine took me on a misty, drippy exploration of sacred stones in the Peak District lying between Sheffield and Manchester. An overnight sail from Hull deposited me on Belgian soil and that evening I slept under the trees of Amnéville.

To unwind from a day of steering down rainswept freeways I took my habitual stroll through the zoo. Nothing quite refreshes the spirit like communion with these creatures who share our physical world but, one could say, in another dimension. I paused long in front of the thick bullet-proof glass wall separating me from the jaguars' jungly compound. As always, I tried to engage their attention to send a psychic greeting.

Suddenly the black jaguar sprang to life, lunging directly at me against the glass wall, standing on his hind legs, mighty forepaws at my shoulders, face to face. Immediately he slid off the wall and stalked away. It was not an attack but a greeting; there was no display of fangs, no intimidating roar. I was not startled, did not budge, continuing to focus on his mind, but he did not deign to notice me after regaining his shady platform. Our animal spirit companions do indeed drift back and forth between our dimension and those secret lands where their souls dwell.

[1]   Joan Parisi Wilcox, *Masters of the Living Energy, the mystical world of the Q'ero of Peru.* Rochester, VT: Inner Traditions, 2004. xvi+336p., index, glossary, bibliography, notes. ISBN 1-59477-012-3.
      This is a revised and expanded edition of the author's *Keepers of the Ancient Knowledge,* 1999.
[2]   At Anneberg my Danish friend Jeanett gave our "Peruvian family" goose feathers she had mounted and provided with a handle and some decorative glass beads. Mine has become an invaluable tool.
[3]   Leonardo "Fibonacci" of Pisa, the preeminent European mathematician of his time, brought an interesting number series back from studies in Egypt. This "summation" series was only a small part of his massive *Liber Abacci,* published in 1202 and 1228.
      His book introduced the decimal system amd Hindu-Arabic numbers to Europe. The Fibonacci series is constructed by adding the two previous numbers to get the next one. Thus: 1, 1, 2, 3, 5, 8,13, 21, 34, 55, 89, 144, and on to infinity.

As the series progresses one can observe that the ratio of one number to the next is close to .618 to 1. Working backward, toward the next lowest number, the ratio is 1.618. This has become known as the "golden ratio", for it is observable in nature. It is the basis of the logarithmic spiral, such as seen in the shells of snails and sea creatures, many botanical forms, whirlpools and hurricanes, atomic particles, the horns of some animals, galaxies in the cosmos. The ratio appears in human DNA, proportions of the human body, the Great Pyramid and some examples of classical architecture. Many painters use it to govern the proportions of their canvases as well as the internal composition. Look for the proportion three-to-five when studying a work of art. The brilliant financial analyst Robert R. Prechter, to whom I am indebted for acquainting me with this natural phenomenon, applies Fibonacci ratios to financial analysis, with considerable success. Find Prechter's books on his website: www.elliottwave. com.

4 Once one of the grandest and richest of England's cathedral-abbeys, Glastonbury was abandoned and allowed to fall into ruin after the "Dissolution" in 1539, when King Henry the Eighth broke from the Catholic Church.

5 In England the tracks made by farm tractors are called "tram lines". These lines cross Wiltshire's cereal fields at regular intervals, providing easy access to the circular formations without breaking down standing crop.

6 There are usually a number of internet sites which cover the crop circle phenomenon. For a comprehensive view of what's new and what's old, year-by-year and country-by-country, it is hard to beat <www.cropcircleconnector. com>.

7 Nigel Pennick and Paul Devereux, *Lines on the Landscape*, p.36. London: Robert Hale, 1989. 288p. maps, illustrations, index, bibliography, glossary. ISBN 0-7090-3704-X
   The authors credit this line to the work in 1904 of Francis J. Bennett.

8 *The Sun and the Serpent*, pp 83, 159.

9 Julian Cope, *The Modern Antiquarian, a pre-millennial odyssey through megalithic Britain*. London: Thorsons, 1998. 438p, copiously illustrated, index, bibliography. ISBN 0-7225-3599-6.
   The author cites the astronomer John North, who called the rooms "star-chambers", p. 203.

10 Cope, *The Modern Antiquarian*, p. 197, quoting A.G.Bradley in "Round About Wiltshire" (1906).

11 There are eight white horses cut into the chalk hills of Wessex, only one of which, the Uffington White Horse, dates back about 2000 years. The remainder, all of them in Wiltshire, have been cut from the 18th to the 20th centuries by horse fanciers, town councils, school boys, a fire brigade. Two of them commemorate royal coronations. They are created by removing grass and topsoil to expose the white chalk rock below. The white horse of Alton Barnes, situated on Milk Hill about a mile north of the village, dates to 1812 and measures 166 feet high by 160 feet long.

Chapter Forty

TAKING FLIGHT

Being a shaman is a path with two parallel tracks.

First comes the understanding that, if it is in your genetic makeup, you never stopped being a shaman in the leap from one lifetime to another. There may be karmic questions that lead to interruptions or delays in recognizing the track, but it is always there. Long after the event I realized that was what Eileen meant when, after the powerful meditation in her hogan, she said "you could be a shaman." In the beginning I took those words to mean that I could learn to become a shaman, it was a possibility I could choose to pursue. Several years later down the path it began to dawn on me that I had no choice; I was born a shaman and neither I nor anyone else close to me knew it until that dramatic first visit to Arizona.

The second track is the education necessary to acquire the tools which allow you to get back to work in this new incarnation. In my case this phase took the better part of ten years, mostly because the geographical distance from my preferred teacher was a real obstacle. During that time I did perform shamanic healings a few times, even at long distance, but I was not yet equipped for the core of the work.

That core is care of the human soul. Shamanic traditions around the planet focus on the soul in one way or another. The essential quality of a shaman is the capacity to enter what we call "non-ordinary reality" and travel within other dimensions of consciousness in search of missing soul pieces or of information that will help our clients heal. It is fashionable to speak of this altered state as being "trance", but it is not that. The great scholar Mircea Eliade called it "ecstasy". He said "shamanism always remains an ecstatic technique at the disposal of a particular elite[1]."

Be careful of that word "ecstasy". The dictionary definition is "a state of being beyond reason and self-control," but that is misleading. Shamanic ecstasy may or may not be "out of control". Many indigenous traditions have rituals in which the shaman goes outside of himself and does lose control while "out there". Many cultures speak of "trance" as the important tool. The tradition in which my teacher was trained and functions prefers "non-ordinary reality". Without losing consciousness, reason, control or memory, we accept leadership by our Guides who take us where we need to go. Once there, in that non-ordinary reality, we act in total self-control. We are fully conscious, but elsewhere, operating under the guidance and protection of our Guides. It's conscious teamwork, my Guide plucking the soul of our client from a thorn tree while I pin the threatening serpent with a forked pole. Should the serpent be a fire-breathing dragon, and it sometimes is, my Guide will have provided me with a heatproof cosmonaut suit beforehand. It's extremely non-ordinary, but it is very real while we are doing it.

These journeys take us into other dimensions, and it is typical of shamanism around the globe that these are organized on three levels. Nomenclature and details change, but the essence is similar from culture to culture.

First there is the Real World, the here and now in which we live, but which is extensible in time. Thus my Guide may fly me to a well-known city, perhaps London, but at some other point in time, such as the eleventh century.

We go up to a higher level, the Light World. Each shaman's perception of the Light World can vary. There is no norm. Typically we push through some lower layers, frequently thick, frequently populated with hostile spirits, emerging into a high, clear domain in which the stars are not far away. My Light World has a lot of towering, snowclad peaks hanging over alpine lakes, sometimes bordered by forests. There are also high arid lands with little foliage, and there is always more to explore. Beyond this semi-familiar topography lie our neighbor planets, their moons, comets and asteroids, and farther out still are the stars and their own moons and planets — other galaxies too.

Below the Real World is a lower level, reached through a tunnel, which is called variously the Lower World or the Dark World. "Dark" does not mean blackness or a place where evil reigns. It can be just as light as up above, but it also contains some challenging, sinister regions.

Our Guides lead us into one of these three dimensions in search of an entity, frequently but not always a person, who holds something that belongs to our client. This missing soul piece may be given to us in symbolic form but it can often be an object which is familiar to the client. As an example, on behalf of a client living in England my Guides took me to Gloucester Cathedral during the eighteenth century. A lady wrapped in a dark cape sat in a pew, praying. When I interrupted her, gently of course, she began to tell me about her son serving with the British "Redcoats" during the American Revolution. When I explained I had come on behalf of my client and asked if she held anything that belonged to her, she reached into the folds of her cloak and pulled out a rag doll. It was small, about eight inches tall, dressed in blue and green with a touch of red, and it had yellow yarn for hair.

When I described this doll to my client she recognized it immediately, saying she used to have a little rag doll just like that. Together with another "piece" brought back during the same journey, she felt she was brought confirmation that England was indeed where she, a foreigner, was supposed to be. The pieces brought a sense of relief that she was in the right place.

The technique for getting into this non-ordinary reality was the core of what Eileen taught during a series of one-week seminars in my sacred space. We began journeying the first day, and our long days were filled with journeys and subsequent dissection of what happened. We needed to work as much as possible so that we could gain confidence in what we experienced. Eileen taught a series of protocols within which we should operate for best results, and all this required endless fine-tuning throughout the week.

Everything is done to the beat of a drum. The beat has to be strong, powerful, steady, echoing the heartbeat of Mother Earth. It is rare that one has the luxury of a live drummer. Most of the time we use recordings, either on compact disk or on tape. On two or three occasions I have profited from the infrequent presence of my friend André, who has learned the beat and the volume. A good live drummer can lend great power and depth to the shaman's movement through the three levels, but the recording I have been working with lately is almost as good as the real thing.

I'll never forget my first journey within these protocols. During the seminar we worked in pairs, partners journeying for one another. Out of the fog of uncertainty in which I seemed to be embarked there developed the image of a tall gray-haired lady in a flowered dress with a white collar. She was part of the scene when some kind of a dark, cloudy commotion surrounded my partner. I sensed her falling.

In the ensuing "debriefing" my partner said her grandmother, tall and gray-haired, wore dresses like that. And the commotion, that was my partner falling and badly hurting her ankle at age eleven, an injury that plagued her with recurrent misery over the years. Bringing back that soul piece — the injury — was a prerequisite to ultimate healing.

Over and over again during that week we learned that we were indeed "going places and doing things", all with a therapeutic thrust. The process and the protocols with which Eileen armed us did indeed function.

After the seminars we continued to work with one another at distance as we tested our wings. Quickly I began journeying for the dead, for as previously pointed out, we spend half our time helping the dead and the dying. We go regularly to the scenes of disasters and catastrophes. Plane crashes, ships that sink, buses rolling off mountain roads, fires, floods, earthquakes, volcanic eruptions, are the daily bread of the serious shaman. The souls of the victims are usually in a state of shock, frequently hovering above the site in a state of confusion. When you die in a hospital bed there is plenty of time for your escorts to the next dimension to gather around and wait for your soul to start slipping out of its failing body. Clairvoyants will see them around the bed. When the earth shakes and great slabs of concrete crush you to instant physical death, your rudely ejected soul may be hanging a few feet over its lost body, traumatized, not yet accepting its new homeless status. They don't understand that they are now spirit, or if they do, they are worried about their families. Shamans have a major role to play in such situations. We have to help souls understand what has happened, what comes next, and how we can help them move toward the Light.

Above the wreckage of the Iranian city of Bam, after a monster earthquake, I met the soul of a man repeating "I have to find my wife, I have to find my wife." I told him that if she had died like him she would go to the Light, and he would find her there quickly. If she was alive in the wreckage the rescue workers would find her, and there would be nothing he could do. It was time to go Home, and I offered to guide him. A female soul gazed sadly down at the ruin of her home, worried for her children. "If they are alive you cannot help them, that's the job of the rescue crews. If they're not alive, you'll find them in the Light," and once again I offered my help.

In such circumstances we often perform rituals of purification, the return of soul pieces and guidance, and I have worked with clouds of souls numbering sometimes as many as fifty. Above these sites of catastrophe one often encounters other shamans busily doing the same thing.

My journey to a plane crash site is illustrative of this work. Roughly fifty souls were milling around aimlessly, half of them adolescents and children. More than one hundred had been killed but my Guide told me the others either followed their bodies in the ambulances or they got to the Light by themselves. I explained the desirability of returning soul pieces they had accumulated from family, friends, associates, even enemies during their lifetimes. We smudged them with smoking sage, then my Guide passed among them with a big sack, receiving all manner of tangible objects which symbolized, at this moment, the frequently intangible soul pieces. Using a gourd rattle, I rattled around the group while my Guide took away the soul pieces for redistribution, then I pointed them toward the Rainbow Bridge, beyond which one could see intense Light. They all went except the Captain, who had hung back and who was clearly upset, agitated, nervous.

"It was so sudden," he said. "A heavy blast, as if a window had been broken by a bird or something punctured the hull. I died instantly, there was no time to take the plane down to lower altitude and save lives." He was clearly grieving, even feeling guilty. I proposed a crystal healing and he agreed. With this specially-chosen quartz crystal I worked to extract anxiety and the feelings of guilt from his heart. Then he turned and left toward the Rainbow Bridge.

For my first dead client I clipped a mortuary notice from the morning newspaper. My Chief Guide gave permission for the journey and off we went to meet the "client". Imagine my surprise when, finding him admiring the view from the balcony of an alpine chalet, I saw bullets tear into his body. It was so unbelievable I asked my Guide to "replay the tape". I saw it all again, and there was no doubt. Unknowingly I had chosen a murder victim, although I never saw the murderer.

Disaster work is, of course, done because it needs to be done. We go to catastrophes in the same spirit of helpfulness that motivates organized rescue crews. They can't see us, but we are there too. Our job, like theirs, is to serve. Eileen emphasized that the shaman's motto is "I serve".

Living souls who come to us pay a fee in the same sense they would pay for energy work, or massage, or reflexology. We have no scruples about being paid well for our time, for journeying is hard work and there is always a danger that something could happen out there in "non-ordinary reality" that could cost us our physical lives.

As I proof-read these lines it has been thirty-four years since Great Spirit began trying to get my attention with a set of well-orchestrated calls for my help, twenty-eight years since I began daily meditation, seventeen years since I was made aware of my shamanic potential, sixteen years since I first began transmitting healing energy with my hands, which led quite naturally to retrieving souls. At each new fork in this path the key word has been "acceptance".

The first step was the hardest. As I wrote in Chapter Four, it took several days to push through the walls of hesitation that held me back from meditation. There were moments when it simply seemed silly to sit and probe a layer of consciousness which was not like ordinary introspection, which I liked, and not like prayer in a church service, which I did not like. A sort of self-consciousness stood in my way. On one level, I suspect, there was a bit of fear about possibly attracting unwelcome spirits of vague origin. I believe there is a lot of fuzzy, indefinable fear blocking the way of people who could benefit from meditation. Some of it has to do with fear of offending "God", whoever or whatever that is, and some of it has to do with fear of unscrupulous gurus.

That first step was successful, in ways that I had not imagined. Visualizing my little Blue Whale gave me a glimpse of the hidden power of mind. From there on my appetite for further spiritual experience became progressively insatiable.

It is now impossible for me to imagine a life which ignores the invisible world around us. It was all a matter of stumbling onto the right path. Early distaste for the Christianity being shoved down my juvenile throat set up a roadblock. Breaking through that invisible barrier set into motion a kind of blind pilgrimage. At that time the direction of the path was unclear. I didn't know where it led, but I knew that I had to follow it.

Brugh Joy's book and his varieties of meditation cast light on the way, and I am eternally grateful to this healer who I have met only through his pages. Those experiments led me to Transcendental Meditation. TM had numerous effects on me ——not all of them good — but which did furnish a few years of "basic training". Robert Monroe's system for synchronizing the two hemispheres of the brain provided a helpful boost. It's a sort of power tool from which many have benefited. Out of these early steps grew my ability to create a personal style of meditation. Intensive exploration of earth energies fostered a particular current of inner power which sustained the solitary path. Then another well-orchestrated "coincidence" took me to Arizona to meet a living guide. She refused the mantle of "teacher", referring me back to that elusive Inner Teacher. She forced me to go ever deeper within myself, but she was there to answer questions and offer occasional suggestions — all by the indirection typical of the native American way.

In the process the physical body in which I am dressed has become chronologically old, but my vision of the path has steadily enlarged. The energy that is "I" will always be alive. The body is transitory; the spirit that wears it goes on forever. It's fascinating to be incarnated at this time in the planet's history, although I won't be afraid to leave when Soul decides my work is done. In the meantime I shall go about this task of serving as intermediary between the visible and the invisible worlds.

Occasionally I have looked back and asked myself "what would this lifetime have been like if I had not taken the path, if I had not accepted the challenge?" The answer always comes back: "dull!"

---

[1]   Mircea Eliade (1907-1986), *Shamanism: Archaic Techniques of Ecstasy*. Princeton University Press: 1964 for the English translation. xxiii+610 p., index, bibliography. ISBN 0-691-01779-4. Originally published in French as "Le Chamanisme et les techniques archaïques de l'extase", Paris, Payot, 1951.

This is without argument the major exposition of worldwide shamanism. Eliade presents examples of shamanic ritual and practice in nearly every indigenous culture on the globe. He does not, of course, tell "how to do it".

EPILOGUE

This true story began on a note of mystification: it seemed as if invisible forces were tugging me somewhere. It took me a few years to connect all the dots and begin to see the vague outline of a design. I had no idea where it all was leading. There are still some holes in my total understanding, because my Virgo nature wants all the facts.

Some information has trickled in since the manuscript was finished. It begins to be clear that the shamanic gene came down through my maternal grandfather's side. A cousin who has been visiting told me a little story about our mutual grandfather. Her father (one of my uncles) directed her at one time to a meditational center in Hollywood, where, he said, his father used to go to meditate in the garden. That place has proved to be a center, inaugurated in 1942, of the Self-Realization Fellowship founded by Paramahansa Yogananda.

We already knew that Grandfather had been a Theosophist in the early years of the 20th century, and that he meditated. It now seems clear that his meditational life may have extended over close to forty years, a fact which supports the presence of a genetic predisposition to the mystic life. And that he followed the way of Yogananda impresses me deeply. It helps explain to me why I was attracted to Yogananda's movement, even if only for a relatively short time.

Even later we learned that another cousin's genealogical research had turned up another interesting lead. Grandfather's own father was a farmer in the American South, and thus served in the Confederate Army during the war of the 1860s. What did he do? He was a "medic". *Why would a farmer suddenly become a medic unless he possessed useful knowledge about plants and healing?*

That lurking gene needed somehow to reach me. We had surmised that the gene simply "slept" in my mother, a phenomenon that appears to happen frequently. There is however one visible symptom: a hummingbird brooch. The hummingbird is a very shamanic creature, one of the strongest animal symbols. My mother selected and bought a hummingbird brooch to wear on her coats and jackets. It is not at all the kind of jewelry that my father would have bought her. It's a piece of upscale costume jewelry: a jaunty little gold-dipped hummingbird with green head feathers and a red eye. It responded to something in her, and she brought it home. Years later she held it out to me, saying "I think you ought to have this, would you like it?" Indeed I did. It graces jackets from time to time, but I hadn't worn it for some time until, recently, I opened an inner compartment of my jewel box. There was this shamanic symbol staring up at me, connecting more of those dots.

So we can see some evidence of how five generations, down to my daughter, have carried on a particular tendency. Will we ever be able to track this shamanic lineage back up the genealogical stream? You can bet I am trying!

BIBLIOGRAPHY

Arya, Pandit Usharbudh, D.Litt., *Mantra and Meditation, Superconscious Meditation, Volume 2.* Honesdale, PA: Himalayan International Institute of Yoga Science and Philosophy, 1981. xxxiii+247p., appendix. ISBN 0-89389-074-X.

Bloomfield, Harold H, M.D., Michael Peter Caine, Dennis T. Jaffe, and Robert B. Kory, *TM: discovering inner energy and overcoming stress.* New York: Dell, 1975. Foreword by Hans Selye, M.D., and introduction by R. Buckminster Fuller. ISBN 440-06048-195.

Bock, Janet, *The Jesus Mystery ("of lost years and unknown travels").* Los Angeles: Aura Books,1980. 231p. appendix "The Legend of Saint Issa", notes, bibliography, ISBN 0-937736-00-7.

Cannon, Dolores, *Jesus and the Essenes ("Fresh insights into Christ's Ministry and the Dead Sea Scrolls").* Bath (UK): Gateway Books, 1992. 272p., bibliography, index. ISBN 0-946551-92-8.

Cranston, Sylvia and Carey Williams, *Reincarnation, a new horizon in science, religion and society.* New York: Julian Press, 1984. xiv+385p., notes, index. ISBN 0-517-55496-8.

Edwards, Betty, *Drawing on the Right Side of the Brain, how to unlock your hidden artistic talent.* Los Angeles: Tarcher, 1979; London: Souvenir Press, 1981. 207p., glossary, bibliography, index. ISBN 0-285-62468-7.

Ferguson, Marilyn, *The Aquarian Conspiracy, personal and social transformation in the 1980s.* Los Angeles: Tarcher, 1980. 448p., references and readings, index. ISBN 0-87447-191-9 (paper).

Grandjean, Geneviève (texte) et René Pierre Bille (photos), *Animaux de Montagne, vie sauvage.* Editions Slatkine, Calligram, 1992, 75p. ISBN 2-88445-099-8 and ISBN 2-05-100916-3.

Hartmann, Ernst, Dr. med., *Krankheit als Standortproblem* ("Illness as a Problem of Location"). Heidelberg: Haug Verlag, 1967.

Head, Joseph and S.L. Cranston, *Reincarnation, an east-west anthology.* New York: Julian Press, 1961, and Wheaton, Ill.: Theosophical Publishing House, 1981. x+342p., preface, appendix, index. ISBN 0-8356-0035-1.

_____. Reincarnation: *The Phoenix Fire Mystery.* New York: Julian Press, 1977, 1979. xix+620p., notes, index. Foreward by Elisabeth Kubler-Ross, M.D. ISBN 0-517-56101-8.

Joy, W. Brugh, M.D., *Joy's Way, A Map for the Transformational Journey, an introduction to the potentials for healing with body energies.* Los Angeles: Tarcher, 1979. 290p., index. ISBN 0-87447-085-8 (paper).

Kubler-Ross, Elisabeth, M.D., *On Death and Dying.* New York: Macmillan, 1960. 289p., bibliography, paper. LC 69-11789.

Maharishi Mahesh Yogi, *On the Bhagavad-Gita, a New Translation and Commentary, Chapters 1-6.* Harmondsworth and Baltimore: Penguin Books, 1969. 494p.

Merz, Blanche, *Les Hauts-Lieux Cosmo-Telluriques, leurs énergies subtiles méconnues* (Cosmic-terrestrial sacred sites, their unrecognized subtle energies.) Genève: Librairie de l'Université, Georg, 1983. 200p., glossary, bibliography. ISBN 2-8257-0104-01. In English: *Points of Cosmic Energy,* translated by Michèle Carter Burdet. Saffron Walden: C. W. Daniel, 1987. 184p., glossary, bibliography. ISBN 0 85207 194 9.

Monroe, Robert A., *Journeys Out of the Body.* New York: Doubleday, 1971, Anchor Books, 1977. 280p. ISBN 0-385-00861-9.

Montgomery, Ruth, *A Search for the Truth.* New York: Ballantine Books, Fawcett Crest, 1966. 256p. ISBN 0-449-24530-6.

_____, *A World Beyond.* New York: Fawcett Crest, 1971. 176p. ISBN 0-449-24085-1.

_____, *The World Before.* New York: Ballantine, Fawcett Crest, 1976. 288p. ISBN 0-449-20319-0.

Moody, Raymond A. Jr. M.D., *Life After Life,* 1977.

Playfair, Guy Lyon and Scott Hill, *The Cycles of Heaven, cosmic forces and what they are doing to you.* London: Souvenir Press, 1978. 368p., illus., references, index. ISBN 0 285 62335 4. Also: London: Pan Books, 1979. 400p, all illustrations and appendices, in paperback, ISBN 0 330 25676 9.

(Pomasanoff, Alex), *The Invisible World, sights too fast, too slow, too far, too small for the naked eye to see.* London: Secker & Warburg, 1981. 160p. ISBN

0-436-37680-6. A collection of scientific photos from dozens of sources, inspired by a National Geographic Society television production.

Prophet, Elizabeth Clare, *The Lost Years of Jesus*. Livingston, MT: Summit University Press, 1984. 401p., notes, bibliography. ISBN 0-916766-61-6.

Russell, Peter, *The TM Technique, A Skeptic's Guide to the TM Program*. Boston: Routledge & Kegan Paul, 1976, 1977. xi+191p., references, index. ISBN 0-7100-8672-5.

Stearn, Jess, *Edgar Cayce — The Sleeping Prophet*. New York: Doubleday 1967, Bantam 1968. 287p.

Steiger, Brad and Francie, *The Star People*. New York: Berkley, 1981. 200p., index. ISBN 0-425-05513-2.

Sullivan, Walter, "The Reign of the 'Terror Bird'", *International Herald-Tribune*, February 2, 1989, p.7.

Wheeler, Peter (comp.), *The Way of Love ("Joseph of Arimathea tells the true story behind the message of Jesus")*. London: The Leaders Partnership, 1996. 255p., genealogical charts. ISBN 90-75635-01-X. A compilation of recorded channelings, the medium remaining anonymous (I have met her; she has channeled for me.)

Wood, Ernest, *Yoga Dictionary*. New York: Philosophical Library, 1956. Pp. 104-105.

22253107R00307

Printed in Great Britain
by Amazon